Fog Computing:
Breakthroughs in Research and Practice

Information Resources Management Association
USA

Published in the United States of America by
IGI Global
Engineering Science Reference (an imprint of IGI Global)
701 E. Chocolate Avenue
Hershey PA, USA 17033
Tel: 717-533-8845
Fax: 717-533-8661
E-mail: cust@igi-global.com
Web site: http://www.igi-global.com

Library of Congress Cataloging-in-Publication Data

Names: Information Resources Management Association, editor.
Title: Fog computing : breakthroughs in research and practice / Information
    Resources Management Association, editor.
Description: Hershey, PA : Engineering Science Reference, [2018] I Includes
    bibliographical references.
Identifiers: LCCN 2017051715I ISBN 9781522556497 (h/c) I ISBN 9781522556503
    (eISBN)
Subjects: LCSH: Cloud computing.
Classification: LCC QA76.585 .F64 2018 I DDC 004.67/82--dc23 LC record available at https://lccn.loc.gov/2017051715

British Cataloguing in Publication Data
A Cataloguing in Publication record for this book is available from the British Library.

For electronic access to this publication, please contact: eresources@igi-global.com.

List of Contributors

Table of Contents

Preface

The ever-changing landscape surrounding decentralized computing infrastructures can make it very challenging to stay at the forefront of innovative research trends. As cloud applications and services are reaching bottlenecks in mobility and location awareness, fog computing is on the rise and is being described as the next big thing due to its ability to support emerging IoE applications that demand real-time and predictable latency.

In support of research and discoveries on fog computing, IGI Global is pleased to offer this comprehensive reference that will empower students, researchers, practitioners, computer engineers, IT professionals, and academicians with a stronger understanding of fog computing and how it can be applied to numerous industries and disciplines.

This compilation is designed to act as a single reference source on conceptual, methodological, and technical aspects, and will provide insight into emerging topics including but not limited to cyber security, smart XSS attack monitoring systems, vehicular fog computing, binary edge detection algorithm, and smart systems. The chapters within this publication encompass the transition from cloud to fog computing and are sure to provide readers with the tools necessary for further research and discovery in their respective fields.

The following paragraphs provide a summary of what to expect from the chapters.

This extensive reference opens by highlighting the foundation of cloud computing and the internet of things (IoT) in advancing current tools and applications for sending and receiving data. Through perspectives on smart systems, wireless technologies, and real-time applications, the first few chapters demonstrate how the emergence of fog computing is helping to improve mobility support, lower latency, and increase location awareness.

The next few chapters within this publication focus on emerging innovations in the application of fog computing for optimizing and improving user experiences. Including discussions on smart environments, CloudFIT, and distributed computing, research is presented on the facilitation of faster networking and computing and data storage. This inclusive information also explores advances in mobile computing and virtualization.

Also presented within this publication is coverage on the theoretical and practical applications of security utilization in fog computing. Through innovative discussions on wireless sensor networks, security platforms, and sensor data, the processes of assuring secure data locating, tracking, and transferring across fog domains to the cloud are also discussed. These perspectives contribute to the available knowledge on security information management in various fields.

As a comprehensive collection of research on the latest findings related to fog computing, this publication provides researchers, practitioners, and all audiences with a complete understanding of critical concepts and issues.

Chapter 1
Internet of Things:
Possibilities and Challenges

Sumit Kumar
Jawaharlal Nehru University, India

Zahid Raza
Jawaharlal Nehru University, India

ABSTRACT

Internet of Things (IoT) is a novel approach of connecting things/objects and thus transmitting information between various entities of the physical world or to the control centers where this information can be interpreted. IoT has been poised as the next evolution of internet promising to change our lives by involving a seamless access to people and devices in a ubiquitous way leading to a smart world. These devices, often referred to as smart items or intelligent things can be home appliances, healthcare devices, vehicles, buildings, factories and almost anything networked and fitted with sensors, actuators, and/or embedded computers. IoT promises to make the world smarter and proactive by enabling things to talk and others to understand. This work first presents an insight into the origin of IoT and its network as well as data centric architecture while listing the major possibilities. The seemingly important role and challenges of using Wireless Sensor Networks (WSN) which acts as the base in sensing and monitoring has been discussed. Since, the future lies in utility computing, best realized in the form of cloud computing, a cloud centric view of IoT is also presented.

1. INTRODUCTION

The Internet of Things (IoT) is a network link of the objects as well as computers, sensors, humans etc. supported by Internet or a collection of clouds to achieve anything and anywhere or everywhere computing and was introduced in 1999 at MIT. Till now, the basic use of the Internet is to connect computational machines to machines while communicating in the form of web pages. IoT goes one step further to connect each and everything useful in this world over the internet using a wireless network of sensors sensing everything in our daily life being aided with the growing presence of open wireless technology like Bluetooth, RFID, Wi-Fi and the promising 4G-LTE. These things can be any type, size, use, and

DOI: 10.4018/978-1-5225-5649-7.ch001

architecture generating various kinds of data along with computational needs varying with respect to place and time (Hwang, Dongarra, & Fox, 2012; Karimi & Atkinson, n.d.; Gubbia, Buyya, Marusic & Palaniswami, 2013; Atzori, Iera, & Morabito, 2010; Zanella, Bui, Vangelista & Zorzi, 2014).

It is an accepted fact that the growth of information technology has not left any part of our life untouched. This is primarily because of the penetration of the smart devices in our day to day life with the situation drastically changing in 2007 with Steve Jobs unveiling the iPhone. As an estimate, approximately 7.6 billion people are expected to be using 50 Billion devices connected to them directly or indirectly which according to the Cisco IBSG is IoT with more number of devices connected to an individual than people (Evans, 2011). Based on these numbers, Cisco IBSG estimates the birth of IoT between the period 2008 and 2009 as shown in Figure 1. The Oxford English Dictionary added a definition for "Internet of Things" in September 2013 as "A proposed development of the Internet in which everyday objects have network connectivity, allowing them to send and receive data" (Hwang, Dongarra, & Fox, 2012).

IoT is a very wide and new research area. Hence, there are not any standard and existing definitions for IoT as of now. Some of the other popular definitions are presented below:

- **Definition by Lu & Neng, (2010):** "Things in IoT have identities and virtual personalities operating in smart spaces using intelligent interfaces to connect and communicate within social, environment, and user contexts;"
- **Definition by the European Commission (2011):** "The basis and semantic concepts is composed by two words: Internet and Thing, where Internet can be explained as the world-wide network of interconnected computer networks, based on a standard and existing communication protocol like TCP/IP. The Thing is an object not exactly identification. Hence, semantically, Internet of Things means a world-wide network of interconnected objects exclusively addressable, based on standard and existing communication protocols;"

Figure 1. Estimated birth of IoT by Cisco IBSG (Evans, 2011)

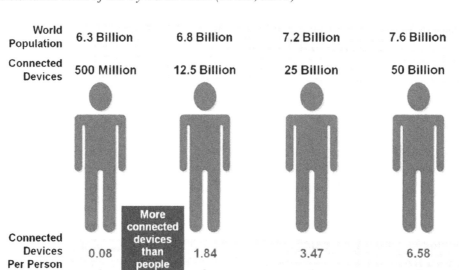

- **Definition by Guillemin and Friess (2009):** "The Internet of Things allows people and things to be connected anytime, anyplace, with anything and anyone, ideally using any path/network and any service."

A spirit of definition by Guillemin & Friess (2009) has been more clearly presented in Figure 2. IoT can therefore, be thought as an evolution of internet and intranet network developments and could be theoretically defined as an active universal network coupled with self-configuring capabilities for interoperable communication protocols identifying things, physical attributes, virtual personalities and uses intelligent interfaces for supporting the information network (Vermesan et al., 2011; Guo Zhang, & Wang, 2011). Another typical IoT scenario has been presented in Figure 3 (http://www.google.co.in/imgres?imgurl=x-raw-image:///002a2a06cab12c973082238b10fcf34f439cdd3ac4703969603a0b5508 1ca7fa&imgrefurl=https://ingenierie.openwide.fr/content/download/1511/17408/file/FC.pdf&h=393 &w=540&tbnid=lyyxygYqKgALzM:&docid=dE_SDhVnIzKRFM&hl=en-IN&ei=SwEBVsG5NsS x0ATuqIngBg&tbm=isch&ved=0CB0QMygBMAFqFQoTCIGLobCNisgCFcQYlAodblQCbA). The illustration depicts IoT as a loosely coupled network of networks connecting a lot of things/objects surrounding us with these things, objects or people connected with one network or the other. Therefore, IoT derives its inspiration from the fact that for the living community to thrive, it is important to closely involve technology with people in order to have context and knowledge aware intelligent decisions. This is important because of the fact that evolution has to be supported by communication. Realization of a true IoT scenario will help us to be more sensory and proactive enabling us to meet the challenges in a better way.

Figure 2. Abstract view of the IoT (Guillemin & Friess, 2009)

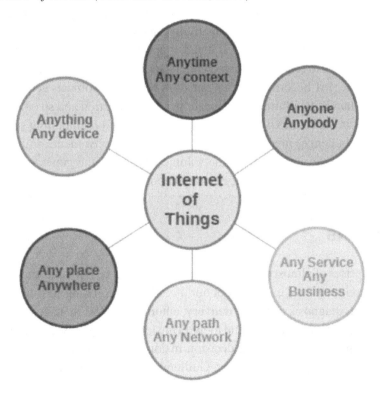

Figure 3. A typical IoT scenario (http://www.google.co.in/imgres?imgurl=x-raw-image:///002a2a06c ab12c973082238b10fcf34f439cdd3ac4703969603a0b55081ca7fa&imgrefurl=https://ingenierie.open-wide.fr/content/download/1511/17408/file/FC.pdf&h=393&w=540&tbnid=lyyxygYqKgALzM:&docid =dE_SDhVnIzKRFM&hl=en-IN&ei=SwEBVsG5NsSx0ATuqIngBg&tbm=isch&ved=0CB0QMygBMA FqFQoTCIGLobCNisgCFcQYlAodblQCbA)

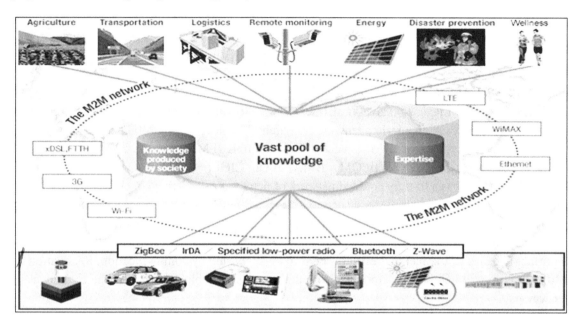

As IoT evolves, it is important to unambiguously address both people and objects. These devices could be active or passive in communication capabilities and demands the involvement of the physical sensors, Radio Frequency IDentification (RFID) and supporting wireless technologies for sensing the information. In addition, it also requires a shared understanding of the user context for autonomous and smart behavior. Therefore, IoT becomes an amalgamation of different objects generating data of various types e.g. temperature, humidity, illumination, location, communication and so on. Although, IoT opens up a lot of possibilities in moving to a smarter world, realizing and maintaining such a scenario poses numerous barriers and challenges involving various aspects of its constituents. Further, the challenge of filtering and retaining the relevant data from the volumes of data being generated makes it even more complex (Vermesen & Friess, 2014; Tedjini, Perret, Deepu, & Bernier, 2009).

2. IoT APPLICATIONS

The vision of IoT comprises of almost everything that surrounds us be it people, processes, data or things indicating its applications in almost every part of our life. Therefore, it ranges from real-time monitoring of patients health report, diagnosis and drug delivery, automatic traffic management, efficient accident and crime handling capabilities, environmental monitoring for calamity prevention with the ultimate goal of closer human machine ties for proactive decision making. Some other conventionally possible IoT contributions are listed as follows (Sundmaeker, Guillemin, Friess, & Woelfflé, 2010; Mayer, Guinard,

& Trifa, 2012; Mayer & Karam, 2012; Atzori, Iera, & Morabito, 2010; Xu, He & Li, 2014; Zanella, Bui, Vangelista & Zorzi, 2014; Ovidiu & Friess, 2014):

- **Personal:** The use of IoT in one's personal space could be the use of Wi-Fi services in sensing and controlling the wireless devices for better home management and ease of living. Google Chromecast can be an example connecting the laptops with the TV's through home Wi-Fi network;
- **Society:** It includes activities concerning the development of smarter societies, cities and people e.g. government initiatives for e-participation and e-inclusion for aging and disabled people, traffic and crowd management etc.;
- **Environment:** Its include the safety, monitoring and expansion of all natural resources like farming & reproduction, recycling, environmental management services, energy management etc.;
- **Industry:** It involves the economic or marketable transactions between companies, organizations and other entities e.g. industrialized, logistics, service sector, banking and bodies of financial governmental etc.;
- **Computational Marketplace:** The applications could even be intra domain as well as inter domain following the collaborative problem solving and addressing. One such example is a computational marketplace which is a web based paradigm in which many algorithms work together (may be one feeding the other in a stateless way) to solve a problem for the user in a transparent way. For e.g. a person wearing a sensor connected to the web relaying information about its heartbeat. The same data can be relayed to many different algorithms which will check for the possibility of any heart attack and in case if its probable rush to send inputs in the form of links to algorithms or medicines required in this case or just to keep a record of the state in the repository if everything is well. This is, in a way, a peer of Information market which is concerned only with gathering information from the user and supplying it to firms/people in order to increase the reach of the business and to get more customers. The essential commodity in both the cases is the Smart devices which generates information / data. In the process many parties/algorithms/ service providers come together and join hands seamlessly to solve a problem while retaining scalability, fault tolerance and change tolerance. Stateless means simply the data will be passed from one algorithm to another without any further requirements for the new algorithm to proceed with execution.

Computational marketplace should facilitate the integration, lookup and interaction with smart devices for efficient services. This brings into picture, many considerations in the process like inclusion of various parties involved, their discovery, selection of appropriate party, optimal route etc. that demands consideration (Mayer, Guinard, & Trifa, 2012; Mayer & Karam, 2012).

3. IoT ARCHITECTURE

IoT should be capable of interconnecting billions or trillions of constituting heterogeneous objects over the Internet. The architectural design of IoT facilitate the processing, routing, storage and retrieval of events and allow for disconnected operations such as: network connectivity in intermittent state. Accordingly, there is a critical need for a flexible layered architecture. The architectural framework of the IoT refers to the description of its various constituents and establishing a commonality between its various domains. It therefore, serves as a reference model for defining the relationships between various verticals considering data abstraction while addressing important Quality of Service (QoS) parameters involved e.g. protection, security, privacy, and safety. Further, it facilitates the processing, routing, storage and retrieval of events. The IoT nodes are needed to connect nearest networks with other nodes, local nodes or remote nodes. In general IoT objects require connection with other networks and with other nodes be it local nodes or remote. Therefore, it is best to be supported through a decentralized, distributed approach of the architecture. Although, the ever-increasing number of proposed architectures has not yet converged to a reference model but still a network centric view and the data centric views are the popular ones. Mostly, the IoT architecture is seen from the wireless sensor networks perspective owing to their significant role. The Representational State Transfer (REST) framework for understanding software architecture via architectural styles is also very useful for such applications.

3.1. Network Centric Architecture

Figure 4 represents a typical internet centric IoT architecture from the wireless sensor network and cloud perspective considering different deployments scenarios such as scalability, modularity and configuration (https://www.google.co.in/search?q=12+The+Internet+of+Things+(IOT)&oq=12+The+Internet+of+Things+(IOT)&aqs=chrome..69i57.1241j0j7&sourceid=chrome&es_sm=93&ie=UTF-8). The middle two layers offering Management Service and Gateway and Network can be clubbed together to have a Cloud centric model of IoT. Here, the layer above the cloud layer belongs to the consumers with their requirements and the bottom one being the physical layer responsible for the generation of data. The middle layer is the cloud layer which effectively deals with the visualization, computation, analytics and the storage of data as per the *aaS model of cloud computing. Similarly, object centric and human centric and semantic oriented models of IoT architecture have been presented (Vermesan et al., 2011; Gubbia, Buyya, Marusic & Palaniswami, 2013; Uckelmann, Harrison, & Michahelles, 2011; https://www.google.co.in/search?q=12+The+Internet+of+Things+(IOT)&oq=12+The+Internet+of+Things+(IOT)&aqs=chrome..69i57.1241j0j7&sourceid=chrome&es_sm=93&ie=UTF-8l; Barnaghi, Wang, Henson, & Kerry, 2012; Atzori, Iera, & Morabito, 2010; Fielding, 2000; Al-Fuqaha, Mohsen, Mehdi, Mohammed, & Moussa, n.d.).

3.1.1. Sensor Layer Architecture

The lower layer in IoT architecture is a group of smart things/objects incorporated through sensors, actuators and embedded communication system. The main work of the sensors is to allow the interconnections between physical and digital worlds and providing the real-time operational information data collection and processing. Accordingly, it can have different types of ubiquitous nodes/sensors for various purposes. The sensors have the ability to measure/read various types of data such as temperature, air quality, movement and electricity etc. that changes the signal output. The connectivity to the sensor aggregators is done using LAN, WAN, Bluetooth or any suitable network.

3.1.2. Gateways and Networks

The big amount of data created by the sensors devices demands an efficient wireless or wired network as a transfer medium for communications. The problem with current networks is their machine to machine

Figure 4. A typical IoT architecture (https://www.google.co.in/search?q=12+The+Internet+of+Thing s+(IOT)&oq=12+The+Internet+of+Things+(IOT)&aqs=chrome..69i57.1241j0j7&sourceid=chrome &es_sm=93&ie=UTF-8

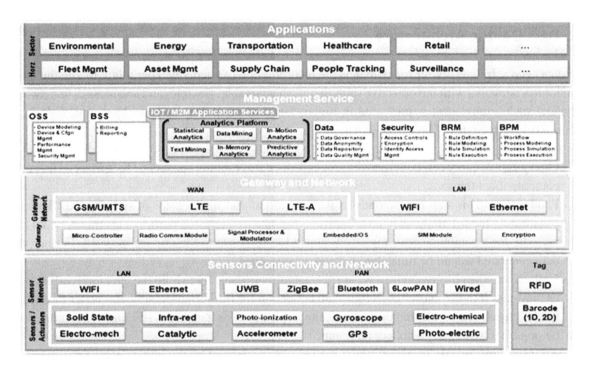

connection model and protocols. Since, IoT involves various devices and objects, this layer should be able to adapt to the extensive range of IoT services and applications using multiple and different networks with different technologies and access protocols.

3.1.3. Management Service Layer Architecture

The management service provides the processing or accessing of information generated by the lower layer through analytics, security controls, process modeling and management of devices. In the cloud centric view, Management Service layer along with the Gateways and Networks layer together form the various services that can be offered either as infrastructure, platform, software or any other *aaS where * could be hardware or even people. Thus, it becomes a combination of on demand storage and computing tools for various service providers viz. sensing, analytical tools, AI tools, visualization tools or any such service provider(s). Cloud programming models such as Map Reduce also comes into picture along with other required features like running services, dynamic provisioning, workload management and billing and reporting to name a few.

3.1.4. Application Layer Architecture

This layer corresponds to the various applications that benefit from the IoT ranging from environment, energy transportation surveillance to even healthcare. Even the applications with overlapping areas are possible cutting through various domains. It is important that the visualization tools are easy to operate and user friendly like the touch screens and be compatible with various platforms. Further, the interpretation of the results should be done presented in an unambiguous way for the associated applications.

3.2. Data Centric Architecture

The data centric framework for IoT demands the incorporation of a federated paradigm to join the independent IoT networks with the objective of realizing an adaptable, flexible, and seamless data network. A typical such arrangement is presented in Figure 5 and discussed as follows (Aggarwal, Ashish, & Sheth, 2013; Abu-Elkheir, Hayajneh, & Ali, 2013):

- **Querying:** A query can be initiated to request the data from the sensors or to retrieve it from the computational things;
- **Production:** This step corresponds to the generation and the transfer of data by the "Things" constituting the IoT framework and reporting this data to interested parties. This transfer could be periodic for a continuous reading or on demand in response to the queries initiated. Further, the data generated should be time-stamped and geo-stamped;
- **Collection:** The objects should have at least a minimum capacity to hold the data for a certain time or may pass it to the master object for data collection for further processing and better flexibility. For example, Wireless communication technologies such as Zigbee, Wi-Fi and cellular are used by objects to send data to collection points;
- **Aggregation/Fusion:** Transmitting all the raw data generated by the objects may consume more bandwidth and requires higher data rate demanding the use of efficient aggregation and compression techniques;
- **Delivery:** The data generated in the processed and/or stored form may be required to be sent to the destination passing many objects in between. This data may correspond to the final response or may be used for analysis temporarily or for final storage;
- **Preprocessing:** Since IoT inherently is heterogeneous with objects varying in nature and data formats and structures, data preprocessing may be required. Preprocessing further serves to handle the missing data to present it in a unified and standard format since the IoT data originates from different sources with varying formats and structures;
- **Store/Update:** This phase corresponds to the requirement of handling the storage of the continuous data being generated or the updates in case of discrete data generated by objects. Since, data too is of many types, the facility should be capable of handling data of various types be it structured or unstructured while deciding the update frequency e.g. NoSQL key-value. Further, the storage can be centralized or decentralized;
- **Processing/Analysis:** This phase involves the processing of the data with proper analysis as per the needs. This processing may be task or user specific and can be done both on instantaneous data or the stored/archived data.

Figure 5. IoT data management and life cycle (Uckelmann, Harrison, & Michahelles, 2011)

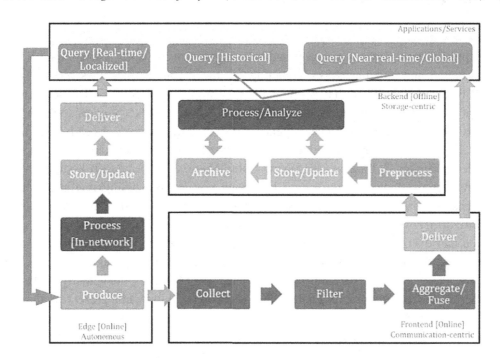

4. BIG DATA ANALYTICS, CLOUD, AND FOG COMPUTING WITH IoT

The connections between a huge amount of physical things/objects like humans, animals, plants, machine to machine, smart phones, etc. furnished with sensors devices to the Internet generates what is popularly known as *big data*. Owing to the enormous generation of data in the IoT, the primary big data requirement becomes a smart and resourceful storage. Evidently, interconnected devices will also need the methods to store, process, and repossess the data. The big data is a very big amount of data and is important to capture, manage and process the data within a suitable slot of time even from the commonly used hardware environments and software tools for the success of IoT or any other paradigm. If any person wants to use software and hardware components of cloud computing services, these are provided by public, private and some authorized companies. The Cloud services are providing the services for researchers and businesses to use and maintain many resources remotely, reliably and at a low cost. Fog computing has also been coined recently viewed as an extension of cloud computing in the sense that rather than computing and storing everything in a cloud, these services are brought closer to the user edge devices. The IoT uses a very large amount of embedded devices like actuators and sensors and these devices are bound to produce big data which in turn requires complex computations to extract knowledge. Accordingly, cloud with or without Fog base form becomes the best option for the IoT for storage space and computing resources to store and process the big data. The following subsection further discusses the overlaps between the IoT and big data analytics with Cloud and Fog computing (Rao, Saluia, Sharma, Mittal & Sharma, 2012; Bryant, Katz, & Lazowska, 2008).

4.1. Big Data Analytics and IoT

Big date concerns with the processing and analytics required to be done on large data repositories generated due to many applications e.g. web documents and indexing, sensor networks, astronomical applications realizing smart cities and social networks on an ongoing basis. Big data becomes very relevant in the context of IoT being an umbrella term covering many such applications. Since, IoT is bound to generate huge data all of which may not be important, it is important that efficient techniques, tools, architectures and algorithms for storage of the useful heterogeneous data be developed which can be used to mine the raw data for valuable information while identifying and discarding the erroneous data. Dang, Wang, & Wu (2013), Heba, Elmogy & Barakat (2015), and Cubo, Nieto, & Pimente (2014) suggests that these algorithms can be grouped into four classes viz. heterogeneous data processing, nonlinear data processing, high dimensional data processing and distributed and parallel data processing. Accordingly, these verticals can be further explored for specialized interests. In addition, since IoT involves a lot of personal data collection and distribution, which can be statistically and semantically correlated to determine the group behavior, the risk of potential discrimination and other harms to the users can become very threatening. Therefore, the IoT algorithms should be capable of handling the velocity of the change in data, data types, data structures and the context based decision making while preserving the privacy of the data in a secured manner.

There are various platforms that are available for big data analytics like Apache Hadoop and SciDB. However, these tools may hardly be strong and sufficient for the big data needs of IoT. Here, mostly the IoT data is a huge amount to be collected and processed by the available tools. For the IoT and as per user demands, these platforms should work in real-time. For example, Facebook has used an improved version of Hadoop to analyze billions of messages per day and offers a real-time statistics of user actions. In the terms of resources, there is a ubiquitous presence of a lot of powerful servers in data centers and smart devices around us. These are also offering the computing capabilities and it can be used to perform parallel and distributed computing for the IoT data analytics. IoT needs a common big data analytic platform which can even be delivered as a service to IoT applications (Tsai, Lai, Chiang & Yang, 2014; Borthakur et al., 2011; Mukherjee, Paul, Dey, & Banerjee, 2014).

A new research area has been proposed for IoT big data analytics service known as TSaaaS. In this area, researchers are using time series data analytics to perform pattern mining on a huge amount of sensors for data collection. Their analytic services relies on the Time Series Database service and is accessible by a set of RESTful interfaces. The study estimates that the TSaaaS can perform pattern searches faster than the accessible systems. The existing approaches can help too in some important fields like Principle Component Analysis (PCA), Pattern reduction, Dimensionality reduction, Feature selection and Distributed computing methods (Tsai, Lai, Chiang, & Yang, 2014; Xu et al., 2014).

4.2. Cloud Computing and IoT

Cloud computing has already proven its worth in providing us the mechanism for big data that permits the processing of data and the extraction of valuable knowledge from it. In the case of IoT it demands the collected data to be aggregated and transmitted to a powerful processing resource(s) for information extraction. Although, both the Cloud and the IoT have been independent evolutions, their integration promises to open new avenues benefiting both. Thus, IoT can rely on the unlimited capacity and structured services offered by the Cloud to be used as the processing and storage centers in a cost-effective manner. Further, the efficient management of these on demand internet services in a reliable manner with less deployment cost too benefits IoT. The Cloud, on the other hand, will gain from the pervasive and real-world reach of the IoT. In general, the Cloud will be used as an intermediate between the things and the applications hiding all the complexity and functionalities required to realize the IoT (Lu & Neng, 2010; Ding, Wang, & Wu, 2013; Heba, Elmogy, & Barakat, 2015; Liu, Dong, Guo, Yang, & Peng, 2015).

The Cloud computing for the IoT needs to address the following issues (Al-Fuqaha, Mohsen, Mehdi, Mohammed, & Moussa, 2015):

- **Synchronization:** This challenge corresponds to the synchronization between various cloud service sellers intending to provide real-time services since services are built on top of various cloud platforms;
- **Standardization:** Standardizing Cloud computing is an important challenge for cloud-based IoT services considering the requirement to interoperate between various vendors;
- **Balancing:** Making a balance among generally used cloud computing services environments and IoT requirements is another issue due to the differences in infrastructure;
- **Reliability:** With the differences in the security mechanisms between the IoT devices and the cloud platforms, reliability becomes a concern which even threatens the security of both applications and the providers;
- **Management:** Cloud computing and IoT both have different resources and components. Managing Cloud computing and IoT systems is an enormous effort becoming even more complex with IoT;
- **Enhancement:** For the customers' expectations, a validating IoT cloud-based service is necessary to ensure good services.

We can use IoT in various cloud platforms with different capabilities and strengths such as ThingWorx, OpenIoT, Google Cloud, Amazon, GENI, etc. For example, Xively (formerly known as Cosm and Pachube) represents one of the first IoT application service providers. This allows the sensor data to be available on the web. The main aims of Xively is to connect devices to applications securely in real-time. Xively provides a Platform as a Service (PaaS) solution for the IoT application developers and service providers. It is capable to contain devices with the platform by complete libraries (such as ARM mbed, Electric Imp and iOS/OSX) and facilitate communication via HTTP(S), Sockets/Websocket, or MQTT. (Verma & Verma, 2014; Yang et al., 2013). As another example, Nimbits is an open source Platform as a Service (PaaS) that stabilizes connection between smart embedded devices and the cloud. It can also perform data analytics on the cloud, generates alerts, and connects with social networks and spreadsheets. Furthermore, it connects to websites and can store, share and retrieve sensors data in various formats including numeric, text based, GPS, JSON or XML. To exchange the data or messages, XMPP is a built-in service in Nimbits. The core of Nimbits is a server that provides REST web services for logging and retrieval of raw and processed data (Nimbits, 2014).

In general, some of the features of Xively and Nimbits which even serves as the requirements for other cloud-based service providers for IoT service offerings can be written as (Doukas, 2012):

- Open source, free and easy to use exposing the accessible Application Programming Interfaces (APIs);
- Interoperability with many internet protocols, environments and an ability to manage the real-time wired and wireless sensors and distributed the data in various formats such as JSON, XML and CSV;
- Support for many Original Equipment Manufacturers (OEM) like Arexx, Nanode, OpenGear, Arduino and mBed.

4.3. Fog Computing in Support of the IoT

Fog Computing is being seen as a bridge between smart IoT devices and large-scale cloud computing and cloud storage services with the potential to increase the cloud computing services to the edge devices of the network. Fog network further strengthens the case of using the cloud based IoT. It is realized with Fog providing the context aware, low latency localization with Cloud providing global centralization. This in turn promises to improve the Quality of Service (QoS) to a good extent. Because of their propinquity to the end-users compared to the cloud data-centers, fog computing promises to offer services for an effective delay performance. It is to be noted that between the fog and the cloud the former has a massive computational, storage and communications capabilities. Figure 6 presents the roles of cloud data-centers and the cloudlets (fog computing) intending to deliver the IoT services to the end-users. Mobile network operators could help in the realization of fog computing having the potential to offer fog services as one of IaaS, PaaS, or SaaS models to the enterprise businesses through their service network or cell towers (Verma & Verma, 2014; Bonomi, Milito, Zhu, & Addepalli, 2012).

Figure 6. Realizing IoT with cloud and fog resources (Al-Fuqaha, Mohsen, Mehdi, Mohammed, & Moussa, 2016)

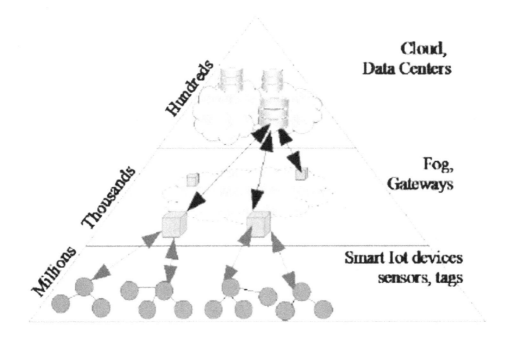

Considering the scale of IoT, managing the network, connectivity while providing a continuous service is challenging. However, techniques such as Software Defined Networks (SDN) can be used to address the problem with network virtualization. Fog computing can serve as a best choice for the IoT designers for the following features (Al-Fuqaha, Mohsen, Mehdi, Mohammed, & Moussa, 2015):

- **Location:** Fog resources are located between smart objects and the cloud data-centers, resulting in better delay performance;
- **Distribution:** Fog computing is based on "micro" centers with limited storage, processing and communication capabilities compared to the cloud. This makes possible to organize many such "micro" centers closer to the end-users as their cost is typically a small fraction compared to cloud data-centers;
- **Scalability:** Fog allows IoT systems to be more scalable such that as the number of end-user increase, the number of deployed "micro" fog centers can increase to cope with the increasing load. Such an increase cannot be achieved by the cloud because the deployment of new data-centers is cost prohibitive;
- **Density of Devices:** Fog helps to provide resilient and replicated services;
- **Mobility Support:** Fog resources can act as a mobile cloud too being located close to the end-users;
- **Real-Time:** Fog has the potential to provide better performance for real-time interactive services;
- **Standardization:** Fog resources needs to be standardized like cloud to enable interoperation with various cloud providers;
- **On the Fly Analysis:** Fog resources can perform data aggregation to send partially processed data as opposed to raw data to the cloud data-centers for further processing.

Fog computing, thus has the potential to increase the overall performance of IoT applications performing a part of the high-level services offered by the cloud, inside the local resources and leading the way to a smarter world.

5. CHALLENGES IN IoT

Internet is the physical layer of the communication network made up of transmitting and routing devices on top of which the application layer known as the World Wide Web operates acting as an interface. IoT represents the next evolution of the internet by making the internet sensory (Evans, 2011). Realizing IoT means several disparate networks coupled with sensors need to operate seamlessly. The requirements of IoT architecture then becomes to maximize the interoperability along with various distributed resources and systems as well as information and services, software, devices or smart objects. To achieve the same, it presents a lot of challenges ranging from the node structure, standards used, architecture to issues related to wireless sensor networks. Further, it is important to develop the new system in parallel with the existing ones and if possible, develop applications on top of the existing system with interoperability facility. For the IoT to be up and running smoothly, there are many potential challenges that need to be addressed affecting both individuals and as a society with some being listed as follows (Hwang, Dongarra, & Fox, 2012; Guillemin & Friess, 2009; Matthias, Huchzer, & Picker, 2010; Aggarwal, Ashish, & Sheth, 2013; Guo Zhang, & Wang, 2011; Atzori, Iera, & Morabito, 2010; Gershenfeld, Krikorian, &

Cohen, 2004; Zanella, Bui, Vangelista & Zorzi, 2014; Vermesen & Friess, 2014; Tedjini, Perret, Deepu, & Bernier, 2009; Demirkol, Alagoz, Deliç, & Ersoy, 2006; Fielding, 2000.

5.1. Characteristics of IoT Resources

IoT faces a great challenge in terms of the number of diverse and heterogeneous participants of extraordinary large number which are geographically dispersed. The deployment of IPv6, as shown in Figure 7, based on 128 bits or its lightweight version can make it possible to address these billions of objects with a unique IP address in contrast to IPv4 that allows for a total of 2^{32} addresses which is just over 4 billion addresses (Kushalnagar, Montenegro, & Schumacher, 2007; https://en.wikipedia.org/wiki/IPv6)

Even multilayered addressing scheme addressing resources in terms of Uniform Resource Names (URN) can be used being accessed through URLs. This result in dynamics in the physical environment in which the resources might be constrained e.g. battery life and signal coverage. Even location of the objects is important in IoT which in this case will have a huge spread. In addition, the sensory resources will have limited computing capabilities with limited memory. Further, the sensory nature even results in disruption of services from time to time because of their placements (Gubbia, Buyya, Marusic & Palaniswami, 2013; Guillemin & Friess, 2009).

5.2. Characteristics of IoT Data

Due to the sensory nature and diverse participation by different objects, the data generated is also different with different abstraction levels e.g. raw, infrared or derived. This data is usually of the transient nature for which quality in many situations cannot be assured depending on the environment. Processing such a data in a common understandable format becomes a big challenge.

In the terms of modality, resource capabilities and data quality the data producers are very different. In the terms of running environments and data needs, the data consumers are heterogeneous. The heterogeneities lead to various challenges for an efficient data management:

Figure 7. IPv6 addressing (https://en.wikipedia.org/wiki/IPv6)

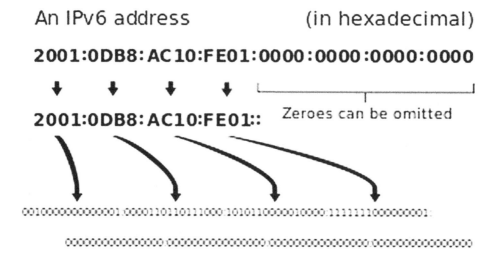

- **Data Collection Architecture:** Two popular different methods of data collection have been reported in the literature one being centralized and the other being self-supported. In the former case, the entire data processing for all the sensing data are performed a specialized server. In the latter case, the data have the ability to get processed into the device by itself;

- **Standards for Communication and Knowledge Representation:** The sensor's data comes from various platforms over different bandwidth and Internet connectivity networks and have different connection technologies. Even, the interfaces used are different. Therefore, it demands a standard sensor gateway interface for all components for seamless operation;

- **Data Uncertainty:** The sensor data is involved in many resources of unstable nature. There can be error in the data due to may be a broken embedded sensor. Another problem is that fact that human being activities can be recognized by RFID-based devices. Therefore, if RFID sensing objects are furnished which are placed close to each other, they sense the human body and detect them concurrently. This results in the final recognition result getting affected by RFID;

- **Data Mining and Extraction:** Owing to the challenging heterogeneous and unpredictable nature of IoT, sensing useful data and its extraction becomes a big challenge. It is a big challenge to simultaneously learn representations of events and activities at various levels of abstraction. It demands another level of learning on top of the shallow learning methods existing today resulting in a deep learning.

5.3. Privacy and Security

Privacy of humans and confidentiality of business processes are two very compelling issues in IoT. Ensuring privacy of the individual parties and maintaining it from the beginning is a must as the system is not designing for restricted resource devices. There are many problems regarding the privacy and security in IoT based environment because people suspect tracking of their data movement, shopping and other sensitive data over the internet deterring them to use the services. The selection of devices, data and data ownership are major challenges for the IoT concept.

It is particularly important to secure the privacy of applicants and objects where the devices consistently contributing data to the community-scale applications and are being monitored invisibly. Data anonymization techniques to hide the personal identity of users can be used when the users are contributing the data in the data set but is not sufficient as it can be derived from the report of the user's data. Thereby, it demands for restricted policies and laws for user's rights to control and access the data and its uses.

The data security issues for IoT corresponds to the same problem for the internet where the data is open and dynamic and thus becoming a security issue though at a much larger scale. The industry is witnessing a lot of tools and technology for better computing, communication and storage but productivity can only be ensured with safeguard against improper use of these advances (Gubbia, Buyya, Marusic & Palaniswami, 2013; Aggarwal, Ashish, & Sheth, 2013; Abu-Elkheir, Hayajneh, & Ali, 2013; Atzori, Iera, & Morabito, 2010).

5.4. Privacy in Data Transmission

The privacy and security issue for data can arise both during data collection and during data transmission and sharing with the extensive use of RFID technology in IoT. This is particularly important when user data is handled in process chains, e.g. on RFID tags where the data protection and privacy concerns have to be taken into account from not only the user-perspective but as well from the enterprise perspective.

The use of the unique identifier for the objects and persons in the RFID tags can lead to severe problems e.g. disclosing the location during transmission. As an example, these tags have the information about the complete manufacturing process and can be misused upon sharing. kill command is generally used for a tag for things/products, which have a short-term lifetime (before point of sale) for tracking purpose and is the simplest and important solution for privacy with RFID data. The kill command is started by a RFID signal, which stops the working of the tag and no longer releases the Electronic Product Code (EPC), which is used to describe it. By inclusion of a small password with the kill command could make it more secure.

The important requirements of new sensor applications are installation and updating or reprogramming. For all devices in the network, this is successfully done by remote wireless reprogramming. Usually, the network reprogramming consists of only a data broadcasting protocol and without authentication the code is distributed on all nodes in the network raising the security concerns while exposing the vulnerabilities (Gubbia, Buyya, Marusic & Palaniswami, 2013; Vermesan & Friess, 2014; Tedjini, Perret, Deepu, & Bernier, 2009).

5.5. Human Centric Sensing

The use of shared data by using the mobile sensing nodes/devices is referred to as the human-centric sensing. The people centric sensing offers the possibility of low cost sensing of the environment localized to the user generating correct and valuable data. In this context, it becomes an issue that what should be the human role in sensing e.g. controlling the condition of a sensing job as accept or stop. Therefore, how much should be the human participatory sensing in decision making and its appropriateness e.g. in deciding how and which application should be accepted becomes important. Another way of human participation is the opportunistic level e.g. when the devices get to meet a new application requests and load shifting of the users. But there are some limitations in both the conditions. In participatory sensing, there are many demands that are concerned from the users. In the opportunistic approaches, there are many issues like possibility the leak of individually sensitive information and high computation cost on decision making.

In human centric sensing, the use of mobile network sensors forms an extremely unstable group of sensing nodes where no static sensing communication is available that can be potentially providing connections. When a huge number of populations of mobile nodes are available, the sensing devices must identify which node(s) may accept the jobs/tasks. Further, relying on users volunteering data and with inconsistent samples because of the user travel path or the degree of participation limits the ability to produce meaningful data and effective decisions.

5.6. Low-Level Sensing Data

The Low-level sensing data depends on the data processing controlled by lab settings and unauthorized users and is a challenge to deal with in IoT. The data generated in IoT needs to be stored and used intelligently for smart monitoring and actuation. Further, storage, ownership and expiry of data become critical (Guillemin & Friess, 2009; Matthias, Huchzer, & Picker, 2010; Aggarwal, Ashish, & Sheth, 2013; Vermesen & Friess, 2014; Tedjini, Perret, Deepu, & Bernier, 2009):

- **Lacking of a Common Model:** The individual and social behavior is usually idiosyncratic. Thus, in the same environmental condition the response of the objects may vary depending on activity factors. For example, a person holds a mobile phone in the pocket or in the hand may impact the correct identification of object when the same activity identification model is used. Therefore, it is important to train dissimilar classifiers for different contexts;

- **Complexity and Ambiguity:** The perfect identification is a very big challenging work in IoT because our daily life activities are much complex and complicated. For this reason, there are a lot of new challenges present in our environment. Human creates more than one activities at the same time and the same place e.g. while walking on the road we can talk with our friend on a mobile call being different and parallel activities. Therefore, similar conditions or even the same one can be interpreted in a different way.

5.7. Network Technology

IoT involves many objects connected to different networks. Ensuring a smooth operation while meeting the QoS is an important issue as the IoT will have different kinds of traffic which can be throughput and delay tolerant elastic traffic or the bandwidth and delay sensitive inelastic real-time traffic. Therefore, it is required to address the challenges emanating from the network issues, RFID technology and as well as due to the use of sensor networks:

- **General Challenges:** To connect the entities in a network is primary goal of the IoT. These things are completely heterogeneous with respect to the application domains functionality. This is a big challenge as IoT requires common standard communication protocols and schemas. Addition or removal of devices must not hamper the performance of the network, functioning of the devices and the reliable and effective use of data over the network. Things/Objects and devices are build together in local ad-hoc networks, which are connected to bigger networks. This makes the topological identification difficult many times. In comparison to established network solutions, the traffic problem in the IoT will be much higher and the network development engineers must develop new high-performance algorithms to solve these types of problem. The data distribution, synchronization and caching in the network are some other challenges. Further, it needs to be ensured that the applicable data is available on any device at any time. In addition, the frequency bands and the availability of broadband is equally important to be considered for successful implementation of IoT;

- **Radio Frequency Identification (RFID):** RFID technique provides IoT the object/things identification and location without the need of storing information. RFID tags uses radio frequency waves for cooperative interactions and information exchanges between one device to another device even though they are not in the same line of sight or close physical contact. An active tag is used majorly for the monitoring applications making battery power a concern. In contrast, an inactive tag does not need a power source because there the power is consumed by the reading device. In general, the widespread use of RFID applications depend on the price incurred by the tags and the reading devices, size of the tags for convenient use on devices and their storage capacities and the price to performance ratio offered. These devices use the wireless technology of Automatic Identification and Data Capture (AIDC). Apart from addressing these challenges, it is required that for the data generated, the duplicate and erroneous readings should be removed and efficient data compression techniques should ensure saving the storage space. Further, the implicit meaning of the data should be conveyed by the RFID sensors. RFID comprises up of the following two components (Tuhin, Uday, & Sugata, 2015):

- ○ **RFID Tags (Transponders):** In a RFID tag, an antenna is embedded in a microchip. The RFID tag is a memory unit, which holds a unique identifier known as Electronic Product Code (EPC) providing a universal numerical data by which that particular tag can be uniquely and universally recognized;
- ○ **RFID Readers (Transceivers):** The RFID reader works as the identification detector of each tag cooperating and communication with the EPC of the tag which it is scanning;

- **Sensor Networks:** Sensor devices work at the core of the IoT by sensing the parameters by monitoring the environment. This information is then processed for reactive actions which might include collecting the data from a group followed by processing. Figure 8 presents a glimpse of the relationship between WSN and the IoT. These sensors are quite efficient as compared to RFID tagged devices having the capability to perform complex computations Therefore, these are more active parts of the information system of the IoT. It is required for the wireless sensor networks to have an efficient mechanism to combine the cyber infrastructure with the Service Oriented Architecture (SOA) with the resources being used by several applications. It is important to have a platform independent middleware for developing sensor applications like Open Sensor Web Architecture (OSWA). The network is expected to have the self-healing capability to heal itself in case of node failures. Wireless Sensor Network (WSN) is group of autonomous nodes whose wireless communication access by limited frequency and bandwidth. In WSN, communicating nodes consists a sensor for sensing the information, a microcontroller for processing of the data part of which can be saved in memory. The radio transceiver section is responsible for the interaction with the external world. The entire operation is powered by an in-house battery (Tuhin, Uday, & Sugata, 2015).

In WSN, for the limited communication range of each sensor node, multi-hop communication of information takes place between the source station and the base station. The wireless sensors collects important data transmitted through a collaboration of one node to other nodes and then sent to the sink node for directed routing towards the base station. As always, price is an important factor here too. But it can be addressed by efficient planning and execution of the deployment of sensors and efficient algorithms to retrieve information with minimum number of sensors used using data oriented integration. There is a relation between data storage, energy utilization, and network traffic and covers both fixed and portable sensing communications as well as continuous and random sampling. Compressive sensing can allow decreasing signal measurements without impacting the signal (Charith & Arkady, 2014; Tuhin, Uday, & Sugata, 2015).

5.8. Software Applications and Cloud Usage

The software application being an essential component of the middleware is another challenging part of IoT. It requires development of specific tools fitting the characteristics of the IoT environment. These tools, depending on the context should be able to perform different types of functions like discovery and recognition of things being compatible with various platforms. Further, it should result in a coherent system that understands how to react to specific events while collaborating.

Figure 8. Relationship between sensor networks and IoT (Charith & Arkady, 2014)

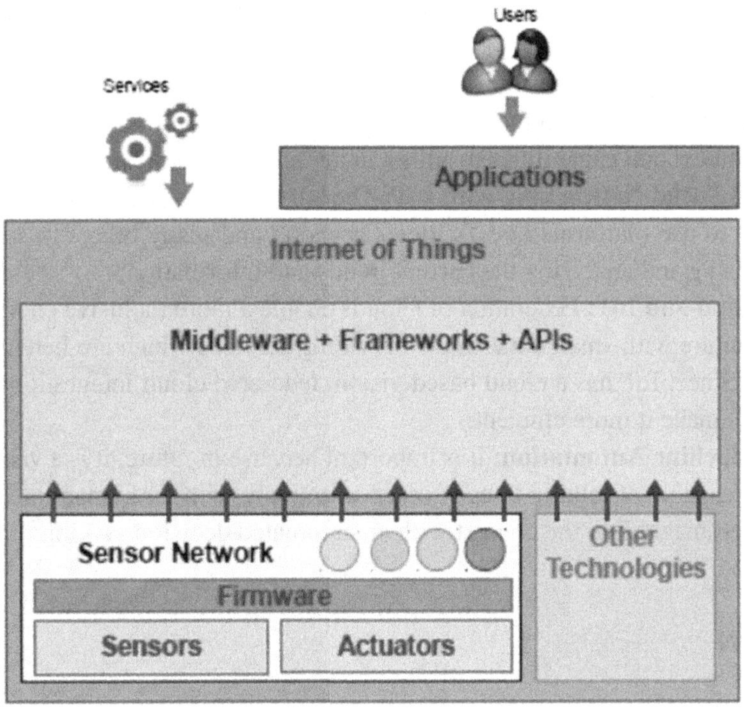

The cloud centric IoT architecture offering various services at the middleware layer has many advantages like reducing the upfront cost and lower cost of on demand services and storage but also brings into picture all the cloud computing challenges (Sajid, & Raza, 2013). Here, the compute algorithms are required to deal with meeting various QoS parameters be it response time, cost of service or maximizing resource utilization. Owing to the financial nature of use of the cloud services and penalties involved in not meeting them in terms of the Service Level Agreements (SLA) makes these issues even more serious that needs to be taken care of. In general sensor networks does not demand IoT for its existence. But for the IoT to realize life, sensor networks are a must.

6. OTHER RESEARCH DIRECTIONS IN IoT

The development of IoT infrastructure and seamlessly blending all the services we vision for our day to day life throws open a number of research directions (Xu, He & Li, 2014; Zanella, Bui, Vangelista & Zorzi, 2014; Gubbia, Buyya, Marusic & Palaniswami, 2013; Atzori, Iera, & Morabito, 2010):

- **Energy Efficient Sensing:** IoT involves a number of sensors for sensing the environment both in the form of continuous or random sensing for a Green IoT. This sensing is both from static and mobile devices. Therefore, the demand for suitable tools and techniques that reduces the transmission power comes into picture e.g. Compressive Wireless Sensing (CWS);

- **Reprogrammable Networks:** Being dynamic, IoT requires a periodic sensor application to be installed and updated. This requires a secure reprogramming tools and techniques to prevent any attack on the system;
- **Use of Context Aware AI Techniques:** This refers to the incorporation of artificial intelligence in the system for efficient decision making for configuration, protection and healing while considering both the context and capabilities resulting in an intelligent and smart IoT environment;
- **Integration of Social Networking with IoT:** The current age being the age of social networking encourages us to use platforms like Twitter, Facebook and many others to sense and develop a context by sensing and analyzing the current trends and information;
- **Federated Cloud and IoT:** Federation of Clouds enable a more inclusive environment and is going to be the future with small datacenters providing services which are better than what offered by the giants. Since, IoT has a cloud based vision, federated cloud integration and combined development will make it more efficient;
- **Machine to Machine Automation:** It is important because in future, it is a vision that the objects in IoT will be capable of talking to each other seamlessly without human intervention. This will provide a better insight into the context with an automated decision making.

7. CONCLUSION

Internet of Things (IoT) promises to change our future influencing our day to day life in an effective way. Coupled with the superior sensor technology, material cost and reliable hardware and software, IoT aims to provide a more proactive world around us for a smarter living environment. But it is a real challenge to implement such a heterogeneous, intelligent, adaptive and autonomous network of networks. With the world moving towards Cloud, IoT can be a step forward offering multitude of services in a collaborative way e.g. a computational marketplace. This work presents an insight into the various possibilities offered by IoT and important challenges to meet this vision from various perspectives. Till now, most of the IoT architecture is based on the wireless sensor networks perspective. But since the user is at the center it should permit the use of data and communications to develop new applications. The biggest challenge for the Internet of Things is its multidisciplinary nature. True realization of the Internet of Things is possible only when the concern of the multidisciplinary objects is taken care of. Different stakeholders with completely different backgrounds are needed in the development process and thus the success of the operation and hence IoT gets decided by their ability, concern and efficiency to work together. In conclusion, IoT will be a success only when it not only represents the technical evolution but brings value to our day today life.

ACKNOWLEDGMENT

The authors would like to acknowledge UPE-II, Jawaharlal Nehru University for the financial support provided in carrying out this work.

REFERENCES

Abu-Elkheir, M., Hayajneh, M., & Ali, N. A. (2013). Data Management for the Internet of Things: Design Primitives and Solution. *Sensors (Basel)*, *13*(11), 15582–15612. doi:10.3390/s131115582 PMID:24240599

Aggarwal, C.C., Ashish, N., & Sheth, A. (2013). The Internet of Things: A Survey from the Data-Centric Perspective. New York: Springer Science+Business Media.

Akyildiz, I., Su, W., Sankarasubramaniam, Y., & Cayirci, E. (2002, August). A survey on sensor networks. *Communications Magazine*, *40*(8), 102-114. doi:10.1109/MCOM.2002.1024422

Al-Fuqaha, A., Guizani, M., Mohammadi, M., Aledhari, M., & Ayyash, M. (2015). Internet of Things-A Survey on Enabling Technologies, Protocols and Applications. *IEEE Communications Surveys and Tutorials*, *17*(4), 2347–2376.

Andrea, Z., Nicola, B., Lorenzo, V., & Michele, Z. (2014, February). Internet of Things for Smart Cities. *IEEE Internet of Things Journal*, *1*(1), 22–32. doi:10.1109/JIOT.2014.2306328

Atzori, L., Iera, A., & Morabito, G. (2010, October). The Internet of Things: A survey. *The International Journal of Computer and Telecommunications Networking*, *54*(15), 2787–2805.

Bin, G., Zhang, D., & Zhu, W. (2011). Living with Internet of Things: The Emergence of Embedded Intelligence. In *Proceedings of the Fourth International Conference on Cyber, Physical and Social Computing (CPSCom)*, Dalian, China, October 19-22 (pp. 297 – 304).

Bonomi, F., Milito, R., Zhu, J., & Addepalli, S. (2012). Fog computing and its role in the internet of things. In *Proceedings of the First Edition of the MCC Workshop on Mobile Cloud Computing* (pp. 13-16). doi:10.1145/2342509.2342513

Borthakur, D., Gray, J., Sarma, J. S., Muthukkaruppan, K., Spiegelberg, N., Kuang, H., & Rash, S. et al. (2011). Apache hadoop goes realtime at Facebook. In *Proceedings of the 2011 ACM SIGMOD International Conference on Management of Data* (pp. 1071-1080). doi:10.1145/1989323.1989438

Bryant, R. Katz R. H. & Lazowska, E. D. (2008). Big-data computing: creating revolutionary breakthroughs in commerce, science and society.

Charith, P., & Arkady, Z. (2014). Context Aware Computing for The Internet of Things: A Survey. *IEEE Communications Surveys and Tutorials*, *16*(1), 414–454.

Cubo, J., Nieto, A., & Pimente, E. (2014). A Cloud-Based Internet of Things Platform for Ambient Assisted Living. *Sensors (Basel)*, *14*(8), 14070–14105. doi:10.3390/s140814070 PMID:25093343

Da Li, X., Wu, H., & Li, S. (2014, November). Internet of Things in Industries: A Survey. *IEEE Transactions on Industrial Informatics*, *10*(4), 2233–2240. doi:10.1109/TII.2014.2300753

Demirkol, I., Alagoz, F., Deliç, H., & Ersoy, C. (2006). Wireless Sensor Networks For Intrusion Detection: Packet Traffic Modeling. *IEEE Communications Letters*, *10*(1), 22–24. doi:10.1109/LCOMM.2006.1576557

Dennis, M., & Huchzer, M. P. D. (2010). Key Problems and Instantiations of the Internet of Things (IoT). In Proceedings of the TKK T-110.5190 Seminar on Internetworking.

Ding, G., Wang, L., & Wu, Q. (2013). Big Data Analytics in Future Internet of Things. Cornell University Library. arXiv:1311.4112

Doukas, C. (2012). *Building Internet of Things with the ARDUINO*. CreateSpace Independent Publishing Platform.

Elnahrawy, E., & Nath, B. (2004). Context-aware sensors. In H. Karl, A. Wolisz, & A. Willig (Eds.), Wireless Sensor Networks, LNCS (Vol. 2920, pp. 77–93). Springer. 6 doi:10.1007/978-3-540-24606-0_6

European Commission. (2008). Internet of things in 2020 road map for the future (Working Group RFID of the ETP EPOSS, Tech. Rep.). Retrieved 2011-06-12 from http://ec.europa.eu/information_society/policy/rfid/ documents/iotprague2009.pdf

Evans, D. (2011). *The Internet of Things: How the Next Evolution of the Internet Is Changing Everything*. Cisco Internet Business Solutions Group.

Fielding, R. T. (2000). Architectural Styles and The Design of Network-Based Software Architectures (The Representational State Transfer (REST)) [Ph.D. dissertation]. Univ. California, Irvine.

Firner, B., Moore, R. S., Howard, R., Martin, R. P., & Zhang, Y. (2011). *Poster: Smart buildings, sensor networks, and the internet of things. In Proceedings of the 9th ACM Conference on Embedded Networked Sensor Systems, ser. SenSys '11* (pp. 337–338). New York, NY: ACM. doi:10.1145/2070942.2070978

Gershenfeld, N., Krikorian, R., & Cohen, D. (2004). The internet of Things. *Scientific American*, *291*(4), 76–81. doi:10.1038/scientificamerican1004-76 PMID:15487673

Gluhak, A., & Schott, W. (2007). A wsn system architecture to capture context information for beyond 3g communication systems. In *Proceedings of the 3rd International Conference on Intelligent Sensors, Sensor Networks and Information ISSNIP '07* (pp. 49 –54). doi:10.1109/ISSNIP.2007.4496818

Guillemin, P., & Friess, P. (2009). Internet of Things- Strategic Research Roadmap.

Uckelmann, D., Harrison, M., & Michahelles, F. (2011). Harrison Mark, Michahelles Florian, Architecting the Internet of Things. London: Springer.

Heba, A., Elmogy, M., & Barakat, S. (2015). Big Data on Internet of Things: Applications, Architecture, Technologies, Techniques, and Future Directions. *International Journal on Computer Science and Engineering*, *4*(6), 300–313.

Hwang, K., Dongarra, J., & Fox, G. (2012). Distributed and Cloud Computing: From Parallel Processing to the Internet of Things. Singapore: Elsevier.

Vermesan, O., Friess, P., & Friess, P. (2011). Internet of Things- Global Technological and Societal Trends. River Publishers.

Gubbi, J., Buyya, R., Marusic, S., & Palaniswami, M. (2013). Internet of Things (IoT): A vision, architectural elements, and future directions. *Future Generation Computer Systems*, *29*(7), 1645–1660. doi:10.1016/j.future.2013.01.010

Karimi, K., & Akinson, G. (2012). What the Internet of Things (IoT) Needs to Become a Reality. Retrieved from http://www.eetimes.com/document.asp?doc_id=1280077

Katasonov, A., Kaykova, O., Khriyenko, O., Nikitin, S., & Terziyan, V. (2008). Smart Semantic Middleware for the Internet of Things. In *Proceedings of the Fifth International Conference on Informatics in Control, Automation and Robotics*, Funchal, Madeira, Portugal.

Kushalnagar, N., Montenegro, G., & Schumacher, C. (2007). *IPv6 Over Low- Power Wireless Personal Area Networks (6LoWPANs)*. Overview, Assumptions, Problem Statement, and Goals.

Liu, Y., Dong, B., Guo, B., Yang, J., & Peng, W. (2015). Combination of Cloud Computing and Internet of Things (IOT) in Medical Monitoring Systems. *International Journal of Hybrid Information Technology*, *8*(12), 367–376. doi:10.14257/ijhit.2015.8.12.28

Lu, T., & Neng, W. (2010). Future internet: The internet of things. In *Proceedings of the 3rd International Conference on Advanced Computer Theory and Engineering (ICACTE) (Vol. 5*, pp. 376-380). doi:10.1109/ICACTE.2010.5579543

Mukherjee, A., Paul, H. S., Dey, S., & Banerjee, A. (2014). ANGELS for distributed analytics in IoT. In *Proceedings of the 2014 IEEE World Forum on Internet of Things (WF-IoT)* (pp. 565-570).

Nimbits. (n.d.). Retrieved from http://www.nimbits.com/

Payam, B., Wei, W., Cory, H., & Taylor, K. (2012, January). Semantics for the Internet of Things: Early Progress and Back to the Future. *International Journal on Semantic Web and Information Systems*, *8*(1), 1–22. doi:10.4018/jswis.2012010101

Rao, B., Saluia, P., Sharma, N., Mittal, A., & Sharma, S. (2012). Cloud computing for internet of things & sensing based applications. In *Proceedings of the 2012 Sixth International Conference on Sensing Technology (ICST)* (pp. 374-380). doi:10.1109/ICSensT.2012.6461705

Sajid, M., & Raza, Z. (2013). Cloud Computing: Issues & Challenges. In *Proceedings of the International Conference on Cloud, Big Data and Trust (ICCBDT - 2013)*, Rajiv Gandhi Proudyogiki Vishwavidyala, Bhopal, India, November 13-15 (pp. 35-41). Retrieved from http://www.google.co.in/imgres?imgurl=x-raw-image:///002a2a06cab12c973082238b10fcf34f439cdd3ac4703969603a0b55081ca7fa&imgrefurl=https://ingenierie.openwide.fr/content/download/1511/17408/file/FC.pdf&h=393&w=540&tbnid=lyyxygYqKgALzM:&docid=dE_SDhVnIzKRFM&hl=en-IN&ei=SwEBVsG5NsSx0ATuqIngBg&tbm=isch&ved=0CB0QMygBMAFqFQoTCIGLobCNisgCFcQYlAodblQCbA

Simon, M., Dominique, G., & Vlad, T. (2012). Searching in a Web-based Infrastructure for Smart Things. In *Proceedings of the Third IEEE International Conference on the Internet of Things*, Wuxi, China, October 24-26 (pp. 119-126).

Simon, M., & Karam, D. S. (2012). A Computational Space for the Web of Things. In *Proceedings of the Third International Workshop on the Web of Things*, New Castle, UK, June 18-22.

Sundmaeker, H., Guillemin, P., Friess, P., & Woelfflé, S. (2010). Vision and Challenges for Realising the Internet of Things. *Cluster of European Research Projects on the Internet of Things*, *3*(3), 34–36.

Tedjini, S., Perret, E., Deepu, V., & Bernier, M. (2009). Chipless Tags, the Next RFID Frontier. In *Proceedings of TIWDC 2009*, Pula, Italy.

Tsai, C., Lai, C., Chiang, M., & Yang, L. T. (2014). Data Mining for Internet of Things: A Survey. *IEEE Communications Surveys and Tutorials*, *16*(1), 77–97. doi:10.1109/SURV.2013.103013.00206

Tuhin, B., Uday, K., & Sugata, S. (2015). Survey of Security and Privacy Issues of Internet of Things. *Int. J. Advanced Networking and Applications*, *6*, 2372–2378.

Uckelmann, D., Harrison, M., & Michahelles, F. (2011). *An Architectural Approach Towards the Future Internet of Things*. Springer-Verlag. doi: Retrieved from https://www.google.co.in/search?q=12+The+Internet+of+Things+(IOT)&oq=12+The+Internet+of+Things+(IOT)&aqs=chrome.69i57.1241j0j7&sourceid=chrome&es_sm=93&ie=UTF-810.1007/978-3-642-19157-2_1

Verma, D. C., & Verma, P. (2014). Techniques for surviving mobile data explosion. John Wiley & Sons, . doi:10.1002/9781118834404

Vermesen, O., & Friess, P. (2014). *Internet of Things: From Research and Innovation to Market Deployment*. River Publishers.

Wikipedia. (n.d.). IPv6. Retrieved from https://en.wikipedia.org/wiki/IPv6

Xu, X., Huang, S., Chen, Y., Browny, K., Halilovicy, I., & Lu, W. (2014). TSAaaS: Time series analytics as a service on IoT. In *Proceedings of the 2014 IEEE International Conference on Web Services (ICWS)* (pp. 249-256). doi:10.1109/ICWS.2014.45

Yang, K., Alkadi, G., Gautam, B., Sharma, A., Amatya, D., Charchut, S., & Jones, M. (2013). Park-A-Lot: An Automated Parking Management System. *Computer Science and Information Technology*, *1*, 276–279.

This research was previously published in the International Journal of Systems and Service-Oriented Engineering (IJSSOE), 7(3); edited by Dickson K.W. Chiu, pages 32-52, copyright year 2017 by IGI Publishing (an imprint of IGI Global).

Chapter 2
A Scalable Big Stream Cloud Architecture for the Internet of Things

Laura Belli
University of Parma, Italy

Gianluigi Ferrari
University of Parma, Italy

Simone Cirani
University of Parma, Italy

Lorenzo Melegari
University of Parma, Italy

Luca Davoli
University of Parma, Italy

Màrius Montón
WorldSensing, Spain

Marco Picone
University of Parma, Italy

ABSTRACT

The Internet of Things (IoT) will consist of billions (50 billions by 2020) of interconnected heterogeneous devices denoted as "Smart Objects:" tiny, constrained devices which are going to be pervasively deployed in several contexts. To meet low-latency requirements, IoT applications must rely on specific architectures designed to handle the gigantic stream of data coming from Smart Objects. This paper propose a novel Cloud architecture for Big Stream applications that can efficiently handle data coming from Smart Objects through a Graph-based processing platform and deliver processed data to consumer applications with low latency. The authors reverse the traditional "Big Data" paradigm, where real-time constraints are not considered, and introduce the new "Big Stream" paradigm, which better fits IoT scenarios. The paper provides a performance evaluation of a practical open-source implementation of the proposed architecture. Other practical aspects, such as security considerations, and possible business oriented exploitation plans are presented.

DOI: 10.4018/978-1-5225-5649-7.ch002

INTRODUCTION

The actors involved in IoT scenarios have extremely heterogeneous characteristics (in terms of processing and communication capabilities, energy supply and consumption, availability, and mobility), spanning from constrained devices, also denoted as "Smart Objects (SOs)," to smartphones and other personal devices, Internet hosts, and the Cloud. Smart Objects are typically equipped with sensors and/or actuators and are thus capable to perceive and act on the environment where they are deployed. By 2020, 50 billions of Smart Objects are expected to be deployed in urban, home, industrial, and rural scenarios (Evans, 2011), in order to collect relevant information, which may be used to build new useful applications.

Shared and interoperable communication mechanisms and protocols are currently being defined and standardized, allowing heterogeneous nodes to efficiently communicate with each other and with existing common Internet-based hosts or general-purpose Internet-ready devices. The most prominent driver for interoperability in the IoT is the adoption of the Internet Protocol (IP), namely IPv6 (Postel, 1981; Deering & Hinden, 1998). An IP-based IoT will be able to extend and interoperate seamlessly with the existing Internet.

In a typical IoT scenario, sensed data are collected by SOs, deployed in and populating the IoT network, and sent uplink to collection entities (servers or the Cloud). In some cases, an intermediate element may support the Cloud, carrying out storage, communication, or computation operations in local networks (e.g., data aggregation or protocol translation). This approach is the basis of the Fog Computing (Bonomi, Milito, Zhu, & Addepalli, 2012) and will be better explained in the "Background" section.

Figure 1 shows the hierarchical structure of layers involved in data collection, processing, and distribution in IoT scenarios.

Figure 1. The hierarchy of layers involved in IoT scenarios: the Fog works as an extension of the Cloud to the network edge to support data collection, processing, and distribution

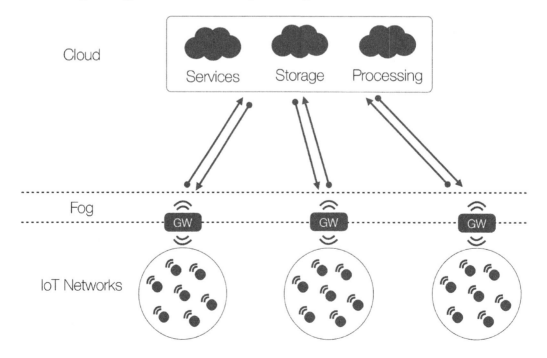

With billions of nodes capable of gathering data and generating information, the availability of efficient and scalable mechanisms for collecting, processing, and storing data is crucial.

Big Data techniques, which were developed in the last few years and became popular due to the evolution of online and social/crowd services, address the need to process extremely large amounts of heterogeneous data for multiple purposes. These techniques have been designed mainly to deal with huge volumes of information (focusing on storage, aggregation, analysis, and provisioning of data), rather than to provide real-time processing and dispatching (Zaslavsky, Perera, & Georgakopoulos, 2013; Leavitt, 2013). Cloud Computing has found a direct application with Big Data analysis due to its scalability, robustness, and cost-effectiveness.

One of the distinctive features of IoT systems is the deployment of a huge amount of heterogeneous data sources collecting data from the environment and sending information through the internet to collectors. The work of all data sources generate, as a whole, streams with a very high frequency. Moreover, several relevant IoT scenarios (such as industrial automation, transportation, networks of sensors and actuators) need real-time or predictable latency.

The number of data sources, on one side, and the subsequent frequency of incoming data, on the other side, create a new need for Cloud architectures to handle such massive information flows.

Big Data approaches typically have an intrinsic inertia because they are based on batch processing. For this reason, they are not suitable to the dynamicity of IoT scenarios with real-time requirements.

To better fit these requirements, the Big Data paradigm is shifted to a new paradigm, which has been denoted as "Big Stream" (Belli, Cirani, Ferrari, Melegari, & Picone, 2014). Big Stream-oriented systems should react effectively to changes and provide smart behavior for allocating resources, thus implementing scalable and cost-effective Cloud services. The Big Stream paradigm is specifically designed to perform real-time and ad-hoc processing in order to link incoming streams of data to consumers. This new paradigm should: have a high degree of scalability and fine-grained/dynamic configurability; and efficiently manage heterogeneous data formats which are not a priori known.

The main differences between Big Data and Big Stream paradigms can be summarized as follows.

- The nature of data sources: Big Stream refers to scenarios with a huge number of data sources sending small amounts of information.
- The real-time or low-latency requirements of consumers: information in Big Stream IoT scenarios is usually short-lived and should be provided to consumers before it becomes outdated (and useless).
- The meaning of the adjective "Big:" for Big Data, it refers to the data volume, whereas for Big Stream it refers to the global aggregate information generation rate of data sources. Moreover, this has an impact on the data that are considered relevant to consumer applications. While for Big Data applications it is important to keep all sensed data, in order to be able to perform any required computation, Big Stream applications might decide to perform local data aggregation/ pruning, in order to minimize the latency in conveying the final processing results to consumers, without persistence needs.

In conclusion, although both Big Data and Big Stream deal with massive amounts of data, they have different purposes (as shown in Figure 2): the former focuses on storage, analysis and interpretation of data, while the latter focuses on data flow management in order to provide informations to interested customers with minimum latency.

From a more general perspective, Big Data applications might be consumers of Big Stream data flows.

For the above observations, the objective of this paper is to propose an architecture targeting Cloud-based applications with real-time constraints, i.e., Big Stream applications, for IoT scenarios. The proposed architecture relies on the concepts of a data listener and data-oriented processing graph in order to implement a scalable, highly configurable, and dynamic chain of computations on incoming Big Streams and to dispatch data with a push-based approach, thus providing the lowest delay between the generation of information and its consumption.

BACKGROUND

The IoT paradigm refers to a huge number of different and heterogeneous SOs connected in a worldwide "Network of Networks." These nodes are envisioned as collectors of information from the environment in order to provide useful services to users. This ubiquitous sensing, enabled by the IoT in most areas of modern living, has led to information and communication systems invisibly embedded in the environment, thus making the technology disappear from the consciousness of the users. The outcome of this trend is the generation of a huge amount of data that, depending on the specific application scenario, should be processed, aggregated, stored, transformed, and delivered to the final users of the system, in an efficient and effective way, with traditional commodity services.

In the next sections, related works regarding Cloud, Big Data, IoT architectures and models are first presented; then, some suitable open-source technologies and protocols are listed.

IoT Architectures

A large number of architectures for IoT scenarios have been proposed in the literature. For instance, most of the ongoing projects on IoT architectures address relevant challenges, particularly from a Wireless Sensor Networks (WSN) perspective. Some examples are given by a few European Union projects, such as SENSEI project (European Community's 7th Framework Programme, 2008-2010) and Internet of Things-Architecture (IoT-A) project (European Community's 7th Framework Programme, 2012-2015).

Figure 2. (a) Data sources in Big Data systems. (b) The multiple data sources and listeners management in Big Stream system

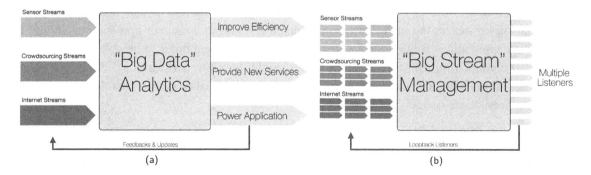

The purpose of the SENSEI project is to create an open and business-driven architecture that addresses the scalability problems for a large number of globally distributed Wireless Sensor and Actuator (WS&A) network devices, enabling interactions with physical environment.

The IoT-A project consortium has focused on the definition of an initial set of key building blocks, aiming at creating open interoperable platforms, connecting vertically closed architectures.

"Connect All IP-based Smart Objects!" (CALIPSO) (European Community's 7th Framework Programme, 2011-2014) is another European project whose main purpose is to build IoT systems with IPv6-connected and low-power consumption SOs, thus providing both high interoperability and long lifetime, entailing three communication protocol stack layers (network, routing, and application).

In (Gubbi, Buyya, Marusic, & Palaniswami, 2013) is proposed an IoT architecture which is not based on WSNs and is focused instead on the user and the Cloud. The consumer is the "center" and drives the use of data and infrastructure to develop new applications. The rest of the work discusses the key enabling technologies and the different future applications domains, describes a Cloud-centric architecture for IoT, and presents a real implementation.

Another Cloud-based IoT architecture is proposed in the FI-WARE project (European Community's 7th Framework Programme, 2011), an open infrastructure with public, royalty-free, and OCCI-compliant API, providing to developers a platform to build innovative products.

As previously stated, the most prominent driver to provide interoperability in the IoT, referring to IP stack, is IPv6. At the application layer, the IoT scenario brings a variety of possible protocols that can be employed according to the specific applications requirements. Relevant options are: (i) HyperText Transfer Protocol (HTTP) (R. Fielding et al., 1999); (ii) Constrained Application Protocol (CoAP) (Shelby, Hartke, Bormann, & Frank, 2014); (iii) Extensible Messaging and Presence Protocol (XMPP) (Saint-Andre, 2004); (iv) MQ Telemetry Transport (MQTT) protocol (Locke, 2010); (v) Constrained Session Initiation Protocol (CoSIP) (Cirani, Picone, & Veltri, 2013, 2014; Cirani, Davoli, Picone, & Veltri, 2014).

Regardless of the selected application-layer protocol, most IoT/M2M applications follow the REpresentational State Transfer Protocol (REST) architectural model presented in (R. T. Fielding, 2000), as this provides simple and uniform interfaces and is designed to build long-lasting, robust, and resilient to changes applications.

Big Data Processing Pattern

From a business perspective, managing and gaining insights from data is a challenge and a key to competitive advantage. Analytical solutions that mine structured and unstructured data are important, as they can help companies to gain cross-related information not only from their privately acquired data, but also from large amounts of data publicly available on the Web, social networks, and Blogs. Big Data opens a wide range of possibilities for organizations to understand the needs of their customers, predict their demands, and optimize the use of evaluable resources.

The work of (McAfee & Brynjolfsson, 2012) illustrates that the Big Data notion is different and more powerful with respect to traditional analytics tools used by companies. As analytics tools, Big Data can find patterns and glean intelligence from data translating that into business advantage. However, Big Data is powered by what is often referred as a multi V model, in which V stands for:

- **Variety:** To represent the data types;
- **Velocity:** To represent the rate at which the data is produced and processed and stored according with further analysis;
- **Volume:** To define the amount of data;
- **Veracity:** Refers to how much the data can be trusted given the reliability of its sources.

Big Data architectures generally use traditional processing patterns with a pipeline approach (Hohpe & Woolf, 2003). These architectures are typically based on a processing perspective where the data flow goes downstream from input to output, to perform specific tasks or reach the target goal.

Typically, the information follows a pipeline where data are sequentially handled with tightly coupled pre-defined processing sub-units (static data routing). The described paradigm can be defined as "process-oriented:" a central coordination point manages the execution of subunits in a certain order and each sub-unit provides a specific processing output, which is created to be used only within the scope of its own process without the possibility to be shared among different processes. This approach represents a major deviation from traditional Service Oriented Architectures (SOAs), where the sub-units are external web services invoked by a coordinator process rather than internal services (Isaacson, 2009). Big Data applications generally interact with Cloud Computing architectures which can handle resources and provide services to consumers.

In (Assunção, Calheiros, Bianchi, Netto, & Buyya, 2014), the authors presents a survey on approaches, environments, and technologies on key-areas for Big Data analytics capabilities, investigating how they can contribute to build analytics solutions for Clouds. A set of gaps and recommendations, for the research community, on future directions on Cloud-supported Big Data computing are also described.

Fog Computing

In the area of user-driven and Cloud IoT architectures, (Bonomi, Milito, Zhu, & Addepalli, 2012) propose Fog Computing as a novel and appropriate paradigm for a variety of IoT services and applications that require mobility support, low latency, and location awareness.

The Fog can be described as a highly virtualized platform that provides computing, storage, and networking services between end-devices and the Cloud. In other words, the Fog is meant to act as an extension of the Cloud, operating at the edge of the network to support endpoints by providing rich services that can fulfill real-time and low-latency consumer's requirements. The Fog paradigm has specific characteristics, which can be summarized as follows:

- Geographical distribution, in contrast with the centralization envisioned by the Cloud;
- Subscriber model employed by the players in the Fog;
- Support for mobility.

The architecture described by (Bonomi, Milito, Zhu, & Addepalli, 2012) is based on the Fog and Cloud interplay: the former provides localization, low latency, and context awareness to endpoints; the latter provides global centralization functionalities. In the presented IoT Fog scenario, collectors at the edge of the network manage the data generated by sensors and devices: the portion of these data that require real-time processing (from milliseconds to tenths of seconds) are consumed locally by the first tier of the Fog. The rest is sent to the higher tiers for operations with less stringent time constraints (from seconds to minutes). The higher is the tier, the wider is the geographical coverage and the longer the time scale. As a result, the Fog must support several types of storage: from ephemeral, at the lowest tier, to semi-permanent, at the highest tier. The ultimate and global coverage is provided by the Cloud, which is used as repository for data with a potential duration of months or years.

Stream and Real-Time Management

The architecture proposed in the current paper is specifically designed for scenarios with low latency and real-time requirements. Other projects related to real-time and stream management are Apache Storm (Apache, n.d-a.) and Apache S4 (Neumeyer, Robbins, Nair, & Kesari, 2010).

Storm is a free and open source distributed real-time computation system to reliably process unbounded streams of data. The system can be integrated with different queueing and database technologies and provides mechanisms to define topologies in which nodes consume data streams and process them in arbitrarily complex ways. S4 is a general purpose, near real-time, distributed, decentralized, scalable, event-driven, and modular platform that allows programmers to implement applications for processing streams of data. Multiple application nodes can be deployed and interconnected on S4 clusters to create more sophisticated systems.

Although there are several similarities between these systems and the architecture proposed here, such as modularity, scalability, latency minimization and the graph topology, there are some notable differences. The most relevant use cases for Storm and S4 are stream processing and continuous computations on data stored in databases (e.g., message processing for database update). The proposed architecture, on the other hand, is specifically designed to work in dynamic IoT scenarios comprising heterogeneous data sources and making no assumption on the repositories (if needed) where data can be retrieved or stored.

Another major difference is related to the nature of the topology of the processing units. While Storm stream management is based on an operator-defined and static graph topology, the architecture proposed in the remainder of this paper is extremely dynamic, as the number of nodes and edges in the Graph Framework can change according to the workload and listener's requirements.

The works described in (Marganiec et al., 2014; Tilly & Reiff-Marganiec, 2011) address the problem to process, procure, and provide information related to the IoT scenario with almost zero latency. The authors consider, as a motivating example, a taxi fleet management system, which has to identify the most relevant taxi in terms of availability and proximity to the customer's location. The core of the publish/subscribe architecture proposed in (Marganiec et al., 2014) is the Mediator, which encapsulates the processing of the incoming requests from the consumer side and the incoming events from the services side. Services are publishers (taxis in the proposed example) which are responsible to inform the Mediator if there is some change in the provided service (e.g., the taxi location or the number of current passengers). Thus, instead of pulling data at consumer's request time, the Mediator knows at any time the status of all services, being able to join user requests with the event stream coming from the taxis, using temporal join-statements expressed through SQL-like expressions.

Cloud Computing

Cloud Computing represents the increasing trend moving to the external deployment of Information Technology (IT) resources, obtaining them as services (Stanoevska-Slabeva, Wozniak, & Ristol, 2009). Cloud Computing enables convenient and on-demand network access to a shared pool of configurable computing resources (e.g., networks, servers, storage elements, applications, and services) that could be rapidly provisioned and released with minimal management effort or service provider interaction (Mell & Grance, 2011).

At hardware level, a number of physical devices, including processors, hard drives, and network devices, fulfill processing and storage needs. Above this, the combination of (i) software layer, (ii) virtualization layer, and (iii) management layer, allows effective management of servers. In Cloud Computing, available service models are the following.

- **Infrastructure as a Service (IaaS):** Provides processing, storage, networks, and other computing resources, allowing the consumer to deploy and run arbitrary software, including OSs and applications. The consumer has control over OSs, storage, deployed applications and, possibly, limited control of select networking components.
- **Platform as a Service (PaaS):** Provides the capability to deploy infrastructure, consumer-created, or acquired applications. The consumer has no control on the underlying infrastructure (e.g., network, servers, OSs, or storage) but only manages deployed applications.
- **Software as a Service (SaaS):** Provides the capability to use the provider's applications, running on the Cloud infrastructure, by accessing from various client devices through proper client interfaces. The consumer does not manage or control the underlying Cloud infrastructure or individual application capabilities, with the possible exception of limited user-specific application configuration settings.

Cloud Computing is generally complementary to the IoT scenario, as it acts (i) as collector of real-time sensed data and (ii) as provider of services built on the basis of collected informations. The main need is to be extremely scalable, allowing the support to large-scale IoT applications.

There are several open source frameworks and technologies which can be used for Cloud IoT systems, such as OpenStack (Rackspace, NASA, n.d.) and OpenNebula (Milojičić, Llorente, & Montero, 2011). The former is an open Cloud OS that controls large pools of computing, storage, and networking resources, while OpenStack can be seen as a framework with a vendor-driven model, the second is an open-source project aiming at delivering a simple, feature-rich, and flexible solution to build and manage enterprise Clouds and virtualized data centers.

ARCHITECTURE

As previously stated, a major difference between Big Data and Big Stream resides in the real-time and low-latency requirements of consumers. The gigantic amount of data sources in IoT applications has mistakenly made Cloud services implementers believe that re-using Big Data-driven architectures would be the right solution for all applications, rather than designing specific paradigms for those scenarios.

IoT application scenarios are characterized by a huge number of data sources, sending small amounts of information to a collector service, typically at a limited data rate. Many services can be built on top of these data, such as environmental monitoring, building automation, and smart cities applications. These applications are typically characterized by low-latency or real-time requirements, in order to provide efficient reactive/proactive behaviors.

Big Stream Oriented Architecture

Applying a traditional Big Data approach for IoT application scenarios might lead to high - even unpredictable - latencies between data generation and its availability to a consumer, since this was not among the main objectives behind the design of Big Data systems.

Figure 3 illustrates the main delay contributions introduced when data, generated by SOs in IoT networks, need to be processed, stored, and then polled by consumers. Clients interested in processed data are extremely heterogeneous, spanning from mobile or desktop applications to Data Warehouse (DW) applications and till other IoT Smart Objects networks.

The total delay required by any data to be delivered to a consumer can be expressed as:

$$T = t_0 + t_1 + t_2$$

where:

- t_0 is the time elapsed from the moment a data source sends information, through an available API, to the Cloud service (1), which dispatches the data to an appropriate queue, where it can wait for an unpredictable time (2), in order to decouple data acquisition from processing;
- t_1 is the time needed for data, extracted by the queue, to be pre-processed and stored into a DW (3): this time contribution depends on the number of concurrent processes that need to be executed and get access the common DW and the current size of the DW;
- t_2 is the data consumption time, which depends on: (i) the remaining time that a polling consumer needs to wait before performing the next fetch (4); (ii) the time for a request to be sent to the Cloud service (5); (iii) the time required for lookup in the DW and post-process the fetched data (6); and (iv) the time for the response to be delivered back to the consumer (7).

Figure 3. Delay contributions in a traditional Big Data architecture for IoT, from data generation to applications information delivery

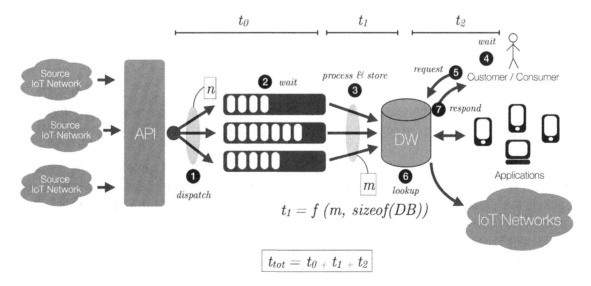

It can be observed that the architecture described is not optimized to minimize the latency and, therefore, to feed (possibly a large number of) real-time applications but, rather, to perform data collection and batch processing. Moreover, it is important to underline and understand that significant data for Big Stream applications might be short-lived, since they are to be consumed immediately, while Big Data applications tend to collect and store massive amounts of data for an unpredictable time.

The main design criteria of the architecture proposed in this paper are:

- The minimization of the latency in data dispatching to consumers;
- The optimization of resource allocation.

The main novelty in the presented architecture lies in the concepts of "consumer-oriented" data flows and "listeners." The former denotes a different approach in retrieving incoming data, rather than being based on the knowledge of collection points (repositories) to which request data. The latter relies on final consumers: data generated by a deployed Smart Object, might be of interest for some consumer application, denoted as listener, which can register itself in order to receive updates (either in the form of raw or processed data) coming from a particular streaming endpoint (i.e., Cloud service). On the basis of application-specific needs, each listener defines a set of rules, which specify what type of data should be selected and the associated filtering operations. For instance, referring to a smart parking scenario, a mobile application might be interested in receiving contents related only to specific events that occur within a given geographical area, in order to accomplish relevant tasks. Specifically, the application can listen for parking sensor status updates, the positions of other cars, or weather conditions, in order to find available parking spots.

The proposed Big Stream architecture guarantees that, as soon as they are available, data will be dispatched to the listener, which is thus no longer responsible to poll data, thus minimizing latencies and possibly avoiding network traffic.

The information flow in a listener-based Cloud architecture is shown in Figure 4.

With the Big Stream paradigm, the total time required by any data to be delivered to a consumer can be expressed as:

$$T = t_0 + t_1$$

where:

- t_0 is the same time delay contribution defined for Figure 3;
- t_1 is the time needed to process data extracted from the queue and be processed (according to the needs of the listener, e.g., to perform format translation) and then deliver it to registered listeners.

It is clear that the perspective inversion introduced by a listener-oriented communication is optimal in terms of minimization of the time that a listener must wait before it receives data of interest. In order to highlight the benefits brought by the Big Stream approach, with respect to Big Data, an alerting application (where an event should be notified to one or more consumers in the shortest possible time) can be considered. The traditional Big Data approach would require an unnecessary pre-processing/storage/post-processing cycle to be executed before the event can be made available to consumers, which would

Figure 4. The delay contributions from data generation to consumers information delivery following the listener-based Big Stream approach

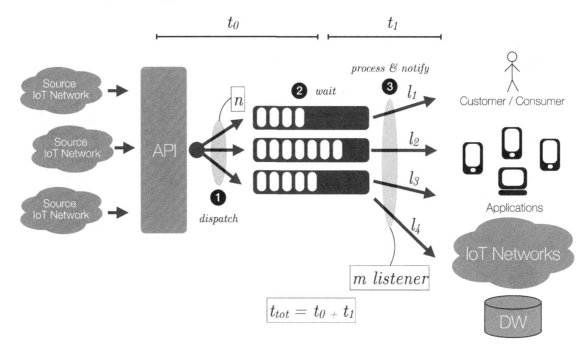

be responsible to retrieve data by polling. The listener-oriented approach, instead, guarantees that only the needed processing will be performed before data are being delivered directly to the listener, thus providing an effective real-time solution.

This general discussion proves that a consumer-oriented paradigm may be better suited to real-time Big Stream applications, rather than simply reusing existing Big Data architectures, which better fit applications that do not have critical real-time requirements.

Graph-Based Processing

In order to overcome the limitations of the "process-oriented" approach described in the previous section and fit with the proposed Big Stream paradigm, the proposed Cloud architecture is based on a Graph Framework. More precisely, we consider a graph composed by basic building blocks that are self-consistent and perform "atomic" processing on data, but that are not directly linked to a specific task. In such a system, the data flows are based on dynamic graph-routing rules determined only by the nature of the data itself and not by a centralized coordination unit. This new approach allows the platform to be "consumer-oriented" and to implement optimal resource allocation. Without the need of a coordination process, the data streams can be dynamically routed in the network by following the edges of the graph and allowing the possibility to automatically switch-off nodes (if some processing units are not required at a certain point) and transparently replicate nodes (if some processing entities are consumed by a significant amount of concurrent consumers).

Figure 5 illustrates the proposed directed Graph-based processing architecture and the concept of listener. A listener is an entity (e.g., a processing unit in the graph or an external consumer) interested in

Figure 5. The proposed listener-based Graph architecture: the nodes of the graph are listeners; the edges refer to the dynamic flow of information data streams

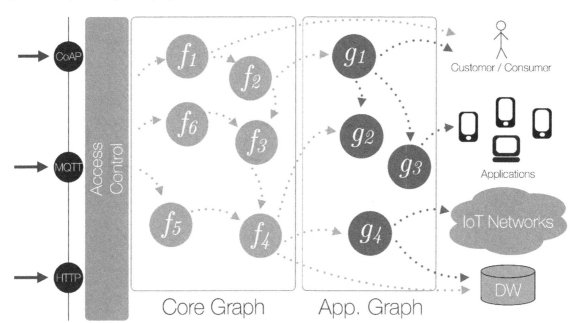

the raw data stream or in the output provided by a different node in the graph. Each listener represents a node in the topology and the presence and combination of multiple listeners, across all processing units, defines the routing of data streams from producers to consumers. More in detail, in this architectural approach:

- Nodes are processing units (processes), performing some kind of computation on incoming data;
- Edges represent flows of information linking together various processing unit, which are thus able to implement some complex behavior as a whole;
- Nodes of the graph are listeners for incoming data or outputs of other nodes of the graph.

The designed Graph-based approach allows to optimize resource allocation in terms of efficiency, by switching off processing units that have no listeners registered to them (enabling cost-effectiveness and scalability) and by replicating those processing units which have a large number of registered listeners. The combination of these two functionalities and the concept of listener allow the platform and the overall system to adapt itself to dynamic and heterogeneous scenarios, by properly routing data streams to the consumers, and to add new processing units and functionalities on demand.

In order to provide a set of commonly available functionalities, while allowing to dynamically extend the capabilities of the system, the graph is composed by concentric layers. Each layer contains two types of nodes, as shown in Figure 6 (a):

- **Core Graph Nodes:** Listeners which perform basic processing operations provided by the architecture (e.g., format translation, normalization, aggregation, data correlation, and other transformations);
- **Application Graph Nodes:** Listeners that require data coming from an inner graph layer in order to perform custom processing on already processed data.

The architecture thus consists of a single Core Layer including many core nodes, and several Application Layers containing application nodes. The complexity of processing is directly proportional to the number of layers crossed by the data. This also means that data at an outer graph layer must not be processed again at an inner layer, which also guarantees that processing loops, due to misconfigurations, are avoided by design.

From an architectural viewpoint, as shown in Figure 6 (b), nodes at inner graph layers cannot be listeners of nodes of outer graph layers. In other words, there can be no link from an outer graph node to an inner graph node, but only vice versa. Same layer graph nodes may be linked together if there is a need to do so.

In particular, a processing unit of the Core Graph layer can be a listener only for other nodes of the same layer (*n* incoming streams) and a source for other Core and Application graph nodes (*m* outgoing streams). A node of an Application Graph layer can be, at the same time:

- A listener of *n* incoming flows from Core and/or Application graph layers;
- A data source only for other *m* nodes of the application graph layers or heterogeneous external consumers.

The overall behavior of a task is generated by following a complete path in the Graph from a data source to a final consumer. Processing units perform operations that can be reused, thus data produced by a node can belong to several different paths and can be forwarded to all interested listeners. For this reason, in order to optimize the workload nodes with a large number of listeners can be replicated and nodes with no listeners can be shut down.

Figure 6. (a) The concentric linked Core and Application Layers. (b) Basic processing nodes build the Core Graph Layer, the outer nodes have increasing complexity

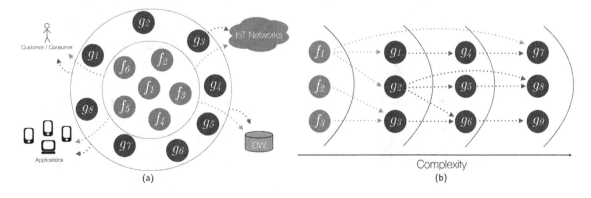

IMPLEMENTATION

In this section, the details of the functionalities and implementation of the proposed architecture by using standard protocols and open-source components are presented (Belli, & al., 2015).

Three main modules concur in forming the entire system:

- Acquisition and normalization of the incoming raw data;
- Graph management;
- Application register entity.

All modules and their relationships are shown in Figure 7. A detailed explanation is given in the following sections.

Acquisition Module

The Acquisition Module represents the entry point, for external IoT networks of SOs, to the Cloud architecture. Its purpose is to receive incoming raw data from heterogeneous sources, making them available to all subsequent functional blocks. As mentioned before, about IoT models, several application-layer protocols can be implemented by SOs; adhering to this idea, the Acquisition Module has been modeled to include a set of different connectors, in order to properly handle each protocol-specific incoming data stream.

Considering the main and most widespread IoT application-layer protocols, the current implementation of the Acquisition Module supports: HTTP, CoAP and MQTT.

In order to increase scalability and efficiency, in the module implementation an instance of NGINX (Reese, 2008) has been adopted as an HTTP acquisition server node. The server is reachable via the default HTTP port, working with a dedicated PHP page, as processing module, which has been configured to forward incoming data to the inner queue server. We have chosen NGINX, instead of the prevailing

Figure 7. Components of the proposed Graph Cloud architecture and relations between each element

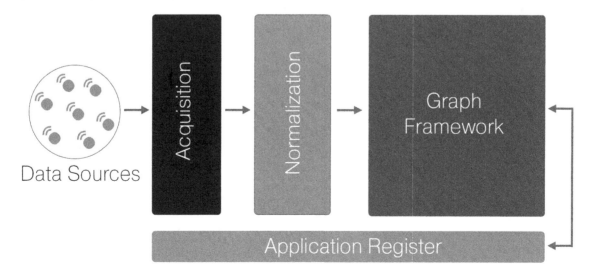

and well-known open source Apache HTTPD Server (R. T. Fielding & Kaiser, 1997), because it uses an event-driven asynchronous architecture to improve scalability and, specifically, aims to guarantee a high performance even in the presence of a critical number of requests.

The CoAP acquisition interface has been implemented using a Java process, based on a mjCoAP server (Cirani, Picone, & Veltri, 2014) instance, waiting for incoming raw messages, and connected to the RabbitMQ queue server (RabbitMQ, n.d.), passing it injected elements. Indeed, since the proposed architecture is Big Stream-oriented, a well-fitting messaging paradigm is given by queue communication; therefore, in the developed platform an instance of RabbitMQ queue broker was adopted.

The MQTT acquisition node is built by implementing an ActiveMQ (Apache, n.d.) server through a Java process which listens for incoming data over a specific input topic (*mqtt.input*).

This solution has been preferred over other existing solutions (e.g., the C-based server Mosquitto) because it provides a dedicated API that allows a custom development of the component. The MQTT acquisition node is also connected to the architecture's queue server. In order to avoid potential bottle-necks and collision points, each acquisition protocol module has dedicated Exchange module and queue (managed by RabbitMQ), linked together with a protocol-related routing key, ensuring the efficient management of incoming streams and their availability to the subsequent nodes.

In the described implementation, an Exchange is a RabbitMQ component which acts as a router in the system and dispatches incoming messages to one or more output queues, following dynamic routing rules.

Normalization Module

Since incoming raw data are generally application- and theme-dependent, a Normalization Module has been designed in order to normalize all the collected information and generate a representation suitable for processing. The normalization procedure is made by fundamental and atomic operations on data such as:

- Suppression of useless information (e.g., unnecessary headers or meta-data);
- Annotation with additional information;
- Translation of the payload to a suitable format.

In order to handle the huge amount of incoming data efficiently, the normalization step is organized with protocol-specific queues and Exchanges.

As shown in the normalization section of Figure 8, the information flow originated by the Acquisition Module is handled as follows.

- All protocol-specific data streams are routed to a dedicated protocol-dependent Exchange, which forwards them to a specific queue.
- A normalization process handles the input data currently available on that queue and performs all necessary normalization operations in order to obtain a stream of information units that can be processed by subsequent modules.
- The normalized stream is forwarded to an output Exchange.

The main advantage of using Exchanges is that queues and normalization processes can be dynamically adapted to the current workload: for instance, normalization queues and processes could be easily replicated to avoid system congestion.

Each normalization node has been implemented as a Java process, which analyzes incoming raw data extracted from a queue identified through a protocol-like routing key (e.g., *<protocol>.event.in*), leaving unaltered the associated routing key, which identifies the originator SO protocol. The received data are fragmented and encapsulated into a JSON-formatted document, which provides an easy-to-manage format.

At the end of the normalization chain, each processor node forwards its new output chunk to its next Exchange that represents the entry-point of the Graph Module, promoting data flows to next layers of the proposed architecture.

Graph Framework

The Graph Framework is composed by an amount of different computational processes representing a single node in the topology; layers are linked together with frontier Exchanges, forwarding data streams to their internal nodes.

Each Graph node i of a specific layer n is a listener, waiting for input data stream on a dedicated layer n Exchange-connected queue. If this node also acts as publisher, after performing its processing on input data, it can deliver computation results to the its layer n Exchange. In order to forward streams, informations generated by node i become available for layer n and layer $n+1$ listeners, interested for this kind of data, thanks to the binding between layer n and layer $n+1$ Exchanges.

Incoming messages are stored into active queues, connected to each Graph Layer's Exchange. Queues can be placed into the Core Graph layers, for basic computation, or into Application Graph Layers, for enhanced computation. Layers are connected, through one-way links, with their successor Exchange by using the binding rules allowed by the queue manager, ensuring proper propagation of data flows and avoiding loops. Each graph layer is composed by Java-based Graph Nodes dedicated to process data

Figure 8. Detailed representation of Acquisition and Normalization blocks

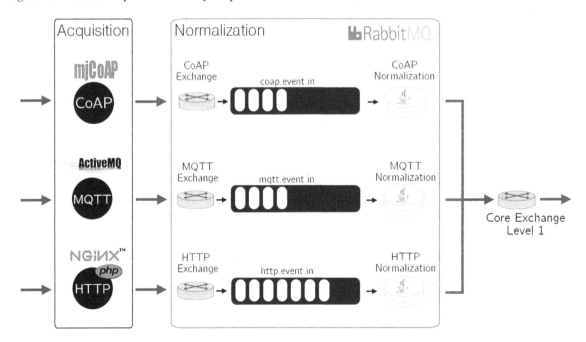

provided by the Graph layer's Exchange. Such nodes can either be Core, if they are dedicated to simple and primitive data processing, or Application, if they are oriented to a more complex and specific data management. Messages, identified with a routing key, are first retrieved from the layer's Exchange, then processed, and finally sent to the target Exchange, with a new work-related routing key, as shown in Figure 9. If the outgoing routing key belongs to the same incoming graph layer, data remain into same Exchange and become available for other local processes. If the outgoing routing key belongs to an outer graph layer, then data are forwarded to the corresponding Exchange and, finally, forwarded adhering to binding rules. Each graph node, upon becoming part of the system, can specify if it acts as a data publisher, capable of handling and forwarding data to its layer's Exchange, or if it acts only as data consumer. A data flow continues until it reaches the last layer's Exchange, responsible to manage the notification to the external entities that are interested in final processed data (e.g., Data Warehouse, browsers, Smart entities, other Cloud Graph processes).

Application Register Module

The Application Register Module has the fundamental responsibilities (i) to manage the processing graph by maintaining all the information about the current statuses of all graph nodes in the system and (ii) to route data across the graph. In more detail, the application register module performs the following operations:

- Attach new nodes or consumer applications interested in some of the streams provided by the system;
- Detach nodes of the graph that are no more interested in streaming flows and eventually re-attach them;
- Handle nodes that are publishers of new streams;
- Maintain information regarding topics of data, in order to correctly generate the routing keys and to compose data flow between nodes in different graph layers.

Figure 9. Interaction between Core and Application layers with binding rule

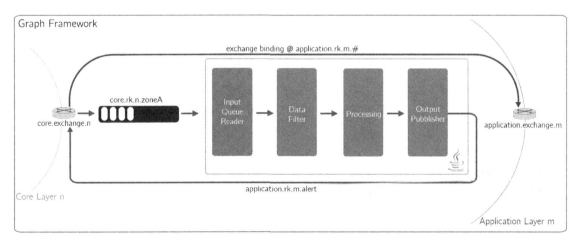

In order to accomplish all these functionalities, the Application Register Module is composed by two main components, as shown in Figure 10.

The first module is the Graph State Database, which is dedicated to store all the information about active graph nodes, such as: their states, layers, and whether they are publishers. The second one is the Node Registration and Queue Manager (NRQM), which handles requests from graph nodes or external processes, and handles queue management and routing in the system. When a new process joins the graph as a listener, it sends an attach request to the Application Register Module, specifying the kind of data which it is interested to. The NQRM module stores the information of the new process in the Graph State Database and creates a new dedicated input queue for the process, according to its preferences. Finally, the NRQM sends a reference of the queue to the process, which becomes a new listener of the graph and can read the incoming stream from the input queue. After this registration phase, the node can perform new requests (e.g., publish, detach, and get status).

The overall architecture is managed by a Java process (Application Register), which has the role to coordinate the interactions between graph nodes and external services, like the RabbitMQ queue server and the MySQL database. It maintains and updates all information and parameters related to processing unit queues. As a first step, the Application Register starts up all the external connections, and then it activates each layer's Exchange, binding them with their successors. At the end, it proceeds with the activation of a Jetty HTTP server, responsible for listening and handling all Core and Application nodes requests, as shown in Figure 10: (A) attach, (B) status request, (C) change publishing policy, (D) detach, and (E) re-attach request, using a RESTful HTTP paradigm.

In Figure 11, all the proposed architecture modules described above, with a detailed indication of the information flows, are shown.

Figure 10. Detailed representation of the Application Register module, with possible actions that may be performed by Graph nodes, highlighting ATTACH request steps needed to include an external node in the Graph

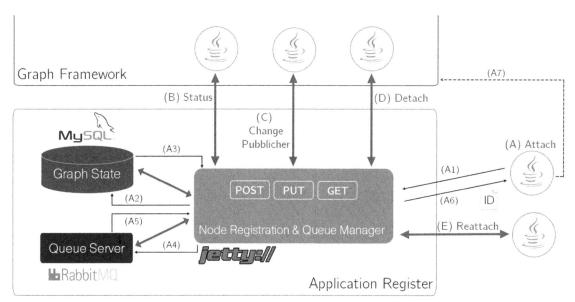

Figure 11. The complete Graph Cloud Architecture, with reference to the data stream flows between all building blocks, from IoT data sources to final consumers

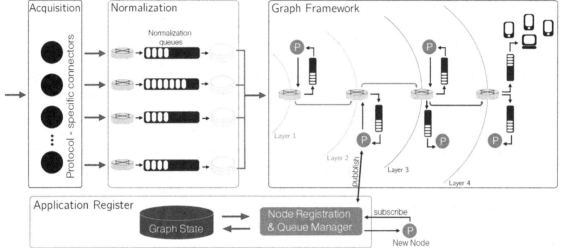

PERFORMANCE EVALUATION

The implementation of the proposed Graph Framework for Big Stream management has been carried out by deploying an Oracle VirtualBox VM, equipped with Linux Ubuntu 12.04 64-bit, 4GB RAM, 2 CPUs and 10GB HDD.

The implemented architecture has been evaluated through the definition of a real use case, represented by a Smart Parking scenario. The data traces used for the evaluation of the proposed architecture have been provided by WorldSensing from one of the company's deployments in a real-life scenario, used to control parking spots on streets. The traces are a subset of an entire deployment (more than 10,000 sensors) with information from 400 sensors over a 3 month period, forming a dataset with more than 604k parking events.

Each dataset item is represented by: (i) sensor ID; (ii) event sequence number, relative to the specific sensor; (iii) event timestamp; and (iv) parking spot status (free/busy). No additional informations about parking zone are provided. Therefore, thus, in order to create a realistic scenario, parking spot sensors are divided into 7 groups, representing different parking zones of a city. This parking spot-city zone association is stored into an external database.

Experimental Setup

The parking dataset has been used in the Cloud infrastructure using a Java-based data generator, which simulates the IoT sensors network. The generator randomly selects an available protocol (HTTP, CoAP, or MQTT) and periodically sends streams to the corresponding acquisition node interface. Once the data has been received by the acquisition layer, they are forwarded to the dedicated normalization Exchange, where corresponding nodes enrich incoming data with platform-specific details. With reference to the selected scenario, the normalization stage adds parking zone details to input data, retrieving the association from an external database. Once the normalization module has completed its processing, it sends the structured data to the Graph Framework, allowing to further process the enriched data stream.

The Graph Framework considered in our experimental set-up is composed by 8 Core layers and 7 Application layers, within which different node topologies are built and evaluated.

Processed data follow a path based on routing keys, until the final external listener is reached. Each Application node is interested in detecting changes of parking spot data, related to specific parking zones. Upon a change of the status, the Graph node generates a new aggregated descriptor, which is forwarded to the responsible layer's Exchange, which has the role to notify the change event to external entities interested in the update (free → busy, busy → free).

The rate of these events, coming from a real deployment in a European city, respects some rules imposed by the company, and for our purposes might seems low. Thus, in order to stress enough the proposed Big Stream Cloud system, the performance is evaluated by varying the data generation rate in a proper range. In other words, we force a specific rate for incoming events, without taking into account real parking spots timestamps gathered from the dataset.

Results

The proposed architecture has been evaluated, using the testbed described in the previous subsection, by varying the incoming raw data from 1 msg/s to 100 msg/s. The evaluation consists in assessing the performance of the acquisition stage and the computation stage.

First, performance is evaluated by measuring the time difference (dimension: [ms]) between the instant at which data are sent from a data generator to the corresponding acquisition interface and the instant at which the data are enriched by normalization nodes, thus becoming available for the first processing Core Node. The results are shown in Figure 12. The acquisition time is slightly increasing but it is around 15 ms at all considered rates.

The second performance evaluation has been carried out by measuring the time (dimension: [ms]) between the instant at which enriched data become ready for processing activities and the time instant at which the message reaches the end of its Graph Framework routes, becoming available for external consumers/customers. In order to consider only the effective overhead introduced by the architecture, and without considering implementation-specific contributions, performance results were obtained by subtracting the processing time of all Core and Application Nodes. Finally, these times have been normalized over the number of computational nodes, in order to obtain the per-node overhead introduced by the architecture, in a way that is independent of the specific routing and topology that were implemented. The results, shown in Figure 13 and Figure 14, have thus been calculated using the following expression:

$$T_{processing_{freq}} = \frac{T_{out} - T_{in} - \sum_{k=1}^{N} GP_k}{N}$$

where: T_{out} is the instant at which parking data reach the last Application layer; T_{in} indicates the instant in which normalized data comes to first Core layer; and GP_k is the processing time of a Graph process $k \in \{1,...,N\}$.

Figure 13 shows how $T_{processing}$ values grow increasing the data generation frequency (from 10 msg/s to 100 msg/s). Each curve is related to a different Graph topology.

Figure 12. Average time (dimension: [ms]) related to the acquisition block

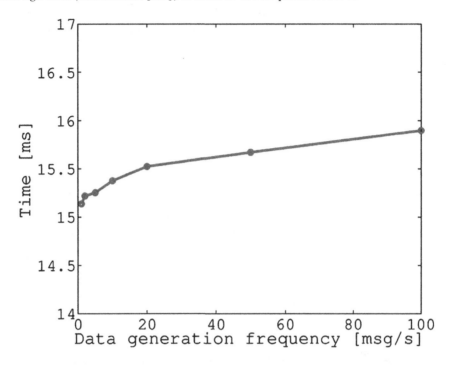

Figure 13. Average times (dimension: [ms]) related to Graph Framework processing block, showing per-node time, varying data generation rate, for each subset of nodes deployed into the Graph topology

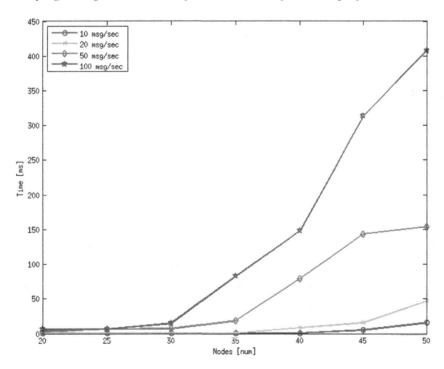

Figure 14. Average times (dimension: [ms]) related to Graph Framework processing block, showing per-node time, varying the subset of nodes deployed into the Graph topology, for each evaluated data generation frequency

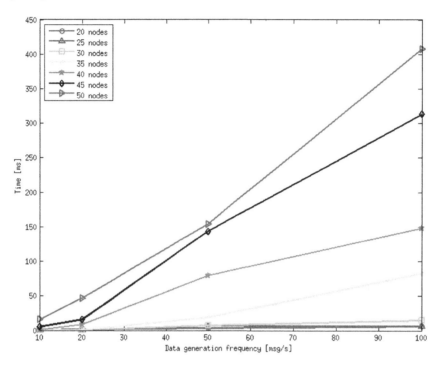

Figure 14 shows how $T_{processing}$ values grow increasing the number of nodes composing the Graph topology (from 20 to 50 nodes). Each curve in Figure 14 is related to a different value of frequency rate.

DISCUSSIONS

Solutions and Security Considerations

The presented architecture is designed with reference to a specific IoT scenario with strict latency and real-time requirements, namely a smart city-related Smart Parking scenario. There are several possible use cases and applications fitting this scenario, alerting or real time monitoring applications.

The work of (Vilajosana et al., 2013) shows how Smart Cities are having difficulties in real deployment, even though obvious factors justify the necessity and the usefulness of making cities smarter. The authors of (Vilajosana et al., 2013) analyze in detail the causes and factors which act as barriers in the process of institutionalization of smart cities, and propose an approach to make smart cities become a reality.

The authors advocate three different stages in order to deploy smart cities technologies and services.

- **The Bootstrap Phase:** This phase is dedicated to offer services and technologies that are not only of great use and really improve urban living, but also offer a return on investments. The important objective of this first step is, thus, to set technological basis of the infrastructure and guarantee the system long life by generating cash flows for future investments.
- **The Growth Phase:** In this phase, the finances generated in the previous phase are used to ramp up technologies and services which require large investments and not necessarily produce financial gains but are only of great use for consumers.
- **The Wide Adoption Phase:** In this third phase, collected data are made available through standardized APIs and offered by all different stakeholders to third party developers in order to create new services. At the end of this step, the system becomes self-sustainable and might produce a new tertiary sector specifically related to services and applications generated using the underlying infrastructure.

With reference to the third phase, (Vilajosana et al., 2013) propose three main different business models to handle the delivery of informations to third parties.

- **The App Store-Like Model:** Developers can build their apps using a set of verified APIs after a subscription procedure which might involve some subscription fee. IoT operators can hold a small percentage of gains of Apps published in Apple and/or Android market.
- **The Google Maps-Like Model:** The percentage fee on apps sales price is scaled according to the number and granularity of the queries to deployed APIs.
- **The Open Data Model:** This model grants access to APIs in a classical open data vision, without charging any fee to developers.

The architecture described in this paper is compatible with the steps described in the work of (Vilajosana et al., 2013) and, more specifically, it can adopt the "Google-Maps-like" where infrastructure APIs make available different information streams with different complexity layers.

The graph architecture, moreover, gives another opportunity to extend the business model, as developers can use available streams to generate a new node of the graph, and publish a new stream for the system.

Another aspect, with a relevant impact on the business model, is security. This entails both processing module and interaction with external entities. It is possible to adopt different policies related to authentication and/or authorization on data sources, e.g., based on well-known and standard solutions such as OAuth (Hammer-Lahav, 2010; Hardt, 2012), avoiding data stream malicious alterations and following negative consequences, that could affect both processing results and platform reliability. At a final stage, security could be applied for consumer accounting and authentication, ensuring appropriate platform access only by authenticated/authorized entities, and providing security transactions, with authorized entities, via secured communications.

Security features, including authorization, authentications and confidentiality, should be integrated into the architecture, in order to make the implementation complete and usable. Details about integration of security features in the proposed Big Stream platform and its further impact on the system performance are not included in this paper. They represent interesting research topics for future work.

Practical Use

In the previous sections, we have detailed the implementation of the Graph-based Cloud architecture for a Big Stream IoT scenario. This section addresses some aspects regarding practical use of the proposed architecture, taking into account its deployment on a Cloud platform.

The proposed architecture is mainly intended for developers, interested in building applications based on data generated by IoT networks, with real-time constraints, low-overhead, customizing paths and informations flows, in order to generate new streams, through the addition of newly developed and deployed Graph nodes.

Analyzing the Cloud components of the platform, the preferred service model seems to be the Software-as-a-Service (SaaS) model, providing useful services for developers.

- Node upload/deletion: to change the Graph Framework topology, loading or removing newly custom processing node;
- Stream status: to get the list of all available streams generated by the graph;
- Data source upload/deletion: to load or remove a new external data source before the Acquisition module of the Graph-based system.

It is important to observe that each developer, accessing the architecture, could operate on data streams coming from IoT networks (already processed or not) which he/she does not own.

The interactions between IoT developers and the proposed Cloud architecture are similar to those provided by Node-RED (IBM Emerging Technology, 2013), a WEB-based application, running on Node.js engine, which allows developers to create IoT graphs, wiring together hardware devices, APIs, and online services.

FUTURE RESEARCH DIRECTIONS

The proposed architecture is oriented to large amounts of incoming raw data, providing to interested consumers an enhanced version of them: this could be useful in scenarios in which consumers are final entities, interested only in retrieving aggregated data. The proposed architecture could also be seen as a first-step processing platform, in which final data could represent an incoming set for other processing entities. This flow could be applied to many scientific fields: for example, since the proposed architecture is not a simulation or emulation platforms, could serve as data provider for instances of those processors types. In medical environments, the proposed platform could be seen as a platform trying to work on an enhanced dataset, looking for some diagnosis. Other possible applications fields, are related to mobility and vehicular simulation and emulation, where simulations platforms (e.g., ns-2, ns-3) could apply their functionalities over enhanced datasets, being able to work properly, looking for a good performance, in terms of processing time and result reliability.

As stated before, security is a central aspect to be taken into account, in order to enhance the architecture reliability and the processing control. To provide guarantees at input stages, an optimal solution could be represented by the introduction of an authorization module, which tokenizes incoming data adopting an asymmetric security paradigm, to sure that raw data providers are authorized to provide information.

Looking for a reliable behavior at the output stage, a good solution could be reached by introducing an Accounting/Authentication/Authorization (AAA) module, which manages and controls the acceptance of consumers, providing some cryptographic functionalities, to check security-level of each entity.

CONCLUSION

In this paper, the authors presented a novel Cloud Graph-based architecture for efficient management of Big Stream Real-time applications in IoT scenarios. After describing the main requirements, in terms of reduced latency between the data creation instant and the instant at which processed data can be delivered to a consumer, the new Big Stream paradigm has been introduced highlighting its differences with respect to the Big Data paradigm. The main components of the designed listener-based architecture are the following: the Acquisition Module, the Normalization Module, the Graph Framework, and the Application Register. The implementation of the overall system and its evaluation on a real-world Smart Parking dataset has been presented. The listener-oriented approach generates several benefits, such as:

- **Decreased Latency:** The push-based approach guarantees that no delays due to polling and batch processing are introduced;
- **Fine-Grained Self-Configuration:** Listeners can dynamically "plug" to streams interest data;
- **Optimal Resource Allocation:** Processing units that have no listeners can be switched off, while those with many listeners can be replicated, thus leading to cost-effectiveness from the Cloud service perspective.

REFERENCES

Apache. (n.d.-a). *Storm*. Retrieved from https://storm.incubator.apache.org/

Apache. (n.d.-b). *ActiveMQ*. Retrieved from http://activemq.apache.org/

Assunção, M. D., Calheiros, R. N., Bianchi, S., Netto, M. A., & Buyya, R. (2014). Big data computing and Clouds: Trends and future directions. *Journal of Parallel and Distributed Computing*.

Belli, L., Cirani, S., Davoli, L., Melegari, L., Mónton, M., & Picone, M. (2015). An Open-Source Cloud Architecture for Big Stream IoT Applications. In I. Podnar Žarko, K. Pripužić, & M. Serrano (Eds.), Interoperability and Open-Source Solutions for the Internet of Things (Vol. 9001, pp. 73-88). Lecture Notes in Computer Science (LNCS). Springer International Publishing. Retrieved from Doi:10.1007/978-3-319-16546-2_7

Belli, L., Cirani, S., Ferrari, G., Melegari, L., & Picone, M. (2014). *A Graph-based Cloud architecture for Big Stream real-time applications in the Internet of Things*. In *2nd International Workshop on Cloud for IoT (CLIoT 2014)*, Manchester, United Kingdom, September 2014.

Bonomi, F., Milito, R., Zhu, J., & Addepalli, S. (2012). *Fog Computing and its role in the internet of things*. In *Proceedings of the First Edition of the ACM Workshop on Mobile Cloud Computing* (p. 13-16). New York, NY, USA. Retrieved from http://doi.acm.org/10.1145/2342509.2342513

Cirani, S., Davoli, L., Picone, M., & Veltri, L. (2014, July). *Performance Evaluation of a SIP-based Constrained Peer-to-Peer Overlay.* In *2014 International Conference on High Performance Computing Simulation (HPCS),* (p. 432-435). Retrieved from doi:10.1109/HPCSim.2014.6903717

Cirani, S., Picone, M., & Veltri, L. (2013). CoSIP: A Constrained Session Initiation Protocol for the Internet of Things. In C. Canal & M. Villari (Eds.), *Advances in Service-Oriented and Cloud Computing* (Vol. 393, pp. 13–24). Springer Berlin Heidelberg. Retrieved from doi:10.1007/978-3-642-45364-9_2

Cirani, S., Picone, M., & Veltri, L. (2014). *A Session Initiation Protocol for the Internet of Things.* Scalable Computing: Practice and Experience, 14 (4), 249-263. Retrieved from doi:10.12694/scpe.v14i4.931

Cirani, S., Picone, M., & Veltri, L. (2015). mjCoAP: An Open-Source Lightweight Java CoAP Library for Internet of Things Applications. In: Interoperability and Open-Source Solutions for the Internet of Things. LNCS, vol. 9001, Retrieved from DOI:, Springer International Publishing Switzerland. doi:10.1007/978-3-319-16546-2_10

Deering, S., & Hinden, R. (1998, December). *Internet Protocol, version 6 (IPv6) Specification (No. 2460).* RFC 2460 (Draft Standard). IETF. Retrieved from http://www.ietf.org/rfc/rfc2460.txt. (Updated by RFCs 5095, 5722, 5871, 6437, 6564, 6935, 6946, 7045, 7112)

Dunkels, A., Gronvall, B., & Voigt, T. (2004). *Contiki - A Lightweight and flexible Operating System for tiny networked sensors.* Local Computer Networks, 2004. 29th Annual IEEE International Conference on (pp. 455-462). IEEE.

Emerging Technology, I. B. M. (2013). *Node-RED.* Retrieved from http://nodered.org/

European Community's 7th Framework Programme. (2007). *OpenIoT - Open Source Cloud solution for the Internet of Things.* Retrieved from http://openiot.eu/. Retrieved from http://openiot.eu/

European Community's 7th Framework Programme. (2008-2010). *SENSEI Project.* Retrieved from http://www.ict-sensei.org/

European Community's 7th Framework Programme. (2011-2014). *CALIPSO - Connect All IP-based Smart Objects.* Retrieved from http://www.ict-calipso.eu/

European Community's 7th Framework Programme. (2011). *FI-Ware Project.* Retrieved from http://www.fi-ware.org/

European Community's 7th Framework Programme. (2012-2015). *Internet of Things - Architecture (IoT - A).* Retrieved from http://www.iot-a.eu/

Evans, D. (2011). *The Internet of Things: How the next evolution of the internet is changing everything.* CISCO white paper, 1.

Fielding, R., Gettys, J., Mogul, J., Frystyk, H., Masinter, L., Leach, P., & Berners-Lee, T. (1999). *Hypertext transfer protocol – http/1.1.* United States: RFC Editor.

Fielding, R. T. (2000). Architectural styles and the design of network-based software architectures (Unpublished doctoral dissertation).

Fielding, R. T., & Kaiser, G. (1997). The Apache HTTP server project. *IEEE Internet Computing, 1*(4), 88–90. Retrieved from doi:10.1109/4236.612229

Gubbi, J., Buyya, R., Marusic, S., & Palaniswami, M. (2013). Internet of Things (IoT): A vision, architectural elements, and future directions. *Future Generation Computer Systems, 29*(7), 1645–1660. Retrieved from http://www.sciencedirect.com/science/article/pii/S0167739X13000241 doi:10.1016/j. future.2013.01.010

Hammer-Lahav, E. (2010). *RFC 5849: The OAuth 1.0 protocol. Internet Engineering Task Force.* IETF.

Hardt, D. (2012). RFC 6749: *The OAuth 2.0 authorization framework-revision.*

Hohpe, G., & Woolf, B. (2003). *Enterprise integration patterns: Designing, building, and deploying messaging solutions.* Boston, MA, USA: Addison-Wesley Longman Publishing Co., Inc.

Isaacson, C. (2009). *Software pipelines and SOA: Releasing the power of multi-core processing* (1st ed.). Addison-Wesley Professional.

Leavitt, N. (2013). Storage challenge: Where will all that big data go? *Computer, 46*(9), 22–25. Retrieved from doi:10.1109/MC.2013.326

Locke, D. (2010). *MQ Telemetry Transport (MQTT) v3. 1 protocol specification.* IBM developer Works Technical Library], Retrieved from https://www.ibm.com/developerworks/webservices/library/ws-mqtt/

Marganiec, S. R., Tilly, M., & Janicke, H. (2014, June). *Low-Latency Service Data Aggregation Using Policy Obligations. In Web Services (ICWS)*, 2014 IEEE International Conference on (pp. 526-533). IEEE.

McAfee, A., & Brynjolfsson, E. (2012). Big data: The management revolution. *Harvard Business Review*, (90): 60–66. PMID:23074865

Mell, P., & Grance, T. (2011). The NIST definition of Cloud Computing. *National Institute of Standards and Technology, 53*(6), 50.

Milojičić, D., Llorente, I. M., & Montero, R. S. (2011). *OpenNebula: A Cloud management tool.* IEEE Internet Computing, 15(2), 0011-14.

Mosquitto. (n.d.). *An Open Source MQTT Broker.* Retrieved from http://mosquitto.org/

MySQL. (n.d.). Retrieved from http://www.mysql.com/

Neumeyer, L., Robbins, B., Nair, A., & Kesari, A. (2010). S4: Distributed stream computing platform. In *2010 IEEE International Conference on Data mining workshops (ICDMW)* (pp. 170–177). doi:10.1109/ ICDMW.2010.172

Postel, J. (Ed.). (1981, September). RFC 791 Internet Protocol - DARPA Internet program, protocol specification [Computer software manual]. Retrieved from http://tools.ietf.org/html/rfc791

RabbitM. Q. (n.d.). Retrieved from http://www.rabbitmq.com/

Rackspace, N. A. S. A. (n.d.). *OpenStack Cloud Software - Open source software for building private and public Clouds.* Retrieved from https://www.openstack.org/

Reese, W. (2008). *NGINX: the high-performance web server and reverse proxy*. Linux Journal, 2008 (173), 2.

Rosenberg, J., Schulzrinne, H., Camarillo, G., Johnston, A., Peterson, J., Sparks, R., & Schooler, E. (2003). *RFC 3261: SIP: Session Initiation Protocol*. IETF, Tech. Rep., 2002. Retrieved from http://www.ietf.org/rfc/rfc3261.txt

Saint-Andre, P. (2004, October). *Extensible messaging and presence protocol (XMPP): Instant messaging and presence*. Internet RFC 3921.

Shelby, Z., Hartke, K., Bormann, C., & Frank, B. (2014). *RFC 7252: The Constrained Application Protocol (CoAP)*. Internet Engineering Task Force.

Stanoevska-Slabeva, K., Wozniak, T., & Ristol, S. (2009). *Grid and Cloud Computing: a business perspective on technology and applications*. Springer Science & Business Media.

Tilly, M., & Reiff-Marganiec, S. (2011, March). Matching customer requests to service offerings in real-time. In *Proceedings of the 2011 ACM Symposium on Applied Computing* (pp. 456-461). ACM. Retrieved from doi:10.1145/1982185.1982285

Vilajosana, I., Llosa, J., Martinez, B., Domingo-Prieto, M., Angles, A., & Vilajosana, X. (2013). Bootstrapping smart cities through a self-sustainable model based on big data flows. Communications Magazine, IEEE, 51(6).

Vinoski, S. (2006, November). *Advanced message queuing protocol*. IEEE Internet Computing, 10 (6), 87–89. Retrieved from .10.1109/MIC.2006.116

Zaslavsky, A., Perera, C., & Georgakopoulos, D. (2013). *Sensing as a service and big data*. Retrieved from http://arxiv.org/abs/1301.0159

KEY TERMS AND DEFINITIONS

Big Data: Paradigms and technologies to handle massive volume of structured and unstructured data which is so large that it's impossible to process using traditional database and software techniques.

Big Stream: Paradigms and technologies to handle with real-time and low-latency requirements, the massive volume of data generated with very high frequency by a huge number of different data sources.

Exchange: In a generic network or graph topology is a component that receives messages from producers and dispatches them to one or more output queue depending on specific routing rules.

Graph: A mathematical model to represent a set of entities connected to each other. The complete topology of a graph is identified by a list of vertices (or nodes) and a list of edges (or links) between two vertices.

Internet of Things: The interconnection of billions of heterogeneous devices called "Smart Objects" through the Internet infrastructure. Smart Objects are typically constrained devices like sensors or actuator and are deployed to collect data and to build useful services to consumers.

Listener: In an event driven system, a process or a component which is able to listen for and to handle it a particular event.

Real-Time System: System required to guarantee responses with hard and strict time constraints.

Smart Object: A device with communication capabilities deployed in IoT systems. Generally has constrained capabilities and is equipped with sensor or actuator to collect data or act in the environment.

This research was previously published in the International Journal of Systems and Service-Oriented Engineering (IJSSOE), 5(4); edited by Dickson K.W. Chiu, pages 26-53, copyright year 2015 by IGI Publishing (an imprint of IGI Global).

Chapter 3
Wireless Enabling Technologies for the Internet of Things

Mahmoud Elkhodr
University of Western Sydney, Australia

Seyed Shahrestani
University of Western Sydney, Australia

Hon Cheung
University of Western Sydney, Australia

ABSTRACT

This Chapter provides several comparable studies of some of the major evolving and enabling wireless technologies in the Internet of Things (IoT). Particularly, it focuses on the ZigBee, 6lowpan, Bluetooth Low Energy, LTE, and the different versions of Wi-Fi protocols including the IEEE 802.11ah. The studies, reported in this chapter, evaluate the capabilities and behaviors of these technologies in terms of various metrics including the data range and rate, network size, RF Channels and Bandwidth, Antenna design considerations, Power Consumption, and their Ecosystem. It is concluded that the requirements of each IoT application play a significant role in the selection of a suitable wireless technology.

INTRODUCTION

The Internet of Things (IoT) was about a vision in which all physical objects are tagged and uniquely identified using RFID transponders or readers (Neil, 2000). Nowadays, research into the IoT has extended this vision to the connectivity of things to anything, anyone, anywhere and at any time. The IoT has grown into multiple dimensions, which encompass various networks of applications, computers, devices, sensors, actuators, smart devices as well as physical and virtual objects (Elkhodr, Shahrestani, & Cheung, 2013). Communication, collaboration and sharing of information between the various facets of the IoT are a keystone for the triumph of the IoT. In the IoT, things are interconnected together using various wireless, wired or mobile communication technologies such as ZigBee, Bluetooth, 4G, Wi-Fi, and other evolving communications technologies. The nature of the IoT communications is no longer restricted to

DOI: 10.4018/978-1-5225-5649-7.ch003

human users but also extends to things-to-things communications. This paradigm of things-to-things and things-to-human communications is a major shift from an essentially computer-based network model to a fully distributed network of connected devices.

The IoT has now more potential to provide a real-world intelligent platform for the collaboration of distributed smart objects via local-area wireless and wired networks, and/or via wide-area heterogeneous network interconnections such as the Internet (Elkhodr et al., 2013). This growth can be attributed to many technological advances. Particularly, it is due to the advance of mobile and wireless communications networks, such as 4G, Wi-Fi and 802.11ah, and their wide-range or low-power wireless capabilities. The rapid development and pervasive evolution of wireless technologies have the potential to grow to accommodate the billions of things envisioned in the IoT. Traditionally, network end-users of the Internet are computers and mobile devices. In the IoT, network users will expand to include humans, things, machines, and a combination or group of them. Thus, the IoT will connect devices that we carry or wear, and devices which we interact with at homes, work, and recreational places; creating an entirely new category of connected devices. The IoT creates a proliferation of devices that until recently very few people would have considered it beneficial to connect to the Internet. Reinventing not only the way we connect to the Internet but the way objects around us are used in everyday activities. Ultimately, wireless technologies and their infrastructures will grow to meet the high demand for connectivity created by the vast amounts of IoT devices joining the Internet. The increase in connectivity demands creates new challenges in terms of communication requirements, device hardware characteristics, software, and resilience capabilities.

Nonetheless, an interesting aspect of the adoption of wireless technologies in the IoT is the incorporation of multiple long range and short range wireless technologies into the designs of IoT applications. In eHealth, for example, applications such as body area networks may develop into an autonomous world of small wireless and networked mobile devices attached to their users. They mostly connect to the Internet using a mobile phone as a gateway or via a wireless access point. Wireless technologies in the IoT need to handle a large degree of ad-hoc growth in device connectivity, structure, organization, and significant change in contextual use, including mobility as well. Many devices will constantly be connected to the energy grid such as smart appliances in the smart home application example. On the other hand, many other IoT devices suffer from limited energy resources as they are powered by small batteries or rely on energy harvesting techniques throughout their lifetime (Vecchio, Giaffreda, & Marcelloni, 2014). Examples of these devices are wireless sensors and those deployed in remote locations. Hence, finding an answer to "Which wireless technology best fits the IoT" is subjective to the application requirements and device capabilities. However, it is established that the need to accommodate the requirements for minimum energy and computation, slim and lightweight solutions in various IoT communication scenarios and applications is essential for the proliferation of the IoT (Vermesan & Friess, 2013). Indeed, most of the future growth in wireless IoT connectivity will stem from these requirements. For the real growth to occur, interactions on the IoT between various industry segments are also needed. To achieve this, interoperability of communications between classic and low-power wireless technologies is fundamental to the success of the IoT.

This Chapter investigates and compares some of the evolving and enabling wireless technologies in the IoT. It provides a brief review of the IEEE 802.15.4 technologies, Bluetooth Low Energy, and Wi-Fi in the section "IoT Wireless enabling protocols". Then the Chapter moves to provide several comparative studies between low-power wireless technologies, particularly, ZigBee, 6Lowpan, and 802.11ah, and the other variants of Wi-Fi technology (802.11a/b/g/n/ac), and LTE in the section "A comparative study of IoT enabling technologies". The comparative studies examine various parameters of these wireless technologies such as their data rates and ranges, network sizes, transmission powers, security, and significantly their ecosystem and suitability of adoption in the IoT. The Chapter concludes by providing some practicals observations from the literature.

Connectivity of Things: The Last Few Meters

The first issue to consider in the IoT is how things will join the Internet. There are two ways for a typical computing device to connect to the Internet:

1. Independently using a mobile broadband connection to an Internet Service Provider (ISP). Two popular examples are a laptop equipped with a mobile broadband modem and a mobile device that connects to the Internet via 3G or 4G that has an inbuilt modem; and
2. Via a local-area wireless or wired network that is connected to a base station or a router. Examples are local area networks (LANs) that connect computers and devices within the same geographical area. Each device on the network is regarded as a node with one of them designated as a gateway. A gateway is a device which shares an Internet connection with other nodes and acts as a router.

In the IoT, an IoT device can connect to the Internet directly, that is it uses the IP suite to exchange data with other devices or servers over the Internet. Alternatively, an IoT device on a local network can use a non-IP protocol to communicate with others devices in a local network setup. Non-IP devices can connect to the Internet via an Internet gateway. Therefore, this gateway has the capability of communicating with non-IP devices in the local network on one hand, and with IP devices on the Internet on the other hand. The gateway is responsible for communicating with the local devices e.g. a sensor, and for the processing of the data it receives. Processing of data may include restructuring and formatting using the TCP/IP stack to enable the communication of these data over the Internet. For example, consider the smart home IoT application example. A wireless sensor can form a local network with another device referred to as a controller. The sensor is responsible for sending some sensory information to the controller. The controller can relay this sensory information to a cloud, mobile device, database or any server on the Internet. Therefore, the controller uses TCP/IP for Internet connectivity. However, the communication between the sensor and the controller is not necessarily based on TCP/IP.

The benefit of connecting IoT devices using IP technology to the Internet enables flexibility. It allows the modification or addition of functionalities to a device without changing the communication requirements. However, the implementation of the TCP/IP stack often requires a fair amount of processing power and energy. The TCP/IP stack is considered to be complex and demanding, implying more development time and more expensive hardware. For these reasons, IP technology might not be suited for devices which have low energy, low communication, and computation capabilities. As a result, many IoT devices, such as the sensor in the smart home example stated above, elect to use simpler protocols.

IoT Wireless Enabling Protocols

The IoT covers a broad range of applications and devices. The 802.11 protocol with its 802.11a/b/g/n/ac variants, popularly known as Wi-Fi, is among the first obvious technology candidates for the IoT. Today, almost every house, workplace, cafe and university has a Wi-Fi network. Wi-Fi has become the de-facto term when referring to connecting to the Internet via a wireless access point. The widespread adoption of Wi-Fi definitely makes it a first technology choice for many IoT applications. However, in some IoT applications, the choice of technology is limited to the device's hardware capabilities, low-power consumption requirement, and the overall cost. Many IoT devices require the use of a low-cost and low-power wireless technology when connecting to the Internet. Traditionally, energy consumption has always been a limiting factor in many wireless sensor network applications. This limiting factor will continue as an important challenge facing the development of many applications in the IoT. In fact, for the growth of the IoT, low-power consumption is an essential requirement that needs to be met.

In addition to low-power consumption, there are other associated requirements that need to be considered as well. For instance, the cost of technology, security, simplicity (easy to use and manage), wireless data rates and ranges, among others, are important requirements that need attention. Many evolving wireless technologies such as ZigBee and Bluetooth are competing to provide the IoT with a low-power wireless connectivity solution. Other wireless technologies such as the IEEE 802.11ah and 6Lowpan protocols are emerging as well. They offer similar low-power wireless connectivity solutions for the IoT. Consequently, there could be many choices of low-power wireless protocols in many IoT applications. Consider, for example, a car-parking system application based on the IoT. A typical IoT-based car-parking system combines many components together. It combines a variety of devices, multiple networking protocols, several sources of data, and various wireless and generations of technologies. Many of the devices involved in the communications are lightweight devices such as sensors which operate on battery. They would require a low-power wireless technology to function effectively.

Essentially, low-power wireless technologies contribute to improving not only the way an IoT device connects to the Internet but the efficiency of the overall IoT application as well. A network consisting of low-cost and lightweight IoT devices can be used to monitor relevant operating and contextual parameters. These devices are also capabale of making useful decisions (based on the occurrence of specific events) while simultaneously communicating with a number of other IoT devices. In general, an heterogeneous setup allows an IoT system to perform many automated tasks by combining the various data gathered from these IoT devices. Recall the smart home IoT application example. In this application, IoT devices such as wireless sensors can report the ambiance temperatures in various locations in a house to an IoT central device, referred to as the controller, which in turns can make a decision on varying the output of the air-conditioning system. Adding more IoT devices to the IoT system will increase the intelligence of the system as well. For instance, if some other sensors are providing information on whether the house is occupied or not (whether the people occupying the house are out or no), then the controller will be able to make a better decision on when the heating system should be turned on or off. In this smart home example, the IoT devices are in the form of simple sensor devices which have a small bandwidth and low-power requirement. Hence, the need for low-power wireless technologies in this and many other similar applications in the IoT.

Bluetooth Low Energy

Bluetooth Low Energy (BLE), also known as Bluetooth Smart and Bluetooth version 4 is an enhancement to the classic Bluetooth protocol (Bluetooth SIG, 2001). BLE is leading a revolution in the areas of wearable technologies, entertainment devices, wireless sensor networks and notably, the Internet of Things. The design of the BLE protocol, which puts the device to sleep when it is not needed, allows low-power consumption by a BLE device (Mackensen, Lai, & Wendt, 2012). It allows a device, communicating through BLE and running on a coin-cell battery, to last for more than a year. The BLE protocol operates in the unlicensed 2.4 GHz Industrial, Scientific, and Medical (ISM) band. It uses the Time Division Multiple Access (TDMA) and Frequency-Division Multiple-Access (FDMA) access technologies (Bluetooth SIG, 2012). To counteract interference and fading, BLE uses a frequency hopping scheme that hops between 40 frequencies separated by 2 MHz. Three of these channels are advertising channels, and the rest are data channels (Ahmed, 2013). TDMA scheme provides different time-slots to different data streams in a repetitive cyclic order. The scheme assigns a specific time slot for each device; which allows a device to send and receive data on a particular frequency at a time. The FDMA scheme is based on the concept of allocating a frequency band or channel to each device. To reduce interference with other 2.4 GHz based wireless technologies, Bluetooth supports adaptive frequency hopping (AFH). AFH determines the available frequency by detecting the frequencies of other devices in the spectrum. This technology provides an efficient transmission scheme within the allocated frequency spectrum and therefore increases the performance of Bluetooth even in the presence of other technologies.

Bluetooth is a packet-based protocol. It implements a master-slave communication architecture. A master is a Bluetooth enabled device which has the capability of communicating with a maximum of seven other Bluetooth-enabled devices, referred to as slaves, at a time. In Bluetooth terms, a master is a device which initiates a connection. By agreements, Bluetooth devices can switch roles from a master to slave and vice versa as well (Bluetooth SIG, 2001). BLE allows devices to communicate with each other when they come in a permitted range, normally up to 100 meters depending on the power classification of the device (more power, longer range). The BLE protocol is designed to have an over the air data rate of 1 Mbps and throughput of around 0.27 Mbps (Bluetooth SIG, 2012). However, in practical implementations, the data rate and throughput are much lower (Gomez, Oller, & Paradells, 2012). The low-power consumption feature of BLE is achieved by putting a BLE device to sleep for a longer period of time. The device will only wake up for a shorter amount of time when it is sending or receiving data. However, the fact that BLE is only sending a small amount of data at a time with efficient energy consumption makes it a favorable technology choice for several light IoT applications. On the contrary, BLE can be judged as impractical to use in many other IoT applications which might require the use of a more capable technology in terms of range and bandwidth.

The throughput, range, data rate, and power consumption parameters of BLE are affected by some other parameters such as the connection parameters. Two important aspects of BLE are the physical channels and events. The physical channel specifies the frequency at which data is sent. In terms of events, an event is the time unit in which data is sent between BLE devices. There are two types of events: advertising events and connection events. Advertising events are used to send advertising packets; while connection events are used to send the actual data. Figure 1 shows an example of two connection events and one advertising event. In these events, the slave and master devices are exchanging some packets. The packets of each of the events are sent on a different frequency given that BLE uses a frequency hopping technique. Other important aspects which relate to the BLE are the connection interval and slave latency. A connection interval is a period of time that occurs between two consecutive connection events (Bluetooth SIG, 2012). The slave latency is a parameter that results in power saving by allowing the slave device to skip a number of connection events if it does not have data to send (Ahmed, 2013). Slave latency specifies the maximum number of connection events that can be skipped (Texas Instruments, 2013).

Figure 1. Bluetooth connection and advertising events

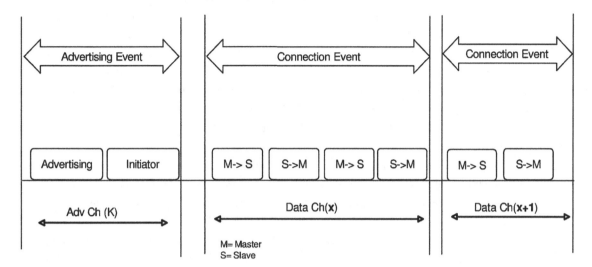

The low-power consumption feature of the BLE protocol enables connectivity, monitoring and sharing of information for many devices, such as home appliances, and wearable devices with a minimal consumption of energy. Significantly, the BLE protocol creates opportunities for a number of IoT applications. It is a strong candidate to be used as a communication protocol in several IoT devices which are limited by their low-power and low-cost characteristics. Examples of these IoT applications and devices range from health monitor devices in e-health, devices in retails applications and in home automation systems ("Bluetooth Smart Technology: Powering the Internet of Things," 2015), and smart appliances in smart grid applications. Additionally, the widespread adoption of smartphones and the advancement made by BLE in terms of energy consumption enable the introduction of many wearables and fitness devices which integrate with smartphones. In addition, BLE has a good potential for becoming an essential technology for the "last 100 meters in low-power and low-cost small devices" of the IoT ("Bluetooth Smart Technology: Powering the Internet of Things," 2015). Using a smartphone or another similar device as a temporary or mobile gateway is increasingly getting popular in numerous IoT applications. Thus, BLE plays a significant role in providing the communication medium needed between this gateway and the IoT devices. There are also some applications where the same IoT device (e.g. a sensor) is used for both mobile and fixed-location applications.

ZigBee

The IEEE 802.15.4 is a protocol designed for low-rate wireless personal area networks (LR-WPANs). It defines the physical and media access control layers (Hackmann, 2006). The IEEE 802.15.4 is the basis for ZigBee (ZigBee Alliance, 2006), WirelessHART (Chen, Nixon, & Mok, 2010), and 6LoWPAN (Kushalnagar, Montenegro, & Schumacher, 2007). The IEEE 802.15.4 operates in the unlicensed 2.4 GHz band which overlaps with other wireless technologies (Wi-Fi, and Bluetooth) sharing the same band. ZigBee is an extension to the 802.15.4 standard. ZigBee is built on top of the 802.15.4's radio layer. It specifies the application, network. and security layers, as described in (ZigBee Alliance, 2014). Often, the terms 802.15.4 and ZigBee are used interchangeably. However, this may not be correct as ZigBee devices are not necessarily compatible with some implementations of the 802.15.4 standard. ZigBee's data rate is considered low when compared with Bluetooth and Wi-Fi. For instance, ZigBee has a data rate that ranges from 20 to 250 kbps (Baker, 2005). On the other hand, Bluetooth has a maximum speed of 3 Mbps and a practical data transfer rate of 2.1 Mbps, whereas Wi-Fi has a data rate that ranges over 54 Mbps. The battery lifetime of Bluetooth classic device is a few days, while that of Wi-Fi is a few hours. In BLE, a battery can last for over a year. However, the battery in a ZigBee device may last for five years before having to be recharged or replaced. Although ZigBee does not have the capability of a high data rate and it is not adequate for real-time applications, it is, per se, serves best in applications where both Wi-Fi and Bluetooth are less suitable.

ZigBee IP is an improvement to the classic ZigBee. ZigBee IP has a layered architecture that makes it suitable to work with other 802.15.4 implementations. The design of ZigBee IP accommodates an IPv6 protocol stack. This stack is developed specifically to operate on low-power and low-cost devices. Moreover, ZigBee IP incorporates technologies, such as 6LoWPAN, that optimize routing and meshing in wireless sensor networks. It supports the requirements of ZigBee Smart Energy version 2.0 as well. This combination of technologies offers a solution that enables the extension of IEEE 802.15.4 based networks to IP-based networks. In terms of the network size, ZigBee IP network is considered to be highly scalable. ZigBee IP protocol does not enforce any limitation on the network size. Theoretically, the size of the network is limited by the hardware specifications of the ZigBee devices such as the available memory and the amount of data exchanged. A typical IEEE 802.15.4 network supports a large number of ZigBee devices. Several ZigBee IP networks can coexist in the same physical area. They can be designed to interconnect at the coordinator level which allows a network to increase the number of connected devices further. The main advantage of ZigBee IP compared to other 802.15.4 technologies is its architecture. ZigBee IP provides a scalable architecture that supports an-end-to end networking based on IPv6. Therefore, many applications in the IoT benefit from this architecture.

ZigBee Network Topology

A typical ZigBee network consists of different types of devices which are the ZigBee coordinator, ZigBee routers and ZigBee end devices (Yang, 2009). Each ZigBee device on the network has a specific functionality that is defined by its operational role. The ZigBee coordinator is responsible for controlling the ZigBee network as it coordinates the messages between the ZigBee routers and ZigBee end devices (Yang, 2009). The ZigBee router acts as a message relay that performs like a bridge for ZigBee networks. The ZigBee end devices are standalone devices that participate in the ZigBee network (Yang, 2009). Figure 2 shows an example of a ZigBee network topology in which the information flow is shown. The coordinator may stand for a smart-home control system. The routers are devices such as an air conditioner or a thermostat, while the end devices can be security sensors and light switches (Jain, 2014), (Yang, 2009).

ZigBee supports different network topologies which include star and mesh topologies (Farahani, 2011). The star topology is used when the devices are close to each other and where the use of one coordinator is sufficient. A star topology can also be a part of a larger mesh network with several routers to each of which several end devices can be connected. A mesh network is a network topology that allows the nodes to communicate via an alternative path in case there is any failure in one of the intermediate devices in an existing path e.g. link redundancy (Yang, 2009). ZigBee has two operational modes, i.e., beacon mode and non-beacon mode. In the beacon node, the nodes are aware of when to communicate with one another and the coordinator periodically sends beacons to all devices on the network. Nodes, including

Figure 2. ZigBee IP network topology example

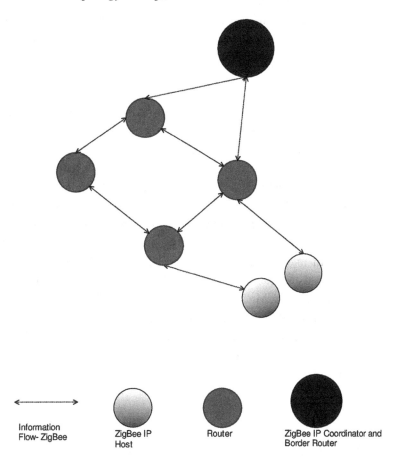

the coordinator, may sleep between beacons. The beacons sent by the coordinator check whether there is a message received or not. If there are no messages received, the nodes can go back to sleep mode. On the other hand, the non-beacon mode is characterized by less coordination between the coordinator and the nodes. Since the nodes only communicate when they need to, the coordinator's receiver is always active which enables it to receive messages from other nodes in real-time. Consequently, in the non-beacon mode, the coordinator consumes more energy since it has to be always listening. In contrast, other ZigBee devices on the network save their power since they do not need to stay awake when they are not engaging in any communication. Therefore, they remain in -sleep for a longer period of time. To better understand the differences between the beacon and non-beacon modes, consider the following simple IoT application scenario where the ZigBee network is configured in a non-beacon mode: A wireless switch is used to turn on/off an appliance e.g. a lamp. The switch is battery operated while the ZigBee node at the lamp is connected to the power supply. Therefore, the lamp (the ZigBee coordinator) is always active; while the switch (the ZigBee end device) remains asleep until someone uses the wireless switch to turn on or off the lamp. In this scenario, the switch wakes up and sends a command to the lamp which is always active and listening. The switch then remains active until it receives an acknowledgment from the lamp and then returns to sleep.

ZigBee offers seamless communications across different domains with significant functions for consumers. It allows communication with excellent interoperability among a broad range of smart and innovative business products that enhance everyday life (Elahi & Gschwender, 2009).

The 6Lowpan Protocol

6LoWPAN refers to IPv6 over Low-power Wireless Personal Area Networks. It is a low-power wireless mesh network protocol. By definition, 6LoWPAN is a protocol which enables IPv6 packets to be carried on top of low-power wireless networks, specifically IEEE 802.15.4 networks. The concept is based on the idea that the Internet Protocol should be extended to even the smallest devices, extending the applications of the IP to lightweight devices with limited processing capabilities in the IoT. 6LowPAN uses 802.15.4 in the un-slotted CSMA/CA mode and relies on beacons for link-layer device discovery (Yibo et al., 2011). Similar to ZigBee, the 6LowPAN protocol is developed based on the IEEE standard 802.15.4-2003. It has low processing and low storage costs. 6LowPAN works by fragmenting IPv6 packets and compressing them into UDP/ICMP headers. The 6LoWPAN group defines the header compression and encapsulation techniques that allow IPv6 packets to be communicated across various IEEE 802.15.4 based networks (Caputo, Mainetti, Patrono, & Vilei, 2012). 6LoWPAN is a competitor for ZigBee and BLE protocols. It has applications in smart metering and smart homes as well. 6LoWPAN supports interoperability with other implementations of the 802.15.4 protocol, and with other IP-based devices as well (Lu, Li, & Wu, 2011). Addressing and adaption mechanism are available for devices that communicate across the two different domains of IPv6 and 802.15.4. An example of a 6Lowpan network is provided in Figure 3.

Figure 3. 6Lowpan network example

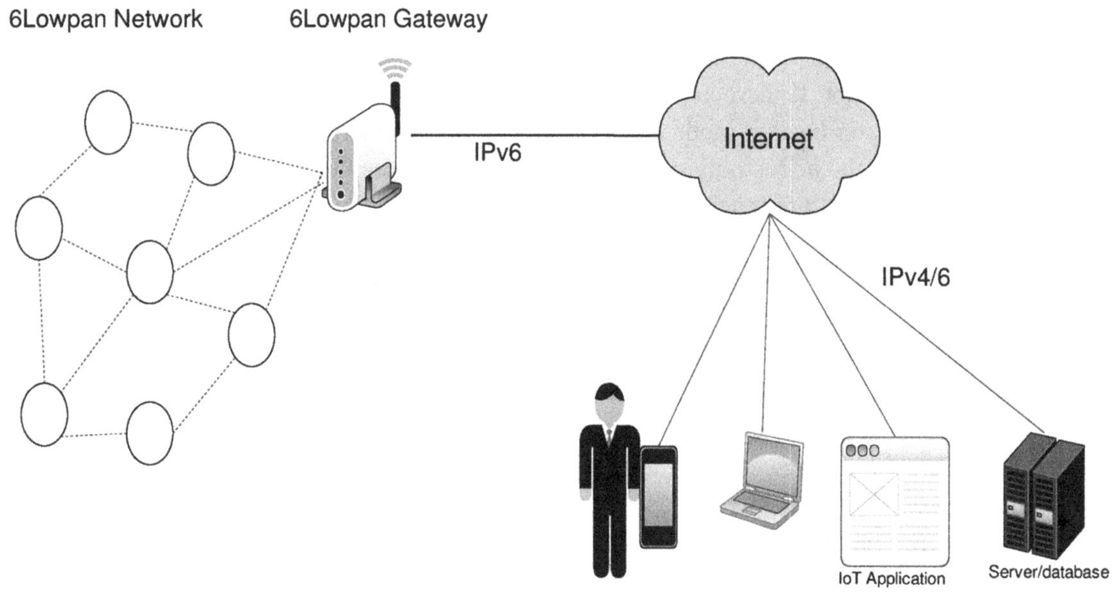

The 802.11 Wireless LAN Protocol

Wireless Local Area Networks (WLANs) is the dominant technology for indoor broadband wireless access. WLAN products have become commodity items used in professional and consumer products alike. Recently, the propagation of WLANs as extensions of wired networks has been increasing dramatically, and thereby, giving devices equipped with wireless interfaces a higher degree of mobility. The two most common WLAN standards are the IEEE 802.11 standard (commonly branded as Wi-Fi) and the European HIPER (High-Performance Radio) LAN (Lemstra, Hayes, & Groenewegen, 2010). The IEEE 802.11 defines two types of configurations, the Infrastructure Basic Service Set (iBSS), and Independent BSS (IBSS). In iBSS, an access point (AP) is the central entity of each coverage area with coordination functionality. Additionally, the AP acts as a bi-directional bridge between the wireless network and the wired infrastructure (i.e., typically Ethernet). Stations (STA) are mostly mobile devices equipped with IEEE 802.11 wireless network interfaces. Communication between the AP and the associated stations occurs over the shared wireless medium that carries the data. A station must associate with an AP in order for it to transmit and receive data to and from the wired infrastructure, and to communicate with other stations on the same WLAN. A Basic Service Set (BSS) is the term used to refer an AP and its associated stations. In large WLANs, multiple BSSs can be joined using a distribution system (DS), thus providing sufficient coverage for a greater number of stations. This setup of having two or more BSSs is referred to as an Extended Service Set (ESS). The DS is the wired backbone connecting APs and allowing the associated stations to access services available on the wired infrastructure. Therefore, Wi-Fi devices can form a star topology with its AP acting as an Internet gateway. The output power of Wi-Fi is higher than other local area network wireless technologies. Full coverage of Internet connectivity is important for Wi-Fi networks so dead spots which may occur are overcome by the use of more than one antenna in the AP.

Wi-Fi operates in the 2.4 and 5 GHz bands. Its operations in the 5 GHz band allow the use of more channels and provide higher data rates. However, the range of 5 GHz radio indoors (e.g. inside buildings) is shorter than 2.4 GHz. The IEEE 802.11b and IEEE 802.11g operate in the 2.4 GHz ISM band. Thus, they encounter interferences from other technologies operating in the same frequency band such as the microwave, cellular and Bluetooth technologies. Interference can be overcome using spectrum technologies like the Direct Sequence Spread Spectrum (DSSS) and orthogonal frequency division (OFDM) methods. The IEEE 802.11 protocol uses the ISM band to achieve good performance with a high or low frequency depending on the environment.

The IEEE 802.11n improves the previous versions of the standard by introducing the multiple input and multiple output methods (MIMO). It operates both in the 2.4 and 5 GHz frequency bands. It supports a data rate ranging from 54 Mbit/s to 600 Mbit/s (Perahia & Stacey, 2013). The IEEE 802.11ac is an improved version of the IEEE 802.11n and it provides high-throughput wireless local area networks (WLANs) in the 5 GHz band with more spatial streams and higher modulation with MIMO yielding data rates up to 433.33 Mbps (Akyildiz, Su, Sankarasubramaniam, & Cayirci, 2002). The IEEE 802.11ac provides a single link throughput of at least 500 Mbps and up to 1 gigabit per second. The IEEE 802.11ac extends the air interface concept defined by the IEEE 802.11n protocol allowing a higher throughput to be achieved. This extension includes a wider RF bandwidth of up to 160 MHz and a higher density modulation up to 256 QAM. It allows more downlink clients, up to 4 clients using multi-user MIMO, and up to eight MIMO spatial streams as well (Akyildiz et al., 2002). The IEEE 802.11ac offers a new range of WLAN use cases. For instance, the mutli-station capability allows the streaming of HD videos simultaneously to multiple clients. The single-link enhancement opens the door to a variety of automated tasks that can be achieved in a rapid and efficient way, such as the rapid synchronization and backup of large files (Bejarano, Knightly, & Park, 2013). Other IEEE 802.11ac usages include a wireless display to HD TVs and monitors, floor automation and large auditorium deployments (De Vegt, 2008). Thus, the IEEE 802.11ac serves as a promising communication technology for many IoT applications, particularly in Multimedia, monitoring and surveillance applications. Also, it is best suited for IoT scenarios that require the real-time exchange of a large amount of data. Examples are Remote Medical Assistance via Wireless Networks (raw surgical camera), Intra-Large-Vehicle Applications (e.g. airplanes, trains), Multi-Media Mesh Backhaul and point to point backhaul as shown in Figure 4. Table 1 highlights the main improvement the IEEE 802.11ac has made to the previous version of the standard, the IEEE 802.11n.

Therefore, the IEEE 802.11ac is a significant improvement in technology and data-carrying capabilities. SU-MIMO (single-user multiple input/multiple output) technology is one of the hallmarks of the older 802.11n standard (Geier, 2014). The IEEE 802.11ac supports multi-user MIMO (MU-MIMO)

Figure 4. The IEEE 802.11ac backhaul capabilities

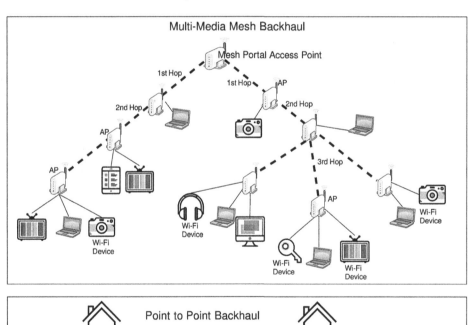

Table 1. Main differences between 802.11n and 802.11ac

	802.11n	**802.11ac**
Frequency band	2.4 and 5 GHz	Only 5 GHz
Spatial Streams	1 to 4(MIMO spatial streams)	1 to 8 (MIMO spatial streams)
Chanel width	20, 40 MHz	20,40,80, [160] MHZ
Mutli-user MIMO	No	Yes
Maximum speed	600 Mbps	3 Gbps +

technology which allows the simultaneous transmission and receiving of multiple separate signals from devices in the same frequency band. As a result, an IEEE 802.11ac router can exchange data at a maximum physical link rate of 1.3Gbps. This can be achieved because the IEEE 802.11ac protocol supports simultaneous operations of up to three streams. In contrast, an IEEE 802.11n router can only support a maximum physical link rate of 150Mbps per stream (Geier, 2014).

At the other end of the spectrum, the IEEE 802.11ah standard operates in the unlicensed 900MHz frequency band. A wireless signal operating on the 900MHz band can penetrate walls, but it would deliver a limited bandwidth ranging from 100Kbps to 40Mbps (Adame, Bel, Bellalta, Barcelo, & Oliver, 2014). One common IoT application of this technology would be sensors and actuators in homes or commercial buildings. Thus, IEEE 802.11ah could be positioned as a competitor to Bluetooth and ZigBee protocols in the IoT space.

The IEEE 802.11ah

Wi-Fi, with its 802.11 a/b/g/n/ac variants, might not be suitable to use in some IoT applications where low-power consumption is a vital requirement for the operation of IoT devices. Wi-Fi was originally designed to offer high throughput to a limited number of devices located indoor at a short distance from each other. Therefore, to meet the IoT low-power requirements, the IEEE 802 LAN/MAN Standards Committee (LMSC) formed the IEEE 802.11ah Task Group (TGah) (IEEE, 2015). The task group objective is to extend the applicability area of 802.11 networks. It aims to design an energy efficient protocol allowing thousands of indoor and outdoor devices to work in the same area (Khorov, Lyakhov, Krotov, & Guschin, 2014). The IEEE 802.11ah aims to support a range of throughput options ranging from 150 Kbps up to 40 Mbps over an 8 MHz band (Adame et al., 2014). In term of wireless range, the proposed IEEE 802.11ah protocol supports a wider coverage range when compared to the IEEE 802.11n/ac protocol. The IEEE 802.11ah supports applications with coverage of up to 1 km in outdoor areas and up to 8191 devices associated with one access point. The IEEE 802.11ah operates in the unlicensed sub-1GHz bands, excluding the TV white-space bands. Sub 1 band provides an extended wireless range when compared to the other bands used by conventional 802.11 Wi-Fi standards which operate in the 2.4 GHz and 5 GHz bands (Qualcomm, 2014). The IEEE 802.11ah relies on the one-hop network topology and employs power saving mechanisms (Adame et al., 2014). Given that the IEEE 802.11ah protocol falls under the overall Wi-Fi umbrella, it is expected that it will be compatible with the existing Wi-Fi infrastructure. The IEEE 802.11ah allows access to more than 8 thousand devices in the range of 1 km within an area with high concentration of small devices such as sensors, and mini controllers. Therefore, the IEEE 802.11ah technology can satisfy the IoT requirements while maintaining an acceptable user experience in parallel with the IEEE 802.11 technologies. One of the interesting functional requirements of the IEEE 802.11ah is to enable coexistence with the IEEE 802.15.4 standard.

The 802.11ah standard includes new PHY and MAC layers grouping devices into traffic induction maps to accommodate small units and machine to machine (M2M) communications (Valerio, 2014). The physical layer allows devices along with the AP to operate over various sub-1GHz ISM bands depending on the regulation of the country (Valerio, 2014). The 900 MHz band is currently used in Europe for GSM 2G cellular facilities. The 900 MHz is used in many devices, and it is suitable for M2M communications specifically in light devices such as wireless sensors. In some countries, the frequency bands vary from 902-928 MHz in the USA, 863-868.6 in Europe, 950.8-957.6 MHz in Japan. Other countries are expected to follow in releasing the spectrum once the 802.11ah standard is finalized.

The 802.11ah Power Saving Mode

The direct advantages of using the sub-1 GHz spectrum, also referred to as Sigsbee, in the IoT is the improvement in the coverage area for IoT devices and applications, in addition to increasing energy efficiency. Nevertheless, Sigsbee plays a significant role in wireless connectivity. It specifically targets wireless sensor networks. Applications can be found in home automation and building automation with intelligent metering instruments (AMI). The IEEE 802.11ah protocol implements energy-saving mechanisms which guarantee that the limited energy resources available for a sensor node are efficiently used. A large number of devices can be accommodated by a single IEEE 802.11ah AP due to the infrequent data exchange in some IoT applications. However, the device' activity needs to be properly distributed over time (Adame et al., 2014).

The IEEE 802.11 standard defines two states for a wireless network interface: awake or sleep. In the awake state, the device's radio is turned on allowing the wireless interface to perform data communications, or just to remain idle (Asha, 2012). In the sleep state, the radio of the device is turned off, and the wireless interface is put to sleep (He, Yuan, Ma, & Li, 2008). This state is specified in the IEEE 802.11 standard as Power Saving Mode (PSM). In PSM, the AP buffers incoming frames destined for mobile stations. It continues doing this until the station wakes up. When the device wakes up, the buffered traffic will be delivered. The station goes back to PSM once the buffered traffic is fully delivered (He et al., 2008). To achieve this, the IEEE 802.11ah standard defines two classes of signalling beacon frames: (a) Delivery Traffic Indication Map (DTIM) which informs which groups of STAs have pending data at the AP, and (b) the Traffic Indication Map (TIM) which specifies which STA in a given STA group has pending data at the AP. Consequently, the PSM, TIM, and Page Segmentation result in a new scheme which improves the overall power efficiency of IEEE 802.11ah devices. For further reading on the new proposed PSM scheme, the reader is referred to (Adame et al., 2013).

On the other hand, the IEEE 802.11af, also called Super Wi-Fi or White-Fi, operates in the unused TV spectrum. 802.11af coverage can extend up to several kilometers as it operates on the frequency bands between 54MHz and 790MHz. It offers a reasonable throughput, estimated at 24Mb/s. It has similar applications as 802.11ah, providing bandwidth for sensors and other devices of the IoT (Mohapatra, Choudhury, & Das, 2014).

A COMPARATIVE STUDY OF IOT ENABLING WIRELESS TECHNOLOGIES

Nowadays, the wireless industry is increasingly adopting the IoT. There is a growing momentum to embrace and design technologies that adhere explicitly to the IoT requirements. This includes the modification of existing technologies e.g. from Bluetooth classic to Bluetooth smart, and from ZigBee to ZigBee IP, as we have seen in the previous sections. Moreover, it also involves the design of new technologies such as the IEEE 802.11ah. These technologies aim at addressing key IoT wireless and devices' requirements, such as low-power consumption, lower computation capabilities, reduced implementation and operational costs, and wider coverage range. The previous section provided a brief review of the IEEE 802.15.4 technologies, Bluetooth Low energy, and the IEEE 802.11ah technology. The IEEE 802.15.4 family of technologies such as the 6Lowpan and ZigBee technologies are currently used in various wireless sensor network applications. These applications are characterized by requirements similar to those encountered in IoT and M2M applications. The Bluetooth Low Energy technology is widely adopted in wearables and consumer products. On the other hand, the IEEE 802.11ah is a new protocol under development. It is designed to operate in the sub-one-gigahertz (900MHz) band. It has an extended range when compared to traditional Wi-Fi, and it is regarded as a competitor for both ZigBee, 6Lowpan, and the other already-established protocols in this sub-one band.

However, all the aforementioned technologies have their positive qualities and obviously have their negatives as well. For instance, the gain in range with the use of the IEEE 802.11ah is lost in bandwidth, whereas with the use of ZigBee the gain in bandwidth is lost in range. Therefore, rather than attempting to nominate the ideal technology for the IoT, this section presents a brief comparison of some of these wireless technologies. The areas of the IoT involve heterogeneous sets of devices which use various communication technologies to share and exchange information. Within the IoT, some IoT applications can be in the form of simple peer-to-peer applications. Other IoT applications can also be based on personal area network setups, involving the use of few devices and users. Other complex applications might involve the use of a variety of heterogeneous devices which communicate using a wide array of technologies, in different setups and topologies. Therefore, a technology that can be deemed suitable for a particular IoT application might not necessarily be suited for adoption in many others. In fact, the ability to connect and coexist amongst various devices operating using several communication technologies is the spirit behind the IoT. Having an ecosystem of coexisted technologies and devices is what enables the IoT vision of extending communications to anything, and anywhere.

Data Rate and Range

The IEEE 802.11ac and LTE advanced have the highest data rate among the wireless technologies in use today. The IEEE 802.11ac specification provides a theoretical maximum data transfer speed of more than 3Gbps. It can provide a transfer speed up to 1.3Gbps as well, and supports up to 8 streams (Siddiqui, Zeadally, & Salah, 2015). On the other hand, LTE Advanced has a1 Gbps fixed speed and a rate of 100 Mbps to mobile users (Stroud, 2015). Figure 5 compares between various wireless technologies in terms of distance coverage in meters, rates, ranges and power consumptions.

In the low-power wireless technology space, Bluetooth Low Energy has the highest data rate of 2.1 Mbps. The ZigBee and 6Lowpan technologies, supported by the IEEE 802.15.4 standard, have a data rate of 250 Kbps in 2.4 GHz frequency band. However, ZigBee's data rate falls to 20 Kbps in the 868 MHz band and to 40 Kbps in the 915 MHz band in some countries (Anitha & Chandrasekar, 2011). On the other hand, the IEEE 802.11.ah has the lowest data rate targeted at 150Kbps with an average of 100 Kbps. In term of the theoretical wireless range, as illustrated in Figure 5, cellular technologies, e.g. LTE, cover a larger area when compared with other Wi-Fi technologies, with IEEE 802.11 variants coming second at an approximate maximum range of a 100 m.

As of the range of low-power wireless technologies, the IEEE 802.11ah rules the chart against 802.15.4 and BLE technologies in terms of range. The 802.11ah coverage range also outperforms that of the other variants of the 802.11 protocol, with a range coverage of approximately 1 km, as shown in Figures 5 and 6. On the other hand, it should be noted that the 802.15.4 supports mesh networking. Meshing in mesh networking is a term used to describe when a message is routed through several nodes on a network until it reaches its destination. As such a ZigBee network's range can be easily extended with the use of repeaters in a mesh formation. Data in a ZigBee network "hops" around a mesh of nodes until a route to the host (usually the Internet) is found. Therefore, repeaters and/or a high density of nodes can be used to extend the coverage of a ZigBee network.

Figure 5. Comparative study of IoT enabling wireless technologies against power consumption, distance coverage in meters, and data rate

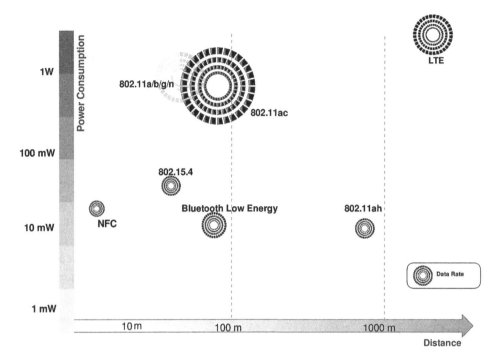

Figure 6. IEEE 802.11 a/b/g/n/ac range comparison in meters

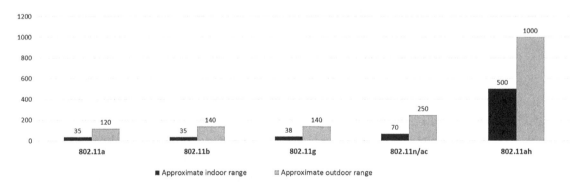

Interestingly, the IEEE 802.11ah is under development with meshing in mind as well. Therefore, the choice of technology in terms of data rate and range come back to the requirements of the IoT applications in hand. Accordingly, if an IoT application requires the use of a larger number of nodes and meshing is an option, ZigBee appears to be a suitable candidate given the data rate edge over its 802.11ah counterpart. On the other hand, in IoT applications that require the deployment of fewer nodes with minimal traffic, 802.11ah is a strong contender to ZigBee. This is due to the reason that 802.11ah has a larger coverage area without relying on any meshing technique, and it is intended to be backward compatible with the variants of 802.11 Wi-Fi technology. However, as we will see in the next subsections, relying on the data rate and range differences only does not provide an efficient measure for the selection of a technology as there are other criteria that should be considered as well.

Network Size

The BLE protocol supports a maximum of 8 nodes per network which include one master device and 7 devices as slaves. ZigBee can have up to 65,000 nodes per network in a star topology (Baker, 2005). Both of these technologies can be extended into more sophisticated networks. For instance, ZigBee can be extended to a cluster tree or mesh network while BLE can be extended to a scatternet network. An interconnected piconet consisting of more than 8 Bluetooth devices is referred to as a scatternet. It is the process of connecting two piconets together. A scatternet can be created when a device belonging to one piconet is elected to be a member of the second piconet as well (McDermott-Wells, 2004).

On the other hand, the baseline IEEE 802.11 standard does not limit the number of devices in the network. However, the limitation can be attributed to the length of some of the fields defined in the management frames of the standard (IEEE 802.11 Working Group, 2010). The Association Identifier (AID) which is a unique value assigned to a station by the AP during an association handshake, is 14 bits long. However, the values other than 1-2007, which are 0 and 2008-16383, are reserved. In particular, AID = 0 is reserved for group addressing traffic (Khorov et al., 2014). Therefore, the AID design limits the number of stations that can be associated with an AP to 2007 (Khorov et al., 2014). Additionally, the Traffic Indication Map (TIM) bitmap enforces the same limit on the number of associated stations as well. The TIM is used for power management mechanisms. It defines the number of buffered frames received from an AP. For these reasons, TGah is extending the range of AID values for 802.11ah's devices from 1-2007 to 0-8191. Also, the IEEE 802.11ah draft standard is increasing the maximal length of the TIM bitmap for 802.11ah's devices from 2008 bits to 8192 bits (Khorov et al., 2014). Therefore, it is quite obvious that ZigBee and the IEEE 802.11ah outperform the classical 802.11a/ac protocol when it comes to the network size requirements. Of course, cellular technologies have an enormous network size. However, cellular connectivity cannot be possible without involving a mobile provider which usually charges a fee per connection. Therefore, while cellular technology can accommodate an enormous network size of devices, the cost involved are dramatically higher than those associated with other technologies such as ZigBee. Table 2 provides a brief comparison between ZigBee, BLE and Wi-Fi in terms of their network size.

RF Channels and Bandwidth

Tables 3 shows some of the main differences between the various wireless technologies. These technologies operate in a broad range of frequencies. For instance, ZigBee operates in the 868/915 MHz, and 2.4 GHz. 6LoWPAN operates in the 900 to 2400 MHz; 802.11a/b/g/n/ac works in the 2.4 and 5 GHz bands. On the other hand, the IEEE 802.11ah is fragmented over various frequency bands based in the

Table 2. Network size comparison of ZigBee, BLE and Wi-Fi

Technology	Network Size
ZigBee	Approximately up to 65,000 nodes
Bluetooth	8 nodes per network/piconet
Wi-Fi (802.11a/ac)	2007 associated with an AP
Wi-Fi 802.11ah	Approximately 8000 nodes

Table 3. Comparative study of various wireless technologies

Wireless Technology	Applications (Example)	Frequency	Range	Data Rate
ZigBee	Home Automation, Industrial Monitoring, Light link.	2.4 GHz	10 to 20 m	250 Kbps
RFID	RFID Tags, Access management, Machine readable documents.	120-150 KHz	10cm-200m	26 Kbps
Bluetooth 4	Bluetooth smart, Fitness tracker, wearable devices.	868/915 2.4GHz	<100m	2.1 Mbps
Cellular e.g. 3G/LTE	Any device with Cellular connectivity capability	Australia: 2100Mhz, 1800MHz, 900Mhz 850MHz	Where signal reach	7.64-100 Mbps up to 1 Gbps fixed in LTE Advanced
802.11 a to ac	Smart Homes	2.4, 3.6, 5, 60 GHz	Up to 100m	Up to 1.3Gbps
NFC	Metro tickets, Mobile payment, Shopping center.	13.56 MHz	< 20 cm	106 to 424 Kbps
6LoWPAN	Smart Homes, Smart Metering	900 to 2400 MHz	10-20 m	200 kbps
Sub-1 GHz 802.11ah	Smart Home Wireless sensor networks, metering automation.	Sub 1 GHz	Up to 1KM	150 Kbps

country. It is observed that most of these technologies, excluding that of the IEEE 802.11ah, operate in the 2.4 GHz band. In addition to Bluetooth, Wi-Fi, and ZigBee, RFID operates in the 2.45 GHz band (microwave) as well.

Another observation is that the IEEE 802.11ah protocol operates in sub-1GHz band for the purpose of saving power and extending the range of Wi-Fi. However, this shifting of bands for Wi-Fi means 802.11ah's frequency band operations will differ from one country to another. For instance, 802.11ah operates at 868 MHz in Europe, 780 MHz in China, and in a range of other frequencies in other countries. The variability in frequency operations of 802.11ah hampers the unification of Wi-Fi products and adds another level of complexity and fragmentation to the already fragmented IoT. As such, 802.11ah's product makers will have to deal with different sets of regulations and certifications for various regions.

In term of modulation, Bluetooth employs frequency hopping (FHSS) with 79 channels and 1 MHz bandwidth; while Wi-Fi uses OFDM modulation in 802.11a/g/n with 14 RF channels and 22 MHz bandwidth, and ZigBee uses direct-sequence spread spectrum (DSSS) with 2 MHz bandwidth and 16 available channels. Refer to Table 4 for a modulation comparison for these technologies. It should be noted that Wi-Fi uses a variety of modulation techniques including BPSK, CCK, OFDM, DSSS, QPSK, and M-QAM.

Table 4. Frequency modulation comparison

Technology	802.11a/n	802.11b	802.11g	802.11ac/ah	ZigBee	Bluetooth
Modulation	OFDM	DSSS	DSSS OFDM	OFDM	BPSK ASK OQPSK	AFH FHSS

Antenna Considerations

Designing antennas for wireless devices is becoming an emerging area of research. Typically, larger antennas are required when the devices are operating over a lower frequency band. Therefore, given that a ZigBee 2.4 GHz device can work well with a 6 cm antenna, a sub-GHz device will require under comparable circumstances a larger antenna (Araiza Leon, 2015). For instance, when standardizing 802.11ac, one of the selling point of .11ac technology in addition to its data rate speed, was the reduced size of antenna requirement given that .11ac operates in the 5 GHz band (Qualcomm, 2012). Therefore, it will be interesting to watch the antenna design TGah will adopt in IEEE 802.11ah. The antenna design of MIMO and other solutions are also evolving. Examples are those based on Steerable Square Loop antenna design such as the one proposed in (Pal, Mehta, Mirshekar-Syahkal, Deo, & Nakano, 2014).

Transmission Power

As shown in Figure 5 and Table 5, the 802.15.4 based technologies; BLE and 802.11ah, all have a low power consumption characteristic. The transmission power of BLE ranges from 1 to 10 mW (Dementyev, Hodges, Taylor, & Smith, 2013). ZigBee transmission power is very low estimated to be under 1 mW, while, the Wi-Fi standard has a transmission power of approximately 100 mW. On the other hand, the IEEE 802.11ah has a transmission power of less than 10 mW. It is targeted to be under 1mW with the new proposed PSM scheme which aims for better energy efficiency.

In (Olyaei, Pirskanen, Raeesi, Hazmi, & Valkama, 2013), it was found that in terms of energy consumption, and in the case of a small number of nodes in a low traffic scenario, the IEEE 802.15.4 consumed more average energy for the successful transmission of a packet compared with IEEE 802.11ah. However, in congested networks, the energy consumption of the IEEE 802.11ah was found to be relatively higher than that of IEEE 802.15.4. Therefore, the study concludes that, in terms of energy consumption, the IEEE 802.15.4 outperformed the IEEE 802.11ah, especially in a dense network and non-saturated traffic. However, in terms of throughput, the IEEE 802.11ah has a better performance when compared to IEEE 802.15.4. Nevertheless, it should be noted that, at the time of writing, the IEEE 802.11ah standard is still under development. Thus, more simulations and experimental studies are required to determine the performance of IEEE 802.11ah effectively.

Table 5. A comparative study of low power wireless technologies

Technology	Bluetooth Low Energy	ZigBee	6Lowpan	Wi-Fi
Standard	IEEE 802.15.1	IEEE 802.15.4	IEEE 802.15.4	IEEE 802.11ah
Data rate	1 Mbps	250Kbps	250kbps	150Kbps
Theoretical Range	100 m	10 to 20 m	~20 m	Up to 1000 m
Bandwidth	1 MHz	2Mhz	0.3/0.6; 2 MHz	1,2,4,8,16 MHz
Power consumption	0.01 to 0.5 W	~1mW	~1mW	~1mW
Security	128-bit AES with Counter Mode CBC-MAC and application layer user defined	TLS1.2 AES-128-CCM X.509 v3 certificates and ECC-256 cipher suite	AES link layer TSL/SSL on	Application layer security similar to 802.11

The Ecosystem

In term of the ecosystem, The IEEE 802.11ah has the potential to stand out amongst its counterparts. Given that the IEEE 802.11ah falls under the overall Wi-Fi umbrella, it is expected that it will be compatible with the existing Wi-Fi infrastructure, specifically to be compatible with IEEE 802.11a/b/g/n/ac standards. The IEEE 802.11ah has the potential to grow the Wi-Fi market from its existing computing and mobile platforms to the IoT market significantly. However, since the IEEE 802.11ah still in its early stage of development, it is yet to establish itself against already recognized technologies such as BLE and ZigBee. However, as shown in Figure 7, the IEEE 802.11ah implements the full TCP/IP stack when compared to 6Lowpan and ZigBee.

Nevertheless, ZigBee has been winning grounds in several IoT consumer based applications including electronics, smart meter infrastructure, and home automation. When meshing can be used, ZigBee's data rate differentiates it against the IEEE 802.11ah. ZigBee's is increasingly being adopted in IoT areas such as automated meter reading, leading to participation in the smart grid push by utility companies. This has become an especially active area for ZigBee. However, implementation of ZigBee remains, in greater parts, within closed ecosystems and applications. For instance, the lack of a native support for ZigBee in the mobile device domain (smartphones, tablets, laptops, smart watches, gadgets, car multimedia etc.), is a major challenge for early IoT adopters, more specifically, in applications where a mobile device is used as a temporary gateway for IoT devices.

On the other hand, Bluetooth Low Energy is a potential competitor in some IoT areas. It might find applications in medical equipment and in remote control applications. BLE has been dominating the consumer electronics market. Additionally, BLE has been increasingly used to eliminate cabling for peripherals. This brings these peripherals closer to the communication networks and allows the management of these devices. Table 6 compares the ecosystems of ZigBee, BLE, and IEEE 802.11ah.

The criteria considered in the rating of technologies provided in Table 6 and the conclusions that can be drawn from Table 6 include the following:

- The wireless technologies surveyed above have built-in link layer authentication and encryption, which most likely need to be completed with an end-to-end security at the application layer.
- Bluetooth low energy has the potential for less power consumption than IEEE 802.15.4 (less overhead).

Figure 7. Comparative study of TCP/IP stack with ZigBee, 6Lowpan, and IEEE 802.11ah

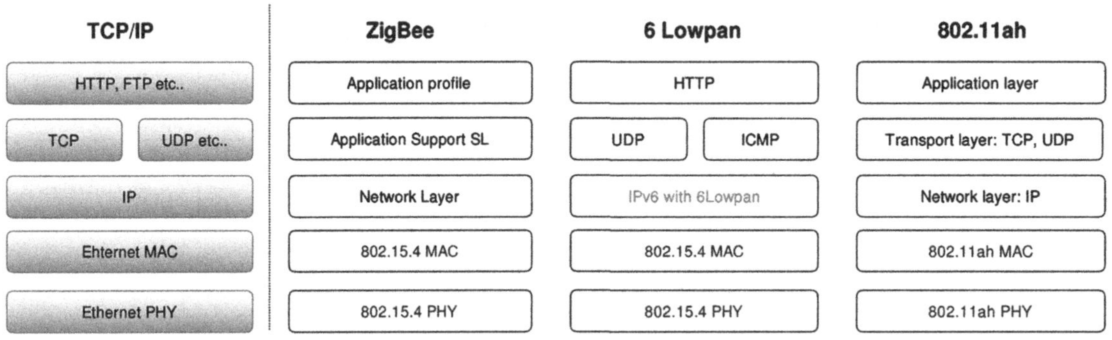

Table 6. Comparative study of ZigBee, BLE and 802.11ah based on various criteria

	Security	Location Detection	Low Cost	Ease of Use	Ecosystem	Low Power	Range	Remote Control	Antenna Size	Networking Size	Frequency Band
802.15.4	✓	✓	✓	✓	✓	✓	✓(✓)	✓	✓	✓	✓
BLE	✓	✗	✓	✓	✓	✓	✗	✓	✓	✗	✓
802.11ah	✓	✓	✓	✓	✓	✓	✓	✓	✓	✓(✓)	✓
Comment			Wi-Fi target: as per ZigBee	Wi-Fi target: as per 802.11	- BLE and 802.11ah have a larger ecosystem. BLE is established in phones, wearables, etc... 802.11ah compatible with 802.11 ZigBee has a closed ecosystem established in some use cases e.g. smart energy	802.11ah target: as per ZigBee	Criteria: 'home'. ZigBee Mesh will improve range. BLE: Room range Wi-Fi: Home range, extendable by mesh		lower freque-ncies require larger antennas	Criteria: >1000 Nodes per network. ZigBee has an edge of networking size of 65,000 device	802.15.4 and BLE operate on 2.4 GHz; while 802.11ah is fragmented by region

- The IEEE 802.15.4 lacks the native support in the important ecosystem of mobile devices.
- The ecosystem with phones, tablets, laptops and phone accessories is driving down the cost of Bluetooth low energy.
- The IEEE 802.15.4 has a data rate advantage over the IEEE 802.11ah. As of coverage, similar to the IEEE 802.11ah, many IEEE 802.15.4 based technologies (e.g. ZigBee) support mesh whereby repeaters can be used to extend the coverage.
- The IEEE 802.11ah can be used in a variety of existing devices which will significantly improve the low-power consumption for these devices.
- 6LoWPAN implementation allows a device to communicate with another device over the Internet without having to go through, for example, a ZigBee-to-IP translation layer/device. At the time of writing, it is not clear as yet if the IEEE 802.11ah is backward compatible with existing IEEE 802.11n/ac infrastructure and if any sort of infrastructure update or upgrade is needed. However, the fact that IEEE 802.11 is widely accepted as the dominant indoor wireless technology including IEEE 802.11 based indoor access points (APs) and stations (Aust, Prasad, & Niemegeers, 2012), makes Wi-Fi's infrastructure compatibility with IEEE 802.11ah is a core aspect for its adoption.
- 6LoWPAN offers interoperability with other wireless IEEE 802.15.4 devices as well as with devices on any other IP network with the use of a simple bridging device. However, bridging between ZigBee and non-ZigBee networks requires a more complex application layer gateway.
- For the IoT scenario that requires the use of thousands of devices, ZigBee has a networking size of 65,000 devices. Similarly, the IEEE 802.11ah can also cater for approximately 8 thousand devices as well. Data rate and the required coverage area play their roles in marking the differences between these two technologies as well.
- The IEEE 802.11ah benefits from the optimal propagation characteristic of sub-1GHz license-exempt frequency bands compared to 2.4 and 5 GHz bands. However, as mentioned before, the IEEE 802.11ah frequency band fragmentation across different countries might be an issue in some IoT applications.

Security

As discussed in the Introduction, the evolution of wireless technologies specifically low-power wireless technologies is driving the growth of the IoT. New devices are increasingly getting connected to the Internet, from connected vehicles to connected homes and cities. This growth in connected devices to the communication networks translates into increased security risks and poses new challenges to security. A device which connects to the Internet, whether it is a constraint or smart device, inherits the security risks of today's computer devices. Almost all security challenges are inherent to the IoT. Hence, some fundamental security requirements in the IoT, such as authorization, authentication, confidentiality, trust, and access control need to be considered. Things should be securely connected to their designated network(s), securely controlled and accessed by authorized entities. Data generated by things need to be collected, analyzed, stored, dispatched and always presented in a secure manner. Notwithstanding, there are security risks associated with things to things communications as well. The heterogeneity of devices and communications in the IoT pose many new security challenges. For instance, the integration of WSNs into the Internet, as part of the IoT, creates new security problems. These security problems are derived from the process of connecting a sensor node with an Internet device. For instance, low-cost and constrained devices that use low-power communication technologies, such as ZigBee or IEEE 802.11ah, need to establish a secure communication channel with more capable devices such as a smartphone. Thus, securing this communication channel requires the use of adequate cryptographic and key management solutions without consuming a lot of bandwidth and energy. This is in addition to the need to employ security protocols which securely connect these devices to the Internet. Add another essential security requirement, such as the need to authorize the devices involved in the communications, and the degree of achieving security for this simple communication scenario increases in complexity.

Significantly, the IoT is vulnerable to the Denial of Service (DoS) attack. Typically, a DoS attack floods a given server with false requests for services. Thus, it prevents legitimate requesters from accessing the server's services (Mirkovic & Reiher, 2004). It attempts to exhaust the computational resources of the server. The IoT vulnerability to the DoS attack is not only limited to things which connect to the Internet directly, but also extended to WSNs. Additionally, the heterogeneous nature and complexity of communications envisioned in the IoT, makes the IoT vulnerable to the distributed denial of service (DDoS) attack. A DDoS attack is a DoS attack made by multiple agents in the network and from various locations (Misra, Krishna, Agarwal, Saxena, & Obaidat, 2011). Therefore, disruptive attacks such as the DoS and DDoS attacks are a serious potential risk to the IoT. Many IoT devices have limited processing capabilities and memory constraints. Therefore, DDoS attacks can easily exhaust their resources. Also, in things- to-things communications, DoS attacks can prove to be difficult to notice before the disruption of the service which could generally be attributed to battery exhaustion (Heer et al., 2011).

In terms of the security features of BLE, ZigBee, 6LowPAN and Wi-Fi, Tables 7 and 8 show the security features supported by these technologies. They show that all the aforementioned technologies support some sort of security. For instance, BLE supports 128-bit AES and ZigBee uses 128-bit keys to implement its security mechanisms. Similarly, 6LowPAN which is based on the IEEE 802.15.4 standard can operate in either secure mode or non-secure mode. The 6lowpan security analysis draft defines two security modes for 6LowPAN: the secure mode and Access Control List. 6LowPAN uses IP at the higher layers. Thus, traditional security protocols which normally are used with Wi-Fi (802.11a/ac) can be used with 6LowPAN. The difference however between Wi-Fi and 6LowPAN is that the later uses a bridge between the end point devices and the router/bridge. This creates a weak intrusion point. For other protocols, depending on the topology of the network, there could be two intrusion points. One at the router or bridge end and one at the gateway end where Internet connectivity is established. The IEEE 802.11ah supports security at the application level. Wi-Fi, in general (IEEE 802.11a/ac), enables unified policy management as the traffic generated from an IoT device can be scanned and secured at the network entry point.

Importantly, 6LowPAN, ZigBee and the rest of low-power wireless protocols have small bandwidth. Thus, adding a security protocol adds to the overhead and reduces the already limited bandwidth available for the communications. For these reasons, the security protocols used by the IEEE 802.15.4 link layer cannot be considered very strong. Thus, technologies based on IEEE 802.15.4 are more vulnerable to intrusions when compared with IEEE 802.11a/ac. Table 8 shows the security suites supported by IEEE 802.15.4. On the other hand, it will be interesting to watch the security mechanism the IEEE 802.11ah is going to adopt once it is finalized.

Table 9 summarizes the implications to security posed by the use of low-power wireless technologies in the IoT including IEEE 802.11ah, and IEEE 802.15.4 based technologies. It shows that lightweight cryptographic security solutions are needed for the IoT.

Henceforth, devices in the IoT are increasingly becoming wireless, often adopting different wireless technologies and RF interfaces. This diversity of devices and technologies create several security threats. Therefore, it is important to understand the capabilities and security vulnerability of low-power wireless technologies. To overcome these vulnerabilities, existing lightweight security solutions need to be further explored and exploited to determine their applicability in the IoT. On the other hand, IoT applications need to account for security right from their design stage.

Table 7. Security features of ZigBee, BLE and Wi-Fi

ZigBee	Bluetooth Low Energy	Wi-Fi
• **Confidentiality:** AES-CTR • **Authentication:** AES-CBC-MAC with 32-, 64-, or 128-bit MAC • **Confidentiality and Authentication:** AES-CCM with 32-, 64-, or 128-bit MAC	• **Security Mode 1:** Is non-secure, with authentication and encryption turned off • **Security Mode 2:** The security manager can implement different security policies and trust levels for different applications. • **Security Mode 3 and 4:** Uses Elliptic Curve Diffie-Hellman (ECDH) public key cryptography for key exchange and link key generation	WPA2: • **Encryption:** Counter Mode with Cipher Block Chaining Message Authentication Code Protocol (CCMP) with 128-bit AES block cipher. • **Data Integrity:** Cryptographic hash function • Support Key Management and reply detection

Table 8. Security suites supported by 802.15.4

Name	Description
AES-CTR	Encryption only, CTR Mode
AES-CBC-MAC-128 AES-CBC-MAC-64 AES-CBC-MAC-32	128 bit MAC 64 bit MAC 32 bit MAC
AES-CCM-128 AES-CCM-64 AES-CCM-32	Encryption with 128 bit MAC Encryption with 64 bit MAC Encryption with 32 bit MAC

Table 9. Security requirements and implication in the IoT

Requirements	Security Implications
Low-Power Consumption Low Bandwidth	• Security traffic should be minimal. • Security establishment should continue during the device sleep time. • Security establishment should not exhaust the device battery. Thus, the computational security establishment's cost should be efficient in term of energy consumption.
Several devices might be connected to a single Access Point (AP)	• APs are vulnerable to single point of failure attack. • APs such as an 802.11ah's AP needs to buffer data for sleeping devices. Thus, Security needs to be maintained at all time.
Devices may be mobile	Initial security establishment needs to be maintained during mobility.

To conclude, the choice between Wi-Fi, including IEEE 802.11ah, Bluetooth, and ZigBee comes back to the IoT application requirements. The cost, data rate, range, network size, ecosystem and importantly the level of security required are the requirements that can be used to select a suitable wireless technology in a given IoT application. Additionally, there are other criteria which have not been fully discussed in this Chapter which might impact on the choice of technologies as well. Examples are the QoS and privacy requirements.

Table 10. Case studies

Name of the Study	Findings
Performance Evaluation of IEEE 802.15.4 for Low-Rate Wireless Personal Area Networks. (Lee, 2006)	• IEEE 802.15.4 has better performance in non-beacon mode • The highest raw data rate achieved is 156 kbps
Performance Evaluation of IEEE 802.15.4 Physical Layer Using MatLab/Simulink. (Alnuaimi, Shuaib, & Jawhar, 2006)	Signal Bit Error Rate (BER) and Signal to Noise Ratio (SNR) values are affected by the data rate and number of bits per symbol.
Comparative assessments of IEEE 802.15.4/ZigBee and 6LoWPAN for low-power industrial WSNs in realistic scenarios. (Toscano & Bello, 2012)	• ZigBee network is greatly influenced by the beacon interval • under low workload, the 6LoWPAN performance is more affected by the duty cycle than by the actual workload • On average, 6LoWPAN protocol provided smaller end-to-end delay when compared with ZigBee • A low-power WSN characterized by low workload should keep the beacon intervals as small as possible • ZigBee network can support smaller duty cycles and provide smaller maximum end-to-end delays and update times slightly closer to the theoretical value than 6LowPAN • 6LoWPAN network shows smaller mean end-to-end delays and higher reliability when compared with ZigBee
A Comparative Study of Wireless Protocols: Bluetooth, UWB, ZigBee, and Wi-Fi. (Pothuganti & Chitneni, 2014)	• The required transmission time is proportional to the data payload size and disproportional to the maximum data rate. • The transmission time ZigBee is longer than BLE and Wi-Fi • In terms of data coding efficiency: for large data sizes, Bluetooth, and Wi-Fi have much better efficiency of over 94%, as compared to 76.52% of ZigBee. • In terms of Power consumption, ZigBee consumed slightly less energy when compared with Bluetooth
Performance comparison between Slotted IEEE 802.15.4 and IEEE 802.11ah in IoT based applications. (Olyaei et al., 2013)	• In congested networks: IEEE 802.11ah outperformed 802.15.4 in terms of throughput. • In some scenarios, the IEEE 802.15.4 slightly outperformed the IEEE 802.11ah in terms of energy consumption.

Observations

Table 10 provides a summary of some relevant studies from the literature. These studies compared and evaluated some technologies which fall under the low-power wireless technology umbrella.

CONCLUSION

In the early days of the Internet which was basically centered on computers, a network of networks was the term used to define the Internet. In the IoT, it seems everything is going to be connected, pants, shoes, shirts, fridges, glasses, washing machines, gardens, dogs, cars, airplanes, cities, you name it. Yet, the term network of networks can still be used to define the IoT. What's new is that connected networks are no longer limited to IP-connected devices/networks in the fashion that we know today. Instead, there are islands of networks using various network technologies. A proliferation of technology protocols has rapidly emerged, with each standard hoping to fill a void or improve on another. This Chapter reviewed and compared some of these enabling technologies particularly, ZigBee, 6lowpan, BLE, and Wi-Fi including the low-power IEEE 802.11ah protocol. It provided comparative studies of these technologies by evaluating their capabilities and behaviours in terms of various metrics including the data range and rate, network size, RF Channels and Bandwidth, antenna design considerations, power consumption, security, and the ecosystem. It is concluded that the choice of a network protocol is greatly influenced by the requirements of the IoT application in hand. Therefore, a technology that might seem right for a particular IoT application might not necessarily be suited for adoption in many others. Ultimately, the challenge remains on how to allow interoperability between these various technologies creating an ecosystem of coexisted devices connecting to the Internet using various wireless protocols, enabling the true IoT vision of extending communications to anything, and anywhere.

REFERENCES

Adame, T., Bel, A., Bellalta, B., Barcelo, J., Gonzalez, J., & Oliver, M. (2013). *Capacity analysis of IEEE 802.11 ah WLANs for M2M communications*. Springer.

Adame, T., Bel, A., Bellalta, B., Barcelo, J., & Oliver, M. (2014). IEEE 802.11 AH: The WiFi approach for M2M communications. *IEEE Wireless Communications*, *21*(6), 144–152. doi:10.1109/MWC.2014.7000982

Ahmed, H. (2013). *Study on the trade off between throughput and power consumption in the design of Bluetooth Low Energy applications*. The University of Tennessee At Chattanooga.

Akyildiz, I. F., Su, W., Sankarasubramaniam, Y., & Cayirci, E. (2002). Wireless sensor networks: A survey. *Computer Networks*, *38*(4), 393–422. doi:10.1016/S1389-1286(01)00302-4

Alnuaimi, M., Shuaib, K., & Jawhar, I. (2006). Performance evaluation of IEEE 802.15. 4 physical layer using MatLab/simulink. *Paper presented at the Innovations in Information Technology*, Dubai, UAE.

Anitha, P., & Chandrasekar, C. (2011). Energy Aware Routing Protocol For Zigbee Networks. *Journal of Computer Applications, 4*(3), 92–94.

Araiza Leon, J. C. (2015). *Evaluation of IEEE 802.11 ah Technology for Wireless Sensor Network Applications* [Master's thesis]. Tampere University of Technology.

Asha, M. M. (2012). Analysis of PS Protocols Using Markov and Cluster Modelin 802.11 WLANS. *Analysis, 2*(2), 298–305.

Aust, S., Prasad, R. V., & Niemegeers, I. G. (2012). IEEE 802.11 ah: Advantages in standards and further challenges for sub 1 GHz Wi-Fi. *Paper presented at the IEEE International Conference on Communications (ICC)*, Ottawa, Canada.

Baker, N. (2005). ZigBee and Bluetooth: Strengths and weaknesses for industrial applications. *Computing & Control Engineering Journal, 16*(2), 20–25. doi:10.1049/cce:20050204

Bejarano, O., Knightly, E. W., & Park, M. (2013). IEEE 802.11 ac: From channelization to multi-user MIMO. *IEEE Communications Magazine, 51*(10), 84–90. doi:10.1109/MCOM.2013.6619570

Bluetooth SIG. (2001). Bluetooth specification version 1.1. Retrieved from http://www.bluetooth.com

Bluetooth, S. I. G. (2012). Bluetooth Core Version 4.0. Retrieved from https://www.bluetooth.org/Technical/Specifications/adopted.htm

Bluetooth Smart Technology. (2015). Powering the Internet of Things. Retrieved from http://www.bluetooth.com/Pages/Bluetooth-Smart.aspx

Caputo, D., Mainetti, L., Patrono, L., & Vilei, A. (2012). Implementation of the EXI schema on wireless sensor nodes using Contiki. *Paper presented at the 2012 Sixth International Conference on Innovative Mobile and Internet Services in Ubiquitous Computing (IMIS)*, Palermo, Italy.

Chen, D., Nixon, M., & Mok, A. (2010). *WirelessHART*. Springer. doi:10.1007/978-1-4419-6047-4

De Vegt, R. (2008). 802.11 ac Usage Models Document. *IEEE 802.11-09/0161r2.*

Dementyev, A., Hodges, S., Taylor, S., & Smith, J. (2013). Power Consumption Analysis of Bluetooth Low Energy, ZigBee and ANT Sensor Nodes in a Cyclic Sleep Scenario. *Microsoft Research.*

Elahi, A., & Gschwender, A. (2009). *ZigBee wireless sensor and control network*. Pearson Education.

Elkhodr, M., Shahrestani, S., & Cheung, H. (2013). The Internet of Things: Vision & Challenges. *Paper presented at the IEEE Tencon*, Sydney, Australia. doi:10.1109/TENCONSpring.2013.6584443

Farahani, S. (2011). *ZigBee wireless networks and transceivers*. Newnes.

Geier, E. (2014). What's next for Wi-Fi? A second wave of 802.11ac devices, and then: 802.11ax. *PC World*. Retrieved from http://www.pcworld.com/article/2366929/what-s-next-for-wi-fi-a-second-wave-of-802-11ac-devices-and-then-802-11ax.html

Gomez, C., Oller, J., & Paradells, J. (2012). Overview and evaluation of bluetooth low energy: An emerging low-power wireless technology. *Sensors (Basel, Switzerland), 12*(9), 11734–11753.

Hackmann, G. (2006). *802.15 Personal Area Networks*. Department of Computer Science and Engineering, Washington University.

He, Y., Yuan, R., Ma, X., & Li, J. (2008). The IEEE 802.11 power saving mechanism: An experimental study. *Paper presented at the IEEE Wireless Communications and Networking Conference*, Las Vegas, USA. doi:10.1109/WCNC.2008.245

Heer, T., Garcia-Morchon, O., Hummen, R., Keoh, S. L., Kumar, S. S., & Wehrle, K. (2011). Security Challenges in the IP-based Internet of Things. *Wireless Personal Communications*, *61*(3), 527–542. doi:10.1007/s11277-011-0385-5

IEEE 802.11 Working Group. (2010). IEEE Standard for Information Technology–Telecommunications and information exchange between systems–Local and metropolitan area networks–Specific requirements–Part 11: Wireless LAN Medium Access Control (MAC) and Physical Layer (PHY) specifications Amendment 6: Wireless Access in Vehicular Environments. *IEEE Std, 802*, 11.

IEEE802.org. (2015). IEEE P802.11 Sub 1GHz Study Group. Retrieved from http://www.ieee802.org/11/Reports/tgah_update.htm

Jain, R. (2014). Wireless Protocols for Internet of Things: Part II–ZigBee. Retrieved from www.cse.wustl.edu/~jain/cse574-14/j_13zgb.htm

Khorov, E., Lyakhov, A., Krotov, A., & Guschin, A. (2014). A survey on IEEE 802.11 ah: An enabling networking technology for smart cities. *Computer Communications*, *2014*, 53–69.

Lee, J. S. (2006). Performance evaluation of IEEE 802.15. 4 for low-rate wireless personal area networks. *IEEE Transactions on Consumer Electronics*, *52*(3), 742–749. doi:10.1109/TCE.2006.1706465

Lemstra, W., Hayes, V., & Groenewegen, J. (2010). *The innovation journey of Wi-Fi: The road to global success*. Cambridge University Press. doi:10.1017/CBO9780511666995

Lu, C.-W., Li, S.-C., & Wu, Q. (2011). Interconnecting ZigBee and 6LoWPAN wireless sensor networks for smart grid applications. *Paper presented at the Fifth International Conference on Sensing Technology (ICST)*, Palmerston North, New Zealand.

Mackensen, E., Lai, M., & Wendt, T. M. (2012). Bluetooth low energy (ble) based wireless sensors. *Paper presented at the IEEE Sensors*, Taipei, Taiwan.

McDermott-Wells, P. (2004). What is bluetooth? *IEEE Potentials*, *23*(5), 33–35. doi:10.1109/MP.2005.1368913

Mirkovic, J., & Reiher, P. (2004). A taxonomy of DDoS attack and DDoS defense mechanisms. *Computer Communication Review*, *34*(2), 39–53. doi:10.1145/997150.997156

Misra, S., Krishna, P. V., Agarwal, H., Saxena, A., & Obaidat, M. S. (2011). A learning automata based solution for preventing distributed denial of service in Internet of things. *Paper presented at the International Conference on Internet of Things (iThings)*, Dalian, China. doi:10.1109/iThings/CPSCom.2011.84

Mohapatra, S. K., Choudhury, R. R., & Das, P. (2014). The Future Directions in Evolving WI-FI: Technologies, Applications, and Services. *International Journal of Next-Generation Networks*, *6*(3), 13–22. doi:10.5121/ijngn.2014.6302

Neil, G. (2000). *When things start to think*. Holt Paperbacks.

Olyaei, B. B., Pirskanen, J., Raeesi, O., Hazmi, A., & Valkama, M. (2013). Performance comparison between slotted IEEE 802.15. 4 and IEEE 802.1 lah in IoT based applications. *Paper presented at the IEEE 9th International Conference on Wireless and Mobile Computing, Networking and Communications (WiMob)*, Lyon, France.

Pal, A., Mehta, A., Mirshekar-Syahkal, D., Deo, P., & Nakano, H. (2014). Dual-Band Low-Profile Capacitively Coupled Beam-Steerable Square-Loop Antenna. *IEEE Transactions on Antennas and Propagation*, *62*(3), 1204–1211. doi:10.1109/TAP.2013.2294866

Perahia, E., & Stacey, R. (2013). *Next Generation Wireless LANs: 802.11 n and 802.11 ac*. Cambridge university press. doi:10.1017/CBO9781139061407

Pothuganti, K., & Chitneni, A. (2014). A Comparative Study of Wireless Protocols: Bluetooth, UWB, ZigBee, and Wi-Fi. In *Advance in Electronic and Electric Engineering* (pp. 2231-1297).

Qualcomm. (2012). IEEE802.11ac: The Next Evolution of Wi-FiTM Standards. Retrieved from www. qualcomm.com/documents/qualcomm-research-ieee80211ac-next-evolution-wi-fi

Qualcomm. (2014). Improving whole home coverage and power efficiency. Retrieved from www.qualcomm.com/invention/research/projects/wi-fi-evolution/80211ah

Siddiqui, F., Zeadally, S., & Salah, K. (2015). Gigabit Wireless Networking with IEEE 802.11 ac: Technical Overview and Challenges. *Journal of Networks*, *10*(3), 164–171. doi:10.4304/jnw.10.3.164-171

Stroud, F. (2015). 802.11ac. *Webpedia*. Retrieved from http://www.webopedia.com/TERM/8/802_11ac. html

Texas Instruments. (2013). Texas Instruments CC2540/41 Bluetooth® Low Energy Software Developer's Guide v1. 4.0. *SWRU271F Version*. Retrieved from http://www.ti.com/lit/ug/swru271f/swru271f.pdf

Toscano, E., & Bello, L. L. (2012). Comparative assessments of IEEE 802.15. 4/ZigBee and 6LoWPAN for low-power industrial WSNs in realistic scenarios. *Paper presented at the 9th IEEE International Workshop on Factory Communication Systems (WFCS)*, Lemgo, Germany.

Valerio, P. (2014). *Can Sub-1GHz WiFi Solve The IoT Connectivity Issues?* The New Global Enterprise.

Vecchio, M., Giaffreda, R., & Marcelloni, F. (2014). Adaptive Lossless Entropy Compressors for Tiny IoT Devices. *IEEE Transactions on Wireless Communications*, *13*(2), 1088–1100. doi:10.1109/TWC.2013.121813.130993

Vermesan, O., & Friess, P. (2013). *Internet of things: converging technologies for smart environments and integrated ecosystems*. River Publishers.

Yang, B. (2009). Study on security of wireless sensor network based on ZigBee standard. *Paper presented at the International Conference on Computational Intelligence and Security*, Beijing, China doi:10.1109/CIS.2009.208

Yibo, C., Hou, K.-m., Zhou, H., Shi, H.-l., Liu, X., Diao, X., ... De Vaulx, C. (2011). 6LoWPAN stacks: a survey. *Paper presented at the 7th International Conference on Wireless Communications, Networking and Mobile Computing (WiCOM)*, Wuhan, China.

ZigBee Alliance. (2006). Zigbee specification. Retrieved from http://www.zigbee.org/zigbee-for-developers/network-specifications/

ZigBee Alliance. (2014). ZigBee architecture and specifications overview. Retrieved from http://www.zigbee.org/zigbee-for-developers/network-specifications/zigbeeip/

KEY TERMS AND DEFINITIONS

6LoWPAN: 6LoWPAN is an acronym of IPv6 over Low power Wireless Personal Area Networks. 6LoWPAN is a low-power wireless mesh network where every node has its own IPv6 address.

Actuators: Actuators are devices responsible for moving or controlling a mechanism or system.

BLE: Bluetooth low energy also known as Bluetooth Smart, Bluetooth LE, Bluetooth 4.0, is a wireless personal area network technology.

IEEE 802.11ah: A wireless networking protocol that is an amendment of the IEEE 802.11-2007 wireless networking standard. It is intended to work with low-power devices.

Internet of Things: The Internet of things is a technology that connects physical objects and not only computer devices to the Internet, making it possible to access data/services remotely and to control a physical object from a remote location.

Location Privacy: The process of using a protecting technique such as location obfuscation for the purpose of protecting the location of a user.

Network Management: Network management refers to the activities and tools that pertain to the operation, administration, maintenance, and provisioning of networked systems.

ZigBee IP: ZigBee IP is a technology that enables Internet connectivity of ZigBee devices using IPv6 protocol.

This research was previously published in Innovative Research and Applications in Next-Generation High Performance Computing edited by Qusay F. Hassan, pages 368-396, copyright year 2016 by Information Science Reference (an imprint of IGI Global).

Chapter 4
Cloud–Based IoT System Control Problems

Sungwook Kim
Sogang University, South Korea

ABSTRACT

Cloud computing and IoT are two very different technologies that are both already part of our life. Their adoption and use are expected to be more and more pervasive, making them important components of the Future Internet. A novel paradigm where Cloud and IoT are merged together is foreseen as disruptive and as an enabler of a large number of application scenarios. In this chapter, we focus our attention on the integration of Cloud and IoT. Reviewing the rich and articulate state of the art in this field, some issues are selected; Cloud Radio Access Network (C-RAN), Mobile Cloud IoT (MCIoT), Social Cloud (SC) and Fog Radio Access Network (F-RAN). C-RAN provides infrastructure layer services to mobile users by managing virtualized infrastructure resources. SC is a service or resource sharing framework on top of social networks, and built on the trust-based social relationships. In recent years, the idea of SC has been gaining importance because of its potential applicability. With an explosive growth of Mobile Cloud (MC) and IoT technologies, the MCIoT concept has become a new trend for the future Internet. MCIoT paradigm extends the existing facility of computing process to different mobile applications executing in mobile and portable devices. As a promising paradigm for the 5G wireless communication system, a new evolution of the cloud radio access network has been proposed, named as F-RANs. It is an advanced socially-aware mobile networking architecture to provide a high spectral and energy efficiency while alleviating backhaul burden. With the ubiquitous nature of social networks and cloud computing, IoT technologies exploit these developing new paradigms.

NEWS-VENDOR GAME BASED RESOURCE ALLOCATION (NGRA) SCHEME

C-RAN has been emerging as a cost-effective solution supporting huge volumes of mobile traffic in the big data era. To exploit next generation C-RAN operations, a main challenging issue is how to properly control system resources. Recently, S. Kim proposed the *News-vendor Game based Resource Allocation* (NGRA) scheme, which is a novel resource management algorithm for C-RAN systems. By employing

DOI: 10.4018/978-1-5225-5649-7.ch004

the news-vendor game model, the NGRA scheme investigates a resource allocation problem with bargaining solutions. In dynamic C-RAN environments, this game-based resource management approach can practically adapt current system conditions while maximizing the expected payoff.

Development Motivation

Modern computation and communication systems operate in a new and dynamic world, characterized by continual changes in the environment and performance requirements that must be satisfied. Dynamic system changes occur without warning and in an unpredictable manner, which are outside the control of traditional operation approaches (Addis, 2013). At the same time, popularity of mobile devices and related applications in various fields are increasing significantly in everyday life. Furthermore, applications become more and more complex, Quality of Service (QoS) sensitive and computation intensive to perform on mobile system. Therefore, new solution concepts need to be developed that manage the computation and communication systems in a dynamically adaptive manner while continuously ensuring different application services (Addis, 2013; Htikie, 2013).

Cloud Radio Access Network (C-RAN) is a new system architecture for the future mobile network infrastructure. It is a centralized, cloud computing based new radio access network to support future wireless communication standards. C-RAN can be implemented based on the concept of virtualization. Usually, virtualization is an enabling technology that allows sharing of the same physical machine by multiple end-user applications with QoS guarantees. Therefore, it helps to reduce costs while improving a higher utilization of the physical resources (Addis, 2013; Zhu, 2014).

No one may deny the advantages of C-RAN services via virtualization technologies. However, there are some problems that need to be addressed. Most of all, next generation C-RAN systems should take into account QoS guarantees while maximizing resource efficiency. However, because of the scarcity of system resource, it is difficult to satisfy simultaneously these conflicting requirements. For this reason, the most critical issue for the next generation C-RAN system is to develop effective resource allocation algorithms (Vakilinia, 2014). But, despite flexibility and great potential applicability, resource allocation problem in C-RAN has received scarce attention as of today.

To design a resource allocation algorithm in C-RAN systems, it is necessary to study a strategic decision making process. Under widely dynamic C-RAN conditions, system agents can be assumed as intelligent rational decision-makers, and they select a best-response strategy to maximize their expected utility with other agents. This situation is well-suited for the game theory. News-vendor game (Malakooti, 2014; William, 2009) is a mathematical game model in operations management and applied economics used to determine optimal inventory levels. Typically, it is characterized by fixed prices and uncertain demand for a perishable product. Therefore, this model can represent a situation faced by a newspaper vendor who must decide how many copies of the day's paper to stock in the face of uncertain demand and knowing that unsold copies will be worthless at the end of the day. The original concept of newsvendor game appeared to date from 1888 where F. Edgeworth used the central limit theorem to determine the optimal cash reserves to satisfy random withdrawals from depositors. The modern formulation dates from the 1951 paper in Econometrica by K. Arrow, T. Harris, and J. Marshak (Arrow, 1951).

Motivated by the aforementioned discussion, the *NGRA* scheme was developed. The main goal of the *NGRA* scheme is to maximize resource efficiency while providing QoS guarantees. In dynamically changing C-RAN environments, the game process in the *NGRA* scheme is divided two stages; the competitive stage and the bargaining stage. At the competitive stage, system resource is allocated in a non-cooperative game manner. Therefore, cloud server controls dynamically the total service request by adjusting the price. When the total service request is larger than the system capacity with the maximum price, system resource can not be distributed effectively in a non-cooperative manner. To effectively handle this case, the *NGRA* scheme adopts a bargaining-based approach. At the bargaining stage, the *NGRA* scheme re-distributes the system resource on the basis of combined bargaining solution.

Cloud Radio Access Network Architecture

In C-RAN systems, there are multiple Cloud Providers (*CPs*), which can generate more revenue from the sharing of available resources. *CPs* have their system resources, such as CPU core, memory, storage, network bandwidth, etc. To ensure the optimal usage of cloud resources, baseband processing is centralized in a Virtualized Baseband units Pool (*VBP*). The *VBP* can be shared by different *CPs* and multiple Base Stations (*BSs*). Therefore, the *VBP* is in a unique position as a cloud brokering between the *BSs* and the *CPs* for cloud services while increasing resource efficiency and system throughput (Checko, 2015).

In the C-RAN architecture, the *BS* covers a small area, and communicates with the Mobile Users (*MUs*) through wireless links. The *BSs* provide the managed connectivity and offer flexibility in real-time demands. To improve *C-RAN* system efficiency, *CPs* can offer their available resources to *BSs* through the *VBP*, and *BSs* can provide services to *MUs* based on their obtained resources. Without loss of generality, each *BS* is assumed to acts as a virtual machine, and *MUs'* applications are executed through the virtualization technology. The general architecture of hierarchical C-RAN system is shown in Figure 1.

Figure 1. Hierarchical C-RAN system structure

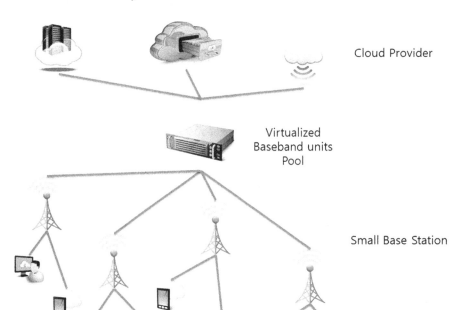

News-Vendor Game Models at the Competitive Stage

The *NGRA* scheme introduces the news-vendor game model ($\mathbb{G}$) for C-RAN systems. $\mathbb{G}$ is a tuple $\left(V, \mathbb{N}, \left(\boldsymbol{S}_i \right)_{i \in \mathbb{N}}, \left(U_i \right)_{i \in \mathbb{N}}, T \right)$ at each time period t of gameplay.

- V is the total amount of available cloud resource in the *VBP*.
- $\mathbb{N}$ is the finite set of players $\mathbb{N} = \left\{ b_0, b_1, \ldots, b_n \right\}$ where b_0 is the *VBP* and $b_{i, 1 \leq i \leq n}$ represents the i th *BS*.
- $\boldsymbol{S}_i$ is the set of strategies with the player i. If the player i is the *VBP*, i.e., $i = 0$, a strategy set can be defined as resource prices. If the player i is a *BS*, i.e., $1 \leq i \leq n$, the strategy set is defined as the amount of requested resource.
- The U_i is the payoff received by the player i. Traditionally, the payoff is determined as the obtained outcome minus the cost to obtain that outcome. For simplicity, the outcome is represented in a general form of *log* function.
- The T is a time period. The $\mathbb{G}$ is repeated $t \in T < \infty$ time periods with competitive and cooperative manner.

To understand the behavior of self-regarding system agents, game models have some attractive features. As a kind of game model, news-vendor game was initially developed for the classical, single-period newsboy problem (Wen, 2009). In the *NGRA* scheme, the traditional news-vendor game is extended as a two-stage repeated game. Initially, the *VBP* dynamically adjusts the price of resource unit, and *BSs* request cloud resources to maximize their payoffs. In this stage, resource allocation procedure is formulated as a non-cooperative game model. If service requests from *BSs* is more than the capacity of the *VBP*, the cloud resource is re-distributed adaptively according to the combined bargaining solution. In this stage, resource allocation procedure is formulated as a bargaining game approach. By a sophisticated combination of these two different game approaches, the *NGRA* scheme attempts to approximate a well-balanced system performance among conflicting requirements.

At the competitive stage, the strategy set for the *VBP* ($\boldsymbol{S}_0$), i.e., available price levels for a resource unit, is assumed as below.

$$S_0 = \left\{ p^t \mid p^t \in \left[p_{\min}, p_{\max} \right] \right\} \tag{1}$$

where p^t is the price at time t. The $p_{\min}, p_{\max}$ are the pre-defined minimum and maximum price levels, respectively. From the viewpoint of *VBP*, the $p_{\max}$ is good to maximize its profit. From the viewpoint of *BSs*, $p_{\min}$ is good to maximize their payoff. The actual price at time t (p^t) is dynamically decided according to the current system conditions. In this model, the p^t is determined as the weighted sum of $p_{\min}$ and $p_{\max}$.

$$p^t = \omega \times p_{\max} + \left(1 - \omega \right) \times p_{\min} \tag{2}$$

where ω is a weighted factor for the both prices. Under diverse system environments, the value of ω should be modified dynamically. In the *NGRA* scheme, *Rubinstein-Stahl* model is adopted to adjust the ω value. *Rubinstein-Stahl* model was proposed as a solution to the problem when two players were negotiating the division of the benefit (Xie, 2010). Therefore, players negotiated with each other by proposing offers alternately. After several rounds of offer and count-offers, players finally come to an agreement. In *Rubinstein-Stahl* model, there exists a unique solution for this negotiation process (Xie, 2010). The *NGRA* scheme assumes that the *Rubinstein–Stahl* model's equilibrium point is obtained through negotiation between the *VBP* stance and *BSs'* stance.

In the *Rubinstein-Stahl* model, the *VBP* is assumed as a supplier, and all *BSs* are assumed as a single customer. Two players, i.e., supplier and customer, have their own bargaining power (δ). The division proportion of the benefits can be obtained according to the negotiation power, which can be computed at each player individually. A more negotiation power player benefits more from the negotiation process. Players negotiate with each other by proposing offers alternately. After several rounds of negotiation, they finally reach an agreement as following (Park, 2015; Zhao, 2002).

$$\left(x_s^*, x_c^*\right) = \begin{cases} \left(\dfrac{1-\delta_c}{1-\delta_s \times \delta_c}, \dfrac{\delta_c \times \left(1-\delta_c\right)}{1-\delta_s \times \delta_c}\right) & \textit{if supplier offers first} \\[3ex] \left(\dfrac{\delta_s \times \left(1-\delta_c\right)}{1-\delta_s \times \delta_c}, \dfrac{1-\delta_s}{1-\delta_s \times \delta_c}\right) & \textit{if customer offers first} \end{cases}.$$

s.t.,

$$\left(x_s^*, x_c^*\right) \in R^2 : x_s^* + x_c^* = 1, x_s^* \geq 0, x_c^* \geq 0 \text{ and } 0 \leq \delta_s, \delta_c \leq 1 \tag{3}$$

where x_s^* and x_c^* are final dividends for supplier and customer, respectively. δ_s and δ_c be the supplier and consumer patience factor. Lower δ (or higher δ) value means lower patience (or more patience). In the *Rubinstein-Stahl* negotiation model, the patience factor strongly affects the negotiation process; the more patience has, the more payoff attains. From a common-sense standpoint, consumers should know the current price as early as possible for the effective service continuity. Under this situation, they lack patience in bargaining. For this reason, the *NGRA* scheme represents the consumer's patience as a monotonous time decreasing function. According to the inverse effect of reciprocal relationship, the supplier's patience is defined vice versa. Therefore, the consumer's patience (δ_c^t) and supplier's patience (δ_s^t) at t^{th} round of negotiation process are defined as follow (Park, 2015; Xie, 2010).

$$\delta_c^t = 1 - \left(\frac{e^{\xi^t} - e^{-\xi^t}}{e^{\xi^t} + e^{-\xi^t}}\right) \text{ and } \delta_s^t = \left(\frac{e^{\xi^t} - e^{-\xi^t}}{e^{\xi^t} + e^{-\xi^t}}\right)$$

s.t.,

$$\frac{d\delta_c^t}{dt} < 0, \ \frac{d\delta_s^t}{dt} > 0, \ \delta_c^0, \delta_s^\infty = 1, \text{ and } \delta_c^\infty, \delta_s^0 = 0 \tag{4}$$

where ξ^t is the patience coefficient at t^{th} round. For the ideal C-RAN system management, the *NGRA* scheme dynamically adjusts the ξ^t value. When the requested service increases (*or* decreases), the price (p) should increases (*or* decreases) to maximize the resource efficiency. To implement this mechanism, the value of ξ^t is defined as the ratio of the current cloud workload to the total system capacity.

$$\xi^t = 1 - \left(\frac{T_Q - C_Q}{T_Q} \right), s.t., 0 < \xi^t < 1 \tag{5}$$

where T_Q and C_Q are the total cloud capacity and the current cloud workload, respectively. If the gap between T_Q and C_Q is larger, the ξ^t decreases using (5) and δ_c (*or* δ_s) increases (*or* decreases), simultaneously. Therefore, according to the ξ^t value, the values of δ_c and δ_s are adjusted adaptively. On the basis of obtained δ_c and δ_s values, the *NGRA* scheme can get the weighted factor (ω). In a realistic negotiation scenario, a supplier offers the price first. Therefore, the values of ω and ($1 - \omega$) are obtained according to (3).

$$\omega = \frac{1 - \delta_c}{1 - \delta_s \times \delta_c} \text{ and } (1 - \omega) = \frac{\delta_c \times (1 - \delta_s)}{1 - \delta_s \times \delta_c} \tag{6}$$

Finally, the price (p) in the competitive game stage is obtained based on the equation (2). When the p is high, cloud service requests are reduced with unsatisfactory payoffs, and vice versa. Therefore, at the competitive stage, the *VBP* can control dynamically the total service request by adjusting the price according to (2)-(6).

News-Vendor Game Models at the Cooperative Stage

When the current cloud workload is controllable through the above price strategy, the news-vender game can be operated only in the competitive game stage. However, in an overloaded situation, i.e., the cloud resource is not sufficient to support all service requests, the cooperative game stage is started. In recent years, cooperative approaches derived from game theory have been widely used for efficient resource allocation problems. The most popular approaches are the *Nash Bargaining Solution* (NBS) and the *Kalai-Smorodinsky bargaining solution* (KSBS) (Kim, 2010; Kim, 2014). Because of their appealing properties, the basic concept of NBS and KSBS has become an interesting research topic in economics, political science, sociology, psychology, biology, and so on (Kim, 2014).

Based on the traditional game theory, the Nash bargaining solution can be formulated as follows (Kim, 2014).

$$\prod_i (u_i^* - d_i) = \max_{u_i \in \mathbb{S}} \prod_i (u_i - d_i), where \ u_i^* \in \mathbb{S} \ and \ d_i \in \boldsymbol{d} \tag{7}$$

where $\mathbb{S} = \{(u_1,\ldots u_n)\} \subset \mathbb{R}^n$ is a jointly feasible utility solution set, and a disagreement point (**d**) is an action vector $\boldsymbol{d} = (d_1,\ldots,d_n) \in \mathbb{S}$ that is expected to be the result if players cannot reach an agreement. In the game theory terminology, an outcome vector $< u_1^*, u_2^*,\ldots,u_n^* >$ is a unique and fair-efficient solution, called the NBS that fulfills the Nash axioms (Kim, 2014).

1. **Individual Rationality:** NBS should be better off than the disagreement point. Therefore, no player is worse off than if the agreement fails. Formally, $u_i^* \geq d_i$ for all player i.
2. **Feasibility:** NBS is reasonable under the circumstances. That is, $\boldsymbol{U}^* \in \mathbb{S}$.
3. **Pareto Optimality:** NBS gives the maximum payoff to the players. Therefore, if there exists a solution $\boldsymbol{U}^* = \left(u_1^*..u_i^*..u_n^*\right)$, it shall be Pareto optimal.
4. **Invariance With Respect to Utility Transformations:** A utility function specifies a player's preferences. Therefore, different utility functions can be used to model the same preferences. However, the final outcome should not depend on which of these equivalent utility representations is used. In other words, for any linear scale transformation of the function ψ, $\psi\left(F\left(\mathbb{S},d\right)\right) = F\left(\psi\left(\mathbb{S}\right),\psi\left(d\right)\right)$. This axiom is also called *Independence of Linear Transformations or scale covariance.*
5. **Independence of Irrelevant Alternatives:** The solution should be independent of irrelevant alternatives. In other words, a reasonable outcome will be feasible after some payoff sets have been removed. If $\boldsymbol{U}^*$ is a bargaining solution for a bargaining set $\mathbb{S}$ then for any subset $\mathbb{S}'$ of $\mathbb{S}$ containing $\boldsymbol{U}^*$, $\boldsymbol{U}^*$ continues to be a bargaining solution. Formally, if $\boldsymbol{U}^* \in \mathbb{S}' \subset \mathbb{S}$ and $\boldsymbol{U}^* = F\left(\mathbb{S},d\right)$, then $\boldsymbol{U}^* = F\left(\mathbb{S}',\mathrm{d}\right)$.
6. **Symmetry:** Symmetry means that if the players' utilities are exactly the same, they should get symmetric payoffs, i.e., equal payoffs. Therefore, payoff should not discriminate between the identities of the players, but only depend on utility functions. For example, if $\mathbb{S}$ is invariant under all exchanges of users, $F_i\left(\mathbb{S},d\right) = F_j\left(\mathbb{S},d\right)$ for all possible players i and j.

Even though the NBS can provide a unique and fair Pareto optimal solution, Nash axioms do not always characterize the situations we encounter in reality. In particular, the *Independence of irrelevant alternatives* has been the source of considerable contention. When a feasible solution set is modified, NBS is unconcerned about a relative fairness. Therefore, the dilemma is an insensitivity to utility translations. In some cases, the outcome of the bargaining process may be the result of reciprocal equality. Therefore, during the 1950-1980s, extensive research had been done to replace the axiom, *Independence of irrelevant alternatives* (Zehavi, 2009).

KSBS is an alternative approach to the bargaining problem proposed by Kalai and Smorodinsky (Kim, 2010; Kim, 2014). While Nash's solution requires the solution to be independence when irrelevant alternatives are modified, the KSBS relaxed this condition. Therefore, Kalai and Smorodinsky replaced the axiom of *Independence of irrelevant alternatives* by *individual monotonicity*. Under *individual monotonicity* condition, if the feasible set is changed in favor of one of the players, this player should not end up losing because of this change (Zehavi, 2009). More formally, *individual monotonicity* axiom is defined as (Kim, 2010; Kim, 2011).

7. **Individual Monotonicity:** A bargaining situation $\left(\mathbb{W}, d\right)$ is better than $\left(\mathbb{S}, d\right)$. if and only if

$$\sup\left\{u_i : \left\{\left(u_1,,, u_n\right)\right\} \in \mathbb{W}\right\} \geq \sup\left\{u_i : \left\{\left(u_1,,, u_n\right)\right\} \in \mathbb{S}\right\}$$

where $1 \leq i \leq n$. A solution function F is individually monotonic for a player if whenever $\left(\mathbb{W}, d\right)$ is better than $\left(\mathbb{S}, d\right)$, then $F\left(\mathbb{W}, d\right) > F\left(\mathbb{S}, d\right)$. F is individually monotonic if the same property holds for all players.

KSBS is a unique solution satisfying the axioms (1)-(4) and (6)-(7). Mathematically, it is defined as

$$\frac{\sup\{u_1\} - d_1}{I_1^* - d_1} = \ldots = \frac{\sup\{u_i\} - d_i}{I_i^* - d_i} = \ldots = \frac{\sup\{u_n\} - d_n}{I_n^* - d_n}$$

s.t.,

$$\sup\{u_i\} = \sup\left\{u_i : \left\{\left(u_1,,, u_n\right)\right\} \in \mathbb{W}\right\}, \ I_i^* = \max\left\{u_i : u_i \in \mathbb{S}\right\}$$

and

$$1 \leq i \leq n \tag{8}$$

where I_i^* is the ideal point of player i. Therefore, players choose the best outcome subject to the condition that their proportional part of the excess over the disagreement is relative to the proportion of the excess of their ideal gains (Kim, 2010; Kim, 2011; Zehavi, 2009).

The *NGRA* scheme develops a new bargaining solution by combining the axioms of *Independence of irrelevant alternatives* and *Individual monotonicity*. To implement this solution, the main issue is how to trade-off between different principles, which can be tackled by cooperative games with transferable utility. The combined bargaining solution (u^α) of the NBS and KSBS is such that:

$$U_i^\alpha = \alpha \times u_i^{NBS} + \left(1 - \alpha\right) \times u_i^{KSBS}$$

$$U_i^\alpha \in \left\{U_1^\alpha .. U_i^\alpha .. U_n^\alpha\right\} \text{ and } 1 \leq i \leq n \tag{9}$$

where α is a control parameter to relatively emphasize the principle of *Independence of irrelevant alternatives* or *Individual monotonicity*. The major feature of *Individual monotonicity* is that increasing the bargaining set size in a direction favorable to a specific player always benefits that player. Therefore, when the bargaining set size of each player is huge different, this feature can keep the relative fairness among players.

The *NGRA* scheme adaptively adjusts the α value in an online decision manner. In dynamic C-RAN environments, a fixed value of α cannot effectively adapt to the changing conditions. When the normalized difference of the bargaining set size is high, the *NGRA* scheme should strongly depend on the axiom of *Individual monotonicity*. In this case, a lower value of α is more suitable. When the normalized difference of the bargaining set size is nearly the same, the *NGRA* scheme can put more emphasis on the axiom of *Independence of irrelevant alternatives*. In this case, a higher value of α is more desirable. Based on this consideration, the value of α is dynamically adjusted according to the current ratio of bargaining set difference.

$$\alpha = \frac{\min_{i,j \in \mathbb{N}} \left(\left| I_i^* - I_j^* \right| \right)}{\max_{i,j \in \mathbb{N}} \left(\left| I_i^* - I_j^* \right| \right)} \, s.t., 1 \leq i, j \leq n \tag{10}$$

With the dynamic adaptation of α value, the *NGRA* scheme can be more responsive to current C-RAN conditions. Finally, the set of resource allocation for BSs at time t, denoted by $\mathbb{R}$, is calculated as

$$\mathbb{R} = \mathcal{R}_i \mid \left\{ \mathcal{R}_1 .. \mathcal{R}_i .. \mathcal{R}_n \right\} \underset{=\!=}{def} \mathcal{R}_i = \left(\frac{U_i^\alpha}{\sum_{i=1}^n U_i^\alpha} \right) \times \mathfrak{R}^t \tag{11}$$

where $\mathfrak{R}^t$ is the available cloud resource at time t. The solution set $\mathbb{R}$ is a possible outcome of the combined bargaining process; $\mathbb{R}$ is adaptively obtained in the cooperative trade-off area.

The Main Steps of the *NGRA* Scheme

In the *NGRA* scheme, both non-cooperative and cooperative game models have been applied to the cloud resource allocation process. This two-stage approach suggests that a judicious mixture of collaboration and competition is advantageous in dynamic C-RAN environments. The main steps of the *NGRA* scheme are given next.

Step 1: At the initial time, the price (p) is set to the initial value, and *BSs* request their cloud service to maximize their payoffs in a non-cooperative game approach.

Step 2: At each game period, the p is decided according to the *Rubinstein-Stahl* model. In the basis of (2)-(6), the p is dynamically adjusted by taking into account the current cloud workload (ξ).

Step 3: After the p decision, δ, ω and ξ values are modified periodically using (4),(5) and (6).

Step 4: When the cloud services are congested at the competitive stage, it is impossible to control the resource allocation through price control strategy. At this time, the bargaining stage is started.

Step 5: At each game period, NBS and KSBS are obtained using (7) and (8). At the same time, the control parameter α is adjusted dynamically using (10).

Step 6: The combined bargaining solution ($U^{\alpha}_{i,1\leq i\leq n}$) of the NBS and KSBS are obtained based on (9), and the set of resource allocation for *BSs* ($\mathbb{R}$) is finally calculated according to (11).

Step 7: Under widely diverse C-RAN environments, the *VBP* and *BSs* are self-monitoring constantly for the next news-vendor game process; proceed to Step 2.

Summary

As a new model of distributed computing, all kinds of distributed resources are virtualized to establish a shared resource pool through C-RAN systems. C-RAN solution enables dynamic on-demand response, combining collaborative radio and real-time cloud infrastructure while providing convenient and configurable resources. Therefore, dynamic and efficient mechanism for rapidly scaling cloud resources is becoming a hot spot in research areas. The NGRA scheme is a novel resource allocation scheme based on the news-vender game model. The main goal of the NGRA scheme is to maximize system performance while ensuring service QoS. To satisfy this goal, the NGRA scheme develops a two-stage game mechanism. The important feature of this approach is its adaptability, flexibility and responsiveness to current C-RAN conditions.

THE HIERARCHICAL GAME BASED RESOURCE SHARING (HGRS) SCHEME

Over the past decade, wireless applications have experienced tremendous growth, and this growth is likely to multiply in the near future. To cope with expected drastic data traffic growth, Cloud computing based new Radio Access Network (*C-RAN*) has been proposed for next generation cellular networks. It is considered as a cost efficient way of meeting high resource demand of future wireless access networks. The Hierarchical Game based Resource Sharing (HGRS) scheme is a novel resource sharing scheme for future *C-RAN* systems. Based on the Indian buffet game, the *Hierarchical Game based Resource Sharing* (HGRS) scheme formulates the *C-RAN* resource allocation problem as a two-level game model, and finds an effective solution according to the coopetition approach.

Development Motivation

In recent years, the Radio Access Network (*RAN*) is commonly used to support the exponential growth of mobile communications. Conceptually, *RAN* resides among network devices such as a mobile phone, a computer, or any remotely controlled machine, and provides connections with core networks. However, traditional *RAN* architecture has been faced with a number of challenges. First, a highly loaded Base Station (*BS*) cannot share processing power with other idle or less loaded *BSs*; it results in a poor resource utilization. Second, a *BS* equipment serves only radio frequency channels in each physical cell, where *BS*'s resources cannot be shared with other *BSs* in different cells. Finally, *BSs* built on proprietary hardware cannot have a flexibility to upgrade radio networks (Htike, 2013; Sigwele, 2014). To overcome these problems, Cloud computing based Radio Access Network (*C-RAN*) is widely considered as a promising paradigm, which can bridge the gap between the wireless communication demands of end-users and the capacity of radio access networks (Sigwele, 2014; Zhu, 2014).

In 2013, C. Jiang introduced the fundamental notion of Indian buffet game to study how game players make multiple concurrent selections under uncertain system states (Jiang, 2013). Specifically, Indian buffet game model can reveal how players learn the uncertainty through social learning and make optimal decisions to maximize their own expected utilities by considering negative network externality (Jiang, 2015). This game model is well-suited for the *C-RAN* resource sharing problem. Motivated by the above discussion, the HGRS scheme is developed based on the Indian game model. The key feature of HGRS scheme is to develop a decentralized mechanism according to the two-level coopetition approach. The term 'coopetition' is a neologism coined to describe cooperative competition. Therefore, coopetition is defined as the phenomenon that differs from competition or cooperation, and stresses two faces, i.e., cooperation and competition, of one relationship in the same situation (Kim, 2015). In the HGRS scheme, the game model consists of two-levels; upper and lower Indian buffet games. At the upper-level game, cloud resources are shared in a cooperative manner. At the lower-level game, allocated resources are distributed in a non-cooperative manner. Based on the hierarchical interconnection of two game model, control decisions can cause cascade interactions to reach a mutually satisfactory solution.

Usually, different *C-RAN* agents may pursue different interests, and act individually to maximize their own profits. This self-organizing feature can add autonomics into *C-RAN* systems and help to ease the heavy burden of complex centralized control algorithms. Based on the recursive best response algorithm, the HGRS scheme draws on the concept of a learning perspective and investigates some of the reasons and probable lines for justifying each system agent's behaviors. The dynamics of the interactive feedback learning mechanism can allow control decisions to be dynamically adjustable. In addition, by employing the coopetition approach, control decisions are mutually dependent on each other to resolve conflicting performance criteria.

Indian Buffet Game Model for *C-RAN* Systems

The HGRS scheme considers a *C-RAN* architecture with one Virtualized Baseband units Pool (*VBP*), 10 Small Base Stations (*SBSs*) and 100 Mobile Users (*MUs*), and system resources, which are the computing capacities of CPU, memory, storage and bandwidth. These resources can be used by the *MUs* through the *VBP* to gain more revenue. *CPs* cooperate to form a logical pool of computing resources to support *MUs'* applications. Each *MU* application service has its own application type, and requires different resources requirements.

Let us consider an Indian buffet restaurant which provides m dishes denoted by $d_1, d_2, ..., d_m$. Each dish can be shared among multiple guests. Each guest can select sequentially multiple dishes to get different meals. The utility of each dish can be interpreted as the deliciousness and quantity. All guests are rational in the sense that they will select dishes which can maximize their own satisfactions. In such a case, the multiple dish-selection problem can be formulated to be a non-cooperative game, called Indian buffet game. In the traditional Indian buffet game, the main goal is to study how guests in a buffet restaurant learn the uncertain dishes' states and make multiple concurrent decisions by not only considering the current utility, but also taking into account the influence of subsequent players' decisions (Kim, 2014; Jiang, 2015).

During the *C-RAN* system operations, system agents should make decisions individually. In this situation, a main issue for each agent is how to perform well by considering the mutual-interaction relationship and dynamically adjust their decisions to maximize their own profits. The HGRS scheme develops a new *C-RAN* system resource sharing algorithm based on the Indian buffet game model. In the HGRS scheme, the dynamic operation of *VBP*, *SBSs* and *MUs* is formulated as a two-level Indian buffet game. At the first stage, the *VBP* and *SBSs* play the upper-level Indian buffet game; the *VBP* distribute the available resources to each *SBS* by using a cooperative manner. At the second stage, multiple *MUs* decide to purchase the resource from their corresponding *SBS* by employing a non-cooperative manner. Based on this hierarchical coopetition approach, the HGRS scheme assumes that all game players (*VBP*, *SBSs* and *MUs*) are rational and independent of gaining the profit as much as possible. Therefore, for the implementation practicality, the HGRS scheme is designed in an entirely distributed and self-organizing interactive fashion.

Mathematically, the upper-level Indian buffet game ($\mathbb{G}^U$) can be defined as

$$\mathbb{G}^L = \left\{ \mathbb{P}, \left\{\boldsymbol{\mathcal{L}}_i\right\}_{i \in \mathbb{P}}, \left\{\boldsymbol{\mathcal{T}}_i\right\}_{i \in \mathbb{P}}, \left\{U_i\right\}_{i \in \mathbb{P}}, T \right\}$$

at each time period t of gameplay.

- $\mathbb{N}$ is the finite set of players $\mathbb{N} = \left\{\boldsymbol{\mathcal{C}}, \boldsymbol{\mathcal{B}}\right\}$ where $\boldsymbol{\mathcal{C}} = \{VBP\}$ represents one *VBP* and $\boldsymbol{\mathcal{B}} = \left\{b_1, \ldots, b_n\right\}$ is a set of multiple *SBSs*, which are assumed as guests in the upper-level Indian restaurant.

- $\mathbb{D}$ is the finite set of resources $\mathbb{D} = \{d_1, d_2, \ldots, d_l\}$ in the *VBP*. Elements in $\mathbb{D}$ metaphorically represent different dishes on the buffet table in the upper-level Indian restaurant.

- $\boldsymbol{S}_i$ is the set of strategies with the player i. If the player i is the *VBP*, i.e., $i \in \boldsymbol{\mathcal{C}}$, a strategy set can be defined as $\boldsymbol{S}_i = \{\delta_i^1, \delta_i^2, \ldots, \delta_i^l\}$ where δ_i^k is the distribution status of kth resource, i.e., $1 \le k \le l$. If the player i is a *SBS*, i.e., $i \in \boldsymbol{\mathcal{B}}$, the player i can request multiple resources. Therefore, the strategy set can be defined as a combination of requested resources

$$\boldsymbol{S}_i = \{\varnothing, \{d_i^1\left(\mathcal{I}_i^1\right)\}, \{d_i^1\left(\mathcal{I}_i^1\right), d_i^2\left(\mathcal{I}_i^2\right)\}, \ldots, \{d_i^1\left(\mathcal{I}_i^1\right), d_i^2\left(\mathcal{I}_i^2\right), \ldots, d_i^l\left(\mathcal{I}_i^l\right)\}\}$$

where $\mathcal{I}_i^k$ is the player i's requested amount for the kth resource; each player's strategy set is finite with 2^l elements.

- The U_i is the payoff received by the player i. If the player i is the *VBP*, i.e., $i \in \boldsymbol{\mathcal{C}}$, it is the total profit obtained from the resource distribution for *SBSs*. If the player i is a *SBS*, i.e., $i \in \boldsymbol{\mathcal{B}}$, the payoff is determined as the outcomes of the distributed resources minus the cost of corresponding resources.

- The T is a time period. The $\mathbb{G}^U$ is repeated $t \in T < \infty$ time periods with imperfect information.

Based on the distributed resources, *SBSs* are responsible to support *MUs*' services while ensuring the required Quality of Service (QoS). Usually, *SBSs* deploy sparsely with each other to avoid mutual interference, and are operated in a time-slotted manner. To formulate interactions between *SBSs* and *MUs*, the lower-level Indian buffet game ($\mathbb{G}^L$) can be defined as

$$\mathbb{G}^L = \left\{ \mathbb{P}, \left\{ \boldsymbol{\mathcal{L}}_i \right\}_{i \in \mathbb{P}}, \left\{ \boldsymbol{\mathcal{T}}_i \right\}_{i \in \mathbb{P}}, \left\{ U_i \right\}_{i \in \mathbb{P}}, T \right\}$$

at each time period t of gameplay.

- $\mathbb{P}$ is the finite set of players $\mathbb{P} = \left\{ \boldsymbol{\mathcal{B}}, \boldsymbol{\mathcal{X}} \right\}$ where $\boldsymbol{\mathcal{B}} = \left\{ b_1, \ldots, b_n \right\}$ is a set of multiple *SBSs*, and $\boldsymbol{\mathcal{X}} = \left\{ x_1, \ldots, x_m \right\}$ is a set of multiple *MUs*, which are assumed guests in the lower-level Indian restaurant.

- $\boldsymbol{\mathcal{L}}_i = \{ \mathcal{R}_i^1, \mathcal{R}_i^2, \ldots, \mathcal{R}_i^l \}$ is the finite set of the player i's resources, i.e., $i \in \boldsymbol{\mathcal{B}}$. Elements in $\boldsymbol{\mathcal{L}}_i$ metaphorically represent different dishes on the buffet table in the ith lower-level Indian restaurant; there are total n lower-level Indian restaurants.

- $\boldsymbol{\mathcal{T}}_i$ is the set of strategies with the player i. If the player i is a *SBS*, i.e., $i \in \boldsymbol{\mathcal{B}}$, the strategy set can be defined as $\boldsymbol{\mathcal{T}}_i = \{ \lambda_i^1, \lambda_i^2, \ldots, \lambda_i^l \}$ where λ_i^k is the price of kth resource in the ith *SBS*. If the player i is a *MU*, i.e., $i \in \boldsymbol{\mathcal{X}}$, the player i can request multiple resources. Therefore, the strategy set can be defined as a combination of requested resources

$$\boldsymbol{\mathcal{T}}_i = \{ \varnothing, \{ \mathcal{R}_i^1 \left(\xi_i^1 \right) \}, \{ \mathcal{R}_i^1 \left(\xi_i^1 \right), \mathcal{R}_i^2 (\xi_i^2) \}, \ldots, \{ \mathcal{R}_i^1 \left(\xi_i^1 \right), \mathcal{R}_i^2 \left(\xi_i^2 \right), \ldots, \mathcal{R}_i^l \left(\xi_i^l \right) \} \}$$

where ξ_i^k is the *MU* i's request amount for the kth resource.

- The U_i is the payoff received by the player i. If the player i is a *SBS*, i.e., $i \in \boldsymbol{\mathcal{B}}$, it is the total profit obtained from the resource allocation for *MUs*. If the player i is a *MU*, i.e., $i \in \boldsymbol{\mathcal{X}}$, the payoff is determined as the outcomes of the allocated resources minus the cost of corresponding resources.

- The T is a time period. The $\mathbb{G}^L$ is repeated $t \in T < \infty$ time periods with imperfect information.

C-RAN Resource Sharing in Upper Indian Buffet Game

First, the upper-level Indian buffet game in the HGRS scheme is addressed. In *C-RAN* systems, there are multiple resource types, and multiple *SBSs* requests different resources to the *VBP*. The HGRS scheme mainly considered four resource types: CPU, memory, storage, and network bandwidth. Let $\mathbb{D}$ denote a set of resources in the *VBP*, $\mathbb{D} = \{ d_1 = \text{CPU}, d_2 = \text{memory}, d_3 = \text{storage}, d_4 = \text{bandwidth} \}$ where each d represents the available amount of corresponding resource. Virtualization technology is used to collect these resources from *CPs*, and they are dynamically shared among *SBSs*. In the upper-level Indian buffet game, there are one *VBP* and *n* *SBSs*. The *VBP* is responsible for the cloud resource control, and distributes resources over multiple *SBSs*. Each *SBS* is deployed for each micro cell, and covers relatively a small area. In general, *SBSs* are situated around high traffic-density hot spots to support QoS ensured applications. To get an effective solution for the upper-level Indian game, the HGRS scheme focused on the basic concept of the *Shapley Value* (*SV*). It is a well-known solution idea for ensuring an equitable division, i.e., the fairest allocation, of collectively gained profits among the several collaborative players (Kim, 2014).

When the requested amount of kth resource (∂_i^k, $1 \leq k \leq 4$) of the the ith *SBS* (SBS_i) is less than the distributed resource ($\mathcal{A}_i^k$), i.e., $\partial_i^k < \mathcal{A}_i^k$, the SBS_i can waste this excess resource, and the property loss is estimated based on the resource unit price ($U\_\mathcal{P}_i^k$). $U\_\mathcal{P}_i^k$ value is adaptively adjusted in the lower-level Indian buffet game. In this case, the value function ($v(SBS_i)$ of the SBS_i becomes

$$v(SBS_i) = -U\_\mathcal{P}_i^k \times \left(\mathcal{A}_i^k - \partial_i^k\right).$$

Conversely, if $\partial_i^k > \mathcal{A}_i^k$, the deficient resource amount $\left(\partial_i^k - \mathcal{A}_i^k\right)$ is needed in the SBS_i. Therefore, the value function becomes

$$v(SBS_i) = U\_\mathcal{P}_i^k \times \left(\partial_i^k - \mathcal{A}_i^k\right).$$

The HGRS scheme assumes that

$$\mathbb{N} = \{\ \mathcal{C} = \{VBP\} \bigcup \mathcal{B} = \left\{b_1, \ldots, b_n\right\}\ \}$$

is a set of upper game players and $v(\cdot)$ is a real valued function defined on all subsets of $\mathcal{B}$ satisfying $v(\varnothing) = 0$. Therefore, in the game model, a nonempty subset (*c*) of $\mathcal{B}$ is called a *coalition*. A set of games with a finite number of players is denoted by " . Given a game $\left(\mathcal{B}, v(\cdot)\right) \in \Gamma$, let $\mathbb{C}^k$ be a *coalition structure* of $\mathcal{B}$ for the kth resource. In particular, $\mathbb{C}^k = \left\{c_1^k, \ldots, c_j^k\right\}$ is a partition of $\mathcal{B}$, that is,

$$c_f^k \bigcap c_h^k = \varnothing \text{ for } f \neq h \text{ and } \bigcup_{t=1}^{j} c_t^k = \mathcal{B}.$$

Let θ be an order on $\mathcal{B}$, that is, θ is a bijection on $\mathcal{B}$. A set of all the orders on $\mathcal{B}$ is denoted by $\Theta(\mathcal{B})$ (Kamijo, 2009; Lee, 2014). A set of game players preceding to the player i for the kth resource at order θ is

$$\mathfrak{A}_i^\theta(k) = \left\{j \in \mathcal{B} : \theta(j) < \theta(i)\right\}.$$

Therefore, $v\left(\mathfrak{A}_i^\theta(k)\right)$ can be expressed as

$$v\left(\mathfrak{A}_i^\theta\left(k\right)\right) = U\_\mathcal{P}_i^k \times \left[\sum_{q \in \mathfrak{A}_q^{\theta'}(k)} \partial_q^k - \sum_{q \in \mathfrak{A}_q^{\theta'}(k)} \mathcal{A}_q^k\right]^+ - U\_\mathcal{P}_i^k \times \left[\sum_{q \in \mathfrak{A}_q^{\theta'}(k)} \mathcal{A}_q^k - \sum_{q \in \mathfrak{A}_q^\theta(k)} \partial_q^k\right]^+$$

s.t.,

$$[x]^+ = \max\left(x, 0\right) \tag{12}$$

A marginal contribution of the player i at order θ in $\left(\mathcal{B}, v(\cdot), k\right)$ is defined by

$$\mathcal{S}_i^\theta\left(\mathcal{B}, v, k\right) = v\left(\mathfrak{A}_i^\theta\left(k\right) \cup \{i\}\right) - v\left(\mathfrak{A}_i^\theta\left(k\right)\right).$$

Then the *SV* of $\left(\mathcal{B}, v(\cdot), k\right)$ is defined as follows (Kamijo, 2009):

$$SV_i\left(\mathcal{B}, v, k\right) = \frac{1}{\left|\Theta\left(\mathcal{B}\right)\right|} \times \sum_{\theta \in \Theta(\mathcal{B})} \left(\mathcal{S}_i^\theta\left(\mathcal{B}, v, k\right)\right), \text{ for all } i \in \mathcal{B} \tag{13}$$

where $|\cdot|$ represents the cardinality of the set. Therefore, the *SV* is an average of marginal contribution vectors where each order $\theta \in \Theta\left(\mathcal{B}\right)$ occurs in an equal probability, that is, $1/\left|\Theta\left(\mathcal{B}\right)\right|$. Under the co-operative game situation, *SV* provide a unique solution with the desirable properties,

1. Efficiency,
2. Symmetry,
3. Additivity,
4. Dummy (Kamijo, 2009).

Although the *SV* is quite an interesting concept, and provides an optimal and fair solution for many applications, its main drawback is its computational complexity: the number of computations will increase prohibitively when the number of game players increases. Therefore, applications that utilize the *SV* remain scarce. In the HGRS scheme, if all possible orderings of *SBSs* ($\Theta\left(\mathcal{B}\right)$) have to be taken into account in calculating equation (12) and (13), the computational complexity of calculating the *SV* can be very high and too heavy to be implemented in real *C-RAN* operations. To resolve this problem, the HGRS scheme adopts the new concept of *Asymptotic Shapley Value* (*A_SV*) approach, which is an approximation method for the *SV* under a large number of players (Kamijo, 2009; Lee, 2014). For the kth resource, let the *A_SV* of player i be ϕ_i^k; it is given as.

$$
\phi_i^k = \begin{cases} \left[U\_\mathcal{P}_i^k \times \int\limits_0^1 erf\left(\dfrac{\sqrt{\mathcal{P}_u^k} \times \tau}{\sqrt{2} \times \eta} \right) dp \right] \times \left(\partial_i^k - \mathcal{A}_i^k \right), & if \ \dfrac{\mu_s^k \times N_s^k}{\mu_B^k \times N_B^k} = 1 \\[20pt] U\_\mathcal{P}_i^k \times \left(\partial_i^k - \mathcal{A}_i^k \right), & if \ \dfrac{\mu_s^k \times N_s^k}{\mu_B^k \times N_B^k} \neq 1 \end{cases}
$$

s.t.,

$$
erf(x) = \frac{1}{\sqrt{\left| \Theta(\mathcal{B}) \right|}} \int\limits_{-x}^x e^{-y^2} dy, \eta = \sqrt{\frac{\mu_B^k \times \left(\sigma_S^k \right)^2 + \mu_s^k \times \left(\sigma_B^k \right)^2}{\mu_B^k + \mu_s^k}}, \tau = \frac{\mu_s^k \times N_s^k - \mu_B^k \times N_B^k}{\sqrt{\mathcal{B}}} \tag{14}
$$

where N_s^k and N_B^k are the number of players with the condition of $\partial^k - \mathcal{A}^k < 0$, and the condition of $\partial^k - \mathcal{A}^k \geq 0$, respectively. μ_s^k and μ_B^k (or $\left(\sigma_S^k \right)^2$ and $\left(\sigma_B^k \right)^2$) are the mean (or variance) of total wasted and needed k^{th} resource, respectively. The method for obtaining the proof of the derivation of *A_SV* value can be found in (Lee, 2014).

Under dynamic *C-RAN* environments, fixed resource distribution methods cannot effectively adapt to changing system conditions. The HGRS scheme treats the resource distribution for multiple *SBSs* as an on-line decision problem. At the time period t, the total amount of available k^{th} resource ($\mathcal{A}\_\mathcal{R}_t^k$) is dynamically re-distributed over *SBSs* according to ϕ^k values. In order to apply the time-driven implementation of resource re-distribution, the HGRS scheme partitions the time-axis into equal intervals of length *unit_time*. At the end of each time period, the re-distributed k^{th} resource amount for the *SBS$_i$* ($\Pi_i^k(t)$) is obtained periodically as follows.

$$
\Pi_i^k(t) = \mathcal{A}\_\mathcal{R}_t^k \times \frac{\phi_i^k + \left| \min\limits_{j \in \mathcal{B}} \left\{ \phi_j^k \right\} \right|}{\sum\limits_{b \in \mathcal{B}} \left(\phi_b^k + \left| \min\limits_{j \in \mathcal{B}} \left\{ \phi_j^k \right\} \right| \right)}, s.t., t \in T \tag{15}
$$

C-RAN Resource Sharing in Lower Indian Buffet Game

In the lower-level Indian game model, multiple *MUs* requests different resources to their corresponding *SBS*. Let MU_i^j are the *MU* j in the area of *SBS$_i$* and $\mathcal{L}_i$ denote a set of resources in the ith *SBS*, $\mathcal{L}_i = \{ \mathcal{R}_i^1 = \text{CPU}, \mathcal{R}_i^2 = \text{memory}, \mathcal{R}_i^3 = \text{storage}, \mathcal{R}_i^4 = \text{bandwidth} \}$. Each $\mathcal{R}_i^k$ represents the available amount of kth resource in the *SBS$_i$*; these resources are obtained from the *VBP* through the upper-level Indian game. Individual *MU* attempts to actually purchase multiple resources based on their unit prices $U\_\mathcal{P}_i^k$, where $1 \leq k \leq 4$ and $i \in \mathcal{B}$.

The lower-level Indian game deals with the resource allocation problem while maximizing resource efficiencies. Based on the reciprocal relationship between *SBSs* and *MUs*, the HGRS scheme adaptively allocates *SBSs'* resources to each *MU*. From the viewpoint of *MUs*, their payoffs correspond to the received benefit minus the incurred cost (Wang, 2005). Based on its expected payoff, each *MU* attempts to find the best actions. The *MU* j's utility function of kth resource (U_j^k) in the ith *SBS* is defined as.

$$U_j^k\left(\xi_j^k(i)\right) = b_j\left(\xi_j^k(i)\right) - c\left(U\_\mathcal{P}_i^k, \xi_j^k(i)\right)$$

s.t.,

$$b_j\left(\xi_j^k(i)\right) = \omega_j^k \times \log\left(\xi_j^k(i)\right) \text{ and } mp^k \leq U\_\mathcal{P}_i^k \leq Mp^k \qquad (16)$$

where $\xi_j^k(i)$ is the *MU* j's requested amount of kth resource in the SBS_i, and $b_j\left(\xi_j^k(i)\right)$ is the received benefit for the *MU* j. ω_j^k represents a payment that the *MU* j would spend for the kth resource based on its perceived worth. The $U\_\mathcal{P}_i^k$ is the unit price for the kth resource unit in the SBS_i, and $c\left(U\_\mathcal{P}_i^k(i), \xi_j^k(i)\right)$ is the cost function of SBS_i. Each *SBS* decides the $U\_\mathcal{P}_i^k$ between the pre-defined minimum (mp^k) and the maximum (Mp^k) price boundaries. In general, a received benefit typically follows a model of diminishing returns to scale; *MU*'s marginal benefit diminishes with increasing bandwidth (Wang, 2005). Based on this consideration, the received benefit can be represented in a general form of *log* function. In a distributed self-regarding fashion, each individual *MU* is independently interested in the sole goal of maximizing his/her utility function as.

$$\max_{\xi_j^k(i) \geq 0} U_j^k\left(\xi_j^k(i)\right) = \max_{\xi_j^k(i) \geq 0} \left\{ b_j\left(\xi_j^k(i)\right) - c\left(U\_\mathcal{P}_i^k(i), \xi_j^k(i)\right)\right\} \qquad (17)$$

From the viewpoint of *SBSs*, the most important criterion is a total revenue; it is defined as the sum of payments from *MUs* (Feng, 2004). Based on the $U\_\mathcal{P}_i^k$ and the total allocated resource amounts for *MU*'s, the total revenue of all *SBSs* (Ψ) is given by

$$\Psi = \sum_{i=1}^{n}\Psi_i = \sum_{i=1}^{n}\sum_{k=1}^{l}\left(U\_\mathcal{P}_i^k \times T_i^k\right) = \sum_{i=1}^{n}\sum_{k=1}^{l}\sum_{j=1}^{m}\left(U\_\mathcal{P}_i^k \times \xi_j^k(i) \times \mathfrak{l}_j^k(i)\right)$$

s.t.,

$$\mathfrak{l}_j^k(i) = \begin{cases} 1, & \textit{if the requested } \xi_j^k(i)\textit{ is actually allocated} \\ 0, & \textit{otherwise} \end{cases} \qquad (18)$$

where n, l, m are the total number of *SBSs*, resources and *MUs*, respectively. Each *SBS* adaptively controls its own $U\_\mathcal{P}^k$ to maximize the revenue in a distributed manner. The traffic model is assumed based on the elastic-demand paradigm; according to the current $U\_\mathcal{P}^k$, *MUs* can adapt their resource requests. It is relevant in real world situations where *MUs'* requests may be influenced by the price (Yang, 1997a; Yang, 1997b). In response to ω_j^k, the *MU* j can derive the $\xi_j^k(i)$ $\left(=\omega_j^k/U\_\mathcal{P}_i^k\right)$. In the SBS_i, the total requested resource amount from corresponding *MUs* is defined as.

$$\sum_{k=1}^{l}\sum_{j=1}^{m}\xi_j^k(i)=\sum_{k=1}^{l}\left(\frac{\sum_{j=1}^{m}\omega_j^k}{U\_\mathcal{P}_i^k}\right) \tag{19}$$

When the price is low, more *MUs* are attracted to participate *C-RAN* services because of the good satisfactory payoff. However, if the price is high, *MUs* requests are reduced because of the unsatisfactory payoff. Therefore, to deal with the congestion problem, a higher price is suitable to match the resource capacity constraint while reducing the potential demands. In order to toward the demand-supply balance, the current price should increase or decrease by $\Delta U\_\mathcal{P}^k$.

In the HGRS scheme, *SBSs* individually take account of previous price strategies to update their beliefs about what is the best-response price strategy in the future. If a strategy change can bring a higher payoff, *SBSs* have a tendency to move in the direction of that successful change, and vice versa. Therefore, *SBSs* dynamically tune their current strategies based on the payoff history. For the kth resource, the SBS_i's price strategy at the time period $t+1$ ($\lambda_i^k(t+1)$) is defined as

$$\begin{cases}\lambda_i^k(t+1)=\Lambda\left[\lambda_i^k(t)+\left|\Delta U\_\mathcal{P}_i^k(t)\right|\right], & If\ \Omega>0\\ \lambda_i^k(t+1)=\Lambda\left[\lambda_i^k(t)-\left|\Delta U\_\mathcal{P}_i^k(t)\right|\right], & If\ \Omega\le 0\end{cases}$$

s.t.,

$$\Delta U\_\mathcal{P}_i^k(t)=\frac{\left(\Psi_i^k(t)-\Psi_i^k(t-1)\right)}{\Psi_i^k(t-1)},\ \Omega=\frac{\left(\lambda_i^k(t)-\lambda_i^k(t-1)\right)}{\Delta U\_\mathcal{P}_i^k(t)}$$

and

$$\Lambda\left[\mathcal{K}\right]=\begin{cases}\Lambda\left[\mathcal{K}\right]=mp^k, & if\ \mathcal{K}<mp^k\\ \Lambda\left[\mathcal{K}\right]=\mathcal{K}, & if\ mp^k\le\mathcal{K}\le Mp^k\\ \Lambda\left[\mathcal{K}\right]=Mp^k, & if\ \mathcal{K}>Mp^k\end{cases} \tag{20}$$

where $\Psi_i^k(t)$ and $\lambda_i^k(t)$ are the SBS_i's revenue and price strategy for the kth resource at the time period t, respectively. $\left|"U\_\mathcal{P}_i^k(t)\right|$ represents the absolute value of $"U\_\mathcal{P}_i^k(t)$. According to (20), the strategy profile of all *SBSs* can be denoted by a $n\times l$ matrix as follows:

$$\mathcal{T}_i(t) = \left\{ \lambda_i^1(t), \lambda_i^2(t), \dots \lambda_i^l(t) \right\} = \begin{bmatrix} \lambda_1^1(t), \lambda_1^2(t), \cdots, \lambda_1^l(t) \\ \lambda_2^1(t), \lambda_2^2(t), \cdots, \lambda_2^l(t) \\ \vdots \quad \vdots \quad \ddots \quad \vdots \\ \lambda_n^1(t), \lambda_n^2(t), \cdots, \lambda_n^l(t) \end{bmatrix}., \text{ s.t., } i \in \mathcal{B} \tag{21}$$

The Main Steps of the HGRS Scheme

The HGRS scheme presents the two-level Indian buffet game model. In the upper-level Indian buffet game, available resources of *CPs* are distributed to *SBSs* based on the concept of *A_SV*. In the lower-level Indian buffet game, Individual *SBS* allocate the distributed resources to *MUs* according to the non-cooperative manner. The main steps of the HGRS scheme are given next.

Step 1: At the initial time, all *SBSs* have same price strategies ($\mathcal{T}$). At the beginning of game, this starting guess is a reasonable assumption.

Step 2: At each game period, the *VBP* collects available resources from *CPs* using the virtualization technology, and distribute these resources to each *SBS* according to (12)-(15).

Step 3: Individual *MU* in each cell attempts to actually purchase multiple resources from corresponding *SBS*. Based on this information, each *SBS* dynamically decide the price strategy ($\mathcal{T}$) using (19) and (20).

Step 4: At each game period, the *VBP* re-distributes periodically the *CP* resources based on the currently calculating ϕ values; it is the upper-level Indian game.

Step 5: Based on the current price ($\mathcal{T}$), each *MUs* dynamically decide the amount of purchasing resources according to (17).

Step 6: Strategy decisions in each game player are made in an entirely distributed manner.

Step 7: Under widely diverse *C-RAN* environments, the *VBP*, *SBSs* and *MUs* are self-monitoring constantly based on the iterative feedback mechanism.

Step 8: If the change of prices in all *SBSs* is within a pre-defined bound (ε), this change is negligible; proceed to Step 9. Otherwise, proceed to Step 2 for the next iteration.

Step 9: Game is temporarily over. Ultimately, the HGRS scheme reaches an effective resource sharing solution. When the *C-RAN* system status is changed, it can re-trigger another game-based resource sharing procedure.

Summary

Efficient and fine-grained resource sharing becomes an increasingly important and attractive control issue for new-generation *C-RAN* systems. The HGRS scheme proposes a novel multi-resource sharing algorithm, which is framed as a two-level Indian buffet game model: upper-level Indian game is played among *VBP-SBSs*, and lower-level Indian game is played among *SBSs-MUs*. Based on the hierarchical interaction mechanism, the *VBP*, *SBSs* and *MUs* are intertwined and make decisions during the step-by-step interactive feedback process. The main novelty of HGRS scheme is to apply a new resource sharing paradigm to control the *C-RAN* environment.

CLOUD-BASED COMPUTATION OFFLOADING (CCO) SCHEME

The *Cloud-based Computation Offloading* (CCO) scheme is designed as an effective MCIoT computation offloading algorithm for Future IoT Platform. Based on the nested game model, each mobile device determines the portion of remote offloading computation based on the Rubinstein game approach. Then, a computation resource in the cloud system is dynamically assigned for the requested offloading computation. The CCO scheme can approach an optimal solution for the offloading computation in MCIoT system.

Development Motivation

Recently, the rapid technology development makes it possible for connecting various smart mobile devices together while providing more data interoperability methods for application purpose. Therefore, the diverse nature of applications has challenged the communication and computation mechanisms to look beyond conventional applications for effective network policies, Quality of Service (QoS) and system performance. The Internet of Things (IoT) paradigm is based on intelligent and self configuring mobile devices interconnected in a dynamic and global network infrastructure. It is enabling ubiquitous and pervasive computing scenarios in a real world (Botta, 2014; Kim, 2010).

In the current decade, a growing number of researches have been conducted to acquire data ubiquitously, process data timely, and distribute data wirelessly in the IoT paradigm. To satisfy this requirement, mobile devices should have a capacity to handle the required processing and computation work. Unfortunately, the desire for rich, powerful applications on mobile devices conflicts with the reality of these devices limitations: slow computation processors, little memory storage and limited battery life. For this reason, mobile devices still lag behind desktop and server hardware to provide the experience that users expect. (Singh, 2014; Vermesan, 2011).

The Mobile Cloud (MC) is emerging as one of the most important branches of cloud computing and is expected to expand the mobile ecosystems. Usually, cloud computing has long been recognized as a paradigm for big data storage and analytics; it has virtually unlimited capabilities in terms of storage and processing power. MC is the combination of cloud computing, mobile computing and wireless networks to bring rich computational resources to mobile users, network operators, as well as cloud computing providers. With an explosive growth of the multimedia mobile applications, MC computing has become a significant research topic of the scientific and industrial communities (Chen, 2015; Sabyasachi, 2013; Zhu, 2014).

The two fields of MC and IoT have been widely popular as future infrastructures and have seen an independent evolution. However, MC and IoT are complementary technologies, and several mutual advantages deriving from their integration have been identified (Singh, 2014). Therefore, a symbiosis has developed between mobile devices and MC, and is expected to be combined for the future Internet. Generally, mobile devices can benefit from the virtually unlimited capabilities and resources of MC to compensate its storage, processing, energy constraints. Specifically, the MC can offer an effective solution to implement IoT service management. On the other hand, the MC can benefit from the IoT system by extending its scope to deal with real world things in a more distributed and dynamic manner (Botta, 2014). Nowadays, the extension of MC over dynamic IoT environments has been referred as a next generation communication and computing paradigm (Sabyasachi, 2013).

The CCO scheme focuses on the integration of MC and IoT, which is call the MCIoT paradigm. MCIoT should support wide variety of multimedia applications with different QoS requirements; these applications need different system resources. However, mobile devices are generally characterized with limited storage and processing capacity. A possible way to dealing with this problem is to remotely execute some computation tasks on a more powerful cloud system, with results communicated back to the mobile devices. This method is the computation offloading (Sinha, 2011). Therefore, the synergy of MC and IoT lies at the junction of mobile devices, different wireless network providers and cloud computing systems.

Although the computation offloading approach can significantly augment computation capability of mobile devices, the task of developing a comprehensive and reliable computation offloading mechanism remains challenging. A key challenge is how to efficiently coordinate multiple mobile devices and MCIoT system. Usually, individual mobile devices locally make control decisions to maximize their profits in a distributed manner. This situation leads us into game theory. In 1988, an American political scientist, George Tsebelis introduced an important new concept, called nested games, to rational choice theory and to the study of comparative politics (Tsebelis, 1988). Using the notion of nested games, he showed that game players are involved simultaneously in several games. He argued that the '*nestedness*' of the principal game explains why a player confronted with a series of choices might not pick the alternative which appears to be optimal. In other words, what seems to be irrational in one arena becomes intelligible when the whole network of games is examined. Originally, the nested game has been used by anyone interested in the effects of political context and institutions on the behavior of political actors. Nowadays, nested game approach can be used to analyze a systematic, empirically accurate, and theoretically coherent account of apparently irrational actions (Jesse, 2002; Pang, 2011; Wang, 2013).

The CCO scheme adopts a nested game approach to address the computation offloading algorithm in the MCIoT platform. Nested game model is a useful framework for designing decentralized mechanisms, such that the mobile devices can self-organize into the mutually satisfactory computation offloading decisions. Usually, different mobile devices may pursue different interests, and act individually to maximize their profits. This self-organizing feature can add autonomics into MCIoT systems and help to ease the heavy burden of complex centralized control algorithms.

Nested Game Model for Computation Offloading

Under competitive or cooperative environments, behaviors of game players have direct influence on each other. Based on rational assumptions, game theory is to study the decision-making mechanism and the balance of decision-making interactions (Kim, 2014). However, game players seem to act irrationally, but if treating the game as a part of a larger game, we can see their behaviors are rational (Pang, 2011). From the view of small independent game, each player's strategy is not the optimal solution. However, from the view of big game, players' reactions are the best responses. Such games are called as nested games, and small games may be used as sub-games nested in the sequential game of a larger game (Jesse, 2002; Pang, 2011; Wang, 2013). In multiple fields of nested game, game players try to optimize their payoffs in the principal game field and also involved a game about the rules of the game. It can lead to apparently suboptimal payoffs as the game player fails to see the other fields that provide context for the small game in the principal field. Several studies use nested game theory to explain political party behavior, budget negotiations, electoral systems and public policy (Park, 2007).

The CCO scheme specifies the nested game to design a new computation offloading algorithm. The key point of MC offloading mechanism hinges on the ability to achieve enough computing resources with small energy consumption. In recent years, this technique has received more attention because of the significant rise of offload-available mobile applications, the availability of powerful clouds and the improved connectivity options for mobile devices. The main challenges to design an effective computation offloading algorithm lies in the adaptive division of applications for partial offloading, the mismatch control mechanism between how individual mobile devices demand and access computing resources, and how cloud providers offer them. To decide what, when and how to be offloaded, the CCO scheme should consider the offload overhead and current MCIoT system conditions.

In the resource-rich MC environment, a mobile device must pay the price to take advantage of computation offloading. To gain an extra benefit, idle computation resources in MCIoT system compete to get the requested offloading task. Therefore, mobile devices can select the most adaptable computation resource to execute their offloaded computations. The MCIoT environment can be described as follows:

1. $\mathbb{D} = \left\{ D_0, D_1, \ldots, D_n \right\}$ is the set of mobile devices, and $A_i, i \in \left[1, n \right]$ is an application, which belongs to the mobile device D_i.

2. Mobile device applications are elastic applications, and can be split. For example, $A_i = \sum_{k=1}^{L} a_k^i$, where a_k^i is the kth module of A_i, and some parts (i.e., coded modules) of A_i can be offloaded.

3. $\mathbb{R} = \left\{ R_0, R_1, \ldots, R_m \right\}$ is the set of idle cloud computing resources in the MCIoT environment, and $R_j, j \in \left[1, m \right]$ has a computation capacity ($\mathcal{F}_{R_j}^R$; CPU cycles per second) and expected price (ψ^{R_j}; price per CPU cycle of the R_j) to accomplish the offloaded computations.

4. Price in each $R_{j, 1 \leq j \leq m}$ can be dynamically adjustable according to the auction mechanism.

5. For simplicity, there is no communication noise and uncertainties in MCIoT environments.

The CCO scheme develops a two-stage nested game model comprised of elastic applications, mobile devices and computation resources in the MC. In the first stage, applications of mobile devices are divided into two parts: one part runs locally and the other part is run on the MC side. In the second stage, offloaded tasks are matched to computing resources in the MCIoT system. Based on the auction mechanism, computation resources submit different offers to get the requested offload task, and the most adaptable offer is selected. According to the two-stage sequential nested game approach, the CCO scheme can make decisions about whether to perform computation offloading, which portion of application should be offloaded to the cloud, and which resource is selected to accomplish the requested offload.

Offloading Communication and Computation Process

By taking into account both communication and computation aspects of MCIoT environments, the CCO scheme formulate a new decentralized computation offloading algorithm. In each mobile device, applications can be computed either locally on the mobile device or remotely on the cloud via computation offloading. For the local computing approach, each mobile device (e.g., D_i) can execute the some computation part of A_i, individually. The local computation execution time ($L\_CT_{comp}^{A_i-D_i}$)) of the application A_i on the mobile device D_i is given as

$$L\_CT_{comp}^{A_i-D_i} = \frac{\sum_{k=1}^{L} \mathfrak{U}\left(a_k^i\right) \times a_k^i}{\mathcal{F}_{D_i}^{L}}, s.t., \mathfrak{U}\left(a_k^i\right) = \begin{cases} 1, & \text{if } a_k^i \text{ is locally computed} \\ 0, & \text{otherwise}\left(a_k^i \text{ is offloaded}\right) \end{cases} \tag{22}$$

where $\mathcal{F}_{D_i}^{L}$ is the computation capability of mobile device D_i. The local computation cost ($L\_CC_{comp}^{A_i-D_i}$) of the application A_i on the mobile device D_i is calculated based on the $L\_CT_{comp}^{A_i-D_i}$ and consumed local computation energy (ρ).

$$L\_CC_{comp}^{A_i-D_i} = \rho^{D_i} \times \left(\mathcal{F}_{D_i}^{L} \times L\_CT_{comp}^{A_i-D_i}\right) \tag{23}$$

where ρ^{D_i} is the coefficient denoting the consumed energy cost per CPU cycle. The evaluation of total local computation overhead ($T\_O_{local}^{A_i-D_i}$) of the application A_i on the mobile device D_i is a non-trivial multi-objective optimization problem. It is addressed as a weighted sum by considering normalized time and energy cost.

$$T\_O_{local}^{A_i-D_i} = \lambda_{D_i}^{A_i} \times \left(\frac{L\_CT_{comp}^{A_i-D_i}}{\frac{1}{\mathcal{F}_{D_i}^{L}} \times \sum_{k=1}^{L} a_k^i}\right) + \left(1-\lambda_{D_i}^{A_i}\right) \times \left(\frac{L\_CC_{comp}^{A_i-D_i}}{\rho^{D_i} \times \sum_{k=1}^{L} a_k^i}\right) \tag{24}$$

where $\lambda_{D_i}^{A_i}$ is a parameter to control the relative weights given to execution time and energy consumption. To satisfy the A_i's demand, $\lambda_{D_i}^{A_i}$ is adaptively decided. In the equation (30), the $\lambda_{D_i}^{A_i}$ value decision process is explained in detail.

Next, the CCO scheme estimates the remote computation overhead through the MC offloading mechanism. Generally, the communication and computation aspects play a key role in MC offload. The CCO scheme considers a delay sensitive Wi-Fi model for offloading services; mobile devices are sensitive to delay and their payoff decreases as delay increases. As a wireless access Base-Station (BS), a WiFi access point manages the uplink/downlink communications of mobile devices. For the computation offloading, the mobile device D_i would incur the extra overhead in terms of time and energy to submit the computation offload via wireless access. Based on the communication model in (Chen, 2015), the offloading communication time ($O\_CT_{off}^{A_i-D_i}$) and energy ($O\_CE_{off}^{A_i-D_i}$) of the application A_i on the mobile device D_i are computed as follows.

$$O\_CT_{off}^{A_i-D_i}\left(\mathbb{D}\right) = \frac{\sum_{k=1}^{L} \mathfrak{I}\left(a_k^i\right) \times a_k^i}{\mathcal{B} \times \log_2\left(1 + \frac{P_i \times H_{i,BS}}{\omega + \sum_{a_k^g \in A_g \backslash \{A_i\}: \mathfrak{I}\left(a_k^g\right)=1} P_g \times H_{g,BS}}\right)}$$

$$s.t., g \in [1,n], D_g \in \mathbb{D} \ and \ \mathfrak{I}\left(a_k^i\right) = \begin{cases} 1, & if \ a_k^i \ is \ offloaded \\ 0, & otherwise \end{cases} \tag{25}$$

$$O\_CE_{off}^{A_i-D_i}\left(\mathbb{D}\right) = \frac{P_i \times \sum_{k=1}^{L} \mathfrak{I}\left(a_k^i\right) \times a_k^i}{\mathcal{B} \times \log_2\left(1 + \frac{P_i \times H_{i,BS}}{\omega + \sum_{a_k^g \in A_g \backslash \{A_i\}: \mathfrak{I}\left(a_k^g\right)=1} P_g \times H_{g,BS}}\right)}$$

where $\mathcal{B}$ is the channel bandwidth and P_i is the transmission power of device D_i. $H_{i,BS}$ denotes the channel gain between the mobile device D_i and the BS, and ω denotes the interference power. From the equation (25), the CCO scheme can see that if too many mobile devices choose to offload the computation via wireless access simultaneously, they may incur severe interference, leading to low data rates. It would negatively affect the performance of MC communication. Therefore, offloading decisions among mobile devices are tightly coupled each other (Chen, 2015). To address this conflicting situation, game theory can be adopted to achieve efficient computation offloading decisions.

After the offloading, the computation time ($C\_T_{remote}^{A_i-R_j}$) and payment ($P_{remote}^{A_i-R_j}$) of remote computation task ($\sum_{k=1}^{L} \mathfrak{I}\left(a_k^i\right) \times a_k^i$) on the assigned computation resource R_j can be then given as

$$C\_T_{remote}^{A_i-R_j} = \frac{\sum_{k=1}^{L} \mathfrak{I}\left(a_k^i\right) \times a_k^i}{\mathcal{F}_{R_j}^R} \ and \ P_{remote}^{A_i-R_j} = \psi^{R_j} \times \mathcal{F}_{R_j}^R \times C\_T_{remote}^{A_i-R_j}. \tag{26}$$

where $\mathcal{F}_{R_j}^R$ is the R_j's computation capability and ψ^{R_j} is the coefficient denoting the price per CPU cycle of the R_j. According to (25) and (26), the total offload overhead ($T\_O_{off}^{A_i-R_j}$) of the application A_i on the computation resource R_j is computed as a weighted sum by considering execution time and consuming cost.

$$T\_O_{off}^{A_i-R_j} = \lambda_{D_i}^{A_i} \times \left(\frac{O\_CT_{off}^{A_i-D_i}\left(\mathbb{D}\right) + C\_T_{remote}^{A_i-R_j}}{\frac{1}{\mathcal{F}_{D_i}^L} \times \sum_{k=1}^{L} a_k^i}\right) + \left(1 - \lambda_{D_i}^{A_i}\right) \times \left(\frac{O\_CE_{off}^{A_i-D_i}\left(\mathbb{D}\right) + P_{remote}^{A_i-R_j}}{\rho^{D_i} \times \sum_{k=1}^{L} a_k^i}\right) \tag{27}$$

According to (24), (25), (26) and (27), the total execution time of A_i ($T\_C_{total}^{A_i-D_i,R_j}$) with partial offloading can be estimated considering between the local and remote computing times.

$$T\_C_{total}^{A_i-D_i,R_j} = \max\left[L\_CT_{comp}^{A_i-D_i},\left(O\_CT_{off}^{A_i-D_i}\left(\mathbb{D}\right)+C\_T_{remote}^{A_i-R_j}\right)\right] \tag{28}$$

Finally, we can compute the total execution overhead of A_i ($\mathcal{S}^{A_i-D_i,R_j}\left(\mathbb{D}\right)$) like as

$$\mathcal{S}^{A_i-D_i,R_j}\left(\mathbb{D}\right) = \lambda_{D_i}^{A_i} \times \left(T\_C_{total}^{A_i-D_i,R_j}\right) + \left(1-\lambda_{D_i}^{A_i}\right) \times \left(\frac{L\_CC_{comp}^{A_i-D_i}+\left(O\_CE_{off}^{A_i-D_i}\left(\mathbb{D}\right)+P_{remote}^{A_i-R_j}\right)}{\rho^{D_i} \times \sum_{k=1}^{L} a_k^i}\right) \tag{29}$$

To meet the application-specific demand, different applications have different evaluation criteria for time and energy consumption. For example, when a mobile device is running an application that is delay sensitive (e.g., real-time applications), it should put more weight on the execution time (i.e., a higher λ) in order to ensure the time deadline, and vice versa. Therefore, a fixed value for λ cannot effectively adapt to the different application demands. In this work, the value of λ for the A_i on mobile device D_i ($\lambda_{D_i}^{A_i}$) is dynamically decided as follows.

$$\lambda_{D_i}^{A_i} = \min\left[1,\left(\frac{\frac{1}{\mathcal{F}_{D_i}^{L}} \times \sum_{k=1}^{L} a_k^i}{T\_D^{A_i}}\right)\right] \tag{30}$$

where $T\_D^{A_i}$ is the time deadline of A_i. Therefore, through the real-time online monitoring, the CCO scheme can be more responsive to application demands.

Application Partitioning Game

An important challenge for partial offloading is how to partition elastic applications and which part of partitioned application should be pushed to the remote clouds. The CCO scheme analyzes how mobile devices can exploit a partial offloading between cloud computation and local computation. To distribute computation tasks for partial offloading, the CCO scheme provides a non-cooperative bargaining game model by considering the consuming cost and computation time. Usually, a solution to the bargaining game model enables the game players to fairly and optimally determine their payoffs to make joint-agreements (Park, 2007; Suris, 2007). Therefore, the bargaining model is attractive for the partitioning problem.

In *Rubinstein-Stahl* model, players have their own bargaining power (δ). They negotiate with each other by proposing offers alternately. After several rounds of negotiation, players finally reach an agreement as following (Pan, 2008; Zhao, 2002).

$$\left(x_1^*, x_2^*\right) = \begin{cases} \left(\dfrac{1-\delta_2}{1-\left(\delta_1 \times \delta_2\right)}, \dfrac{\delta_2 \times \left(1-\delta_1\right)}{1-\left(\delta_1 \times \delta_2\right)}\right) & \textit{if the player\_1 offers first} \\[4mm] \left(\dfrac{\delta_1 \times \left(1-\delta_2\right)}{1-\left(\delta_1 \times \delta_2\right)}, \dfrac{1-\delta_1}{1-\left(\delta_1 \times \delta_2\right)}\right) & \textit{if the player\_2 offers first} \end{cases}$$

s.t.,

$$\left(x_1^*, x_2^*\right) \in \mathbf{R}^2 : x_1^* + x_2^* = 1, x_1^* \geq 0, x_2^* \geq 0 \text{ and } 0 \leq \delta_1, \delta_s \leq 1 \tag{31}$$

It is obvious that

$$\frac{1-\delta_2}{1-\left(\delta_1 \times \delta_2\right)} \geq \frac{\delta_2 \times \left(1-\delta_1\right)}{1-\left(\delta_1 \times \delta_2\right)}$$

and

$$\frac{\delta_1 \times \left(1-\delta_2\right)}{1-\left(\delta_1 \times \delta_2\right)} \leq \frac{1-\delta_1}{1-\left(\delta_1 \times \delta_2\right)}.$$

Traditionally, the bargaining power in the *Rubinstein-Stahl's* model is defined as follows (Pan, 2008).

$$\delta = e^{-\xi \times \Phi}, \text{ s.t., } \xi > 0 \tag{32}$$

where Φ is the time period of negotiation round. Given the Φ is fixed, δ is monotonic decreasing with ξ. Therefore, ξ is an instantaneous discount factor to adaptively adjust the bargaining power.

In the CCO scheme, the *Rubinstein-Stahl* bargaining game model is formulated to solve the application partitioning problem. In the game model, cloud computation resource and mobile device are assumed as players, which are denoted as the *player_1* (i.e., mobile device for local computation) and *player_2* (i.e., cloud resource for remote computation). In the scenario of the *Rubinstein-Stahl* model, each player has different discount factor (ξ). Under various MCIoT situations, the CCO scheme dynamically adjusts ξ values to provide more efficient control over system condition fluctuations. When the current local computation overhead is heavy, the mobile device does not have sufficient computation capacity to support the local computation service. In this case, a higher value of the *player_1*'s discount factor (ξ_I) is more suitable. If the reverse has been the case (i.e., the remote computation overhead is heavy), a higher value of the *player_2*'s discount factor (ξ_{II}) is suitable. At the end of each game period, the *player_1* and *player_2* adjust their discount factor values (ξ_I and ξ_{II}) as follows.

$$\xi_I = 1 - \xi_{II}, s.t., \xi_{II} = \frac{T\_O_{off}^{A_i\_R_j}}{S^{A_i\_D_i, R_j}(\mathbb{D})} \tag{33}$$

For simplicity, the CCO scheme assumes that the ξ values are fixed within an offloading procedure for each application, while they can be changed in different applications. Therefore, as system situations change after application partitioning, each player can adaptively adjust their ξ_I and ξ_{II} values for the next application execution while responding current MCIoT system conditions.

Cloud Resource Selection Game

Recently, researchers have proposed various auction models to optimally match up the buyer and seller according to their desires. It is a significant and efficient market-based approach to solve the allocation problem with more requisitions. Therefore, the auction game model can provide a resource selection mechanism in MC systems. In the computation resource selection scenario, there are a requested offload task (i.e., buyer) and computation resources (i.e., sellers). Based on the sequential offloading requests, the action model is designed as the one-to-many auction structure. As sellers, computation resources ($\mathbb{R}$) in MC system offer bids (i.e., the expected selling prices) for the remote offload computation. To show their preference to get the offloading computation, sellers ($\mathbb{R}$) can adjust their selling prices, periodically. For the tth auction stage, the seller (i.e., $R_j \in \mathbb{R}$) bids his price ($\psi^{R_j}(t)$) per CPU cycle is defined as follows.

$$\psi^{R_j}(t) = \begin{cases} \psi^{R_j}(t-1) + \left(1 - \dfrac{1}{\left(\exp\left(\max\left[5-0, \varepsilon_{R_j}\right]\right)\right)}\right), & \text{if } R_j \text{ is selected at } t-1 \\ s.t., \varepsilon_{R_j} \sim N\left(\mu_{R_j}, \sigma^2_{R_j}\right) \\ \psi^{R_j}(t-1) - \left(1 - \dfrac{1}{\left(\exp\left(\max\left[0, \varepsilon_{R_j}\right]\right)\right)}\right), & \text{otherwise} \end{cases} \tag{34}$$

where ε_{R_j} is a random variable to presents the price adjustment. Because the sellers are not interrelated, the random variable (ε) of each seller is independent of each other. According to (34), each seller (i.e., $R_j \in \mathbb{R}$) bids his offer (ψ^{R_j}, $\mathcal{F}_{R_j}^R$) at each auction round, and then the buyer (i.e., $D_i \in \mathbb{D}$) select the most adaptable offer. In the CCO scheme, the minimum price offering resource while satisfying the computation deadline ($T\_D^{(\cdot)}$) is selected. This dynamic auction procedure is repeated sequentially serial auction round. In each auction round, sellers can learn the buyer's desire with incoming information, and can make a better price decision for the next auction.

The Main Steps of the CCO Scheme

The CCO scheme presents a two-stage nested game model for the interaction of game players such as elastic applications, mobile devices and MC computation resources. Applications are involved in the application partitioning game in the first stage, and mobile devices and MC resources are involved in the resource selection game in the second stage. This two-stage nested game reflects the sequential dependencies of decisions in each stage. The main steps of the CCO scheme are given next.

Step 1: At the initial time, applications in each mobile devices are equally partitioned for local and remote offloading computations. At the beginning of game, this starting guess is useful to monitor the current MCIoT situation.

Step 2: According to (22)-(30), mobile devices can estimate their total offload overhead ($T\_O_{off}^{(\cdot)}$) and the total execution overhead ($\mathcal{S}^{(\cdot)}\left(\mathbb{D}\right)$), individually.

Step 3: Based on the (31)-(33) equations, each mobile device adaptively re-partitions its application based on the *Rubinstein-Stahl* bargaining game model.

Step 4: One part is computed locally on the mobile device. In MC side, the other part is computed remotely on the computation resource, which is selected according to the auction game.

Step 5: For the next resource selection process, computation resources periodically adjust their selling prices ($\psi^{(\cdot)}$) according to (34).

Step 6: As game players, elastic applications, mobile devices and MC computation resources are interrelated, and interact with each other in a two-stage nested game. In each stage game, game players try to maximize their payoffs while they are involving in a bigger game.

Step 7: Under widely diverse MCIoT environments, mobile devices and computation resources are self-monitoring constantly for the next iterative feedback processing. This iterative feedback procedure continues under MCIoT system dynamics.

Step 8: When a new application service is requested, it can re-trigger another computation offloading process; proceeds to Step 1 for the next game iteration.

Summary

Over recent past years, a novel paradigm where Cloud and IoT are merged is expected to be an important component of the Future Internet. The CCO scheme reviews the integration of MC and IoT, and designs a new computation offloading algorithm in the MCIoT platform. Based on the nested game model, the main goal of the CCO scheme is to maximize mobile device performance while providing service QoS. To satisfy this goal, the CCO scheme consists of application partitioning game and cloud resource selection game. In the partitioning game, applications are adaptively partitioned according to the *Rubinstein-Stahl* bargaining model. In the resource selection game, computation resources in MC system are selected based on the one-to-many auction game model. Based on the nested game principle, these game models are interrelated to each other, and operated as a two-stage sequential game.

DYNAMIC SOCIAL CLOUD MANAGEMENT (DSCM) SCHEME

The *Dynamic Social Cloud Management* (DSCM) scheme is developed with a view of game theory model and reciprocal resource sharing mechanism. In particular, the DSCM scheme devises a new transformable Stackelberg game to coordinate the interdependence between social structure and resource availability for individual users. The DSCM scheme constantly monitors the current SC system conditions and adaptively exploits the available resources while ensuring mutual fairness.

Development Motivation

Digital relationships between individual people become more and more embedded in our daily actions, and they can be powerful influences in our real-life. Moreover, we are now connected with all our social networks through mobile devices. The increasing ubiquity of social networks is evidenced by the growing popularity of social network services. A social network service consists of a representation of each user, his or her social links, and a variety of additional services. Usually, social networks provide a platform to facilitate communications and resource sharing between users while modelling real-world relationships. Therefore, a variety of social network services have extended beyond simple communication among users (Hemmati, 2010; Jang, 2013; Zhang, 2014).

With the advent of social networks, cloud computing is becoming an emerging paradigm to provide a flexible stack of computing, software, and storage services. In a scalable and virtualized manner over networks, cloud users can access to fully virtualized hardware resources. The adoption of cloud computing technology is attractive; users obtain cloud resources, whose management is partly automated and can be scaled almost instantaneously. However, with the rapid development of cloud computing, critical issues of cloud computing technology have emerged. In general, modern cloud applications are characterized by assuming a constant environment. But, real-world environments are open, dynamic and unpredictable (Chen, 2015; Liu, 2015).

In social networks, individual users are bound by finite resource capacity and limited capabilities. However, some users may have surplus resource capacity or capabilities. Therefore, the superfluous resource could be shared for a mutual benefit. Within the context of a social network, users may wish to share resources without payment, and utilize a reciprocal credit based on the trust model (Chard, 2010; Chard, 2012). To satisfy this goal, a new concept, Social Cloud (SC) was introduced by combining the methodologies of social networks and cloud computing. SC is a novel scalable computing model where resources are beneficially shared among a group of social network users. From (Chard, 2010), the formal definition of SC can be defined like as; *A social cloud is a resource and service sharing framework utilizing relationships established between members of a social network*. Based on the cloud computing technique, SC model is used to enable virtualized resource sharing through service-based interfaces.

To construct the SC system in a real-world environment, there are many challenges that need to be carefully considered. First of all, the concept of SC focuses on the sharing rather than sale of resources. Using sharing preferences, the social context of exchange is accentuated along with the social ties of individual users. However, social relationships are not simply edges in a graph. There are many different types of relationship; different users will associate different levels of trust to different relationship contexts, and have different reliability, trustworthiness and availability. Therefore, users may have very specific preferences with whom they interact. To design an effective SC control scheme, it is necessary to take into account the preferences and perceptions of users towards one another (Caton, 2014).

Under widely dynamic SC system conditions, end users can be assumed as intelligent rational decision-makers, and they select a best-response strategy to maximize their expected payoffs. This situation is well-suited for the game theory. In 1934, German economist H. V. Stackelberg proposed a hierarchical strategic game model based on two kinds of different decision makers. Under a hierarchical decision making structure, one or more players declare and announce their strategies before the other players choose their strategies. In game theory terms, the declaring players are called as leaders while the players who react to the leaders are called as followers.

Originally, Stackelberg game model was developed to explain the monopoly of industry. The leader is the incumbent monopoly of the industry and the follower is a new entrant; it can be the static bilevel optimization model (Kim, 2014). The DSCM scheme has further extended the classical Stackelberg model and developed a novel game mode, called Transformable Stackelberg (TS) game model. In the TS game, each player can be a leader or a follower as the case may be. Therefore, the position of game players is dynamically transformable according to current conditions.

TS game model is a useful framework for designing decentralized mechanisms, such that users in SC systems can self-organize into the mutually satisfactory resource sharing process. This self-organizing feature can add autonomics into SC systems and help to ease the heavy burden of complex centralized control algorithms. Especially, the DSCM scheme pays serious attention to trust evaluation, repeated interactions and iterative self-learning techniques to effectively implement the resource sharing process. In the DSCM scheme, such techniques have been incorporated into the TS game model, and work together toward an effective system performance.

Transformable Stackelberg Game Model

Social cloud is a form of community cloud and is designed to enable access to elastic compute capabilities contributed by socially connected community (Caton, 2014). To avoid the social dilemma such as '*Tragedy of the Commons*', social incentives motivate users to participate in, and contribute to, SC systems in different ways. Motivation is generally categorized as either intrinsic or extrinsic. Extrinsic motivation represents that users are motivated by an external reward, e.g., virtual currency. Therefore, they will contribute to the SC while the expected benefits exceed the cost of contribution. Intrinsic motivation represents an internal satisfaction obtained from the task itself rather than the rewards or benefits. In realities, people incline to cooperate with others for reciprocation and altruism. These factors rationalize non-economic behaviors and motivates users to contribute to SC (Chard, 2012).

The DSCM scheme leverages social incentives to create ad hoc clouds without incurring the overhead of central complex processes. In the DSCM scheme, these techniques have been incorporated into the TS game model, which is developed to let distributed players learn the best strategy in the step-by-step interactive online manner. This approach can induce all SC users to share resources as much as possible and ensure a good tradeoff between the implementation complexity for real-world SC operations and an effective system performance. Therefore, the DSCM scheme can be used to overcome one of the major limitations of traditional SC monitoring methods.

In a realistic SC scenario, each user, i.e., network device, can be a resource supplier or demander. Suppliers make their decisions by considering the possible reactions of demanders. Demanders react dependently based on the decision of suppliers while attempting to maximize their satisfaction. Therefore, in the TS game model ($\mathbb{G}$), suppliers plays the role of leaders and demanders become followers. Based on these assumptions, $\mathbb{G}$ is defined as a tuple $\mathbb{G} =$

$$\left(\mathbb{N}, \left(V_i\right)_{i \in \mathbb{N}}, \left(\boldsymbol{S}_i\right)_{i \in \mathbb{N}}, \left(\Lambda_i\right)_{i \in \mathbb{N}}, \left(U_i\right)_{i \in \mathbb{N}}, T\right)$$

at each time period t of gameplay.

- $\mathbb{N}$ is the finite set of players, $\mathbb{N} = \{p_1, \dots, p_n\}$ where $p_{i,1 \leq i \leq n}$ represents the ith user. A player can be a supplier or a demander at times. Therefore, the position of each player would be dynamically changeable as a leader or a follower.
- V_i is the amount of exchangeable resources of the player i. In this scheme, V is the computing capacity, e.g. CPU cycles.
- $\boldsymbol{S}_i$ is the set of strategies with the player i. If the player i is a supplier, $\boldsymbol{S}_i$ can be defined as the amount of sharing resource. If the player i is a demander, $\boldsymbol{S}_i$ is defined as the amount of requested resource.
- Λ_i is the contribution level of the player i in the SC community.
- The U_i is the payoff received by the player i. Traditionally, the payoff is determined as the obtained outcome minus the cost to obtain that outcome.
- The T is a time period. The $\mathbb{G}$ is repeated $t \in T < \infty$ time periods with competitive and cooperative manner.

In the SC system, each network device has its own computation resources and executes elastic applications. Applications can be divided into two parts: one part runs locally and the other part can be executed on the cloud side. Therefore, applications in each network device can be computed either locally or remotely via computation offloading. In general, the main challenges to design an offloading mechanism are to decide what, when and how to be offloaded. In the DSCM scheme, available resources in suppliers are matched to demanders based on the supplier-demander interactive relationship. According to the TS game model, network devices can self-organize into the mutually satisfactory computation offloading decisions.

Resource Sharing Process in Social Cloud Systems

Different users may pursue individually to maximize their profits. From the viewpoint of demanders, the payoff corresponds to the resource sharing benefit minus the incurred cost to share the remote resource. Therefore, the utility function of demander i (U_i^D) is defined as follows:

$$U_i^D\left(x_i, \Lambda_i\right) = \mathcal{B}_i\left(j, x_i\right) - \mathcal{C}_i(j, x_i), \text{ s.t., } j \text{ is a supplier} \in \mathbb{N} \text{ and } i \neq j \tag{35}$$

where x_i is the requested resource amount, and $\mathcal{B}_i(\cdot)$ and $\mathcal{C}_i(\cdot)$ are the benefit and cost functions for the demander i. Usually, elastic applications have concave benefit function, which provides monotone increasing values in proportion to the assigned resource amounts. According to the amount of assigned resource, $\mathcal{B}_i(\cdot)$ and $\mathcal{C}_i(\cdot)$ are given by

$$\mathcal{B}_i\left(j,x_i\right) = \sin\left(\frac{\pi}{2}\times\frac{b_j^i}{x_i}\right) \text{ and } \mathcal{C}_i(j,x_i) = \zeta\times\left(\varrho\times\frac{b_j^i}{\mathcal{MX}}\right)$$

s.t.,

$$\zeta = \frac{b_j^i}{\max\left\{\Lambda_i,b_j^i\right\}} \text{ and } \varrho = \frac{\varepsilon\left(b_j^i\right)}{\varepsilon\left(\mathcal{MX}\right)} \tag{36}$$

where b_j^i is the assigned resource amount from the supplier j. ζ is a cost control parameter, and $\mathcal{MX}$ is the total resource amount to process the corresponding application. $\varepsilon\left(\mathcal{MX}\right)$ and $\varepsilon\left(b_j^i\right)$ are the energy consumption to execute $\mathcal{MX}$ and b_j^i amount resources, respectively. In the DSCM scheme, $\varepsilon\left(\cdot\right)$ is a linear function. Λ_i is the accumulated contributiveness of the demander i. After the remote execution, Λ_i is decreased by b_j^i, i.e., $\Lambda_i = \Lambda_i - b_j^i$. Based on the expected payoff $U^D\left(\cdot\right)$, demanders can try to find the best actions, i.e., the decision of x_i amount.

From the viewpoint of suppliers, the payoff also corresponds to the received benefit minus the incurred cost to assign the sharing resource. However, in contrast to the demanders' interest, the sharing benefit is defined according to the reciprocal cooperation, more generally, the combination of evolution, altruism, and reciprocity. In the DSCM scheme, users can be altruistic toward others and react to other users' altruism. Therefore, the received benefit function is developed based on the simple reciprocal mechanism. By considering the service cost, the supplier j's utility function to the demander i ($U_j^S\left(\cdot\right)$) is defined as follows:

$$U_j^S\left(\mathcal{Z}_j,\Lambda_j,i\right) = \mathbb{B}_j\left(\mathcal{Z}_j,\Lambda_j,i\right) - \mathbb{C}_j\left(\mathcal{Z}_j\right) \tag{37}$$

where $\mathcal{Z}_j$ is the amount of sharing resource of the supplier j, and $\mathbb{B}_j\left(\mathcal{Z}_j,\Lambda_j,i\right)$ and $\mathbb{C}_j\left(\mathcal{Z}_j\right)$ are the benefit and cost functions for the supplier j, respectively. To get the optimal payoff, suppliers try to maximize their benefit function while minimizing their cost function. According to the $\mathcal{Z}_j$ and Λ values, $\mathbb{B}_j\left(\cdot\right)$ and $\mathbb{C}_j\left(\cdot\right)$ are given by.

$$\mathbb{B}_j\left(\mathcal{Z}_j,\Lambda_j,i\right) = \left[\left(\theta_j^i\times e^{\mathcal{Z}_j}\right) + \mathcal{F}_j\left(\Lambda_j\right)\right] \text{and } \mathbb{C}_j\left(\mathcal{Z}_j\right) = \lambda\times\left(\frac{\varepsilon\left(\mathcal{Z}_j\right)}{\varepsilon\left(\mathfrak{T}\right)}\right)$$

s.t.,

$$\theta_j^i = \frac{\varphi_j + \left(\varphi_j \times \left(\Lambda_i \Big/ \left(\Lambda_i + \Lambda_j\right)\right)\right)}{1 - \left(\Lambda_i \Big/ \left(\Lambda_i + \Lambda_j\right)\right)} \text{ and } \mathcal{F}_j\left(\Lambda_j\right) = \left(\mathcal{Z}_j \Big/ \max\left\{\Lambda_j, \mathcal{Z}_j\right\}\right) \tag{38}$$

θ_j^i is the supplier j's altruistic parameter to the demander i, and φ_j is the supplier j's general altruistic propensity. $\varepsilon\left(\mathfrak{T}\right)$ and $\varepsilon\left(\mathcal{Z}_j\right)$ are the energy consumption to execute the supplier j's total resource ($\mathfrak{T}$) and $\mathcal{Z}_j$, respectively. λ is the cost control parameter. After the resource sharing process, Λ_j is increased by $\mathcal{Z}_j$, i.e., $\Lambda_j = \Lambda_j + \mathcal{Z}_j$.

Under dynamically changing SC environments, a fixed altruistic propensity cannot effectively adapt to the current SC condition. Therefore, the φ value should be dynamically adjustable. In order to implement the φ value adjustment process, suppliers should learn how to perform well by interacting with demanders and dynamically adjust their φ levels. Based on the exponential weight learning algorithm (Gajane, 2015), suppliers in the TS game model can constantly adapt each φ level to get an appropriate attitude to their corresponding SC environments. Let $\mathbb{K}$ be the set of all possible altruistic propensity levels, i.e., $\varphi \in \mathbb{K}$. In the DSCM scheme, the probability of choosing the k's propensity level in $\mathbb{K}$ at time t ($P_k^\varphi\left(t\right)$) is defined by.

$$P_k^\varphi\left(t\right) = \left(1 - \gamma\right) \times \left(\omega_k\left(t\right) \Big/ \sum_{j=1}^K \omega_j\left(t\right)\right) + \frac{\gamma}{\|\mathbb{K}\|}$$

s.t.,

$$\omega_j\left(t\right) = \omega_j\left(t-1\right) \times \exp\left(\gamma \times \left(\mathcal{U}_j\left(t-1\right) \Big/ \left(P_j^\varphi\left(t-1\right) \times \|\mathbb{K}\|\right)\right)\right) \tag{39}$$

where $\gamma \in [0,1]$ is an egalitarianism factor, which tunes the desire to pick an action uniformly at random. That is, if $\gamma = 1$, the weights have no effect on the choices at any step. $\|\mathbb{K}\|$ is the total number of propensity levels, and $\mathcal{U}_j\left(t-1\right)$ is the obtained payoff ($U_j^s\left(\cdot\right)$) at time $t-1$. According to the distribution of $P\left(t\right)$, suppliers can modify their φ levels without any impractical rationality assumptions. During the step-by-step iteration, suppliers individually adjust the φ value by using the dynamics of feedback-based repeated process. Therefore, under dynamic SC situations, the main advantage of DSCM scheme is a real-world practicality.

During real-world SC operations, multiple demanders can request the resource sharing from the same supplier. In this case, the role of supplier is to distribute dynamically the limited resource for each demander. To get a fair-efficient resource allocation, the DSCM scheme develops a new resource distribution algorithm based on the relative utilitarian bargaining model (Kim, 2014); it can be applicable and useful in a SC system with a frequently changing situation. In the DSCM scheme, demanders' Λ values are considered as asymmetric bargaining powers. Therefore, the bargaining solution ($\mathcal{R}\_\mathcal{B}$) for resource distribution is given by.

$$\mathcal{R}\_\mathcal{B} = \max_{b_j^i,\ i\in\mathcal{N}_j} \left(\sum_{i\in\mathcal{N}_j} \mathfrak{U}_i\left(b_j^i,\Lambda_i\right) \right), s.t., \mathfrak{U}_i\left(b_j^i,\Lambda_i\right) = \left(\frac{b_j^i}{x_i}\right)^{\eta_i} \text{ and } \eta_i = \left.\Lambda_i\middle/\sum_{j=1}^K \Lambda_j\right. \tag{40}$$

where $\mathcal{N}_j$ is the set of all resource requesting demanders to the supplier j. $\mathcal{R}\_\mathcal{B}$ is a vector, which corresponds to the resource distribution amounts to each demander.

In general, traditional game models have focused on investigating *which* decisions are made or *what* decisions should be made. Therefore, an equilibrium point is a well-known solution concept in classical game models. The strategy in equilibrium is the best response to the strategies of the other users. In the TS game model, an equilibrium point of suppliers and demanders are can be defined as follows:

$$U^*\left(U^{D*},U^{S*}\right) =$$
$$\begin{cases} \begin{bmatrix} U^{S*} = \arg \max_{\mathcal{Z}_j \in S_j} \left\{ U_j^S\left(\mathcal{Z}_j,\Lambda_j,i\right)\right\}, & \textit{if } j \textit{ is a supplier with single demander } i \\ \arg \max_{i\in\mathcal{N},\mathcal{Z}_j^i\in S_j} \left\{ U_j^S\left(\mathcal{Z}_j,\Lambda_j,\mathcal{N}\right)\right\}, & \textit{if } j \textit{ is a supplier with multiple demanders } N \end{bmatrix} \\ U^{D*} = \arg \max_{x_i\in S_i} \left\{ U_i^D\left(x_i,\Lambda_i\right)\right\}, & \textit{if } i \textit{ is a demander} \end{cases} \tag{41}$$

In recent decades, there had been many conceptual and empirical critiques toward the equilibrium concept. First, in the scenario of equilibrium, the players are assumed to be fully rational. This perfect rational assumption requires complete information; all factors of the game should be common knowledge. However, in reality, this assumption is actually disputable, and rarely holds. In particular, the hypothesis of exact rationality does not apply to many interactive situations. Second, the idea of equilibrium has mostly been developed in a static setting. Under the dynamic changing SC environments, it cannot capture the adaptation of players to change their strategies and reach equilibrium over time.

The DSCM scheme introduces a new solution concept for the TS game model; it is the obtained consensus with reciprocal advantage. Such a consensus in multi-player decision making process is defined as *Cooperative Consensus Equilibrium* (*CCE*). During TS game operations, game players may adjust their altruistic propensities when outcomes contradicts their beliefs, and adaptively modify their altruistic propensities in an attempt to reach a mutually acceptable decision vector. Therefore, the solution concept of *CCE* presents a dynamic learning interpretation to adapt the current SC situations.

Definition: *CCE* is a system status that can be obtained through repeating the TS game with receiving feedbacks. When all the accumulated contributiveness (Λ) of users are balanced, i.e., the relative contribution differences of users are less than a pre-defined maximum bound (Γ_Λ), this state is defined as the *CCE*. That is formally formulated as

$$\max_i \left\{ i \in \mathbb{N} \left| \left(\frac{\left(\Lambda_i \Big/ T_i^M \right)}{\left(\sum_{k \in \mathbb{N}} \Lambda_k \Big/ T_k^M \right)} \right) \right\} < \Gamma_\Lambda \tag{42}$$

where T_k^M is the maximum resource capacity of user k's device. Therefore, the main idea of *CCE* is to minimize the maximum unbalanced behavior degree of users.

The Main Steps of the DSCM Scheme

The DSCM scheme present a new TS game model for the interaction of multiple users with elastic applications. In the TS game, a sophisticated combination of the reciprocal relationship and incentive mechanism can provide much more suitable resource sharing algorithm. Based on the real-time interactive feedback process, each user can adapt its behavior and act strategically to achieve a better profit. The DSCM scheme is described by the following major steps.

Step 1: At the start, all Λ values are set to the relatively same initial values, e.g., zero, and each altruistic propensity φ is randomly chosen from $\mathbb{K}$. When reciprocal interaction history is unavailable, it is a proper initialization. Control parameters, i.e., γ, λ and Γ_Λ, are listed in Table1.

Step 2: When an individual device needs an additional resource, it becomes a demander, and asks the x amount resource to maximize the expected payoff $U^D(\cdot)$ according to equation (35).

Step 3: If the neighboring nodes of a demander have enough available resources, they can be suppliers. Suppliers provide the $\mathcal{Z}$ amount resource to maximize the expected payoff $U^S(\cdot)$ according to equation (37). When multiple demanders request the resource simultaneously, a supplier distributes the available resource using the equation (40).

Step 4: Using the simple two-sided matching algorithm, a demander selects the most adaptable supplier, and the resource is effectively shared. After the resource sharing process, Λ is adjusted dynamically.

Step 5: In each game stage game, φ of each mobile device is periodically modified according to the exponential weight learning algorithm. Based on the adjusted $P^\varphi_{k,k \in \mathbb{K}}$ in equation (39), an actual φ value of each device is selected stochastically.

Step 6: As game players, mobile devices are interrelated with elastic applications, and interact with each other in the TS game. Under widely diverse SC environments, this iterative feedback procedure continues to reach the *CCE* status.

Step 7: Mobile devices self-monitors the current SC situation in a distributed online manner; the next iteration resumes at Step 2.

Summary

The ever increasing use of social networks and arrival of new computing paradigms like cloud computing has urged the need to integrate these platforms for the better and inexpensive usage of resources. Sharing cloud resources in such environments would be very helpful. The DSCM scheme addresses a new resource control algorithm for SC systems. Using the TS game model, users iteratively observed the received payoffs and repeatedly modified their altruistic propensities to effectively manage SC resources. The DSCM scheme enables the sharing of SC resources between users via reciprocal cooperative relationships, and can effectively approach the *CCE* status using a step-by-step feedback process.

EMBEDDED GAME BASED FOG COMPUTING (EGFC) SCHEME

The *Embedded Game based Fog Computing* (EGFC) scheme is developed as a novel Fog Radio Access Networks (F-RAN) system control scheme based on the embedded game model. In the EGFC scheme, spectrum allocation, cache placement and service admission algorithms are jointly designed to maximize system efficiency. By developing a new embedded game methodology, the EGFC scheme can capture the dynamics of F-RAN system and effectively compromises the centralized optimality with decentralized distribution intelligence for the faster and less complex decision making process.

Development Motivation

In the past decade, the evolution toward 5G is featured by the explosive growth of traffic in the wireless network, due to the exponentially increased number of user devices. Compared to the 4G communication system, the 5G system should bring billions of user devices into wireless networks to demand high bandwidth connections. Therefore, system capacity and energy efficiency should be improved to get the great success of 5G communications. Cloud Radio Access Network (C-RAN) is an emerging architecture for the 5G wireless system. A key advantage of C-RAN is the possibility to perform cooperative transmissions across multiple edge nodes for the centralized cloud processing. However, the cloud processing comes at the cost of the potentially large delay entailed by fronthaul transmissions. It may become a major performance bottleneck of a C-RAN system per critical indicators such as spectral efficiency and latency (Hung, 2015; Park, 2016; Tandon, 2016).

As an extension of C-RAN paradigm, fog computing is a promising solution to the mission critical tasks involving quick decision making and fast response. It is a distributed paradigm that provides cloud-like services to the network edge nodes. Instead of using the remoted cloud center, the fog computing technique leverages computing resources at the edge of networks based on the decentralized transmission strategies. Therefore, it can help overcome the resource contention and increasing latency. Due to the effective coordination of geographically distributed edge nodes, the fog computing approach can meet the 5G application constraints, i.e., location awareness, low latency, and supports for mobility or geographical distribution of services. The most frequently referred use cases for the fog computing concept are related to the IoT (Borylo, 2016; Dastjerdi, 2016).

Taking full advantage of fog computing and C-RANs, Fog Radio Access Networks (F-RAN) has been proposed as an advanced socially-aware mobile networking architecture in 5G systems. F-RANs harness the benefits of, and the synergies between, fog computing and C-RAN in order to accommodate the broad range of Quality of Service (QoS) requirements of 5G mobile broadband communication (Tandon, 2016a). In the F-RAN architecture, edge nodes may be endowed with caching capabilities to serve the local data requests of popular content with low latency. At the same time, a central cloud processor allocates radio and computational resources to each individual edge nodes while ensuring as much as various applications (Tandon, 2016). To maximize the F-RAN system performance, application request scheduling, cache placement, and communication resource allocation should be jointly designed. However, it is an extremely challenging issue.

In the architecture of F-RANs, multiple interest relevant system agents exist; they are the central Cloud Server (CS), Edge Nodes (ENs) and Mobile Users (MUs). The CS provides contents to download, allocates radio and communication resources to ENs. ENs, known as Fog-computing based Access Points (F-APs), manage the allocated radio resource, and admit MUs to provide application services. MUs wish to enjoy different QoS services from the F-RAN system. Different system agents have their own benefits, but their benefits could conflict with each other, and each agent only cares about its own profit. Therefore, it is necessary to analyze the interactions among these conflicting system agents and design proper solutions. Although dozens of techniques have been proposed, a systematic study on the interactions among CS, F-APs and MUs is still lacking (Hu, 2016).

The traditional game theoretic analysis should rely on the perfect information and idealistic behavior assumptions. Therefore, there is a quite general consensus to say that the predicted game solutions are useful but would be rarely observed in real world situations. Recently, specialized sub-branches of game theory have been developed to encounter this problem. To design a practical game model for the F-RAN system management, the EGFC scheme adopts an online dynamic approach based on the interactive relationship among system agents. This approach exploits a partial information on the game, and obtains an effective solution under mild and practical assumptions. From the standpoint of algorithm designers, this approach can be dynamically implemented in the real-world F-RAN environments.

Embedded Game Model for F-RAN Systems

In the C-RAN architecture, all control functions and application storage are centralized at the CS, which requires a lot of MUs to transmit and exchange their data fast enough through the fronthaul link. To overcome this C-RAN's disadvantage with the fronthaul constraints, much attention has been paid to mobile fog computing and the edge cloud. The design of fog computing platform has been introduced to deliver large-scale latency-sensitive applications. To implement the fog computing architecture, traditional edge nodes are evolved to the Fog-computing based Access Point (F-AP) by being equipped with a certain caching, cooperative radio resource and computation power capability (Peng, 2016; Tandon, 2016a).

The main difference between the C-RAN and the F-CRAN is that centralized storage cloud and control cloud functions are distributed to individual F-APs. Usually, F-APs are used to forward and process the received data, and interface to the CS through the fronthaul links. To avoid all traffic being loaded directly to the centralized CS, some local traffic should be delivered from the caching located in F-APs. Therefore, each F-AP integrates not only the front radio spectrum, but also the locally distributed cached contents and computation capacity. This approach can save the spectral usage of constrained fronthaul while decreasing the transmission delay. In conclusion, the main characteristics of F-RAN include ubiquity, decentralized management and cooperation (Peng, 2016; Tandon, 2016a).

During the F-RAN system operations, system agents, i.e., CS, F-APs, MUs - should make decisions individually by considering the mutual-interaction relationship. Under the dynamic F-RAN environments, system agents try to maximize their own profits in a competitive or cooperative manner. The EGFC scheme develops a new game model, called embedded game, for the F-RAN system. According to the decision making method, the embedded game procedure can be divided two phases. At the first phase, the CS and F-APs play a superordinated game; the CS distribute the available spectrum resource to each F-APs by using a cooperative manner. At the second phase, F-APs and MUs play subordinated games. By employing a non-cooperative manner, an individual F-AP selectively admits its corresponding MUs to provide different application services. Taken as a whole, multiple subordinated games are nested in the superordinated game.

Formally, the EGFC scheme defines the embedded game model $\mathbb{G} = \{ \mathbb{G}^{super}, \mathbb{G}^{sub}_{i,1 \leq i \leq n} \}$ where $\mathbb{G}^{super}$ is a superordinated game to formulate interactions between CS and F-APs, and $\mathbb{G}^{sub}_i$ is a subordinated game to formulate interactions between the ith F-AP and its corresponding MUs. Firstly, the $\mathbb{G}^{super}$ can be defined as

$$\mathbb{G}^{super} = \left\{ \mathbb{N}, \mathcal{R}_{CS}, \boldsymbol{S}^{\mathcal{R}}_{CS}, U_{i,1 \leq i \leq n}, T \right\}$$

at each time period t of gameplay.

- $\mathbb{N}$ is the finite set of $\mathbb{G}^{super}$ game players

$$\mathbb{N} = \{ \text{CS}, F\text{-}AP_1, F\text{-}AP_2 ... F\text{-}AP_n \}$$

where the total $n+1$ number of $\mathbb{G}^{super}$ players; one CS and n F-APs.

- The total spectrum resources of CS is $\mathcal{R}_{CS}$, which would be distributed to n F-APs.
- $\boldsymbol{S}^{\mathcal{R}}_{cs} = \{ \delta_1, \delta_2, ... \delta_n \}$ is the sets of CS's strategies for the spectrum resource allocation. δ_i in $\boldsymbol{S}^{\mathcal{R}}_{cs}$ is the allocated spectrum amount for the $F\text{-}AP_{i,1 \leq i \leq n}$.
- The $U_{i,1 \leq i \leq n}$ is the payoff received by the $F\text{-}AP_i$. It is estimated as the obtained outcome minus the cost from the spectrum resource allocation.
- The T is a time period. The $\mathbb{G}^{super}$ is repeated $t \in T < \infty$ time periods with imperfect information.

Secondly, the $\mathbb{G}^{sub}_i$ is the ith subordinated game, and it can be defined as

$$\mathbb{G}^{sub}_i = \left\{ \mathbb{M}_i, \Re_i, \boldsymbol{S}^{\delta_i}_{F-AP_i}, \boldsymbol{S}^{\mathcal{C}^i}_{F-AP_i}, \boldsymbol{S}^{\sigma^i}_{F-AP_i}, \mathcal{U}^i_{j,1 \leq j \leq m}, T \right\}$$

at each time period t of gameplay.

- $\mathbb{M}_i$ is the finite set of $\mathbb{G}^{sub}_i$ game players

$$\mathbb{M}_i = \{F\text{-}AP_i, MU_1^i, \ldots, MU_m^i\}$$

where $MU_{j,1 \le j \le m}^i$ is the jth MU in the area covered by the $F\text{-}AP_i$.

- The set of $F\text{-}AP_i$'s resources is $\mathfrak{R}_i = \{\delta_i, \mathcal{C}_i, \sigma_i\}$ where δ_i, $\mathcal{C}_i$, σ_i are the allocated spectrum resource, the computation capacity, and the placed cache files in the $F\text{-}AP_i$, respectively.
- $\boldsymbol{S}_{F-AP_i}^{\delta_i}$, $\boldsymbol{S}_{F-AP_i}^{\mathcal{C}_i}$ and $\boldsymbol{S}_{F-AP_i}^{\sigma_i}$ are the sets of $F\text{-}AP_i$'s strategies for the spectrum allocation for MUs, the computation capacity assignment for MUs, and cache placement in the $F\text{-}AP_i$, respectively.
- The $\mathcal{U}_{j,1 \le j \le m}^i$ is the payoff received by the $F\text{-}AP_i$.
- The T is a time period. The $\mathbb{G}_i^{sub}$ is repeated $t \in T < \infty$ time periods with imperfect information.

Solution Concept for the Superordinated Game

In the superordinated game, game players are CS and F-APs, and they are rational to reach a win-win situation. In many situations, each rational agent is able to improve his objectives without preventing others from improving their objectives. Therefore, they are more prone to coordinate and willing to play cooperative games (Qiao, 2006). Usually, solution concepts are different in different games. For the CS and F-APs interactions, the *Kalai and Smorodinsky Bargaining Solution* (KSBS) is an interesting solution concept. Like as the well-known *Nash Bargaining Solution* (NBS), the KSBS also provides a fair and optimal solution in a cooperative manner. In addition, the KSBS can be used when the feasible payoff set is not convex. It is the main advantage of KSBS over the NBS. Due to this appealing property, the KSBS approach has been practically implemented to solve real-world problems (Kim, 2014).

In order to show the effectiveness of the KSBS, it is necessary to evaluate each player's credibility. The EGFC scheme obtains the KSBS based on the F-APs' trustworthiness. This information can be inferred implicitly from the F-APs' outcome records. Therefore, the EGFC scheme can enhance the effectiveness of KSBS while restricting the socially uncooperative F-APs. At time t, the $F\text{-}AP_i$'s trust assessment $\left(\mathcal{T}_i(t)\right)$ for the spectrum allocation process is denoted by

$$\mathcal{T}_i(t) = \left\{(1-\beta) \times \mathcal{T}_i(t-\Delta t)\right\} + \left\{\beta \times \left[\left(\cfrac{\left(\cfrac{U_i(\Delta t)}{\sum_{j=1}^n U_j(\Delta t)}\right)}{\left(\cfrac{\delta_i(t-\Delta t)}{\mathcal{R}_{CS}}\right)}\right)\right]\right\}$$

s.t.,

$$\beta = \frac{\left(\phi \times \mathcal{T}_i\left(t\right)\right)}{\left(1 + \left\{\phi \times \mathcal{T}_i\left(t\right)\right\}\right)} \text{ and } \phi \geq 0 \tag{43}$$

where $U_i\left(\Delta t\right)$ is the throughput of the $F\text{-}AP_i$ during the recent Δt time period, and $\delta_i\left(t - \Delta t\right)$ is the δ_i value at the time period $[t - \Delta t]$. The parameter β is used to weigh the past experience by considering a trust decay over time. In addition, the EGFC scheme introduces another parameter ϕ to specify the impact of past experience on $\mathcal{T}_i\left(t - \Delta t\right)$. Essentially, the contribution of current information increases proportionally as ϕ increases. In this case, the EGFC scheme can effectively adapt to the currently changing conditions while improving resiliency against credibility fluctuations (Bao, 2012).

Under the dynamic F-RAN environment, F-APs request individually their spectrum resource to the CS at each time period. To adaptively respond the current F-RAN system conditions, the sequential KSBS bargaining approach gets the different KSBS at each time period. It can adapt the timely dynamic F-RAN situations. At time t, the timed KSBS ($\mathfrak{F}_{KSBS}^t$) for the spectrum resource problem is mathematically defined as;

$$\mathfrak{F}_{KSBS}^t\left(\boldsymbol{S}_{cs}^{\mathcal{R}}\right) = \left\{\delta_1\left(t\right), \delta_2\left(t\right), \ldots \delta_n\left(t\right)\right\} =$$

$$\left|\frac{\sup\left\{U_1^t\left(\delta_1\left(t\right)\right)\right\} - d_1}{\omega_1^t \times \left(\mathbb{O}_1^t - d_1\right)} = \ldots = \frac{\sup\left\{U_i^t\left(\delta_i\left(t\right)\right)\right\} - d_i}{\omega_i^t \times \left(\mathbb{O}_i^t - d_i\right)} = \ldots = \frac{\sup\left\{U_n^t\left(\delta_n\left(t\right)\right)\right\} - d_n}{\omega_n^t \times \left(\mathbb{O}_n^t - d_n\right)}\right|$$

s.t.,

$$\mathbb{O}_i^t = \max\left\{U_i^t\left(\delta_i\left(t\right)\right) \mid U_i^t\left(\delta_i\left(t\right)\right) \in \mathbb{R}^n\right\}, \quad \omega_i^t = \frac{\mathcal{T}_i\left(t\right)}{\sum_{j=1}^n \mathcal{T}_j\left(t\right)}$$

and

$$\sup\left\{U_i^t\left(\delta_i\left(t\right)\right)\right\} = \sup\left\{U_i^t\left(\delta_i\left(t\right)\right) : \left\{\left(U_i^t\left(\delta_1\left(t\right)\right), \ldots, U_n^t\left(\delta_n\left(t\right)\right)\right)\right\} \subset \mathbb{R}^n\right\} \tag{44}$$

where $U_i^t\left(\delta_i\left(t\right)\right)$ is the $F\text{-}AP_i$'s payoff with the strategy δ_i during the recent time period (Δt). $\mathbb{R}^n$ is a jointly feasible utility solution set, and a disagreement point ($\boldsymbol{d}$) is an action vector $\boldsymbol{d} = (d_1, .. d_n) \in \mathbb{R}^n$ that is expected to be the result if players, i.e., F-APs, cannot reach an agreement (i.e., zero in the system). ω_i^t ($0 < \omega_i^t < 1$) is the player $F\text{-}AP_i$'s bargaining power at time t, which is the relative ability to exert influence over other players. $\mathbb{O}_i^t$ is the ideal point of player $F\text{-}AP_i$ at time t. Therefore, players choose the best outcome subject to the condition that their proportional part of the excess over the disagreement is relative to the proportion of the excess of their ideal gains. Simply, the EGFC scheme can think that the KSBS is the intersection point between the Pareto boundary and the line connecting the disagreement to the ideal gains (Kim 2016). Therefore, in the EGFC scheme,

$$\boldsymbol{S}_{cs}^{\mathcal{R}} = \mathfrak{F}_{KSBS}^{t}\left(\boldsymbol{S}_{cs}^{\mathcal{R}}\right) = \left\{\delta_1\left(t\right),\delta_2\left(t\right),\ldots\delta_n\left(t\right)\right\}$$

is a joint strategy, which is taken by the CS at time t.

In non-deterministic settings, $\mathfrak{F}_{KSBS}^{t}\left(\boldsymbol{S}_{cs}^{\mathcal{R}}\right)$ is a selection function to define a specific spectrum allocation strategy for every F-APs. Due to the main feature of KSBS, the increasing of bargaining set size in a direction favorable to a specific F-AP always benefits that F-AP. Therefore, in the superordinated game, self-interested F-AP can be satisfied during the F-RAN system operations. To practically obtain the $\mathfrak{F}_{KSBS}^{t}\left(\boldsymbol{S}_{cs}^{\mathcal{R}}\right)$ in the equation (44), the EGFC scheme can re-think the KSBS as a weighted max-min solution like as;

$$\mathfrak{F}_{KSBS}^{t}\left(\boldsymbol{S}_{cs}^{\mathcal{R}}\right)=\left\{\delta_1\left(t\right),\delta_2\left(t\right),\ldots\delta_n\left(t\right)\right\} = \arg\max_{\left\{\delta_1(t),\delta_2(t),\ldots\delta_n(t)\right\}}\left\{\min_{\delta_{i,1\le i\le n}(t)}\left(\frac{\sup\left\{U_i^t\left(\delta_i\left(t\right)\right)\right\}-d_i}{\omega_i^t\times\left(\mathbb{O}_i^t-d_i\right)}\right)\right\} \tag{45}$$

Solution Concept for the Subordinated Games

Edge processing is the key emerging trends in the F-RAN system. It refers to the localization of computing, communication, and storage resources at the F-APs. In the F-RAN architecture, F-APs are connected to the CS through fronthaul links. Under this centralized structure, the performance of F-RANs is clearly constrained by the fronthaul link capacity; it incurs a high burden on fronthaul links. Therefore, a prerequisite requirement for the centralized CS processing is the high bandwidth and low latency fronthaul interconnections. However, during the operation of F-RAN system, unexpected growth of service requests may create a traffic congestion. It has a significant impact on the F-RAN performance. To overcome the disadvantages of F-RAN architecture imposed by the fronthaul constraints, new techniques have been introduced with the aim of reducing the delivery latency by limiting the need to communicate between the CS and MUs (Tandon, 2016b).

Currently, there are evidences that MUs' downloading of on-demand multimedia data is the major reason for the data avalanche over F-RAN; numerous repetitive requests on the same data lead to redundant transmissions. Usually, multimedia data are located in the CS and far away from MUs. To ensure an excellent QoS provisioning, an efficient solution is to locally store these frequently-access data into the cache memory of F-APs while reducing the transmission latency; it is known as caching. This approach can effectively mitigate the unnecessary fronthaul overhead caused by MUs' repetitive service requests. Therefore, CS, F-APs and MUs are all the beneficiaries from the local caching mechanism (Li, 2016).

In the subordinated game, an efficient caching mechanism is designed by carefully considering the relations and interactions among CS, F-APs and MUs. Therefore, it not only can the heavy traffic load be relieved at fronthaul links, but also the request latency can be decreased, which results in better QoS (Tandon, 2016b). A practical caching mechanism is coupled with the data placement. In the F-RAN architecture, the EGFC scheme assumes that a multimedia file set $\mathbb{M} = \{ \mathcal{M}_1, ..., \mathcal{M}_L \}$ consists of L popular multimedia files in the CS, and files in $\mathbb{M}$ can be possibly cached in each F-AP. The popularity distribution among $\mathbb{M}$ is represented by a vector $\mathcal{Q} = [g_1, ..., g_L]$. Generally, the vector $\mathcal{Q}$ can be modeled by a Zipf distribution (Li, 2016);

$$g_l = \left(\frac{1}{l^\tau} \right) \Bigg/ \left(\sum\nolimits_{f=1}^{L} \frac{1}{f^\tau} \right), \text{ s.t., } 1 \leq l \leq L \text{ and } \tau > 0 \tag{46}$$

where τ factor characterizes the file popularity. In the EGFC scheme, MUs in each F-AP area are assumed to request independently the lth file $\mathcal{M}_{l, 1 \leq l \leq L}$. Therefore, the τ value is different for each F-AP. According to (46), $\mathcal{M}_1$ (*or* $\mathcal{M}_L$) has the highest (*or* lowest) popularity. The CS intends to rent a frequency-accessing fraction of $\mathbb{M}$ for caching to maximize the F-RAN system performance. The EGFC scheme denotes the caching placement strategy as a two-dimensional matrix $\mathbb{I} = \left[0,1 \right]^{n \times L}$ consisting of binary entries where 1 is indicating the caching placement in a F-AP, and 0 is not. $\mathbb{I}$ is defined as

$$\mathbb{I} \triangleq \begin{bmatrix} I_1^1 & \cdots & I_1^L \\ \vdots & \ddots & \vdots \\ I_n^1 & \cdots & I_n^L \end{bmatrix} \in \left[0,1 \right]^{n \times L} \tag{47}$$

where $I_i^l = 1$ means that the file $\mathcal{M}_l$ is cached at the $F\text{-}AP_i$ and $I_i^l = 0$ means the opposite. For the $F\text{-}AP_i$, the profit ($\mathfrak{R}_i^c$) gained from the local caching mechanism can be defined as follows;

$$\mathfrak{R}_i^c = \sum_{l=1}^{L} \left(g_l^i \times \mathcal{L}^i \times \mathcal{Z}_l^i \times I_i^l \right) - \sum_{l=1}^{L} \left(\mathfrak{C}_l^i \times I_i^l \right), s.t., g_l^i \in \mathcal{Q}^i \tag{48}$$

where $\mathcal{Q}^i$ is the vector $\mathcal{Q}$ of $F\text{-}AP_i$ and $\mathcal{L}^i$ is the total number of service requests on average. $\mathcal{Z}_i^l$ and $\mathfrak{C}_i^l$ is the revenue and cost from the caching in the $F\text{-}AP_i$, respectively. From the viewpoint of $F\text{-}AP_i$, the fraction $[I_i^1 ... I_i^L]$ of $\mathbb{I}$ ($\mathcal{Q}^i$) needs to be optimized for maximizing the $\mathfrak{R}_i^c$.

Based on the current caching placement, Service Admission Control (SAC) algorithm should be developed to make admission decisions to maximize their spectrum efficiency while maintaining a desirable overhead level. Especially, when the requested services are heavy, that is, the sum of the requested resource amount exceeds the currently available system capacity, the SAC comes into act whether to accept a new service request or not. Based on the acceptance condition, such as the current caching status and resource capacity, the SAC problem can be formulated as a joint optimization problem. In this problem, the EGFC scheme takes into account the maximization of spectrum efficiency while minimizing the fronthaul overhead.

The EGFC scheme set out to obtain fundamental insights into the SAC problem by means of a game theoretic approach. Therefore, the subordinated game is designed to formulate the interactions of the F-AP and MUs while investigating the system dynamics with imperfect information. To implement the subordinated game, the EGFC scheme adopts the concept of dictator game, which is a game in experimental economics, similar to the ultimatum game, first developed by D. Kahneman et al (Daniel, 1986). In the dictator game, one player, called *the proposer*, distributes his resource, and the other players, called *the responders*, simply accept the decision, which is made by *the proposer*. As one of decision theory, the dictator game is treated as an exceptional non-cooperative game or multi-agent system game that has a partner-feature and involves a trade-off between self- and other-utility. Based on its simplicity, the dictator game can capture an essential characteristic of the repeated interaction situation (Kim, 2014).

In the subordinated game model, each F-AP is *the proposer* and MUs are *the responders*. They interact with each other and repeatedly work together toward an appropriate F-RAN performance. To effectively make SAC decisions, *the proposer* considers the current system conditions such as the available spectrum amount, the current caching placement and fronthaul overhead status. By a sophisticated combination of these conflicting condition factors, *the proposer* attempts to approximate a temporary optimal SAC decision. The SAC decision procedure is shown in Figure 2.

According to the SAC procedure, each $F\text{-}AP_i$ can maintain the finest SAC solution while avoiding the heavy computational complexity or overheads. For the subordinated game, the EGFC scheme proposes a new solution concept, *Temporal Equilibrium* (*TE*). In the EGFC scheme, all MUs follow compulsorily the decision of *F-APs*, and the outcome profile of SAC process constitutes the *TE*, which is the current service status.

$$TE = \overrightarrow{\mathcal{T}\varepsilon}_i \mid \left(\mu_i \cup \psi_i\right) \rightarrow \left(\Theta^i_{j,1 \leq j \leq m} \in \left(\mu_i \cup \psi_i\right)\right) \underline{\underline{def}} \; \overrightarrow{\mathcal{T}\varepsilon}_i = \begin{cases} \Theta^i_j \in \mu_i, & if \; \Theta^i_j \; is \; accepted \\ \Theta^i_j \in \psi_i, & otherwise \end{cases} \tag{49}$$

The Main Steps of the EGFC Scheme

In the EGFC scheme, the superordinated game for spectrum allocation and the subordinated game for SAC decisions are interlocked and serially correlated. The subordinated game depends on the outcome of superordinated game, and the result of subordinated games is the input back to the superordinated game process. Structurally, the multiple subordinated games are nested in the superordinated game, and they are linked based on the step-by-step interactive feedback process. The main steps of the EGFC scheme are given next.

Step 1: At the initial time, the spectrum resource allocation $S^{\mathcal{R}}_{cs} = \{\delta_1, \delta_2, \ldots \delta_n\}$ and trustworthiness ($\mathcal{T}$) for F-APs are equally distributed. This starting guess guarantees that each F-AP enjoys the same benefit at the beginning of the game.

Step 2: Control parameters $\mathcal{C}$, n, m, σ, β, $\mathcal{R}_{CS}$, Δt, ϕ, $\mathcal{Z}$, $\mathfrak{C}$, τ, L, $\mathfrak{M}$ and ϵ are given from the simulation scenario (refer to the Table I).

Step 3: At each superordinated game period, $S^{\mathcal{R}}_{cs} = \{\delta_1, \delta_2, \ldots \delta_n\}$ is dynamically adjusted according to (43)-(45); it is the timed KSBS while taking into account the current F-RAN situations.

Figure 2. Service admission control procedure

Define:

Θ_j^i : a new service request of MU_j^i,

Min_S(Θ_j^i**)**, **Min_C(**Θ_j^i**)** : the minimum spectrum and computation requirement of Θ_j^i

χ^i, y^i : the currently using spectrum and computation amount in the F-AP_i

X^i, M^i : the current and maximum fronthaul transmission rate

When the Θ_j^i is requested in the F-AP_i,

 If Θ_j^i request is cached in the F-AP_i, // *no computation offloading task*

  { *If* $\left(\chi^i + \textbf{\textit{Min\_S}}\left(\Theta_j^i \right) \le \boldsymbol{S}_{F-AP_i}^{P^i} \right)$, it is accepted

   Otherwise, it is rejected }

 Else {

 If Θ_j^i is computation offloading task,

  { *If* $\left(\left(\chi^i + \textbf{\textit{Min\_S}}\left(\Theta_j^i \right) \le \boldsymbol{S}_{F-AP_i}^{P^i} \right) \text{and} \left(y^i + \textbf{\textit{Min\_C}}\left(\Theta_j^i \right) \le \boldsymbol{S}_{F-AP_i}^{X^i} \right) \right)$,

   it is accepted

  Else if $\left(\left(\chi_j^i + \textbf{\textit{Min\_S}}\left(\Theta_j^i \right) \le \boldsymbol{S}_{F-AP_i}^{P^i} \right) \text{ and } \left(X^i + \textbf{\textit{Min\_S}}\left(\Theta_j^i \right) \le \grave{o} \times M^i \right) \right)$

   it is accepted,

  Otherwise, it is rejected }

  Else if $\left(\left(\chi_j^i + \textbf{\textit{Min\_S}}\left(\Theta_j^i \right) \le \boldsymbol{S}_{F-AP_i}^{P^i} \right) \text{ and } \left(X^i + \textbf{\textit{Min\_S}}\left(\Theta_j^i \right) \le \grave{o} \times M^i \right) \right)$

   it is accepted,

  Otherwise, it is rejected

 }

Step 4: The trustworthiness ($\mathcal{T}$) for each F-AP is modified periodically by using (43).

Step 5: In a distributed manner, the caching placement in each F-AP occurs while maximizing the $\mathfrak{R}^c$ according to the equation (48).

Step 6: Based on the assigned δ value, each F-AP performs a subordinated game. By considering the current system conditions such as χ, y, $\mathfrak{R}^c$ and $\mathfrak{X}$, the SAC procedure is executed in a real-time online manner.

Step 7: The superordinated and subordinated games are interlocked and serially correlated. Based on the interactive feedback mechanism, the dynamics of embedded game can cause cascade interactions of game players and players can make their decisions to quickly find the most profitable solution.

Step 8: Under widely diverse F-RAN environments, the CS and F-APs are self-monitoring constantly for the next embedded game process; proceed to Step 3.

Summary

As a promising paradigm for the 5G communication system, the F-RAN has been proposed as an advanced socially-aware wireless networking architecture to provide the higher spectral efficiency while maximizing the system performance. In the EGFC scheme, the SAC algorithm is nested in the spectrum allocation algorithm to effectively control the conflict problem of F-RAN system agents. Based on the interactive feedback mechanism, the EGFC scheme has the potential to handle multiple targets without using more complex multi-target tracking algorithm.

REFERENCES

Addis, B., Ardagna, D., Panicucci, B., Squillante, M. S., & Zhang, L. (2013). A Hierarchical Approach for the Resource Management of Very Large Cloud Platforms. *IEEE Transactions on Dependable and Secure Computing*, *2*(1), 253–272. doi:10.1109/TDSC.2013.4

Arrow, K. A., Harris, T. E., & Marschak, J. (1951). Optimal inventory policy. *Econometrica*, *19*(3), 250–272. doi:10.2307/1906813

Bao, F., & Chen, I. (2012). Trust management for the internet of things and its application to service composition. *IEEE WoWMoM*, *2012*, 1–6.

Borylo, P., Lason, A., Rzasa, J., Szymanski, A., & Jajszczyk, A. (2016). Energy-aware fog and cloud interplay supported by wide area software defined networking. *IEEE ICC*, *2016*, 1–7.

Botta, A., Donato, W., Persico, V., & Pescape, A. (2014). On the Integration of Cloud Computing and Internet of Things. *IEEE FiCloud*, *2014*, 23–30.

Caton, S., Haas, C., Chard, K., Bubendorfer, K., & Rana, O. F. (2014). A Social Compute Cloud: Allocating and sharing infrastructure resources via social networks. *IEEE Transactions on Services Computing*, *7*(3), 359–372. doi:10.1109/TSC.2014.2303091

Chard, K., Bubendorfer, K., Caton, S., & Rana, O. F. (2012). Social cloud computing: A vision for socially motivated resource sharing. Services Computing. *IEEE Transactions on Service Computing,* *5*(4), 551-563.

Chard, K., Caton, S., Rana, O. F., & Bubendorfer, K. (2010). Social cloud: Cloud computing in social networks. In *Cloud Computing* (pp. 99–106). IEEE. doi:10.1109/CLOUD.2010.28

Checko, A., Christiansen, H. L., Ying, Y., Scolari, L., Kardaras, G., Berger, M. S., & Dittmann, L. (2015). Cloud RAN for Mobile Networks - A Technology Overview. *IEEE Communications Surveys and Tutorials*, *17*(1), 405–426. doi:10.1109/COMST.2014.2355255

Chen, X. (2015). Decentralized Computation Offloading Game for Mobile Cloud Computing. *IEEE Transactions on Parallel and Distributed Systems*, *26*(4), 974–983. doi:10.1109/TPDS.2014.2316834

Daniel, K., Jack, L. K., & Richard, H. T. (1986). Fairness and the assumptions of economics. *The Journal of Business*, *59*(4), 285–300.

Dastjerdi, A. V., & Buyya, R. (2016). Fog Computing: Helping the Internet of Things Realize Its Potential. *Computer*, *49*(8), 112–116. doi:10.1109/MC.2016.245

Feng, N., Mau, S. C., & Mandayam, N. B. (2004). Pricing and power control for joint network-centric and user-centric radio resource management. *IEEE Transactions on Communications*, *52*(9), 1547–1557. doi:10.1109/TCOMM.2004.833191

Gajane, P., Urvoy, T., & Clérot, F. (2015). A Relative Exponential Weighing Algorithm for Adversarial Utility-based Dueling Bandits. *Proceedings of the 32nd International Conference on Machine Learning*, (pp. 218-227).

Hemmati, M., Sadati, N., & Nili, M. (2010). Towards a bounded-rationality model of multi-agent social learning in games. *IEEE ISDA*, *2010*, 142–148.

Htikie, Z., Hong, C. S., & Lee, S. W. (2013). The Life Cycle of the Rendezvous Problem of Cognitive Radio Ad Hoc Networks: A Survey. *Journal for Corrosion Science and Engineering*, *7*(2), 81–88.

Hu, Z., Zheng, Z., Wang, T., Song, L., & Li, X. (2016). Game theoretic approaches for wireless proactive caching. *IEEE Communications Magazine*, *54*(8), 37–43. doi:10.1109/MCOM.2016.7537175

Hung, S. C., Hsu, H., Lien, S. Y., & Chen, K. C. (2015). Architecture Harmonization Between Cloud Radio Access Networks and Fog Networks. *IEEE Access*, *3*, 3019–3034. doi:10.1109/ACCESS.2015.2509638

Jang, I., Pyeon, D., Kim, S., & Yoon, H. (2013). A Survey on Communication Protocols for Wireless Sensor Networks. *Journal for Corrosion Science and Engineering*, *7*(4), 231–241.

Jesse, N., Heo, U., & DeRouen, K. Jr. (2002). A Nested Game Approach to Political and Economic Liberalization in Democratizing States: The Case of South Korea. *International Studies Quarterly*, *46*(3), 401–422. doi:10.1111/1468-2478.00239

Jiang, C., Chen, Y., Gao, Y., & Liu, K. J. R. (2013). Indian Buffet Game with non-Bayesian social learning. *IEEE GlobalSIP*, *2013*, 309–312.

Jiang, C., Chen, Y., Gao, Y., & Liu, K. J. R. (2015). Indian Buffet Game With Negative Network Externality and Non-Bayesian Social Learning. *IEEE Transactions on Systems, Man, and Cybernetics. Systems*, *45*(4), 609–623.

Kamijo, Y. (2009). A two-step Shapley value in a cooperative game with a coalition structure. *International Game Theory Review*, *11*(02), 207–214. doi:10.1142/S0219198909002261

Kim, K., Uno, S., & Kim, M. (2010). Adaptive QoS Mechanism for Wireless Mobile Network. *Journal for Corrosion Science and Engineering*, *4*(2), 153–172.

Kim, S. (2010). Dynamic Online Bandwidth Adjustment Scheme Based on Kalai-Smorodinsky Bargaining Solution. *IEICE Transactions on Communications*, *E93-B*(7), 1935–1938. doi:10.1587/transcom.E93.B.1935

Kim, S. (2011). Stackelberg Game-Based Power Control Scheme for Efficiency and Fairness Tradeoff. *IEICE Transactions on Communications, E94-B*(8), 2427–2430. doi:10.1587/transcom.E94.B.2427

Kim, S. (2014). *Game Theory Applications in Network Design*. Hershey, PA: IGI Global. doi:10.4018/978-1-4666-6050-2

Kim, S. (2014). Intervenient Stackelberg Game based Bandwidth Allocation Scheme for Hierarchical Wireless Networks. *Transactions on Internet and Information Systems (Seoul), 8*(12), 4293–4304.

Kim, S. (2015). Learning based Spectrum Sharing Algorithms by using Coopetition Game Approach. *Wireless Personal Communications, 82*(3), 1799–1808. doi:10.1007/s11277-015-2314-5

Kim, S. (2016). News-vendor game-based resource allocation scheme for next-generation C-RAN systems. *EURASIP Journal on Wireless Communications and Networking*, (1), 1–11.

Lee, W., Xiang, L., Schober, R., & Wong, V. W. S. (2014). Direct Electricity Trading in Smart Grid: A Coalitional Game Analysis. *IEEE Journal on Selected Areas in Communications, 32*(7), 1398–1411. doi:10.1109/JSAC.2014.2332112

Li, J., Sun, J., Qian, Y., Shu, F., Xiao, M. & Xiang, W. (2016). A Commercial Video-Caching System for Small-Cell Cellular Networks using Game Theory. *IEEE Access*. (forthcoming)

Liu, Y., Sun, Y., Ryoo, J. W., Rizvi, S., & Vasilakos, A. V. (2015). A Survey of Security and Privacy Challenges in Cloud Computing: Solutions and Future Directions. *Journal for Corrosion Science and Engineering, 9*(3), 119–133.

Malakooti, B. (2014). *Operations and Production Systems with Multiple Objectives*. New York, NY: John Wiley & Sons.

Pan, M., & Fang, Y. (2008). Bargaining based pairwise cooperative spectrum sensing for Cognitive Radio networks. *IEEE MILCOM, 2008*, 1–7.

Pang, Y., Xie, S., & Jiang, S. (2011). The application of nested-game theory in the public participation mechanism in the decision-making of large engineering projects. *Systems Engineering Procedia, 1*, 142–146. doi:10.1016/j.sepro.2011.08.024

Park, H., & van der Schaar, M. (2007). Bargaining Strategies for Networked Multimedia Resource Management. *IEEE Transactions on Signal Processing, 55*(7), 3496–3511. doi:10.1109/TSP.2007.893755

Park, S., Simeone, O., & Shamai, S. (2016). Joint optimization of cloud and edge processing for fog radio access networks. *IEEE ISIT, 2016*, 315–319.

Park, Y., & Kim, S. (2015). Bargaining based Smart Grid Pricing Model Demand Side Scheduling Management. *ETRI Journal, 37*(1), 197–202. doi:10.4218/etrij.15.0114.0007

Peng, M., Yan, S., Zhang, K., & Wang, C. (2016). Fog-computing-based radio access networks: Issues and challenges. *IEEE Network, 30*(4), 46–53. doi:10.1109/MNET.2016.7513863

Qian, M., Hardjawana, W., Shi, J., & Vucetic, B. (2015). Baseband Processing Units Virtualization for Cloud Radio Access Networks. *IEEE Wireless Communications Letters, 4*(2), 189–192. doi:10.1109/LWC.2015.2393355

Qiao, H., Rozenblit, J., Szidarovszky, F., & Yang, L. (2006). Multi-Agent Learning Model with Bargaining. *Proceedings of the 2006 Winter Simulation Conference*, (pp. 934-940). doi:10.1109/WSC.2006.323178

Sabyasachi, A.S., De, S. & De, S. (2013). On the Notion of Decoupling in Mobile Cloud Computing. *IEEE HPCC_EUC'2013*, (pp. 450-457).

Sigwele, T., Pillai, P., & Hu, Y. F. (2014). Call Admission Control in Cloud Radio Access Networks. *IEEE FiCloud, 2014*, 31–36.

Singh, D., Tripathi, G., & Jara, A. J. (2014). A survey of Internet-of-Things: Future Vision, Architecture, Challenges and Services. *IEEE World Forum on Internet of Things (WF-IoT' 2014)* (pp. 287-292).

Sinha, K., & Kulkarni, M. (2011). Techniques for fine-grained, multi-site computation offloading. *IEEE CCGRID, 2011*, 184–194.

Suris, J. E., DaSilva, L. A., Han, Z., & MacKenzie, A. B. (2007). *Cooperative Game Theory for Distributed Spectrum Sharing. IEEE, ICC*, 5282–5287.

Tandon, R., & Simeone, O. (2016a). Harnessing cloud and edge synergies: Toward an information theory of fog radio access networks. *IEEE Communications Magazine, 54*(8), 44–50. doi:10.1109/MCOM.2016.7537176

Tandon, R., & Simeone, O. (2016b). Cloud-aided wireless networks with edge caching: Fundamental latency trade-offs in fog Radio Access Networks. *IEEE ISIT, 2016*, 2029–2033.

Tsebelis, G. (1988). Nested Games: The Cohesion of French Electoral Coalitions. *British Journal of Political Science, 18*(2), 145–170. doi:10.1017/S0007123400005044

Vakilinia, S., Qiu, D., & Ali, M. M. (2014). Optimal multi-dimensional dynamic resource allocation in mobile cloud computing. *EURASIP Journal on Wireless Communications and Networking*, 1–14.

Vermesan, O., & Friess, P. (2011). *Internet of Things - Global Technological and Societal Trends*. River Publishers.

Wang, X., & Schulzrinne, H. (2005). Incentive-Compatible Adaptation of Internet Real-Time Multimedia. *IEEE Journal on Selected Areas in Communications, 23*(2), 417–436. doi:10.1109/JSAC.2004.839399

Wang, Y., Lin, X., & Pedram, M. (2013). A Nested Two Stage Game-Based Optimization Framework in Mobile Cloud Computing System. *IEEE SOSE, 2013*, 494–502.

Wen, J. (2009). No-centralize Newsvendor Model with Re-distributed Decision-making Power. *IEEE IITA, 2009*, 237–240.

William, J. S. (2009). *Operations Management* (10th ed.). New York, NY: McGraw-Hill.

Xie, B., Zhou, W., Hao, C., Ai, X., & Song, J. (2010). A Novel Bargaining Based Relay Selection and Power Allocation Scheme for Distributed Cooperative Communication Networks. *IEEE Vehicular Technology Conference (VTC 2010)*, (pp. 1-5). doi:10.1109/VETECF.2010.5594320

Yang, H. (1997a). Sensitivity analysis for the elastic-demand network equilibrium problem with applications. *Transportation Research*, *31*(1), 55–70. doi:10.1016/S0191-2615(96)00015-X

Yang, H., & Bell, M. G. H. (1997b). Traffic restraint, road pricing and network equilibrium. *Transportation Research Part B: Methodological*, *31*(4), 303–314. doi:10.1016/S0191-2615(96)00030-6

Zehavi, E., & Leshem, A. (2009). Alternative Bargaining Solutions for the Interference Channel. *IEEE CAMSAP*, *2009*, 9–12.

Zhang, S. (2014). Influence of relationship strengths to network structures in social network. *IEEE ISCIT*, *2014*, 279–283.

Zhao, Y., & Zhao, H. (2002). Study on negotiation strategy. *International Conference On Power System Technology 2002*, 1335-1338.

Zhu, W. Z., & Lee, C. H. (2014). A New Approach to Web Data Mining Based on Cloud Computing. *Journal for Corrosion Science and Engineering*, *8*(4), 181–186.

KEY TERMS AND DEFINITIONS

Baseband Processing: Baseband processor is used to process the down-converted digital signal to retrieve essential data for the wireless digital system.

Cloud Radio Access Network (C-RAN): C-RAN is a centralized, cloud computing-based architecture for radio access networks that supports 2G, 3G, 4G and future wireless communication standards.

Computation Offloading: The transfer of certain computing tasks to an external platform, such as a cluster, grid, or a cloud.

Kalai-Smorodinsky Bargaining Solution: A solution to the Bargaining problem. It was suggested as an alternative to Nash's bargaining solution. The main difference between the two solutions is that the Nash solution satisfies independence of irrelevant alternatives while the KS solution satisfies monotonicity.

Mobile Cloud IoT: A kind of platform which supports diverse and geographically dispersed devices to work together. Cloud Computing plays a significant role in combining services offered by heterogeneous devices and scaling up to handle large number of users in a reliable manner.

Nash Bargaining Solution: A Pareto efficient solution to a Nash bargaining game. According to Walker, Nash's bargaining solution was shown by John Harsanyi to be the same as Zeuthen's solution of the bargaining problem.

Rubinstein-Stahl Model: Provide a possible solution to the problem that two players are bargaining with the division of the benefit.

Shapley Value: A solution concept in cooperative game theory. To each cooperative game it assigns a unique distribution among the players of a total surplus generated by the coalition of all players. The Shapley value is characterized by a collection of desirable properties.

Social Cloud: A scalable computing model wherein virtualized resources contributed by users are dynamically provisioned amongst a group of friends.

Tragedy of the Commons: An economic theory of a situation within a shared-resource system where individual users acting independently according to their own self-interest behave contrary to the common good of all users by depleting that resource through their collective action.

This research was previously published in Game Theory Solutions for the Internet of Things edited by Sungwook Kim, pages 13-77, copyright year 2017 by Information Science Reference (an imprint of IGI Global).

Chapter 5
Extending IoTs Into the Cloud–Based Platform for Examining Amazon Web Services

Jagdeep Kaur
The NorthCap University, India

Meghna Sharma
The NorthCap University, India

ABSTRACT

The public cloud Amazon Web Service (AWS) provides a wide range of services like computation, networking, analytics, development and management tools, application services, mobile services, and management of Internet-of-Things (IoT) devices. The Amazon Web Services (AWS) IoT is an excellent IoT cloud platform and is exclusively responsible for connecting devices into various fields like healthcare, biology, municipal setup, smart homes, marketing, industrial, agriculture, education, automotive, etc. This chapter highlights many other initiatives promoted by AWS IoT. The main motive of this chapter is to present how AWS IoT works. The chapter starts with the design principles of AWS IoT services. Further, the authors present a detailed description of the AWS IoT components (e.g., Device SDK, Message Broker, Rule Engine, Security and Identity Service, Thing Registry, Thing Shadow, and Thing Shadow Service). The chapter concludes with a description of various challenges faced by AWS IoT and future research directions.

INTRODUCTION

Internet-of-things (IoT) consists of internetworking of physical devices, objects embedded with sensors, actuators, software, electronics, network connectivity that allow these objects to collect and exchange data. This term was first used by (Ashton, 2011) to connect RFID and supply-chain through internet. Over the past few years due to various factors like cheap sensors, cheap bandwidth, cheap processing, smartphones, ubiquitous wireless computing, big data etc. IoT has emerged as the most promising technology to connect the different devices. It is helping to achieve the goal of smart homes and smart cities. Few examples of IoT based applications are:

DOI: 10.4018/978-1-5225-5649-7.ch005

- **Hydroponic System:** It is used for automated watering the plants and taking care of all the needs of plants for optimal growth.
- **Smart Waste Management System:** It takes care of full garbage bins and unattended garbage. It sets up the right route and timely schedule.
- **Smart Sprinkler Control:** With the help of smartphone the sprinkler can be controlled from anywhere.
- **Blood Pressure Monitor:** With a wearable cuff and health mate app one can hassle free monitor his/her blood pressure.
- **Fitness Tracker Devices:** Many wearable devices like FitBit, Jawbone allows to monitor physical activities, sleep pattern etc.
- **Smart Homes:** With the help of devices like Nest Thermostat to regulate temperature according to surroundings and Amazon echo to control light, music and other house hold appliances with the voice control.

This tremendous increase in the IoT devices is draining the computing resources required to maintain the connectivity and data collection required by these devices. The data generated by these devices is putting strain on internet infrastructure. The industry is working in different ways to solve this data problem. The cloud computing provides a right solution to this problem. The IoT and Cloud computing are two complementary technologies. The large amount of data generated by IoT can be easily managed by Cloud computing.

Since 2005, when the cloud computing has emerged it has changed our life style and work style (Armbrust, 2010). Cloud computing is supported by various processing engines like Apache spark(Zaharia, 2010), Apache Hadoop (Shvachko, 2010), Google File System (Ghemawat, 2003)etc.The cloud computing can be categorized into different types like public cloud, private cloud, hybrid cloud, Software as Service (SasS), Infrastructure as Service (IasS) and Platform as Service (PasS). The public cloud are owned by companies and they provide access to users over public network. The private cloud is like the public cloud except that there is a single access by user/organization/company etc. The hybrid cloud is a mix of two. In SaaS, the user/organizations run the applications in the cloud which connect to the other users through web browsers. Whereas, PaaS is used to build and deliver cloud based application. It eliminates the need to buy and maintain hardware, software, hosting etc. The cloud IoT is a type of PaaS which helps to interconnect the devices. Some of the popular cloud IoT are Amazon Web Services AWS Cloud, GE Predix, Google Cloud IoT, Microsoft Azure IoT Suite, IBM Watson, and Salesforce IoT Cloud. Each of the cloud offers a different range of services.

The main purpose of this chapter is to present an insight into how AWS IoT works. In order to achieve this following objectives are formulated:

- The state-of-art of Cloud IoT.
- To study the design principles of AWS.
- How the various AWS IoT components AWS IoT Components viz. Device Gateway, Message Broker, Rule Engine, Security and Identity Service, Thing Registry, Thing Shadow and Thing Shadow Service interact?
- The challenges faced by AWS IoT.

These objectives are explained in the subsequent sections.

STATE-OF-ART OF CLOUD IOT

With the emergence of cloud computing and Internet-of-Things making contributions for creating the smart world many researchers have made studies in these areas (Mohammad, 2009). According to (Josyula, 2016) an interoperable platform for IoT devices and cloud services is proposed. It has been demonstrated that without using a separate application server how an android application can be used to save efforts and cost. Another work by (Weisong, 2016) introduced the concept of edge computing and addressed the various issues like response time requirement, battery life constraint, bandwidth cost saving etc. at the edge of the network. Suciu et al. (George, 2013) proposed a generic platform for IoT and cloud computing interoperability study. They worked on the interoperability of RFID, NFC, M2M, sensor, actuators, context aware services etc.

AWS IOT

The AWS IoT can be further studied in terms of the design principles its components.

Design Principles

AWS platform is popular among the consumer, commercial and industrial ends. The design principles are responsible for the success of IoT platform. The core principles are: Standard protocols, security, scalability, Quality of Service, usability and cost reduction. These are explained as follows:

1. **Standard Protocols:** There is a flexibility to integrate variety of devices and machines to internet using standard protocols. Even the different data sources and enterprise systems are connected through standard protocol. The protocols work effectively for all the operating systems. Moreover, the customer can easily make transition to some other competitor technology if he/she is not satisfied.
2. **Security:** As the devices are generating large amount of data and the users can directly control a device hence security is prime concern. AWS IoT provides a secure duplex translation between device protocols.
3. **Scalability:** IoT applications require the ability to scale across different location in order to maintain data consistency and lower latency for better response from devices.'
4. **Quality of Service:** High performance of the IoT applications is expected due to guaranteed message delivery. Before the cloud technology came into picture, the organizations used to hire extra hardware to handle immense amount of data generated by the devices. But now it can be easily handled with cloud and IoT devices.
5. **Usability:** For the developers using modern technology it should be easy to develop the cloud based IoT solutions.
6. **Cost Reduction:** The AWS platform offers consumption based pricing model. Hence the total cost can be directly estimated from the infrastructure required and efforts required to process, store and analyze the sensor data received from IoT solutions.

AWS IOT COMPONENTS

AWS IoT delivers a duplex and highly secure communication between the IoT applications and its associated devices and the AWS cloud. It helps to collect, store and analyze data from these devices. Moreover, mobile applications are also made to control these devices through mobiles or tablets. The main components are: Device Gateway, Message Broker, Rule Engine, Security and Identity Service, Thing Registry, Thing Shadow and Thing Shadow Service. These are described briefly here:

1. **Device SDK:** It facilitates secure and efficient communication of devices with the cloud IoT.
2. **Message Broker:** It delivers a way for publishing and receiving messages between devices and IoT applications. It uses Message Queue Telemetry Transport (MQTT) protocol. With MQTT over Web socket every browser becomes MQTT device. It also make use of HTTP REST to publish, subscribe and receive messages
3. **Rule Engine:** It associates AWS IoT to peripheral devices and and other AWS services like AWS Lambda, Amazon S3 and Amazon DynamoDB.
4. **Security and Identity Service:** It is responsible for keeping the credentials safe for secure communication between the devices and message broker & rule engine.
5. **Thing Registry:** The devices are allocated resources like certificates, MQTT client ids etc. for easy management and troubleshooting of the devices.
6. **Thing Shadow:** The existing state information of a device or app is stored in the form of a JSON (Java Script Object Notation) document. It gives consistent information of the devices connected to the AWS cloud.

WORKING OF AWS IOT

The AWS IoT connects the devices to the cloud and the applications in the cloud interact with the devices. Most of the IoT applications allow users to control the devices remotely through the mobile apps or collect and analyze the sensor data produced by it (Guide, 2017). The connected devices report their states by publishing messages in MQTT topics. When a message is published it is sent to the MQTT message broker that forwards messages to all the clients subscribed for that topic. The Thing registry maintains the entries of all the connected devices of AWS IoT, describing the certificates used by the devices for secure communication. The rules can be formulated based on the data in the message received. The thing registry also maintain information consisting of last reported state and the desired state requested by an application. The thing shadow respond to the application by providing the JSON document and then it can control the thing by requesting the change in state. The messages can be delivered to various AWS services such as Lambda, DynamoDB, Firehose, Kinesis, S3, Simple Queue Service (SQS), and Simple Notification Service (SNS) without any extra fees.

The working of AWS IoT components can be understood better by viewing the interaction between the components as schematically presented as in Figure 1.

Each of the components is explained in detail in this section.

Figure 1. AWS IoT components

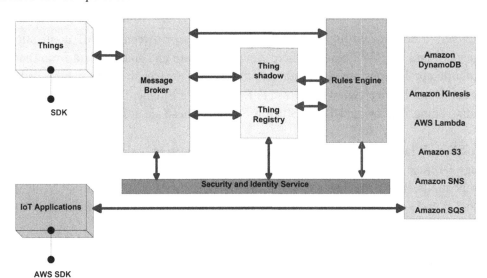

1. **Device SDK:** This component helps to quickly connect the device and the applications to AWS IoT. The Software Development Kit consists of open-source libraries, developer manuals with examples to develop innovative IoT product based on different hardware platform. This component provides SDK for connecting the hardware platform like Raspberry Pi to AWS IoT. The different SDKs provided are:
    a. AWS SDK for Mobile (Android and IoS)
    b. AWS SDK for Arduino Library (Arduino Yun)
    c. AWS IoT SDK for embedded OS (C SDK)
    d. AWS IoT SDK for Java
    e. AWS IoT SDK for embedded Linux Platform(Java Script SDK)
    f. AWS IoT SDK for Python
2. **Message Broker:** With the increase in the number of connected devices in IoT and the number messages generated by them a robust messaging service is required. In a computer network, a message broker is an intermediate program that translates the formally-defined messages from the sender to the formally-defined messages for the receiver. It is the core of the AWS IoT Components. It works on the basis of publish-subscribe model. The connected devices, say the sensors send the measurement values to the message broker. The message broker in turn sends this information to all the subscribers, say apps or tablets, who have listed to receive messages for this topic. Hence, the publishing consists of process of sending messages to the message broker and subscribing is the process of receiving messages from the publishers through the message broker. It can be represented by Figure 2. It communicates through MQ Telemetry Type protocol (for publishing and subscription) and HTTP (for publishing only). The message broker maintains the list of all the subscribers. The protocols used are described as follows:
    a. **MQTT Protocol:** It is a light-weight transport protocol used for publishing and subscription of all devices in the AWS IoT. It is used in resource–sensitive scenarios. There are two aspects of MQTT:

> i.   **CLIENT:** The MQTT client consists of publishers and subscribers. It can be any device where the MQTT library is running and is connected to MQTT broker over any kind of network.
>
> ii. **BROKER:** As described above the MQTT broker can handle many connected clients. It is responsible for message receiving, filtering and sending the messages to subscribed clients. It also take cares of authentication and authorization of clients.

b. **HTTP:** It is a TCP/IP based protocol for delivering data on the World Wide Web. The HTTP specification specifies how clients request data will be constructed and sent to the server and how the server respond to these requests. The REST API is used to link clients using HTTP protocol with the message broker. The MQTT protocol is better than the HTTP protocol in the following ways:

> i.   It is having 93 times faster throughput.
>
> ii. It requires 11.89 times less battery power to send the data.
>
> iii. It requires 170.9 times less battery to receive data.
>
> iv. It needs 50% less power to keep connected.
>
> v.   It is using eight times less network overhead.

3. **Rule Engine:** The rule engine evaluates the messages received form the publishers (Guide,2017). It further deliver the messages to the AWS service based on certain business rules. It is shown in the Figure 3. The rule engine performs the following tasks:

a. It filters the data received from a connected device.

b. It writes data received from a device to an Amazon DynamoDB database.

c. It publishes data to an Amazon SQS queue.

d. It also sends the data from an MQTT message to Amazon Machine learning to make predictions based on an Amazon ML model.

4. **Security and Identity Service:** The Transport Layer Service (TLS) encrypts the data to and from AWS IoT to the connected devices, as depicted in Figure 4. The data is protected in AWS IoT using strong security features. Moreover, the identity principals of authentication are used with mobile apps, web-based applications and desktop applications. For example, X.509 certificates are used by AWS IoT devices, IAM users, groups and roles are used by desktop applications and web applications, Amazon cognito identities are used by mobile applications.

5. **Thing Registry:** A thing is a representation of a device on the AWS cloud. In the Thing registry all the connected devices in the AWS IoT are represented by things. It is shown in Figure 5. It maintains records of the associated devices to the AWS IoT account. The mobile apps provided alongside, will create the required AWS IoT resources. The functions like emails generation, text messages or deployment of other services can be easily started.

6. **Thing Shadow:** Its main task is to store and recover present state of the thing or device. The thing shadow can be used to get and set the state of the device over HTTP or MQTT irrespective of its connection with the internet. The thing report the present state to other shadows and get the preferred result from the shadow. The shadow reports the difference, if any, between the desired and the reported state along with the version number and meta-data. The last reported state of the device can be retrieved in the mobile app. The JSON document service has the following property: state, metadata, timestamp, client token and version.

Figure 2. The message broker

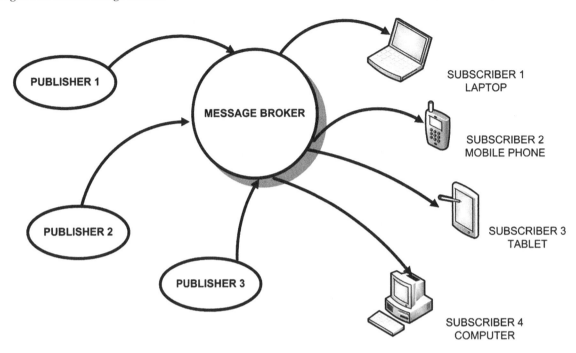

Figure 3. The rule engine

The three main driving factors for the success of the AWS IoT are: firstly anyone can connect a device, secondly any device can connect securely and thirdly it is easy to start. Apart from these the consumption based model allows for the payment to be based on the usage. There is no minimum amount charged per device. These features make it quite popular among many organizations. The most attractive feature of AWS IoT is its pricing. Usage based payment is done and there is no minimum charges to be paid.

Figure 4. Security and identification in AWS IoT

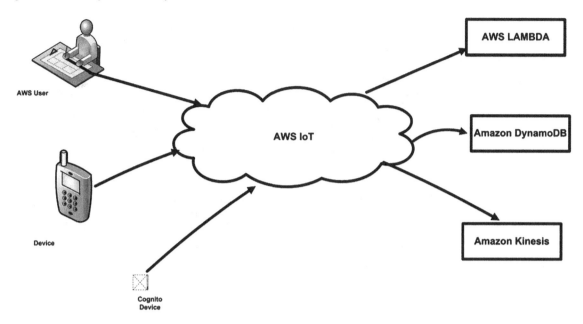

Figure 5. Thing registry

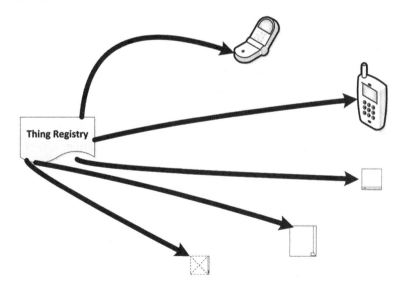

CHALLENGES

Although AWS IoT is gaining popularity all over but there are some challenges that need to be addressed. The authors identified the following challenges:

- **Availability of Variety of SDKs and Tools:** Due to availability of large number of SDKs for different hardware platforms, it becomes difficult to make a choice.

Figure 6. Thing shadow

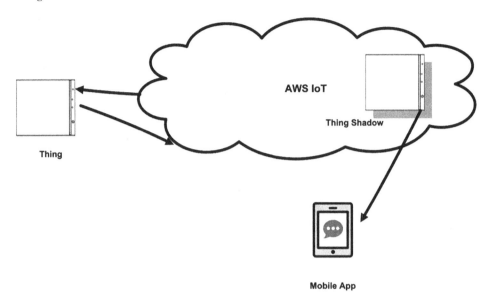

- **Variety of Communication and Application Protocols:** Considering the large variety of protocols available for communication, it becomes difficult for the developer to choose an appropriate protocol.
- **Scalability:** It is a major challenge to scale the applications for large number of devices.
- **Security and Management:** With the explosion of large number of devices and associated data on the IoT cloud it becomes cumbersome to maintain the security.
- **Integration of Cloud and Mobile Applications:** The connection between the two becomes difficult and may vary case to case.
- **Cultural Differences:** Due to the cultural differences existing among different parts of the world it is not possible to use the same set of solution for the same problem across the world.

CONCLUSION

The internet is used today for information processing, social networking and for availing different services. There are some devices that can be readily connected to the internet like the ATMs and the mobile phones. According to an estimate, by 2025 there will be approximately 80 billion devices connected to the internet. The cloud computing paradigm offers ubiquitous access to configurable resources like servers, storage, application and services. The IoT and cloud computing together offers various advantages. They together can be used as Software as Service, Platform as a Service or Infrastructure as a Service. Here, in this chapter the authors will explore the Platform as a Service aspect of this combination. The term Internet-of-things consists of network of connected components where the world wide web is the network and the components are all the devices that can be connected to it. Initially, RFID was the main technology later on with the advent of wireless sensor networks and Bluetooth enabled device the current trend has now shifted towards the Internet-of-Things. The public cloud AWS provides a wide range of services like computation, networking, analytics, development and management tools, application services, mobile services and management of IoT devices. This chapter presents the detailed study of AWS IoT platform. It starts with the introduction of cloud computing and IoT. It covers the various applications of this technology. It presented a detailed description of the AWS IoT components and how they work together. It also highlighted the various challenges and the research directions in this area.

REFERENCES

Armbrust, M., Fox, A., Griffith, R., Joseph, A. D., Katz, R., Konwinski, A., & Zaharia, M. (2010). A view of cloud computing. *Communications of the ACM, 53*(4), 50–58. doi:10.1145/1721654.1721672

ASD Guide. (n.d.). Available online: http://docs. aws. amazon. com/AutoScaling/latest. DeveloperGuide/ as-dg. pdf

Ashton, K. (2011). That 'internet of things' thing. *RFiD Journal, 22*(7).

Ghemawat, S., Gobioff, H., & Leung, S. T. (2003, October). The Google file system. *Operating Systems Review, 37*(5), 29–43. doi:10.1145/1165389.945450

Josyula, S. K., & Gupta, D. (2016, October). Internet of things and cloud interoperability application based on Android. In *Advances in Computer Applications (ICACA), IEEE International Conference on* (pp. 76-81). IEEE. doi:10.1109/ICACA.2016.7887927

Mohamed, A. (2009). A history of cloud computing. *Computer Weekly*, 27.

Shi, W., Cao, J., Zhang, Q., Li, Y., & Xu, L. (2016). Edge computing: Vision and challenges. *IEEE Internet of Things Journal, 3*(5), 637–646. doi:10.1109/JIOT.2016.2579198

Shvachko, K., Kuang, H., Radia, S., & Chansler, R. (2010, May). The hadoop distributed file system. In *Mass storage systems and technologies (MSST), 2010 IEEE 26th symposium on* (pp. 1-10). IEEE. doi:10.1109/MSST.2010.5496972

Suciu, G., Halunga, S., Vulpe, A., & Suciu, V. (2013, July). Generic platform for IoT and cloud computing interoperability study. In *Signals, Circuits and Systems (ISSCS), 2013 International Symposium on* (pp. 1-4). IEEE. doi:10.1109/ISSCS.2013.6651222

Zaharia, M., Chowdhury, M., Franklin, M. J., Shenker, S., & Stoica, I. (2010). Spark: Cluster computing with working sets. *HotCloud, 10*(10-10), 95.

This research was previously published in Examining Cloud Computing Technologies Through the Internet of Things edited by Pradeep Tomar and Gurjit Kaur, pages 216-227, copyright year 2018 by Information Science Reference (an imprint of IGI Global).

Chapter 6

Strategies to Implement Edge Computing in a P2P Pervasive Grid

Luiz Angelo Steffenel
University of Reims Champagne-Ardenne, France

Manuele Kirsch Pinheiro
Pantheon-Sorbonne University, France

Lucas Vaz Peres
Federal University of Western Pará, Brazil

Damaris Kirsch Pinheiro
Federal University of Santa Maria, Brazil

ABSTRACT

The exponential dissemination of proximity computing devices (smartphones, tablets, nanocomputers, etc.) raises important questions on how to transmit, store and analyze data in networks integrating those devices. New approaches like edge computing aim at delegating part of the work to devices in the "edge" of the network. In this article, the focus is on the use of pervasive grids to implement edge computing and leverage such challenges, especially the strategies to ensure data proximity and context awareness, two factors that impact the performance of big data analyses in distributed systems. This article discusses the limitations of traditional big data computing platforms and introduces the principles and challenges to implement edge computing over pervasive grids. Finally, using CloudFIT, a distributed computing platform, the authors illustrate the deployment of a real geophysical application on a pervasive network.

DOI: 10.4018/978-1-5225-5649-7.ch006

INTRODUCTION

Big data and data analytics have become essential tools for the strategic planning of any company. While data analysis is not a new topic, it was boosted by the development of large-scale computing platforms, notably the clouds. While cloud computing relies on distant resources, several works try to leverage the use of proximity resources as effective computing platforms (Garcia Lopez, 2015; Parashar & Pierson, 2010; Steffenel & Kirsch-Pinheiro, 2015).

Indeed, the number and nature of proximity computing devices (smartphones, Internet of Things - IoT, etc.) is growing exponentially, and it is important to understand how to exploit the power of these computing resources. For this reason, new approaches like edge or fog computing aim at delegating part of the work to devices in the "edge" of the network (Lopez, 2015). Because several strategies can be used to implement edge computing, this work specifically focus on the use of pervasive grids to leverage such challenges. Indeed, pervasive grids (Parashar & Pierson, 2010) associate classical and volatile computing resources. We believe that organizations can perform big data analytics with minimal costs by associating IoT and mobile devices as well as idle or unused resources in the enterprise network.

Therefore, in this paper, we discuss the limitations of traditional big data computing platforms and introduce the principles and challenges to implement edge computing over pervasive grids. To illustrate this, we present CloudFIT, a distributed computing platform based on a P2P overlay, and discuss how it can be improved to efficiently deploy edge/pervasive computing applications, especially those related to big data analytics. Indeed, after presenting the main architecture of CloudFIT, we focus on the required strategies to ensure data proximity and context awareness, two factors that impact the performance of big data analysis in distributed systems.

For conducting this research, we adopted a two-fold approach, combining a conceptual research method with a case study a case study. Indeed, according to research method categories pointed out by Mora et al. (2008), a conceptual research corresponds to the study of ideas related to real objects including designing of new conceptual artifacts such as a framework/model, a method/model, or a system/component. For these authors, a "conceptual design research is the purposeful design of conceptual artifacts", in which the design artifact is dictated by the design goals. The principles and challenges we discuss in this paper represent, in our research, these design goals that guided the application of CloudFIT platform. The results of this conceptual research are then confronted to a case study issue from a real geophysical problem. Peres, 2013 conduct a case study analysis of the detection of Ozone Secondary Events (OSE) problem and Peres et al., (2017) present a detailed description of TOC monitoring by Brewer spectrophotometer in Southern Space Observatory SSO/CRS/INPE – MCTI (29.4 °S; 53.8°O; 488.7m) station for more than twenty years (1992 - 2014). Through this two-fold approach, we search for confronting our design goals with results from an empirical research proposed by the case study. Thus, we deploy the OSE detection algorithm over different scenarios representing edge and pervasive computing networks, both to validate the algorithm and to infer its execution performance.

This remain of this paper is organized as follows: we start presenting big data, the limitations of traditional computing platforms and the notions of edge computing and pervasive grids. The next section introduces the distributed computing platform CloudFIT and explain its main features. This section is followed by a case study that illustrates the usage of CloudFIT with a real application. Finally, we conclude this paper and explore future research directions.

BACKGROUND

Handling Big Data in Traditional and Pervasive Environments

Big data is research area presenting several definitions as it can be used in countless domains (Babiceanu & Seker, 2016). Even though, the literature often characterizes big data through a set of dimensions (Jagadish et al., 2014; Hashem et al., 2015; Gartner 2011; Babiceanu & Seker, 2016): *Volume, Variety, Velocity, Veracity* and *Value*. These 5 V's push big data to much more than a simple volume threshold as pointed out by Hashem et al. (2015), who stands that big data refers to "the increase in the volume of data that are difficult to store, process, and analyze through traditional database technologies". Indeed, the main challenges in big data processing are related to the complexity of the data itself, as for example one Terabyte of satellite images cannot be explored in the same way than 1 TB of structured text data.

As all five V dimensions have an impact on the way information should be handled, it is important to understand how traditional and pervasive computing platforms can be employed and what are their limitations.

Constraints and limitations of traditional infrastructures for big dataTraditional big data tools like Apache Hadoop (2016) were particularly designed for dedicated infrastructures like clusters or datacenters, relying on fast network connections and high-performance hardware, as underlined by Wright (2014). However, the usage of such infrastructures represent a significant investment, both on the acquisition of the dedicated equipment and its maintenance cost (human and material).

Public cloud platforms are often presented as a low-cost and scalable alternative to cluster infrastructures, thanks to their on-demand model. In a cloud platform, there is no need for investment on material or maintenance, as these costs are assumed by the cloud provider. Although less expensive than cluster infrastructures, public cloud platforms have some drawbacks that must be evaluated when deploying big data applications.

One of the limitations of public cloud platforms we can cite is the transfer cost of a large volume of data through the network. Not only most cloud providers charge for large inbound/outbound traffic, but the connection speed may be a barrier on zones disposing of a poor or limited network access. In addition, transferring data to an external public cloud platform can represent a confidentiality risk that may prevent some applications to rely on public cloud platforms.

Because of these issues, some organizations may refrain to adopt high performance infrastructures like clusters and public cloud platforms for their applications. In the next section, we present a possible alternative platform for big data analysis for such organizations.

Proximity Services With Edge Computing and Pervasive Grids

The dissemination of proximity devices with non-negligible processing capacities (smartphones, tablets, laptops and nanocomputers like the Raspberry Pi) encourages the integration of these devices in the computing effort. Today, several works try to leverage the use of these proximity resources, and we strongly believe this can be achieved through the use of edge computing over pervasive grids.

Edge computing is a concept that aims at migrating part of the computation to devices in the "edge" of the network (Garcia Lopez et al., 2015). The main reason for this migration is the recent rise in computing power from mobile and proximity devices, transforming close base stations into "intelligent service hubs that are capable of delivering highly personalized services directly from the very edge" (Vermesan et al., 2014). Similar concepts like mobile edge computing (Dey et al., 2013; ETSI, 2014), edge-centric computing (Garcia Lopez et al., 2015) or fog computing (CISCO, 2013; Bonomi et al., 2012) also try to deploy applications and services closer to the final user, and can therefore be considered as variants of the edge computing concept.

Among the typical examples of edge computing we can cite fog services (Bonomi et al., 2012) and cloudlets (Satyanarayanan et al., 2009), all proposing the deployment of proximity servers offering enough computing power to perform complex computations (services) with a reduced service latency. In most cases, tasks are migrated from the cloud to the edge thanks to containers and microservice components (Pahl & Lee, 2015), but this is not a rule. In the same way, the computer power that can be offered by IoT devices, nanocomputers or even tablets and smartphones is often underestimated. With a few exceptions like (Dey et al., 2013), these works limit the role of edge devices by considering them as a frontend layer, connected to a bigger and more powerful "core" network that performs most of the work.

In our understanding, the notion of pervasive grid can be employed to unleash the latent computing power of proximity devices. Indeed, the concept of Pervasive grids (Parashar & Pierson, 2010) aims at transparently integrate sensing/actuating instruments and devices together with classical high-performance systems in a dynamic network. These grids can be composed by idle and under-explored resources in the enterprise network, by small Raspberry Pi or TV set-top devices, but also interconnect them to virtual machines deployed on cluster infrastructures. More than all, pervasive grids represent an opportunity to deploy computing tasks over local computing resources, minimizing data transfer over distant network.

Due to the heterogeneous nature of devices in a pervasive grid, tasks must be assigned according to the capabilities of each device, exploring the diversity of resources and improving the usage of proximity nodes. One example of such usage is presented by (Ramakrishnan et al., 2014), in which the computing resources of a home (laptops, tablets or nanocomputers) are associated to perform a preliminary analysis on sensor data concerning the movement of the residents, triggering an alarm or calling for an external action if necessary.

Of course, adopting pervasive grids for big data analysis implies considering several questions such as data processing, data distribution and tasks scheduling, all while efficiently matching the resources capabilities (Shekar & Gokhale, 2017). In order to illustrate these challenges, we present in the next section a platform for pervasive grids, and discuss how it can be improved to deploy big data applications under the edge computing approach.

DEVELOPING A PLATFORM FOR EDGE AND PERVASIVE COMPUTING

The distributed computing concept accelerates in the 90's, as an extension on the Internet of the cycle stealing principle. Former applications aimed to crack RC5 or DES keys by exhaustive search thanks to the aggregation of hundreds of PCs to solve a problem. Web-based Computing projects arose at the end of the 90's like SETI@home (Anderson et al., 2002) and Boinc (Anderson, 2005), and were soon followed by P2P-based middleware (Brasileiro et al., 2007). However, the fast spread of clusters, grids and cloud infrastructures stalled the development of such middlewares, which were relegated to niche domains like those related to computing-intensive applications (combinatorial research, cryptography, etc.).

In this section, we present CloudFIT, a distributing computing middleware adapted to both computing and data-intensive applications. CloudFIT is structured around collaborative nodes connected over a P2P overlay network that provides communication, fault-tolerance and distributed storage, while its scheduling mechanism is based on the FIIT (Finite Independent Irregular Tasks) paradigm. For instance, applications that can be parallelized in a finite number of tasks and executed in batches are fit for this platform, like for example combinatorial problems (Krajecki & Jaillet, 2004) or ETL (Extract-Transform-Load) steps in a big data application. Hence, the well-known map-reduce paradigm used in several big data applications can be considered as a subset of the FIIT problems.

Instead of relying on containers and microservices, CloudFIT is written in Java and packed in a small jar file so that it can be easily deployed over a wide range of devices, from dedicated servers to low-end devices like Raspberry Pi. Because CloudFIT relies on P2P overlays, it is extremely elastic as nodes can join or leave the platform according to the availability of the resources or the variation in the demand. Also, inner services for replication and decentralized management of tasks ensure the completion of the tasks even in situations of high volatility or network partition (see Figure 1).

An application running on CloudFIT must simply implements two methods: how many tasks to solve and how to compute an individual task. These methods guide the deployment of tasks and their execution. Furthermore, each node receives the parameters of the current job and is able to locally decide which tasks still need to be computed and how to proceed, carrying the work autonomously if no other node can be contacted. Access to a distributed storage facility is also provided by the P2P overlay, allowing nodes to obtain input data and store their partial results. The status of completed tasks is distributed among the nodes, contributing therefore to the coordination of the work and to form a global view of the execution.

As nodes in a pervasive cluster may leave the network for different reasons (failure, low battery, network disconnection, etc.), CloudFIT supports by default a robust distributed scheduling with no "task reservation", allowing nodes to execute different tasks in parallel when they are able to communicate to each other or, in the worst case, to complete all the computation by itself. This scheduler mechanism also allows idle processes to speculatively execute incomplete tasks, reducing the "tail effect" when a task is computed by a slow node. The scheduling mechanism supports task and job dependencies (allowing the composition of DAGs and workflows) and can be also be driven by a context module (Cassales et al., 2016) with additional information about the nodes capacities.

The next sections give some details on the implementation strategies employed in CloudFIT.

Coordination and Clustering

One of the major challenges with edge computing is to coordinate which tasks are assigned to each resource in order to efficiently perform operations and reduce the communication latency (Shekar & Gokhale, 2017). When using a P2P overlay, however, we observe that nodes are often organized indistinctly from their real location, preventing therefore a good use of close-range devices to provide a low latency service. We consider that P2P overlays must be enriched through the use of clustering, organizing nodes in computing layers that provide bounded communication latencies, context-awareness or trustworthiness/isolation.

Several clustering approaches are proposed in the literature (Johnen & Mekhaldi, 2011), with both manual or automatic clustering depending on specific metrics, so in CloudFIT we decided to implement clustering through the concept of community. As presented by Lim and Conan (2014), a community is a group ID to which nodes subscribe in order to share tasks and data or interconnect different communities in a multi-layered architecture. For instance, all applications in CloudFIT share a baseline community used for task distribution and wide-range communication, while the creation or subscription to additional communities can be managed directly by the applications.

Figure 1. CloudFIT architecture stack

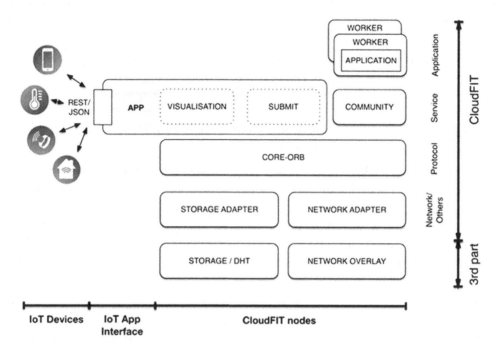

Data Access

Another important aspect to consider of is how data is accessed, as big data applications involve the gathering, the transformation and the analysis of data. While these applications can rely on an external storage servers/services (like a cloud storage service), this solution is not always adapted to their needs as it incurs extra latencies or transfer fees.

In a previous work (Steffenel & Kirsch-Pinheiro, 2015), we conducted performance tests comparing the performance of Hadoop and CloudFIT when running the well-known *WordCount* application in a cluster platform. While these tests show that CloudFIT can reach performances at the same level than Apache Hadoop, we also observed the need to reinforce the *data locality,* i.e., the optimal data access for the computing tasks. Indeed, part of the success of Apache Hadoop is its capability to start tasks where the data is stored, avoiding therefore unnecessary network transfers.

Unfortunately, traditional P2P systems favor data spread and replication (to prevent the loss of data in the case of churn) at the expense of losing data locality (Wu et al., 2005). Indeed, P2P storage APIs are often based on distribute hash tables (DHT), which are conceived to spread and replicate the data across the network, sometimes storing data on nodes really far from the original source (or the clients). In a DHT, the data is identified by a *hash id* that maps to a *node id* the entire P2P network. While this node may hold the primary data replica, it can also be a simple directory service pointing to the node where the data is really stored, making hard the mapping between tasks and data (Wang et al., 2015).

While CloudFIT is still based on a P2P overlay that lacks data locality information, we designed a solution to reinforce through *data proximity.* Indeed, our approach helps preventing too much dispersion of the data over the network, keeping therefore data close to the nodes that will perform the tasks.

For such, we rely on the TomP2P overlay (Bocek, 2015), which contrarily to most P2P overlays offers several hash keys (instead of a single hash key). While a typical P2P storage uses a simple mapping where the data is indexed in the node with ID closes to the hash key of the data, TomP2P identifies resources with up to four keys $\{k_l, k_d, k_c, k_v\}$, namely k_l (*location key*, which determines the node ID closest to the hash key), k_d (domain key, used for namespacing), k_c (content key, which identifies different resources stored in the same location) and k_v (version key, which allows the managing of different versions of the same resource).

In order to implement data proximity, we manipulate the location key so that it is not randomly spread among all nodes but specifically attached to a set of nodes. Thanks to a double hashing function, we decouple the location key and the content key for a resource: in a first moment, the content key is obtained through a traditional hashing method. Later, the location key is computed to map only among the community nodes.

Figure 2 shows an example of such mapping that reinforces the data proximity. Hence, in a traditional P2P storage with a single location key, a resource r_3 could be stored in any node in the network, depending on the hash result (like for example $hash(r_3)=k_{17}$). By using a location and a content key and a community-aware hash function $hash_{ca}()$, we can bound the location key to the nodes in the community, all while properly identifying a resource. Hence, for a resource r_3 and a community C_1 composed by nodes with IDs k_{12}, k_{13} and k_{14}, we can compute a community-aware location key k_l' that points to a node from the community. Hence, the primary copy of the resource r_3 will be located in the node k_l' with the content key k_{c3}. Even if the community is small data is preserved as each resource has its own content key. The domain key and version key can also be used to improve this resiliency.

As a consequence, this mapping improves the probability that the primary copy of a resource is stored in a node from the community, all while allowing the storage overlay to perform replication on other nodes, even those outside the community.

Context and Scheduling

While the previous factors help improving the performance in a distributed computing platform, we shall address a last issue in order to offer a really scalable pervasive support. As the computing performance varies a lot from device to device, context information such as processing power, available memory and storage space or even current CPU load can be useful to improve the execution performance, as demonstrated by Dey et al. (2013). Also, efficiently matching the tasks with the resources capabilities and their locations is a key element on the optimization of performance-sensitive edge application (Shekar & Gokhale, 2017).

As presented before, the default scheduler on CloudFIT implements a best-effort algorithm that has the advantage of being totally distributed, i.e., all nodes collaborate to consume the tasks without a central coordinator. This scheduler currently performs a basic matching according to the tasks expressed requirements (minimum requested memory, disk space, etc.), but it can be enriched with additional context elements such as the CPU or network speeds (Celaya & Arronategui, 2011). This way, nodes can decide whether it is important to prioritize one single task at time in order to avoid memory swap (like in memory-intensive applications) or how to balance the available cores in the machine with the relative performance of its processors (a 4-core Raspberry Pi is still less powerful than a single core in an Intel i7 processor). Such context information is collected by a context collector as the one presented in Figure 3, which is integrated into the CloudFIT stack.

Figure 2. Computing the Location key to implement data-proximity

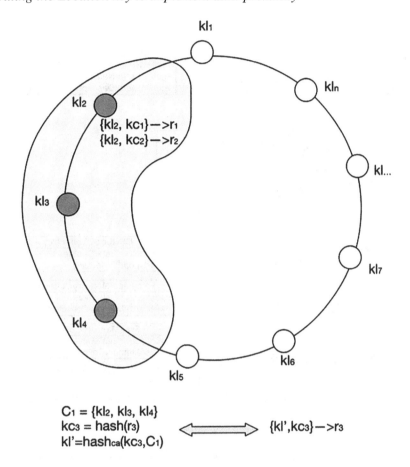

$C_1 = \{kl_2, kl_3, kl_4\}$
$kc_3 = hash(r_3)$
$kl' = hash_{ca}(kc_3, C_1)$

$\Longleftrightarrow$

$\{kl', kc_3\} \rightarrow r_3$

While the execution performance is a key component of context information, we also try to use it to improve the data access performance in the storage layer. Indeed, we observed in our experiments that data access performance is the result of both data access on the nodes (both on memory and disk) and the overhead caused by the storage management, affecting especially devices with low capacity. For example, a Raspberry Pi is highly penalized by the speed access of its SD card, in spite of having a good computing power. To circumvent such limitation, CloudFIT allows nodes to choose between acting as full storage nodes or simply as remote data clients. This way, low-end nodes can keep saving/reading data through the network but do not need to manage the storage, alleviating both the disk usage and the storage processing.

The next section presents a case study in which we design and deploy a data intensive application over a pervasive cluster using CloudFIT.

CASE STUDY: MONITORING OZONE EVENTS FOR UV ALERTS

In order to better validate design assumptions proposed on CloudFIT, we have decided to confront those with an empirical environment, through a case study issue from a reality situation. Thus, in this section,

Figure 3. Context collector structure (Cassales et al., 2016)

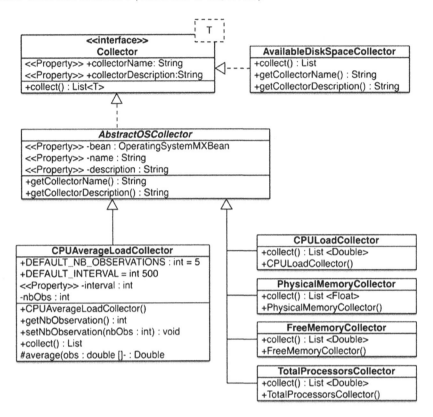

we present a real application developed over CloudFIT and deployed over a pervasive cluster, initially presented in (Steffenel et al., 2016). This application implements a surveillance and alert system for ultra-violet risks due to ozone-layer events all while relying on already existing computational resources, representing no additional cost to the institution.

Indeed, it is well known that the discovery of the Antarctic Ozone hole (Farman et al., 1985) raised the interest of the scientific community, with several studies monitoring the variation in the density of the ozone layer on polar regions (Salby et al., 2012). Inhabited zones can also be affected due to both movements of the polar vortex borders over these regions (Marchand et al., 2002) or by the influx of air masses with reduced concentration of ozone detached from the polar vortex. The latter case, known as Ozone Secondary Effects (OSE), may cause a temporary reduction in the total column ozone (TCO) over populated areas (Manney et al., 1994; Pinheiro et al., 2011) and trigger important public health subjects as a reduction of 1% in the total ozone column may lead to an increase of 1.2% in the ultraviolet radiation (Guarnieri et al., 2004).

Today OSE can only be detected *a posteriori*, as satellite and ground instruments can at most inform the current status of the TCO over an area. To create an effective monitoring and public health alert system, we need to forecast OSE. Unfortunately, most of the climatic models are limited to the lower atmosphere layers (especially those associated to the weather forecast), and do not explore the interactions in higher layers, like those associated to the Ozone layer.

Instead of adapting a simulation model, our approach to forecast OSE relies in the analysis of historical data, looking for correlation patterns that can lead to a good forecast. Using CloudFIT, we created a pervasive HPC platform out of existing computational resources, minimizing the operational costs as there is no need to investment in the acquisition of dedicated machines or in the leasing of cloud resources.

Experiment Methodology

In the case of the Ozone Secondary Events detection, the problem was defined as a set of different tasks to be performed, each one exploring the CloudFIT distributed computing environment to its advantage. These tasks are described in Table 1.

Each step can be parallelized and the dependency between different jobs can be represented as a DAG, as illustrated in Figure 4. Furthermore, we can set different communities for different parts of the workflow. For instance, low-entry devices gathered at community C1 can be used to pre-process and store the data from ground-based Brewer or Dobson spectrophotometers as well as those readings from the OMI sensors from the satellites.

The newly entered data can trigger the OSE detection procedure, or in the case of a deeper analysis, launch an historical search for recurrent patterns that could be useful for event forecasting. This step, covering both filtering and time series analysis, requires more computing resources, so a community C2 composed by more powerful nodes can ensure this work.

Figure 4 also includes two other communities, C3 and C4, used to perform the last steps associated to the detection and forecasting of OSE.

Input Preprocessing

The total ozone column can be measured by ground equipment but also counts with a worldwide satellite coverage, the OMI instrument, which produces a global measurement once a day. TOMS/OMI website offers different datasets, from raw data to final analyzed products. In our case, we use access raw data to extract all the necessary information to our calculations. The file format provided by OMI, presented in Figure 5 (at the left side) is not really adapted for parallel processing. Each file corresponds to the measures of a day and contains a header that specifies the basic information for that file (date, coordinates grid, step), followed by the measurements for each latitude (indicated at the end of the line) and for all covered longitudes. Each measure in Dobson Units (UD) is represented as a 3 digits integer that

Table 1. Detail of OSE analysis steps

Step	Actions
Input preprocessing	transform raw OMI data files for the analysis
Filtering and aggregation	select data corresponding to a given geographical zone and time window, performing aggregation if needed
Time series analysis	extract of correlation parameters for the target period and zone
Event detection	identification of abnormal ozone values and eventual alert generation
Event forecast	application of parameters to forecast OSE over inhabited areas

Figure 4. Workflow for the OSE detection framework

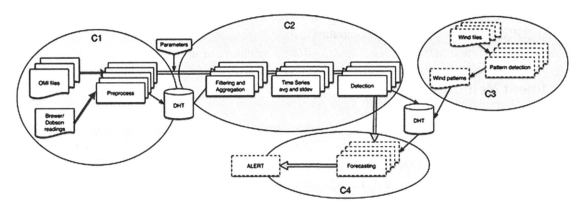

must be parsed from the other readings. For example, in Figure 5, the coordinates (-89.5, -179.5) has a value 280, (-89.5, -178.5) has a value 280, and so on.

As this format is difficult to manipulate, we preferred to preprocess it and store the data as JSON entries using the template presented in Figure 5 (at the right side). JSON is a well-known format that is easy to parse and also compatible with document-oriented NoSQL databases. The preprocessing is highly parallelizable as each input file containing the measures of a given day can be treated independently from each other and distributed over all the nodes using the DHT.

A similar procedure is implemented for other atmospheric parameters like wind currents. NetCDF files containing U and V components of wind currents at different altitudes are transformed in JSON entries for each coordinate pairs. As a result, the analysis of TCO concentration and dominant wind currents can be performed in the next task.

Time-Series Analysis, OSE Detection and Forecast

As presented above, OSE are defined by abnormal drops in the total ozone column that are not directly related to the expansion of the Antarctic Ozone Hole. The detection of the ozone concentration reduction is made by comparing the measured values for a given day with and the historical average for that zone. The current approach used by Vaz Peres (2013) relies on the historical average by month, i.e., measures are compared to the corresponding month average. For example, the October 22, 2013 values would be compared to the historical average for the October month. While this approach allows the detection of

Figure 5. OMI Ozone raw data file for a given day and its JSON representation

```
Day:  1 Jan  1, 2013   OMI TO3   STD OZONE   GEN:13:003 Asc LECT: 01:44 pm
Longitudes:  360 bins centered on 179.5 W to 179.5 E  (1.00 degree steps)
Latitudes :  180 bins centered on  89.5 S to  89.5 N  (1.00 degree steps)
280280280280280280280280280280280280280280280280280280280279279279279279279
279279279279279279279279279279279279279279279279279279279279279279279279279
279279279279279279279279279279279279279279279279279279279279279279279279279
279279279279279279279279279279279279279279280279280280280280280280280280280
280280280280280280280280280280280280280280280280280280280279279279280280280
280280280280280280280280280280280280280280281281281281281281281281281281281
(...)
282282282282282282282282282282  lat = -89.5
(...)  lat = -88.5
(...)  lat = -87.5
(...)
```

```
{
"date":"20130101",
"step":"1.0",
"latitudes":{
"-89.5":["-179.5":"280","-178.5":"280",(...)],
"-88.5":["-179.5":"272","-178.5":"272",(...)],
(...)
}
}
```

OSE, it lacks precision as the natural ozone concentration varies from year to year and also from the beginning to the end of the month, especially in transition months like July or November. Using a standardized average for each month would result in false-positive alerts that we wish to minimize. Therefore, in order to make more precise estimations, our implementation uses a sliding window approach that computes averages and standard deviations for a time series of 15 days. This solution is more realistic as it allows natural variations in a given period to be taken into account.

Once the average and standard deviation for a given coordinate (in a given time period) is computed, we can proceed with the detection of OSE. One easy formula, applied on the experiment presented in the next section, considers the occurrence of an OSE if the measure for a given coordinate is less than the expected lower bound (1.5× the standard deviation) with respect to the last 15 days average.

While OSE detection is important, to implement an OSE forecast model is a major objective of this project. As developing a specific atmosphere modeling for the Ozone layer is beyond our scope, we decided to implement forecasting by detecting recurrent patterns leading to OSEs. For this, an extensive correlation analysis between OSE occurrences and atmospheric factors like wind currents must be performed. Hence, the use of different communities on CloudFIT allows the computation of an historical correlation database, all while online OSE detection/forecast is performed on the most recent Ozone readings. We believe that with such approach even a single low-end machine can ensure a daily forecast report, relying on patterns previously computed by a large community on the CloudFIT network.

Experimental Results

In order to evaluate the effectiveness of deploying the OSE detection application on top of CloudFIT, we considered the first analysis steps (preprocessing to OSE detection) for the period between October 15th, 2013 and October 31st, 2013 over different devices, both individually and in a pervasive cluster mode. This scenario considers an area spanning 50°x55° (2750 coordinate points) on the south of South America that coincides with the area covered by the analysis from Vaz Peres (2013) and used to validate our results. For instance, in Figure 6, the upper part contains the Total Column Ozone (TCO) concentration from October 18th to October 22, 2013 over the South Pole according to the NASA *Ozone Hole Watch* Web site (http://ozonewatch.gsfc.nasa.gov/), while the lower part shows the progression of the OSE front as detected by our framework. The main advantage of our method is that instead of simply observing the Ozone concentration we are able to highlight the zones that experience a TCO drop, emphasizing the impact of OSE and allowing a more precise evaluation of the health risks.

Also, in order to evaluate the execution performance of our algorithms, we conducted the same experiment over three different platform configurations. In the first one, 3 Raspberry Pi 2 (900MHz 4-core ARM Cortex-A7, 1GB RAM) collaborate in a small network; in the second configuration, we created a heterogeneous network composed by one Raspberry Pi 2, one Macbook Air (Intel i7-4650U, 2 cores, 8GB RAM) and one Lenovo U110 (Intel Core2 Duo). Finally, the algorithm was run in a single Dell Precision T5610 server (Intel Xeon E5-2620, 12 cores, 32GB RAM). The first two configurations aim to represent edge/pervasive computing platforms that could be found in a real situation: the pure Raspberry Pi network may represent the low-end devices that serve as a first computing layer to the edge computing network, while the heterogeneous network represents a voluntary computing network composed by devices available at a given moment. The Xeon server, on the other hand, is used as a control reference to infer the performance of the algorithm in a more classical infrastructure.

Figure 6. Absolute Ozone concentration and the OSE progression between October 18 to October 22, 2013

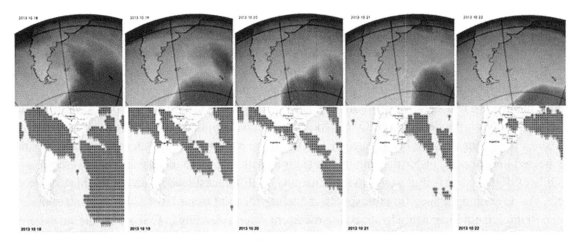

Hence, the analysis of the OMI data from satellites in the Raspberry Pi 2 network took around 30 minutes, while the pervasive cluster required about 10 minutes. By comparison, the Xeon server required less than 7 minutes. Furthermore, in the case the application shall perform a global coverage (65000+ coordinates) or requires more data intensive operations (historical analysis, forecast), new nodes can join CloudFIT at any moment and thus provide the elasticity required to perform the tasks under different loads.

CONCLUSION

The digital economy that marked the turn of this century changed in deep the way companies plan and manage their business models, and big data analytics is one of the major tools supporting this revolution. It is an error, however, to think that big data requires massive investments and the usage of large-scale resources like those found in a dedicated datacenter or in a cloud computing facility. Some organizations are more prone to lightweight and less expensive platforms, we strongly believe that these organizations can boost their efficiency with minimal costs by relying on edge computing over pervasive grids. For this reason, this paper shows how edge computing and pervasive grids can be used to develop efficient and flexible big data analytic tools and applications.

To illustrate this approach, we present a distributed computing platform that implements the concepts of both edge computing and pervasive grids. We demonstrate its utilization to deploy an atmospheric surveillance system developed for a governmental institution.

The works presented in this paper represent only the first steps towards the generalization of big data on edge and pervasive environments. Indeed, additional research concerning context awareness is essential, as several advances can be obtained through it: better usage of resources, energy awareness (green computing), proximity services, etc.

It is worth noting that the increasing number and nature of proximity devices (IoT, smartphones, etc.) represents an unprecedented computing power at the reach of our hands, and that edge and pervasive computing are tools that can help unleash that computing power. Indeed, efficiently exploring these new resources is a valuable asset for any organization, both in cost reductions and in the sustainable usage of the resources.

REFERENCES

Anderson, D. (2004) BOINC: A system for public-resource computing and storage. In *Proceedings of the 5th IEEE/ACM International Workshop on Grid Computing*. doi:10.1109/GRID.2004.14

Anderson, D., Cobb, J., Korpela, E., Lebofsky, M., & Werthimer, D. (2002). SETI@home: An experiment in public-resource computing. *Communications of the ACM, 45*(11), 56–61. doi:10.1145/581571.581573 PMID:12238525

Apache Hadoop. (2016). Retrieved from http://hadoop.apache.org/

Babiceanu, R. F., & Seker, R. (2016). Big Data and virtualization for manufacturing cyber-physical systems: A survey of the current status and future outlook. *Computers in Industry, 81*, 128–137. doi:10.1016/j.compind.2016.02.004

Bocek, T. (2015). TomP2P, a P2P-based high performance key–value pair storage library. Retrieved from https://tomp2p.net/

Bonomi, F., Milito, R., Zhu, J., & Addepalli, S. (2012). Fog computing and its role in the internet of things. In *Proceedings of the 1st MCC Workshop on Mobile Cloud Computing, MCC '12*, New York, NY. doi:10.1145/2342509.2342513

Brasileiro, F., Araujo, E., & Voorsluys, W., Oliveira & M. Figueiredo, F. (2007) Bridging the High Performance Computing Gap: the OurGrid Experience. *7th IEEE International Symposium on Cluster Computing and the Grid (CCGrid '07)* (pp. 817-822). doi:10.1109/CCGRID.2007.28

Cassales, G. W., Charao, A., Kirsch-Pinheiro, M., Souveyet, C., & Steffenel, L. A. (2016). Improving the performance of Apache Hadoop on pervasive environments through context-aware scheduling. *Journal of Ambient Intelligence and Humanized Computing, 7*(3), 333–345. doi:10.1007/s12652-016-0361-8

Celaya, J., & Arronategui, U. (2011) A Highly Scalable Decentralized Scheduler of Tasks with Deadlines. In *Proceedings of the IEEE/ACM 12th International Conference on Grid Computing* (pp. 58-65).

Cisco. (2013). *Cisco Research Center Requests for Proposals (RFPs)*. Retrieved from http://research.cisco.com/research#rfp-2013078

Dey, S., Mukherjee, A., Paul, H. S., & Pal, A. (2013). Challenges of using edge devices in IoT computation grids. In *Proceedings of the Int. Conf. on Parallel and Distributed Systems* (pp. 564–569). doi:10.1109/ICPADS.2013.101

ETSI. (2014). *Mobile-edge computing - introductory technical white paper*. Retrieved from http://bit.ly/2bzLQ8m

Farman, J., Gardiner, G., & Shanklin, J. (1985). Large losses of total ozone in Antarctica reveal seasonal clox/nox interaction. *Nature, 315*(6016), 207–210. doi:10.1038/315207a0

Garcia Lopez, G., Montresor, A., Epema, D., Datta, A., Higashino, T., Iamnitchi, A., & Riviere, E. et al. (2015). Edge-centric computing: Vision and challenges. *Computer Communication Review, 45*(5), 37–42. doi:10.1145/2831347.2831354

Gartner. (2011, June 27). *Gartner Says Solving 'Big Data' Challenge Involves More Than Just Managing Volumes of Data*. Newsroom. Retrieved from http://www.gartner.com/newsroom/id/1731916

Guarnieri, R., Padilha, L., Guarnieri, F., Echer, E., Makita, K., Pinheiro, D., & Schuch, N. et al. (2004). A study of the anticorrelations between ozone and UV-B radiation using linear and exponential fits in southern Brazil. *Advances in Space Research, 34*(4), 764–776. doi:10.1016/j.asr.2003.06.040

Hashem, I. A. T., Yaqoob, I., Anuar, N. B., Mokhtar, S., Gani, A., & Khan, S. U. (2015). The rise of "big data" on cloud computing: Review and open research issues. *Information Systems, 47*(January), 98–115. doi:10.1016/j.is.2014.07.006

Jagadish, H., Gehrke, J., Labrinidis, A., Papakonstantinou, Y., Patel, J. M., Ramakrishnan, R., & Shahabi, C. (2014). Big Data and Its Technical Challenges. *Communications of the ACM, 57*(7), 86–94. doi:10.1145/2611567

Johnen, C., & Mekhaldi, F. (2011). Self-stabilization versus robust self-stabilization for clustering in ad-hoc network. In *Proceedings of the 17th International Conference on Parallel Processing* (pp. 117-129). Springer. doi:10.1007/978-3-642-23400-2_12

Krajecki, M., & Jaillet, C. (2004). Solving the Langford problem in parallel. In *Proceedings of the 3rd International Workshop on Parallel and Distributed Computing* (pp. 83-90). IEEE.

Lim, L., & Conan, D. (2014). Distributed event-based system with multiscoping for multiscalability. In *Proceedings of the 9th Workshop on Middleware for Next Generation Internet Computing*. ACM. doi:10.1145/2676733.2676736

Manney, G. L., Zurek, R. W., O'Neill, A., & Swinbank, R. (1994). On the motion of air through the stratospheric polar vortex. *Journal of the Atmospheric Sciences, 51*(20), 2973–2994. doi:10.1175/1520-0469(1994)051<2973:OTMOAT>2.0.CO;2

Marchand, M., Bekki, S., Pazmino, A., Lefèvre, F., Godin-Beekmann, S., & Hauchecorne, A. (2005). Model simulations of the impact of the 2002 Antarctic ozone hole on the midlatitudes. *Journal of the Atmospheric Sciences, 62*(3), 871–884. doi:10.1175/JAS-3326.1

Mora, M., Gelman, O., Paradice, D., & Cervantes, F. (2008). The case for conceptual research in information systems. In Proceedings of the CONF-IRM 2008 (p. 52).

Pahl, C., & Lee, B. (2015) Containers and Clusters for Edge Cloud Architectures – a Technology Review. In *Proceedings of the 3rd IEEE International Conference on Future Internet of Things and Cloud (FICloud)* (pp. 379-386). doi:10.1109/FiCloud.2015.35

Parashar, M., & Pierson, J. M. (2010). Pervasive grids: Challenges and opportunities. In K. Li, C. Hsu, L. Yang et al. (Ed.). Handbook of Research on Scalable Computing Technologies (pp. 14–30). Hershey, PA: IGI Global.

Peres, L. V., Bencherif, H., Mbatha, N., Schuch, A. P., Toihir, A. M., Bègue, N., & Schuch, N. J. et al. (2017). Measurements of the total ozone column using a Brewer spectrophotometer and TOMS and OMI satellite instruments over the Southern Space Observatory in Brazil. *Ann. Geophys., 35*, 25–37. doi:10.5194/angeo-35-25-2017

Pinheiro, D., Leme, N., Peres, L., & Kall, E. (2011). *Influence of the Antarctic ozone hole over South of Brazil in 2008 and 2009*. National Institute of Science and Technology.

Ramakrishnan, A., Preuveneers, D., & Berbers, Y. (2014). Enabling self-learning in dynamic and open IoT environments. In *Proceedings of the 5th International Conference on Ambient Systems, Networks and Technologies (ANT-2014)* (pp. 207–214).

Salby, M. L., Titova, E. A., & Deschamps, L. (2012). Changes of the Antarctic ozone hole: Controlling mechanisms, seasonal predictability, and evolution. *Journal of Geophysical Research, D, Atmospheres*, *117*(D10). doi:10.1029/2011JD016285

Satyanarayanan, M., Bahl, P., Caceres, R., & Davies, N. (2009). The case for vm-based cloudlets in mobile computing. *IEEE Pervasive Computing*, *8*(4), 14–23. doi:10.1109/MPRV.2009.82

Shekhar, S., & Gokhale, A. (2017) Dynamic resource management across cloud-edge resources for performance-sensitive applications. In *Proceedings of the 17th IEEE/ACM International Symposium on Cluster, Cloud and Grid Computing*. doi:10.1109/CCGRID.2017.120

Steffenel, L. A., & Kirsch-Pinheiro, M. (2015). When the cloud goes pervasive: approaches for IoT PaaS on a mobiquitous world. In *Proceedings of the EAI International Conference on Cloud, Networking for IoT systems (CN4IoT 2015)*.

Steffenel, L. A., Kirsch-Pinheiro, M., Kirsch-Pinheiro, D., & Vaz Peres, L. (2016). Using a Pervasive Computing Environment to Identify Secondary Effects of the Antarctic Ozone Hole. In *Proceedings of the 2nd Workshop on Big Data and Data Mining Challenges on IoT and Pervasive (Big2DM)*. doi:10.1016/j. procs.2016.04.215

Vaz Peres, L. (2013). *Efeito Secundário do Buraco do Ozônio Antártico Sobre o Sul do Brasil* [Msc in Meteorology dissertation]. Universidade Federal de Santa Maria, Brazil.

Vermesan, O., Friess, P., Guillemin, P., Giaffreda, R., Grindvoll, H., Eisenhauer, M., & Tragos, E. Z. et al. (2014). Internet of Things beyond the hype: Research, innovation and deployment. In *Internet of Things - From Research and Innovation to Market Deployment*. River Publishers.

Wang, W., Barnard, M., & Ying, L. (2015). Decentralized scheduling with data locality for data-parallel computation on peer-to-peer networks. In *Proceedings of the Annual Allerton Conference on Communication, Control, and Computing*, Monticello, IL. doi:10.1109/ALLERTON.2015.7447024

Wright, A. (2014). Big Data Meets Big Science. *Communications of the ACM*, *57*(7), 13–15. doi:10.1145/2617660

Wu, D., Tian, Y., & Ng, K.-W. (2005) Aurelia: Building locality-preserving overlay network over heterogeneous P2P environments. In *Proceedings of the International Conference on Parallel and Distributed Processing and Applications*. Springer.

This research was previously published in the International Journal of Information Technologies and Systems Approach (IJITSA), 11(1); edited by Manuel Mora, pages 1-15, copyright year 2018 by IGI Publishing (an imprint of IGI Global).

Chapter 7

APT:
A Practical Tunneling Architecture for Routing Scalability

Dan Jen
Center for Naval Analyses, USA

Michael Meisel
ThousandEyes, USA

Daniel Massey
Colorado State University, USA

Lan Wang
The University of Memphis, USA

Beichuan Zhang
The University of Arizona, USA

Lixia Zhang
University of California – Los Angeles, USA

ABSTRACT

The global routing system has seen a rapid increase in table size and routing changes in recent years, mostly driven by the growth of edge networks. This growth reflects two major limitations in the current architecture: (a) the conflict between provider-based addressing and edge networks' need for multihoming, and (b) flat routing's inability to provide isolation from edge dynamics. In order to address these limitations, we propose A Practical Tunneling Architecture (APT), a routing architecture that enables the Internet routing system to scale independently from edge growth. APT partitions the Internet address space in two, one for the transit core and one for edge networks, allowing edge addresses to be removed from the routing table in the transit core. Packets between edge networks are tunneled through the transit core. In order to automatically tunnel the packets, APT provides a mapping service between edge addresses and the addresses of their transit-core attachment points. We conducted an extensive performance evaluation of APT using trace data collected from routers at two major service providers. Our results show that APT can tunnel packets through the transit core by incurring extra delay on up to 0.8% of all packets at the cost of introducing only one or a few new or repurposed devices per AS.

DOI: 10.4018/978-1-5225-5649-7.ch007

INTRODUCTION

The Internet routing scalability problem reflects a fundamental limitation of the current Internet routing architecture: the use of a single, inter-domain routing space for both transit provider networks and edge sites. A natural solution is to separate these two fundamentally different types of networks into different routing spaces. As estimated by Massey et al. (2007), removing edge-site prefixes from the inter-domain routing system could reduce the global routing table size and update frequency by about one order of magnitude.

In addition to improve scalability, this separation can provide other benefits. End hosts will not be able to directly target nodes within the routing infrastructure, and this topology hiding feature will increase the difficulty of DoS (Denial of Service) and other attacks against the Internet core. Edge networks will enjoy benefits such as better traffic engineering and the ability to change providers without renumbering. The idea of separating end customer sites out of inter-domain routing first appeared in Deering (1996) and Hinden (1996), in which the scheme was named "Map & Encap": the source maps the destination address to a provider that serves the destination site, encapsulates the packet, and tunnels it to that provider. This idea started to attract attention from vendors and operators after the recent IAB report (Meyer et al., 2007) and has been actively discussed at the IRTF Routing Research Group (IRTF RRG Working Group, n.d.; Li, 2011). However, the original proposal was only an outline. It did not solve a number of important issues such as how to distribute the mapping information, how to handle failures, how to ensure security, and how to incrementally deploy the system.

In this chapter, we present *APT (A Practical Tunneling architecture)*, a design for a concrete realization of the Map & Encap scheme that addresses all of these above issues. APT uses a hybrid push-pull model to distribute mapping information, a data-driven notification mechanism to handle physical failures between edge sites and their providers, and a lightweight public-key distribution mechanism for cryptographic protection of control messages. APT can be incrementally deployed with little to no new hardware, and incurs extra delay on no more than 0.8% of all packets, according to our trace-driven evaluation.

Note that separating core and edge networks only redefines the scope of inter-domain routing; it does not change any routing protocols. Therefore, other efforts of designing scalable routing protocols, e.g., compact routing (Krioukov et al., 2007) and ROFL (Caesar et al., 2006), are orthogonal and are not affected by the change in architecture.

BACKGROUND

Since APT is a realization of the Map & Encap scheme, we begin with an explanation of how Map & Encap works.

There are two types of networks in the Internet: *transit networks* whose business role is to provide packet transport services for other networks, and *edge networks* that only function as originators or sinks of IP packets. As a rule of thumb, if the network's AS number appears in the middle of any AS path in a BGP (Rekhter et al., 2006) route today, it is considered as a transit network; otherwise it is considered as an edge network. Usually Internet Service Providers (ISPs) are transit networks and end-user sites are edge networks (e.g., corporate networks and university campus networks). The IP addresses used by transit networks are called *transit addresses* and the IP addresses used by edge networks are called *edge addresses*. The corresponding IP prefixes are called *transit prefixes* and *edge prefixes*.

Map & Encap does not change any underlying routing protocols. It changes the *scope* of routing announcing only transit prefixes into the global routing system. In other words, the inter-domain routing protocol for transit networks maintains reachability information only to transit prefixes, resulting in smaller routing tables and fewer routing updates. To deliver packets from one edge network to another, border routers between the edge networks and the core network need to tunnel the packets across the transit core, as illustrated in Figure 1. When a host in *Site1* sends a packet to a host in *Site2*, the packet first reaches *Site1*'s provider, *ISP1*. However, routers in *ISP1* cannot forward the packet directly to *Site2* since their routing tables do not have entries for any edge prefixes. Instead, *ISP1*'s border router, *BR1*, maps the destination address to *BR2*, a border router in *ISP2* that can reach *Site2*. Then the packet is encapsulated by *BR1*, tunneled through the transit core, decapsulated by *BR2* and delivered to *Site2*.

We call a border router that performs encapsulation when tunneling packets an *Ingress Tunnel Router (ITR)*, and one that performs decapsulation an *Egress Tunnel Router (ETR)*. A border router connecting a transit network to an edge network usually serves as both ITR and ETR, and can be referred to as a *Tunnel Router (TR)* in general. Internal ISP routers or routers connecting two ISPs do not need to understand the tunneling mechanism; they function the same way as they do today, only with a smaller routing table.

Related Work

There have been a number of efforts to address the scalability problem of global routing system (Li, 2011). We briefly describe these designs and highlight APT's differences in comparison.

Subramanian et al. proposed HLP (2005) to address the routing scalability problem. HLP divides the Internet routing infrastructure into many trees, each with tier-1 providers as the root. The design goal is to confine local routing instability and faults to each tree. However, as noted by the HLP designers, Internet AS connectivity does not match well to a model of non-overlapping trees. In fact, multihoming practices have been increasing rapidly over time, which stands in direct opposition to HLP's attempt to divide the routing infrastructure into separable trees. In contrast, as demonstrated in the next section (*The APT Protocol*), APT separates the transit core of the routing infrastructure from the edge networks, greatly facilitating edge multihoming.

CRIO (Zhang et al., 2006) represents another effort to address routing scalability. In order to reduce the global routing table size, CRIO proposes to aggregate otherwise non-aggregatable edge prefixes into "virtual prefixes." The routers that advertise these virtual prefixes become the proxy tunnel ends for traffic going to the prefixes they aggregate. Thus, some traffic may take a longer path.

On the operational Internet, the inherent conflict between provider-based addressing and site multihoming has long been recognized (Meyer et al., 2007). Two solutions to the problem, Map & Encap and GSE (O'Dell, 1997) were proposed more than ten years ago. Both proposals separate edge networks from the transit core in the routing system. GSE uses the low-order bytes of IPv6 addresses to represent the address space inside edge networks, and the high-order bytes for routing in the transit core. Like Map & Encap, GSE needs a mapping service to bind the two address spaces. They propose storing the mapping information in DNS. This approach avoids the need for a mapping system such as APT, but brings up a number of other issues. Zhang (2006) provides an overview of open issues with GSE, some of which are shared by any routing separation design, e.g., handling border link failures and edge-network traffic engineering, which are addressed in APT.

Since 2007, the IRTF Routing Research Group has been actively exploring the design space for a scalable Internet routing architecture and the working group has recently produced a recommendation (Li, 2011). Among the proposed solutions, a notable one is LISP (Farinacci et al., 2012). LISP defines a service interface between ITR/ETR and mapping resolvers and mapping servers, so that different mapping systems can be implemented without impacting ITR/ETR operations. The mapping system that is under active development is called LISP Alternative Topology (ALT) (Farinacci et al., 2011). Collectively LISP and ALT represent another realization of the Map & Encap scheme, which differs in a number of significant ways from APT. One difference is in mapping information distribution. APT distributes a full mapping table to every transit AS, allowing each AS to decide how many mapping servers to deploy to balance the tradeoff of cost versus performance. ALT keeps the mapping information at the originating edge networks, and builds a global hierarchy of servers to forward mapping requests and replies. Another major difference is the location of TRs: APT prefers provider-edge routers to align cost with benefit as well as facilitate incremental deployment, while LISP prefers TR deployment at customer-edge routers.

Iannone and Bonaventure (2007) reported the results of an evaluation of ITR caching performance in LISP using traffic traces collected between a university campus and its ISP. It demonstrated the effects of cache size, lifetime, and cache miss rate, and the impact on traffic. We also evaluated APT performance using data traces collected from operational networks. While Iannone and Bonaventure (2007) use data from one edge network (which is appropriate for LISP), our evaluation is based on data traces from provider-edge routers that typically serve multiple edge-network customers.

Another approach to reduce routing table size is to use compact routing, i.e., trade longer paths for less routing state. However, a recent study determined that this type of routing cannot handle routing dynamics very well (Krioukov et al., 2007).

Figure 1. Separating transit and edge networks

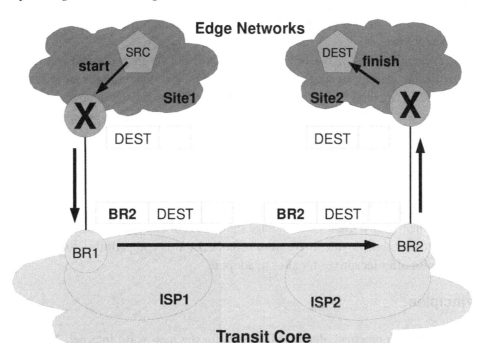

THE APT PROTOCOL

Challenges to Realization

There are a number of significant challenges that we must face when designing a practical realization of the Map & Encap scheme. These challenges define a number of tradeoffs that must be kept in careful balance when developing a concrete design.

TR Placement: In order to ensure all traffic is properly tunneled, a TR must be on the path between an edge network and its provider. Thus, we should pick the router at one end of the link connecting an edge network to its provider in the transit core. But the question is which of these two routers is more suitable for becoming a TR. From a technical standpoint, a provider-side router will generally serve many edge-side routers. As a result, there are fewer provider-side routers, but each one handles a greater quantity of traffic. From an economic standpoint, someone has to pay for the new infrastructure, but edge networks and transit networks have different incentives to do so.

Making Mapping Information Available at TRs: Mapping information describes a relationship between a transit network and an edge network, which is not necessarily known by other parties on the Internet. In order to avoid service quality degradation, it is important to minimize potential data loss and delay introduced by the extra step of retrieving this mapping information. Ideally speaking, if all mapping information were to be pushed to all ITRs, delay and loss would be minimal. However, the mapping table size would start with approximately the size of the current default-free zone (DFZ) routing table, and potentially grow quickly by one or two orders of magnitude. On the other hand, not equipping ITRs with the full mapping table would require pulling mapping information from a remote location. This implies a lookup delay, during which packets will incur additional latency and/or loss.

Scalability: Since the main goal of Map & Encap is to solve the routing scalability problem, any realization of the Map & Encap scheme must itself be scalable. Due to the high cost of deployment, any change to the Internet architecture must be designed not to merely postpone the problem, but to counteract it as best we can.

Maintaining Reliability: Today, the Internet often relies on the inter-domain routing protocol to discover failures in connectivity to edge networks. Once edge networks are removed from the transit core's routing tables, this method of discovering edge network failures will no longer be possible. Thus, a Map & Encap scheme must provide a new way to discover these failures if we intend to maintain the reliability of the current network.

Security: Mapping solution can provide new opportunities to improve network security, but can also provide new opportunities for attackers to hijack or redirect traffic. A good design should exploit the former, and provide lightweight methods to prevent the latter.

Incremental Deployment: On the Internet, one simply cannot set a flag day when all sites will switch to a new design, no matter how great an advantage the design offers. As a result, any design must explicitly assume incremental deployment. We must offer backwards compatibility for sites that are slow to adopt APT and also offer incentives for sites to adopt it.

Design Principles

We intend for APT to be a practical, deployable design for the real-world Internet. To ensure that our design meets this goal, we adhere to the following design principles.

- *Do no harm* to Internet services or service quality. Improve scalability while causing as little disruption as possible to current Internet services.
- *Align cost with benefit* by ensuring that no one is paying so that someone else can profit. We must acknowledge that the Internet infrastructure is owned and managed by a number of independent entities that operate on a for-profit model.
- *Allow flexibility* for operators to make tradeoffs between performance and resources. Different administrative domains that make up the Internet will want to make such tradeoffs in different ways, and will only deploy a new system if it is flexible enough to allow this.

How APT Works

APT places TRs at the provider-side of the link between edge networks and their providers (see Figure 2). There are two main reasons for this, derived from our design principles. First, since Map & Encap is intended to solve the routing scalability problem and release the pressure on ISP routers, it is natural that ISPs should pay the cost. This is one way in which APT aligns cost with benefit. Second, a tunnel has two ends, the ITR and the ETR. A solution should allow, but not require, both ends to be placed in the same administrative domain, such as within the network of a single ISP. This allows unilateral deployment of APT by a single ISP. Had we chosen to place TRs at the customer-side, no single edge network would be able to benefit from unilateral deployment.

To distribute mapping information, APT uses a hybrid push-pull model. All mapping information is pushed to all transit networks. However, within each transit network, only a small number of new devices called *default mappers (DMs)* store the full mapping table. ITRs store only a small cache of recently used mappings. When an ITR receives a data packet, it looks for an appropriate mapping in its cache. If such a mapping is present, it can encapsulate the packet and forward it directly to an appropriate ETR. Otherwise, it forwards the packet to a DM (the xTR is configured with the anycast address of the local DMs). The DM treats the packet as an implicit request for mapping information. In response, it sends an appropriate mapping to the requesting ITR, which stores the mapping in its cache. Meanwhile, the DM encapsulates and forwards the packet on behalf of the ITR. This process is illustrated in Figure 2.

Default mappers and tunnel routers have very different functionality. DMs are designed to manage the large mapping table, but only need to forward a relatively small amount of data traffic. This is because tunnel routers cache recent mapping results and DMs only need to handle cache misses. TRs have small routing tables, but need to forward very large volumes of traffic. This distinction will become even more prominent in the future as the Internet grows larger to include more edge networks and the traffic volume continues to increase. Since DMs and TRs are likely to be implemented in separate devices, both their hardware and software can be engineered for their specific purposes and both can scale appropriately for their specific tasks.

The association between an edge and a transit network may change due to either provider changes or border link failures. Provider changes occur when an edge network switches providers – an event that occurs in human time scale, likely measured in weeks or months. Physical failures of the links between transit and edge networks, however, can occur more frequently. In APT, only infrequent provider changes will trigger updates to the mapping table and be propagated to all transit networks. APT does not update the mapping table due to physical failures. Rather, APT takes a data-driven approach to edge-network unreachability notification. APT only informs certain senders of the failure, i.e., only those senders that are attempting to communicate with an unreachable edge network will receive the failure notification. This greatly reduces the scale of the physical failure's impacts.

Thanks for not storing the entire mapping table at every ITR, APT requires drastically less storage than a pure push model. By using data-driven local queries, APT mitigates the delay and prevents the loss associated with a pure pull model. By propagating the mapping table to all transit networks, APT allows individual networks the flexibility to manage their own mapping systems. A transit network can install more DMs to increase robustness and decrease latency, or fewer DMs to decrease the cost of deployment. By using data-driven failure notifications, APT notifies senders of edge-network unreachability while still eliminating the traffic caused by current edge-network routing updates. All of these design decisions honor our principles of doing no harm, aligning cost with benefit, and allowing for flexibility.

Default Mappers

In APT, a default mapper, or DM, performs the following functions:

- Maintaining the full mapping table. More specifically, it authenticates new mapping entries before accepting them, and removes entries that have exceeded their Lifetime value (see "Mapping Distribution Protocol").
- Propagating mapping information to other DMs in neighboring ASes. DMs in different networks peer to form a DM overlay network via which mapping information is propagated throughout the entire transit core.
- Providing local ITRs with mapping information as needed. DMs provide a central management point for local traffic engineering policies. When an ITR requests mapping information, a DM can direct traffic by deciding which ETR address to provide in response.
- Forwarding packets in the event of an ITR cache miss.
- Handling transient failures without updating the mapping table. When long-term changes such as provider changes happen, mapping table entries are updated by the originating network's operator. Routing churns, on the other hand, will not cause changes in the mapping table.

Although APT can work with just one DM in each transit AS, an AS may install multiple DMs for high robustness and load balancing, with each DM maintaining the full mapping table. To efficiently manage and communicate with multiple DMs, an AS configures an internal multicast group, *DMall*, and an internal anycast group, *DMany*. Packets sent to *DMall* will be forwarded to all of the DMs in the same AS, and any router in the AS can reach the nearest DM by sending packets to *DMany*. Thus, adding or removing DMs is transparent to other routers in the same AS.

Note that *DMany* (*DMall*) is an anycast (multicast) group local to a single AS. To prevent potential abuse, *DMany* and *DMall* are configured for internal use only. Any packet coming from outside of the AS destined to *DMany* or *DMall* will be dropped at the AS border. In the case that anycast is useful for external communication, a separate address, *DMany_ext* is set up for external use. There is no multicast group for external use. If some external information needs to reach all DMs in an AS, it is always sent to one specific DM or to *DMany_ext* for authentication and verification before being sent to *DMall*.

Mapping Information

The mapping information in APT associates each edge prefix with one or more transit addresses, each belonging to an ETR in an ISP that serves the particular edge network. The ETR must have a direct connection to the edge network owning the prefix. For example, if a university owns the address prefix a.b/16 and has two Internet service providers ISP1 and ISP2, then a.b/16 will be mapped to the ETRs in ISP1 and ISP2 that directly connect to the university network.

To support traffic engineering, APT associates two values with each ETR address: a priority and a weight. When an ITR looks up the mapping information for an edge prefix, the ETR with the highest priority is picked. When multiple addresses have the same priority, they will be used in proportion to their weight. If an edge network wants to have one provider as a primary entry point for its incoming traffic and another as a backup, it can simply assign a lower priority to the address(es) of the ETR(s) at its backup provider. If the network wants to load balance its incoming traffic between multiple providers, it can assign the same priority to multiple ETRs and use appropriate weights to split the traffic.

Mapping information for an edge prefix is generated in the following way. First, the edge network owning the prefix sends priorities and weights to each of its providers. Next, a default mapper in each provider announces a *MapSet* containing the edge prefix, its own ETR addresses for that prefix, and the edge network's priorities and weights.

Formally speaking, for an edge prefix p and its provider network N, MapSet$(p, N) = \{(d,w) \mid d$ is an ETR address in N **and** d is directly connected to p, and w is the priority and weight information for d $\}$. Note that one edge prefix may be mapped to multiple ETRs in the same provider network. If p is multihomed to m providers to m providers $N_1, N_2, ..., N_m$, MapSet$(p) = \cup_{i=1}^{m}$ MapSet(p, N_i). To distinguish MapSet(p,N) from MapSet(p), we call the former a *Provider-Specific MapSet* and the latter a *Complete MapSet*, or simply a *MapSet*. Furthermore, we use the term *MapRec* to refer to the mapping from an edge prefix to any *single* ETR address.

Data Forwarding

Recall that an edge prefix's MapSet can contain many ETR addresses. When tunneling a packet to such a prefix, one of these ETR addresses must be selected as the tunnel egress. In order to keep TRs as simple as possible, we place all ETR selection logic in default mappers, including enforcement of the MapSet's priorities and weights. This allows ITRs to avoid any decision-making when forwarding high volumes of data and allows centralization of policy decisions.

To enable this, APT ITR caches contain only MapRecs. MapRecs contain mappings from an edge prefix to a *single* ETR address. When an ITR receives a packet from an edge network, it first tries to find a MapRec matching the destination address in its cache[1]. If the lookup is successful, the packet is tunneled from the ITR to the ETR address contained in the MapRec, just like in Figure 1. When the ITR has a cache miss, it tunnels the packet to *DMany*, the anycast address of the local DMs.

ITRs also maintain a *cache idle timer (CIT)* for each MapRec in their cache. The CIT for a MapRec is reset whenever the MapRec is accessed. Once a MapRec has been idle for an amount of time greater than the CIT value, the MapRec is flushed from the ITR's cache. The CIT is important for the performance of APT under edge-network reachability failures (see "Failure Detection and Recovery").

Upon receiving a tunneled packet from a local ITR, a DM first performs a longest-prefix match in its mapping table to find the MapSet for the destination address. It then selects one ETR address from the MapSet based on the priority, the weight value, and local policy. The DM then creates a MapRec and sends it to the ITR who sent the data packet. Other than the edge prefix and selected ETR address, the MapRec contains a CIT value assigned by the DM. Finally, the DM tunnels the packet to the selected ETR address, with the tunnel source address set to the original ITR.

Until the ITR receives the DM's response, it will continue to forward packets with the same destination prefix to the DM. The DM will continue to forward these packets, but will suppress duplicate control messages to the ITR using a *Deaf Timer* for the (ITR, edge prefix) pair. It will retransmit the MapRec only when the timer expires.

To illustrate the above process, Figure 2 shows a simple topology, where *Site1* and *Site2* are two edge networks, each owning edge prefix P_1 and P_2, respectively. *ISP1*, *ISP2* and *ISP3* are transit networks. A node in *Site1* sends a packet to a node in *Site2*. When this packet arrives at *ITR1*, it looks up the destination address *d* in its MapRec cache. There is no matching prefix, so *ITR1* sends the packet to a default mapper (*M1* in this case) by encapsulating the packet with *DMany* (*ISP1*) as the destination address. When this packet arrives at *M1*, it decapsulates the packet and performs a longest-prefix match in its mapping table using the destination address *d*. Since *d* matches the prefix P_2, it will find the MapSet for P_2 containing *ETR1* and *ETR2*. *M1* selects *ETR1* based on the priority value, responds to *ITR1* with a MapRec that maps P_2 to *ETR1*, and then encapsulates the packet with *ETR1* as the destination address and sends it out.

Figure 2. Example topology for data forwarding

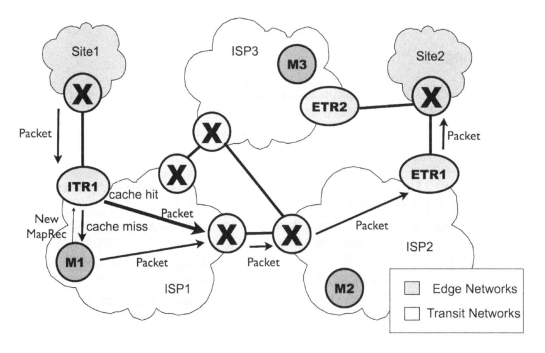

Failure Detection and Recovery

In today's Internet, edge networks achieve higher reliability through multihoming. When connectivity to one provider fails, packets can be routed through other providers. Today, when such a connectivity failure occurs, this information is pushed into the global routing table via BGP. In APT, edge network connectivity is reflected in a mapping table that does not adjust to physical failures. Thus, an ITR may attempt to tunnel packets to an ETR that has failed or has lost connectivity to the edge network. APT must be able to detect such failures and route the affected traffic through an alternate ETR. Generally speaking, there are three types of failures that APT must handle:

1. The transit prefix that contains the ETR has become unreachable.
2. The ETR itself has become unreachable.
3. The ETR cannot deliver packets to the edge network. This can be due to a failure of the link to its neighboring device in the edge network, or a failure of the neighboring device itself.

Handling Transit Prefix Failures: An ITR will not necessarily be able to route traffic to all transit prefixes at all times. If an ITR attempts to tunnel a packet to an ETR in a transit prefix that it cannot currently reach, it treats this situation much like a cache miss and forwards the packet to a local default mapper. In Figure 3, *ITR1* has no route to *ETR1*, so it will forward the packet to its default mapper, *M1*. In its forwarding table, *M1* will also see that it has no route to *ETR1*, and thus select the next-most-preferred ETR for *Site2*, *ETR2*. Then *M1* tunnels the packet to *ETR2* and replies to *ITR1* with the corresponding MapRec. *M1* can assign a relatively short CIT to the MapRec in its response. Once this CIT expires, *ITR1* will forward the next packet destined for *Site2* to a default mapper, which will respond with the

Figure 3. An example of a transit prefix failure

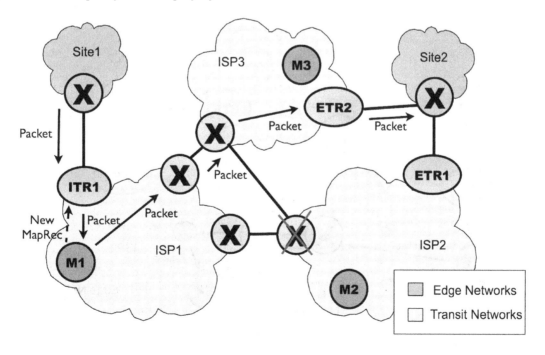

most-preferred MapRec that is routable at that time. This allows *ITR1* to quickly revert to using *ETR1* once *ETR1* becomes reachable again.

Handling ETR Failures: When an ETR fails, packets heading to that ETR are redirected to a local DM in the ETR's transit network. This redirection is achieved through the intra-domain routing protocol (IGP); each DM in a transit network announces a high-cost link to all of the ETRs it serves. When an ETR fails, the normal IGP path to the ETR will no longer be valid, causing packets addressed to the ETR to be forwarded to a DM. The DM will attempt to find an alternate ETR for the destination prefix using its mapping table and tunnel the packet to that ETR.[2] The DM also sends an *ETR Unreachable Message* to the ITR's DM, informing the ITR's DM that the failed ETR is temporarily unusable. How the ETR's DM determines the ITR's DM address will be discussed in the following section.

To avoid sending the address of an unreachable ETR to any subsequently requesting ITRs, default mappers also store a *Time Before Retry (TBR)* timer for each ETR address in a MapSet. Normally, the TBR timer for each ETR is set to zero, indicating that it is usable. When an ETR becomes unreachable due to a failure, its TBR timer is set to a non-zero value. The DM will not send this ETR address to any ITR until the TBR timer expires. We will refer to the action of setting a MapRec's TBR to a non-zero value as "invalidating a MapRec."

In Figure 4, traffic entering *ISP2* destined for *ETR1* should be directed to *M2*, the default mapper in *ISP2*, according to *ISP2*'s IGP. When *M2* receives such a data packet, *M2* will tunnel the packet to *ETR2*, and notify *M1*, the default mapper in *ISP1*, of *ETR1*'s failure by sending an ETR Unreachable Message to *DMany_ext(Site1)*, the external anycast address for *ISP1*'s DMs (obtained via the Mapping Distribution Protocol). M1 can then send a new MapRec containing ETR2 to ITR1. Similar to the previous case, the CIT for this MapRec will be relatively short.

Figure 4. An example of a single ETR failure

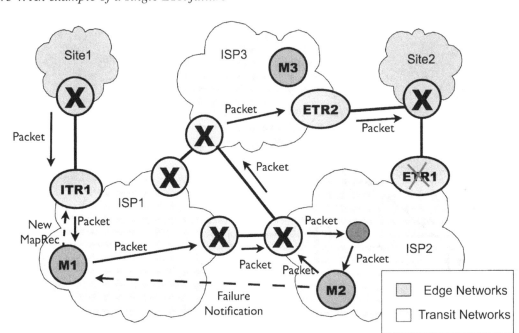

Handling Edge Network Reachability Failures: The final case involves a failure of the link connecting an ETR to its neighbor in an edge network or the failure of the neighbor itself. This case is handled similarly to the previous case, except that the message sent to the ITR's default mapper will be of a different type, *Edge Network Unreachable*. In Figure 5, when *ETR1* discovers it cannot reach *Site2*, it will send packets destined for *Site2* to its DM, *M2*, setting the *Redirect Flag* when encapsulating the packet. The Redirect Flag signals to *M2* that the packet could not be delivered and should be re-routed. *M2* will redirect the packet to *ETR2* and then send an Edge Network Unreachable Message to *M1*.

Mapping Distribution Protocol

Making mapping information available to ITRs is one of the most important challenges in realizing a Map & Encap scheme. APT adopts a hybrid push-pull approach: it pushes the mapping information to DMs in all transit networks, but lets ITRs pull the mapping information from DMs.

DM Mesh: In APT, mapping information is distributed via a mesh of overlay connections between DMs. These overlay connections are configured manually based on contractual agreement, just as how links are set up in BGP. Two neighboring APT ASes should establish at least one DM-DM connection between them. They can also choose to have multiple DM-DM connections for reliability. An AS can configure one or multiple DMs to connect to external DMs, but it is not required that all of its DMs have external connections. The DMs that have external connections will forward incoming mapping information to their local *DMall* group, from which DMs without external connections will learn the mapping information.

Having the DM Mesh congruent to the AS topology facilitates incremental deployment and aligns maintenance and setup cost with benefit. Mapping information is just a small amount of additional data

Figure 5. An example of a failure of the link connecting an ETR to its edge network

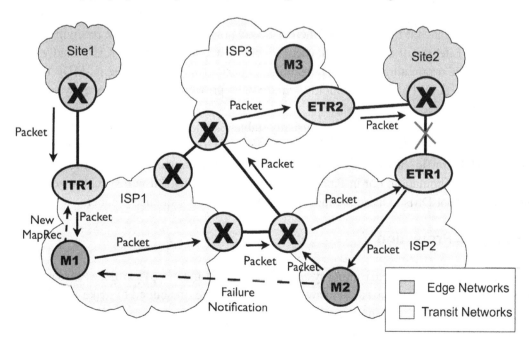

transmitted between two neighboring ASes that already have a contractual agreement for exchanging traffic. Since mapping exchange is bi-directional, it should benefit both parties equally. This means that both parties have incentives to maintain the connection well and fix any problems quickly.

The Dissemination Protocol: DMs exchange MDP messages using an OSPF-style flooding protocol, without the topology and path computation parts of OSPF. An MDP message has a header and a payload. Different payload types are supported. For mapping dissemination, the payload is provider-specific MapSets and the provider's *DMany_ext* address. For security purposes, MDP is also used to propagate public keys and prefix lists for provider networks, which will be discussed below.

A DM originates MDP messages to push its own provider-specific MapSets to other provider networks. For instance, a customer network with prefix p is dual-homed through providers X and Y. Provider X's DM(s) would generate an MDP message containing *MapSet(p,X)* and *DMany_ext(X)* and send this message to its neighboring DMs. After this message propagates throughout the transit core, DMs in other networks will know the addresses of the ETRs in X's network via which prefix p can be reached. In case they need to send feedback information to X, they will use the address *DMany_ext(X)* to reach X's DMs. Similarly, provider Y will announce *MapSet(p,Y)* and its own *DMany_ext(Y)*. After receiving the provider-specific MapSets *MapSet(p,X)* and *MapSet(p,Y)*, DMs combine them to get the complete MapSet for prefix p, including ETRs from both networks X and Y. Putting all MapSets together, a DM gets the complete mapping table to reach all edge prefixes.

The header of an MDP message contains control information necessary for efficient data dissemination. It includes (1) the AS number of the originator of the message, (2) a sequence number, and (3) a Lifetime. The combination of the AS number and the sequence number uniquely identifies a message. It is used by a receiver to determine whether an incoming message is new. The Lifetime is used to make sure an outdated message will expire at certain time.

When a DM receives an MDP message from a neighboring DM, it will check whether this is a new message and make sure that the message has a Lifetime greater than one. Outdated, expired, or duplicate messages will be dropped. Accepted messages will be forwarded to all neighboring DMs except the one from which the message was received. Message transmission is acknowledged at every hop. The sending DM will retransmit the message if there is no acknowledgment from the receiving DM within certain time. The Lifetime of a received Mapset is decremented as time goes by. Eventually, a MapSet will expire. It is the originating DM's responsibility to periodically re-generate its MDP messages to refresh other DMs. A DM can also explicitly withdraw its previous announcements by sending out a withdrawal message onto the DM mesh.

Since customer-provider relationships are usually stable for at least a month due to contractual obligations, the message Lifetime and the refresh frequency can be set to the scale of days or weeks, which mean the volume of MDP traffic should be easily manageable. Other techniques in OSPF are also incorporated to help efficient dissemination. For instance, every time a DM reboots, it will synchronize its mapping table with its neighbor DMs to learn the most recent MapSets and sequence numbers.

Cryptographic Protection

While our design makes the global routing system more scalable and more flexible, we also need to make sure its security is not compromised. In answering this challenge, we intend to make APT as secure as the current Internet at least, making improving where practical.

APT adds new control messages that attackers could forge to manipulate packet forwarding. This constitutes a major security threat. For instance, a forged failover notification message could prevent ITRs from using certain ETRs, and a forged MapRec or MapSet could divert large quantities of traffic to arbitrary ETRs.

In APT, we add cryptographic protection to all control messages. We assume that every transit network has its own public-private key pair and signs all APT control messages that it generates. Receivers verify the signature before accepting a message. As in many other large scale systems, the main challenge in enabling cryptographic protection is how to distribute public keys in the first place. APT does not rely on a Public Key Infrastructure (PKI) for key distribution, since a PKI would require a significant amount of effort and coordination among all transit networks. The slow progress or lack of progress in deploying PKI-based solutions in the Internet (e.g., DNSSEC (Arends et al., 2005) and SBGP (Kent et al., 2000)) suggests the need for an alternative that does not require a rigid delegation infrastructure.

Key Distribution: APT employs the DM Mesh to propagate every transit network's public key to all other networks in the transit core. To prevent attackers from forging someone else's public key, we require that every network have its neighbors verify and sign its key. For instance, if X has two neighbors, Y and Z, then X should have both neighbors verify X's public key and sign it. X will announce its key together with Y and Z's signatures through the DM Mesh. Similarly, X will also vouch for Y and Z's public keys.

Once every network announces its own key together with its neighbors' signatures, this information forms a web of trust, which a receiver can use to determine whether to trust a public key. For instance, assume X already trusts the public keys of networks Z and R. If X receives a message carrying W's public key and signatures from Z and R, then X can verify these signatures. If the two signatures indeed belong to Z and R, respectively, X will trust this message, record W's public key, and forward the message to its peers. Each network can configure its threshold for trusting a key, as long as this threshold is greater than one. Later, X can also use W's signature to verify other messages. If an attacker announces a false public key for W, he will not be able to forge the signatures of Z and R. In this case, X will discard the attacker's forged key.

Neighbor signatures are done when two neighbor ASes configure their DM connections. They verify the keys and signatures offline. Keys have a finite time-to-live after which they will expire. Keys can be replaced or revoked via a Rollover message or a Withdrawal message, respectively. These messages are signed by the old keys as well as the new keys if there are any. ASes should periodically rollover their keys, obtaining signatures from their neighbors for the new keys.

Attack Detection: Recall that APT adds cryptographic protection to all control messages. If private keys are compromised or networks misbehave, they can pose security threats that signatures cannot prevent. For instance, a misbehaving network, due to either operational errors or malicious acts, may inject mapping information for prefixes belonging to other networks, effectively hijacking other's traffic. This problem exists in the current Internet. In APT, we take advantage of the DM mesh and the flooding protocol to quickly detect such incidents, which is a significant improvement over the current Internet.

In APT, edge networks do not participate in the mapping dissemination process. However, they can still check the correctness of their mapping information by setting up an MDP monitoring session with their providers.[3] MDP ensures that a message will reach every provider network without changes. If there is an announcement of a false mapping for some edge prefix, the transit network(s) legitimately associated with that edge prefix will receive the message. Yet, since each provider only announces its own provider-specific MapSet, it cannot know whether another provider-specific MapSet for the same edge prefix is legitimate. A rogue network announcing a forged provider-specific MapSet for the same edge prefix would go undetected. Thus, the burden of detecting false announcements falls on edge networks. If the edge network is monitoring MDP messages, it can quickly detect the false announcement and take action. If the edge network is not monitoring MDP messages, the situation is no worse than it is today. In the current Internet, edge prefixes are announced in BGP. BGP is a path-vector routing protocol, which does not propagate every announcement everywhere. If a prefix is hijacked, the real owner of the prefix may not receive the false announcement, and the attack will go undetected.

A serious attack that a rogue network can launch is to map a large number of edge prefixes to a single ETR. This would redirect a large amount of traffic to that ETR, effectively constituting a distributed denial-of-service (DDoS) attack. To prevent this, DMs sign and announce the list of their own transit prefixes in MDP, propagating the message to every transit network. Receivers can verify the signature and record the list of transit prefixes. To understand how this prevents the aforementioned type of DDoS attack, assume X announces the transit prefix containing ETR e, which is verified and accepted by all other transit networks. If rogue AS Z attempts to map edge prefixes $a/8$ and $b/8$ to e, other transit networks can detect that Z does not own the transit prefix containing e, and will reject the false mapping information.

If Z tries to defeat this scheme by signing and announcing one of X's prefixes in MDP, it will be quickly detected by X. Other networks will detect this conflict as well. They can use past history to help decide which announcement to trust before the problem is resolved. If a network has trusted X's announcement for a long time in the past, it can continue to trust X until the conflict is resolved, likely due to actions X will take.

Evaluation

In this section, we present an evaluation of APT's feasibility using real traffic traces. Whether APT is feasible depends on its data delivery performance and hardware requirements, which in turn are affected by traffic characteristics, since APT uses a data-driven approach to pull mapping information from DMs. We therefore used data-driven simulation to evaluate the packet delay introduced by caching at ITRs, the cache size at ITRs, and the amount of data traffic redirected to DMs. Below, we first describe our simulator and data sources, and then present our results.

The TR Cache Simulator: The cache hit rate at ITRs is critical to overall APT performance. A high hit rate will ensure that few packets will experience redirection delay and each default mapper can serve multiple TRs without being overburdened. To evaluate the TR cache hit rate, and therefore the load placed on default mappers, we simulated TR caching using traces from real provider-edge (PE) routers. We used a number of different cache and network parameters to determine their effect on the cache hit rate.

Our cache simulator examines destination address d of each packet in a traffic trace and attempts to perform a longest-prefix-match lookup of d in its prefix cache, C. If a match is found, this is counted as a cache hit. If no match is found, this is counted as a cache miss and a new cache entry is added for d after a certain delay. The delay is a configurable parameter used to emulate the round-trip time between the ITR and a DM. The prefix used for the new cache entry is determined by a real BGP routing table. This is feasible only when the address d is not anonymized. Otherwise, the simulator uses $d/24$ as the prefix. Note that we are underestimating our cache performance in the latter case, as most prefixes in the BGP routing table are shorter than/24. In reality, we could use a smaller cache and have a lower miss rate.

A maximum cache size m can also be specified. If there is a cache miss when C already contains m entries, the least-recently used prefix is removed from C before the new cache entry is added. Prefixes can optionally be removed from *C* once they have remained inactive for a specified interval of time, or cache inactivity timeout (CIT).

Data Sources: We ran the simulator on packet-level traces from two real PE routers.

*FRG:*This trace was collected at the FrontRange Gigapop in Colorado. It consists of all traffic outbound to a tier-1 ISP during the period 09:00 to 21:00, Mountain Standard Time, on November 7, 2007. In our analysis, we used a list of actual prefixes retrieved from the RIBs at RouteViews Oregon, also on November 7, 2007. When using a limited-size cache with this data set, the maximum size was 4,096 entries, less than ten percent of the total number of prefixes seen in the trace (52,502).

*CERNET:*This trace was collected at Tsinghua University in Beijing, China. It consists of all traffic outbound from the university through a particular PE router into the CERNET backbone from 09:00 to 21:00, China Standard Time, on January 23, 2008. This data was anonymized using a prefix-preserving method before analysis, so, though addresses remain in the same prefix after anonymization, they cannot be mapped to a real BGP prefix list. Instead, every prefix is assumed to be a/24. This provides us with a worst-case estimate, assuming/24 continues to be the longest prefix length allowed in the network. Since this results in a significantly larger number of total prefixes in the trace (985,757), we used a larger maximum when simulating a limited cache size: 65,536.

Results: In our simulations, we used four different combinations of cache size and CIT value. The cache size was either unlimited or an order of magnitude smaller than the total number of prefixes seen in the trace. The CIT value was either infinity or 30 minutes. During each run, the simulator emulated four different latencies for retrieving mapping information from a default mapper: zero (an instantaneous cache add), 10ms, 30ms, and 50ms. We selected 50ms as our worst-case delay based on (AT&T) and (Keynote Systems), which show that a single, carefully placed default mapper in the network of most tier-1 ISPs in the United States would be reachable from any hypothetical TR in that network within approximately 50ms.

Table 1 shows cumulative cache miss rates. "Optimal" refers to a cache with unlimited size and an infinite CIT. "With CIT" refers to a cache with unlimited size and a CIT of 30 minutes. "With Limit" refers to a cache with limited size and a CIT of infinity or 30 minutes – the results are the same regardless of the CIT value. This suggests that entries are replaced before their CIT timer expires. Only the best and worst case delays (zero and 50 ms) are shown.

We can make the following two observations. First, the miss rate is well below 1% in all cases. In other words, less than 1% of the traffic was redirected to the local DM. The worst case miss rate is 0.810% for the CERNET data set with a fixed cache-size limit and 50ms delay to receive new mappings. As stated above, we predicted this data set to be a worst case based on our use of/24 prefixes for all addresses.

Table 1. Cumulative cache miss rates for both data sets with three different cache types and best- and worst-case default-mapper latencies.

Data Source	% Miss Rate					
FRG	0.001	0.002	0.004	0.005	0.537	0.687
CERNET	0.054	0.059	0.198	0.207	0.756	0.810
Delay (ms)	0	50	0	50	0	50
Type	Optimal		With CIT		With Limit	

Figure 6. ITR cache size (FRG). The first data point was sampled two minutes into the trace.

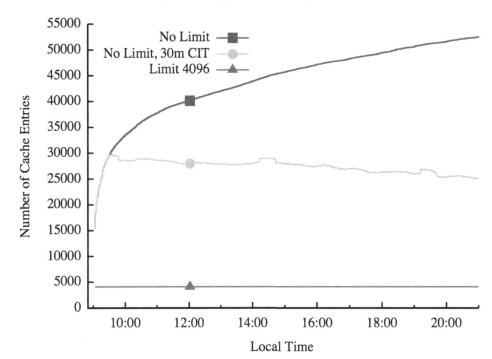

Figure 7. Default mapper load (FRG). The first data point was sampled two minutes into the trace.

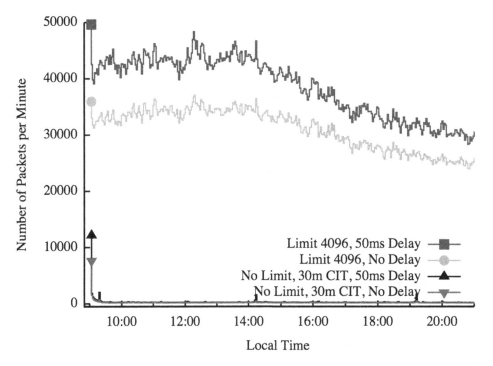

Second, a 50 ms delay in adding new cache entries had a mostly negligible effect on the miss rate, compared with no delay. One explanation is that the inter-packet delay for initial packets to the same destination prefix is longer than 50 ms most of the time. This is plausible considering that initial packets are usually for TCP connection setup or DNS lookup, which takes one round-trip time before the next packet is sent.

These results suggests that moving the mapping table from the ITRs to a local DM has negligible impact on overall performance, providing strong support for our design decisions.

Figure 6 shows cache sizes in number of entries and Figure 7 shows the number of packets that would be forwarded to a default mapper per minute, both for the FRG data set. We omit the figures for CERNET, as they are similar to those for FRG.

Two things are apparent from these results. First of all, latency between TR and default mapper has a minimal or, in most cases, undetectable effect on the default mapper load. This is consistent with our earlier results on cache miss rate.

Second of all, the packet-forwarding burden placed on default mappers is quite manageable. Even a TR at a high-traffic, provider-edge router would place a load on the default mapper of less than 1,000 packets per minute in the normal case with a cache size above 30,000 entries. In a more extreme case where such a TR had only a 4,096-entry capacity, the load placed on the default mapper would still be under 50,000 packets per minute. Using this data, we can make a conservative estimate of the number of TRs that a single default mapper can support. Assuming the worst case from our simulations of 50,000 redirected packets per minute per TR, even a default mapper running on commodity 2001 PC hardware would have enough forwarding capability to support hundreds of TRs (Morris et al., 1999).

Incremental Deployment

On the Internet, one simply cannot set a flag day when all sites will switch to a new design, no matter how great an advantage the design offers. As a result, APT explicitly assumes incremental deployment. Our design offers incentives for sites that adopt APT. An APT-capable ISP will be able to reduce the routing table size in its internal routers. Moreover, our design allows backwards compatibility for sites that are slow to adopt APT by converting mapping information in APT networks to BGP routes that can be used by legacy networks.

Before we delve into the details, we define the following terms. If a transit AS has adopted APT, it is called an *APT AS*. Otherwise, it is called a *non-APT AS*. A topologically connected set of APT ASes form an *APT island*. Note that our design allows individual ISPs to deploy APT unilaterally, without any coordination with other ASes. Such an ISP would simply form a new APT island. Unconnected APT islands do not exchange mapping information with each other.

Edge Networks: APT offers various incentives for edge networks to use APT providers. The Map N Encap solution allows all edge networks to use provider-independent addressing, which eliminates forced renumbering due to provider change, and also eases multihoming. In addition, APT mappings are a powerful tool for traffic engineering. Currently, an edge network may use AS-path padding or address de-aggregation for load balancing. However, these techniques provide only rudimentary control over which route is selected by a traffic source. In APT, an edge network can clearly specify traffic preferences among all of its APT providers. This explicit approach to managing inbound traffic greatly simplifies existing practices and achieves more effective results.

These benefits come at minimal to no cost for edge networks. Because the APT design focuses on placing new functionality in transit networks, all changes go virtually unnoticed by edge networks. The only new task for an edge network is to provide traffic preference information to its providers. If necessary, a transit provider can generate this traffic engineering information on behalf of its edge-network customers, and APT can be incrementally deployed *without any changes* to edge networks.

Transit Networks: All transit ASes will continue to use BGP to reach transit prefixes, even if all of them adopt APT. Edge prefixes are handled differently. APT islands configure their border routers as TRs so that their customers' data packets will be encapsulated and decapsulated as they enter and exit the AS. An APT island can then remove all customer edge prefixes from their BGP routing tables.

APT ASes must still allow their customers to interact with the rest of the existing system. To explain how this is done, we must answer three questions:

What information do APT ASes use to reach their customer edge prefixes? Inside an APT island, the APT ASes exchange mapping information with each other (see "Mapping Distribution Protocol"). This allows their default mappers to maintain a mapping information table for the entire island. We will call this the *island mapping table*.

How can an APT AS reach edge prefixes served by non-APT ASes? All transit ASes will continue to use BGP to reach those edge prefixes connected to non-APT ASes. Note the following differences from the current Internet: (a) APT ASes do not run BGP sessions with their customer networks in edge address space, and (b) the BGP routing tables maintained by routers in APT ASes do not contain those edge prefixes that are already in the island mapping table (unless a prefix is connected to both an APT AS and a non-APT AS.

How can an edge network connected to a non-APT AS reach an edge prefix connected to an APT AS? APT ASes at the border of an APT island must advertise the edge prefixes in their island mapping table to their non-APT neighbors via BGP.

An APT island grows larger by connecting one of its DMs to a DM in another APT island. When two APT islands merge, their island mapping tables merge into a single, larger island mapping table. As a result, each router in the merged island can remove the island mapping table prefixes from their BGP tables, offsetting the increase in mapping table size. Furthermore, the increase in mapping table size will affect only a small set of devices (default mappers), while essentially all routers can benefit from the reduction in BGP table size. As the APT island grows, the BGP tables of the island routers will continue to shrink, providing incentive for non-APT ASes to join the island (and for APT islands to merge). APT providers can also offer their customers all of the benefits mentioned above.

Interoperation Under Partial Deployment: We now describe how to enable communication between APT and non-APT networks, or between two different islands, using the topology in Figure 8. Suppose edge network *Site1* is a customer of *ISP1*, and thus is a part of *APT Island 1*. *Site3* and *Site4* are customers of *ISP3* and *ISP4* respectively. They are part of *APT Island 2*. *Site2* is a customer of *ISP2*, which is a non-APT network. *Site3* is also a customer of *ISP2*.

How can a non-APT site like *Site2* reach an APT site, such as *Site1*? Recall that *Site1*'s prefixes are not in the BGP tables of any router in *APT Island 1*, but they *are* in the *APT Island 1* mapping table. Thus, ISPs at the border of Island 1 need to convert the mapping information for *Site1* into a BGP route and inject it into non-APT networks. Since default mappers maintain a complete island mapping table, they can do the conversion – the converted BGP route will contain only the announcing DM's own AS number (the AS where traffic will enter the island) and *ISP1* (the AS where traffic will exit the island towards *Site1*). In addition, if *Site1* has an AS number, its AS number will appear at the end of the BGP

Figure 8. Example topology for incremental deployment

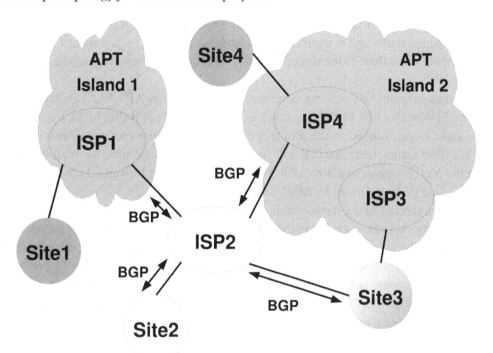

path in order to be consistent with current BGP path semantics. The details of the path taken within the APT island are not relevant to the BGP routers in the legacy system. DMs will advertise these routes to their networks' non-APT neighbors in accordance with routing policies. Eventually, *Site2* will receive the BGP route to *Site1*. These APT BGP announcements will include a unique community tag X so that other BGP speakers in *APT Island 1* can ignore them.

The above works fine for sites whose providers are all from the same APT island, but what about sites that multihome with ISPs both inside and outside of the island? To support this type of multihoming, we require that all APT routers check their BGP tables *before* attempting to encapsulate a packet. Otherwise, packets would always route through APT providers to the destination site, never using the non-APT provider. Furthermore, the DMs at island border ISPs will still announce these sites' prefixes into BGP, but will tag these announcements with a unique community tag Y(different from X) telling other BGP speakers in the island that the destination sites are multihomed to ASes inside and outside the island. Note that Y must differ from X. BGP announcements with community tag X can be ignored by non-DM routers in the APT Island. However, announcements with community tag Y cannot be ignored by island nodes.[4]

To see how these requirements support the above multihoming, we will go through an example. In Figure 8, *Site3* multihomes with an APT AS(*ISP3*) as well as a non-APT AS(*ISP2*). Thus *Site3* will have 2 types of routes announced into BGP – a traditional BGP route announced by *ISP2*, and an injected BGP route announced by APT ISPs at the border of *APT Island 2*. The injected BGP route will include a unique community tag Y telling other BGP speakers in *APT Island 2* that *Site3* is multihomed to ASes inside and outside *APT Island 2*. Receivers of the announcements will choose one route to store in their loc-RIB, using standard BGP route selection. When a border router in *APT Island 2* receives packets destined to *Site3*, it first checks its BGP table *before* looking in its cache. It will find one of the 2 BGP routes in its loc-RIB. It then checks the route community attribute value. If the value is Y, then it knows the route is an injected route, and it attempts to encapsulate the packet via standard APT practices. If the value is anything other than Y, the router does not encapsulate the packet and routes the packet via standard BGP.

We now explain how an APT site can communicate with an non-APT site. For example, how can *Site1* reach *Site2*? When an ITR in *ISP1* receives a packet from *Site1*, it first looks for the prefix in its BGP routing table (as mentioned in the previous example). Since the prefixes of non-APT ASes are stored in a TR's BGP routing table, the ITR will find a match, check the route's community attribute, and discover that the prefix belongs to a non-APT AS. The packet is then forwarded toward the destination using the forwarding table generated by BGP.

How do two unconnected APT islands communicate with each other? In our figure, *Site4* is a customer of *ISP4*, an APT network, but *ISP4* is not in the same island as *Site1*'s provider, *ISP1* (i.e. there are some non-APT networks in between). Unconnected APT islands do not exchange mapping information with each other, so *Site4*'s prefixes will not be in *APT Island 1*'s mapping table, and *Site1*'s prefixes will not be in *APT Island 2*'s mapping table. However, the two islands will still receive each other's BGP routes injected using the method described previously. As a result, *Site1* will communicate with *Site4* just as it would with the customer of a non-APT network using BGP routing information, and vice versa.

Routing Policy and Mapping

As previously noted, the inter-domain routing protocol is outside the scope of the APT design. If APT were deployed on the current Internet, BGP would continue to serve this purpose. In other words, BGP will still be used to find paths between ITRs and ETRs that are in different ASes.

However, an ETR is a necessary hop in any APT routing path, but multihomed destinations have more than one ETR to choose from. Therefore, APT ETR selection can have an effect on routing paths. In this section, we intend to clarify how APT can affect BGP routing paths, and what kinds of policies are both possible and necessary to support in APT to maintain the flexibility of current routing policy.

One might believe that there are three situations in which policy can be applied to mapping information in APT: (1) When a provider-specific MapSet is created, (2) when a default mapper selects an ETR from a MapSet, and (3) when propagating MapSets to other transit networks. However, APT chooses to make policy applied in situation 1 take first priority and use situation 2 only to break ties. We believe that source-specific mappings are too expensive to support; they would defeat our hybrid push-pull approach. Therefore, APT negates the usefulness of situation 3.

To understand why, consider the following. Since the path taken by a BGP update determines the path of data flow, the path of each BGP update must be carefully managed through policy. This is not the case for MapSet announcements. MapSets do not change based on the path by which they are propagated. In fact, APT guarantees this – any modification made to a MapSet during propagation will cause signature verification to fail and propagation to end. Furthermore, it is in the interest of the party owning an ITR, or sending party, to have access to *all* MapSets in the network. This will allow the sending party to provide the most robust service to their customers.

The result is that applying policy along the path via which a MapSet is propagated will not have any desirable effect. For example, assume, for the sake of argument, we used a policy-rich protocol, such as BGP, for MapSet update propagation. Accordingly, some transit network *X* withholds an update for some MapSet *m* from their peer *Y*. *Y* wants to receive all updates for all MapSets, so *Y* simply peers with *Z*, who *is* willing to send updates for *m*. The MapSet updates for *m* that *Y* receives from *Z* are *identical* to the updates that it would have received from *X*, were *X* willing to forward them. Therefore, all that *X* has accomplished by withholding MapSet updates from *Y* is to force *Y* to find an additional peer. More importantly, *X*'s application of policy does not have any effect on the routing paths between *X* and *Y*. This is due to the fact that the method by which *Y* selects an ETR for any given destination edge address is entirely unrelated to the method by which it received the corresponding MapSet.

CONCLUSION

In this chapter, we have presented a practical design for a new tunneling architecture to solve the routing scalability problem. APT deploys default mappers in transit networks to maintain the full table of mappings from edge prefixes to the addresses of their transit providers, so that data packets can be tunneled over the transit core. The DMs form a mesh congruent to the underlying network topology and use the mesh to flood mapping information. To secure mapping data distribution and all control messages, DMs cryptographically sign messages and use a novel scheme based on neighbor signatures to distribute public keys. To minimize control overhead, data delay, and data loss, APT adopts a data-driven approach to handle cache misses at ITRs as well as temporary unreachability of ETRs; data packets are used both to signal DMs to provide mapping information to ITRs and to allow DMs to forward these data packets in the meantime.

Looking at the bigger picture, APT necessarily brings additional complexity into the Internet architecture. Thus, a question naturally arises: why is it necessary to change the existing routing architecture?

We believe the answer lies in the fact that the Internet has grown by orders of magnitude. In an article by J. B. S. Haldane, "Being the right size" (Haldane, 1928), the author illustrated the relationship between the size and complexity of biological entities using a vivid example. As stated in the article, "a typical small animal, say a microscopic worm or rotifer, has a smooth skin through which all the oxygen it requires can soak in." However, "increase its dimensions tenfold in every direction, and its weight is increased a thousand times, so ... it will need a thousand times as much food and oxygen per day. Now if its shape is unaltered its surface will be increased only a hundredfold, and ten times as much oxygen must enter per minute through each square millimeter of skin." This is why every large animal has a lung, an organ specialized for soaking up oxygen. The author concludes that, "for every type of animal there is a most convenient size, and a large change in size inevitably carries with it a change of form." It would be unimaginable for small insects to have lungs. On the other hand, it is also impossible for big animals to live without lungs.

Table 2.

Mapping Distribution	Push from origin network to all ASes, pull from ITRs from local DMs.
Mapping Security	Sign each mapping entry; distribute keys over the DM mesh.
Failure Handling	Redirect packets to DMs to find alternative ETRs to use.
Deployment	Incrementally deployable and can interoperate with legacy networks.

In the case of the Internet, the existing architecture, where all autonomous systems live in the same routing space, was designed more than a decade ago when the Internet was very small in size. Today, not only has the Internet grown beyond its designers' wildest imaginations, but the goals of individual networks have diverged. Edge networks are multihomed for enhanced reliability and performance, while ISPs are specialized for high-performance, yet economical, packet delivery service. The different goals of different parties have brought different and conflicting requirements to the shared address and routing space. Thus, the original architecture can no longer meet the functional requirements of today's grown-up Internet. A new routing architecture is needed to accommodate the growth of the Internet and the differentiation of individual networks, and APT is exactly such an attempt.

REFERENCES

Arends, R., Austein, R., Larson, M., Massey, D., & Rose, S. (2005). Internet engineering task force. *DNS Security Introduction and Requirements*. AT&T. (n.d.). *U.S. network latency*. Retrieved from http://ipnetwork.bgtmo.ip.att.net/pws/network_delay.html

Brim, S., Chiappa, N., Farinacci, D., Fuller, V., Lewis, D., & Meyer, D. (2008). *LISP-CONS: A content distribution overlay network service for LISP*. Retrieved from http://tools.ietf.org/html/draft-fuller-lisp-cons-04

Caesar, M., Condie, T., Kannan, J., Lakshminarayanan, K., Stoica, I., & Shenker, S. (2006). ROFL: Routing on Flat Labels. In *Proc. of the ACM SIGCOMM*.

Deering, S. (1996, March). *The map & encap scheme for scalable IPv4 routing with portable site prefixes*. Presented at Xerox PARC.

Farinacci, D., Fuller, V., & Meyer, D. (2011). *LISP alternative topology (LISP-ALT)*. Retrieved from http://tools.ietf.org/html/draft-fuller-lisp-alt-10

Farinacci, D., Fuller, V., Oran, D., & Meyer, D. (2012). *Locator/ID separation protocol (LISP)*. Retrieved from http://tools.ietf.org/html/draft-farinacci-lisp-23

Fuller, V., & Farinacci, D. (2012). *LISP map server interface*. Retrieved from http://tools.ietf.org/html/draft-ietf-lisp-ms-16

Haldane, J. B. S. (1928). *Being the right size*. Retrieved on May 12, 2008, from http://irl.cs.ucla.edu/papers/right-size.html

Hinden, R. (1996). *RFC 1955: New scheme for internet routing and addressing (ENCAPS) for IPNG*. Retrieved from http://tools.ietf.org/html/rfc1955

Iannone, L., & Bonaventure, O. (2007). On the cost of caching locator/ID mappings. In *Proceedings of the CoNext Conference*.

IRTF RRG Working Group. (n.d.). *Website*. Retrieved from http://www.irtf.org/charter?gtype=rg&group=rrg

Kent, S., Lynn, C., & Seo, K. (2000). Secure border gateway protocol. *IEEE Journal on Selected Areas in Communications, 18*(4). doi:10.1109/49.839934

Keynote Systems. (n.d.). *Internet health report.* Retrieved from http://www.internethealthreport.com/

Krioukov, D., Claffy, K. C., Fall, K., & Brady, A. (2007, July). On compact routing for the Internet. *ACM SIGCOMM CCR, 37*(3), 43–52. doi:10.1145/1273445.1273450

Li, T. (2011). Internet research task force. *RFC 6115: Recommendation for a Routing Architecture.*

Massey, D., Wang, L., Zhang, B., & Zhang, L. (2007, August). A scalable routing system design for future Internet. In *Proceedings of the ACM SIGCOMM Workshop on IPv6 and the Future of the Internet.*

Meyer, D., Zhang, L., & Fall, K. (2007). Internet engineering task force. *RFC 4984: Report from the IAB Workshop on Routing and Addressing.*

Morris, R., Kohler, E., Jannotti, J., & Kaashoek, M. F. (1999). The click modular router. *SIGOPS Operating Systems Review, 33*(5), 217–231. doi:10.1145/319344.319166

O'Dell, M. (1997). *GSE - An alternate addressing architecture for IPv6.* Retrieved from http://tools.ietf.org/html/draft-ietf-ipngwg-gseaddr-00

Rekhter, Y., Li, T., & Hares, S. (2006). Internet engineering task force. *RFC 4271: A Border Gateway Protocol.*

Subramanian, L., Caesar, M., & Ee, C. T., Handley, M., Mao, Z. M., Shenker, S., & Stoica, I. (2005). HLP: A next generation inter-domain routing protocol. In ACM SIGCOMM.

Zhang, L. (2006). An overview of multihoming and open issues in GSE. *IETF Journal, 2.*

Zhang, X., Francis, P., Wang, J., & Yoshida, K. (2006). Scaling IP routing with the core router-integrated overlay. In *Proceedings of ICNP.*

ADDITIONAL READING

Bu, T., Gao, L., & Towsley, D. (2004, May). On characterizing BGP routing table growth. *Computer Networks, 45*(1), 45–54. doi:10.1016/j.comnet.2004.02.003

Feamster, N., Gao, L., & Rexford, J. (2007). How to lease the Internet in your spare time. *ACM SIGCOMM CCR, 37*(1), 61–64. doi:10.1145/1198255.1198265

Huston, G. (2001). Analyzing the Internet BGP routing table. *Internet Protocol Journal, 4*(1).

Li, J., Guidero, M., Wu, Z., Purpus, E., & Ehrenkranz, T. (2007, April). BGP routing dynamics revisited. *ACM SIGCOMM CCR, 37*(2), 7–16. doi:10.1145/1232919.1232921

Meng, X., Xu, Z., Zhang, B., Huston, G., Lu, S., & Zhang, L. (2005, January). IPv4 address allocation and BGP routing table evolution. In ACM SIGCOMM CCR.

Oliveira, R., Izhak-Ratzin, R., Zhang, B., & Zhang, L. (2005). Measurement of highly active prefixes in BGP. In IEEE GLOBECOM.

Xu, W., & Rexford, J. (2006). MIRO: Multi-path inter-domain routing. In ACM SIGCOMM.

Yang, X., Clark, D., & Berger, A. (2007, August). NIRA: A new routing architecture. *IEEE/ACM Transactions on Networking, 15*(4). doi:10.1109/TNET.2007.893888

ENDNOTES

[1] In practice, the ITR would maintain a small BGP table and check this before the cache. This is done for backwards compatibility.

[2] If the alternate ETR is in a different network, whether to forward packets in this situation is determined by the contractual agreement between the edge network and its providers.

[3] Note that the monitor does not make any announcements, it simply passively examines all incoming MDP messages.

[4] More specifically, the announcements cannot be ignored by ITRs and island border routers that peer with non-island neighbors. Other island routers can still ignore the announcements.

This research was previously published in Solutions for Sustaining Scalability in Internet Growth edited by Mohamed Boucadair and David Binet, pages 60-82, copyright year 2014 by Information Science Reference (an imprint of IGI Global).

Chapter 8
Image Mosaicing Using Binary Edge Detection Algorithm in a Cloud–Computing Environment

Abdullah Alamareen
Jordan University of Science and Technology, Jordan

Omar Al-Jarrah
Jordan University of Science and Technology, Jordan

Inad A. Aljarrah
Jordan University of Science and Technology, Jordan

ABSTRACT

Image Mosaicing is an image processing technique that arises from the need of having a more realistic view of the real world wider than the view captured by the lenses of the available cameras. In this paper, a sequence of images will be mosaiced using binary edge detection algorithm in a cloud-computing environment to improve processing speed and accuracy. The authors have used Platform as a Service (PaaS) to provide a number of nodes in the cloud to run the computational intensive image processing and stitching algorithms. This increased the processing speed as most of image processing algorithms deal with every single pixel in the image. Message Passing Interface (MPI) is used for message passing among the compute-nodes in the cloud and a MapReduce technique is used for image distribution and collection, where the root node is used as reducer and the others as mappers. After applying the algorithm on different sequence of images and different machines on JUST cloud, the authors have achieved high mosaicing accuracy, and the execution time has been improved when comparing it with sequential execution on the images.

DOI: 10.4018/978-1-5225-5649-7.ch008

1. INTRODUCTION

In the field of image processing, image mosaicing, also known as panoramic imaging is the process of finding the exact overlapping area between two images and combining them to form a single image (Sharma, et al., 2013). The main step of image mosaicing is the stereo pairs matching, which is finding pairs of points in the two images that refer to the same vision. After finding these points and determining the overlapping region, the stitching process of the two images in one image is performed.

Most of the mosaicing algorithms are constructed to mosaic only two images, but nowadays the need of mosaicing sequence of images has increased and become one of the important topics in the image processing field. For example, it can be used to build a full map of a country for the purpose of a virtual tour. The process of mosaicing images comprises four steps: feature extraction, finding the corresponding points, establishing the homography between those points, and finally stitching the images in one image (Murali, & Madanapalle, 2012; Cho, YunKoo & Jaeyeon, 2003). The extraction of the stereo pairs is called image alignment. There are different methods to implement image alignment such as the correlation that uses the pixels values in each image (Kim, & Jeffrey, 2004), the frequency domain coefficient (Reddy, Srinivasa & Biswanath, 1996), corner or edge detection (Rocha, Ricardo, & Aurélio, 2000), features description that use high level feature to match the images (Szeliski, 2010) and binary edge detection (Aljarrah, et al., 2014).

Mosaicing sequence of images takes a long time to produce the final image when the mosaic algorithm is implemented on a single node because most of the image processing algorithms deal with every single pixel in the image (Giess, et al., 2014). Consequently, there is a need to parallelize the mosaic algorithm to speed-up the computational time and reduce the waiting time.

Cloud computing is a new computing paradigm that dynamically provides various resources using self-services over the internet in a pay-as-you-go basis. It allows on demand dynamic provisioning of infrastructure, platform, and software resources from any location over the world (Plummer, et al., 2008). Clouds can be classified as public, private, and hybrid. Cloud computing can offer Hardware as a Service (HaaS), Software as a Service (SaaS), and Platform as a Service (PaaS) (Plummer, et al., 2008). It provides a good solution to distribute the computations on a set of nodes.

There are many techniques to distribute and collect data among different nodes in the cloud; MapReduce is considered as one of the most widely used techniques (Yamamoto, 2012). MapReduce is a programing model used for processing large data set, which consists of three main steps: map, shuffle, and reduce. In MapReduce, the data is distributed to all mappers and each one works alone.

After the mappers complete their work, the results are sent with their keys to the reducer, which will produce the final result. There are many ways to exchange data between mappers and the reducer and one of these ways is Message Passing Interface (MPI) (Barney, 2009). It is a library designed for message passing between different nodes in a parallel computing environment.

(Bay, et al., 2008) presented SURF (Speeded up Robust Feature), which introduces a feature detector and a descriptor to detect key points and to stitch images. They used Hessian matrix approximation to reduce the number of computations in detecting the key points using convolution filters. (Bhosle, Chaudhuri, & Roy, 2002). proposed a new method using Geometric Hashing for automatic generation of mosaics, which leads to finding the matching points quickly.

(Qiu, Liang, & Rong, 2013) proposed a new algorithm to mosaic images with different scales, where most of the traditional mosaic algorithms cannot deal with different scale images. They used the SIFT algorithm to extract the features' points. After that, they extract transformation parameters and then the mosaiced image will be obtained.

(Jain, Saxena, & Singh, 2012) proposed a new algorithm to mosaic images using random corner methods. Their algorithm works in three steps: the first step is finding the corners in the two inserted images, the second step is disposal of the false corners in each image, and finally similar corners will be found using homographs to produce the final output mosaic. (Singh, 2013) presented an implementation of SIFT algorithm to extract the invariant features from the images.

This paper presents a new algorithm for mosaicing images using binary edge detection in a cloud-computing environment. The proposed algorithm performs the mosaicing process in three methods. In the first method, the binary edge detection algorithm is used to mosaic a sequence of images but it is slow in producing the final image because it deals with every single pixel in the images to find the overlapping area for stitching. In the second method, the binary edge detection algorithm is used with SURF algorithm to speed-up the mosaicing process where in this method the overlapping area is found using some key points. In the third method, the binary edge detection algorithm is used with SURF algorithm in iterative mode for additional speed-up to produce the mosaiced image.

This paper shows how the mosaic algorithms work in a cloud computing environment and how to parallelize the load in the cloud. In addition, the MapReduce technique is used to distribute and collect data on the cloud where the MPI is used to exchange the data between the machines. In addition, it provides a comparison between SURF algorithm and binary edge detection with SURF algorithms. Our results show that the binary edge detection with SURF algorithm is faster than SURF algorithm, but the best result was when we applied the binary edge detection with SURF algorithm in iterative mode.

The work proposed in this paper arose from the need of having a more realistic view of the real world wider than the view captured by the lenses of the available cameras. There are already some image mosaicing algorithms, but they only mosaic a limited number of images with low speed, which motivated us to build a real-time algorithm for mosaicing any number of images in high speed and with high accuracy. The proposed algorithm can be used to build full maps of countries for navigation purpose and to build aerial maps for spacecraft.

The rest of the paper is organized as follows. The second section presents an overview of cloud computing. The third section describes the proposed system. Experimental results and discussion are presented in the fourth section. Finally, the paper is concluded in the fifth section.

2. BACKGROUND

Cloud computing is a new computing paradigm that dynamically provides various resources using self-services over the Internet in a pay-as-you-go basis. It allows on demand dynamic provisioning of infrastructure, platform, and software resources from any location over the world. In addition, cloud computing aims to exploit the difference in the time zones between different regions in the world such that, the same infrastructure may be used by different users in different countries. Most of the new companies face a challenging problem in the cost of the infrastructure, platform, and software resources, so by using the cloud, the company can focus on its business, while using resources on demand in a pay-as-you-go basis.

(Rodero-Merino, et al., 2010). present the importance of cloud nowadays and the growth in using it, especially the IaaS and the importance of having an automated system to manage the cloud services. They proposed a new abstraction layer (Claudia) to manage the cloud and allow automatic deployment for services. (Johnson, 2010) presents the infrastructure as s service in cloud computing and focuses on some of the considerations that the user needs to put into account before migrating the work to the cloud.

(Dawoud, Ibrahim, & Christoph, 2010) present a study to enhance the security in cloud computing, especially IaaS layer. They present a new model to protect the cloud. They proposed a model to enhance the security in Iaas layer. This model has three main entities; the first entity is Secure Configuration Policy (SCP) to protect the hardware and software in the cloud, the second entity is a Secure Resources Management Policy (SRMP), and the third one is the Security Policy Monitoring and Auditing (SPMA) to track the system life cycle.

(Ji, et al., 2012) proposed several techniques to process big data from system and application aspects using cloud computing. In addition, they presented an optimization algorithm for the MapReduce technique to improve processing of big data, where they added a Merge step after Reduce step to combine the outputs of two MapReduce jobs and to minimize the cost of data transmission. Furthermore, they improved the MapReduce technique to process big data online, while traditional algorithms failed to do so.

(Sweeney, et al., 2011) proposed an open-source Hadoop Image Processing Interface (HIPI) to solve the problem of the Hadoop Mapreduce platform system for large distributed processing. The main purpose of HIPI is to create interface for computer vision with MapReduce technology and to create a tool that makes the development of large-scale image processing extremely accessible.

(Wu, et al., 2012) presented a modified MapReduce algorithm on integrated 2D to 3D using Hadoop to enhance the response time. In traditional MapReduce algorithm, the reducer must wait for all mappers to complete their work, and then it starts integrating the data processed by mappers for the final image. Therefore, they proposed a new algorithm that allows the reducer to start working with the achieved percentage of data. They improved the waiting and computing times so the user can quickly get final images.

(Zhang, et al., 2013) present MK-means algorithm, where they apply the clustering in the parallel environment using MPI. K-means algorithm spilt M observations into N clusters and each observation goes to the cluster with its nearest mean, but by using MPI, it is called MK-means. By using MPI with K-means, the overhead time is reduced on large data set when compared with the K-means.

(Ruan, et al., 2012) present an implementation of MPI for security purposes. Nowadays, the number of clusters has been increased and some clusters are connected with others via public networks. Therefore, sensitive parallel applications running on the clusters have to be secured. They encrypt and decrypt the messages between different nodes.

3. IMAGE MOSAICING USING BINARY EDGE DETECTION ALGORITHM IN A CLOUDE COMPUTING ENVIRONMENT

The proposed algorithm is designed to mosaic sequence of images using binary edge detection algorithm. The binary edge detection algorithm deals with every single pixel in the colored image in the spatial domain. Consequently, the process of mosaicing a sequence of images will take a long time that may reach to hours or days. By using a cloud-computing environment and distributing the images to a set of nodes in the cloud as shown in Figure 1, the time complexity will be less than the sequential mosaicing in one node. The technique that is used in this algorithm to distribute the images to the compute nodes, to gather the mosaiced images from the nodes, and to produce and display the final result is a MapReduce based on MPI.

Figure 1. General view of the algorithms on Cloud

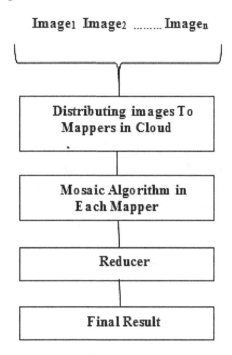

After specifying the number of images and nodes, each mapper (node) will take a certain number of images as shown in Equation (1), where each image has a unique key <image, key>. Then, each mapper needs to know which images it will mosaic. We assume that the images are presented in a sequence related to their order in final mosaiced image. Therefore, each mapper needs only to know the keys of the first and last images in its share as shown in Equations (2) and (3).

$$\text{ni} = Floor\left(\frac{Ni}{Nn}\right) \tag{1}$$

where:

ni: Number of images in each node,
Ni: Number of all images, and
Nn: Number of nodes.

If Ni Mod Nn is more than zero, there are extra images that have not been distributed to any node, so that those images have to be redistributed to the nodes.

$$Fi = 1 + nID * ni \tag{2}$$

$$Li = Fi + ni - 1 \tag{3}$$

where:

Fi: First image in each node,
nID: The node ID, and
.ni: Number of images in each node.
Li: Last image in each node,

3.1. Image Mosaicing Using Binary Edge Detection Algorithm in a Cloude Computing Environment

We have applied different approaches to mosaic a sequence of images in a cloud computing environment to speed up the mosaicing process. The first approach uses the "Binary Edge Detection Algorithm" as shown in Figure 2. After distributing the images to the N mappers, each mapper will mosaic its assigned images and the reducer will be locked until all mappers complete their work. The mosaicing process is based on binary edge detection as shown in Figure 3, which is implemented using MPI with OPENCV.

In binary edge detection algorithm, each image will be converted into gray scale and then into a binary image. After that, the binary images are converted into images that only contain the edges using Soble filter, where those edges are the main parameter to find the overlapping area between every two consecutive images. The overlapping area is found by setting a fixed block in the beginning of the middle row of the second image of every two consecutive images, and this block will be compared with all blocks in the first image to find the matching block.

Figure 2. Binary edge detection algorithm

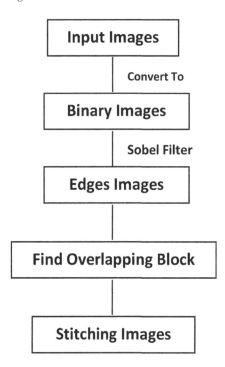

The block size is (L/20)*(W/20) where L and W are the length and width of the second image, respectively. After finding the overlapping block, the stitching technique will be applied. These steps will be repeated until the mapper mosaics all its assigned images and produces one image with a unique key that will be sent to the reducer (root node).

Once the reducer received all the mappers' images with their keys, it will call the mosaic function to mosaic the received images and to produce the final image.

3.2. Mosaicing Images Using Binary Edge Detection Algorithm and Surf Algorithm

The second approach for mosaicing a sequence of images is to combine the binary edge detection algorithm with SURF, which is shown in Figure 4. In the binary edge detection algorithm, each image will be converted into gray scale and then into a binary image. After that, the binary images are converted into images that only contain the edges using Soble filter, then the SURF algorithm will be applied on every two consecutive images to find the key points in each one. The key points will be compared to extract the most similar key points between the two images, which will be called the main key points, where those key points are the main parameter to find the overlapping area between every two consecutive images.

Figure 3. Pseudo code of binary edge detection algorithm

```
Approach one: mosaic sequence of images using Binary
Edge Detection Algorithm
1. DEFINE Number Of Images to mosaic
2. DEFINE Number_Of_Nodes (Mappers)
3. DISTRIBUTE images to all Mappers :< Image, unique
   _number>
4. LOCK the reducer until RECEIVE all mosaiced images
from mappers
5. IF processor ID != 0 THEN
6. IN each processor(mapper): processor _images(x) = floor
(Number_Of_Images / Number_Of_Nodes)
7. First_Image_In_Each_Processor = 1- (processor ID*x)
8. Last_Image_In_Each_Processor=First_Image_In_Each_Proce
ssor + x
9. DO mosaic for images using binary edge detection algorithm
10. MPI_SEND the mosaiced image TO reducer with its key
<Image, key>
11. ELSE
12. FOR each mosaiced image
13. MPI_RECEIVE the mosaicked images from mappers
with its keys <Image, key>
14. END FOR
15. DO mosaic for Mappers results to gain the final image using
binary edge detection algorithm
16. ENDIF
```

Figure 4. Binary edge detection algorithm with SURF

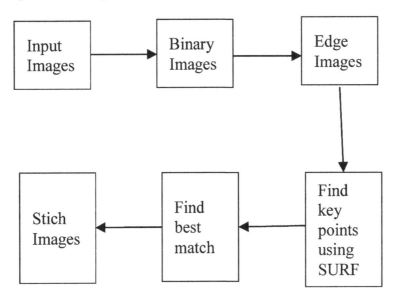

After distributing the images to N mappers, each mapper will mosaic its assigned images and the reducer will be locked until all mappers complete their work. The mosaicing process is based on binary edge detection and SURF algorithms as shown in Figure 5, which is implemented using MPI with OPENCV.

The overlapping area is found by setting a block around each main key point and comparing it with the corresponding one in the other image to find the distance between them, where the two blocks that give the minimum distance will be the most similar and the overlapping area at their key points. After finding the overlapping area, the stitching technique will be applied. These steps will be repeated until the mapper mosaics all its assigned images and produces one image with a unique key that will be sent to the reducer (root node). Once the reducer received all the mappers' images with their keys, it will call the mosaic function to mosaic the received images and to produce the final image.

3.3. Mosaicing Images Using Binary Edge Detection Algorithm and Surf Algorithm in Iterative Mode

We have applied different approaches to mosaic sequence of images in cloud computing environment to speed up the mosaicing process. In this section, an interactive mode is added to the second algorithm. After the root node distributes the images (M) to the N nodes, where N < = M/2, each node will mosaic its assigned images and the root will be locked until all nodes complete their work. In this approach, the iterative mode is used as shown in Figure 6. When the root node receives the mosaiced images (K) from other nodes, it will re-distribute them to L nodes, where L < = K/2. This process will be repeated until the root receives only two images, and at this step, the root will call the mosaic function to produce the final image.

After converting the binary images into images that only contain the edges using Soble filter, the SURF algorithm will be applied on every two consecutive images to find the key points in each one. The key points will be compared to extract the most similar key points between the two images, which will

Figure 5. Pseudo code of binary edge detection algorithm and SURF

```
Approach two: mosaic sequence of images using Binary Edge
Detection and SURF

1. DEFINE Number_Of_Images to mosaic

2. DEFINE Number_Of_Nodes (Mappers)

3. DISTRIBUTE images to all Mappers :< Image, unique_number>

4. LOCK the reducer until RECEIVE all mosaiced images from
mappers

5. IF processor ID != 0 THEN

6. IN each processor(mapper): processor_images(x) = floor
(Number_Of_Images / Number_Of_Nodes)

7. First_Image_In_Each_Processor = 1 + (processor ID*x)

8. Last_Image_In_Each_Processor = First_Image_In_Each_Processor +
x

9. FIND the images key_points

10. Extract the main_key_points between every two consecutive
images
```

be called the main key points, where those key points are the main parameter to find the overlapping area between every two consecutive images, and stitch the images.

4. EXPERIMENTAL RESULTS AND COMPARISON

In this research, Jordan University of Science and Technology (JUST) IBM Cloudburst is used to implement the mosaic algorithms, and message passing interface (MPI) is used for communication between the machines in this cloud. JUST IBM Cloudburst is a model of private cloud computing, where it is a complete package of software, hardware, and services that work correctly in any environment.

Ten machines have been allocated on JUST IBM Cloudburst to distribute the work on it and to improve the performance of the mosaic algorithms, where the machines have the following specifications:

- The operating system is Ubuntu 12.4-LTS-64 bit.
- The RAM is 4 GB.
- The processor is 4 Cores.
- The Hard Disc is 20 GB.

Figure 6. Pseudo code of binary edge detection algorithm and SURF in iterative mode

```
Approach Three: mosaic sequence of images using Binary
Edge Detection and SURF In iterative Mode.
1.DEFINE Number_Of_Images to mosaic

2.DEFINE Number_Of_Nodes (Mappers)

3.DISTRIBUTE images to all Mappers :< Image, unique
_number>

4.LOCK the reducer until RECEIVE all mosaiced images from
mappers

5.IF processor ID != 0 THEN

6.IN each processor(mapper): processor_images(x) = floor
(Number_Of_Images/Number_Of_Nodes)
7.First_Image_In_Each_Processor= 1+ (processor ID*x)

8.Last_Image_In_Each_Processor=First_Image_In_Each_Proces
sor + x

9. FIND the images key points

10. Extract the main key points between every two consecutive
images

11.Compare the main key points to find the overlapping area

12.DO mosaic for images using binary edge detection algorithm

13.MPI_SEND the mosaiced image TO reducer with its key
<Image, key>

14.ELSE

15.FOR each mosaiced image
```

By using MPI, one of the allocated nodes should act as a master node to control the other nodes (slaves), and all machines must have the following requirements:

- The MPI library is installed.
- The nodes Connected via TCP/IP network.
- The nodes have the same processor architecture to share the executable file.
- Each node has a common user name, where in our work the user name for all nodes is justcbuser.
- SSH server must install in each slave node.
- The master node must have the SSH client.
- The slave nodes are authorized at the master node.

All mosaic techniques presented here are implemented using OpenCV with MPI in a cloud computing environment. The efficiency of the algorithms has been tested using a sequence of 20 images [28]. Figures 7 and 8 show the sequence of images were used to test the three algorithms. Figure 9 shows the final result by the reducer.

Table 1 shows the execution time for image mosaicing using binary edge detection algorithm, where the parallel execution is faster than sequential execution (one node), but it does not mean that any increase in the nodes number will decrease the elapsed time in the execution.

Table 2 shows the execution time for image mosaicing using binary edge detection and SURF algorithm. When the binary edge detection algorithm and SURF in Iterative Mode algorithm was used to mosaic the 20 image by four nodes, the elapsed time was 0.9349 second. By comparing our algorithm with SURF algorithm, we find that our algorithm is faster than SURF algorithm and the SURF could not mosaic large images, while in our algorithm, we did not face any problem in image size, and consequently, the proposed algorithm is able to mosaic any number of images. The two systems were tested on the test images, SURF can only handle up to 7 images in the tested image sequence, namely image 1 through 7; the elapsed time to mosaic the images in the binary edge detection with SURF algorithm and in SURF was 0.39 and 1.3 second, respectively.

In terms of quality and accuracy of the final image, our algorithm gives the exact size of the stitched images in the result. However, the result image in SURF always has a black area at the end of the image, which is equal in size to the overlapping area. This is because when it stitches the images after finding the overlapping area, it will shift one of the overlapping areas to the end of the result image and replace its values with zeros.

Figure 7. The Images 1-4 in the sequence

Figure 8. The Images 5-20 in the sequence

Figure 9. The mosaiced images

Table 1. The execution time for image mosaicing using binary edge detection algorithm

Number of Nodes	Elapsed Time in Seconds
1	163.6080
2	73.4213
3	75.6985
4	67.9751
5	69.4937
6	75.4365
7	87.8052
8	92.2606
9	98.1732
10	100.9031

Table 2. The execution time for image mosaicing using binary edge detection and SURF algorithm

Number of Nodes	Elapsed Time in Seconds
1	3.4795
2	1.8431
3	1.5231
4	1.3743
5	1.56005
6	1.4508
7	1.7628
8	1.9686
9	2.1153
10	2.2192

5. CONCLUSION

In this research, a new algorithm to mosaic sequence of images is presented using binary edge detection algorithm in a cloud-computing environment based on MapReduce technique. The algorithm is implemented in C++ using OpenCV and MPI libraries. The aim of this study is to mosaic any number of overlapping images and to get the result in high speed, accuracy, and quality. The algorithm is tested on a set of 20 images; the results are better in comparison with sequential execution, where the execution time of image mosaicing in one node using binary edge detection algorithm is 163.608 seconds, but after parallelizing the algorithm using 4 nodes the execution time is reduced to 67.9751 seconds. The previously mentioned algorithm is improved by using SURF key points to find the matching block. By this enhancement, the execution time in one node is reduced to 3.4795 seconds, where in 4 nodes is reduced to 1.3743 seconds. Finally, the binary edge detection and SURF algorithm are constructed in iterative mode and the execution time is reduced to 0.9349 second. By comparing our algorithm with SURF algorithm, we found that our algorithm is faster in mosaic process.

REFERENCES

Aljarrah, I., Abdullah, A., Abdelrahman, I., & Osama, A. (2014). Image Mosaicing Using Binary Edge Detection. *Proceedings of the International Conference on Computing Technology and Information Management (ICCTIM2014)* (pp. 186-190). The Society of Digital Information and Wireless Communication.

Barney, B. (2009). Message passing interface (mpi). Lawrence Livermore National Laboratory. Retrieved from https://computing.llnl.gov/tutorials/mpi/

Bay, H., Ess, A., Tuytelaars, T., & Gool, L. V. (2008). Speeded-Up Robust Features (SURF). *Computer Vision and Image Understanding, 110*(3), 346–359. doi:10.1016/j.cviu.2007.09.014

Bhosle, U., Chaudhuri, S., & Roy, S. D. (2002). A Fast Method for Image Mosaicing using Geometric Hashing. *Journal of the Institution of Electronics and Telecommunication Engineers, 48*(3-4), 317–324. doi:10.1080/03772063.2002.11416292

Cho, S. YunKoo C., & Jaeyeon L. Automatic Image Mosaic System Using Image Feature Detection and Taylor Series. Proceedings of DICTA (pp. 549-560).

Dawoud, W., Ibrahim, T., & Christoph, M. (2010). Infrastructure as a service security: Challenges and solutions. *Proceedings of the 2010 the 7th International Conference on Informatics and Systems (INFOS)* (pp. 1-8). IEEE.

Giess, C., Mayer, A., Evers, H., & Meinzer, H. (1998). Medical image processing and visualization on heterogenous clusters of symmetric multiprocessors using MPI and POSIX threads. *Proceedings of the First Merged International Parallel Processing Symposium and Symposium on Parallel and Distributed Processing.* doi:10.1109/IPPS.1998.669916

Jain, D. K., Saxena, G., & Singh, V. K. (2012). Image Mosaicing Using Corner Techniques. *Proceedings of the 2012 International Conference on Communication Systems and Network Technologies.* doi:10.1109/CSNT.2012.27

Ji, C., Li, Y., Qiu, W., Awada, U., & Li, K. (2012). Big Data Processing in Cloud Computing Environments. *Proceedings of the 2012 12th International Symposium on Pervasive Systems, Algorithms and Networks.* doi:10.1109/i-span.2012.9

Johnson, K. (2010). *Spotlight on Cloud Computing Series, Infrastructure as a service.* EDUCAUSE.

Kim, J., & Fessler, J. (2004). Intensity-Based Image Registration Using Robust Correlation Coefficients. IEEE Transactions on Medical Imaging IEEE Trans. *Med. Imaging, 23*(11), 1430–1444. doi:10.1109/TMI.2004.835313

Murali, Y., & Madanapalle, M. (2012). Image Mosaic Using Speeded Up Robust Feature Detection. *Image, 1*(3).

Plummer, Daryl C., David W., & David M. (2008). Cloud computing confusion leads to opportunity. Gartner Report.

Qiu, P., Liang, Y., & Rong, H. (2013). Image Mosaics Algorithm Based on SIFT Feature Point Matching and Transformation Parameters Automatically Recognizing. *Proceedings of the 2nd International Conference on Computer Science and Electronics Engineering (ICCSEE 2013).* doi:10.2991/iccsee.2013.392

Reddy, B., & Chatterji, B. (1996). An FFT-based technique for translation, rotation, and scale-invariant image registration. *IEEE Transactions on Image Processing IEEE Trans. on Image Process., 5*(8), 1266–1271. doi:10.1109/83.506761 PMID:18285214

Rocha, A., Ricardo, F., & Aurélio, C. (2000). Image mosaicing using corner detection. *Proceedings of the SIARP2000-V Ibero-American Symposium on Pattern Recognition.*

Rodero-Merino, L., Vaquero, L. M., Gil, V., Galán, F., Fontán, J., Montero, R. S., & Llorente, I. M. (2010). From infrastructure delivery to service management in clouds. *Future Generation Computer Systems, 26*(8), 1226–1240. doi:10.1016/j.future.2010.02.013

Ruan, X., Yang, Q., Alghamdi, M. I., Yin, S., & Qin, X. (2012). ES-MPICH2: A Message Passing Interface with Enhanced Security. *IEEE Transactions on Dependable and Secure Computing IEEE Trans. on Dependable and Secure Comput., 9*(3), 361–374. doi:10.1109/TDSC.2012.9

Sharma, S., Hitesh, T., Shivam, N., Tanuj, D., & Sumit, T. (2009). Using Self-Organizing Neural Network for Image Mosaicing. In *Advanced Applications of Electrical Engineering* (pp. 76-80).

Singh, J. (2013). Image Mosaicing with Invariant Features Detection using SIFT. *Global Journal of Computer Science and Technology, 13*(5).

Sweeney, C., Liu, L., Sean, A., & Jason, L. (2011). *HIPI: a Hadoop image processing interface for image-based mapreduce tasks.* University of Virginia.

Szeliski, R. (2010). Feature-based alignment. In *Texts in Computer Science Computer Vision* (pp. 273-301). doi:10.1007/978-1-84882-935-0_6

Wu, T., Chen, C., Kuo, L., Lee, W., & Chao, H. (2012). Cloud-based image processing system with priority-based data distribution mechanism. *Computer Communications, 35*(15), 1809–1818. doi:10.1016/j.comcom.2012.06.015

Yamamoto, M. (2012). Parallel image database processing with mapreduce and performance evaluation. in pseudo distributed mode. *International Journal of Electronic Commerce Studies, 3*(2), 211–228. doi:10.7903/ijecs.1092

Zhang, J., Wu, G., Hu, X., Li, S., & Hao, S. (2013). A Parallel Clustering Algorithm with MPI – MKmeans. *JCP Journal of Computers, 8*(1). doi:10.4304/jcp.8.1.10-17

This research was previously published in the International Journal of Information Technology and Web Engineering (IJITWE), 11(3); edited by Ghazi I. Alkhatib, pages 1-14, copyright year 2016 by IGI Publishing (an imprint of IGI Global).

Chapter 9
Fog Computing:
Applications, Concepts, and Issues

Chintan Bhatt
Charotar University of Science and Technology, India

C. K. Bhensdadia
Dharnsinh Desai University, India

ABSTRACT

The Internet of Things could be a recent computing paradigm, defined by networks of extremely connected things – sensors, actuators and good objects – communication across networks of homes, buildings, vehicles, and even individuals whereas cloud computing could be ready to keep up with current processing and machine demands. Fog computing provides architectural resolution to deal with some of these issues by providing a layer of intermediate nodes what's referred to as an edge network [26]. These edge nodes provide interoperability, real-time interaction, and if necessary, computational to the Cloud. This paper tries to analyse different fog computing functionalities, tools and technologies and research issues.

1. INTRODUCTION

At a really generic level of understanding it is said that Internet of Things (IoT) may be the network infrastructure where the physical and virtual objects are all equipped with sensing and communication capabilities in order that they will use the Pervasive Internet for data transmission and other controlling and monitoring purposes. This definition could seem rather dubious at the primary scan. The inferences and the implications of the definition are going to be clearer as we have a tendency to move forward with the content of this text.

To put this simply, "IoT is a scenario in which objects, animals or people are provided with unique identifiers and the ability to automatically transfer the data over a network without requiring human-to-human or human-to-computer interaction". Explosive growth of Smart Devices and PCs brought the amount of devices connected to the Internet to 12.5 billion in 2010, while the world's human population exaggerated to 6.8 billion. It is estimated by CISCO that IoT was "born" between 2008 and 2009 (see Figure 1).

DOI: 10.4018/978-1-5225-5649-7.ch009

Figure 1. The Internet of Things - Next Evolution of the Internet (CISCO)

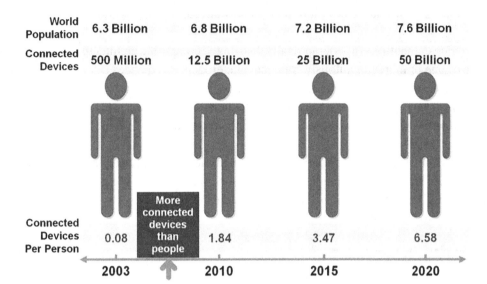

'Fog Computing' is the computing directly at the edge of the network, which might deliver new applications and services particularly for the longer term of web. This computing relies on the basis that process jobs, which can be executed on edgy nodes (located in between the cloud and user devices) to reduce communication latencies. Thus, fog computing provides higher Quality of Service (QoS).

In fog computing, fog nodes offer resources/services at the edge of the network. They will be devices with limited capability like set-top boxes, access points, routers, switches, base stations, and end devices, or devices with lots of capability i.e. machines like Cloudlet and IOx.

"IOx (product from Cisco) works by hosting applications during a Guest software system (GOS) running throughout a hypervisor directly on the Connected Grid Router (CGR)." Python scripts can be run, own code can be compiled, and operation system can be replaced with their own on IOx platform.

This paper presents a survey on fog computing specializing in its ideas, applications and underlying problems one could encounter in coming up with and implementing fog system.

2. FOG COMPUTING BASICS

There are not any unanimous definitions of fog computing considering it's in its immature state. This has junction rectifier to several definitions of the fog, relying upon completely different views as follows:

Definition 1: "Fog computing is a scenario where a huge number of heterogeneous (wireless and sometimes autonomous) ubiquitous and decentralized devices communicate and potentially cooperate among them and with the network to perform storage and processing tasks without the intervention of third parties. These tasks can be for supporting basic network functions or new services and applications that run in a sandboxed environment. Users leasing part of their devices to host these services get incentives for doing so (Vaquero & Rodero-Merino, 2014)".

This definition, nonetheless, is still debatable because it fails to address the unique connection to the cloud (S. Yi et al., 2015). Thus, a new definition is introduced:

Definition 2: "Fog computing is a geographically distributed computing architecture with a resource pool consists of one or more ubiquitously connected heterogeneous devices (including edge devices) at the edge of network and not exclusively seamlessly backed by cloud services, to collaboratively provide elastic computation, storage and communication (and many other new services and tasks) in isolated environments to a large scale of clients in proximity (Yi et al., 2015)".

The fog computing can include a variety of sensors in the network (reducing the need to act with distant resources) with low latency. For example, various sensors in smart cities are generating huge volume of data so called "Big Data". Such data will be processed nearer to the source while not transferring huge amounts of data across the internet.

2.1. Big Data Analytics in IoT

What makes huge information a very important quality to businesses is the "potential to extract analytics and accordingly information"; by that, any professional can do financial benefit. Some of the platforms for big data analytics are Apache Hadoop, Cloudera, Hortonworks, MapR etc. But, these tools are not enough for big data requirements of IoT. The quantity of information generated by IoT is too massive to be fed and processed by these tools. Big data platforms should work in real-time to attend the users expeditiously in IoT. For example, enhanced version of Hadoop is used in Facebook for the analysis of billions of messages per day and give real-time statistics.

2.2. Fog Computing in IoT

Cloud Computing is related to "…on-demand services for users, elasticity of resources and measurable services for transparency…" Few challenges in Cloud Computing for the IoT are "Synchronization, Standardization, Balancing, Reliability, Management and Enhancement". IoT utilizes various platforms like ThingWorx, OpenIoT, Google Cloud, Amazon, GENI, etc. with different abilities and assets. Xively (one in all the primary IoT application hosting service suppliers) is letting sensor data to be available on Internet. Objective of Xively is to handle IoT applications securely in fixed time span. It is the example of Platform as a Service (PaaS). It is able to integrate devices with the platform with the help of libraries like ARM mbed, electrical Imp and iOS/OSX and guide communication via HTTP(S), Sockets/Websocket, or MQTT. Simple IoT application of Xively is the automated car-parking zone. Xively is popular due to these characteristics:

- Open source, free and easy to use
- Interoperability with many protocols and environments
- Good visualization
- Support from Original Equipment Manufacturers like OpenGear, Arduino, mBed, etc.

Fog computing/Cloudlets/Edge computing acts as a connection between devices and cloud computing. Fog computing offer services that deliver higher delay performance due to nearness to the end-users

Figure 2. Cloud and Fog resources in IoT

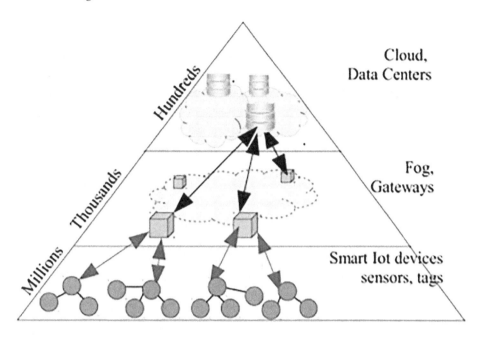

compared to the cloud data-centers. Cloud has large machine, storage and communications abilities compared to the fog. Roles of the cloud data-centers and cloudlets for IoT services are shown in Figure 2. Mobile network operators are the potential suppliers of fog computing as they can provide fog services in form of IaaS/PaaS/SaaS.

Fog computing will function as for the IoT designers for these features: "Scalability, On the fly analysis, Location, Mobility Support (Mobile Cloud), Real-time interactive services," etc. This field desires a lot of care to resolve different problems like reliability and security of data on the edge devices. Cloud Computing and Fog Computing are compared in Table 1:

3. DEVELOPMENT PROCESS IN FOG

There are several ways that for IoT code to store and analyse huge amount of information generated by sensors within the cloud. Developing and deploying code for IoT applications to edge locations/devices is time consuming, and expensive. To unravel these issues, ioFog was created (see Figure 3).

ioFog can be put in on any hardware which is running UNIX system. It provides a universal runtime for micro services to run on the edge. ComSat element provide automated interconnection of ioFog instances. It relieves developers from writing code to transfer information from one place to a different. ioAuthoring provides Orchestration and management of micro services.

Fog Computing layers:

Table 1. Comparison of Cloud Computing with Fog Computing

Parameter	Cloud Computing	Fog Computing
Latency	High	Low
Delay Jitter	High	Low
Location of service	Within Internet	On edge of local network
Geo-distribution	Centralized	Distributed
Support for Mobility	Low	High

Figure 3. Components of Fog

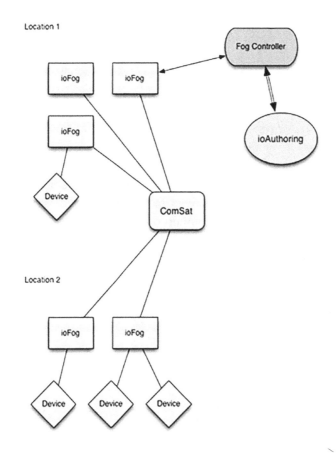

1. Software agent "ioFog" runs on numerous operating systems and provides a universal runtime for IoT micro services.
2. Node controller "Fabric Controller" runs on UNIX. Its associate API permits for numerous tooling to be designed for fog computing fabric.
3. The internetworking utility "ComSat" runs on UNIX and provides the way for ioFog instances to interconnect, in case of non-public network layers and firewalls.

4. A design-time interface "ioAuthoring" is for making, saving, editing, and deploying micro services. It runs on UNIX and uses the Fabric Controller API to do its work.

5. The convenience of programming to the developers against objects rather than exploitation the native REST API is given by Software Development Kits (SDKs).

6. A local software development tool "Test Message Generator" provides developers the way to check their code against simulated things before creating the hassle to package their code as a micro service.

4. EXPERIMENTATION

Install Java Runtime 8 or higher

User need to accept the license agreement for the Oracle edition of Java 8
sudo add-apt-repository ppa:webupd8team/java
sudo apt-get update
sudo apt-get install oracle-java8-installer
Install Docker
Install the latest version of Docker with following command:
curl -fsSL https://get.docker.com/ | sh
ioFog installation
Use command line to install ioFog. Some commands that need to be entered.
Add the iotracks package repository to your system
curl -s https://packagecloud.io/install/repositories/iotracks/iofog/script.deb.sh | sudo bash
Install ioFog (it will automatically detect your system architecture, such as ARM or AMD64)
sudo apt-get install iofog
Start the ioFog daemon service
sudo service iofog start
Result
marsian@localhost:~$ sudo iofog config -n ens33
Change accepted for Parameter: -n, Old value was:eth0, New Value is: ens33
marsian@localhost:~$ sudo iofog info
Instance ID: not provisioned
IP Address: 192.168.1.2
Network Interface: ens33
ioFog Controller: https://iotracks.com/api/v2/
ioFog Certificate: /etc/iofog/cert.crt
Docker URL: unix:///var/run/docker.sock
Disk Usage Limit: 50.00 GiB
Message Storage Directory: /var/lib/iofog/
Memory RAM Limit: 4096.00 MiB

CPU Usage Limit: 80.00%

Log Disk Limit: 10.00 GiB

Status Update Frequency: 30

Get Changes Frequency: 60

Log File Directory: /var/log/iofog/

Log Rolling File Count: 10

marsian@localhost:~$

marsian@localhost:~$ sudo iofog status

ioFog daemon: RUNNING

Memory Usage: about 65.14 MiB

Disk Usage: about 0.00 MiB

CPU Usage: about 0.00%

Running Elements: 1

Connection to Controller: ok

Messages Processed: about 0

System Time: 22/04/2017 10:25 PM

marsian@localhost:~$ sudo iofog provision g8BQtb8m

Provisioning with key "g8BQtb8m"...

Success - instance ID is rhCbFRC4FXqwF43ypgxrMX

Access the ioAuthoring in a Web browser

Sign up here https://iotracks.com/signup

Login here https://iotracks.com/login

Create a new ioFog instance (drag and drop a fog instance on Fog page) and generate a provisioning key (see Figure 4).

Go to Linux command line, type 'sudo iofog provision ABCDWXYZ' and replace the ABCDWXYZ with your provisioning key (it is case sensitive) and verify the results

The output will show a success message if the process is successful and will show an instance ID

If provisioning process was successful, type 'sudo iofog status' and verify that the 'controller connection' value is now listed as 'ok'

The output will show an error if provisioning process was not successful (a common problem is having the wrong network adapter set in the configuration)

A. Check which network adapters are available on your machine with 'sudo ifconfig' command
B. Enter 'sudo iofog config -n YourNetworkAdapter' command (replace the 'YourNetworkAdapter' with your adapter)
C. Enter 'sudo iofog info' command and verify that it returns correct values of 'IP Address' and 'Network Interface'
D. Repeat 'sudo iofog provision ABCDWXYZ' command (replace the ABCDWXYZ with your provisioning key)

Figure 4. Generating provisioning key

5. CONCLUSION

Processing information nearer to wherever it's made and required solves the challenges of exploding information volume, variety, and rate. Fog computing accelerates alertness and response to events by eliminating a trip to the cloud for analysis. It avoids the requirement for expensive bandwidth additions by offloading gigabytes of network traffic from the core network. Ultimately, organizations that adopt fog computing gain deeper and quicker insights, resulting in accumulated business agility, higher service levels, and improved safety.

REFERENCES

Al-Fuqaha, A., Guizani, M., Mohammadi, M., Aledhari, M., & Ayyash, M. (2015). Internet of Things: A Survey on Enabling Technologies, Protocols and Applications. *IEEE Communications Surveys and Tutorials*, *17*(4), 2347–2376. doi:10.1109/COMST.2015.2444095

Augur, H. (2016, March 21). Is fog computing the future of the cloud. *Dataconomy*. Retrieved from http://dataconomy.com/2016/03/fog-computing-future-cloud/

Bhatt, C., & Bhensdadia, C.K. (2016). Mining Big Data Using Modified Induction Tree Approach. *International Journal of Intelligent Engineering and Systems*, *9*(2), 14-20.

Bonomi, F., Milito, R., Zhu, J., & Addepalli, S. (2012). *Fog computing and its role in the internet of things. In workshop on Mobile cloud computing*. ACM.

Bonomi, F., Milito, R., Zhu, J., & Addepalli, S. (2012). Fog Computing and Its Role in the Internet of Things. In *Proceedings of the Workshop on Mobile Cloud Computing* (pp. 13–16). doi:10.1145/2342509.2342513

Bonomi, F., Milito, R., Zhu, J., & Addepalli, S. (2012). Fog computing and its role in the Internet of Things. In *Proc. 1st Edition MCC Workshop Mobile Cloud Comput.* (pp. 13–16). doi:10.1145/2342509.2342513

Borthakur, D., Gray, J., Sarma, J. S., Muthukkaruppan, K., Spiegelberg, N., Kuang, H., ... & Schmidt, R. (2011). Apache Hadoop goes realtime at Facebook. In *Proc. 2011 ACM SIGMOD Int. Conf. Management Data* (pp. 1071–1080). doi:10.1145/1989323.1989438

Chang, H., Hari, A., Mukherjee, S., & Lakshman, T. V. (2014). Bringing the cloud to the edge. In *Proc. of the IEEE Conf. INFOCOM WKSHPS '14* (pp. 346–351). doi:10.1109/INFOCOMW.2014.6849256

Cisco. (2014). Iox overview. Retrieved from http://goo.gl/n2mfiw

Dastjerdi, A. V., & Buyya, R. (2016). Fog Computing: Helping the Internet of Things Realize Its Potential. *Computer*, *49*(8), 112–116. doi:10.1109/MC.2016.245

Eclipse. (n. d.). ioFog (Proposal). Retrieved from https://projects.eclipse.org/proposals/iofog

Cisco. (2015Fog Computing and the Internet of Things.

Butterfield, E.H. (2016Fog Computing with Go: *A Comparative Study*.

Hromic, H., Le Phuoc, D., Serrano, M., Antonic, A., Zarko, I. P., Hayes, C., & Decker, S. (2015). Real Time Analysis of Sensor Data for the Internet of Things by Means of Clustering and Event Processing. In *Proceedings of the IEEE International Conference on Communications* (pp. 685–691). doi:10.1109/ICC.2015.7248401

Bhayani, M., Patel, M., & Bhatt, C. (2016). Internet of Things (IoT): In a way of smart world. In M. Bhayani, M. Patel & C. Bhatt (Eds.), *Proceedings of the International Congress on Information and Communication Technology* (pp. 343–350).

Luan, T. H., Gao, L., Li, Z., Xiang, Y., & Sun, L. (2015). Fog Computing: Focusing on Mobile Users at the Edge. Retrieved from http://arxiv.org/abs/1502.01815

Madsen, H., Albeanu, G., Burtschy, B., & Popentiu-Vladicescu, F. L. (2013). Reliability in the utility computing era: Towards reliable fog computing. In *Proc. 20th IWSSIP '13* (pp. 43–46). doi:10.1109/IWSSIP.2013.6623445

Mukherjee, A., Paul, H. S., Dey, S., & Banerjee, A. (2014). ANGELS for distributed analytics in IoT. In *Proc. IEEE WF-IoT* (pp. 565–570).

Rahman, M. N., & Sruthi, P. (2015). Real Time Compressed Sensory Data Processing Framework to Integrate Wireless Sensory Networks with Mobile Cloud. In *Proceedings of the Online International Conference on Green Engineering and Technologies (IC-GET)*. doi:10.1109/GET.2015.7453835

Satyanarayanan, M., Bahl, P., Caceres, R., & Davies, N. (2009). *The case for vm-based cloudlets in mobile computing*. Pervasive Computing, 8(4).

Satyanarayanan, M., Simoens, P., Xiao, Y., Pillai, P., Chen, Z., Ha, K., & Amos, B. et al. (2015, April). Edge Analytics in the Internet of Things. *IEEE Pervasive Computing / IEEE Computer Society [and] IEEE Communications Society*, *14*(2), 24–31. doi:10.1109/MPRV.2015.32

Shah, T., & Bhatt, C. M. (2012). The Internet of things: technologies, communications and computing. CSI Communications, 7.

Tsai, C. W., Lai, C. F., Chiang, M. C., & Yang, L. T. (2014). Data mining for Internet of Things: A survey. *IEEE Commun. Surveys Tuts.*, *16*(1), 77–97.

Verma, D. C., & Verma, P. (2014). *Techniques for Surviving Mobile Data Explosion*. New York, NY: Wiley. doi:10.1002/9781118834404

Willis, D. F., Dasgupta, A., & Banerjee, S. (2014). Paradrop: a multi-tenant platform for dynamically installed third party services on home gateways. In *Proceedings of the SIGCOMM workshop on Distributed cloud computing*. ACM. doi:10.1145/2627566.2627583

Xu, X., Huang, S., Chen, Y., Browny, K., Halilovicy, I., & Lu, W. (2014). TSAaaS: Time series analytics as a service on IoT. In *Proc. IEEE ICWS '14* (pp. 249–256). doi:10.1109/ICWS.2014.45

Yang, K. et al.. (2013). Park-a-lot: An automated parking management system. *Comput. Sci. Inform. Technol.*, *1*(4), 276–279.

This research was previously published in the International Journal of Grid and High Performance Computing (IJGHPC), 9(4); edited by Emmanuel Udoh, Ching-Hsien Hsu, and Mohammad Khan, pages 105-113, copyright year 2017 by IGI Publishing (an imprint of IGI Global).

Chapter 10
Fog Computing and Virtualization

Siddhartha Duggirala
Bharat Petroleum Corporation Limited, India

ABSTRACT

The essence of Cloud computing is moving out the processing from the local systems to remote systems. Cloud is an umbrella of physical/virtual services/resources easily accessible over the internet. With more companies adopting cloud either fully through public cloud or Hybrid model, the challenges in maintaining a cloud capable infrastructure is also increasing. About 42% of CTOs say that security is their main concern for moving into cloud. Another problem which is mainly problem with infrastructure is the connectivity issue. The datacenter could be considered as the backbone of cloud computing architecture. As the processing power and storage capabilities of the end devices like mobile phones, routers, sensor hubs improve we can increasing leverage these resources to improve your quality and reliability of services.

INTRODUCTION

Cloud computing has completely transformed how businesses function and handle their IT infrastructures. By consolidating all the available resources and providing software defined resources based on the demand has been an efficiency driver. The main reasons the cloud computing really took of are the resource utilisation, efficiency, on demand resource delivery and financial benefits associated with them.

Up until the recent years the processing power, storage available at the end points like user PCS, embedded devices room mobile phones are limited. So, it made logical sense to move the burden of processing and storage to the cloud. An effective example of this is Chromebook from Google or any one of the plethora of cloud services we use every day. The only big disadvantage of these services or products is that they are completely network dependent. Heavy usage of network bandwidth and latency expectations place higher demands on the network infrastructure. This sometimes reduces the quality of experiences for the end users and in extreme cases can even be fatal.

DOI: 10.4018/978-1-5225-5649-7.ch010

Right now in 2017, there are about 2 devices connected to internet per every human on Earth and the number of devices estimated to be connected to internet is estimated to be 50 billion by 2020. These include the mobile phones, smart routers, home automation hubs, smart industrial machines, sensors smart vehicles (Hou, Li, Chen et al., 2016) and the whole gamut of smart devices. To give an idea of how much needs to be pushed through the Internet due to these devices, Boeing flight generate about 1 TB of data or even more for one hour of operation, the weather sensors generate about 500gb of data per day. Our mobile phone sensors are capable of generating more than 500mb of logs per data and that multiplied by number of smart phones is staggering amount of data. This along with the increasing rich media usage in the Internet will be a huge challenge for the next generation networks.

As the processing power and storage capabilities of the end devices like mobile phones, routers, sensor hubs improve we can increasing leverage these resources to improve your quality and reliability of services. Processing or even caching the data near wherever it is generated or utilised frequently not only of loads of the burden on the networks but also improves the decision making capabilities for commercial or industrial instalments, quality of experience for personal usage.

Handling this new generation of requirements of volume, variety and velocity in IOT data requires us to evaluate the tools and technologies. For effective implementation of these use cases places the following requirements on the infrastructure:

1. **Minimise Latency:** Milliseconds, even microseconds matter when you are trying to prevent a failure at a nuclear power station, or preventing of some calamity or to make a buyable impression on a customer. Analyzing data and gaining actionable insights are near as the device itself makes all the difference between a cascading system failure and averting disaster.

2. **Optimising Network Utilisation:** Data generated by the sensors is huge. And not all the data generated is useful. It is not even practical to transport this vast amount of data to centralised processing stations/Data centre nor is it necessary.

3. **Security and Privacy:** Data needs to be protected both in transit and at rest. This requires efficient encryption, monitoring and automated response in case of any breach (Stojmenovic & Wen, 2014).

4. **Reliability:** As more and more intelligent systems are deployed, their effect on the safety of citizens and critical infrastructure cannot be undermined.

5. **Durability:** As the devices themselves can be deployed across wide area of environment conditions. The devices themselves need to be durable and made rugged to work efficiently in harsh environments likes railways, deep oceans, utility field substations and vehicles (Hou, Li, Chen et al., 2016).

6. **Geographic Distribution and Mobility:** The Fog devices should be dispersed geographically as to provide the storage and processing resources to the sensors/actuators producing and acting based on the decisions made. The sensors themselves can be highly mobile. The fog environment should be able to provide consistent resources even in this highly dynamic scenarios. This is especially the case with Wireless sensor area networks, Personal body area networks, Vehicular area network (MANET/VANET).

7. **Interoperability**: The fog devices are intended to be connected to all sorts of devices. Many of these devices have proprietary communication protocols and are not based on IP. In these cases, the fog nodes should be able to communicate and even translate them to IP protocols incase the data needs to be pushed to cloud.

FOG COMPUTING

In simple terms, Fog computing (Yi, Li, & Li, 2015) or Edge computing extends the cloud to be closer to the things that produce, act on and consume data. The devices at the edge are called fog nodes can be deployed anywhere with network connectivity, alongside the railway track, traffic controllers, parking meters, or anywhere else. Any device with sufficient network, storage and computing resources can be a Fog nodes. For example, network switches, embedded servers, CCTV cameras, industrial controllers.

Analyzing data close to where it is collected/generated minuses network latency and offloads gigabytes of less valuable data from the core network, keeping the critical, sensitive data inside the network.

Cisco coined the term Fog computing and defined it as an extension of cloud computing paradigm from the core of network to the edge of network, a highly virtualized platform providing computation, storage (Wu & Sun, 2013) and networking services between end devices and tradition cloud servers. In other work authors defined "Fog computing as a scenario where a huge number of heterogeneous ubiquitous and decentralized devices communicate and potentially cooperate among themselves and with the network to perform storage and processing tasks without any third-party intervention. These tasks can be basic network functions or sophisticated, novel services and applications that run in a virtualized environments. Users leasing a part of their devices to host these services get incentives for doing so,". Although the exact definition of Fog computing is still being constructed it is essential to separate this from related technologies.

Similar concepts such as Mobile cloud computing and Mobile Edge computing overlap with Fog computing. In Mobile Edge computing (Hu, Patel, Sabella et al., 2015), cloud server running at the edge of the mobile network performs specifics tasks that cannot be accomplished with traditional network infrastructure. While Mobile Cloud computing refers to infrastructure in which data storage and processing occurs outside the mobile devices. MCC pushes the data and computation to the cloud making it feasible for the non-smartphone users to use mobile applications and services. Fog computing is a more generalized platform with virtual resources and application aware processing.

Applications of Fog computing is as diverse as IoT and Cloud computing itself. What IoT and Fog computing have in common is to monitor and analyse real-time data from network connected things and acting on them. Machine-to-machine coordination or human-machine interaction can be a part of this action. Unlimited possibilities,

As we have seen in earlier sections, the following scenarios make a good case for Fog computing:

1. Data is generated from thousands or millions of things/sensors distributed geographically.
2. Data is collected at the extreme edges of the infrastructure: factory floors, warehouses, roadways, etc.
3. The time taken to analyse, take a decision and act on the data is in range of milliseconds.

Difference between Fog computing and Cloud computing:

The core difference comes in the way resources are organized. In cloud computing the resources are centralized whereas in Fog computing the resources are scattered and available possibly nearer the client. Cloud service providers are generally single tiered organizations whereas the fog ecosystem as such is multi-tiered. Fog computing supports dynamic, mobility better than cloud computing as the resources allocated are near-by the usage itself. Due to the service locality and geographic distribution of resources the latency in transmission of data is highly reduced. This mode of processing has an added benefit of

Figure 1. Fog platform high level architecture

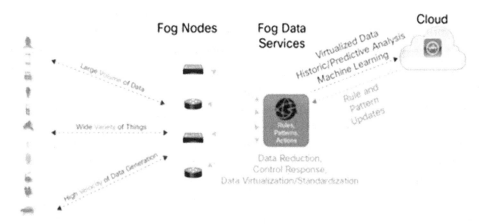

adhering to local security and privacy norms. The differences are highlighted in the succeeding table (Figure 2).

If you look at the financial side of implementing fog computing, a study at Wikibon found that cloud-only infrastructure is costlier to maintain as compared to Cloud with Fog/Edge computing infrastructure. One of the main reasons for this is the average life cycle of a cloud server is a measly 2 years. In proper Fog computing infrastructure the servers' life time is upto 8 years. This would make a huge difference for companies small and large in both short term and long term technology infrastructures.

As we have already seen the major demerit with cloud computing is latency (Bonomi, Milito, Zhu et al., 2012). Latency in feeding the data into the system to analyzing it and producing tangible insights. These insights in many cases help in making split-second decisions. Some data is valuable at the moment

Figure 2. Cloud computing vs. Fog Computing

Requirement	Cloud Computing	Fog Computing
Latency	High	Low
Delay Jitter	High	Very low
Location of server nodes	Within the internet	At the edge of the local network
Distance between the client and the server.	Multiple hops	One hop
Security	Undefined	Can be defined
Attack on data enroute	High probability	Very low probability
Location awareness	No	Yes
Geographical distribution.	Centralized	Distributed
Number of server nodes	Few	Very large
Support for mobility	Limited	Supported
Real time interactions	Supported	Supported
Type of last mile connectivity.	Leased line	Wireless

it is recorded. For example, a pressure gauge going critical in a manufacturing plant, or a security breach at a critical site or Complex event processing. Fog computing helps in analysing at the sources and give results with-in milliseconds range. And the insights are fed to visualisation tools to communicate and coordinate with other systems, the data is then sent to cloud for archiving, aggregation and further batch analysis can be done at the cloud level. As shown in Figure 3. As we move on to transactional analytics and Historical analysis cloud become the ideal choice to do run the analyses.

Another advantage in analyzing the data near the source is all the data generated need to be fed into cloud system. The data generated will have a lot of noise or unnecessary data which doesn't provide us with any significant insight. So, pushing the data just wastes precious network bandwidth and cloud storage.

Data thinning removes this unnecessary data and strips away all the noise just leaving us with only the data that really matters. For example, a driverless car might generate Petabytes of image data a year of bumpers or speed breakers or any line it crosses and that generated data in entirety is so useful. A Boeing jet generates 2.5TB data per 1 hour of flight operation. An oil drill sensors generate more than 10 GB of data per second.

As the minimalist principle states "More is not always better." The processing of the data at the fog nodes not only reduce the time to insight but they in-turn help in making emergency responses more efficient.

Application Scenarios Healthcare Monitoring

One of important ways the Fog computing might help in Health care is to take conservative snap decisions and escalate the risky situations for deep analysis which can further help in reducing the risk of false negatives. One such effective implementation is for alerting doctor of cardiac arrests (Stantchev, Barnawi, Ghulam et al., 2015).

Earlier notification systems required users to wear unfriendly chest straps and needed extensive monitoring. Not to mention expensive and often obstructive to the normal flow of life of patients. The implementations based on wearable solved this problem. They are relatively cheap and are used friendly. Data is pushed to the cloud or remote servers from these devices for analysis. On the software side,

Figure 3. Processing latency from Fog computing to Cloud computing

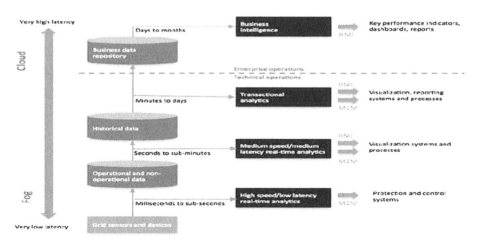

many implementations based on statistical models do not have required positive detention. Rates. To eliminate these errors sophisticated neural network based techniques were employed. Although these techniques provided with high levels of detection rates, they are slow. The simple statistical model scored points in this regard. In addition with the latency of networks to push the data to cloud for processing they couldn't provide analysis within required time frame. To circumvent these problems one can look at processing primary analysis nearer to the patient and push the processed data to the cloud for further analysis. Through this a quick response can be given in a way to avert a possible emergency or handle it in a more efficient manner.

These analyses also come under the broad class of Mobile Big Data analytics use cases. Fog computing provides elastic resources to large scale systems without the latency concerns of cloud computing (Buyya, Yeo, Venugopal et al., 2009). As explained in the health care monitoring case, federation of cloud and fog will take care of data acquisition, aggregation and pre-processing, reducing bandwidth overload and data processing. Bonomi, et al. (Bonomi, Milito, Zhu et al., 2012).

Content Delivery and Caching

Traditional caching or content delivery techniques are heavily server dependent. Even they provide a sense of geo-graphic locality for multi-datacenter implementations. Delivering content to end-users is a not-optimally efficient. What a particular client or set of client want and network level statistics are only available at a local level. This knowledge can be leveraged to optimise the web performance. Since fog nodes lie in the vicinity of the user it can gather statistics and usage knowledge to optimise the user experience. And this reduces the requirement of bandwidth as the data most required will most probably in the vicinity of the user itself. J. Zhu, et al. consider web optimisation from this new perspective in the context of fog computing (Zhu, Chan, Prabhu et al., 2013).

Software Defined Networking

In broadest terms, the network is connection between various servers and storage clusters inside as well as outside a datacenter. This is the fundamental contributor to QoS and delivery performance of applications. Businesses creating their cloud environments should have a keener look at their whole infrastructure mainly the network which glues every component together. Many of the large enterprises work in distributed geographical locations, while the applications that are pre-dominantly media based, time-sensitive. This puts pressure on QoS (Quality of Service) for applications delivered over the network. (Nunes, Mendonca, Nguyen et al., 2014).

Networking has traditionally been completely about hardware. With almost all the major functions are hardcoded in the hardware making it difficult and expensive to upgrade firmware. With the sophistication of software, these functionalities are slowly moved into the software layer, this is called network function virtualization (Martins, Ahmed, Raiciu et al., 2014). Software defined networking is a complete reproduction of physical network at software level, while being more flexible and can be customised according to the application's requirements. The applications can run exactly the same as if they are run on physical network. (Barroso, Clidaras, & Hölzle, 2013).

A protocol is a set of rules governing communications. Networking protocols lay down the format of message, how they will be identified and what actions need to be taken.

Figure 4. Network packet

8 Bytes	6 bytes	6 Bytes	2 Bytes	0-1500 Bytes	0-46 Bytes	4 Bytes
Preamble	Destination Address	Source Address	Frame Length	Data	Pad	Checksum

NETWORK FUNCTION VIRTUALIZATION

If Overlay networks gives the capability of creating network tunnels per flow. The next logical step is offload the functions of hardware based networking services like Firewalls, Load Balancers and provide them as a service on the tunnel. This is Network Function Virtualization. Network function Virtualization proposes to virtualise entire classes of network node functions in to building blocks using virtualization. The popular functions for this are firewalls and IDS/IPS systems from companies like PLUMgrid or Embrane (Wu & Sun, 2013).

Network Function Virtualization runs on x86 platforms, instead of having its own hardware appliance. The NFV architecture has the following three important components:

1. **Virtualized Network Function:** Software implementation of network functions.
2. **Network Function Virtualization Infrastructure:** The combination of software+ hardware on which VNFs are deployed.
3. Network Function virtualization management and Orchestration architecture.

Figure 5. Virtual Network

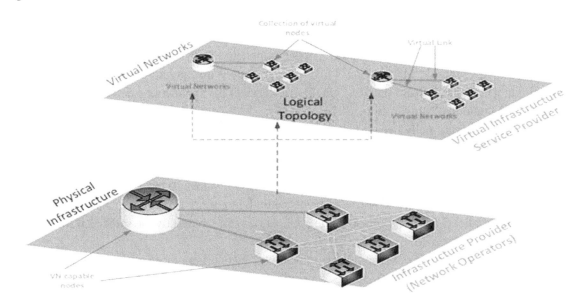

Instead of buying huge, expensive IDS for handling the whole network, one can simply buy specific functions to be deployed.

Software Defined Networking

SDN simply is about making datacenter networking infrastructure pooled and automated resource which can be configured and maintained through software and can seamlessly extend across public/private cloud boundaries. How will this help? Centralized control of networking infrastructure, optimum utilisation of existing physical network, workload optimisation to name a few benefits.

The key of computing trends driving the need of network programmability and a new network paradigm include: changing traffic patterns of applications, big-data computations, consumerisation of IT (Jain & Paul, 2013).

SDN starts with abstracting applications form underlying physical networks. Then it provides consistent platform to specify and enforce policy across all clouds. And finally it provides with a standards based mechanism for automatic deployment of networks while being extensible (Barroso, Clidaras, & Hölzle, 2013).

By separating the control plane from the data plane, SDN makes it possible to build programmable network. It relies on network switches which can be programmed through an SDN controller. Unlike the Overlay networks and NFVs which work on top of physical networks, SDN changes the physical network itself. SDN is implemented on network switches unlike other network virtualization (Jain, & Paul, 2013) techniques. BigSwitch and Pica8 are two notable names selling SDN products. This reduces the necessity to buy black proprietary box switches which are expensive. Instead one can easily buy a cheap white box switches and install SDN controller.

Few characteristics of SDN architecture are: Network control is directly programmable, agile as it is easy for the network manager to enforce changes in policies efficiently and quickly, software based SDN controllers centrally manage the network, the networking resources can be configured programmatically.

Figure 6. Software Defined Networking architecture

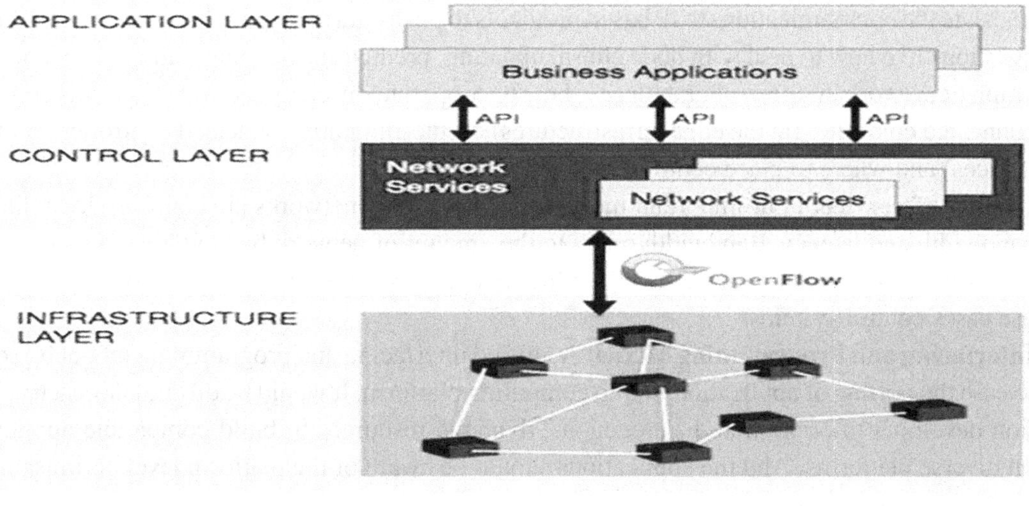

Figure 7. Control and Forwarding element separation within a router

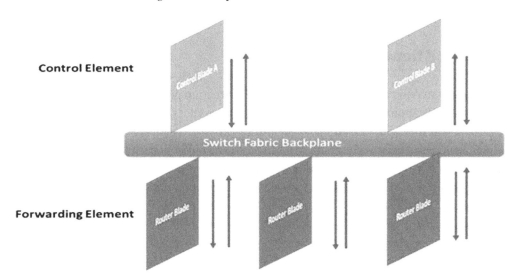

RESEARCH CHALLENGES IN FOG COMPUTING

The fog computing is slowly clutching its way into mainstream. There are still several issues that needs to be tackled. The Fog layer should be interoperable and fault resilient. To achieve this goal in a non-compromising way we need to work on security protocols which don't flood the Fog or create any bottleneck. As the emphasis on standardisation evolves, surely certain challenges will be tackled. we will identify issues and research challenges in implementing and realising full potential of fog computing.

4. **Networking and Interconnectivity:** The Fog nodes are located at the edge of the networks. They are the interlink between the sensor layer and internet infrastructure. Because of that the Fog network is predominantly heterogenous. It needs to support various communication protocols which are not necessarily IP based. The sensor and IoT devices (Aazam & Huh, 2014) for example support ZigBee, MQTT and various other protocols. The fog nodes need to understand and possibly translate the communications to IP based protocols to push data to cloud. There are other interesting questions like how to deal with node churn, updating, predicting and maintaining the connectivity graph of network in different granularity; how to cooperate different controllers such as constantly connected controller (at the edge infrastructures) or intermittently connected controller (at the end devices) and where to place controllers in fog network.

5. **Quality of Service:** Four important metrics for QoS in Fog networks are connectivity, reliability, bandwidth and latency. Bandwidth refers to the amount of network bandwidth and storage bandwidth at the individual nodes. The reliability and latency requirements are especially critical for use cases control systems.

6. **Interfacing and Programming Model:** A unified interfacing and programming model is required to ease the porting of applications to fog computing platform. It would be difficult for each application developer to orchestrate heterogenous, dynamic resources to build compatible applications on diverse platforms. And the applications should be aware of the platform level optimisations.

7. **Security and Privacy:** The main advantage of Fog computing is the data locality. This reduces the effect of privacy leakage. However, machine to machine authentication and authorization, user client access control and enforcement of policies is a challenge. This can be rectified using privacy preserving techniques and end-to-end encryption of data. However, this needs more to be done (Stojmenovic & Wen, 2014).

8. **Provisioning and Resource Management:** The challenges lie in the mobility of end node since metrics such as bandwidth, storage, computation and latency will be changed dynamically. Resource discovery and sharing Resource discovery and sharing is critical for application performance in fog. The dynamic provisioning of resources and application aware hardware provisioning also is one interesting challenge.

9. **Accounting, Billing and Monitoring:** Sustainable business model with sufficient incentives and benefits for the fog services providers and users to make Fog computing viable. How are the incentives decided and how the pricing polices are set is going to one challenge for widespread adoption of Fog computing. And how the pricing policies are enforced. Research directions looks at the similar pricing models of cloud computing (Buyya, Yeo, Venugopal et al., 2009). However, they pose additional challenges on Fog computing platforms.

CONCLUSION

Fog computing will help businesses be more agile and efficient in their operations, help in decluttering and reduces information overload at the higher decision making levels. Fog computing is an extension to the cloud bringing the virtual resources called fog nodes nearby the data generation and consumption. It's application areas are as vast as IoT deployment, 5G network deployment, SDN, Personal Area network, Plant management. Cisco IoX platform is pioneer in this domain providing production level platform for the companies to introduce fog in their environments. The major research challenges include the deployment of fog nodes, International device communication protocols.

REFERENCES

Aazam, M., & Huh, E.N. (2014, August). Fog computing and smart gateway based communication for cloud of things. *Proceedings of the 2014 International Conference on Future Internet of Things and Cloud (FiCloud)* (pp. 464-470). IEEE.

Barroso, L. A., Clidaras, J., & Hölzle, U. (2013). The datacenter as a computer: An introduction to the design of warehouse-scale machines. *Synthesis lectures on computer architecture, 8*(3), 1-154.

Bonomi, F., Milito, R., Zhu, J., & Addepalli, S. (2012, August). Fog computing and its role in the internet of things. *Proceedings of the first edition of the MCC workshop on Mobile cloud computing* (pp. 13-16). ACM. doi:10.1145/2342509.2342513

Buyya, R., Yeo, C. S., Venugopal, S., Broberg, J., & Brandic, I. (2009). Cloud computing and emerging IT platforms: Vision, hype, and reality for delivering computing as the 5th utility. *Future Generation Computer Systems*, *25*(6), 599–616. doi:10.1016/j.future.2008.12.001

Hou, X., Li, Y., Chen, M., Wu, D., Jin, D., & Chen, S. (2016). Vehicular fog computing: A viewpoint of vehicles as the infrastructures. *IEEE Transactions on Vehicular Technology*, *65*(6), 3860–3873. doi:10.1109/TVT.2016.2532863

Hu, Y. C., Patel, M., Sabella, D., Sprecher, N., & Young, V. (2015). Mobile edge computing—A key technology towards 5G (no. 11). ETSI White Paper.

Jain, R., & Paul, S. (2013). Network virtualization and software defined networking for cloud computing: A survey. *IEEE Communications Magazine*, *51*(11), 24–31. doi:10.1109/MCOM.2013.6658648

Martins, J., Ahmed, M., Raiciu, C., Olteanu, V., Honda, M., Bifulco, R., & Huici, F. (2014, April). ClickOS and the art of network function virtualization. *Proceedings of the 11th USENIX Conference on Networked Systems Design and Implementation* (pp. 459-473). USENIX Association.

Nunes, B. A. A., Mendonca, M., Nguyen, X. N., Obraczka, K., & Turletti, T. (2014). A survey of software-defined networking: Past, present, and future of programmable networks. *IEEE Communications Surveys and Tutorials*, *16*(3), 1617–1634. doi:10.1109/SURV.2014.012214.00180

Stantchev, V., Barnawi, A., Ghulam, S., Schubert, J., & Tamm, G. (2015). Smart items, fog and cloud computing as enablers of servitization in healthcare. *Sensors & Transducers*, *185*(2), 121.

Stojmenovic, I., & Wen, S. (2014, September). The fog computing paradigm: Scenarios and security issues. *Proceedings of the 2014 Federated Conference on Computer Science and Information Systems (FedCSIS)* (pp. 1-8). IEEE. doi:10.1145/2757384.2757397

Wu, F., & Sun, G. (2013). *Software-defined storage. Report*. Minneapolis: University of Minnesota.

Yi, S., Li, C., & Li, Q. (2015, June). A survey of fog computing: concepts, applications and issues. *Proceedings of the 2015 Workshop on Mobile Big Data* (pp. 37-42). ACM.

Zhu, J., Chan, D. S., Prabhu, M. S., Natarajan, P., Hu, H., & Bonomi, F. (2013, March). Improving web sites performance using edge servers in fog computing architecture. *Proceedings of the 2013 IEEE 7th International Symposium on Service Oriented System Engineering (SOSE)* (pp. 320-323). IEEE.

ADDITIONAL READING

Feng, D. G., Zhang, M., Zhang, Y., & Xu, Z. (2011). Study on cloud computing security. *Journal of software*, *22*(1), 71-83.

Joshi, Y., & Kumar, P. (Eds.). (2012). *Energy efficient thermal management of data centers*. Springer Science & Business Media. doi:10.1007/978-1-4419-7124-1

Sotomayor, B., Montero, R. S., Llorente, I. M., & Foster, I. (2009). Virtual infrastructure management in private and hybrid clouds. *IEEE Internet Computing, 13*(5), 14–22. doi:10.1109/MIC.2009.119

Wikibon.org. (n. d.). Cloud. Retrieved from http://wikibon.org/wiki/v/Cloud

Zhang, Q., Cheng, L., & Boutaba, R. (2010). Cloud computing: state-of-the-art and research challenges. *Journal of internet services and applications, 1*(1), 7-18.

KEY TERMS AND DEFINTIONS

DAS: Direct attached storage.
DR: Disaster recovery.
NAS: Network attached storage.
SAN: Storage Area Network.
TCO: Total Cost of Ownership.
VM: Virtual Machine.

This research was previously published in Design and Use of Virtualization Technology in Cloud Computing edited by Prashanta Kumar Das and Ganesh Chandra Deka, pages 100-114, copyright year 2018 by Engineering Science Reference (an imprint of IGI Global).

Chapter 11

Vehicular Fog Computing:
Challenges Applications and Future Directions

Varun G. Menon
Sathyabama University, India

Joe Prathap
RMD Engineering College, India

ABSTRACT

In recent years Vehicular Ad Hoc Networks (VANETs) have received increased attention due to its numerous applications in cooperative collision warning and traffic alert broadcasting. VANETs have been depending on cloud computing for networking, computing and data storage services. Emergence of advanced vehicular applications has led to the increased demand for powerful communication and computation facilities with low latency. With cloud computing unable to satisfy these demands, the focus has shifted to bring computation and communication facilities nearer to the vehicles, leading to the emergence of Vehicular Fog Computing (VFC). VFC installs highly virtualized computing and storage facilities at the proximity of these vehicles. The integration of fog computing into VANETs comes with a number of challenges that range from improved quality of service, security and privacy of data to efficient resource management. This paper presents an overview of this promising technology and discusses the issues and challenges in its implementation with future research directions.

INTRODUCTION

Mobile Ad Hoc Networks (MANETs) (Chlamtac, 2003; Conti & Giordano, 2014) are a collection of wireless devices like mobile phones, laptops and iPads that can dynamically form a wireless network for communication in emergency situations, disaster recovery operations (Menon et al., 2016) battlefields etc. These networks are deployed without the support of any fixed infrastructure like access points and does not have any centralized control. It is an autonomous system of mobile device in which every device can join or leave the network at any time leading to a highly dynamic and unpredictable topology. Vehicular

DOI: 10.4018/978-1-5225-5649-7.ch011

Ad Hoc Networks (Li & Wang, 2007; Dua, 2014; Chen et al., 2015) are specific type of MANETs in which the mobile nodes are moving vehicles. In VANETs every vehicle is equipped with an on-board unit and a group of sensors. The radio interfaces or on-board unit enables short range wireless ad hoc networks to be formed. VANETs often has multiple Road Side Units (RSUs) deployed as intermediary servers near the vehicles to process the data. VANETs offer both vehicle to vehicle and vehicle to road-side unit communication (Harsch et al., 2007). Every vehicle in the network plays the role of a sender, receiver and a router to broadcast data to the vehicular network and the roadside units which then uses the data to ensure safe and free flow of traffic. VANETs are used in the design and development of Intelligent Transportation Systems (ITS) that offers improved safety and better transportation. VANETs are currently being used for traffic monitoring, emergency services, safe driving, infotainment services, location detection services, automated toll payment etc.

VANETs have been depending primarily on cloud computing (Vouk, 2008; Rountree & Castrillo, 2014) services for communication, computing and storage facilities. Cloud computing offers computation and storage facilities using a central cloud server or a group of remote servers. Cloud computing provides users with scalable virtual networks, virtual servers for remote storage space and computing facilities. Data stored can be accessed from any place without the trouble of keeping large storage and computing devices in the vehicles. Users could share and distribute large amount of data between the vehicles. One of the major areas of concern in cloud computing is the delay in transfer of data and information from the vehicles to the remote cloud server and back to the vehicles after storage and processing. With tremendous rise in the number of connected vehicles and with their ever-increasing mobility, the demand for applications that support low latency, uninterrupted services is rising day by day. It has become quite difficult to meet the challenges of efficient communication and computation with the emergence of latest and advanced vehicular applications. Providing required Quality of Service (QoS) is another important challenge faced by Vehicular Cloud Computing (VCC) (Whaiduzzaman et al., 2014; Shojafar et al., 2016; Mekki et al., 2016). Various vehicular applications designed for latest high-speed vehicles will require powerful communication and computational support. Apart from cloud computing, the other solutions used to provide communication and computational support was Fourth Generation Cellular Networks (Hampel et al., 2003) and Road Side Units. However, these technologies suffered from many limitations. Cellular networks were controlled by their respective service providers, thus limiting the flexibility of communication in VANETs (Hampel et al., 2003). Also, there were many difficulties in deploying Road Side Units at a larger scale (Kuo et al., 2013).

Fog computing is a paradigm that extends cloud computing services to the edge of the network (Bonomi et al., 2012; Vaquero & Rodero-Merino 2014; Dastjerdi & Buyya, 2016; Chiang & Zhang, 2016; Shin et al., 2016). It introduces an intermediate fog layer between the cloud and the mobile devices. Devices with computing and communication capabilities (fog nodes) are deployed in this fog layer near to the user devices. As computing and storage facilities are provided on the edge (very near to the user), applications offer better QoS with fog computing. Extending fog computing to vehicular networks (Vehicular Fog Computing) (Hou et al., 2016; Kai et al., 2016) helps to provide powerful communication and computational support to the latest applications in vehicular networks. Vehicular Fog Computing uses the devices on the vehicles or deploys devices near to the vehicles to form an intermediary fog layer. These devices then collect the data from the sensors installed on the vehicles, processes them and communicates the result as alerts or messages to the vehicles in its network and with the road side units. This provides immediate alert or data to other vehicles with very less latency. The road side units could then send this data to centralized cloud servers to free the storage space. Cloud servers having high storage and processing capacity may keep this historical data for any analysis in the future. This article initially discusses the limitations with vehicular cloud computing and then presents the issues and challenges involved in integrating fog computing into vehicular ad hoc networks.

VEHICULAR FOG COMPUTING

Fog computing provides a virtual platform for local computing, storage and processing in end user devices rather than in centralized data servers. Fog computing deploys a network of fog servers between the underlying networks and the clouds. In Vehicular Fog Computing the computing, communication and storage services are provided at near user edge devices. A fog server layer is deployed between the vehicles and the cloud server. Vehicular Fog Computing uses the devices on the vehicles or deploys devices near to the vehicles to form this intermediary fog layer. End users and vehicles are also considered part of the "fog". In contrast to the cloud computing services which are more centralized, fog computing targets applications with widely distributed deployments. The sensors and other devices in the vehicles gather data and this data is stored and processed at intermediate fog servers. Thus, the services provide low-latency communication and more context awareness. Figure 1 shows the architecture of Vehicular Fog Computing. The fog could be multiple road side units or devices in vehicles or near the vehicles or it can be an aggregation of the abundant resources from the group of vehicles. Using this fog layer most of the data from the vehicles are processed and immediate response is provided to the vehicles in the network. Communication from the fog layer to the cloud server takes place only when required. Fog computing is highly beneficial for low latency applications such as video streaming and gaming. Proximity to users and the continuous support for mobility have been the two unique advantages that have led to the growing popularity of VFC in research and industry.

Figure 1. Architecture of vehicular fog computing

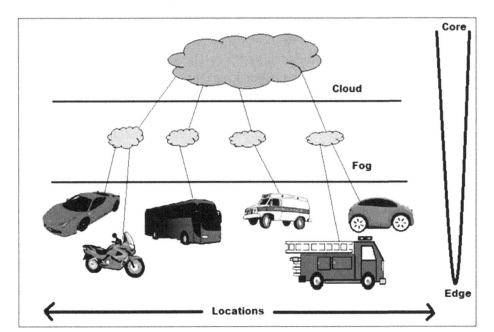

Table 1 shows the comparison of Vehicular Fog Computing (VFC) with Vehicular Cloud Computing (VCC). Although cloud computing offered good performance to vehicular applications, the long distance between mobile devices, vehicles and the remote data centers hindered provision of real-time service to these applications. This led to much higher delay in communication and resource sharing with Vehicular Cloud Computing. Moreover, VFC offers excellent support for mobility while VCC, supports only applications that are less mobile. Vehicular Cloud Computing is bandwidth constraint with high cost of deployment. Vehicular Fog Computing on the other hand has low cost of deployment with real time load balancing and local decision making.

Advantages of Vehicular Fog Computing

- **Low Latency:** Real time processing of data takes place on the edge, much closer to the vehicle. This provides faster results that can be send as messages to other vehicles and road side units. Reduced delay in data transmission is one of the primary advantages with vehicular fogs. With devices inside and near the vehicles acting as fog servers, the delay in communication, computation and data processing will come down drastically leading to high performance of the latest applications installed in vehicles and user devices. With the new generation of Internet of Things, (Deshkar et al. 2017; Philip et al., 2017) reduced delay in data transmission is extremely vital in determining the success all advanced applications installed on these smart devices and vehicles;
- **Pooling of Local Resources:** Idle processing power and sensing ability within the devices at the edge can be pooled for better services in a fog network. Often various devices in the vehicles

Table 1. Vehicular fog computing vs. vehicular cloud computing

Computing Type / Features	Vehicular Fog Computing	Vehicular Cloud Computing
Location of computing, communication and storage facilities	At the proximity of users	Remote locations away from the users
Latency of real time applications	Low	High
Mobility support	High mobility support	Limited mobility support
Service Type	Localized Information Service specific to the fog region	Global Information Collected
Architecture	Distributed	Centralized
Decision making	Local	Remote
Communication	Real Time Load Balancing	Constraints in Bandwidth
Storage	Limited storage space	Highly scalable storage space
Computing Capabilities	Medium Computing Capabilities	Higher Computing Capabilities
Cost of Deployment	Low	High
Number of Server Nodes	Large	Few

might not be utilized to its full potential. These devices can be grouped to generate better computation facility for vehicular networks leading to efficient utilization of resources and reduced costs;

- **Vehicles as Infrastructures:** Hou et al. (2016) proposed a variation of using vehicles as infrastructures to carry out communication and computation and also aggregation of underutilized vehicular resources. Using the vehicles and underutilized devices within the vehicles for computation and communication will help in improving the efficiency of applications using the fog network;

- **Better Quality of Service:** With fog computing, applications offer much faster data rates with minimum latency and response time. Compared to Vehicular Cloud Computing, VFC offers much higher speed in data transmission with reduced delay. This helps to provide better quality of service to applications using the vehicular fog network;

- **Improved Efficiency of Network and Improved Agility of Services:** Fog computing avoids the back-and-forth traffic between cloud servers and devices in vehicles. This saves the bandwidth in the network. Fog computing fosters rapid innovation and affordable scaling. Instead of waiting for changes to be made to the cloud servers and services, users can customize new applications that are available much nearer to them.

APPLICATIONS OF VEHICULAR FOG COMPUTING

Vehicular Fog Computing offers numerous advantages for communication and resource sharing between the vehicles. These advantages can be utilized for designing efficient applications in vehicular networks. We discuss the working of one of the latest application that uses fog servers to monitor the condition of roads. This application for road surface condition monitoring (Basudan et al., 2017) used the fog devices deployed in vehicular networks for data processing. The application consisted of a control center (CC), mobile sensors, e.g., vehicles and smart devices, RSUs as the fog devices, and cloud servers. Figure 2 shows the architecture of the road surface condition monitoring system with vehicular fog computing. The control server (CC) is a trustable entity in charge of the entire system and is responsible for initializing, monitoring and securing the system. Here the mobile sensors that are attached to the vehicles collects data from surface of the road that may include potholes. This real-time data is then immediately transferred to the Road Side Units (RSU's). RSU's are considered as an efficient computational and storage device that can extend the cloud services to the edge. RSUs have the ability to react and make decisions close to the end users. RSU'S processes this data and send alerts to other vehicles regarding the condition of the road including potholes and thus preventing accidents. RSU's may send their data to cloud servers at any point of time to free their storage space. Cloud servers could store this data and can utilize them at a later stage for any require research or analysis.

This application using vehicular fog computing has a number of advantages. The most important being the use of RSU's as the fog servers for computation and in processing data. As the road side units are nearer to the vehicles, the delay in delivering the processed information to the other vehicles in the network would be very less. Also, the application uses a cloud server without compromising on the quality of service. The cloud server helps the road side units to free their storage space. Also, the cloud server may collect data from multiple road side units and process information when required. The constraints or difficulty in the deployment of RSUs in large scale might be a major limitation for this application.

Figure 2. Architecture surface condition monitoring system with vehicular fog computing

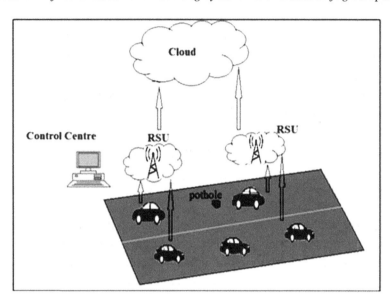

CHALLENGES AND OPEN PROBLEMS

Most of the latest applications in vehicular networks require powerful computational and communication support for efficient functioning. Many applications such as gaming, video streaming etc. always demand low latency communication. These demands are met by deploying fog servers near to the vehicles. But extending fog computing into vehicular ad hoc networks have led to a number of open issues and challenges. We present and discuss these challenges and open problems in Vehicular Fog Computing. Many advanced applications could be designed for vehicles with this very latest and powerful technology.

Quality of Service

Quality of Service is one of the most important performance parameter for any communication network. With application users demanding better Quality of Service, it's vital for Vehicular Fog Computing to satisfy the demands. We focus on transmission delay and reliability as the two important Quality of Service parameters for VFC networks (Yi et al., 2015). With highly mobile vehicles, the topology of VANETs remains dynamic throughout. So, it's very important to design a routing mechanism that would ensure minimum delay in communication between the vehicles and the fog nodes. Also, the delay caused by route failures and retransmissions has to be minimized. The routing mechanism has to take care of the fog nodes deployed near to the users. These devices might be manufactured by different vendors with limitations in mobility and power. The routing mechanism must be supported by the fog nodes and also by the sensors in the vehicles. The fog nodes and the fog computing platform must be able to provide 24*7 support to the application users. Reliability of communication is another major area of concern in VFC. The communication framework should be designed to maintain continuous and reliable communication between the vehicles and fog nodes. With the distributed framework of VFC, it's highly challenging to detect and repair the fog nodes. VFC need to address the major issues in reliability that includes detection of transmission failures, rescheduling failed tasks and recovering from failures in the system.

Resource Management

Efficient utilization of available computation and storage resources in vehicles is a major area of research in VFC. Many techniques used for resource sharing in ad hoc networks (Buttyan & Hubaux, 2000; Zhong et al., 2003) is being tried and tested in VFC. A set of protocols or agreements have to be designed for efficient resource sharing between the vehicles. VFC must make sure that every connected vehicle in the network authorizes the transfer of messages and sharing of resources with one other. A number of efficient protocols have to be devised to detect the idle resources in vehicles and the distribution of tasks among the vehicles. This is an area very less explored by researchers.

Vehicular Mobility Models

Prediction and analysis of vehicular movements are very important factors in designing routing protocols and resource management mechanisms in VFC. With tremendous rise in the number of connected vehicles and with their ever-increasing mobility, it has been very difficult to arrive at a near accurate mobility model. Many mobility models (Viriyasitavat et al., 2009; Naboulsi & Fiore, 2013) have been suggested for VFC. But a much accurate mobility model is required to design efficient applications in VFC. Accurate knowledge of vehicular mobility patterns will help in designing efficient routing protocols for communication and computation in VFC. With precise mobility models, it's easier to design the right protocols for communication and resource sharing.

Security and Privacy

Many recent works have been done on security issues in vehicular ad hoc networks (Maglaras, 2015; Feray et al., 2016; Wei et al., 2016). But very few works have focused on security and privacy issues in vehicular fog computing. With large amount of resources and data being shared in the network, it's important to have stringent and clear security mechanisms in VFC. Lack of proper authentication mechanism can lead to security attacks in the network. With information transmitted between the vehicles being used for safe driving and traffic monitoring, any tampering on data can be fatal. The network has to be protected from misuse of information, resources and protocols by intruders. Considering the sensitivity of user data being distributed in such a dynamic network, it's important to ensure data integrity and privacy. Privacy protection and data confidentiality in VFC is an area very less studied.

CONCLUSION

In this article, we discussed the integration of fog computing into Vehicular Ad Hoc Networks termed as Vehicular Fog Computing. Initially we discussed about vehicular cloud computing and its limitations in supporting advanced applications for highly mobile vehicles in vehicular ad hoc networks. With increasing number of connected vehicles, and continuously increasing mobility, vehicular cloud computing is unable to meet the demand from the latest vehicular applications. The new opportunities and possibilities brought in by fog computing in these highly dynamic vehicular networks were then presented. We discussed the deployment of fog layer between the vehicles and the cloud servers. We highlighted and discussed the advantages of Vehicular Fog Computing over Vehicular clod computing. VFC provides user applications with high mobility support and low latency communication. VFC also has low cost of deployment with real time load balancing and local decision making. Finally, we discussed the issues and challenges that arises with Vehicular Fog Computing and provided future research directions. Future research may focus on improving the quality of service of communication between the vehicles and the fog devices. Security and privacy of data transferred between the vehicles and the fog devices is yet another unexplored area of research.

REFERENCES

Bonomi, F., Milito, R., Zhu, J., & Addepalli, S. (2012). Fog Computing and Its Role in the Internet of Things. In *Proceedings of ACM Mobile cloud computing (MCC '12)*, New York, NY (pp. 13-16). doi:10.1145/2342509.2342513

Buttyan, L., & Hubaux, J. P. (2000). Enforcing service availability in mobile ad-hoc WANs. In *Proceedings of the First Annual Workshop on Mobile and Ad Hoc Networking and Computing, (MobiHOC-2000)*, Boston, MA (pp. 87-96).

Chen, R., Zhong, Z., Chang, C., Ai, B., & He, R. (2015). Performance analysis on network connectivity for vehicular ad hoc networks. *International Journal of Ad Hoc and Ubiquitous Computing*, *20*(2), 67. doi:10.1504/IJAHUC.2015.071692

Chiang, M., & Zhang, T. (2016). Fog and IoT: An Overview of Research Opportunities. *IEEE Internet Of Things Journal*, *3*(6), 854–864. doi:10.1109/JIOT.2016.2584538

Chlamtac, I., Conti, M., & Liu, J. (2003). Mobile ad hoc networking: Imperatives and challenges. *Ad Hoc Networks*, *1*(1), 13–64. doi:10.1016/S1570-8705(03)00013-1

Conti, M., & Giordano, S. (2014). Mobile ad hoc networking: Milestones, challenges, and new research directions. *IEEE Communications Magazine*, *52*(1), 85–96. doi:10.1109/MCOM.2014.6710069

Dastjerdi, A., & Buyya, R. (2016). Fog Computing: Helping the Internet of Things Realize Its Potential. *Computer*, *49*(8), 112–116. doi:10.1109/MC.2016.245

Deshkar, S., Thanseeh, R. A., & Menon, V. G. (2017). A Review on IoT based m-Health Systems for Diabetes. *International Journal of Computer Science and Telecommunications*, *8*(1), 13–18.

Dua, A., Kumar, N., & Bawa, S. (2014). A systematic review on routing protocols for Vehicular Ad Hoc Networks. *Vehicular Communications*, *1*(1), 33–52. doi:10.1016/j.vehcom.2014.01.001

Ferrag, M. A., Maglaras, L., & Ahmim, A. (2016). Privacy-preserving schemes for Ad Hoc Social Networks: A survey. arXiv:1610.06095.

Hampel, G., Clarkson, K. L., Hobby, J. D., & Polakos, P. A. (2003). The tradeoff between coverage and capacity in dynamic optimization of 3G cellular networks. In *Proceedings of VTC—Fall*, Orlando, FL (pp. 927–932). doi:10.1109/VETECF.2003.1285156

Harsch, C., Festag A. & Papadimitratos, (2007). Secure position-based routing for VANETs. In *Proceedings of the 2007 IEEE 66th Vehicular Technology Conference*, Baltimore, MD (pp. 26-30).

Hou, X., Li, Y., Chen, M., Wu, D., Jin, D., & Chen, S. (2016). Vehicular Fog Computing: A Viewpoint of Vehicles as the Infrastructures. *IEEE Transactions on Vehicular Technology*, *65*(6), 3860–3873. doi:10.1109/TVT.2016.2532863

Kai, K., Cong, W., & Tao, L. (2016). Fog computing for vehicular Ad-hoc networks: Paradigms, scenarios, and issues. *Journal of China Universities of Posts and Telecommunications*, *23*(2), 56–96. doi:10.1016/S1005-8885(16)60021-3

Kiess, W., & Mauve, M. (2007). A survey on real-world implementations of mobile ad-hoc networks. *Ad Hoc Networks*, *5*(3), 324–339. doi:10.1016/j.adhoc.2005.12.003

Kuo, W., Tung, Y., & Fang, S. (2013). A node management scheme for R2V connections in RSU-supported Vehicular ad-hoc networks. In *Proceedings of ICNC*, San Diego, CA (pp. 768–772).

Li, F., & Wang, Y. (2007). Routing in vehicular ad hoc networks: A survey. *IEEE Vehicular Technology Magazine*, *2*(2), 12–22. doi:10.1109/MVT.2007.912927

Maglaras, L. A. (2015). A novel distributed intrusion detection system for vehicular ad hoc networks. *International Journal of Advanced Computer Science and Applications*, *6*(4), 101–106.

Mekki, T., Jabri, I., Rachedi, A., & Jemaa, M. (2016). Vehicular cloud networks: Challenges, architectures, and future directions. In Proceedings of Vehicular Communications. doi:10.1016/j.vehcom.2016.11.009

Menon, V., Pathrose, J., & Priya, J. (2016). Ensuring Reliable Communication in Disaster Recovery Operations with Reliable Routing Technique. *Mobile Information Systems*, *2016*, 1–10. doi:10.1155/2016/9141329

Naboulsi, D., & Fiore, M. (2013). On the instantaneous topology of a large-scale urban vehicular network: The Cologne case. In *Proceedings of the ACM MobiHoc*, Bangalore, India (pp. 167–176). doi:10.1145/2491288.2491312

Olariu, S., Khalil, I., & Abuelela, M. (2011). Taking VANET to the clouds. *International Journal of Pervasive Computing and Communications*, *7*(1), 7–21. doi:10.1108/17427371111123577

Philip, V., Suman, V. K., Menon, V. G., & Dhanya, K. A. (2017). A Review on latest Internet of Things based Healthcare Applications. *International Journal of Computer Science and Information Security*, *15*(1), 248–254.

Rountree, D., & Castrillo, I. (2014). *Basics of cloud computing* (1st ed.). Amsterdam: Elsevier Syngress.

Shin, S., Seo, S., Eom, S., Jung, J., & Lee, K. H. (2016). A Pub/Sub-Based Fog Computing Architecture for Internet-of-Vehicles. In *Proceedings of the 2016 IEEE International Conference on Cloud Computing Technology and Science (CloudCom)*, Luxembourg (pp. 90-93). doi:10.1109/CloudCom.2016.0029

Shojafar, M., Cordeschi, N., & Baccarelli, E. (2016). Energy-efficient Adaptive Resource Management for Real-time Vehicular Cloud Services. *IEEE Transactions on Cloud Computing*, *99*, 1–1.

Vaquero, L., & Rodero-Merino, L. (2014). Finding your Way in the Fog. *Computer Communication Review*, *44*(5), 27–32. doi:10.1145/2677046.2677052

Viriyasitavat, W., Tonguz, O. K., & Bai, F. (2009). Network connectivity of VANETs in urban areas. In *Proceedings of IEEE SECON*, Rome, Italy. doi:10.1109/SAHCN.2009.5168949

Vouk, M. (2008). Cloud Computing-Issues, Research and Implementations. *Journal of Computing and Information Technology*, *16*(4), 235. doi:10.2498/cit.1001391

Wei, Z., Yu, F. R., Tang, H., Liang, C., & Yan, Q. (2016). Security Schemes in Vehicular Ad hoc Networks with Cognitive Radios. arXiv:1611.06905.

Whaiduzzaman, M., Sookhak, M., Gani, A., & Buyya, R. (2014). A survey on vehicular cloud computing. *Journal of Network and Computer Applications*, *40*, 325–344. doi:10.1016/j.jnca.2013.08.004

Yi, S., Li, C., & Li, Q. (2015). A survey of fog computing: concepts, applications and issues. In *Proceedings of the 2015 Workshop on Mobile Big Data (MoBiData'15)*, New York, NY (pp. 37–42). doi:10.1145/2757384.2757397

Zhong, S., Chen, J., & Yang, Y. R. (2003). Sprite: a simple, cheat-proof, credit-based system for mobile ad-hoc networks. In *Proceedings of the Twenty-Second Annual Joint Conference of the IEEE Computer and Communications INFOCOM 2003* (Vol. 3, pp. 1987-1997).

This research was previously published in the International Journal of Vehicular Telematics and Infotainment Systems (IJVTIS), 1(2); edited by Daxin Tian, Zhengguo Sheng, and Jianming Ma, pages 15-23, copyright year 2017 by IGI Publishing (an imprint of IGI Global).

Chapter 12
An Extension of the MiSCi Middleware for Smart Cities Based on Fog Computing

Jose Aguilar
Universidad de los Andes, Venezuela

Manuel B. Sanchez
Universidad Nacional Experimental del Táchira, Venezuela

Marxjhony Jerez
University of the Andes, Venezuela

Maribel Mendonca
Universidad Centroccidental Lisandro Alvarado, Venezuela

ABSTRACT

In a Smart City is required computational platforms, which allow environments with multiple interconnected and embedded systems, where the technology is integrated with the people, and can respond to unpredictable situations. One of the biggest challenges in developing Smart City is how to describe and dispose of enormous and multiple sources of information, and how to share and merge it into a single infrastructure. In previous works, we have proposed an Autonomic Reflective Middleware with emerging and ubiquitous capabilities, which is based on intelligent agents that can be adapted to the existing dynamism in a city for, ubiquitously, respond to the requirements of citizens, using emerging ontologies that allow the adaptation to the context. In this work, we extend this middleware using the fog computing paradigm, to solve this problem. The fog extends the cloud to be closer to the things that produce and act on the smart city. In this paper, we present the extension to the middleware, and examples of utilization in different situations in a smart city.

DOI: 10.4018/978-1-5225-5649-7.ch012

INTRODUCTION

Smart Cities should integrate information and communications technology (ICT) in their spaces, in order to exploit the wealth of information and knowledge generated, to improve their planning and public services offered to their citizens. ICT can computerize, interconnect and automate virtually all processes that occur in a city: infrastructure management, power consumption, communication system, traffic, health, etc., ubiquitously integrated (with sensors and actuators) in all elements of the city. This allows a more sophisticated resource management, and emergent behaviors from the interrelationships of these systems.

Applications that run on smart cities, must consider that the context changes continually: situations, availability of services (based on ICT), as well as the requirements and preferences of its citizens. They must, therefore, react to this changing environment at runtime, considering that there are emerging situations, new needs, emerging interactions, and new availability of services, which cannot be predicted a priori. The continuous awareness of context, and the gradual adaptation, become the key to deliver value-added services based on ICT, to address the dynamics of continuously changing environment.

Some of the biggest challenges in developing a Smart City is how to dispose of the enormous and multiple sources of information and services in a given time and in the right way. Cloud Computing is an alternative to use in Smart Cities, since it is a group of computers and servers connected together over the Internet, to form a network for the storage of large amounts of data and services.

In Aguilar, Jérez, Mendonca, and Sánchez, (2016) we have proposed an Autonomic Reflective Middleware for Smart Cities, called MiSCi, based on these ideas. MiSCi is composed by a multi-layer architecture based on a Multi-Agent System (MAS), allowing it having capabilities of such systems, like: sociability, proactivity, adaptability, intelligence, etc. Its architecture is based on web services, allowing its services to be consumed by the applications (in our case, agents), aware of context or not. Agents can create temporary or permanent emerging ontologies, which allow solving a particular situation, according to context.

In a smart city, where there are multiple nodes and applications that interact to offer services to citizens, high quality and low latency are of great importance. The deployment of MiSCi, and classical middleware for smart cities based on a cloud computing paradigm, can become a problem for applications that require real-time response, mobility support and/or Geo-distribution.

The need in the Smart Cities for large amounts of data to be accessed more quickly, and locally, is ever-growing. A new platform is needed to meet these requirements. The Fog Computing paradigm can be the solution. Fog Computing is a distributed infrastructure, in which certain application processes, or services are managed, at the edge of the network by a smart device, but others are still managed in the cloud. Fog Computing enables a new breed of applications and services, and there is a fruitful interplay between the Cloud and the Fog, particularly when it comes to data management and analytics (Bonomi, Milito, Zhu, & Addepalli, 2012).

Fog Computing can offer data, compute, storage and service to the end-user in the edge of the network. This paradigm has characteristics that make it an appropriate platform for critical services and applications, such as those presented in a Smart City. The distinguishing fog characteristics are its proximity to end-users, its dense geographical distribution, and its support for mobility.

In this work, we propose an extended version of the MiSCi architecture proposed in Aguilar et al., 2016, based on the Fog Computing paradigm. The extension is, essentially, a middle layer between the cloud and the hardware, to enable more efficient data processing, analysis and storage, which is achieved by reducing the amount of data that needs to be transported to the cloud. In this way, the Fog Computing extends the Cloud Computing paradigm to the edge of the network, thus enabling new applications and services.

This new layer, called Fog Layer, is the key feature of the extended architecture of MiSCi, because it enables the fog computing paradigm in MiSCi, what is important to meet the requirements of quality of service, latency, data processing, among others, of the users in a Smart City.

This study aims to show the characteristics of the Fog Computing paradigm and its benefits when it is included in MiSCi, since due to the large volume of data processed in a smart city and the real-time needs of users, it is not always possible to store and process the data in the cloud, instead it must be processed locally. Thus, it can alleviate issues the smart cities are expected to produce, such as reducing service latency and improving QoS.

The next section presents a state of the art about architectures for smart cities and fog computing. Next, in section 3 we describe the theoretical aspects base of our extension; in section 4 is described the extended architecture of MiSCi; the Section 5 describes the case study used to test MiSCi, and finally, some conclusions are presented in section 6.

RELATIVE WORKS

The Smart cities involve the Internet of Thing (IoT), Wireless Sensors and Actuator Network (WSAN), which are using a novel paradigm called fog computing to address problems such as unreliable latency, lack of mobility support and location awareness, by providing elastic resources and services to end user at the edge of the network. Yi, Li, and Li, (2015) expose that Fog computing is a novel paradigm that bring the cloud advantage to the edge of network, which has been used in several scenarios, such as Content Delivery and Caching, Real-time video analysis, Augmented Reality, and Mobile Big Data Analysis. Despite the new opportunities and challenges of Fog Computing, Yi et al., (2015) think that is necessary joint efforts to converge the techniques to fog Computing.

The Fog computing extends the Cloud Computing paradigm to the edge of the network (Tang et al., 2015). Tang et al., (2015) introduce a hierarchical Fog Computing architecture for big data analysis in the smart cities. Fog computing parallelizes data processing, in order to satisfy location awareness and low latency. In this work, Tang et al., (2015) implement a 4-layer architecture based on the ideas of scale (component, neighborhood, Community and City) and latency (milliseconds to Seconds, Minute to hours and Days to years), and propose a Smart Pipeline Monitoring as prototype of the architecture. The experience was satisfactory to control and monitor smart cities.

Babu, Lakshmi, and Rao, (2015) propose a Cloud architecture for an agent-oriented IoT platform, which integrates the characteristics of Cloud and IoT paradigms. Babu et al. (2015) use the agent-oriented Model (for autonomy) and Cloud Computing model (For adaptability and flexibility). The Architecture contains three components: The Smart Interface Agent, the Smart User Agent and the Smart Object agent. In this paper, Babu et al., (2015) propose the use of the architecture in diverse scenarios: healthcare, Agriculture, Smart Mobility, Video Surveillance, Smart Home and Smart City. Additionally, they propose to use fog computing in future works.

On the other hand, Aazam and Huh, (2014) present a Smart Gateway, which is an integration of Cloud Computing and IoT using fog computing paradigm, in order to process the data. They propose to create better services, for real time and sensitive applications. The architecture present six layers: Physical and

Virtualization Layer, Monitoring Layer, Preprocessing Layer, temporary Storage Layer, Security Layer, and Transport Layer.

Giordano, Spezzano, and Vinci, (2016) present Rainbow, a three-layer architecture (Cloud, Distributed Middleware, Physical). The distributed Middleware is composed of an agent that offer the intelligence to the IoT through Virtual Objects. The Middleware allows Local Views, Decentralization, and emergent behaviors.

In the architectures presented in this section, some of them have the problems of latency and Geo-distribution, the issues than fog computing solves. Additionally, these architectures lack of context awareness and knowledge representation. With MiSCi, we propose an architecture that offers these last services for smart cities, but it does not offer the capabilities generated by the fog computing paradigm.

THEORETICAL FRAMEWORK

In this section, we are going to introduce some concepts that we use in this research. Initially, we present the original conceptual bases of MiSCi, such as Multiagent Systems (MAS), Context awareness, and Ontological Emergence; and finally, the new concept introduced in this extension: Fog Computing.

Concepts of Base of MiSCi

MiSCi, has three concepts of base: MAS, Context awareness, and Ontological Emergence.

MAS is an emerging subfield of AI that provide principles for the construction of complex systems, involving multiple agents and mechanisms for the coordination of the agents (Stone, 2000). An agent is an entity, such as a robot, with goals, actions, and domain knowledge, situated in an environment (Aguilar, Ríos, Hidrobo, & Cerrada, 2013). The way it acts is called its "behavior".

Context-awareness is an essential component of systems developed in areas like Intelligent Environments, Pervasive & Ubiquitous Computing and Ambient Intelligence (Alegre, Augusto, and Clark, 2016). Alegre et al., (2016) define a system as context-aware if "it uses Context to provide relevant information and/or services to the user, where relevancy depends on the user's task". Independently from this definition, the adjective "context-aware" is generally used in the literature to describe any type of system that is able to use context.

The emergence is used to describe the apparition of new properties that arise when a system overcomes a certain level of complexity, and its properties are not available in its system components (Aguilar, 2014). In this context, an ontology emergent must have some new types of properties, behaviors and laws that are somehow autonomous from, and irreducible to, the sum of the individual properties, behaviors and laws of its parts (Santos, 2015). To make possible an ontology emergent, there are services for the automatic creation of ontologies, based on the analysis of the needs of the system and the context information. In this case, the purpose of the ontological emergence is to manage all the information and knowledge that can be generated in the system, in order to create new emerging knowledge models and adapt the ontological framework to the dynamics and the evolution of the environment, with the purpose of representing the new behaviors, needs and services of the system (Mendonça, Aguilar & Perozo, 2016).

Fog Computing

Several applications are generating large volume and variety of data. Using the classical cloud computing paradigm, where the data is moved to the cloud for analysis, maybe make lose the opportunity to act based on the data. Handling the volume, variety, and velocity of data for these applications, requires a new computing model. Some of the main requirements of these new applications are:

- **Move Data to the Best Place for Processing:** Which depends on how quickly a decision is needed.
- **Minimize Latency:** For example, some of the new applications have real time requirements, which implies analyzing data close to the device that collected the data.
- **Conserve Network Bandwidth:** There are a lot of data generated in real time (for example, a commercial flight can generate more than 10 TB for every 30 minutes of flight). To transport this vast amount of data from thousands of edge devices to the cloud is not practical.

Traditional cloud computing architectures do not meet all of these requirements. Fog Computing is an extension of the Cloud Computing paradigm to the edge of the network, which meets all of these requirements (Yi et al., 2015; Bonomi et al., 2012).

Fog Computing is a model in which data and application processing are concentrated on devices at the edge of the network, instead of being completely in the cloud, so that the data is processed locally on a smart device, instead of being sent to the cloud for it. Thus, enabling a new breed of applications and services. Fog computing paradigm allows:

- Analyze the most time-sensitive data close to where it is generated, at the network edge, instead of sending vast amounts of data to the cloud
- Act on data in milliseconds
- Send selected data to the cloud for longer-term storage and historical analysis
- Some characteristics of Fog computing are:
  - Strong presence of streaming and real-time applications
  - Low latency and location awareness
  - Wide-spread geographical distribution
  - Mobility
  - Very large number of nodes
  - Predominant role of wireless access

Bonomi et al., (2012) argues that the above characteristics make the Fog the appropriate platform for a number of critical IoT services and applications, such as Smart Cities, Connected Vehicle, Smart Grid, and Wireless Sensors. Fog Computing paradigm must be used when:

- Large amount of data is collected at the extreme edge.
- Millions of applications/devices are generating data.
- It is necessary to analyze the data in real time.

Fog computing paradigm works according to the next idea: the cloud is extended to be closer to the things that produce and act, with devices, called fog nodes. Any device with computing, storage, and network connectivity can be a fog node. The fog nodes are deployed anywhere with a network connection: in a vehicle, on top of a power pole, on a factory, alongside the railway track, etc. The fog applications are deployed in the fog nodes closest to the network edge that ingest the data from the devices. Then, the fog application directs the different types of data to the optimal place for their analysis (Giordano et al., 2016):

- The most time-sensitive data are analyzed on the fog node closest to the things generating the data.
- Data that can wait seconds or minutes is passed to an aggregation node for analysis (node that executes several requests from different close fog nodes).
- Data that is less time sensitive is sent to the cloud for historical analysis, big data analytics, and long-term storage.

EXTENDED ARCHITECTURE OF MISCI

This section describes the extensions to the architecture of MiSCi proposed in (Aguilar et al., 2016).

Multilayer Architecture of MiSCi

The core of MiSCi is based in a MAS composed by a multi-layer architecture. The agents of MiSCi perceive the interactions of the users (monitoring the environment, using the sensors available on it), thinks in an appropriate solution (services to be offered to the user) according to the context, plans and deploys the solution in the environment (using the effectors), thus improving the activities carried out by the citizens of the city, with the main objective of improving the quality of life and the comfort of the citizens (see Figure 1).

The architecture of MiSCi contains 9 layers. Each element of this architecture provides essential features to the middleware, enabling the ubiquity, the context awareness, the ontological emergence, smart decisions, fog, and cloud computing, among others. In general, the layers of MiSCi are:

- **MAS Management Layer (MMAL):** This layer is an adaptation of the FIPA standard (Aguilar et al., 2013; FIPA, 2013) what defines the rules that allow a society of agents to coexist and be administered, encouraging the interoperability with other technologies. The Agents in this layer are: Agents Manager (AMA), CCA (Communication Control Agent) and DMA (Data Management Agent), they are specifically defined in (Aguilar et al., 2013).
- **Service Management Layer (SML):** This is an essential layer in the architecture of MiSCi, because it makes possible the integration between the MAS and SOA paradigm in a bidirectional way; that means that agents can register, discover and consume web services in the cloud, and vice versa (agent's tasks are offered as web services). This feature makes possible to use the SaaS model of the cloud computing in MiSCi, which is fundamental in a Smart City. This layer is able to integrate with XML Web Services (using SOAP protocol), and with RESTful web services by using the translation features of the Enterprise Service Bus (ESB). In this layer, the Services Management Agent (SMA), the Web Service Agent (WSA), the Web Service Oriented Agent

Figure 1. MiSCi Architecture: layers and components of the Middleware for Smart Cities

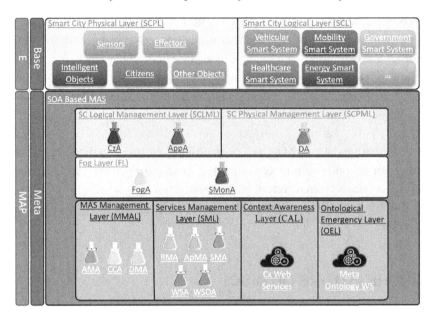

(WSOA), the RMA (Resource Manager Agent) and the ApMA (Applications Manager Agent) are defined. See (Sánchez et al., 2016; Sánchez, Aguilar, Cordero, & Valdiviezo, 2015) for more details about these agents.

- **Context-Awareness Layer (CAL):** The purpose of this layer is to offer context services, allowing agents of MiSCi to manage important information about location, time, and devices, among others. This information is managed in a cycle that is conformed by: the discovering and modeling of the context, reasoning based on the context, and the distribution of the context. Also, it is important to know the quality of the information in the context (quality of the context). For this layer, we take as reference the services defined in Aguilar, Jerez, Exposito, and Villemur, (2015), where is proposed a Context-Aware Reflective Middleware based on the Cloud Computing, with a range of services to manage the context information. See (Aguilar et al., 2016) for details about this layer.

- **Ontological Emergence Layer (OEL):** The objective of this layer is to provide a set of services with very specific tasks for handling ontologies. These services have been proposed in Mendonça et al., (2016). In this work, a defined group of services for Ontology Registration, for Ontology Search, for the Integration of Ontologies, for Update of Ontologies, among others. Also, the structure of the meta-ontologies defined in this layer, are the same proposed in the same work. They propose three meta-ontologies and the procedure to integrate them: a component meta-ontology, a context meta-ontology, and a domain meta-ontology. The meta-ontologies provide an adequate conceptual model of the context of the Smart City. See (Mendonça et al., 2016) for details about this layer.

- **SC Logical Management Layer (SCLML):** It is responsible for providing intelligence to the Smart City. This layer is where all the applications (software, virtual objects, etc.) and persons present in the Smart City are characterized. Basically, each element/person is characterized by an agent (is an abstraction of it), which contains metadata that define its properties. This layer contains agents like CzA (it characterizes each citizen of the Smart City) and AppA (it characterizes

236

useful applications in the smart city, such as the Vehicular Smart System, the Healthcare Smart System, etc.). Those agents are coordinated and cooperate with each other, to take decisions that are needed in a particular situation, to help real people to perform their tasks in the smart city, encouraging the comfort and improving the quality of life of the citizens. This layer is detailed in Aguilar et al., (2016).

- **SC Physical Management Layer (SCPML):** It allows to manage the physical devices in the Smart City. In this layer, all the physical elements of the environment are characterized thought the DA (Device Agent), allowing the interaction between agents and devices of MiSCi. Thus, each physical device is characterized by one DA (is an abstraction of it), which contains meta-data that define its properties. Some of these physical devices are intelligent (smart objects), so that the properties of learning, autonomy, reasoning, among others, are critical to characterize in them. This layer communicates with the real physical device that is in the SCPL layer, because it's through SCPL that agents have access to the physical hardware of the devices. See (Aguilar et al., 2016) for details about this layer.

- **Smart City Physical Layer (SCPL):** This layer is the smart city itself. It is in this layer where all the physical components of the smart city are deployed, such as: a) Sensors, to capture the useful information for services and smart objects in the environment b) Effectors, to modify the physical conditions of the environment c) Smart Objects, which are components of the smart city that may adapt and respond to situations in the current context. See (Aguilar et al., 2016) for details about this layer.

- **Smart City Logical Layer (SCL):** This layer includes the main sub-systems of a smart city, which are responsible for managing the elements of the city in a global way, such as: Vehicular Smart System, responsible for control the traffic; Mobility Smart System, responsible of facilitating the mobility of citizens (public transport); Smart Healthcare System, in charge of facilitating the access to health services, among others. The agents of MiSCi can communicate with these systems through the AppA agents, because they characterize the applications of the smart city in the architecture. In this way, the global systems can be coordinated with the local systems, to meet the needs of the citizens in a given time.

- **Fog Layer (FL):** This layer enables the Fog computing paradigm in MiSCi. The agents in this layer help to decide whether the data will be processed locally or in the cloud, being the Fog Agent (FogA) responsible for this task. FogA uses a meta-ontology provided by the OEL Layer, context information provided by the CAL layer, and system information collected by the System Monitor Agent (SMonA), about the level of occupation in terms of processing and communication (bandwidth) of the agents and local web services, to decide whether or not the data should be processed locally or in the cloud. The fog layer is the extension that we propose in this work, and is detailed in section 4.2.

Fog Computing Paradigm in MiSCi

The Fog Layer is a key feature of the extended architecture of MiSCi, because it enables the fog computing paradigm in MiSCi, what is important to meet the requirements of quality of service, latency, data processing, among other characteristics of performance, of the users in a Smart City. That is due to the large volume of data processed in a smart city and the real-time needs of users, which makes it is not always possible to store and process the data in the cloud, instead they must be processed locally.

The FogA agent is charged to decide what information should be processed locally or in the cloud. Specifically, the data are collected by the DA's and sent to the FogA, each DA characterizes one sensor (contains metadata necessary to communicate with the physical device) of the environment. The FogA takes decisions by using the Fog-ontology described in Figure 2; in this ontology, a weight is assigned to each concept or element of the ontology, so the FogA can know what elements have high priority to be processed locally. Moreover, this information is combined with context information allowing the agents to identify what concepts of the fog-ontology is going to be used. In the other hand, the information collected by the SMonA about the level of the load of the agents is very important, in order to determine if the fog elements have the capacity to process the actual requirement or not. This level is determined in terms of processing and communication; all this information helps the FogA agent to decide what data will be processed locally or in the cloud. The rule that uses the FogA agent to make the decisions is:

- If the SMonA agent informs that the local services and agents are overloaded, the FogA agent will decide to require to the cloud more power of processing;
- Otherwise, if the ontology marks the information with a high weight (according to the context and the domain), and if the SMonA agent informs that the agents or local services are in the capacity to process the data, the FogA agent decides to process the information locally.

As we can see, the ontology is key to take this decision, because it has the rules that defines how the data will be processed, but the data to take the decisions is provided by the DA and the SMon agents, and the Context Services of the CAL layer. Particularly, the axioms defined in the meta-ontologies establish the basic guidelines for the ontologies of the domain. The axioms are statements or rules that define the concepts and their relations, so that the definition of the domain terms is more precise (in this case, the ontology concepts). The axioms determine the categories, the disjoint classes, the complementary classes, among other things. The OWL is used as the knowledge representation language (Mendonça et al., 2016).

Together with the rules, the ontological analysis service processes the semantic information collected to discover new knowledge (new patterns, concepts or properties), in order to determine if they are on the same domain or of different domains, and the level of correspondence between them. Then, based on this analysis, it defines the most appropriate ontological mining tasks (e.g., fusion or linked of ontologies) for the generation of emerging ontologies. See (Mendonça et al., 2016) for more details.

The Fog Ontology is used to define the general model of the components and domains present in the Smart City, and their priorities. This meta-ontology defines general concepts that refer to the domain and context ontologies, and organizes the semantic information from different data sources that arise in the Smart City, by the incorporation of new devices, agents, services, etc. Additionally, it has an attribute, called "priority", that represents a weight of each concept and that can be updated whenever services are requested on the Smart City ontologies. Additionally, the general ontological framework is composed of distributed ontologies that are managed by different agents and services involved in the Smart City, which are heterogeneous (different data structures, languages, data types, etc.). The meta-ontologies managed on the OEL, links and structures the domain and context ontologies, and organizes the semantic information from different data sources that arise in the Smart City, by the incorporation of new devices, agents, services, etc. Agents of the Smart City use their local ontologies for their services, to interact with other agents, etc. The agents involved in the Smart City register information about the system events, and about the ontologies that handle, making semantic annotations of the sources of knowledge used in the Smart City. Also, they relate their concepts and ontologies with the meta-concepts in the

Figure 2. Fog Ontology

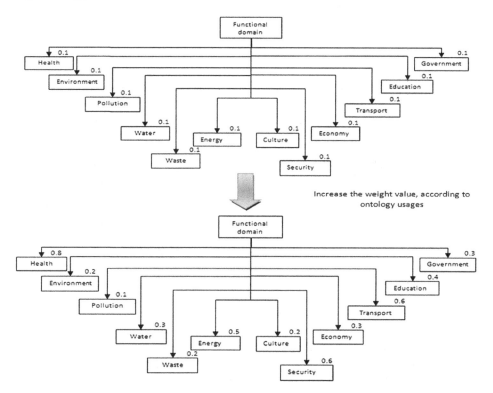

meta-ontologies. When they detect the need to update their knowledge (e.g., a new service, changes in behavior patterns of components, context change, etc.), the agents request the services of the OEL. It is at this moment when the weight of the meta-concept associated with the requested services is updated. This implies that the concepts increase their weights according to the use of the ontologies. This gives us indications of the domains of greater priority in Smart City, and where the fog nodes can be more useful.

The Figure 3 shows how all the elements of the extended MiSCi collaborate to take the decision about where the information should be processed. This figure is detailed as follows:

1.   The process starts with the DA agents, which are collecting data from the sensors and devices of the Smart City. In parallel, the SMonA agent is collecting information about the workload of the agents and local services, and about the bandwidth of the network.
2.   The data collected by the DA agents are sent to the FogA agent.
3.   FogA agent combines the data received from the DA agents with the context information, the fog ontology and the system information received from the SMonA agent, in order to decide whether the data will be processed locally or in the cloud, using the rules given in the fog ontology.
4.   The decision taken by FogA agent is informed to the corresponding agents of the SCLML layer.

Figure 3. Collaboration process to activate the Fog computing

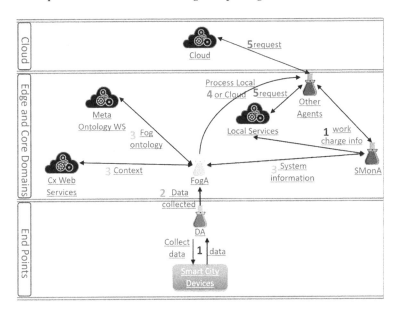

The CzA or AppA agents use this result and invoke the corresponding services locally or in the cloud, according to the information provided by the FogA agent. In this way, MiSCi is able to deal with the requirements of latency, availability of resources and the real-time needs, of the Smart City.

Geospatial Deployment of MiSCi Within the Smart City

As was described in (Aguilar et al., 2016), MiSCi is distributed along the Smart City (see Figure 4). In each block of the city should exist one instance of MiSCi, in which all the physical elements present in that sector are characterized. Each instance of MiSCi manages its own ontologies (context, components, domain, fog, etc.); moreover, each block contains its own local services, while the global services are located in the cloud (global services are shared by all the instances of MiSCi). Each $MiSCi_j$ can share important local information (e.g. context information) with its neighbors, allowing to increment the fog computing capabilities in all the city because it is not necessary to contact the global services to get that information (e.g. information about traffic can be very complex to recover (Zubillaga, Cruz, Aguilar, Zapotécatl, Fernández, Aguilar, Rosenblueth & Gershenson, 2014).

The main sub-systems of the Smart City (like Vehicular Smart System, Healthcare Smart System, etc.) are invoked through an AppA agent. The main sub-systems make part of the global services that manage the elements of the city on a global way, and receive the data from each block when it is necessary.

The FogA agent decides that information should be processed in the cloud, and allows the interaction between the local and global services. The FogA agent manages the behavior of each block, to decide when to use the Fog or the Cloud, according to the needs of the users of the block where it belongs. In the manner how MiSCi is distributed along the city (by blocks), allows it to deal with the high quantity of devices of the Smart City.

Figure 4. Geospatial deployment of MiSCi

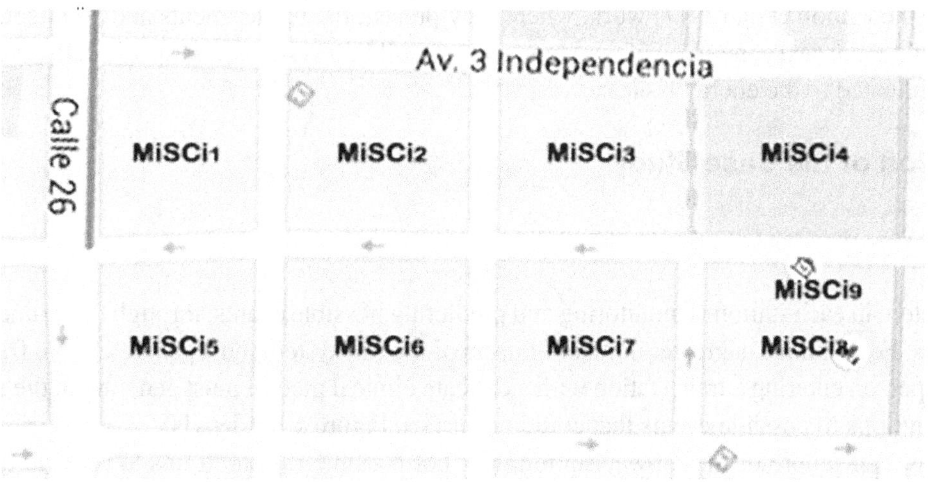

CASE STUDY

Definition of the Case Study

In this section, we present the case study used to test the utility of the fog computing paradigm in the extended architecture of MiSCi, and as the fog layer acts to guarantee the quality of the services, in the situations where the response time is very important.

The case study was divided into three scenarios happening in parallel (see Figure 5), this will allow to demonstrate the capabilities of MiSCi to handle those kind of situations, and show that the fog is a suitable platform for the attention of critical situations.

The first scenario arises in the subway station, in which a system failure happens, making impossible to send trains to this place. The smart city will have the capability to deal with this kind of situations, and activate another mobility system, to allow citizens to reach their destination without major problems. This scenario is similar to the real scenario of the Bilbao Metro station in Spain, defined in Aguirre et al. (2017), which described a context aware application supported by a Wireless Sensor Network (WSN), in an intelligent Transportation system (ITS).

At the same time that the subway fails, a citizen located a few blocks away is suffering a heart attack (his body sensors activate the alert). The smart city should be able to provide priority services to this citizen, and transport him to the closest hospital as soon as possible; however, this situation is complicated because citizens are leaving the subway to go to an alternative transport system, so there is more traffic in this part of the city. This situation represents a difficulty to the ambulance that goes to pick up the patient. This part of the experiment is based on the Islam et al (2015) work, which shows a Health Care infrastructure based on the IoT paradigm. They give examples about how the smartphone can be used as an auxiliary health care application to support diagnosis, give references of drugs, among other things.

The third scenario is given in a nearby shopping center, where some citizens who left the subway due to the failure, decided to stay in this mall for shopping. Because the shopping center is receiving an amount of people greater than normal, it will activate some services to provide environmental and energy conditions necessary for citizens to feel comfortable in that place. Similarly, this part of the experiment is based on the Minoli et al. (2017) work, where they present the requirements and architectures of the Smart Building, the next generation of the Management Building systems, and specifically, they describe the layer dedicated to the energy issues

Description of the Case Study

Scenario 1

The rail system in each station is monitoring and predicting possible events, through the connection with other agents. For example, a greater number of users of the rail system must generate more frequency of trains, or a person entering a train station with a delicate clinical picture must generate in the rail system possible solutions to possible events that could occur (see Figure 5 for details).

At the time of failure of the subway station, it is not possible to send trains to provide the service. MiSCi must activate other mobility systems for citizens to reach their destination.

1. Some DA (sensor) agent detects a failure on the segment of the road that connects to this subway station.
2. The DA agent communicates with the FogA agent to report the fault. The FogA agent determines if the information will be processed in a local node (Fog Node) or if it should access the cloud. FogA agent has already previously determined the Fog Nodes, the information provided by the SMonA agent about the storage capacity, bandwidth, as well as the weight of the meta-ontology domain (see Figure 2) that will give indications of the priority of this application.

Figure 5. Behavior of MiSCi in each scenario

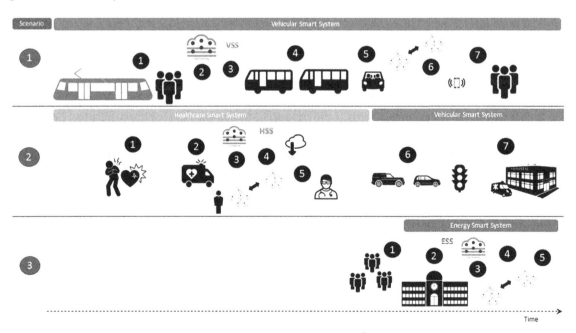

3. The FogA agent informs the failure to the AppA agent that characterizes the Vehicular Smart System (VSS).

4. The VSS determines to send buses to the subway station to mobilize passengers, and further, requires information of context to determine other mobility systems available.

5. The services of context inform about the Carpooling services available, and determines the need to activate a daemon application that can suggest transportation options for the CzA agents.

6. The daemon application requires the "search ontologies" service of carpooling. A FogA agent determines the Fog Node where the search of the ontology will be carried out. A strong fusion is done locally with the transport system ontology, to generate a complete ontology (temporary emerging ontology) with all types of transportation available, which is used by the application in order to suggest to the CzA agents the options available.

7. The citizens will have the option to accept or reject the suggestions of the application.

Scenario 2

The agents of the citizens (CzA) have the personal preferences of each citizen in their cell phones. These agents can monitor their health data, to be processed later. A FogA agent previously determined that the health domain has a high priority through the weights in the fog meta-ontology, thus storing information of citizens of a block in the Fog Node. This information is supplied by the CzA agent. The information supplied by the SMonA agent, such as the storage capacity, is also considered.

When a citizen suffers a heart attack near the subway station, the smart city must provide the best service to attend the citizen, e.g. organize vehicular traffic to move it quickly by ambulance to the medical center. MiSCi must activate its systems to reach this goal in the next way:

1. The CzA agent detects vital signs of the citizen and generates the alarm signal to the Healthcare Smart System (HSS), through the AppA that characterizes that system.

2. The HSS actives the ambulance service to treat the patient, and moves it to the closest medical center.

3. The HSS must obtain context information regarding vital signs, obtained by the sensors (blood pressure, respiration, temperature), as well as the information about the patient's history. The FogA agent performs the search in the HSS (cloud) of the previous illnesses, diseases ancestors, current treatments, habits, allergies, etc.

4. The HSS requests the service of contextual information about possible diagnosis and treatment suggestions that may provide the medical agent that comes in the ambulance. The FogA agent determines that this search must be carried out in the Fog Nodes, since previously it was considered that the area of Health is of high priority. For this, it is requested "ontologies search" service of the health domain, concerning the pathology presented by the patient. If it is necessary to complement the Fog Node information, FogA agent determines the need to update this information through the cloud search.

5. The "Ontological Emergence" Service determines the need to align the "patient's vital signs" ontology (which is a new ontology based on the information of the CzA and the information of the vital signs of the patient at that moment), with the "diseases and symptoms" ontology, obtained by

the previous service, to be used by a recommender system, which provides the information to the paramedics about of possible treatments or immediate steps to treat the patient. It is carried out in the Fog Nodes.

6. The HSS requests the VSS the traffic management, for a rapid transfer of the ambulance to the Medical Center.
7. The VSS synchronizes the semaphores, and alerts the vehicles and buses for clearing the way to the medical center.

Scenario 3

The Mall agent suggests possible actions to customer that access to the mall, and communicates with other agents, like the agents of the different stores in the Mall (e.g., restaurants), and especially, with the smart energy grid system, to give them information about the new users of the Mall (the group of citizens leaving the subway station that decide to enter into this shopping center). MiSCi acts in the next way.

1. The AppA agent that characterizes the Shopping Center (SC) detects the increase in the number of customers in the SC, and requires adapting the environment to provide better and adequate services to the citizens: air conditioners, more lighting, advertising, etc.
2. The AppA (SC) agent determines the need to negotiate with the Energy Smart System (ESS), to get more energy to offer these services for. ESS activates the context services of the MiSCi, to deal with this trouble.
3. The MiSCi, through the context services, requests to the ESS information of the available energy suppliers, to make the negotiation for additional energy. The FogA agent based on the information provided by the SMonA agent, determines whether the information will be processed in the Fog Node, depending on the storage capacity, bandwidth, as well as the priority that it has in the meta-ontology the power domain, to provide higher quality services.
4. The "ontologies search" service is requested in the energy domain, to have information about the energy components. The FogA agent determines whether the information is searched in the cloud or in the local nodes.
5. The "Ontological Emergence" Service, considering that only part of the information is needed, in this case about the energy suppliers, makes a weak fusion (temporary) between the ontology about the components of energy and the AppA (SC) ontology, to generate the necessary knowledge about what would be the best options about the energy suppliers, and perform negotiations to request in a smart way the energy required.

Evaluation of Performance

To compare the performance of the proposed Middleware (with fog computing) with the Middleware without fog computing, simulations have been carried out (see Table 1). We have used the GALATEA Simulator Platform (Uzcátegui, Dávila & Tucci. 2007) for the simulation. We analysis the total service time changes in each case (the total service time is the time from the start of a requirement until obtaining a response from the service), as well as the service processing time (both, for local and cloud services), measured in centiseconds (cs).

In both simulations, we have considered entities like CzA (starts the request), DA (collects data from sensors) and WSA (process the request), as well as FogA (decides if the data should be processed in the cloud or in the fog) and SMonA (has information about internet latency and message routing resources) only when Fog Computing is enabled. Also, we have considered some resources like internet latency and message routing. We have established distributions for service requests (exponential), data collection from sensors (exponential), message routing (exponential), internet latency (exponential), service processing time (Gaussian) and probability of time real or QoS (Bernoulli).

In order to determine the behavior of the system, the latency of internet upload and download has been varied from 0.01 to 5, in the case where fog computing is disable. With fog computing activated, the probability of real-time or QoS has also been varied to 60%, 50% and 40%, so we can establish comparisons that allow to determine if the introduction of fog computing paradigm improves or not the quality of the services offered. The results of the simulations have been resumed in the Table 1.

From the simulations, it's possible to see that in the case of simulations for MiSCi without fog computing, when the latency of internet increases (DL and UL), the total service time increases as well in a considerable way, this produces that the download and upload times increase accordingly (The network becomes congested); the total service time mean reaches values of the order of the 5000 cs (see Figure 6).

In the case of simulations of MiSCi with fog computing, when the latency increases, the total service time increases in an acceptable value, being 15 cs the maximum value, when the latency is 5. We also can see that the processing service time (in local and in the cloud) is not so affected by latency, remaining virtually constant (see Figure 7 and Figure 8).

Table 1. MiSCi Simulation Experiment (Fog enabled/disabled)

		Total Service Time Mean (TST)	Upload Time Mean (UpTM)	Download Time Mean (DoTM)	Time of Processing in Cloud (TPC)	Time of Processing in Local (TPL)
Fog Disabled	UL Mean: 0.01 DL Mean: 0.01	39.970	0.010	0.010	38.806	N/A
	UL Mean: 1.2 DL Mean: 1.2	52.970	1.700	3.890	48.810	N/A
	UL Mean: 5 DL Mean: 5	5.855.127	5.535.424	393.553	9.942	N/A
Fog Enabled	UL Mean: 0.01 DL Mean: 0.01 PB(fog): 60%	7.258	0.010	5.922	5.043	6.171
	UL Mean: 1.2 DL Mean: 1.2 PB(fog): 60%	7.993	1.410	1.228	5.051	6.271
	UL Mean: 5 DL Mean: 5 PB(fog): 60%	15.154	10.008	9.317	5.059	6.535
	UL Mean: 5 DL Mean: 5 PR(fog): 50%	19.128	12.729	12.013	5.581	5.627
	UL Mean: 5 DL Mean: 5 PB(fog): 40%	32.203	22.706	18.539	6.511	5.074

Upload latency: (UL), Download latency (DL), Probability of real time or QoS (PB(fog)).

Figure 6. MiSCi without fog: latency vs total service time

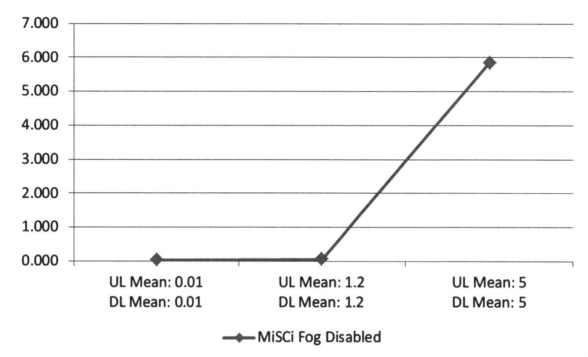

Figure 7. MiSCi with fog: latency vs total service time

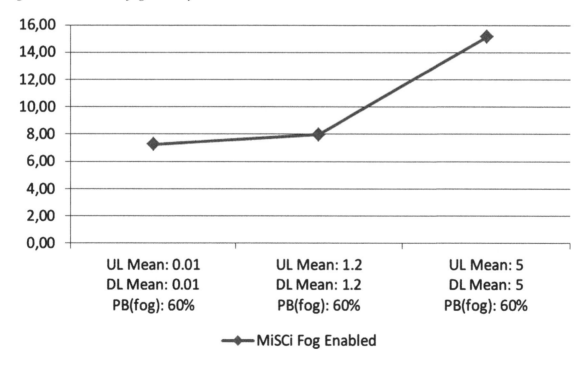

Figure 8. MiSCi with fog: latency vs processing service time

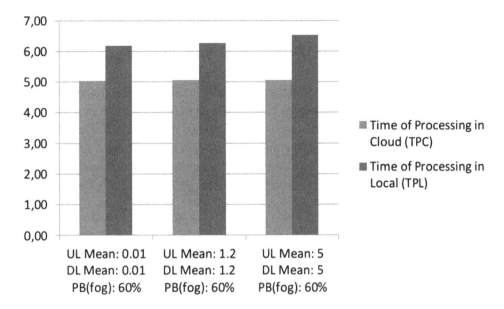

When the probability of real-time or QoS is decreased, we can see that the total service time is affected; this behavior is reasonable because, like the system has a low probability of time real or QoS, most data are processed in the cloud and not in the fog. However, the system is not so affected as in the case of MiSCi without fog computing, reaching 32.20 cs for total service when the probability of time real-time or QoS is 40%, this value is lower than the 5855.12 cs of the model of MiSCi without fog computing.

CONCLUSION

The MiSCi architecture has been extended with the fog computing paradigm, in order to improve the quality of the services to be offered to users of the city. Particularly, in a smart city is collected a large amount of data, generated by thousands of applications/devices. Additionally, this data must be analyzed in real time, in order to be used at the correct moment in the city. With our extension, MiSCi can cover these requirements.

Now, MiSCi has the capacity to respond to situations in real time, through the use of emerging ontologies and contextual awareness. In this way, can provide services adapted to the current situation. The cloud and fog paradigms are perfectly combined in MiSCi, allowing that a smart city can adapt and responds to the needs of its citizens in real time.

The case studies show how MiSCi can manage different situations, allows its adaptation to the existing dynamism in a city, offering their services anywhere, anytime, to anyone, to ubiquitously respond to the requirements of the smart city, adapted to the context of the moment, in real time.

The experiments show that incorporating fog computing in MiSCi is fundamental, in order to deal with the requirements of time real and QoS of a Smart City.

The major drawbacks of our approach are the initial deployment of our middleware in a real scenario (smart city) where we need to define all its components as agents, and the customization of the different levels that requires a learning phase in order to adapt their parameters. Future directions of our research aimed at solving these drawbacks with an automatic generation of the agents and the definition of an initial learning phase for each level

In addition, we are going to introduce in future works, the analysis of the trust of the data collected in different sensors, trust models and emergent coordination mechanism, in order to manage the incertitude of the smart cities. Additionally, we are going to design the main data analysis tasks required in a smart city, based on the idea of the autonomic cycle of data analysis tasks, inspired by works like (Aguilar, 2016b), to be included in MiSCi, in order to generate the knowledge required for a smart city. This extension of MiSCi allows an easy incorporation of services, without a hard-computational cost, guaranteeing an excellent quality of services.

ACKNOWLEDGMENT

Dr. Aguilar has been partially supported by the Prometeo Project of the Ministry of Higher Education, Science, Technology and Innovation of the Republic of Ecuador.

REFERENCES

Aazam, M., & Huh, E.-N. (2014). Fog computing and smart gateway based communication for cloud of things. In *Proceedings of the 2014 International Conference on Future Internet of Things and Cloud (FiCloud)* (pp. 464-470). IEEE.

Aguilar, J. (2014). *Introducción a los Sistemas Emergentes* (1st ed.). Mérida: Talleres Gráficos, Universidad de Los Andes.

Aguilar, J., Buendia, O., Moreno, K., & Mosquera, D. (2016b). *Autonomous Cycle of Data Analysis Tasks for Learning Processes, CICIS* (Vol. 658, pp. 187–202). Springer International Publishing; doi:10.1007/978-3-319-48024-4_15

Aguilar, J., Jerez, M., Exposito, E., & Villemur, T. (2015). CARMiCLOC: Context Awareness Middleware in Cloud Computing. In Proceedings of Computing Conference (CLEI). Latin American: IEEE.

Aguilar, J., Jérez, M., Mendonca, M., & Sánchez, M. (2016). MiSCi: Autonomic Reflective Middleware for Smart Cities. In Technologies and Innovation (pp. 241-253). Springer International Publishing. doi:10.1007/978-3-319-48024-4_19

Aguilar, J., Ríos, A., Hidrobo, F., & Cerrada, M. (2013). *Sistemas Multiagentes y sus aplicaciones en Automatización Industrial* (2nd ed.). Mérida: Talleres Gráficos, Universidad de Los Andes.

Aguirre, E., Lopez-Iturri, P., Azpilicueta, L., Redondo, A., Astrain, J. J., Villadangos, J., & Falcone, F. (2017). Design and implementation of context aware applications with wireless sensor network support in urban train transportation environments. *IEEE Sensors Journal, 17*(1), 169–178. doi:10.1109/JSEN.2016.2624739

Alegre, U., Augusto, J. C., & Clark, T. (2016). Engineering context-aware systems and applications: A survey. *Journal of Systems and Software, 117*, 55–83. doi:10.1016/j.jss.2016.02.010

Babu, S. M., Lakshmi, A. J., & Rao, B. T. (2015). A study on cloud based Internet of Things: CloudIoT. In *Proceedings of the 2015 Global Conference on Communication Technologies (GCCT)* (pp. 60-65). IEEE.

Bonomi, F., Milito, R., Zhu, J., & Addepalli, S. (2012). Fog computing and its role in the internet of things. In *Proceedings of the first edition of the MCC workshop on Mobile cloud computing* (pp. 13-16). ACM. doi:10.1145/2342509.2342513

FIPA. (2013). (IEEE) Revised on 2016, de http://www.fipa.org

Giordano, A., Spezzano, G., & Vinci, A. (2016). Smart Agents and Fog Computing for Smart City Applications. In *Proceedings of the International Conference on Smart Cities* (pp. 137-146). Springer International Publishing. doi:10.1007/978-3-319-39595-1_14

Islam, S. R., Kwak, D., Kabir, M. H., Hossain, M., & Kwak, K. S. (2015). The internet of things for health care: A comprehensive survey. *IEEE Access, 3*, 678–708. doi:10.1109/ACCESS.2015.2437951

Mendonça, M., Aguilar, J., & Perozo, N. (2016). MiR-EO: Reflective Middleware for Ontological Emergency in Intelligent Environments. *Latin American Journal of Computing, 3*(2), 25–39.

Minoli, D., Sohraby, K., & Occhiogrosso, B. (2017). IoT Considerations, Requirements, and Architectures for Smart Buildings–Energy Optimization and Next Generation Building Management Systems. *IEEE Internet of Things Journal, 4*(1), 269–283.

Sánchez, M., Aguilar, J., Cordero, J., & Valdiviezo, P. (2015). A Smart Learning Environment based on Cloud Learning. *International Journal of Advanced Information Science and Technology, 39*(39), 39-52. Retrieved from http://ijaist.com/index.php/pub/item/404-a-smart-learning-environment-based-on-cloud-learning

Sánchez, M., Aguilar, J., Cordero, J., Valdiviezo, P., Luis, B.-G., & Chamba-Eras, L. (2016). Cloud Computing in Smart Educational Environments: application in Learning Analytics as Service. In *New Advances in Information Systems and Technologies* (Vol. 444, pp. 993-1002). Springer International Publishing. doi:10.1007/978-3-319-31232-3_94

Santos, G. C. (2015). Ontological Emergence: How is that possible? Towards a new Relational Ontology. *Foundations of Science, 20*(4), 429–446. doi:10.1007/s10699-015-9419-x

Stone, P., & Veloso, M. (2000).. . *Autonomous Robots, 8*(3), 345–383. doi:10.1023/A:1008942012299

Tang, B., Chen, Z., Hefferman, G., Wei, T., He, H., & Yang, Q. (2015). A hierarchical distributed fog computing architecture for big data analysis in smart cities. In *Proceedings of the ASE BigData & SocialInformatics 2015*.

Uzcátegui, M., Dávila, M., & Tucci, K. (2007). Galatea: Plataforma de Simulación de Sistemas Multi-Agentes. VI Jornadas Científico técnicas de la Facultad de Ingeniería. Mérida, Venezuela.

Yi, S., Li, C., & Li, Q. (2015). A survey of fog computing: concepts, applications and issues. In *Proceedings of the 2015 Workshop on Mobile Big Data* (pp. 37-42). ACM. doi:10.1145/2757384.2757397

Zubillaga, D., Cruz, G., Aguilar, L., Zapotécatl, J., Fernández, N., Aguilar, J., & Gershenson, C. et al. (2014). Measuring the complexity of self-organizing traffic lights. *Entropy*, *16*(5), 2384–2407. doi:10.3390/e16052384

This research was previously published in the Journal of Information Technology Research (JITR), 10(4); edited by Francisco José García-Peñalvo, pages 23-41, copyright year 2017 by IGI Publishing (an imprint of IGI Global).

Chapter 13

Enablement of IoT Based Context–Aware Smart Home With Fog Computing

Maggi Bansal
Thapar University, India

Inderveer Chana
Thapar University, India

Siobhan Clarke
Trinity College, Ireland

ABSTRACT

The recent advent of Internet of Things (IoT), has given rise to a plethora of smart verticals- smart homes being one of them. Smart Home is a classic example of IoT, wherein smart appliances connected via home gateways constitute a local home network to assist people in activities of daily life. Smart Home involves IoT-based automation (such as smart lighting, heating, surveillance etc.), remote monitoring and control of smart appliances. Besides automation, human-in-the-loop is a unique characteristic of Smart home to offer personalized services. Understanding the human behavior requires context processing. Thus, enablement of Smart home involves two prominent technologies IoT and context-aware computing. Further, local devices lying in the smart home have the implicit location and situational information, hence fog computing can offer real-time smart home services. In this paper, the authors propose ICON (IoT-based CONtext-aware) framework for context-aware IoT applications such as smart home, further ICON leverages fog-based IoT middleware to perform context-aware processing.

1. INTRODUCTION

The concept of Smart home aptly justifies the popular thought by (Weiser, 1999) about technology becoming an integral and indistinguishable part of everyday life. Making everyday life easier with the help of technology dates back with notable works in embedded electronics e.g. washing machines,

DOI: 10.4018/978-1-5225-5649-7.ch013

ovens, dishwashers etc., followed by innovations in wireless sensor networks (WSN) e.g. senor based things- taps, doors etc., which in present time is being endowed by the upcoming technology Internet of Things (IoT). In IoT, sensor based everyday devices communicate with the computing platforms (Fog computing, Cloud Computing platforms) for processing the raw sensor data to take wise and smart actions Atzori (2010) and Gubbi (2013). The distinct feature of IoT which differentiates it from its precursor technologies, is the use of a middleware to support processing and long-term analysis of sensor big data stream to take wise actions.

The IoT middleware (computing infrastructure to enable IoT data storage, processing and analysis) can be cloud based Gubbi et al. (2013) or fog computing based Bonomi et al. (2012), Dastjerdi et al. (2016). Per the cloud based IoT middleware, the Cloud platform offers its IaaS, PaaS and SaaS services to perform data storage, processing and analysis for IoT applications, and after the analysis meaningful results or actions are carried back to the user or actuator, in this way the cloud act as middleware for IoT wherein, the IoT data flow occurs in the loop as: user-cloud-user to realize sense-process-actuate sequence for IoT applications. Alike cloud computing, fog computing also offers storage and compute capacity, though bounded by limited resource capacity of fog nodes, but at a nearer distance (in terms of number of network hops) resulting in significant reduction in latency and communication cost. In contrast to the centralized resource pool in cloud computing, the resources in fog computing are distributed in nature and include all sort of potential storage and compute devices encountered across the network between end-user and the cloud and such fog nodes may include nearby idle PCs, servers, access points, routers, and also end-user devices etc. Bonomi et al. (2012). In simpler words, fog computing is the distributed computing paradigm, which provisions data storage, compute and networking on resources occurring between end-device and the cloud server, preferably choosing the resources nearer to the end-devices lying within the local edge network. Hence, it can be concluded that cloud is the centralized on-demand computing infrastructure, while fog is distributed opportunistic computing infrastructure. In fog computing, the management of IoT data within edge network helps to reduce latency, saves cloud communication bandwidth and enables capturing of context information by implicit location and situation awareness. Hence, this paper suggests using fog computing-based IoT middleware to perform IoT data storage and processing on devices such as home gateways, routers, desktop and other computing devices which exist near to the end devices. With sensing-processing-actuating loop, IoT enables enormous applications like smart home, smart healthcare, smart grid etc. However, IoT based smart home is the focus of this paper.

In addition to IoT, smart home has been discussed widely in literature in the field of ubiquitous computing, particularly in the field of context-aware computing. Researchers applied context-aware computing approaches to realize smart home scenario in order to understand the user context and learn user habits for providing personalized smart home services. Models, architectures for context-aware smart home has been discussed in Wang (2005), Zhang (2005), and Klimek (2015). Various works Si (2005), Baralis (2011), Al-Muhtadi (2003), Ellenberg (2011), Vlachostergiou (2016), and Gu (2004) have performed context-aware computing in smart home scenario. Context-aware processing, when applied to smart home enables- modeling user's current context, incorporating user-defined policies, understanding user preferences, and providing context services, thereby providing ambient intelligence to enjoy a comfortable life inside home.

Smart home enablement has been addressed by both the technologies- IoT and context-aware computing. It is quite interesting to note that the two technologies are complementary to each other as, IoT deals with tangible hardware aspect involving the inter-networking of sensors, computation middleware, actuators, smart devices etc. to enable the sensing-processing-actuating control loop while, context-aware computing deals with the intangible software aspect involving various approaches and methods to process and understand the context for taking high-level decisions. With this view, this paper take initiative to propel this upcoming context-aware IoT paradigm. A recent survey on context-aware IoT can be found in Perera et al. (2014), however the authors did not propose any framework or layered architecture for context-aware IoT, which the authors attempt to address here. In this paper, the authors propose ICON (IoT-based Context-aware) framework for context-aware IoT applications such as smart home, which leverages fog computing as the IoT middleware to perform context-aware processing.

The rest of this paper is organized into six sections. Section 2 discuss the literature work related to smart homes. Further, Section 3 gives a description of considered smart home scenario and the undertaken use cases. Then in Section 4, the proposed framework-ICON for context-aware IoT applications has been discussed. In Section 5, the context-processing for the considered scenarios has been described. Finally, the paper is concluded with discussion on implementation in Section 6.

2. RELATED WORK

2.1. IoT Based Smart Home

A general discussion on IoT based smart home is given in Li (2011). A smart home using Raspberry Pi is discussed in Vujovic et al. (2015). Another IoT based smart home has been investigated in Li et al. (2015). The proposed smart home Li et al. (2015) is based on fog platform to provide various smart features in the home like smart energy, healthcare, safety, entertainment etc. The authors showed the benefits of fog over cloud when applied in smart home scenario. An Ambient Assistant Living (AAL) system proposed in Craciunescu et al. (2015) has capabilities like tracking location of in-house persons, fall detection of users and leakage of harmful gases like LPG, natural gas and CO etc. in the smart home. A perspective on fog computing for living has been discussed in McMillin and Zhang (2017) while Varghese et al. (2017) discussed the feasibility of fog computing.

2.2. Context-Aware Computing Based Smart Home

A theoretical model CASSHA for context-aware smart home system has been proposed in Wang et al. (2005). Another layered model CONON is proposed in Zhang et al. (2005) and Klimek et al. (2015) used web services to propose SOA based architecture for context-aware smart home. Other researchers applied various learning-based or rule-based approaches for context-processing. For example, Si et al. (2005) applied learning based Hidden Markov Model (HMM) for context processing and creating context history to learn about user habits and predict services based on user's current context. Majority of context-processing approaches are rule-based approaches as they encode if-then rules to define user policies. Further rule-based approaches for context-processing in smart home include- association rule mining Baralis (2011), predicate rule approach for authentication and access control in smart spaces Al-Muhtadi (2003), ontology based work has been done in Zhang (2005) and Ellenberg (2011), hybrid approaches using fuzzy rules and ontology is proposed in Vlachostergiou et al. (2016) and predicate rules and ontology in Gu et al. (2004).

In this paper, the authors have chosen rule-based context-processing. Further, for rule-based context-processing the first-order predicate logic has been chosen for various reasons: Firstly, personalization policies can be efficiently represented by predicate rules. Secondly, predicate logic offers light-weight processing than ontology, suitable for fog environment. Thirdly, ontology is static in nature- once created it is difficult to update however, the predicate rules are dynamic in nature which can be defined and updated easily.

3. SMART HOME SCENARIO

This section discusses the Smart home use cases considered in this paper:

- **Smart Environment:** Smart environment involves monitoring and control of surroundings and home appliances to provide a sustainable living while minimizing reckless use of home appliances. In this paper, smart environment includes smart temperature control, smart detection of hazards due to LPG leakage or smoke and smart lighting. All these use cases involve various sensors, actuators, smart appliances like smart thermostats, smart lights etc. All these devices constitute acquisition layer of the proposed ICON framework (discussed in next section) for provisioning smart environment services to home residents;
- **Smart Healthcare:** People with heart diseases are at high risk when their heart rate exceeds some threshold, hence their heart rate needs to be constantly monitored to tackle with abnormal situations in real-time. A fall detection system based on acceleration data for heart patients within smart home utilizing fog computing is proposed in Craciunescu et al. (2015), however they do not perform any processing for the heart rate. Hence, in this paper, holistic care for heart patients is provided via heart rate monitoring as well as fall detection, such that the doctor and registered family members are contacted when, either the resting heart rate reaches dangerous range or the patient falls.

An overview of the considered use cases examining the IoT and context perspectives are presented in Table 1. For the sake of simplicity and understanding, the authors have considered only two domains, but the proposed ICON framework is generalized enough for enabling other smart home scenarios.

3.1. ICON: A Layered Framework for IoT Based Context-Aware Computing Applications

In this section, the proposed layered framework for IoT based context-aware computing- ICON has been described; wherein IoT constitutes the tangible hardware ecosystem comprising of sensors, computation middleware and actuators while context-aware computing is intangible software part to process and understand the context to direct action via IoT devices. The authors have chosen a layered framework, since it helps in separation of concerns by clearly defining the functions of each layer. The proposed ICON framework is shown in Figure 1.

In Figure 1, the extreme left side behind the dotted line shows the context-aware computing stack applicable to any context-aware computing application while, the extreme right section shows the generalized IoT stack and the middle section represents the *ICON* framework for IoT-based Context-aware applications, depicting the amalgamation and interplay of two diverse yet complimentary technologies. The context-aware computing stack and the IoT stack are self-explanatory and included here for the sake

Table 1. Smart home use cases with IoT and context perspectives

IoT Perspective		Context Perspective	
Application	Use Case Description	Context Parameters Required	Context Utilization/ Action to Be Taken
Smart Environment (includes air quality, lights and temperature)	Home temperature control using smart thermostat	Season, Presence, TimeofDay	SetThermostat
	Inside air quality monitoring including detection of LPG, smoke etc.	LPGlevel, Smokelevel	For LPG: OpenVentilator For Smoke: SprayWater, SetFireAlarm
	Smart lighting control based on presence or absence of persons in the area	Presence, Posture, TimeofDay, CurrentLightLevel	SetLightLevel
Smart Healthcare	Elderly Care to monitor heart-rate for COPD/ stroke patients	Heartrate	CallDoctor, CallEmergencyContact
	Fall Detection for COPD/ stroke patients	Posture	CallDoctor, CallEmergencyContact

Figure 1. ICON framework

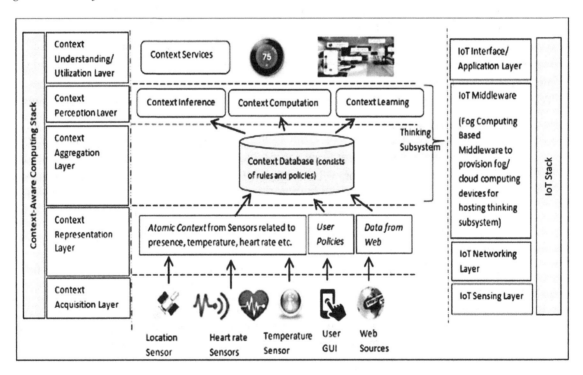

of completeness and understanding, however the framework of these two independent technologies is discussed below briefly, followed by layer-wise detailed explanation of the proposed ICON framework:

- **Context-Aware Computing Stack:** It comprises of layered framework that represent the general steps and functions involved for context-aware computing applications. For context-aware applications, the acquisition layer captures the raw data ie. atomic context via some physical or virtual sensors, upon which the representation layer formats or deduce medium-level context and passes it to aggregation layer to store it into the context database, the context database comprises of rules and personalization policies in addition to the derived contextual data. The context database is used by the perception layer to carry out core context-processing functions such as, context computation- computation of high-level context information, context inference- inferring action-able context-based decisions, and context learning- learning about changes in user preferences and habits to update the context database accordingly. Finally, based on inferences drawn by the perception layer, the context-utilization or understanding layer provides context-aware services to user applications;

- **IoT Stack:** The 4-layer IoT stack has been discussed by Xu et al. (2014). The acquisition layer comprises of sensors, smart devices, web interfaces etc. which provide raw sensor data, which is then transmitted to the IoT middleware by the network layer. Upon the middleware IoT-based stream of data is stored, processed and analyzed to derive meaningful decisions and actionable knowledge, such that these actions or extracted knowledge is transmitted to the actuators or us-ers via the application layer. It is worth to note that, the IoT middleware is the core storage and processing engine to enable IoT applications, where the Big Data stream generated by IoT devices can be stored, processed and analyzed. As discussed earlier in the paper, the IoT middleware can be cloud-based ie. entire data storage and processing done on the cloud platform or fog-based ie. data storage and processing done on Fog-to-cloud continuum. In this paper, the authors suggest fog-based IoT middleware that can leverage home gateways, routers as Fog nodes to provide im-plicit context information;

- **The ICON Framework:** The proposed IoT-based Context-aware framework has been discussed layer-wise below:
    - ○ **Acquisition Layer:** It comprises of various sensors like location, temperature, passive infra-red, heart rate etc. which generate raw sensor data. In addition, this layer can acquire data/information from user GUIs or web interfaces. In ICON framework, user GUI is used to define user personalization policies, and web interfaces are used to access some data from internet such as access weather information, current geographic information, access social networks etc. The raw data acquired by this layer denotes the atomic context, which is being gathered continuously in real-time;
    - ○ **Representation Layer:** The data from acquisition layer is transmitted, by the networking devices, to the IoT middleware for further storage and processing. This layer is responsible for representing the continuous stream of data in appropriate format on the middleware, it may also include aggregating the data over time intervals or some sort of processing to deduce medium-level context etc. Hence, the main functions of this layer include data pre-processing, aggregation, formatting and representation;
    - ○ **Processing Layer:** Processing layer embodies the core "thinking subsystem", being hosted by the IoT middleware. It is worth to mention that, fog computing does not rule out the role of cloud platform rather it suggests to use local fog nodes for immediate storage and process-ing, while using the cloud platform for permanent data storage and long-term analysis. In the

proposed ICON framework, local fog nodes can be leveraged for minimal context-processing which involves storing a local copy of context rules along with real-time computation and inference of context information while, the permanent storage of context database and long-term context learning suits the cloud platform. Hence, fog and cloud go hand-in-hand to enable the overall context processing. The functions of this layer include context-storage and processing, such that fog serves the transient real-time storage and processing while cloud serves for the permanent storage and long-term processing of contextual data. Further, for the smart home scenario considered in this paper the authors used first-order predicate logic for context-processing, which is described in more detail in the next section;

° **Application Layer:** This layer interfaces with actuators, smart appliances etc. either to take action determined by the processing layer or to display notifications and other visualizations. In other words, the context understood from processing layer is utilized here either via mobile/ web interfaces through e-mail, SMS etc. or via actuations to control smart devices.

4. CONTEXT PREDICATE LOGIC

This section discusses the application of predicate logic for context-processing to facilitate the smart home use cases, which were discussed in section 3. The context has been represented in the form of first-order predicate. The predicate name indicates the context type, which is being represented such as Season, Presence, TimeofDay, SetThermostat, Location, Heartrate etc. Use-case wise predicate names are listed in Table 1. Further, relational operators like $<$, $>$ etc. can be used as predicate arguments. Boolean operations such as conjunction ($\wedge$), disjunction ($\vee$) and negation ($\neg$) can be defined over context predicates. Quantification over contexts is done using existential ($\exists$) and universal ($\forall$) quantifiers. The formulation of context-predicate rules for the use case context-aware home temperature control, is shown in Table 2.

Table 2 shows context-rules for smart temperature control use case. Similarly, context rules for smart healthcare and smart lighting are defined in Tables 3 and 4 respectively.

Table 2. Context-aware home temperature control scenario

IoT Based Automation: "Home Temperature Control Using Smart Thermostat"
User Personalization Policy: A. Winter Thermostat settings: 　　1. If someone is at home, set it to 68° F 　　2. If everyone is away from home in the daytime, or it's sleeping time, set it to 66° F B. Summer Thermostat setting: 　　1. If someone is at home, set it to 78° F 　　2. If everyone is away from home in the daytime, or it's sleeping time, set it to 85° F
Context Parameters: Season, Presence, TimeofDay, SetThemostat
Context Predicate Rules: For A.1, winter setting for rule number 1 will be as: *Season(winter)* $\wedge$ $\exists_{Person}$ *x Presence(x, inside-home)* $\Rightarrow$ *SetThermostat(68 F)* For A.2, winter setting for rule number 2 will be as: *Season(winter)* $\wedge$ *($\forall_{Person}$ x ¬Presence(x, inside-home)* $\vee$ *(TimeofDay(currentTime,">", 22:00:00)* $\wedge$ *TimeofDay(currentTime,"<", 06:00:00)))* $\Rightarrow$ *SetThermostat(66 F)* Similarly, rules can be defined for B.1 and B.2

Table 3. Context-aware smart healthcare scenario

IoT Based Automation: "Smart Healthcare to Inform the Doctor and Family Member in Case of Emergency"

User Personalization Policy:
A. Abnormal Heartrate settings:
    1. If the user's heartbeat is abnormal, call the Doctor and EmergencyCcontact.
B. Fall detection setting:
    1. If the user fell down, call the Doctor and EmergencyCcontact.

Context Parameters: HeartRate, Posture
Context Predicate Rules: For A.1, abnormal heart rate setting for rule number 1 will be as: *HeartRate(currentHeartRate, "<", 60) $\wedge$ HeartRate(currentHeartRate, ">", 100) $\Rightarrow$ Call (Doctor, EmergencyContact)* For B.1, fall detection setting for rule number 1 will be as: *HeartRate(currentHeartRate, "<", 60) $\wedge$ HeartRate(currentHeartRate, ">", 100) $\wedge$ Posture(FallDown) $\Rightarrow$ Call (Doctor, EmergencyContact)*

Table 4. Context-aware smart lighting scenario

IoT Based Automation: "Smart Lighting Based on User's Context to Save Electricity"

User Personalization Policy:
A. Daytime Smart Light settings:
    1. If someone is in room and the person is not lying down on the bed, set light ON
    2. If someone is in room and the person is lying down on the bed (ie. sleeping or relaxing), set light OFF
B. Nighttime Smart Light settings:
    1. If someone is in room and the person is lying down on bed, set light OFF
    2. If someone is in room and the person is not lying down on the bed, set light ON *//The person may have woken up to go to bathroom – turning light ON will assist the user or // The person/child may be working/studying- in that case too, the context should be automatically sensed and light should be turned ON.*
C. Anytime Smart Light settings:
    2. If no one is in room and the light is ON, set light OFF *//Turn OFF light to save electricity when not in use*

Context Parameters: TimeofDay, Presence, Posture, CurrentLightLevel, SetLightLevel
Context Predicate Rules: For A.1, daytime setting for rule number 1 will be as: *(TimeofDay(currentTime, ">", 06:00:00) $\wedge$ TimeofDay(currentTime, "<", 22:00:00)) $\wedge$ $\exists_{Person}$ x (Presence(x, inside-bedroom) $\wedge$ $\neg$Posture(x, LieDown)) $\Rightarrow$ SetLightLevel(ON)* For A.2, daytime setting for rule number 2 will be as: *(TimeofDay(currentTime, ">", 06:00:00) $\wedge$ TimeofDay(currentTime, "<", 22:00:00)) $\wedge$ $\exists_{Person}$ x (Presence(x, inside-bedroom) $\wedge$ Posture(x, LieDown)) $\Rightarrow$ SetLightLevel(OFF)* For B.1, nighttime setting for rule number 1 will be as: *(TimeofDay(currentTime, ">", 22:00:00) $\wedge$ TimeofDay(currentTime, "<", 06:00:00)) $\wedge$ $\exists_{Person}$ x (Presence(x, inside-bedroom) $\wedge$ Posture(x, LieDown)) $\Rightarrow$ SetLightLevel(OFF)* For B.2, nighttime setting for rule number 2 will be as: *(TimeofDay(currentTime, ">", 22:00:00) $\wedge$ TimeofDay(currentTime, "<", 06:00:00)) $\wedge$ $\exists_{Person}$ x (Presence(x, inside-bedroom) $\wedge$ $\neg$Posture(x, LieDown)) $\Rightarrow$ SetLightLevel(ON)* For C.1, smart light setting for rule number 1 will be as: *$\forall_{Person}$ x $\neg$Presence(x, inside-bedroom) $\wedge$ CurrentLightLevel(ON) $\Rightarrow$ SetLightLevel(OFF)*

5. IMPLEMENTATION AND DISCUSSION

This section discusses the working of ICON based smart home enabled by fog computing. First, the system architecture has been discussed followed by data collection and processing methodology. The system architecture for ICON based smart home enabled by fog computing is shown in Figure 2, wherein

Figure 2. System architecture for ICON-based smart home enabled by fog computing

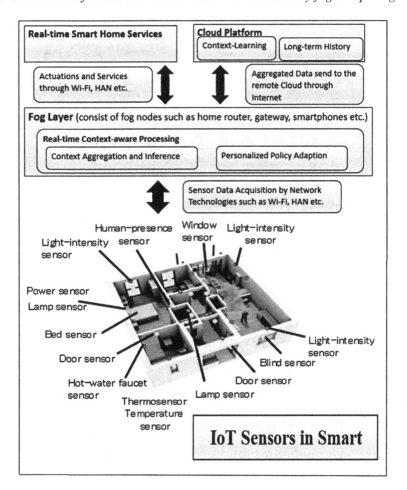

context-processing done on the fog layer enables real-time actuations and services for smart home users while the cloud platform enables continuous long-term learning of user preferences and habits.

In the proposed ICON based smart home solution, various smart appliances such as thermostat, lights etc. transmit their real-time state data for example- current temperature, status of lights etc. to the home gateway via short-range communication protocols such as Wi-Fi, XBee, HAN (Home Area Network) etc. Further, the home gateway is acting as fog node for local processing to provision context-aware personalized services. It is worth to mention that real-time data processing done on the fog device (gateway), is augmented by the long-term processing being done on the cloud. Data processing on the cloud includes tasks such as context-learning and history maintenance. The role of various entities like home sensors, fog gateways and the cloud along with flow of information between these entities is shown in the system architecture described in Figure 2.

After the clear illustration of constituent elements of the proposed smart home, the information processing pipeline depicting data-to-information transformation i.e. Data collection and processing methodology is shown in Figure 3.

Figure 3. Data collection and processing methodology in fog and ICON-based smart home

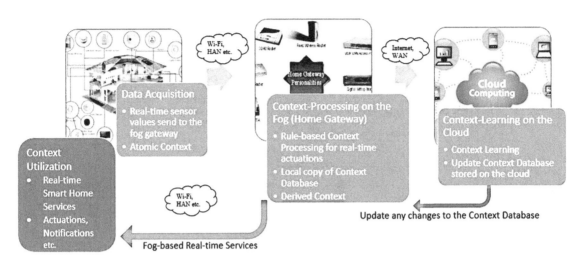

The Figure 3 shows the transition of data through various stages. The raw sensory data from smart appliances and sensors deployed in the smart home represents the atomic context such as current temperature, PIR (Passive Infra-red) status, current value of heart-rate etc. which are sent to the home gateway for fog-based computing where, rule based context-processing is done by referring the context database to derive the context in order to take real-time actions or decisions. The derived context is then utilized by the smart devices and appliances, in the form of real-time actions manifested in smart appliances or in the form of notifications displayed to the intended users. The sense-process-actuate loop runs through "smart devices-to-fog layer-to-smart devices" such that the physical smart devices provision initial sensing and receive post-processing actuations while, the fog nodes process the sensed data to direct the real-time actuations back onto physical smart devices. However, in reality the process stage is shared among the fog and cloud platform such that, fog layer processes incoming real-time contextual data in accordance to the database it already has and further, it can do the processing confined within its resource power, while the cloud does processing for the tasks/data for which fog resources fall short, in addition, the cloud performs long-term learning of context to learn user's habits over time and update its database and perpetuate the updates to fog's context database to incorporate the user preferences. The whole scenario is explained with the help of an example as follows: (the example taken here is the smart lighting scenario whose context-predicate rules are described in Table 4 in preceding sections).

5.1. Case I: Context-Processing on the Fog Node

The fog node processes the data received from various sensors then, process the data to derive the context and take decisions w.r.t context database stored on the fog node. In the smart lighting example of Table 3, all the context-rules viz. A.1, A.2, B.1, B.2, and C.1 are already stored in the context database residing on the fog node. The sensors used in this example are PIR motion sensor- to detect presence of a person inside room, Accelerometer- to detect whether the person is lying down on bed or not, Luminosity sensor- to sense the current light level in the room, and the time readings are taken from system time of fog node. Based on the current values from these sensors, the fog node ie. home router/gateway takes the smart action whether to turn the smart light ON/OFF.

5.2. Case II: Context-Learning on the Cloud

Suppose Michael is the child living with his parents in the considered smart home. Michael is currently doing his high school study and he usually prefers to study during night hours, especially in exam days. So, the user-context for Michael studying late night is such that, current time is night hours, the PIR sensor detects human presence, posture is not lying down (it can be easily calculated from accelerometer readings), thus, the fog node will apply rule B.2 ie. turn ON the light, so that Michael can study and need not worry about turning ON/OFF the light. Now, further suppose that while studying Michael felt exhausted and lie down for a 15 minutes power nap, owing to the current context and lying down posture, the fog node computes the context and applies rule B.1 to turn OFF the light. However, since Michael is having exam next day, he does not want to turn OFF light during power nap in fear of going to deep sleep state, hence, Michael again turns ON light and lies down, this overriding of actuation by user interrupt when sent to the fog gateway would be communicated to the cloud also. Context-learning at the cloud platform, will learn that if Michael overruled the already coded rule to keep light ON during lying down posture, it will record this event, and such event repeated for few days will help the cloud learn that Michael is having exams these days, if Michael sleeps after study during night it is perhaps a power nap and do not turn OFF the light. Once this learnt context is updated in fog's context database, Michael can take power naps with light kept ON by the fog node without manually turning it ON.

The practical implementation of the discussed use cases of context-aware IoT smart home has be done in two phases- in the first phase the IoT based smart home infrastructure was set-up and in the second phase predicate logic on the IoT middleware for context-processing was implemented. The authors plan to extend the functionality of proposed ICON based context-aware IoT based smart home in further works.

6. CONCLUSION

Ambient assisted living and intelligent homes are gaining a huge momentum. In this continuum, the authors presented a holistic smart home solution which includes both, home automation and user adaption via IoT and context-aware processing respectively. In this regard, ICON framework has been proposed for context-aware IoT applications which captures the essence of both IoT and context-aware computing and addresses how context can be handled for IoT systems. Further based on ICON framework, smart home domain has been discussed where the context is processed using predicate logic.

REFERENCES

Al-Muhtadi, J., Ranganathan, A., Campbell, R., & Mickunas, M. D. (2003, March). Cerberus: a context-aware security scheme for smart spaces. In *Pervasive Computing and Communications* (pp. 489-496). IEEE. doi:10.1109/PERCOM.2003.1192774

Atzori, L., Iera, A., & Morabito, G. (2010). The Internet of Things: A survey. *Computer Networks*, *54*(15), 2787–2805. doi:10.1016/j.comnet.2010.05.010

Baralis, E., Cagliero, L., Cerquitelli, T., Garza, P., & Marchetti, M. (2011). CAS-Mine: Providing personalized services in context-aware applications by means of generalized rules. *Knowledge and Information Systems*, *28*(2), 283–310. doi:10.1007/s10115-010-0359-z

Bonomi, F., Milito, R., Zhu, J., & Addepalli, S. (2012). Fog computing and its role in the internet of things. In *Proceedings of the first edition of the MCC workshop on Mobile cloud computing - MCC '12*. doi:10.1145/2342509.2342513

Craciunescu, R., Mihovska, A., Mihaylov, M., Kyriazakos, S., Prasad, R., & Halunga, S. (2015, November). Implementation of Fog computing for reliable E-health applications. In *Proceedings of the 2015 49th Asilomar Conference on Signals, Systems and Computers,* (pp. 459-463). IEEE. doi:10.1109/ACSSC.2015.7421170

Dastjerdi, A. V., & Buyya, R. (2016). Fog Computing: Helping the Internet of Things Realize Its Potential. *Computer*, *49*(8), 112–116. doi:10.1109/MC.2016.245

Ellenberg, J., Karstaedt, B., Voskuhl, S., von Luck, K., & Wendholt, B. (2011, September). An environment for context-aware applications in smart homes. In *Proceedings of the International Conference on Indoor Positioning and Indoor Navigation (IPIN)*, Guimaraes, Portugal.

Gu, T., Pung, H. K., & Zhang, D. Q. (2004). Toward an OSGi-based infrastructure for context-aware applications. *IEEE Pervasive Computing / IEEE Computer Society [and] IEEE Communications Society*, *3*(4), 66–74. doi:10.1109/MPRV.2004.19

Gubbi, J., Buyya, R., Marusic, S., & Palaniswami, M. (2013). Internet of Things (IoT): A vision, architectural elements, and future directions. *Future Generation Computer Systems*, *29*(7), 1645–1660. doi:10.1016/j.future.2013.01.010

Klimek, R., & Rogus, G. (2015, June). Proposal of a Context-Aware Smart Home Ecosystem. In *Proceedings of the International Conference on Artificial Intelligence and Soft Computing* (pp. 412-423). Springer International Publishing. doi:10.1007/978-3-319-19369-4_37

Li, B., & Yu, J. (2011). Research and application on the smart home based on component technologies and internet of things. *Procedia Engineering*, *15*, 2087–2092. doi:10.1016/j.proeng.2011.08.390

Li, J., Jin, J., Yuan, D., Palaniswami, M., & Moessner, K. (2015, November). EHOPES: Data-centered Fog platform for smart living. In *Proceedings of the Telecommunication Networks and Applications Conference (ITNAC), 2015 International* (pp. 308-313). IEEE. doi:10.1109/ATNAC.2015.7366831

McMillin, B., & Zhang, T. (2017). Fog Computing for Smart Living. *IEEE Computer*, *50*(2), 5–5. doi:10.1109/MC.2017.57

Perera, C., Zaslavsky, A., Christen, P., & Georgakopoulos, D. (2014). Context aware computing for the internet of things: A survey. *IEEE Communications Surveys and Tutorials*, *16*(1), 414–454. doi:10.1109/SURV.2013.042313.00197

Si, H., Kawahara, Y., Morikawa, H., & Aoyama, T. (2005). A stochastic approach for creating context-aware services based on context histories in smart home (Cognitive Science Research Paper). University of Sussex.

Varghese, B., Wang, N., Nikolopoulos, D. S., & Buyya, R. (2017). Feasibility of Fog Computing. arXiv:1701.05451

Vlachostergiou, A., Stratogiannis, G., Caridakis, G., Siolas, G., & Mylonas, P. (2016). User Adaptive and Context-Aware Smart Home Using Pervasive and Semantic Technologies. *Journal of Electrical and Computer Engineering, 2016*, 1–20. doi:10.1155/2016/4789803

Vujović, V., & Maksimović, M. (2015). Raspberry Pi as a Sensor Web node for home automation. *Computers & Electrical Engineering, 44*, 153–171. doi:10.1016/j.compeleceng.2015.01.019

Wang, W. Y., Chuang, C. C., Lai, Y. S., & Wang, Y. H. (2005, December). A context-aware system for smart home applications. In *Proceedings of the International Conference on Embedded and Ubiquitous Computing* (pp. 298-305). Springer Berlin Heidelberg. doi:10.1007/11596042_31

Weiser, M. (1999). The Computer for the Twenty-First Century. *Mobile Computing and Communications Review, 3*(3), 3–11. doi:10.1145/329124.329126

Xu, L. D., He, W., & Li, S. (2014). Internet of Things in Industries: A Survey. *IEEE Transactions on Industrial Informatics, 10*(4), 2233-2243.

Zhang, D., Gu, T., & Wang, X. (2005). Enabling context-aware smart home with semantic web technologies. *International Journal of Human-friendly Welfare Robotic Systems, 6*(4), 12–20.

This research was previously published in the Journal of Cases on Information Technology (JCIT), 19(4); edited by Andrew Borchers, pages 1-12, copyright year 2017 by IGI Publishing (an imprint of IGI Global).

Chapter 14
Proactive Mobile Fog Computing Using Work Stealing:
Data Processing at the Edge

SANDER SOO
University of Tartu, Estonia

Chii Chang
University of Tartu, Estonia

Seng W. Loke
Deakin University, Australia

Satish Narayana Srirama
University of Tartu, Estonia

ABSTRACT

A common design of the Internet of Things (IoT) system relies on distant Cloud for management and processing, which faces the challenge of latency, especially when the application requires rapid response in the edge network. Therefore, researchers have proposed the Fog computing architecture, which distributes the computational data processing tasks to the edge network nodes located in the vicinity of data sources and end-users to reduce the latency. Although the Fog computing architecture is promising, it still faces a challenge in mobility when the tasks come from ubiquitous mobile applications in which the data sources are moving objects. In order to address the challenge, this article proposes a proactive Fog service provisioning framework, which hastens the task distribution process in Mobile Fog use cases. Further, the proposed framework provides an optimization scheme in task allocation based on runtime context information. A proof-of-concept prototype has been implemented and tested on real devices.

DOI: 10.4018/978-1-5225-5649-7.ch014

INTRODUCTION

The information systems designed for integrating the Internet of Things (IoT) (Gubbi et al., 2013) are usually applying the global centralized model, in which the IoT devices rely on distant management systems. Such a model is considered to be a drawback in terms of agility (Bonomi et al., 2012). In many real-time ubiquitous applications such as augmented reality, environmental analytics, ambient assisted living, etc., mobile device users require rapid responses. However, the latency caused by the distant centralized model is too high, even though the mobile Internet speed has improved significantly during the last few years. To address this problem, Fog Computing (Fog) (Bonomi et al., 2012) introduces data pre-processing with the computers in the vicinity of the data sources and end-user applications located in the edge network of IoT systems.

In general, Fog computing resources, which are known as Fog nodes, are mediating devices that connect the edge network with the Internet. Some typical examples are industrial integrated routers (e.g., Cisco 829 Industrial Integrated Services Routers), home hubs or set-top boxes that are employed as wireless Internet access points together with embedded virtualization technologies (e.g., Virtual Machines) or containerization technologies (e.g., Docker containers (https://www.docker.com)), which allow clients to deploy software onto them. Compared to the traditional distant Cloud computing model, which requires sending all the data to the Distant Data Center (DDC) for the processing, Fog can provide much better agility.

Although Fog-driven IoT system provides explicit enhancement in performance, it also faces numerous challenges in terms of connectivity (Zhang et al., 2015), discoverability (Troung-Huu et al., 2014), efficient deployment (Ravi & Peddoju, 2014; Guo et al., 2016; Ceselli et al., 2017; Lin & Shen, 2017) and so on. While many of the previous works focused on Fog deployment for specific use cases, this paper aims to address the mobility issue raised in the case of integrating Fog with ubiquitous mobile applications.

Imagine a mobile ubiquitous care application that needs to provide real-time environmental information to its user by continuously collecting and processing data derived from the surrounding environment while its user is moving in outdoor areas. For improving the efficiency, the mobile device (i.e. delegator) is distributing its computational tasks to vicinal Fog servers (i.e. workers). However, the delegator may need to repeatedly resend the tasks to different Fog nodes, due to the dynamic nature of the mobile environment, where the limited wireless signal coverage of the Fog nodes could cause failure in delivering results.

Consequently, it raises a question:

How can the system avoid the situation that requires the delegator to re-send tasks to the other workers due to the failed process result delivery?

In order to address the question, this paper proposes a proactive task distribution framework for mobile Fog environments. The proposed framework consists of two core schemes:

- Proactive task distribution, which is an extension of the Work Stealing scheme (Loke et al., 2015) that provides the mechanism to hasten the speed of task distribution.
- Context-aware Work Stealing, which provides an optimal decision-making mechanism that helps workers (Fog nodes) to decide how they should participate in the distributed processes.

In essence, the contribution of the paper is to study the potential of applying context-aware Work Stealing scheme in Fog computing towards improving the mobility-awareness. The study provides new insights about how distributed systems can achieve the high-performance process migration in the edge networks. Although the study is based on a specific ubiquitous application use case, the involved theoretical design still provides an important foundation for the discipline of mobile distributed computing.

This paper is organized as follows. In the next section, the authors provide an overview and comparison of the related works. Afterwards, the details of the proposed system design are described. This is followed by the Evaluation section that provides detailed analysis of the performed experiments. Finally, this paper is concluded along with future research directions.

RELATED WORKS

Computation Offloading

Computation offloading is a common strategy to reduce the resource consumption and to improve the overall performance of ubiquitous mobile applications. Specifically, earlier works such as MAUI (Cuervo et al., 2010) or Cuckoo (Kemp et al., 2012) have introduced the schemes that assist the system in offloading the process from mobile devices to central surrogates such as the Cloud.

Considering the latency caused by the centralized offloading schemes, recent strategies have introduced the utilization of vicinal computational resources such as Virtual Machine (VM)-based Cloudlet (Satyanarayanan et al., 2009). In general, Cloudlet represents the VM-enabled server machines located on the same network as the mobile application nodes. For example, a local business may provide a Cloudlet machine to their customers to improve the Quality of Experience (QoE) of the mobile applications used by the customers.

In order to optimize the efficiency of the Cloudlet-based computation offloading, a number of researchers have proposed the machine learning algorithms to help the mobile applications' decision in whether or not to offload the tasks (Zhang et al., 2015; Troung-Huu et al., 2014).

Similarly, the offloading optimization is also an imperative research question in terms of balancing the workload between Cloud and Fog (Lin & Shen, 2017) and optimizing the task distribution in mobile ad hoc Clouds (Shi et al., 2015; Yousafzai et al., 2016).

Although existing works described above have proposed numerous strategies for distributing the computational tasks from mobile devices to external resources, most of them have assumed the communication between the delegator and the workers is fairly stable, thus they did not fully address the challenge raised in this paper.

Result Routing

An important aspect in mobile Fog is how to route the process result back to the delegator. In particular, the delegator may have moved out from the wireless network coverage of the Fog node, which has taken the computational tasks.

Instead of assuming the connectivity between the delegator and workers is fairly stable, a number of related research projects have proposed corresponding strategies. For example, Zhang et al. (2016) and Su et al. (2015) propose opportunistic collaborative caching with proximal peers. Further, Fernando et al. (2013; 2016) and Shi et al. (2012) utilize the Time-To-Live (TTL) policy, which defines the work expiring time, i.e. the time before the delegator restarts its delegation process. However, these approaches can potentially cause extra latency. Hence, Ravi et al. (2014) have proposed the interconnected Cloudlet scheme in which the delegator can establish a data routing network among multiple Cloudlet machines on the move.

Load Balancing and Efficient Deployment

A lot of work (Ceselli et al., 2017; Lin & Shen, 2017; Guo et al., 2016; Hong et al., 2013) has introduced approaches for optimizing the workload or discussed the efficiency of deployment for applications that could be improved via Fog. Specifically, Ceselli et al. (2017) have proposed a scheme for the optimized placement of Virtual Machines (VM) that provides improved computation support; Hong et al. (2013) proposed a process placement algorithm based on utilizing the customized scaling policy acquired from the user.

Existing works (Huerta-Canepa & Lee, 2010; Marinelli, 2009) did not consider the heterogeneous device capabilities of the worker nodes. Consequently, this raises the issue of assuming that heterogeneous and unknown devices have uniform capabilities. However, in the case of uniformly distributing the works, some nodes may be overloaded and cannot accept more works. Further, the weaker nodes may not be able to effectively complete the tasks they received in time and thereby result in the bottleneck issue.

Different to the previous works that were based on reactive strategies, the approach proposed in this paper is a proactive task distribution scheme that combines the Work Stealing scheme with context-awareness.

Mobility-Aware Edge Computing

Prior works have considered the mobility-awareness of task distribution (Bittencourt et. al., 2017; Chamola et al., 2017). Bittencourt et. al. (2017) propose policy-based task scheduling to improve the mobility-awareness of Cloudlet services. Chamola et al. (2017) propose a framework that allows mobile devices to offload computationally intensive tasks to Cloudlets, where the decision of which Clouldet handles the task is made by a central Cloudlet manager.

Existing works (Alam et al., 2016; Chamola et al., 2017; Lee & Shin, 2013) have also attempted to address the mobility-awareness of computation offloading. Specifically, Alam et al. (2016) proposed a mobility-aware extension to Fog, based on reinforcement learning. Lee & Shin (2013) proposed a mobile computation offloading scheme based on user mobility models, offering improved mobility support by predicting user movement and future network conditions.

Although previous research has considered mobility-awareness in various contexts, several of these works have only considered the strategies for task allocation in the context of a single computational node and have not focused on utilizing vicinal nodes. Furthermore, various assumptions, e.g., the offloadable application will be initially executed on the mobile device in order to analyze the execution beforehand, may not be applicable for real-world applications and tasks. Similarly, having a centralized manager in place to handle the decision of computation offloading or task allocation makes the system less adaptive and increases overall latency.

SYSTEM DESIGN

Overview

Figure 1 illustrates an overview of the proposed system based on an Ambient Assisted Living (AAL) scenario in which the user Alice's mobile device is operating an AAL service that is continuously collecting and processing the data derived from the surrounding IoT devices in order to provide useful information to Alice while she is walking in an urban area. Considering that the application includes a large volume of data processing, the Cloud backend management system of the AAL application has utilized Fog services to provide rapid responses.

One assumption is that Alice's route has been pre-defined using the corresponding mechanism based on the historical records (Rahaman et al., 2017) or Google Maps API.

Another assumption is that the Cloud backend has gained access to the Fog servers before Alice starts moving. In general, the Fog servers either belong to the same provider as the AAL service or the collaborative providers provide them.

Cloud backend selects the candidate Fog servers based on the route of the user (see the Candidate Worker Selection section). Further, it also deploys the software to the Fog servers to trigger the proactive behavior.

In Figure 1, T1 to T5 represent the timestamps of the user's route. In general, while Alice is moving, the AAL application (i.e., delegator) advertises its existence to Fog nodes (i.e., workers) by sending any of them a registration message. Specifically, the message contains the information of the tasks in the delegator's queue, including the type of the computational tasks. For example, the task can be CPU-intensive, GPU-intensive, RAM-intensive and so on. This information is updated periodically via the Work Stealing requests.

Figure 1. Overview of proactive Fog

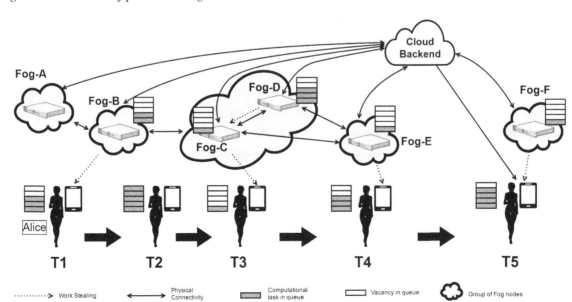

As Figure 1 shows, in T1, a chosen candidate Fog-B actively 'steals' two work items from the delegator. While Alice is moving, the AAL application has generated more tasks (T2). At T3, the delegator has encountered a new worker Fog-C. Since there are two workers in the group where Fog-C belongs, both of them will assist the AAL application.

As can be seen from the figure, Fog-C and Fog-D have acquired a different number of tasks (Fog-D has stolen some tasks from the delegator via Fog-C). In summary, the number of works they acquire is based on the runtime context (e.g., resource availability, workload and bandwidth) of the Fog nodes. The details are described in the Context-aware Work Stealing Scheme section.

There is an inevitable situation, where the Cloud backend does not find any direct connection between two Fog nodes on the user's moving route. For example, Fog-E does not have the connection to Fog-F. In such a case, Fog-E may deliver the process result to the delegator via the Cloud backend. Afterwards, the Cloud backend can either directly send the results to the delegator or indirectly deliver the results via Fog-F. The corresponding strategy of the result delivery is described in the Results Delivery section.

Candidate Worker Selection

Based on the route of Alice, the Cloud backend can identify the candidate Fog nodes needed in assisting Alice's AAL application. The Cloud backend selects the Fog servers based on the scheme below.

Let $E = \{E_1, \ldots, E_n\}$ be the set of all possible encounter Fog nodes on the end user's path. $E_k = \{e_i : 1 \leq i \leq N\}$ denotes the current encounter node(s) and E_{k+1} denotes the next encounter node(s) after E_k. E_1 are the closest encounter nodes to the starting point of the user.

Let E_x be one of the members of E. Then each of the $e_i \in E_x$ (denoted by e_i^x) would be included based on the following considerations:

- If e_i^x has a route through network infrastructure to e_i^{x+1} without utilizing the Cloud, then e_i^x is considered as a priority candidate.
- Let e_y^x to be one of the e_i^x. If e_y^x has a direct route to a priority candidate, it is also considered as a candidate.
- An isolated Fog node, with high computational capabilities and on the moving path of the user, where there are no alternatives, is also considered as a candidate.

Once the Cloud backend has selected the candidate Fog servers, it will deploy the corresponding software to the Fog servers in order to trigger the proactive behavior.

The Worker Network

The Cloud backend forms a worker network for the AAL application based on configuring the candidate Fog nodes into non-overlapping subgroups beforehand, such that all the members of the group are aware of the other Fog nodes in their group. The Work Stealing process among Fog nodes only takes place within the boundaries of the group.

The members of the group receive updates on various characteristics of their peers, such as the current CPU usage, RAM usage, bandwidth usage, etc., delivered by a resource-efficient publish-subscribe protocol such as MQTT (Bank & Gupta, 2014). MQTT also offers a *Last Will and Testament* feature, to notify peers when a node unexpectedly goes offline. Such information is useful in the optimization process.

Upon receiving information from the delegator, the Fog node also notifies the group members about the number of work items available per type (e.g., CPU intensive, GPU intensive, RAM intensive, etc.).

Once the Fog node steals the task(s) from the delegator, the Fog node will also register to a topic of the delegator's events (e.g., an update of the current location). Thus, the Fog nodes would have the knowledge of the delegator's currently connected Fog node and could transmit the results to the delegator accordingly.

Transmitting the results back to the user via the network of Fog nodes could still cover as many Fog nodes as needed.

The grading value to partition the tasks indicates the expected number of tasks a Fog node will handle. This value can be used as an estimate for the initially stolen tasks. Any Fog node will effectively make the final decision on whether or not to take some tasks for processing.

Context-Aware Work Stealing Scheme

Basic Multi-Layered Work Stealing

Loke et. al. (2015) introduce an extension of the original Work Stealing approach for mobile ad-hoc Cloud computing. In addition to the workers and delegators (i.e. distributors of tasks), there exist intermediaries, who can act as workers for some nodes and delegators to others. This enables the delegator to distribute the works to the workers beyond the direct connection range, thereby increasing the resources available for handling tasks and creating a multi-layered view of the system. As the workers finish their tasks, they steal more work from each other and via the delegator.

Context-Awareness Extension

The context-aware extension of the Work Stealing scheme optimizes the multi-layered work item distribution within the worker network, considering the current capabilities of the workers. The scheduled work items (tasks) contain information about the primary hardware resource required for processing the tasks. Such information helps the workers to steal works based on their resource availability. For example, a worker will steal CPU-intensive tasks if it has available CPU resources. Fog nodes would also query for runnables to process the work, either directly from the delegator (e.g., jar files or offline Docker images) or from the Internet (e.g., Docker Hub).

To extend the basic possibility of stealing one task for each resource type, the proposed framework includes a rating for each of the primary resources of a Fog node. Further, the ratings will be fetched by each of the Fog nodes (e.g., at the start of every day from an external service) and would show the capability of the Fog node in the given context of the resource (e.g., CPU), thus enabling different Fog nodes to be mutually comparable based on these values. An example of such external service could be www.cpubenchmark.net for the ratings of CPUs.

The proposed framework aims to allow the Fog nodes to steal work until their resources are properly utilized. However, it is not sensible to steal much more work than what can be currently processed by the adjacent Fog nodes, due to the overhead of routing the computed results back to the continuously moving user.

A key aspect is thus to consider the estimation of the number of work items that should be stolen by a specific Fog node.

A set of context parameters considered in the performance measurement of Fog node can include values such as CPU capability, RAM capability, network speed capability and so on. As a basis, it requires a normalized value for each context element of each Fog node in a given group. The calculation for the case when a higher raw value is better is illustrated below.

$$v_l^x = \frac{raw_l^x \times uw_l^x}{\sum_{i=0}^{|O|} raw_l^i \times uw_l^i}$$ (1)

where:

- v_l^x denotes the normalized value of context element *l* of Fog node *x*.

- raw_l^x denotes the raw value of context element *l* of Fog node *x*. This is the rating value for the resource of the Fog node that denotes the capability of the Fog node, usually in regards to an execution of a common algorithm or a benchmark.

- uw_l^x denotes the utilization weight of context element *l* of Fog node *x*. The weight can be used to account for the actual unutilized percentage of a resource on a Fog node. In this case, the weight would be equal to the idleness of the Fog node in the given context *l* (i.e. 1-U_l, where U_l denotes the current load).

- denotes the set of all Fog nodes, which belong to the same group.

For the case when a lower raw value is better (e.g., the number of intermediate hops involved in delivering the result to the delegator), simply the formula ($1 - v_l^x$) is used.

Based on the data from Equation 1, one can calculate the overall grade per resource context, in order to gain a preliminary estimate on the ratio of the work items to be taken by any given Fog node. This concept is illustrated as follows.

$$grade_l^x = \frac{\sum_{l=0}^{|C|} v_l^x \times cw_l}{\sum_{i=0}^{|O|} \sum_{l=0}^{|C|} v_l^i \times cw_l}$$ (2)

where:

- $grade_l^x$ denotes the preliminary estimate of the ratio of all work items to be taken by Fog node *x* that utilize the resource of context *l*.

- v_l^x denotes the normalized value of context element *l* of Fog node *x*.

- *O* denotes the set of all Fog nodes, which belong to the same group.

- C denotes the union set of the current context and common contexts. Common contexts are the ones that impact the performance of all the contexts (e.g. the network speed capability).
- cw_l denotes the context weight of context element l in the overall perspective. Not all contexts may be equally important, e.g., number of hops to the delegator may be considered less important than the actual CPU capability of the Fog node.

The estimate on the actual number of work items for fog_x to handle (denoted by $\#FW_l^x$) is thus deducible from the grading value and the number of work items. This concept is also illustrated as follows.

$$\#FW_l^x = \left[grade_l^x \times |W_l| \right] \tag{3}$$

where:

- W_l denotes the set of all work items with the given context as the primary resource.

The formulae have been validated experimentally and the results are reported in the Evaluation section.

Results Delivery

In general, there is a possibility that the delegator node has moved out from the range of the worker node before the worker node has completed the tasks and delivered the result to the delegator. Fundamentally, there are two basic approaches for handling the situation.

1. Worker Network Routing. As mentioned previously, Cloud backend has chosen the Fog nodes based on the priority of the connectivity (see Candidate Worker Selection). Hence, the workers can always attempt to route the process result to the node that is currently connected with the delegator.
2. Cloud-assisted Routing. In the case of missing routing path to the currently connected Fog node or due to heavy traffic among the nodes within the routing path, the worker can choose to route the process result to the delegator via Cloud backend.

In order to identify the best approach for the process result delivery, the workers may need to continuously update the network status. Considering the status needs to be up-to-date, the workers will only keep the information in the vicinity (i.e. within the group). When a Fog node in the group should transmit data to the Cloud backend, it would also keep a record of the communication speed. Hence, if any node has a choice to possibly transmit data to the Cloud (or alternatively use the Fog node network), it would aggregate the communication speed data, and compute the weighted average of the times to the Cloud, where the most recent communications have the highest weight. For optimization reasons, some of the calculation results may be cached, in order to improve the performance of the system.

Another crucial aspect would be the distance of hops from the original worker, which handles the computation, to the current Fog node that the delegator is connected to.

The distance in hops could be statically calculated, assuming that each Fog node would know at least the Fog nodes in its vicinity (i.e. a subgraph of the vicinal network of Fog nodes) or a similar approach as for the Cloud context can be used. As the user is constantly moving, at each timestamp when the user connects with a Fog node, this node would send an MQTT message to the topic of the user's location. Only the Fog nodes that have some in-progress tasks from the delegator would subscribe to the topic.

EVALUATION

Reactive and Proactive Task Handling Performance

This section aims to evaluate the performance between the proposed proactive approach and a reactive approach. In the reactive approach, the delegator's work items are expired upon disconnection with one Fog node and retransmitted upon connection with a new Fog node. Conversely, in a proactive approach, the Fog nodes can transmit the results back to the user via the local network between Fog nodes.

The devices involved in the experiment were as follows:

- Fog-1 and Fog-2 — HP Elitebook Folio 9470m (Intel i5-3437U, 8GB RAM).
- Delegator — Nexus 5 smartphone (LG-D821).

The experiment begins with the delegator transmitting a registration message to Fog-1. Fog-1 then steals work item(s) and also the runnable from the delegator. In our current experiment, only a single work item exists. As soon as Fog-1 begins the computation, the delegator disconnects from Fog-1 and connects with Fog-2.

The sizes of the runnable and result are constant values of 25MB. The computation time is a fixed value of 5 seconds on both of the Fog nodes. The work item data is a varying unit with a size of 25MB, 50MB, 75MB or 100MB.

Figure 2 illustrates the differences in time in the context of utilizing the Fog with either a reactive or a proactive approach.

In the reactive case, the delegator transmits the work item and runnable initially to Fog-1 and upon delegator disconnection from Fog-1, the same data is transmitted again to Fog-2. No data is transmitted between the Fog nodes and the computation is simply terminated by Fog-1.

In the proactive case, the work item and runnable data is transmitted once to Fog-1. When the delegator connects with Fog-2, there is nothing left for Fog-2 to steal since the only task has been taken by Fog-1, and the task has not yet expired. When Fog-1 finishes the processing, results are transmitted back to the delegator via Fog-2 (i.e. the Fog node where the delegator is currently connected).

A lot of data needs to be retransmitted when the system utilizes the reactive approach. Therefore, the proactive approach is shown to perform better under the circumstances.

Docker Image Transfer Performance

This section aims to evaluate the performance of using Docker in the local scenario, where the user transmits the Docker image via smartphone using Wi-Fi, and also in the scenario, where the image is downloaded from Docker Hub, via image name and Docker provided API(s).

Figure 2. Comparison of reactive and proactive approach of utilizing Fog

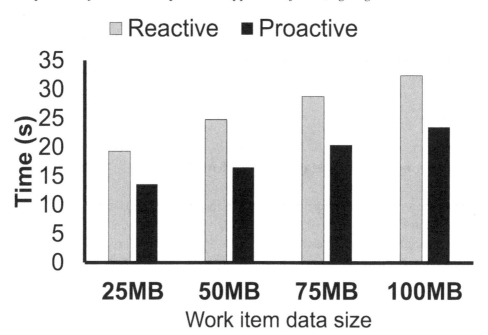

The experiments were conducted using Gigabit Ethernet connection for the Fog node to the Internet and 802.11n Wi-Fi network for smartphone communication.

The Docker images were chosen from the popular Docker Hub images listing, so that the file sizes (not compressed) would be near-linearly increasing (php:alpine 57.3MB, maven:alpine 115.7MB, python:slim 198.6MB).

The devices used in the experiments were as follows:

- Fog-1 — HP Elitebook 840 (Intel i5-4200U, 12GB RAM).
- Delegator — Nexus 5 smartphone (LG-D821).

Local Docker Image Transfer

The process starts with downloading the image file from the delegator and ends with loading the image into the Docker infrastructure running on a Fog node.

The compression used in the experiment was 7-zip normal preset with the standard deflate compression method.

Docker Image File Transfer

Figure 3 illustrates the Docker image transmission times for different images for both with and without the use of compression. This shows that the transmission times can still be quite high, even in the local network. The relatively low speeds were most likely influenced by the Wi-Fi adapter hardware, especially that of the delegator.

Figure 3. Docker image transmission time

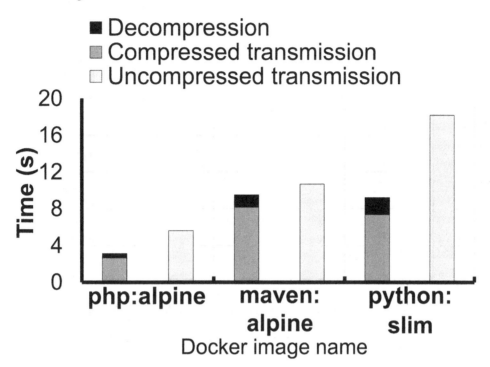

In the case of transmission with using compressed files, the image files would have to be decompressed on the Fog node before they are used. Therefore, this experiment also includes the decompression time. It is important to note that the time improvement from compression may or may not be substantial, depending on the exact image. For example, in our specific case, the compressed sizes of the files did not turn out to be linear. The compressed maven:alpine image was larger than the compressed python:slim image, which reduced the benefit of compression to under a second for maven:alpine. The sizes of the compressed images were approximately between 30-65% smaller than their uncompressed counterparts (php:alpine 25.3MB, maven:alpine 77.5MB, python:slim 70.3MB).

Loading Image Into the Docker Infrastructure

Figure 4 illustrates the time taken to load the Docker image into the Docker infrastructure running on a Fog node. When this action completes, the Docker infrastructure will contain the new image that can be used to run a Docker container.

Total Latency of Local Docker Image Loading Into the Docker Infrastructure

Figure 5 illustrates the overall comparison of time spent utilizing the compressed and uncompressed approaches. This involves all the intermediary tasks required to migrate the Docker image from the delegator to the Fog node in a local network and is completed when the loaded image is ready to be deployed as a container on the Fog node.

Figure 4. Loading time of Docker image to Docker infrastructure

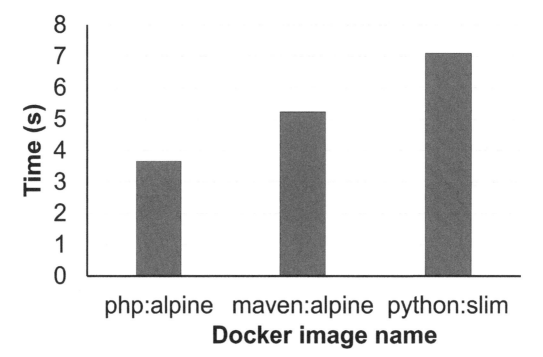

Docker Image Transfer via Docker Hub

Instead of transferring the runnable directly from the delegator to the Fog node, the system can choose to utilize a remote repository. For example, the delegator can specify the link of a Docker Hub image as the runnable. Such an option can reduce the file transmission overhead for the delegator.

Figure 6 illustrates the complete time to download the image with all its layers from Docker Hub and loading the image into Docker infrastructure. This is the over-the-Internet equivalent of Figure 5. Even though the local network has the reduced latency due to the devices being in close physical proximity, the physical hardware limitations become very relevant when the devices have constrained resources.

Task Execution Performance

This subsection aims to compare the performance of task execution by using direct node execution (tasks are not distributed, but solely processed by the directly connected Fog node), Work Stealing approach or a simple round-robin task assignment (even number of tasks distributed to all nodes).

The devices that were involved in this analysis were as follows:

- Fog-1 — HP Elitebook 840 (Intel i5-4200U, 12GB RAM), where approximately 50% RAM and 50% CPU were utilized before the start of the experiment, in order to simulate a Fog node that is already busy with some other tasks beforehand.
- Fog-2 — HP Elitebook Folio 9470m (Intel i5-3437U, 8GB RAM), where the OS utilized approximately 10-15% of RAM by default.

Figure 5. Total latency of local Docker image loading into Docker infrastructure

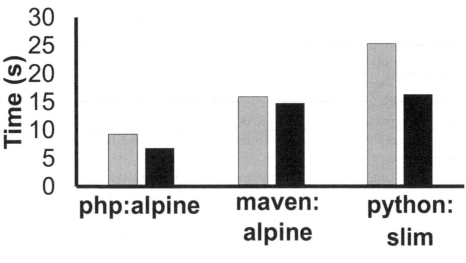

Figure 6. Total Docker image transfer and loading via Docker Hub (Internet)

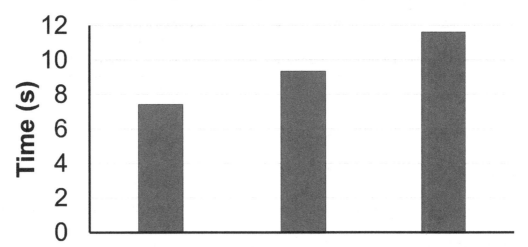

- Fog-3 — Lenovo V570 (Intel i7-2670QM, 16GB RAM), where the OS utilized approximately 10-15% of RAM by default.
- Delegator — Nexus 5 smartphone (LG-D821).

The work items were either CPU-intensive or RAM-intensive tasks, where each category utilized mainly the CPU or RAM resources respectively.

CPU-intensive tasks were further subcategorized as small-cpu and large-cpu tasks, where the time to process small-cpu task was approximately equivalent to half of the large-cpu task. The tasks were designed such that the CPU would be kept utilized at about 70-80% usage level by one task on average.

RAM-intensive tasks were further subcategorized as small-ram and large-ram tasks, where the time to process small-ram task was approximately equivalent to half of the large-ram task. The tasks were designed such that approximately 3-3.5GB of RAM would be utilized by one task on average.

The size of the inputs for the tasks was 5MB for the small tasks and 10MB for the large-tasks. The size of the result data was 1MB.

The evaluation was conducted in the scenario of completing 30 tasks and 60 tasks. In the case of having 30 tasks in total, 20 tasks were CPU-intensive (10 small-cpu and 10 large-cpu tasks) and 10 were RAM-intensive (5 small-ram and 5 large-ram tasks). The case of 60 tasks in total followed the same overview as the 30 tasks variant, except there was exactly twice the number of each type of task. The delegator of the work was connected to Fog-1. Since there were tasks with CPU type and RAM type, then the formula used for estimated distribution of works also contained these main context values.

Task Execution Time

Figure 7 illustrates the differences of task execution times for the three approaches. Firstly, the direct node execution approach performs the worst, because it relies on one node to handle all the tasks, which is already partially utilized beforehand. Secondly, the round-robin approach statically assigns tasks to workers, which produced better performance than the direct node execution approach. Finally, the Work Stealing approach, which considered the runtime context factors, has outperformed the other two approaches.

The experimental results indicate the importance of considering the heterogeneous specification and the runtime context factors of the Fog nodes in the mobile Fog computing.

Partition of Tasks Allocated to Fog Nodes

Figure 8 shows the partition of all the tasks that were executed at any Fog Node, for all the task distribution methods.

The direct node execution approach relies on one single Fog node to handle all the tasks, and the Fog node does not distribute the works further. Hence, it has taken all the tasks.

Since the round-robin approach does not consider the different capabilities of the Fog nodes, the works are distributed uniformly over all the Fog nodes.

The Work Stealing approach, on the other hand, considers the heterogeneous capabilities of the workers. Therefore, the Fog node with the highest characteristics has handled the greatest number of work items and the one with the lowest current capabilities has handled the least work items.

Figure 7. Task execution time

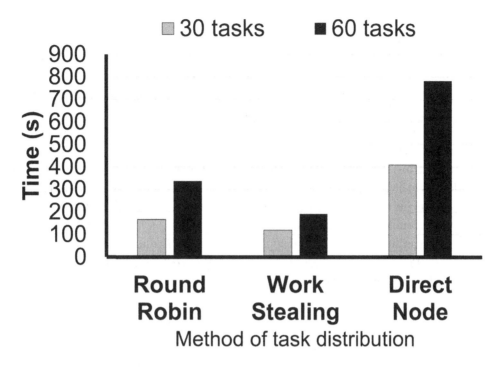

Figure 8. Partition of tasks distributed to Fog nodes

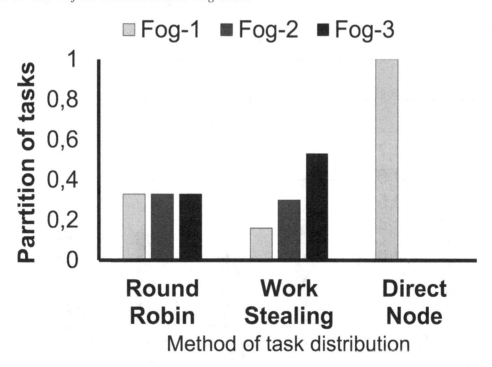

Task Distribution

Figure 9 illustrates the partitioning of types of work between Fog nodes, e.g., how were the small-cpu type of tasks partitioned between Fog nodes.

Since Fog-3 has a much more capable CPU than the other Fog nodes, it has taken the majority of both the small-cpu and large-cpu typed tasks. Since Fog-1 is already considerably utilized both in the CPU and RAM categories, it has taken the least amount of work items. The context of the RAM follows a similar approach. The reason for the partitions to not differ as greatly in this context is most likely because CPU-intensive tasks also use up a part of the RAM. Therefore, if a Fog node is busy with many CPU-intensive work items, then it directly affects the amount of available RAM and thus influences the amount of RAM tasks to be processed. The CPU usage by the RAM-intensive work items is comparably smaller, thus not producing the opposite effect in the other context. This is yet another aspect that cannot be easily taken into account by the static task distribution methods.

A similar figure regarding the round-robin approach was omitted, due to the fact that it would show a uniform distribution of all types of work items between all Fog nodes. Similarly, the direct node execution approach would show everything executing on Fog-1.

CONCLUSION

This paper introduced a mobility-aware framework for proactive Fog service provisioning. In contrast to the previous works that assumed the stable connectivity between the delegator and worker nodes, or required prior analysis of historical data in order to provide an efficient offloading approach; the proposed scheme of this paper enables mobile ubiquitous applications to perform computation offloading with

Figure 9. Work Stealing task distribution by task type

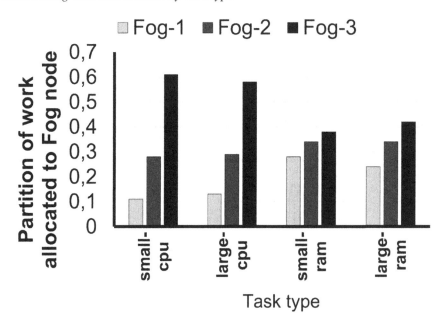

Fog computing servers with minimal prerequisite analysis. Further, the approach provides for an adaptable environment in which stable connectivity need not be guaranteed. Specifically, the Fog nodes can deliver the computational results to the mobile delegator node either through the local worker network or via the assistance of the Cloud, depending on the performance analysis of the approaches. Moreover, the proposed system utilizes an extended Work Stealing paradigm with worker groups, which considers heterogeneous capabilities of Fog nodes and the heterogeneous nature of incoming tasks to be distributed amongst these Fog nodes. The elements of the framework were evaluated on real devices.

In the future, the authors plan to address additional optimizations, where work items that share a runnable would preferably be distributed to Fog nodes that already possess the runnable to further improve efficiency. In addition, it would be interesting to research the pre-scheduling or reservation of Fog nodes in a given area, where a higher priority of execution and a more aggressive variant of freeing up resources (or executing fewer tasks) for the reservation would be used. Additionally, analysis of the energy efficiency of the proposed approach, along with an exploration of network fluctuations of mobile scenarios are also considered as future research directions.

ACKNOWLEDGMENT

This research is supported by Study IT in Estonia.

References

Alam, M. G. R., Tun, Y. K., & Hong, C. S. (2016). Multi-agent and reinforcement learning based code offloading in mobile fog. In *Proceedings of the International Conference on Information Networking (ICOIN)* (pp. 285–290). doi:10.1109/ICOIN.2016.7427078

Banks, A., & Gupta, R. (2014). MQTT Version 3.1.1. OASIS standard. Retrieved from http://docs.oasis-open.org/mqtt/mqtt/v3.1.1/csprd02/mqtt-v3.1.1-csprd02.html

Bittencourt, L. F., Diaz-Montes, J., Buyya, R., Rana, O. F., & Parashar, M. (2017). Mobility-aware application scheduling in fog computing. *IEEE Cloud Computing*, 4(2), 26–35. doi:10.1109/MCC.2017.27

Bonomi, F., Milito, R., Zhu, J., & Addepalli, S. (2012). Fog Computing and Its Role in the Internet of Things. In *Proceedings of the First Edition of the MCC Workshop on Mobile Cloud Computing* (pp. 13-16). New York: ACM. doi:10.1145/2342509.2342513

Ceselli, A., Premoli, M., & Secci, S. (2017). Mobile Edge Cloud Network Design Optimization. *IEEE/ACM Transactions on Networking*.

Chamola, V., Tham, C. K., & Chalapathi, G. S. S. (2017). Latency aware mobile task assignment and load balancing for edge cloudlets. In *Proceedings of the IEEE International Conference on Pervasive Computing and Communications Workshops (PerCom Workshops)*. (pp. 587–592). IEEE. doi:10.1109/PERCOMW.2017.7917628

Cuervo, E., Balasubramanian, A., Cho, D.-k., Wolman, A., Saroiu, S., Chandra, R., & Bahl, P. (2010). Maui: Making smartphones last longer with code offload. In *Proceedings of the 8th International Conference on Mobile Systems, Applications, and Services*, New York, NY (pp. 49–62).

Fernando, N., Loke, S. W., & Rahayu, W. (2013). Honeybee: A Programming Framework for Mobile Crowd Computing. In *Proceedings of the 2012 International Conference on Mobile and Ubiquitous Systems: Computing, Networking, and Services* (pp. 224–236). Springer Berlin Heidelberg. doi:10.1007/978-3-642-40238-8_19

Fernando, N., Loke, S. W., & Rahayu, W. (2016). Computing with nearby mobile devices: a work sharing algorithm for mobile edge-clouds. *IEEE Transactions on Cloud Computing*.

Gubbi, J., Buyya, R., Marusic, S., & Palaniswami, M. (2013). Internet of things (IoT): A vision, architectural elements, and future directions. *Future Generation Computer Systems*, *29*(7), 1645–1660. doi:10.1016/j.future.2013.01.010

Guo, P., Lin, B., Li, X., He, R., & Li, S. (2016). Optimal deployment and dimensioning of fog computing supported vehicular network. In *Proceedings of the 2016 IEEE Trustcom/BigDataSE/ISPA* (pp. 2058–2062). IEEE. doi:10.1109/TrustCom.2016.0315

Hong, K., Lillethun, D., Ramachandran, U., Ottenwalder, B., & Koldehofe, B. (2013). Mobile fog: A programming model for large-scale applications on the Internet of things. In *Proceedings of the Second ACM SIGCOMM Workshop on Mobile Cloud Computing* (pp. 15–20). New York: ACM. doi:10.1145/2491266.2491270

Huerta-Canepa, G., & Lee, D. (2010). A virtual cloud computing provider for mobile devices. *Proceedings of the 1st ACM Workshop on Mobile Cloud Computing & Services: Social Networks and Beyon* (pp. 6:1–6:5). New York: ACM. doi:10.1145/1810931.1810937

Kemp, R., Palmer, N., Kielmann, T., & Bal, H. (2012). Cuckoo: A Computation Offloading Framework for Smartphones. In *Proceedings of the Second International ICST Conference on Mobile Computing, Applications, and Services* (pp. 59–79). Springer Berlin Heidelberg. doi:10.1007/978-3-642-29336-8_4

Lee, K., & Shin, I. (2013). User mobility-aware decision making for mobile computation offloading. In *Proceedings of the IEEE 1st International Conference on Cyber-Physical Systems, Networks, and Applications (CPSNA).* (pp. 116– 119). IEEE.

Lin, Y., & Shen, H. (2017). Cloudfog: Leveraging fog to extend cloud gaming for thin-client mmog with high quality of service. *IEEE Transactions on Parallel and Distributed Systems*, *28*(2), 431–445. doi:10.1109/TPDS.2016.2563428

Loke, S. W., Napier, K., Alali, A., Fernando, N., & Rahayu, W. (2015). Mobile computations with surrounding devices: Proximity sensing and multilayered work stealing. *ACM Transactions on Embedded Computing Systems (TECS)*, *14*(2), 22:1–22:25.

Marinelli, E. E. (2009). Hyrax: Cloud Computing on Mobile Devices using MapReduce. *Science*, *0389*(September).

Rahaman, M. S., Mei, Y., Hamilton, M., & Salim, F. D. (2017). Capra: A contour-based accessible path routing algorithm. *Information Sciences*, *385*, 157–173. doi:10.1016/j.ins.2016.12.041

Ravi, A., & Peddoju, S. K. (2014). Mobility managed energy efficient Android mobile devices using cloudlet. In *Proceedings of the 2014 IEEE Students' Technology Symposium (TechSym)* (pp. 402-407). Kharagpur, India: IEEE.

Satyanarayanan, M., Bahl, P., Caceres, R., & Davies, N. (2009). The case for VM-based cloudlets in mobile computing. *IEEE Pervasive Computing*, *8*(4), 14–23. doi:10.1109/MPRV.2009.82

Shi, C., Lakafosis, V., Ammar, M. H., & Zegura, E. W. (2012). Serendipity: Enabling remote computing among intermittently connected mobile devices. In *Proceedings of the Thirteenth ACM International Symposium on Mobile Ad Hoc Networking and Computing* (pp. 145–154). New York: ACM. doi:10.1145/2248371.2248394

Shi, H., Chen, N., & Deters, R. (2015). Combining mobile and fog computing: Using CoAP to link mobile device clouds with fog computing. In *Proceedings of the 2015 IEEE International Conference on Data Science and Data Intensive Systems* (pp. 564–571). IEEE. doi:10.1109/DSDIS.2015.115

Su, J., Lin, F., Zhou, X., & Lu, X. (2015). Steiner tree based optimal resource caching scheme in fog computing. *China Communications*, *12*(8), 161–168. doi:10.1109/CC.2015.7224698

Truong-Huu, T., Tham, C. K., & Niyato, D. (2014). To Offload or to Wait: An Opportunistic Offloading Algorithm for Parallel Tasks in a Mobile Cloud. In *Proceedings of the 2014 IEEE 6th International Conference on Cloud Computing Technology and Science* (pp. 182-189). Singapore: IEEE.

Yousafzai, A., Chang, V., Gani, A., & Noor, R. M. (2016). Directory-based incentive management services for ad-hoc mobile clouds. *International Journal of Information Management*, *36*(66, Part A), 900–906. doi:10.1016/j.ijinfomgt.2016.05.019

Zhang, C., Sun, Y., Mo, Y., Zhang, Y., & Bu, S. (2016). Social-aware content downloading for fog radio access networks supported device-to-device communications. In *Proceedings of the 2016 IEEE International Conference on Ubiquitous Wireless Broadband*. IEEE. doi:10.1109/ICUWB.2016.7790392

Zhang, Y., Niyato, D., & Wang, P. (2015). Offloading in Mobile Cloudlet Systems with Intermittent Connectivity. *IEEE Transactions on Mobile Computing*, *14*(12), 2516–2529. doi:10.1109/TMC.2015.2405539

This research was previously published in the International Journal of Mobile Computing and Multimedia Communications (IJMCMC), 8(4); edited by Agustinus Waluyo, pages 1-19, copyright year 2017 by IGI Publishing (an imprint of IGI Global).

Chapter 15
Fog Caching and a Trace–Based Analysis of Its Offload Effect

Marat Zhanikeev
Tokyo University of Science, Japan

ABSTRACT

Many years of research on Content Delivery Networks (CDNs) offers a number of effective methods for caching of content replicas or forwarding requests. However, recently CDNs have aggressively started migrating to clouds. Clouds present a new kind of distribution environment as each location can support multiple caching options varying in the level of persistence of stored content. A subclass of clouds located at network edge is referred to as fog clouds. Fog clouds help by allowing CDNs to offload popular content to network edge, closer to end users. However, due to the fact that fog clouds are extremely heterogeneous and vary wildly in network and caching performance, traditional caching technology is no longer applicable. This paper proposes a multi-level caching technology specific to fog clouds. To deal with the heterogeneity problem and, at the same time, avoid centralized control, this paper proposes a function that allows CDN services to discover local caching facilities dynamically, at runtime. Using a combination of synthetic models and real measurement dataset, this paper analyzes efficiency of offload both at the local level of individual fog locations and at the global level of the entire CDN infrastructure. Local analysis shows that the new method can reduce inter-cloud traffic by between 16 and 18 times while retaining less than 30% of total content in a local cache. Global analysis further shows that, based on existing measurement datasets, centralized optimization is preferred to distributed coordination among services.

INTRODUCTION

Traditional Content Delivery Networks (CDNs) (Buyya, 2008) have recently started migrating to clouds (Frank, 2013). Traditional CDNs implement a range of caching (Sivasubramanian, 2007) and request routing (Chen, 2005) techniques in order to optimize the Quality of Service (QoS) of content delivery. QoS in this paper is defined as the ability to sustain a given target data rate (throughput) from a given content replica to each of its end users (simply "users" from this point on). Network congestion at a

DOI: 10.4018/978-1-5225-5649-7.ch015

CDN node directly and negatively affects QoS. Moreover, the whole point of a distributed CDN is to distribute replicas over a global network of storage/server nodes in such a way that a number of users at each node/server is below its congestion point. For more details on the QoS aspects of content delivery refer to a recent study in (Zhanikeev, 2015).

Having migrated to clouds, most of these techniques have to be revisited and in some cases replaced with cloud-compatible alternatives. For example, traditional CDNs would normally treat each location as a single node in a distributed network of replicas (Sivasubramanian, 2007). While this approach remains applicable in clouds at the global scale, cloud platforms can offer multiple kinds of caching at each location, which leads to more complex structures that represent the entire storage and distribution network. Recent literature discusses the MiniCache technology (Kuenzer, 2013) which can be used by individual Virtual Machines (VMs) to maintain an internal cache on a local physical hard-disk. With multiple virtual caches per hard-disk and multiple Physical Machines (PMs), each location can maintain a large number of independent replicas. The Local Hardware Awareness (LHA) technology (Zhanikeev, May 2015) used as part of the proposal in this paper is an alternative to the MiniCache technology. The difference in LHA is that apart from VM- and PM-based caching, it also offers the new DC-based (DC: Data Center) option which can help multiple PMs and VMs share a single replica at a given location.

The central point in this paper is that traditional clouds at network core are aware of the cloudification process and strive to extend their services to devices at network edge. Aggregates of DCs from multiple cloud providers into a single (virtual) cloud are referred to as federated clouds. Clouds that aggregate either both DCs and devices at network edge, or only devices at network edge, are referred to as fog clouds. Cloud-based Content Delivery Networks (CDNs), by the nature of the service, are striving to build fog clouds consisting of a relatively small number of large DCs and a large number of small clouds at network edge. Given the variety and scale of devices at network edge, managing such CDNs becomes a challenge. This paper discusses the recent literature on the subject (Manco, 2014; Frank, 2013) and shows how LHA-compatible fog clouds can drastically improve efficiency in such CDNs.

Apart from the flexibility problem above, fog clouds introduce another new challenge to the traditional caching methods. While in traditional CDNs, locations for replication are assumed to be roughly the same in performance – estimated as a combination of capacity of network access and performance of the storage facilities proper, fog-based distribution has to work with a collection of extremely heterogeneous locations. For example, some fog locations can have fast network connections but offer only a small storage volume. Others may offer much volume but have relatively slower network connections (slow is a bad choice of words – network performance is a nontrivial combination of end-to-end delay and throughput, the two only loosely related to each other). The LHA technology introduced further in this paper helps with this problem as well. Since each service can discover local storage facilities at each fog cloud location, the service has a chance to adjust accordingly. Part of the adjustment is to measure end-to-end network performance and use it to optimize the topology of the global distribution network. This topic is discussed in the measurement study in (Zhanikeev, 2016) and a recent paper on CDN service accountability in (Coileain, 2015). It is also revisited in the next section when reviewing the related literature.

This paper proposes and analyzes a recently defined technology called fog cloud caching – or fog caching for short – for CDNs running on federated/fog clouds. The main premise is that CDN maintains local storage at each small cloud at network edge in a fully distributed manner, without needing or resorting to centralized optimization of physical storage resources. While any hierarchical depth can be supported in principle, this paper discussed the 3-layer technology where caches are maintained at (1)

VMs (same as MiniCache (Manco, 2014)), (2) a location-local storage that can be shared by all VMs hosted at a given small cloud and (3) in a traditional centralized storage service (Frank, 2013). Analysis performed using the hotspot model (Zhanikeev, 2012) for realistic modeling of content popularity, shows that traffic exchange with the main storage can be reduced by up to 18 times. The proposed technology is also found superior to the MiniCache-based technology discussed in recent literature (Kuenzer, 2013; Frank, 2013).

Analysis in this paper is split into two parts. The above analysis focuses on the caching technology itself and is local in nature, as it is limited in scope to a single location. The other part is global analysis which simplifies the model for an individual location but instead focuses on optimization within the entire CDN infrastructure. The infrastructure is modeled using two real measurement datasets which means that the resulting conclusion is applicable to practical conditions available in existing cloud-based CDNs. Additional predictions are made on the direction of further evolution of fog-centric ecosystems.

This paper has the following structure. Section 2 reviews existing literature. Section 3 explains the basic assumptions of the fog caching technology. Section 4 presents the core proposal of this paper in form of the 2-level caching each cloud location. Section 5 introduces essential features used in further analysis. Sections 6-7 and Sections 8-9 contain details of the local and global analysis, respectively, each pair first introducing the specific setup and then presenting the results.

RELATED RESEARCH

Basics of CDN as well as a good collection of the traditional methods can be found in (Buyya, 2008). Traditionally, methods are split into caching and routing. Apart from (Buyya, 2008), a good overview of the various caching strategies can be found in (Sivasubramanian, 2007). The various methods for forwarding requests and, otherwise, optimizing the network between end users and content replicas, can be found in (Chen, 2005).

The core CDN methodology has grown based on several well-established recent technologies. Two of them warrant special attention. Adaptive streaming (Bouten, 2015) is a method that attempts to maintain the necessary performance of realtime streaming (mostly video) by adapting to changes in end-to-end (e2e) network performance. HTTP adaptive streaming, DASH protocol, etc., are several other names for the same basic technology. Specifically, to HTTP, i.e. web delivery, WebSockets are used to implement adaptive streaming in practice (Zhanikeev, 2014).

The other new method is multisource aggregation (Zhanikeev, 2015) which is a new paradigm of content delivery. Multisource aggregation is generic and can be applied to any kind of content and any method of delivery, including realtime (video) streaming. The paper in (Zhanikeev, 2015) has good analysis of the aggregation approach and its comparison with its closest rival – the P2P streaming. In fact, P2P streaming is a specific case of the generic multisource aggregation formulation. There are also hybrid methods which combine both the adaptive streaming and multiple sources within the same method in recent literature (Zhanikeev, 2015).

Note that these two recent methods are complimentary to the research in this paper. Adaptive streaming benefits from offloading content to the edge (just like the traditional delivery) while multisource aggregation benefits from multiple replicas of the same content spread across the delivery network. In both cases, a larger number of cloud locations at network edge has a positive effect. This paper puts all the actual delivery methods out of scope and focuses on the caching part of the technology and its offload effect at network edge.

The above core CDN technologies continue to be discussed in current literature. Optimization and theory of caching has recently been revisited in (Maddah-Ali, 2013). Routing methods as geographically-aware (Narayana, 2013) and multi-level (Calder, 2015) methods have also been proposed recently.

There is also a large body of current academic literature that focuses on CDN migration to clouds (Frank, 2013). The main focus of such research is the new requirements that are raised for cloud-based CDNs, such as higher flexibility (Manco, 2014), better performance of storage technology (Kuenzer, 2013), and others. Several actual cloud-based CDNs can be found in recent papers, such as Akamai (Frank, 2013), Telco (Quoc, 2011), and smaller/virtual providers like Netflix, Hulu, and others (Adhikari, 2015).

Offload is a primary feature of a cloud-based CDN. Clouds located at network edge are referred to as fog clouds (Zhanikeev, 2015). CDNs running on a core cloud would normally strive to offload part of its requests to fog clouds. This paper formulates fog caching as a technology in which CDN-related services run on fog clouds at network edge. The terms fog cloud and network edge are synonyms. Discussion of offload technologies has recently expanded to wireless (4G+) technologies where the offload technology is discussed, literally, as attaching storage (hard disks) to 4G+ base stations or their 5G equivalents (eNB, smallcells, etc.) (Paschos, 2016).

Fog clouds bring new challenges. Traditional replication assumed a roughly uniform hardware infrastructure (Buyya, 2008). Fog clouds run on non-uniform hardware, by definition (Zhanikeev, 2015). Moreover, fog clouds are richer environments with several new roles, namely network provider, cloud provider, cloudlet (local) provider, service provider, etc. Cloudlets are defined in recent literature as small clouds installed at network edge (Frank, 2013) – the term has been popularized initially by Akamai but has since become a common term.

Recent literature focuses on many of the new challenges raised by fog clouds. A good overview can be found in (Lopez, 2015). Infrastructure integration for CDN purposes is discussed in (Liu, 2016). Wireless fog-based content delivery is discussed in (Paschos, 2016). Theoretical problems like coordination (Liu, 2012) and accountability (Coileain, 2015) are also discussed.

Accountability specifically requires special attention. It is a known issue and is defined as the ability of the CDN to measure performance (accounting) and provide an optimal level of performance for each service (accountability). At a deeper level, this discussion is in part about openness, that is whether performance measurements collected by CDN provider are made public or accessible to specific services.

In a broad sense, the topic of accountability exists in several cloud-related areas of research. For example, Virtual Network Embedding (VNE) problem in virtual networking (including clouds) is created as a means of distributing the process of optimization of service-specific topology and allowing for a certain level of coordination across services (Zhanikeev, 2015). Similarly, the method called Cloud Probing is a full-fledged DiY approach to topology optimization of cloud services (Zhanikeev, 2016). Incidentally, the latter method provides one of the two datasets for trace-based analysis further in this paper.

Clouds are based on the virtualization technology. In CDN, virtualization applies mainly to storage. Here, MiniCache (Kuenzer, 2013; Frank, 2013) is a practical technology for virtual storage discussed in recent literature. A more generic technology is the Local Hardware Awareness Platform (LHA) in (Zhanikeev, 2015). This paper builds on top of LHA and assumes that at least two storage modes are possible at each fog location. The term fog location will refer to a local fog cloud facility (rack, small room, or another sub-DC unit of cloud computing).

At yet a deeper level, the storage virtualization technology is often discussed as part of the SSD vs HDD argument (Zhanikeev, 2013), where a hybrid storage facility is built from SSD and/or HDD units in such a way that performance is maximized. Note that the academic viewpoint is that the best optimization is one that is based on realtime measurements of read/write operations. Also, note that this argument is out of scope of this paper due to space limitations. However, when added, this discussion should have an additional positive effect on the ability to offload content delivery.

The main rival of the proposal in this paper is the MiniCache technology (Kuenzer, 2013). In (Frank, 2013), it is used in the settings of an ISP + Cloud hybrid infrastructure. The alternative offered in this paper is a more flexible local hardware discovery technology called LHA (Zhanikeev, 2015) (earlier work), which supports a higher degree of flexibility in caching.

At global scale, the focus of recent research is on centralized optimizations (Liu, 2016; Quoc, 2011; Paschos, 2016). Some resent works show that distributed coordination performs better than a centralized algorithm (Coileain, 2015; Liu, 2012). This paper compares between the two approaches using trace-based analysis based on real measurement datasets.

Fog Caching Basics

Figure 1 shows a generic ecosystem for cloud-based CDNs, with all the roles and technologies discussed in recent literature (Manco, 2014; Frank, 2013).

Network Provider (NP) normally comes between core clouds and users. Ideally, a CDN would strive to maintain local caches at fog clouds which are located within the same NP. In fact, if a fog cloud is a relatively simple rack of hardware installed at a small-size business location, there can be virtually no difference between such a fog cloud and users, in terms of network capacity. However, congestion within the NP should normally be much smaller than at a DC in the core cloud. Using the LHA technology (Zhanikeev, 2015), fog clouds can support two distinct kinds of caching points marked as Cache 1 and Cache 2 – their meaning is explained further in this paper.

Figure 1. Ecosystem of roles and technologies for a cloud-based CDN

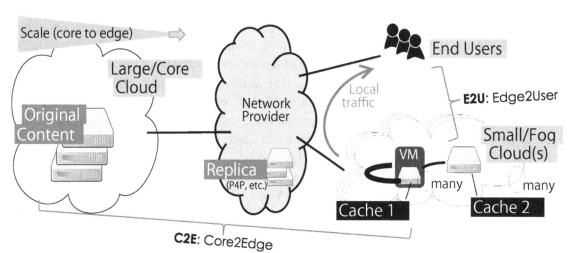

The offload aspects of the CDN in Figure 1 are shown as the Cloud-to-User (C2U) versus Edge-to-User (E2U) spans of the delivery. Since C2U delivery can quickly congest the core CDN, the objective is to move some of the popular content to fog clouds and delivery it via E2U connections.

Note that it is common nowadays for NPs to keep their own replicas of content as is shown in Figure 1. This cache can be maintained independently from CDNs simply by monitoring frequency of requests from local users and caching the most frequent items. P4P is a version of this technique applied specifically to P2P content delivery (Buyya, 2008).

Recent literature discusses new developments in NP-based caching (Frank, 2013), where Akamai (20% of peak traffic), Google (10%) and Netflix (30%) all coordinate with NPs when delivering content. Review in (Frank, 2013) specifically discusses the NetPaaS design that has both CDN (clouds) and ISP components. It should be noted that Net- PaaS relies on the old and well-known technique called DNS forwarding (Chen, 2005) for load balancing – refer to (Zhanikeev, 2014) for a review of the various load balancing techniques. Note that, according to (Frank, 2013), modern CDNs are already cloud-based with core storage and processing performed in Data Centers (DCs).

The role of fog clouds in CDNs is obvious. They help CDNs create and maintain caching locations very close to users. However, the main problem with fog clouds is the heterogeneity (also can be referred to as non-conformity) of hardware or/and network capabilities (Zhanikeev, 2015), which makes centralized optimization of resources very difficult in practice. Moreover, fog clouds would be reluctant – virtualization assumes that the physical resource is hidden – to share their physical parameters with CDNs. Akamai overcame this problem by having its own network of 30k+ cloudlets (Frank, 2013) where each cloudlet is a standardized rack of hardware. Since Akamai is in control of the entire network, centralized optimization is feasible. However, this is not a solution for federated/fog clouds at network edge which are to become flexible ecosystems that would be able to support multiple CDNs. This problem is already discussed in literature as superfluid cloud (Manco, 2014), where the LHA technology in (Zhanikeev, 2015) is offered as a practical solution to this problem.

The MiniCache technology (Manco, 2014) only partially solves the problem of fog caching for CDNs. MiniCache helps individual VMs to perform local caching but the cache is not persistent and is destroyed with the VM itself. The other side of the MiniCache technology is virtualization of physical devices (Kuenzer, 2013), which makes it similar to the RAM+SSD+HDD optimization engines discussed in literature (Zhanikeev, 2013).

The Local Hardware Awareness (LHA) technology, on the other hand, is a better solution (Zhanikeev, 2015). The name of the technology spells out its function – it allows for VMs to detect (become aware of) local hardware (specifically storage for CDNs), at runtime. Using a cloud platform that implements LHA, VMs can break out of the traditional black box of virtualization and discover how much storage can be procured at a given fog cloud at a given time. The technology is explained in (Zhanikeev, 2015) where it is implemented as APIs added to a conventional cloud platform. The technology is not limited to caching and storage in general, and can work for any generic service, including Hadoop environments, sensors, etc. Study in (Zhanikeev, 2015) shows that LHA is a key technology for achieving feasibility of federated/fog clouds in practice.

Proposal: The Two Local Caching Modes

Fog Caching from this point on is defined as hierarchical (layered) caching within an individual fog cloud. This paper focuses on the immediately implementable 3-layer case, where the top layer in the original copy and two bottom layers are maintained by each participant fog cloud. A MiniCache-based technology supports only two layers – the original copy at core cloud plus a VM-based cache in each fog cloud.

Figure 2 shows the design of a cloud-based CDN with layered/fog caching. Cache 1 is an in-VM storage, implemented as files on virtual disk or technologies like MiniCache (Manco, 2014). The problem with the in-VM caching is its volatility where VMs, having to migrate or appear/disappear as part of CDN population management (Zhanikeev, 2014), either have to migrate with their caches (infeasible) or destroy them at each population upgrade. The term population refers to a large number of VMs used as sources in a distributed network of delivery nodes (web or streaming servers, etc.) (Zhanikeev, 2014).

Cache 2 is a storage facility outside of VM but inside a given fog cloud. It requires LHA for discovery – the prototype platform already exists (Zhanikeev, 2015). The pros of this cache are two-fold. First, it can be much larger than the in-VM cache. Secondly, the contents are persistent for the population in that fog cloud. This paper will study more complex dynamics where each newly added VM can rely on Cache 2 to fill its own in-VM cache, where the respective traffic exchange is internal to that fog cloud (no traffic to the core cloud).

The role of CDN manager in the model is as follows. The Manager maintains the main body of content in the traditional manner – using a large-scale storage or CDN facilities (S3, Akamai, etc. (Frank, 2013)). However, at the same time the Manager also has access to a large number of regionally distributed fog clouds at network edge each with its own local storage and can balance the inter-cloud traffic load by keeping a portion of popular content at each local cloud. Further on, this paper proposes a simple model for automatic syncing between the main storage and multiple local storages called lazy caching.

ANALYSIS SETUP: MODELS AND TRACES

Modeling in this paper is based on a synthetic model of popularity of content coupled with a realistic CDN representation based on real datasets.

Figure 2. Design of layered caching using the Local Hardware Awareness (LHA) feature (Zhanikeev, 2015) in federated/ fog clouds

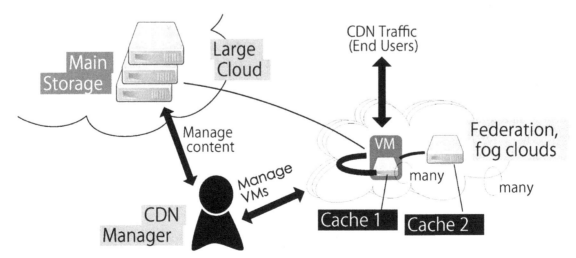

Both the tradition and recent advances in popularity modeling are described in (Traverso, 2013). The traditional methods are:

- Independent Reference Model (IRM) (Traverso, 2013) which detects popular content simply by assigning a counter to each item and counting the number of requests;
- Shot-Noise Model (SNM) is a more recent method which has been shown to outperform IRM – this method achieves higher level of modeling accuracy by adding temporal properties to individual requests (the unit of modeling and an item of content).

The paper in (Traverso, 2013) itself proposes a version of SNM which classifies requests and assigns different temporal properties to each class, thus, further improving modeling accuracy. The new method was shown to work well for video content but has not been tested on other types.

This paper places temporal aspects of popularity out of scope and focuses on the modeling of the popularity level itself. This viewpoint is related to the well-known Zipf model (Traverso, 2013), which is simply a distribution from which one samples popularity as a number of requests per unit of time.

Without the temporal component, the best way to model a generic pool of content is to use a hotspot distribution whose generation process is described in detail in (Zhanikeev, 2012). The model produces normal, pop (for popular), hot and flash sets of numbers – used as numeric evaluations of popularity. The normal set can be discarded as unimportant in this paper – in most CDNs this content would never be replicated and offloaded to network edge. The pop set forms the baseline of content popularity and has the potential to be offloaded. The hot and flash sets describe the same item in the two respective states. The flash state stands for popularity of an item during a Flash Crowd (viral video, etc.).

These sets map perfectly to the CDN usecase. The normal set is for content that is almost never used/ delivered – and therefore not used for analysis in this paper. The pop set is delivered rarely yet CDN has to keep it in mind. The main focus is on the hot/flash sets which contain items which are both popular and experience extreme fluctuations in popularity (a Flash/viral event). Note that despite the name, not all items in the hot/flash sets experience Flash events and the magnitude of fluctuation is different for each item.

Yet, even in the simplified sets-only form above (the full version of the generation process has many tuning parameters) (Zhanikeev, 2012), the resulting hotspot distributions are difficult to apply in simulation. For practical use, it is helpful to classify distributions based on their curvature. The following classification method is applied. First, imagine the log values of the sets plotted in decreasing order of value, as is shown in Figure 3. Given the nature of the distribution, hotspots – there are normally only a few of them – would be plotted at the head of the distribution and then the curve would drop for the rest of values. Note that the drop would be experienced even on the log scale. Here, the only way to classify such a distribution is to evaluate the size of its head.

So, classification in this paper uses the following ranges of values for classification, all in log scale:

- If values at 80% and deeper into the list are 0.15 or above, then Class A is assigned;
- If values at 60% and deeper into the list are 0.6 or above, then Class B is assigned;
- If values at 40% and deeper into the list are 1.3 or above, then Class C is assigned;
- If values at 30% and deeper into the list are 1.8 or above, then Class D is assigned;
- If no class is assigned by this point, the Class E is assigned.

Figure 3. A randomly selected set of curves for each hotspot class, A through E. Class E distributions have more hotspots then class A, on average. The vertical scale is in log while horizontal scale is simply the decreasing order of values.

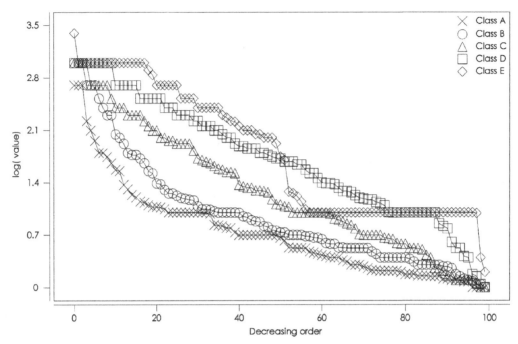

The classification above removes the need to discuss the internal generation parameters. Instead, many hotspot distributions can be generated using a random selection of parameters and the resulting curve would be classified into one of the above classes. As the final minor simplification, each hotspot distribution is converted into two separate curves by combining popular + hot and popular + flash set, each classified and used separately. Only 100 values were generated for each distribution, but this is sufficient as values during simulation are selected randomly from the list, which means that relatively low values are selected much more frequently than the large items.

Figure 3 shows several randomly selected hotspot distributions marked in accordance with its representative class. We can see that the classification is successful by assigning a higher letter to a curve with a relatively higher number of hotspots. Note that the generation process has no maximum value, but, in order to avoid extremely long processing sessions, all values exceeding 1000 are brought back to 1000. The values (not logs, but the original number behind) are translated into the number of requests per day (more details are provided further in this paper).

Hotspot distributions are the synthetic part of the modeling used in analysis further in this paper. The two below traces/datasets come from real-life measurements and are used to emulate realistic conditions both at local (each fog location) and global (entire CDN) scales.

Real-life datasets related to CDNs are rare. Several papers discussed in Section 2 above are based on real traces but do not share them publicly. Some of the traces from traditional CDN research are available but are not useful in cloud environments (Buyya, 2008). After lengthy consideration, the below two traces where selected as the two components of the trace-based analysis in this paper:

- Cloud Measurement Project in (WISC), from this point on referred to as the WISC dataset;
- The paper on the Cloud Probing method (Zhanikeev, 2016) whose trace will be referred to as the CloudProbing dataset.

Cloud Measurement Project (WISC) is a large measurement project run on Amazon EC2 cloud. All 8 regions (currently, there are 9 regions with the new DC added in Europe) were used both as sources and destinations of measurements. The other side of the connections to these DCs were a large number of nodes across the globe. A subset of about 800 nodes are the PlanetLab nodes but the total count of nodes is much larger. The dataset includes both delay and throughput measurements in both DC-node and node-DC directions. These measurements will be used to emulate connections between end users and the cloud.

The CloudProbing dataset (Zhanikeev, 2016) also comes from a measurement project run on Amazon EC2 cloud. However, the measurement target was connections between regions, i.e. DC-DC connections. The paper in (Zhanikeev, 2016) argues that services can measure the network between its own locations and optimize its own performance by migrating to locations which provide a more optimal service overall.

Note that the two datasets are complementary. Namely, the CloudProbing dataset provides the DC-DC measurements missing in the WISC dataset. The merged dataset contained real measurement data for all the possible aspects of a global-scale CDN.

This section was a rough sketch of the analysis setup. Further details are provided later in this paper, when describing each of the two analysis situations.

ANALYSIS OF LOCAL EFFECT: SETUP

This and the next section perform the local part of the analysis. The focus is on a single fog location backed by the core CDN cloud. Performance in question is that of the storage facilities installed at the fog location. The comparison is between the proposed layered caching and the single option offered by the MiniCache technology.

Figure 4 shows 50 randomly selected items from the popularity trace (explained further) in which pop items are mixed with hot/flash. The class of distribution (as was explained above) was ignored in this analysis, so, values were picked from all classes. Note that the vertical axis users logarithmic scale (base 10). Flash and hot states for the same item are connected by a line to show dynamics during simulation, where the item toggles between hot and flash states at random intervals.

For this analysis, a list of 20k items (flash + hot pairs) was sampled from all the available distributions. Half of the items were selected from the pop range of distributions whose popularity does not change during simulation, by definition. The other half were sampled from the truly hot/flash items. An item was set to toggle between the two states (hot/flash) at random periods selected between 1 and 10 hours.

Figure 5 shows the simple model for the layered caching implemented in this analysis. At any given point of time we have access to the list of items ordered by decreasing popularity. A given top percentage of items (top in the list ordered by descending popularity) is assigned as the effective range of Cache 1 (in-VM). Yet a larger percentage of items from the top is assigned as the range of Cache 2 whose size is always strictly larger than Cache 1.

Figure 4. A random sample of the hotspot distribution used for analysis in this paper

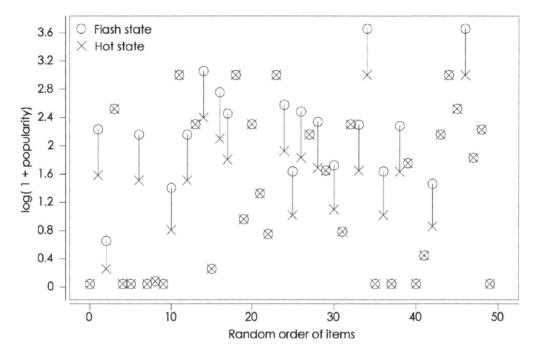

The simple yet effective caching logic is as follows. Each VM only maintains its own Cache 1 but can fill it using items stored in Cache 2, if present. If an item is not found in Cache 2, then VM downloads it from the main storage and uses it to fill both its own Cache 1 and the local Cache 2. This logic can be referred to as lazy caching in respect to Cache 2 (lazy because Cache 2 does not download all its items in a regular/scheduled manner). Size of both caches is defined by a simulation parameter, i.e. 0:1 would mean top 10%. Cache size overflows for both Cache 1 and Cache 2 are resolved by discarding (forgetting) the oldest items.

The overall simulation setup is as follows. 2400 hours (100 days) are simulated, at least 25 times for each unique permutation of simulation parameters, to average out differences introduced by randomness. Only one pair of a large/core and small/fog cloud is analyzed. However, the fog cloud is assumed to host multiple VMs, where a new/blank VM is added every 100 hours of simulation time. No VMs are removed, but, given the presence of Cache 2, removal of VMs has no impact on inter-cloud traffic and can therefore be neglected. Content is assumed to be uniform (all files are of the same size), so instead of presenting the total volume of traffic, analysis is based on monitoring of transfer counts of items as the measure of traffic volume. Comparison between traditional (MiniCache) and the proposed (layered) methods is based on visualizing the offload effect from having the Cache 2 at the fog location.

The sizes of in-VM (Cache 1) and in-cloud (Cache 2) storage are simulation parameters, ranging from 0.05/0.1 (5% in-VM, 10% in-cloud – note that this is not a fraction but a pair of parameters) to 0.1/1.0 (10% in-VM, 100% in-cloud).

Figure 5. Connection between distribution of content popularity and caching layers. Traditional technology (MiniCache) does not use Cache 2.

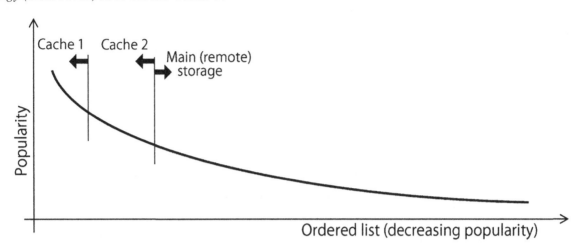

ANALYSIS OF LOCAL EFFECT: RESULTS

The top plot of Figure 6 shows the performance of traditional technology (MiniCache), which uses the 2-layer combination of in-VM caching and remote main storage. The plot shows that inter-cloud exchange (VM to main storage) grows rapidly between 0.05 and 0.1 and slightly less between 0.1 and 0.2. The slowing (note that the virtual scale is log of base 10) is due to gradually fewer changes in popularity as VM digs increasingly deeper into the decreasing list of popularity. The bottom plot of Figure 6 also shows that transfer count will saturate above 0.2, with no more changes in the popularity beyond that position in the list of items.

The main analysis result is shown in the bottom plot of Figure 6 which presents the numeric estimates for the extent of traffic offload achieved by the proposed layered caching method. The offload is visualized simply by plotting the inner/outer ratio between the respective file transfer counts. Higher values correspond to better offload as VMs find increasingly more files in local cache rather than having to download them from the remote main storage. The plot refers to the two transfer counts as inner (in-cloud) versus outer (inter-cloud).

The bottom plot specifically shows the inner/outer line. Only the 0.05/0.1 configuration results in a ratio of < 1. However, note that even at this low ratio the offload is still happening because some files are still found in local cache (inner). In other words, all the data points in the bottom plot of Figure 6 represents the various levels of improvement over the traditional technology in the upper plot.

All the configurations above 0.05/0.1 result in strictly > 1 inner/outer ratios. The growth is linear until 0.1/0.2 at which point the curve saturates, with only a minor improvement offered past 0.2/0.4 points on the horizontal scale, where perfect saturation is achieved. In fact, the lack of change between the last two configurations shows that saturation is achieved when 40% of content is stored in Cache 2 and further growth in size of that cache does not contribute to further improvement in performance.

Figure 6. Analysis results showing inter-cloud transfer count under the traditional technology (top) and the benefit from using layered caching (bottom). Note that ticks on the horizontal scale of the bottom plot are not the division but rather represent pairs of the two setup parameters.

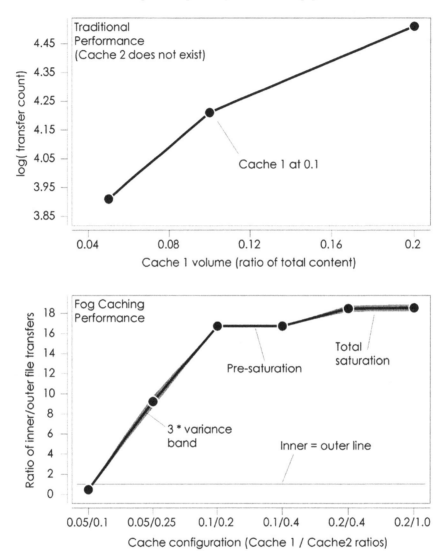

The bottom plot in Figure 6 also shows the 3σ band (three times the variance) around the main curve but scattering due to randomness was found to be so small that it is mildly evident only for a subset of configurations. All in all, the effect of randomness can be considered negligible.

The single important outcome in Figure 6 is that, given the hotspot dataset used for simulation, the maximum factor of between 16 and 18 is achievable in terms of traffic offload, simply by adding an additional storage facility at the fog cloud and make it accessible by all VMs running in that fog cloud. Maximum performance is achieved with only 10% of content stored in Cache 1 (in-VM) and 20% of content stored in Cache 2 (in-cloud). The latter is shared by all the VMs running at that cloud, by design.

ANALYSIS OF GLOBAL EFFECT: SETUP

This and the next section are part of the global analysis. Based on the previous two sections, it is assumed that local offload effect is present. This analysis can then focus on the global effect. Fog locations in this section are simplified (no layered caching) and represented as a non-divisible unit in emulation. Since emulation is based on traces, fog locations are represented by the regions (Data Centers, DCs) of Amazon EC2 services. The focus in this analysis is on distribution of content across all the locations based popularity distribution and its dynamics in time.

The core components were introduced in Section 5, including the hotspot model for popularity synthesis and the two real datasets. The classified version of hotspot distributions is used in this analysis. An ordered set of hotspot conditions is created by applying a gradually increasing range of classes, randomly selected from a large set of randomly generated hotspot distributions. Specifically, configurations A, AB, ABC, ABCD, ABCDE, represent an increasing range of hotspot classes. Statistically, the larger the range, the higher is the average number of hotspots in the total mix of content in the CDN.

The two datasets, WISC (WISC) and CloudProbing (Zhanikeev, 2016) are used to emulate realistic global conditions in the analyzed CDN infrastructure. As was explained earlier, both datasets come from measurements conducted on Amazon EC2 cloud and therefore have the same set of regions (DCs). Even the measurement time period is roughly the same (mid-2015).

The focus of this analysis is on optimization of replica distribution across all the locations (regions, DCs) within the emulated CDN. Existing literature on the subject offers several distinct angles at this problem. There is the energy-efficient approach, which in (Zhanikeev, 2014) was applied to migrations of VMs within the cloud, but is applicable to the CDN settings as well. Energy in CDNs is represented by in-location and cross-location traffic (its volume, cost, etc.), which is limited by traffic shaping (on cloud provider's side), traffic quotas and even naturally by capacity limitations. Pricing for cross-location transfers can also be an issue as well as a numerical means of representing the energy in such optimizations.

This analysis places such optimization methods out of scope and instead selects a simple method represented in Figure 7. The simple approach is to assume that local is always better than global – this, in fact, is the motto of the offload technology as such (Coileain, 2015; Liu, 2012). To emulate a global CDN with different time belts, locations are tied to time belts using the actual GMT offset for each EC2 region. Each location has the same daily curve of request density that peaks at 8AM and 6PM – this assumption is supported statistically from available public surveys (Olympics). At 8AM, 10% of the popular content is replicated and sent to the appropriate DC. At 6PM, the peak is higher which is modeled as replicating and distributing 20% of the popular content to the given location. Note that although the same daily dynamics are applied to all locations, globally the peak access times are not synchronized because of the different GMT offsets at each location. For example, as Figure 7 shows, Oregon location (us-west-2) is GMT -7 hours. Ireland (eu-west-1) is GMT+1, and so on.

End users of CDN services are modeled as follows. E2U (edge-to-user) and C2U (cloud-to-user) is modeled using the WISC dataset (WISC), which provides both throughput and delay measurements between the various domains and EC2 regions (locations). C2C (cloud-to-cloud or DC-DC) is modeled suing the CloudProbing dataset (Zhanikeev, 2016) which provides additional throughput values representing cross-location traffic.

Figure 8 compares throughput values between the two datasets. Each plot is for one location (EC2 region). In case of the WISC dataset, each plot aggregates measurements from all the domain prefixes to that DC. In case of the CloudProbing dataset, each plot aggregates throughput between the location in

Figure 7. Model of a global CDN with several of actual Amazon EC2 DCs selected for descriptor purposes

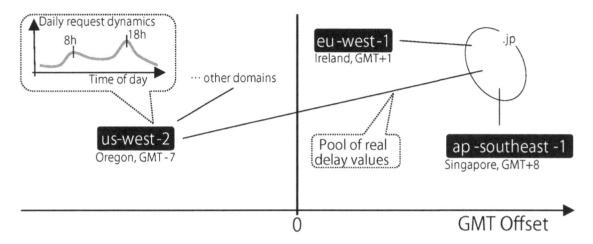

question and all other locations. Vertical scale is the density distribution of throughput values, clustered in 0.2 bins on the log (horizontal) scale. The following simple reading of the figure is offered. There is a constant difference between location-users and cross-location traffic, at the level of between 0.5 and 1 orders of magnitude. Smaller difference is found in US-based locations – this is probably because the majority of end-user domains in the measurement study had excellent network connections (almost on par with the EC2 itself). The gap is larger for locations outside of US. Note that this difference will directly affect the performance in the analysis below. However, since the values come from real measurement traces, this effect represents the actual state of affairs.

The (modeling) story behind Figure 7 is as follows. There is a global CDN represented by 8 locations – for lack of a better dataset, these locations are assumed to represent a fog cloud, where each location is (relatively) closer to end users. There are also services, each has its own content and a home represented by a randomly selected country prefix from the WISC dataset. Figure 7 shows the example of a Japan-based CDN service. Each fog location has its own GMT time offset and therefore knows its own 8AM and 6PM peaks. Using the delay measurements from the WISC dataset, one can easily identify which fog location is the closest to which domain. This makes it possible for each home domain to identify its home fog cloud. This home concept is as an evaluation technique as well, by distinguishing between requests to a home/local cloud versus the long-haul connection to the core cloud. Note that the WISC dataset also provides us with throughput measurements from all domains to all locations, which means that it is possible to estimate how much time it will take to upload or download content to/from services and end users.

Within this story, the following two CDN models are compared:

- **Centralized Model:** The one in which the service uploads all its content to its home location and delegates the task of optimizing its distribution to the CDN. For each location, the CDN migrates replicas of content from home location to all other locations at 8AM (10% of top content) and 6PM (20%), respectively. Transfers start at 8AM and 6PM of local time at each respective location and take as much time as is allowed by the throughput from the CloudProbing dataset. Content

Figure 8. Comparison of throughput measured between EC DCs and end users (WISC dataset), and between EC2 DCs (Cloud Probing Dataset). Throughput on the horizontal scales is in log scale. Each plot represents data selected for a specific DC. US-east-1 region has no counterpart in the WISC dataset.

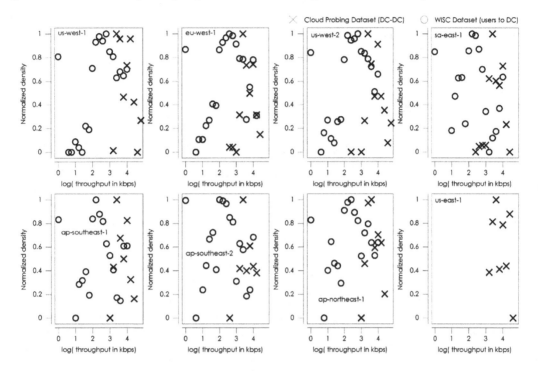

is replicated and moved in accordance to the decreasing order of popularity, i.e. the most popular content is moved first;

- **Distributed Model:** When each service is in charge of replicating and distributing its own content (close to the coordination model in existing research). The same daily peaks at 8AM and 6PM (the same 10% and 20% top content) are used. However, this time the content is uploaded to each location by the service itself. This means that the throughput values from the WISC dataset are used to evaluate completion times for each upload. Note that this model is very close to reality since the actual EC2 framework does not encourage cross-region operations and, in fact, links operations to regions (each AWS command has to tell the platform at which region it is to be run). Other examples in practice – like Rackspace CDN (RackspaceCDN) – show clear pricing for in-location storage but are extremely unclear on pricing and means of cross-location transfers of content (CDN pricing).

One emulation run is conducted as follows. 100 services are mapped to randomly selected domains (countries). Each identifies its home location based on delay values from the DISC dataset. All other locations are deemed remote. Each service gets its own hotspot distribution selected randomly from the allowed range of classes. The distribution represents all the requests per location, per day (between 5k and 10k for most distributions), distributed at uniform time gaps for each content item, further modulated by the daily density curve. Emulation is therefore run for one day, starting at 0th hour, passing through the peaks (and distribution triggers) at 8AM and 6PM, and finally ending at 23:59. When location gets the requests, they do not care where the requests come from (it is assumed that all the traffic is local). Instead, the emulation simply checks whether the requested content is cached locally. Depending on the answer to this question, either Edge-to-User (E2U) or Cloud-to-User (C2U) counter is incremented. Naturally, higher E2U counts represent a stronger offload effect.

ANALYSIS OF GLOBAL EFFECT: RESULTS

Evaluation of performance for the global CDN can be simplified to the simple offload effect metric represented as the ratio of E2U (edge-to-user) to C2U (cloud-to-user) counts. The counts themselves are obtained using the emulation describes in the previous section.

Figure 9 shows the combined results for both Centralized and Distributed models. The Centralized model performs better (in fact, above the psychological 1.0 threshold) than the Distributed model roughly by the factor of 2. Both models show poorer performance as the range of hotspot classes increases (larger number of popular items) where the Distributed model degrades at a higher rate. These effects are to be expected.

Note that the x2 better performance on the part of the Centralized model has to be placed in the context of the difference in throughput between the two datasets. As was shown in the previous section, the difference between location-user (=E2U) and cross-location throughput was found to be 0.5 to

Figure 9. Average offset performance represented as offload effect for distributed and centralized models of caching

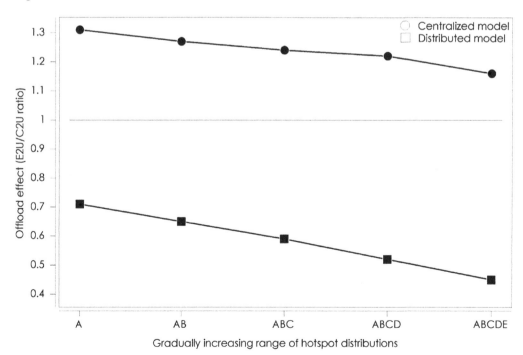

1 orders of magnitude. However, this major gap in performance only translated into the x2 difference in the offload effect. This means that, if content providers (services) improve their network capability (for example, by using multisource aggregation (Zhanikeev, 2014)), the gap between Distributed and Centralized models will quickly disappear.

CONCLUSION

This paper is fully set in the world where CDN services are fully cloudified. This means that both the storage and servers are cloudified, i.e. have become virtual. For storage, it means that CDN services running on clouds get access to virtual blocks of storage facilities. Servers run on Virtual Machines as normal applications or, even more commonly, as container apps (Heroku, Docker, etc.).

In these settings, this paper proposed a layered design of local storage. The MiniCache technology – the default in current literature and practice – only supports in-VM storage and has other limitations (lack of parallel control, quotas, etc.). This is a major flaw as VMs burdened by content cannot quickly migrate to other clouds and the entire cache is lost when VM is destroyed (to be created anew at another location).

The Local Hardware Awareness technology proposed in this paper allowed for in-location but out-VM type of storage. The virtual storage facility is created by the cloud and is shared by all the VMs running at the cloud. VMs still keep their in-VM cache but the negative effect from destroyed VMs is almost completely eliminated – the content can be quickly recovered from the in-location cache.

The ultimate goal of the proposed technology is to achieve the level of flexibility required by CDNs running on fog clouds. The unique feature of fog clouds is the heterogeneity of hardware across numerous small locations. The proposed technology helps by making it possible for VMs to detect storage capabilities at each location at runtime. In the larger scheme of things, this technology supports coordination between services and CDNs and across services, the topic familiar from recent literature on the subject.

Analysis in this paper answered two separate questions pertaining to fog-based CDNs. Local analysis showed that the in-location caching can help by decreasing cross-location traffic by 16-18 times while keeping only 20% of content in the in-location cache.

The global part of the analysis was based on two measurement datasets and answered the question of whether the fog-based CDN has to be run in the centralized versus the distributed manner. Results show that centralized operation of such CDNs should be preferred as the present level of technology. This is mainly because the datasets showed that bulk transfer capabilities are much higher for cross-location transfers within the EC2 framework then when the content is uploaded in a Do-it-Yourself manner by each service to each separate fog cloud.

However, it was also shown that the difference between centralized and distributed models is about the factor of 2, while the difference in throughput between internal cross- EC2 traffic and domain-to-cloud traffic is between 0.5 and 1 orders of magnitude. This means that services should invest into improving networking to their fog locations in order to compete with the centralized management. It is likely that, in several coming years, competition in this area will intensify.

Future research in this topic will help identify key technologies that can make distributed fog-based CDNs compatible even at the present level of technology. For example, multisource aggregation proposed in (Zhanikeev, 2014) (earlier work) can help services boost transfer throughputs as the number of replicas increase. This factor will be considered in future publications.

REFERENCES

Adhikari, V., Guo, Y., Hao, F., Hilt, V., Zhang, Z., Varvello, M., & Steiner, M. (2015). Measurement Study of Netflix, Hulu, and a Tale of Three CDNs. *IEEE/ACM Transactions on Networking*, *23*(6), 1984–1997. doi:10.1109/TNET.2014.2354262

Arunkumar, G., & Venkataraman, N. (2015). A Novel Approach to Address Interoperability Concern in Cloud Computing. *Elsevier Procedia Computer Science*, *50*, 554–559. doi:10.1016/j.procs.2015.04.083

BBC. (2012). The story of the digital Olympics: streams, browsers, most watched, four screens (blog post). Retrieved from http://www.bbc.co.uk/blogs

Bouten, N., Schmidt, R., Famaey, J., Latre, S., & Pras, A., De Turck, F. (2015). QoE-driven in-network optimization for Adaptive Video Streaming based on packet sampling measurements. *International Journal of Computer and Telecommunications Networking*, *81*(C), 96–115.

Buyya, R., Pathan, M., & Vakali, A. (Eds.). (2008). *Content Delivery Networks. Lecture Notes in Electrical Engineering (LNEE)* (Vol. 9). Springer. doi:10.1007/978-3-540-77887-5

Calder, M., Flavel, A., Katz-Bassett, E., Mahajan, R., & Padhye, J. (2015). Analyzing the Performance of an Anycast CDN. *Proceedings of the ACM Internet Measurement Conference (IMC)* (pp. 531–537). doi:10.1145/2815675.2815717

CDN Pricing Calculator. (2016). Retrieved from http://www.cdncalc.com

Chen, C., Ling, Y., Pang, M., Chen, W., Cai, S., Suwa, Y., & Altintas, O. (2005). Scalable Request-Routing with Next-Neighbor Load Sharing in Multi-Server Environments. *Proceedings of the 19th IEEE International Conference on Advanced Information Networking and Applications* (pp. 441–446). doi:10.1109/AINA.2005.303

Coileain, D., & OMahony, D. (2015). Accounting and Accountability in Content Distribution Architectures: A Survey. *ACM Computing Surveys*, *47*(4), 1–35. doi:10.1145/2723701

Data Sets for the Cloud Measurement Project. (2015). Retrieved from http://pages.cs.wisc.edu/~keqhe/cloudmeasure_datasets.html

Frank, B., Poese, I., Lin, Y., Smaragdakis, G., Feldmann, A., Maggs, B., & Weber, R. et al. (2013). Pushing CDN-ISP Collaboration to the Limit. *Computer Communication Review*, *43*(3), 34–44. doi:10.1145/2500098.2500103

Kuenzer, S., Martins, J., Ahmed, M., & Huici, F. (2013). Towards minimalistic, virtualized content caches with minicache. *Proceedings of the 13th Workshop on Hot Topics in Middleboxes and Network Function Virtualization (HotMiddlebox)* (pp. 13–18). doi:10.1145/2535828.2535832

Liu, H., Viswanathan, R., Calder, M., Akella, A., Mahajan, R., Padhey, J., & Zhang, M. (2016). Efficiently delivering online services over integrated infrastructure. *Proceedings of the 13th USENIX Symposium on Networked Systems Design and Implementation (NSDI)* (pp. 77–90).

Liu, X., Dobrian, F., Milner, H., Jiang, J., Sekar, V., Stoica, I., Zhang, H. (2012). A Case for a Coordinated Internet Video Control Plane. In *ACM SIGCOMM* (pp. 359–370).

Lopez, P., Montresor, A., Epema, D., Datta, A., Higashino, T., Iamnitchi, A., & Riviere, E. et al. (2015). Edge-centric Computing Vision and Challenges. *ACM Computer Communication Review*, *45*(5), 37–42. doi:10.1145/2831347.2831354

Maddah-Ali, M., & Niesen, U. (2013). Fundamental Limits of Caching. *Proceedings of the IEEE International Symposium on Information Theory* (pp. 1077–1081).

Manco, F., Martins, J., & Huici, F. (2013). Towards the super fluid cloud. *Computer Communication Review*, *44*(4), 355–356. doi:10.1145/2740070.2631449

Narayana, S., Jiang, W., Rexford, J., & Chiang, M. (2013). Joint Server Selection and Routing for Geo-replicated Services. *Proceedings of the 6th IEEE/ACM International Conference on Utility and Cloud Computing (UCC)* (pp. 423–428). doi:10.1109/UCC.2013.84

Paschos, G., Bastug, E., Land, I., Caire, G., & Debbah, M. (2016). Wireless Caching: Technical Misconceptions and Business Barriers. *IEEE Communications Magazine*, *54*(8), 16–22. doi:10.1109/MCOM.2016.7537172

Quoc, T., Perkuhn, H., Catrein, D., Naumann, U., & Anwar, T. (2011). Optimization and evaluation of a multimedia streaming service on hybrid Telco cloud. *International Journal on Cloud Computing: Services and Architecture*, *1*(2), 1984–1997.

Rackspace. (2016). CDN Pricing. Retrieved from https://www.rackspace.com/cloud/cdn-content-delivery-network

Sivasubramanian, S., Pierre, G., Steen, M., & Alonso, G. (2007). Analysis of Caching and Replication Strategies for Web Applications. *IEEE Internet Computing*, *11*(1), 60–66. doi:10.1109/MIC.2007.3

Traverso, S., Ahmed, M., Garetto, M., Giaccone, P., Leonardi, E., & Niccolini, S. (2013). Temporal Locality in Todays Content Caching: Why it Matters and How to Model it. *Computer Communication Review*, *43*(5), 5–12. doi:10.1145/2541468.2541470

Zhanikeev, M. (2013). *Can We Benefit from Solid State Drives in Rich Multimedia Content Processing, Storage and Streaming? (Technical Report)*. ITE-MMS.

Zhanikeev, M. (2014). Multi-Source Stream Aggregation in the Cloud. In Advanced Content Delivery, Streaming, and Cloud Services. Wiley.

Zhanikeev, M. (2014). Optimizing Virtual Machine Migration for Energy-Efficient Clouds. *IEICE Transactions on Communications*, *E97-B*(2), 450–458. doi:10.1587/transcom.E97.B.450

Zhanikeev, M. (2015). A Cloud Visitation Platform to Facilitate Cloud Federation and Fog Computing. *IEEE Computer*, *48*(5), 80–83. doi:10.1109/MC.2015.122

Zhanikeev, M. (2015). H*ow variable bitrate video formats can help P2P streaming boost its reliability and scale. Springer Journal of Electronic Commerce Research*, *15*(1), 22–47.

Zhanikeev, M. (2015). A New VNE Method for More Responsive Networking in Many-to-Many Groups. *Proceedings of the 7th International Conference on Ubiquitous and Future Networks (ICUFN) (pp. 438–443).* doi:10.1109/ICUFN.2015.7182582

Zhanikeev, M. (2016). Performance Management of Cloud Populations via Cloud Probing. *IPSJ Journal of Information Processing, 24*(1), 99–108. doi:10.2197/ipsjjip.24.99

Zhanikeev, M., & Tanaka, Y. (2012). Popularity-Based Modeling of Flash Events in Synthetic Packet Traces. *IEICE Technical Report on Communication Quality, 112*(288), 1–6.

This research was previously published in the International Journal of Information Technologies and Systems Approach (IJITSA), 10(2); edited by Manuel Mora, pages 50-68, copyright year 2017 by IGI Publishing (an imprint of IGI Global).

Chapter 16
Communication and Security Technologies for Smart Grid

Imed Ben Dhaou
Qassim University, Saudi Arabia & University of Monastir, Tunisia

Aron Kondoro
Royal Institute of Technology, Sweden & University of Dar es Salaam, Tanzania

Amleset Kelati
Royal Institute of Technology, Sweden & University of Turku, Finland

Diana Severine Rwegasira
Royal Institute of Technology, Sweden & University of Turku, Finland

Shililiandumi Naiman
University of Dar es Salaam, Tanzania

Nerey H. Mvungi
University of Dar es Salaam, Tanzania

Hannu Tenhunen
Royal Institute of Technology, Sweden & University of Turku, Finland

ABSTRACT

The smart grid is a new paradigm that aims to modernize the legacy power grid. It is based on the integration of ICT technologies, embedded system, sensors, renewable energy and advanced algorithms for management and optimization. The smart grid is a system of systems in which communication technology plays a vital role. Safe operations of the smart grid need a careful design of the communication protocols, cryptographic schemes, and computing technology. In this article, the authors describe current communication technologies, recently proposed algorithms, protocols, and architectures for securing smart grid communication network. They analyzed in a unifying approach the three principles pillars of smart-gird: Sensors, communication technologies, and security. Finally, the authors elaborate open issues in the smart-grid communication network

DOI: 10.4018/978-1-5225-5649-7.ch016

1. INTRODUCTION

Smart grid is a new paradigm that aims at making the legacy utility grid, efficient, green, reliable and secure. The term was coined in 2007 by the US congress in a bid to modernize the US power grid system (Energy Independence and Security Act of 2007, 2007). As stated in the 2007 Act on energy Independence and Security, a smart grid should have the following ten features: (1) Wide-scale deployment of ICT (Information and communication technologies) to shape-up performance, reliability, and trustworthiness of the utility grid, (2) dynamic optimization of grid operations and resources, (3) integration of effective renewable energy resources, (4) endorsement of advanced demand response scheme, (5) amalgamation of smart technologies for controlling and monitoring the grid operations, (6) consolidation of intelligent appliances, (7) integration of cutting-edge electricity storage and peak-abatement technologies, (8) purveying consumers with timeous information and control options, (9) development of standards for communication and interoperability of appliances and equipment, and (10) battling barriers and obstacles that prevent the adoption of smart grid technologies, practices, and services.

As explained (Korzun & Gurtov, 2015) in (Dutt, Jantsch, & Sarma, 2016) and in (Glesner & Philipp, 2013), smart system should take intelligent decision, has a mechanism for situation awarness, elastic, proactive, etc. The enabling technologies for smart system are determined by the intended functionality. As stated in (Glesner & Philipp, 2013), control and cybersecurity are the cornerstones for smart grid. The recent trend in the process automation is the deployment of sensors for data collection, actuators for control and multi-agent system for solving complex problem.

During recent years, discernible efforts have been put forward to establish a smart grid with the characteristics stated heretofore. A good survey that summarizes the research effort on the permissive technologies for the smart grid until the year 2011 is reported in (Fang, Misra, Xue, & Yang, 2012). The authors reviewed advances in the following three axes: infrastructure, management, and protection. Finally, the researchers digested the omnifarious projects, legislations, programs, standards and trials worldwide in the area of smart grid. Figure 1 elaborates the three essential ingredients in a smart grid.

Communications is a key enabling technology for the smart grid infrastructure. It is believed that the smart grid will integrate multifarious communication technologies like cellular communication, fiber-optic, short-range communication, wireless mesh networks, power-line communication, and satellite communication. The assorted deployment of communication technologies in the smart grid is attributed to factors like the application requirements, the geographic locations, environments, legislations, cost, and so forth. In (Gungor, et al., A Survey on Smart Grid Potential Applications and Communication Requirements, 2013), the authors summarized the communication requirements for fourteen smart grid applications. They further road mapped future smart grid services and applications.

The intensive deployment of communication technologies in the smart grid has precipitated the need for cyber security. The cyber security solution aims to preserve the confidentiality of the consumers, to protect the data against eavesdropping and to prevent embedded systems, used along the smart grid, from running malicious software. The authors of (Yan, Qian, Sharif, & Tipper, 2012) wrapped up the cyber security demands and surveyed the solutions for cyber security elaborated prior to the publication date of their report.

Figure 1. Smart grid ingredients proposed in (Fang, Misra, Xue, & Yang, 2012)

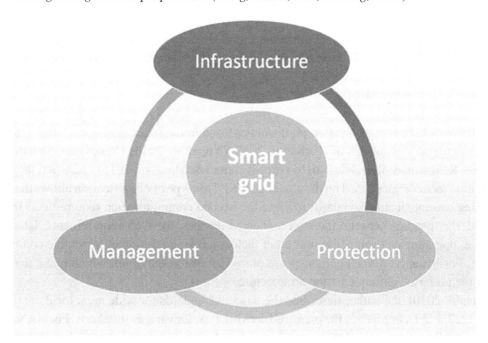

To increase the reliability of the grid and to integrate advanced control and monitoring operations, smart grid will include a variety of smart interconnected sensors. Smart grid sensors render the implementation of a multitude of applications such as situation awareness, fast healing, advanced demand-response schemes, and the monitoring of electrical equipment (voltage transformers, circuit breakers, power cables, arrestors, etc.)

This paper describes state of the art published techniques, schemes, and algorithms in communication technology, cyber-security and wireless sensor networks for the smart grid. It highlights the important latest trends in these aspects of smart grid technologies. Many previous surveys have been done individually on the communication technologies, security and wireless sensor networks enabling the smart grid. However, to the best of our knowledge, there are no surveys that considered these aspects together, and analyzed how they relate to each other. The main contributions of this paper are to provide a holistic overview of communication, security and sensor networks technologies powering the smart grid, highlight recent developments in each aspect and how they affect each other. In addition, the paper also describes recent developments that have occurred since previous surveys were done. The paper is organized as follows: Section 2 summarizes the latest communication protocols and architectures proposed for wide-area network (WAN), neighboring area network (NAN), and home area network (HAN). Section 3 discusses contemporary cryptographic algorithms and protocols for smart grid (key-management, tamper resistance devices, network, and system). Section 4 sums up the latest research results in the design of wireless sensor networks for the smart grid. Finally, section 5 summarizes and provides open issues in the covered areas.

2. COMMUNICATION TECHNOLOGIES

Data communication is a key enabler for the smart grid. Various factors determine the communication technology. These factors include environment, coverage area, data-rate, security, and latency.

2.1. Network Classifications

The classification of the communication platform deployed in the smart grid is essential to identify the competing solutions. The authors of (Farhangi, 2010) (Yu, et al., 2011) (Yan, Qian, Sharif, & Tipper, 2013) (Khan, Rehmani, & Reisslein, 2016) (Erol-Kantarci & Mouftah, 2015) classified the smart grid communication technologies based on the coverage area. This type of classification allows the projection of the existing communication standards to serve the needed communication requirements in the smart grid. Indeed, the distance between the interconnected devices, the QoS requirements, latency, power consumption, operating environments, and other factors guide the design of a suitable communication architecture. For instance, home appliances are placed close to each other, which make the local area network as the preferred communication architecture.

In (Farhangi, 2010), the author described the nascent standards for wide area, local area, and home area networks. Table 1 summarizes the preferred network type for various standards. For HAN, the author claimed that ZigBee is a potential winner as a standard for home energy system, however, recently an emerging standard, named oneM2M, is purging its way (Elmangoush, Steinke, Al-Hezmi, & Magedanz, 2014). The third column in Table 1 summarizes the application and preferred communication protocol for oneM2M.

The generic communication architecture presented in (Yan Y., Qian, Sharif, & Tipper, 2013) is inspired from (Yu, et al., 2011). The architecture engenders home area networks (HANs), business area network (BANs), neighborhood area networks (NANs), and wide area networks (WAN). The survey paper written by the authors of (Erol-Kantarci & Mouftah, 2015) added field area networks (FAN) and argued that the topology of FAN is similar to NAN.

The works by (Gungor, Sahin, Kocak, & Ergut, Smart grid technologies: communication technologies and standards, 2011) and (Fang, Misra, Xue, & Yang, 2012) categorized the grid communication platform based on the communication medium. This type of classification permits to select further the communication architecture based on the QoS requirements, cost, and the environments. For instance, wireless communication in local area network is preferred over wired LAN in case the application needs flexible connectivity, shorter installation time, high mobility (Wickelgren, 1996).

Table 1. Preferred communication for HAN, NAN and WAN

Standard	Network type	Preferred Communication	Application
IEC 61850	WAN	fiber optic	Substation
		WiMax	automation
ANSI C12.22	LAN	IEEE 802.11	Smart meter
		PLC	
oneM2M	HAN	BLE, RFID/NFC,	Home
		WiFi	automation

In (Gungor, Sahin, Kocak, & Ergut, Smart grid technologies: communication technologies and standards, 2011), the authors compared and contrasted six available communication technologies: GSM, GPRS, 3G, WiMax, PLC and ZigBee. They also described five communication requirements security, system reliability, robustness and availability, scalability, and QoS.

(Fang, Misra, Xue, & Yang, 2012) Surveyed the interoperability between the various communication technologies to meet end-to-end requirements and described open research problems.

(Nafi, Ahmed, Gregory, & Datta, 2016) also categorized the smart grid communication architecture based on the standard model of a smart grid as identified in the IEEE 2030 standard (IEEE Std 2030-2011, 2011). This resulted in a three-layer communication network architecture. The core network covers the generation and transmission domains, the wide area network covers the distribution network, and the private network that operates in the customer domain.

(Ma R., Chen, Huang, & Meng, 2013) described categories of communication technologies depending on the task they perform in the overall process of delivering power from the supply to the demand side. In this way, an electric grid can be viewed as consisting of two systems, transmission and distribution. The authors discussed recent communication technologies such as wide area frequency monitoring networks and cognitive radio based regional area networks in the transmission domain, and 802.15 based smart utility networks, TV white space and Hybrid (WiMAX/Wireless Mesh Networks) in the distribution domain.

While many surveys have categorized the smart grid communication infrastructure and technologies in terms of various smart grid application requirements and supported features (Anzar, Nadeem, & Sohail, 2015) (Kabalci, 2016) (Khan & Khan, 2013), other studies have taken a different perspective. (Ancillotti, Bruno, & Conti, 2013) have taken a data-centric approach. The authors have categorized the smart grid communication technologies according to their abilities to facilitate the collection, transmission, and storage of critical data for smart grid applications. They described the communication sub-system of a smart grid as being made up of mainly two parts. The first part is the communication infrastructure responsible for providing the pathway through which different components can connect. The second part is the middleware platform which sits on top of the communication network, abstracting away the underlying details, and providing a user-friendly API for distributed smart grid applications.

2.2. Communication Technologies for NAN and WAN

The wide area network in smart grid is used to ensure data communication between HANs and the utility company. It can also be used to connect the substations to the control center. Both WAN and NAN can be implemented using similar technologies. Figure 2 shows typical applications engendered by WAN (Gobena, Durai, Birkner, Pothamsetty, & Varakantam, 2011).

Table 2 summarizes the latency and bandwidth requirements for smart grid services reported by (Gobena, Durai, Birkner, Pothamsetty, & Varakantam, 2011). The WAN for a smart grid can be private or commercial, the former is solely owned by the utility company. The table shows further the preferred type of communication (private or commercial) for each service (Martin & Schmidt, 2014).

The comparison between private and public WAN for smart grid favors the former, furthermore (Martin & Schmidt, 2014) suggests a few directions to address the shortcomings of private networks. However, a sparkling choice in WAN is to use virtual private networks.

In the sequel, we will describe communication technologies and protocols for WAN proposed from 2014 onwards.

Figure 2. Domains of WAN in smart grid

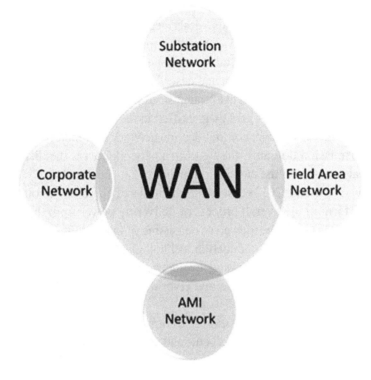

Table 2. QoS for typical WAN applications

Substation				
Service	**Latency**	**Bandwidth**	**Main Drivers**	**Preferred Network**
Synchrophasor	25-100 ms	2-5 Mbps	PMUs	private
Physical security	2 sec	4Mbps	Surveillance cameras	private
SCADA	2-4 sec	10-30 Kbps	number of points	private
AMI				
Connects and disconnects	5 sec	500 Kbps	Grid status	private
Meter Readings	variable	10 Kbps / meter	number of meters	private
Distribution				
FLIR	2-4 sec	10-30 Kbps	circuit complexity	private
Volt/ var optimization	25-100 ms	2-5 Mbps	feeders	private
Asset management	2 sec	5 Mbps	number of assets	private
Workforce access	150 ms	250 Kbps	cameras	commercial
Corporate				
Business Video	250 ms	10-150 Mbps	cameras	commercial
IP Telephony	150 ms	1-5 Mbps	employees	commercial
Wireless	1 sec	variable	employees	commercial
IP Radio	200 ms	250 Kbps	field employees	commercial

Using PLC as communication technologies in AMI, (Sanz, Pinero, Idiago, Esteban, & Garcia, 2014) argued that the deployment of a data concentrator in every transformer substation in case the subnetwork contains a low number of meters is an inefficient solution. They devised a new PLC AMI configuration using a higher frequency and reported real-life evaluation of the PLC. The results showed that the attenuation is inversely proportional to the PLC frequency.

Green communication using cellular networks is an attractive research area that aims to guarantee QoS requirements at the lowest possible energy consumption. The reader who is interested in the application of green communication and data centers for the smart grid is advised to read (Erol-Kantarci & Mouftah, 2015). There are hardware and software solutions that can be used at the base-station to reduce the energy consumption per call. Some of these techniques are using a low-power amplifier, sleep-mode techniques, adaptive coverage area, multi-hop relaying, the integration of renewable energy resources, and so forth.

To address the issues raised due to the growing concern of base-station power consumption and the increasing number of cellular subscribers (dual-sim smartphones, tablets, wireless internet, and so forth), (Lee & Choi, 2014) formulated a mixed integer nonlinear programming problem that seeks to reduce the energy consumption for multi-hop cellular networks. The solution accounts for the spectrum, energy storage, routing, and link scheduling.

Software defined network, SDN, is a new communication paradigm that is based on the publisher-subscribe concept (Nunes, Mendonca, Nguyen, Obraczka, & Turletti, 2014). To address the complexity of network managements in the smart grid, (Kim, He, Thottan, & Deshpande, 2014) elaborated an SDN architecture for the utility network. The architecture supports self-configuration, scalability, and security. The SDN is based on a ramification of the IEEE 802.1Q standard and has been demonstrated using Openflow.

(Saputro, Akkaya, & Guvenc, 2015) argued that communication at the various smart grid segments (HAN, NAN, WAN) has been well studied and investigated. Their work has focused on resolving the inter-networking issues between WAN and HAN. They proposed a hybrid communication architecture that uses LTE to build a wide area network and IEEE 802.11s mesh network to construct a NAN. To ensure privacy and direct access to a smart meter, the researchers suggested a layer for network address translation. The layer was designed for the gateway with the task to ensure end-to-end communication protocol, seamless communication, and to preserve privacy.

To address the problem of unconnected smart meters, (Sha, Alatrash, & Wang, 2016) used an overlay architecture that consists of a WiMAX network to build FAN and a commercial fiber-optic to connect the smart meters to the data center.

The smart city is a new vision for future cities that is based on the heavy integration of ICT in every corner that affects citizens in their daily life (transportation, education, electricity, environment, health care, shopping, communication, public services, and the like). The Internet of Things, IoT, is the vehicle for the development of the smart city and the creation of pervasive applications (Zanella, Bui, Castellani, Vangelista, & Zorzi, 2014). Starting from the big picture of the smart city, (Filho, Filho, & Moreli, 2016) assert that smart grid should be approached from the smart city standpoint to create a convergent communication platform. The authors further compared two popular open IoT standards for the smart city: RF mesh and LoRaWAN. Both standards are capable of building private and public networks. The authors concluded that LoRaWAN is the technology of choice for building three smart grid networks (HAN, NAN, and WAN) as the standard supports three classes of devices. Table 3 summarizes the smart grid applications that can be engendered by each class of devices. However, for advanced distribution

Table 3. Application of LoRaWAN in smart grid

Class	Services
A	street light, AMI, assets management
B	AMI, substation automation
C	SCADA

automation, the authors discounted LoRaWAN and suggested to use other alternative communication technologies like WiMAX and LTE.

2.3. Network Technologies for HAN

The Home Area Network, HAN, is a categorization of all communication technologies that enable smart grid applications in the customer domain part of the power grid. It is characterized by technologies that facilitate the communication between components such as smart meters, smart appliances, and energy management systems, EMS. This allows the realization of applications such as home automation, demand response, the integration of local renewable resources, the reduction of energy costs and the reduction of individual carbon footprints.

Due to the nature of components existing in the customer domain of the power grid, the communication requirements and characteristics of HANs are unique. The communication technologies used have a relatively shorter range compared to the ones used in NAN and WAN. This is due to the close proximity of components found in this domain. These components are also resource constrained. They exist in devices that are typically low-powered with minimal storage and computational abilities. As such, communication protocols that have been employed tend to be lightweight in terms of power usage and processing capabilities.

In addition to considering all communication technologies in the customer domain as one homogeneous network, previous studies have further divided the technologies into three more categories (Kuzlu, Pipattanasomporn, & Rahman, 2014). In addition to the Smart Home Area Network (SHAN), there are also Building Area Networks (BANs) and Industrial Area Networks (IANs). These correspond to the different types of customer premises in which they are implemented. This can be either an individual home, a residential building area or an Industrial setting. The characteristics and features of the communication technologies in these categories differ from each other, due to the different application requirements that exist. Recent studies have highlighted this distinction more by focusing on the unique challenges of each of the sub-categories

2.3.1. SHAN

The main goal of the communication technologies in this area, in the context of the smart grid, is to facilitate the concept of smart homes (Zhou, et al., 2016). This refers to the automation of the different energy components inside a home, in order to manage and control energy use. This includes smart appliances and smart meters that are able to communicate together and coordinate their functions using a communication infrastructure. This is also facilitated by smart home management systems (SHEMs) that integrate all components together, and provide an interface for customers, for monitoring and control purposes (Nanda & Panigrahi, 2016).

Due to the proliferation of the concept of the Internet of Things (IoT), the communication architecture and infrastructure in this category has been dominated by these technologies. Authors in (Stojkoska & Trivodaliev, 2017) describe a novel communication architecture for smart homes based IoT. This architecture is articulated around the cloud technology that connects smart IoT-based appliances, management systems, and third-party analysis tools. These appliances collect and send information directly to the cloud. They also receive commands directly through the communication platform provided by the cloud. In addition, the cloud also provides data storage and processing facilities. Private companies have also recently introduced their own unique communication technologies for their products in this area (Feiler, 2016). As a consequence of this communication architecture, one of the main challenges has been the explosion of data, as more and more devices collect and send energy-related data (Song, Zhou, & Zhu, 2013). Various research efforts have gone into techniques to manage this situation (Diamantoulakis, Kapinas, & Karagiannidis, 2015). However, this remains as an open issue with the need for more innovative solutions (Hu & Vasilakos, 2016).

2.3.2. BAN

Building Area Networks, consist of communication technologies that facilitate the newly emerging concept of smart buildings, and in a broader way smart city. Smart buildings are modern versions of residential buildings with automated energy management systems. Important functions that are supported include demand response, outage management, remote metering and the integration of distributed renewable energy resources. The communication technologies are focused on efficiently supporting these functions.

There are previous studies (Kuzlu, Pipattanasomporn, & Rahman, 2016) that have also looked into and reviewed BAN communication technologies for smart buildings. (Ndjiongue, Ferreira, & Shongwe, 2016) proposed a new communication protocol in the physical layer that combines power line communications (PLC) and visible light communications (VLC). The new technique was able to achieve a much higher throughput for reliable communication especially in inter-building use cases.

(Zhang & Baillieul, 2016) proposed a new communication protocol based on packeted load control messages for smart buildings. The authors developed two new communication protocols based on two scenarios: when there is complete information from sensors in the environment, and in constrained environments where binary information is carried.

(Nguyen, Nguyen, Cuong, & Nguyen, 2016) designed a new wireless-based network for a smart building that transmitted data in the 868 MHz frequency range. The network utilizes a hierarchical architecture with coordinators on each floor of the building, collecting data, and forwarding it upwards through a gateway to a remote server. The gateway and the remote server are linked through the 3G network. This architecture, with the low frequency of transmission, was able to implement a reliable smart building network with low cost and low power consumption.

2.3.3. IAN

In the industrial setting, one of the main concerns is the use of heavy equipment that consumes a lot of power, usually a big portion of that generated in the grid. Therefore, important applications in the context of the grid include demand response (Taqqali & Abdulaziz, 2010), load control (Koutsopoulos & Tassiulas, 2011) and load scheduling (Ma J., Chen, Song, & Li, 2016). The Industrial Area Network (IAN) is a collection of communication technologies, architecture, and algorithms that support these functions.

(Ding & Hong, 2013) proposed a generic demand response model for industrial facilities that can easily help a facility shave off power consumption during peak demand without adversely affecting operations. The model's communication infrastructure is divided into two main parts: the utility side and the Industrial demand side. The utility gateway/meter acts as the bridge between these two main parts, passing messages and commands back and forth. One unique feature of this model is the inclusion of an energy management agent (EMA) which is a conceptual entity that represents a specific industrial task. This includes a monitoring component that measures consumption and control functions for that specific task.

(Wang, Wang, Sun, Guo, & Wu, 2016) proposed a new energy efficient communication system based on IoT technology. The authors also proposed two new novel communication protocols; sleep and wake up scheduling protocols that automatically schedule sleep and wake cycles of communicating nodes, and thus lower energy consumption.

On the other hand, (Wei, Hong, & Alam, 2016) introduced a new communication strategy based on IoT that improves the connectivity of energy-related nodes in industrial facilities. Based on the TCP/IP network model, the authors selected appropriate open lightweight protocols in each layer to facilitate efficient communication. This helps standardization efforts and promotes interoperability. The strategy is also demonstrated to reduce peak energy use in a simulated industrial environment.

2.4. Emerging Technologies for Distributed Intelligence: Peer-to-Peer Computing, IP/MPLS, and Fog Computing

To manage and control the operations of the various assets and equipment within the smart-grid, several techniques from the industrial control system, ICS, have been promoted to create an autonomous and self-healing smart-grid. Distributed intelligence, DI, is a paradigm shift in ICS that enables the integration of large-scale systems (Mahalik, 2003).

Recently, several authors showed the effectiveness of DI in to achieve the objectives of smart-grid. The essential components to create DI are smart nodes and communication technologies. The smart node should have the ability to make a local decision and to cooperate with similar nodes to achieve a global objective. A multi-agent system is one supporting technologies for creating distributed intelligence.

Distributed intelligence in the smart grid has gained momentum (Mues, Alvarez, Espinoza, & Garbajosa, 2011) (Werbos, 2011) as it has enabled a multitude of applications such as feeder automation (Baker & Meisinger, 2011), volt-var control (Ibrahim & Salama, 2015), fault localization and isolation (Ghorbani, Choudhry, & Feliachi, 2013), the interoperability in microgrid (Vukojevic, Laval, & Handley, 2015), seamless integration of smart meter (Vyatkin, Zhabelova, Yang, McComas, & Chouinard, 2012), distributed protection (Yang, Zhabelova, Vyatkin, Nair, & Apostolov, 2012), and control of wind energy conversion system (Moness & Moustafa, 2016).

A couple of communication technologies support the distributed intelligence in the energy sector. On top of that, peer-to-peer computing has been widely accepted both in industry and in academia. (Campos, Matos, Pereira, & Rua, 2014) devised a service-oriented architecture to solve device heterogeneity and interoperability while guaranteeing both reliability and scalability. The peer-to-peer communication is based on the gossip protocol. Web technology has been adopted for the communication between constrained devices and mainframes. In industry, a number of proprietaries and open standard peer-to-peer communication platforms have been proposed. The commercial system of (S&C electric company, 2017) has been devised to build peer-to-peer communication for distributed intelligence in feeder automation. The system operates in ISM band, deploys 128-AES for data encryption, supports over the air configuration, uses frequency hopping spread spectrum technology with 4-GFSK modulation, etc. Other companies such as Siemens and ABB have constructed a peer-to-peer communication network for substation automation in compliance with the IEC 61850 standard (Siemens, 2017) (ABB, 2017).

IP/MPLS is a standard that was designed to, but not limited to, enable ATM and IP integration, prioritize traffic, accommodate different levels of QoS, and guarantee data security. In smart-grid, a proof of concept for teleprotection using secure IP/MPLS has been demonstrated (Blair et al., 2016).

As part of the efforts to reduce latency and delays in the transmission and processing of real-time data for critical smart grid applications, a new paradigm known as fog computing has emerged (Yi, Hao, Qin, & Li, 2015). This new architecture takes advantage of cloud computing technologies while bringing the computing processes closer to the edge of the network. This allows the scalability of large sensor networks without sacrificing response times of critical data exchanges. (Al Faruque & Vatanparvar, 2016) described a novel energy management system that relies on fog computing to provide a scalable solution for controlling energy production and consumption in a microgrid. An architecture that depends on low powered devices found in customer homes allows creating a system that can handle data from a large number of smart devices in a fast and efficient way. This is demonstrated by home and microgrid level energy management systems that were successfully implemented.

2.5. Discussions

Communication technology is an important aspect to the realization of smart grid and its assorted services. There are wide varieties of communication technologies that can be used at the various areas in the smart-grid architecture. These areas are identified as WAN and HAN. In each area, a number of private and commercial solutions exist. Each communication architecture has its drawbacks and advantages. For instance, public cellular communication technologies (WiMAX, LTE, and UMTS) are affordable for the utility company, however, the latency of these technologies, as well as the security, prohibit the adoption of these technologies in critical services like distributed intelligence and SCADA.

The challenges in designing secure and efficient HAN are significantly lower than for WAN. Privacy is one critical feature that the HAN should guarantee. The existing solutions for the realizations of HAN include ZigBee, WLAN, LoRaWAN, and 6LoWPAN.

3. SECURITY AND PRIVACY FOR SMART GRIDS

According to the National Institute of Standards and Technology, NIST, a smart grid is composed of four major segments: energy production and distribution, communication infrastructure, information technology, and industrial control system (NIST Special Publication 1108, 2014). Figure 3 depicts these four segments.

Security for the operations of the smart grid has been identified as a vital requirement by NIST. The three ICT pillars for the smart grid (communication, information technology, and industrial control system) should be protected against known security threats. Because of its widespread geographic area, the diversity of equipment, the proliferation of stakeholders and the wide-spectrum of operation environments, NIST has proposed an N-tier and overlay security architecture. The architecture covers the following areas: device, cryptography and key management, system, and network (The Smart Grid Interoperability Panel, 2010).

Figure 3. Smart-grid segments

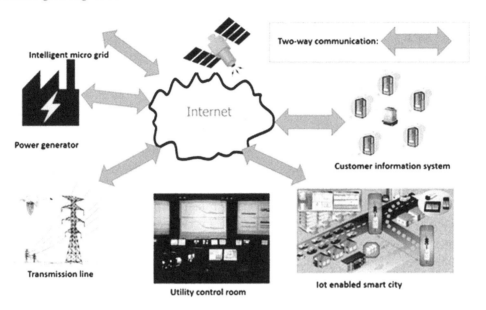

3.1. Key Management

(Kim, Kolesnikov, Kim, & Thottan, 2011) analyzed the communication requirements for the smart grid using an IP-based network and proposed a scalable, lightweight and secure transport protocol, SSTP. The protocol overcomes the weakness present in current transport layer protocols (stream control transmission protocol and transmission control protocol). The SSTP uses a symmetric-key algorithm for authentication and privacy. SSTP is designed for asymmetric security requirements in which the node keys are derived, at the server side, using a master key and a pseudo-random function generator. The Diffie-Hellman key exchange protocol is used to establish an SSTP connection between a utility server and a node.

Motivated by the lack of veracious, secure and scalable communication infrastructure for the smart grid, (Kim, Lee, Atkinson, Kim, & Thottan, 2012) proposed a secure data-centric application extensible, SeDax, platform. SeDax supports end-to-end security and uses RSA and AES cryptosystems for authentication and encryption. The X509 certificate is used to authenticate SeDax nodes. The topic-group authentication messages are encrypted using AES and its scheme is identical to SSTP.

(Dan, Lui, Tabassum, Zhu, & Nahrstedt, 2013) devised lightweight and scalable security protocols for the establishment of shared keys between measurement devices and power system operators via unsecure data-collectors.

Using the security requirements for smart meters (SMs) in advanced metering infrastructure reported in (Cleveland, 2008), (Liu, Chen, Zhu, Zhang, & He, 2013) proposed a key management scheme (KMS) suitable for resource constraint devices and accounts for three communication modes: unicast, multicast and broadcast. The authors used the key graph algorithm to build the KMS. Finally, yet importantly, the KMS is designed for both simple and complex AMI applications. However (Wan, Wang, Yang, & Shi, 2014) asserted that KMS described is unscalable and vulnerable to desynchronization attack. Afterwards, the authors devised a scalable key management scheme, SKM, using identity-based encryption (IBE) and key-tree architecture.

(Yu, Arifuzzaman, Wen, Zhang, & Sato, 2015) elaborated an AMI architecture using information centric networking (ICN-AMI). The architecture aims to reduce traffic congestion and to guarantee secure operation. Inspired from (Liu, Chen, Zhu, Zhang, & He, 2013), the authors further devised a KMS for the ICN-AMI.

3.2. Tamper Resistant Device

Electricity theft represents a major challenge to utility companies and has a profound effect on energy cost, utility revenue, and reliability of the grid. As pointed out by (Smith, 2004), a malicious consumer can steal electricity using a variety of ways such as meter tampering, unpaid bills, irregular payment and illegal electricity connection. The latter is a life-threatening practice. To address electricity theft and blackouts, the smart grid should integrate a secure hardware and software system.

To protect the smart meter gateway from ICT attacks (Detken, Genzel, Rudolph, & Jahnke, 2014), proposed a trusted core network architecture. The network uses a trusted platform module, a trusted neighborhood discovery protocol, and a trustworthy boot process. The driving forces behind the development of the security solution are the "chameleon" malware and the security standards elaborated by the German Federal Office for Information Security for the smart meter gateway.

3.3. Network and System

Advanced metering infrastructure (AMI) is an IoT architecture that connects consumer side smart-meters to the utility meter data management system. AMI is the corner stone for the realization of smart grid applications like dynamic pricing, demand-response scheme, load balancing, and so forth. The security of the AMI at the various levels (software, hardware, communication, and system) is critical for a trustworthy system. (Yan Y., Qian, Sharif, & Tipper, 2013) emphasized that the prevailing cryptographic schemes do not meet the security requirements for AMI networks. Subsequently, the authors elaborated an integrated authentication and confidentiality, IAC, protocol that has three processes: (1) authentication, (2) data confidentiality, and (3) control message confidentiality. (Fan, et al., 2014) identified the weakness of the IAC protocol and advocated a cryptographic protocol with auto-correcting capability that eliminates a suspicious meter. The protocol was designed for a wireless sensor network deployed to monitor the transmission line. The authors further used low-energy encryption and authentication schemes.

(Ye, Qian, & Hu, 2014) questioned the security strength of the IAC protocol and identified six security holes. Further, they elaborated an AMI protocol that addresses the shortcomings of the IAC protocol. However, the authors' scheme does not detect intrusion.

3.4. Discussions

Security in the smart grid is a complex and evolving issue. Security architecture, protocols, and primitives are shaped by multiples factors such as smart grid applications, communication protocols, geographic locations, and implementation constraints. Security and privacy of smart grid can benefit from developments in key areas such as wireless sensor network, trusted platform module, network, database, crypto analysis, IoT, cryptographic algorithms, data security, web-design, and cloud computing. Most existing security solutions aim to address the following issues: smart-meter authentication, security protocols for advanced metering infrastructure, secure demand-response scheme, homomorphic encryption, lightweight authentication protocols, a secure vehicle to grid communication, and interoperable security architecture.

4. WIRELESS SENSOR NETWORKS FOR THE SMART GRID

Sensors are the cornerstone for advanced smart grid applications like distributed generation, situation awareness, demand-response schemes, dynamic line rating, and energy management. The wireless sensor network has been deployed at the energy production units, the transmission and distribution side, business sector, customer premises, service provider, and operator. ZigBee and wirelessHART are two popular WSN technologies used in smart-grid (Liu, 2012).

(Mossé & Gadola, 2012) elaborated a WSN platform to control the conversion of wind energy according to the load. (Mabusela, Kruger, Silva, & Hancke, 2015) used a WSN to control solar thermal power plants. The control and real-time monitoring of PV park using WSN were the focus of (Moreno-Garcia, et al., 2015).

A practical and low-cost WSN using ZigBee technology has been proposed in (Vo, Nguyen, Nguyen, Le, & Huynh, 2013). The system comprises low cost smart power outlets that work both as sensors and as actuators. These outlets are connected to router nodes using a mesh network. A ZigBee coordinator is deployed to control and maintain the network. The energy management software is implemented on a mini-web server. Figure 4 depicts the low-cost WSN system for home energy management proposed in (Vo, Nguyen, Nguyen, Le, & Huynh, 2013). The results show that the system has a delay less than 300ms for a distance shorter than 40m. For higher distances, the delay increases drastically due to the increased packet error rate.

In the utility grid, the transmission line has some special electrical properties that determine its capacity, commonly known as *ampacity* (Farzaneh, Farokhi, & Chisholm, 2013). There exist two popular standards for the determination of the ampacity for the overhead conductors used for power transmission. These industrial standards are IEEE and CIGRE (Schmidt, 1999). To increase the efficiency of the grid and to maximize the energy flow, a dynamic line rating (DLR) process has been proposed as an alternative to static line rating (Yang, Lambert, & Divan, 2007). DLR depends on the electrical properties of the overhead conductor, ambient temperature, conductor heat, and geographic location. Currently, advanced utility companies deploy smart sensors to evaluate the ampacity of the transmission line. Figure 5 depicts a commercial sensor used to monitor a 35kV transmission line. The sensor is a Linux-powered embedded system that uses EM energy for energy harvesting. The sensor uses a GPS signal to append the measured data with the location and supports secure Bluetooth for short-range communication. For long-range communication, the mote has a multi-standards radio interface (LTE/4G, 3G, 2G, GPRS/GSM, CDMA fallback, L+G Gridstream, and Silver Spring Networks). The management of the sensors and data-analyses is done at the utility data center.

The study reported in (Fateh, Govindarasu, & Ajjarapu, 2013), showed that a WSN in combination with wireless and wired communication technology is a cost-efficient solution for the monitoring of a transmission line. The authors further described algorithms to optimally place the cellular network to optimize the cost while satisfying latency and throughout requirements. They further showed the existent technology enables the monitoring of a transmission line using a WSN.

Figure 4. ZigBee based home energy management system proposed by (Vo, Nguyen, Nguyen, Le, & Huynh, 2013)

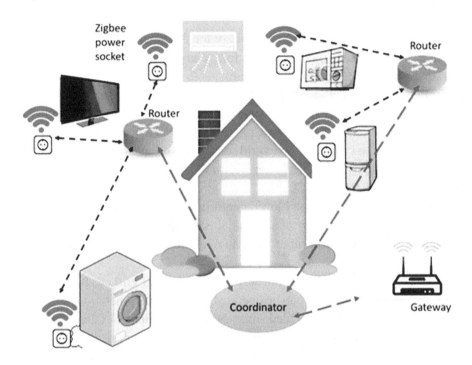

Figure 5. A commercial sensor for transmission line monitoring (Sentient Energy, 2017)

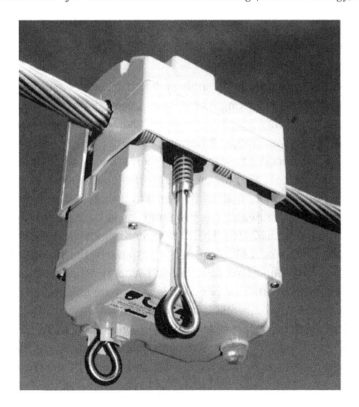

Smart grid sensors and other devices, such as smart meters, can monitor the power consumption of home appliances and facilitate the scheduling of non-critical loads so as to reduce the cost and avoid the peak times (Yang, Lambert, & Divan, 2007).

The smart grid sensor is also the enabling technology for distributed monitoring of the electricity demand and response. The distributed monitoring platform can detect, for instance, equipment failures, blackouts, and power outages in the distribution system.

The new generation of distributed monitoring platforms consists of smart grid sensors with flexible communication modules that perform measuring operations. The measures include electric field strength, fault current, load current, power factors, phase angles, voltage sag, wire temperature, surges and harmonics of the distribution system. A smart grid sensor network uses real-time data to monitor the overhead transformers in the substation, checks the health of vital circuits and schedules maintenance work (Salazar-Llinas, Ginart, & Restrepo, 2014).

WSN is also used for monitoring the load level, controlling the distributed switches, for powering the meter, etc. It can also predict and notify of a potential pending failure before it occurs. A WSN offers plenty of advantages like cost reduction of the grid operation, improving the system up time and reliability (Paoletti & Herman, 2015).

A WSN adds reliability and self-healing characteristics to the smart grid electricity (Gungor, Lu, & Hancke, 2010). The process of automation can be operated on either the generation, transmission or the utilization part of the system. In a WSN enabled smart-grid most equipment failures and damages can be monitored and controlled with devices such as wireless automatic meter reading (WAMR).

The study by (Sood, Fischer, Eklund, & Brown, 2009) mentioned the challenges on how to apply the sensor nodes in the implementation. (McDaniel & McLaughlin, 2009) and (Glaser, 2004) explained that a WSN can be applied in smart grid environments, IoT, Machine to Machine and the communication network.

4.1. WSN Routings in Smart Grid

Routing is an important design factor that determines the efficiency, scalability, and robustness of the WSN. The popular metrics for WSN routing include, but are not limited to, latency, energy efficiency, network lifetime, goodput, scalability, security, coverage, and connectivity (Yamunadevi, Vairam, Kalaiarasan, & Vidya, 2012) (Sangwan, Singh, & Sawant, 2016).

Energy consumption is one important aspect that WSN routing protocols try to optimize. One of the main constraints of a WSN is access to abundant energy (Titouna, Aliouat, & Gueroui, 2016). Sensor devices are typically low power devices that are designed to operate using an energy storage system or energy harvesting. As such, a lot of research has gone into designing energy-efficient routing protocols for WSNs (Sarkar & Senthil Murugan, 2016). There are several approaches that have been used to achieve this (Ari, Yenke, Labraoui, Damakoa, & Gueroui, 2016), inspired by the biological phenomenon of honeybees designed a cluster-based routing mechanism that is energy efficient. By mimicking the fast and efficient clustering mechanisms of artificial bees, the authors were able to design an improved routing protocol that is better performance wise, while still efficient in terms of energy consumption. The authors of (Kumar & Kumar, 2016) proposed a position based routing protocol that achieved energy efficiency by trying to balance the energy consumption of individual sensor nodes across the whole network. They did these using selected parameters such as the remaining sensor energy, the distance between the nodes from the destination and so on. Other authors (Rani, Malhotra, Talwar, & Ahmed, 2017) (Mohemed, Saleh, Abdelrazzak, & Samra, 2016) have also proposed energy-efficient routing protocols for WSN for different use-cases. In the smart grid arena, the RPL routing protocol has been investigated in the context of advanced metering infrastructure (Ancillotti, Bruno, & Conti, 2013). A few enhancements such as auto-configuration, a multi-channel operation have been added to the RPL for AMI (Kulkarni, Gormus, Fan, & Motz, 2011).

A key performance measure related to the energy consumption of a WSN is the network lifetime. Lifetime is the period in which all sensors operational. The death time is the instant of time in which one or more sensor nodes runs out of power. Since WSN, routing protocols consume a considerable amount of power, one of the key challenges that remains is optimizing network lifetime. The goal is to maximize this value as much as possible. An important parameter is used to evaluate the effectiveness of new approaches used for routing protocols. (Chatterjee & Mukherjee, 2014) proposed a novel WSN routing protocol that tried to maximize network lifetime by using a new approach. The WSN was divided into tree based density-varied clusters with a higher density of nodes in the higher levels of the network. This enabled the authors to optimize power usage in the higher traffic levels and provide reliability. (Guo, Yao, Song, Hu, & Liu, 2015) also proposed new routing mechanisms that use sleep mode approach in order to maximize the network lifetime of a WSN. In the context of the smart grid, several routing schemes to extend WSN lifetime have been proposed. The authors considered a routing scheme that accounts for the charging status, the remaining energy, and the transmission power consumption of the nodes. Packet-size optimization combined with transmission power control has been shown as an effective solution to maximize WSN lifetime (Kurt, Yildiz, Yigit, Tavli, & Gungor, 2017).

4.2. Energy Harvesting for WSN

One of the main challenges in WSN is to sustain the power supply at the node. To this end, energy harvesting is an enabling technology, whereby the sensor scavenges power from ambient sources. The most popular sources for energy harvesting are electromagnetic, solar cells, piezoelectric, acoustic, and thermal. Energy harvesting, EH, for WSN in the smart grid is an active research field. The selection of the harvester circuits is determined by factors like cost, location, and application. Most of the recent works on EH (2014-2016) focused on the sensors that are used in the high-voltage domain. (Semedo, Oliveira, & Cardoso, 2014) devised a solar energy harvesting circuit for sensors scattered in high-voltage disconnected switches. The harvested energy is stored in supercapacitor cells. Energy harvesting for sensors deployed along AC lines has its own design bottlenecks because of the low frequency of the EM field (50-60 Hz). To address the problem, a number of schemes have been proposed. J. Han et al., devised a nonintrusive energy harvester circuit using cantilever-structured magneto electric composite (Jinchi, et al., 2015). The experiments showed that the double cell harvester can generate a power of 9.40 mW at 40 A. The work reported in (Moghe, Iyer, Lambert, & Divan, 2015), elaborated an energy harvester for medium and high-voltage, using an electric field. The circuit used two parallel plates to form a storage capacitor. The circuit was able to generate 17 mW using 35-kV AC line. Energy scavenging circuit reported in (Hosseinimehr & Tabesh, 2016) uses miniaturized linear permanent magnet synchronous generator to harvest energy from EM field that surrounds the AC line carrying high-voltage. The results showed that the circuit has a power density of 3.2 mW/kA.

4.3. Discussions

Wireless sensor network is a vital technology for designing robust, secure, self-healing and efficient grid. WSNs have been deployed at the energy generation site, the transmission and distribution side, and consumer premises. The technologies for building WSN are diverse which create an interoperability problem. Middleware is an effective solution that can help to remedy the problem. The processing capabilities and the battery management of the sensor add another dimension to the problem.

5. SUMMARY AND OPEN ISSUES

Smart grid technology is an emerging area of multidisciplinary research. ICT technologies and real-time embedded systems are key enabler for the realization of self-healing, efficient, green and secure smart grid. Recent works in communication technologies have gone in interoperability, secure aggregation, network analyses, self-configuring network, improvements of PLC enabled communication, green communication, and the integration of IoT with the smart grid. However, there are still some open issues that need further investigations. These issues, in general, can be categorized into three main aspects: security/privacy, efficiency, and interoperability.

Security and privacy are still hot issues that continue to affect the underlying communication technologies. These issues have become more prominent as the Internet of Things (IoT) technology has become the backbone technology for the smart grid. IoT devices are vulnerable to cyber-attacks and are used to form bot nets to conduct Distributed Denial of Service Attacks (DDoS). Research into security mechanisms that are lightweight is still an open issue that needs to be tackled.

Due to the stringent communication requirements of smart grid functions and applications, efficiency is an important feature across all aspects of the communication infrastructure and technologies. A number of issues are still open for further research. One area, in particular, is concerned with spectrum utilization. Power line communication (PLC), which is one of the preferred communication technologies, still has to be fully utilized in terms of bandwidth capacity. Research into new techniques such as multi-armed bandit channel selection requires further investigation. Due to the power constraints of different nodes of a smart grid system, a new energy efficient communication protocol has to be investigated further. There are already some interesting proposal and research directions in this area. For smart grid applications that involve complex communication operations, end-to-end latency is still also an open problem. Other open issues related to efficiency include better network traffic characterization mechanisms, which would allow more efficient use of available communication infrastructure, low-cost communication infrastructure, and interference-free communication protocols that minimize packet loss and increase bandwidth efficiency.

The new direction in smart sensor technology is the development of low cost, low maintenance and self-powered sensors to assist realization of a flexible monitoring system. This new type of sensor is referred to as a smart stick-on sensor, which addresses the shortcomings of the current smart sensor technology. The open issues in WSN include the miniaturization of sensors, lightweight protocols, middleware design, interoperability, scalability, healing, energy harvesting, low-power communication protocols, and security.

ACKNOWLEDGMENT

The Swedish government through the SIDA project supports this work. The authors thank the following people: Cleverson Takiguch from S&C electric company for his valuable comments and suggestions to improve the content of the paper and Christine Mwase from Dar es Salam for her effort to improve the paper.

REFERENCES

ABB. (2017). *ABB company*. Retrieved from http://new.abb.com/substation-automation

Al Faruque, M. A., & Vatanparvar, K. (2016, April). Energy Management-as-a-Service Over Fog Computing Platform. *IEEE Internet of Things Journal, 3*(2), 161–169. doi:10.1109/JIOT.2015.2471260

Ancillotti, E., Bruno, R., & Conti, M. (2013, January). The role of the RPL routing protocol for smart grid communications. *IEEE Communications Magazine, 51*(1), 75–83. doi:10.1109/MCOM.2013.6400442

Ancillotti, E., Bruno, R., & Conti, M. (2013, November). The role of communication systems in smart grids: Architectures, technical solutions and research challenges. *Computer Communications, 36*(17-18), 1665–1697. doi:10.1016/j.comcom.2013.09.004

Anzar, M., Nadeem, J., & Sohail, R. (2015, January). A review of wireless communications for smart grid. *Renewable & Sustainable Energy Reviews, 41*, 248–260. doi:10.1016/j.rser.2014.08.036

Ari, A. A., Yenke, B. O., Labraoui, N., Damakoa, I., & Gueroui, A. (2016, July). A power efficient cluster-based routing algorithm for wireless sensor networks: Honeybees swarm intelligence based approach. *Journal of Network and Computer Applications, 69*, 77–97. doi:10.1016/j.jnca.2016.04.020

Baker, J., & Meisinger, M. (2011, December). Experience with a distributed-intelligence, self-healing solution for medium-voltage feeders on the Isle of Wight. In *Proceedings of the 2011 2nd IEEE PES International Conference and Exhibition on Innovative Smart Grid Technologies*, (pp. 1-4). doi:10.1109/ISGTEurope.2011.6162646

Blair, S. M., Booth, C. D., Valck, B. D., Verhulst, D., Kirasack, C., Wong, K. Y., & Lakshminarayanan, S. (2016, March). Validating secure and reliable IP/MPLS communications for current differential protection. In *Proceedings of the 13th International Conference on Development in Power System Protection 2016 (DPSP)* (pp. 1-6). doi:10.1049/cp.2016.0070

Campos, F., Matos, M., Pereira, J., & Rua, D. (2014, September). A peer-to-peer service architecture for the Smart Grid. In *Proceedings of the 14-th IEEE International Conference on Peer-to-Peer Computing* (pp. 1-5). IEEE. doi:10.1109/P2P.2014.6934315

Chatterjee, A., & Mukherjee, D. (2014). Reliable multipath wireless sensor network routing protocol scheme for network lifetime maximization. In *Proceedings of the 2014 2nd International Conference on Business and Information Management (ICBIM)* (pp. 64-68). IEEE.

Cleveland, F. M. (2008, July). Cyber security issues for Advanced Metering Infrastructure (AMI). In *Proceedings of the Power and Energy Society General Meeting - Conversion and Delivery of Electrical Energy in the 21st Century* (pp. 1-5). IEEE. doi:10.1109/PES.2008.4596535

Dan, G., Lui, K.-S., Tabassum, R., Zhu, Q., & Nahrstedt, K. (2013, October). SELINDA: A secure, scalable and light-weight data collection protocol for smart grids. In *Proceedings of the 2013 IEEE International Conference on Smart Grid Communications (SmartGridComm)* (pp. 480-485). doi:10.1109/SmartGridComm.2013.6688004

Detken, K. O., Genzel, C. H., Rudolph, C., & Jahnke, M. (2014, September). Integrity protection in a smart grid environment for wireless access of smart meters. In *Proceedings of the 2014 2nd International Symposium on Wireless Systems within the Conferences on Intelligent Data Acquisition and Advanced Computing Systems* (pp. 79-86). doi:10.1109/IDAACS-SWS.2014.6954628

Diamantoulakis, P. D., Kapinas, V. M., & Karagiannidis, G. K. (2015). Big Data Analytics for Dynamic Energy Management in Smart Grids. *Big Data Research*, 2(3), 94–101. doi:10.1016/j.bdr.2015.03.003

Ding, Y., & Hong, S. H. (2013). A model of demand response energy management system in industrial facilities. In *Proceedings of the 2013 IEEE International Conference on Smart Grid Communications (SmartGridComm* (pp. 241-246). IEEE. doi:10.1109/SmartGridComm.2013.6687964

Dutt, N., Jantsch, A., & Sarma, S. (2016). Toward Smart Embedded Systems: A Self-aware System-on-Chip (SoC) Perspective. *ACM Transactions on Embedded Computing Systems*, 15(2), 22.

Elmangoush, A., Steinke, R., Al-Hezmi, A., & Magedanz, T. (2014, February). On the usage of standardised M2M platforms for Smart Energy management. In *Proceedings of the International Conference on Information Networking 2014 (ICOIN2014)* (pp. 79-84). doi:10.1109/ICOIN.2014.6799669

Energy Independence and Security Act of 2007. (2007). Retrieved from https://www.gpo.gov

Erol-Kantarci, M., & Mouftah, H. T. (2015). Energy-efficient information and communication infrastructures in the smart grid: A survey on interactions and open issues. *IEEE Communications Surveys and Tutorials*, 17(1), 179–197. doi:10.1109/COMST.2014.2341600

Fan, S., Ye, F., Guo, J., Liang, Y., Xu, G., Zhang, X., & Qian, Y. (2014, August). A security protocol for wireless sensor networks designed for monitoring smart grid transmission lines. In *Proceedings of the 2014 23rd International Conference on Computer Communication and Networks (ICCCN)* (pp. 1-7). doi:10.1109/ICCCN.2014.6911789

Fang, X., Misra, S., Xue, G., & Yang, D. (2012). Fourth). Smart Grid- The New and Improved Power Grid: A Survey. *IEEE Communications Surveys and Tutorials*, 14(4), 944–980. doi:10.1109/SURV.2011.101911.00087

Farhangi, H. (2010). The path of the smart grid. *IEEE Power and Energy Magazine*, 8(1), 18–28. doi:10.1109/MPE.2009.934876

Farzaneh, M., Farokhi, S., & Chisholm, W. A. (2013). *Electrical design of overhead power transmission lines* (1st ed.). McGraw-Hill.

Fateh, B., Govindarasu, M., & Ajjarapu, V. (2013, June). Wireless Network Design for Transmission Line Monitoring in Smart Grid. *IEEE Transactions on Smart Grid*, *4*(2), 1076–1086. doi:10.1109/TSG.2013.2241796

Feiler, J. (2016). Working with HomeKit Accessories. In *Learn Apple HomeKit on iOS* (pp. 51–71). Berkeley, CA: Apress. doi:10.1007/978-1-4842-1527-2_5

Filho, H. G., Filho, J. P., & Moreli, V. L. (2016, September). The adequacy of LoRaWAN on smart grids: A comparison with RF mesh technology. In *Proceedings of the 2016 IEEE International Smart Cities Conference (ISC2)* (pp. 1-6). doi:10.1109/ISC2.2016.7580783

Ghorbani, J., Choudhry, M. A., & Feliachi, A. (2013, February). Fault location and isolation using multi agent systems in power distribution systems with distributed generation sources. In *Proceedings of the 2013 IEEE PES Innovative Smart Grid Technologies Conference (ISGT)* (pp. 1-6). doi:10.1109/ISGT.2013.6497805

Glaser, S. D. (2004). Some real-world applications of wireless sensor nodes. In *Proceedings of SPIE Symposium on Smart Structures and Materials* (pp. 344-355). doi:10.1117/12.539089

Glesner, M., & Philipp, F. (2013). Embedded Systems Design for Smart System Integration. In *Proceedings of the IEEE Computer Society Annual Symposium on VLSI (ISVLSI)* (pp. 32-33). doi:10.1109/ISVLSI.2013.6654611

Gobena, Y., Durai, A., Birkner, M., Pothamsetty, V., & Varakantam, V. (2011, March). Practical architecture considerations for Smart Grid WAN network. In *Proceedings of the 2011 IEEE/PES power systems conference and exposition* (pp. 1-6). doi:10.1109/PSCE.2011.5772481

Gungor, V. C., Lu, B., & Hancke, G. P. (2010). Opportunities and Challenges of Wireless Sensor Networks in Smart Grid. *IEEE Transactions on Industrial Electronics*, *57*(10), 3557–3564. doi:10.1109/TIE.2009.2039455

Gungor, V. C., Sahin, D., Kocak, T., & Ergut, S. (2011). Smart grid technologies: communication technologies and standards. *IEEE transactions on Industrial Informatics*.

Gungor, V. C., Sahin, D., Kocak, T., Ergut, S., Buccella, C., Cecati, C., & Hancke, G. P. (2013, February). A Survey on Smart Grid Potential Applications and Communication Requirements. *IEEE Transactions on Industrial Informatics*, *9*(1), 28–42. doi:10.1109/TII.2012.2218253

Guo, J., Yao, J., Song, T., Hu, J., & Liu, M. (2015, Dec). A routing algorithm to long lifetime network for the intelligent power distribution network in smart grid. In *Proceedings of the 2015 IEEE Advanced Information Technology, Electronic and Automation Control Conference (IAEAC)* (pp. 1077-1082). IEEE. doi:10.1109/IAEAC.2015.7428724

Hosseinimehr, T., & Tabesh, A. (2016, August). Magnetic Field Energy Harvesting from AC Lines for Powering Wireless Sensor Nodes in Smart Grids. *IEEE Transactions on Industrial Electronics*, *63*, 4947–4954. doi:10.1109/TIE.2016.2546846

Hu, J., & Vasilakos, A. V. (2016, September). Energy Big Data Analytics and Security: Challenges and Opportunities. *IEEE Transactions on Smart Grid*, *7*(5), 2423–2436. doi:10.1109/TSG.2016.2563461

Ibrahim, M., & Salama, M. M. (2015). Smart distribution system volt/VAR control using distributed intelligence and wireless communication. *IET Generation, Transmission Distribution*, *9*(4), 307–318. doi:10.1049/iet-gtd.2014.0513

Jinchi, H., Jun, H., Yang, Y., & Zhongxu, W. (2015, July). A nonintrusive power supply design for self-powered sensor networks in the smart grid by scavenging energy from AC power line. *IEEE Transactions on Industrial Electronics*, *62*(7), 4398–4407. doi:10.1109/TIE.2014.2383992

Kabalci, Y. (2016, May). A survey on smart metering and smart grid communication. *Renewable & Sustainable Energy Reviews*, *57*, 302–318. doi:10.1016/j.rser.2015.12.114

Khan, A. A., Rehmani, M. H., & Reisslein, M. (2016). Cognitive radio for smart grids: survey of architectures, spectrum sensing mechanisms, and networking protocols. *IEEE Communications Surveys and Tutorials*, *18*(1), 860–898. doi:10.1109/COMST.2015.2481722

Khan, R. H., & Khan, J. Y. (2013, February). A comprehensive review of the application characteristics and traffic requirements of a smart grid communications network. *Computer Networks*, *57*(3), 825–845. doi:10.1016/j.comnet.2012.11.002

Kim, Y. J., He, K., Thottan, M., & Deshpande, J. G. (2014, November). Virtualized and self-configurable utility communications enabled by software-defined networks. In *Proceedings of the 2014 IEEE International Conference on Smart Grid Communications (SmartGridComm)* (pp. 416-421). doi:10.1109/SmartGridComm.2014.7007682

Kim, Y. J., Kolesnikov, V., Kim, H., & Thottan, M. (2011, Oct). SSTP: A scalable and secure transport protocol for smart grid data collection. In *Proceedings of the 2011 IEEE International Conference on Smart Grid Communications (SmartGridComm)* (pp. 161-166). doi:10.1109/SmartGridComm.2011.6102310

Kim, Y. J., Lee, J., Atkinson, G., Kim, H., & Thottan, M. (2012, July). SeDAX: A Scalable, Resilient, and Secure Platform for Smart Grid Communications. *IEEE Journal on Selected Areas in Communications*, *30*(6), 1119–1136. doi:10.1109/JSAC.2012.120710

Korzun, D. G., & Gurtov, I. N. (2015). Service Intelligence and Communication Security for Ambient Assisted Living. *International Journal of Embedded and Real-Time Communication Systems*, *6*(1), 76–100. doi:10.4018/IJERTCS.2015010104

Koutsopoulos, I., & Tassiulas, L. (2011). Challenges in demand load control for the smart grid. *IEEE Network*, *25*(5), 16–21. doi:10.1109/MNET.2011.6033031

Kulkarni, P., Gormus, S., Fan, Z., & Motz, B. (2011, June). A self-organising mesh networking solution based on enhanced RPL for smart metering communications. In *Proceedings of the 2011 IEEE International Symposium on a World of Wireless, Mobile and Multimedia Networks* (pp. 1-6). doi:10.1109/WoWMoM.2011.5986178

Kumar, V., & Kumar, S. (2016, December). Energy balanced position-based routing for lifetime maximization of wireless sensor networks. *Ad Hoc Networks*, *52*, 117–129. doi:10.1016/j.adhoc.2016.08.006

Kurt, S., Yildiz, H. U., Yigit, M., Tavli, B., & Gungor, V. C. (2017, March). Packet Size Optimization in Wireless Sensor Networks for Smart Grid Applications. *IEEE Transactions on Industrial Electronics*, *64*(3), 2392–2401. doi:10.1109/TIE.2016.2619319

Kuzlu, M., Pipattanasomporn, M., & Rahman, S. (2014). Communication network requirements for major smart grid applications in HAN, NAN and WAN. *Computer Networks*, *67*, 74–88. doi:10.1016/j.comnet.2014.03.029

Kuzlu, M., Pipattanasomporn, M., & Rahman, S. (2016, January). Review of communication technologies for smart homes/building applications. In Proceedings of the 2015 IEEE Innovative Smart Grid Technologies - Asia (ISGT ASIA) (pp. 1-6). IEEE.

Lee, J. Y., & Choi, S. G. (2014, Feb). Linear programming based hourly peak load shaving method at home area. In *Proceedings of the 16th International Conference on Advanced Communication Technology* (pp. 310-313). doi:10.1109/ICACT.2014.6778971

Liu, N., Chen, J., Zhu, L., Zhang, J., & He, Y. (2013, October). A Key Management Scheme for Secure Communications of Advanced Metering Infrastructure in Smart Grid. *IEEE Transactions on Industrial Electronics*, *60*(10), 4746–4756. doi:10.1109/TIE.2012.2216237

Liu, Y. (2012). Wireless sensor network applications in smart grid: recent trends and challenges. *International Journal of Distributed Sensor Networks*, *8*(9), 492819. doi:10.1155/2012/492819

Ma, J., Chen, H., Song, L., & Li, Y. (2016, March). Residential Load Scheduling in Smart Grid: A Cost Efficiency Perspective. *IEEE Transactions on Smart Grid*, *7*, 1–1.

Ma, R., Chen, H.-H., Huang, Y.-R., & Meng, W. (2013). Smart Grid Communication: Its Challenges and Opportunities. *IEEE Transactions on Smart Grid*, *4*(1), 36–46. doi:10.1109/TSG.2012.2225851

Mabusela, K., Kruger, C. P., Silva, B. J., & Hancke, G. P. (2015, September). Design of a wireless heliostat system. *AFRICON*, *2015*, 1–5. doi:10.1109/AFRCON.2015.7332011

Mahalik, N. P. (2003). Fieldbus Technology: Industrial Network Standards for Real-Time Distributed Control (1st ed.). Springer-Verlag Berlin Heidelberg.

Martin, M., & Schmidt, R. A. (2014, May 31). *Communications: The smart grid enabling technology*. SmartGrid.gov. Retrieved from https://www.smartgrid.gov/files/NRECA_DOE_Communications_1.pdf

McDaniel, P., & McLaughlin, S. (2009). Security and privacy challenges in the smart grid. *IEEE Security and Privacy*, *7*(3), 75–77. doi:10.1109/MSP.2009.76

Moghe, R., Iyer, A. R., Lambert, F. C., & Divan, D. (2015, March). A Low-Cost Electric Field Energy Harvester for an MV/HV Asset-Monitoring Smart Sensor. *IEEE Transactions on Industry Applications*, *51*(2), 1828–1836. doi:10.1109/TIA.2014.2354741

Mohemed, R. E., Saleh, A. I., Abdelrazzak, M., & Samra, A. S. (2016, December). Energy-efficient routing protocols for solving energy hole problem in wireless sensor networks. *Computer Networks*.

Moness, M., & Moustafa, A. M. (2016, April). A Survey of cyber-physical advances and challenges of wind energy conversion systems: prospects for internet of energy. *IEEE Internet of Things Journal, 3*(2), 134–145. doi:10.1109/JIOT.2015.2478381

Moreno-Garcia, I. M., Pallares-Lopez, V., Gonzalez-Redondo, M., Lopez-Lopez, J., Varo-Martinez, M., & Santiago, I. (2015, March). Implementation of a real time monitoring system for a grid-connected PV park. In *Proceedings of the 2015 IEEE International Conference on Industrial Technology (ICIT)* (pp. 2915-2920). doi:10.1109/ICIT.2015.7125528

Mossé, D., & Gadola, G. (2012, June). Controlling wind harvesting with wireless sensor networks. In *Proceedings of the 2012 International Green Computing Conference (IGCC)* (pp. 1-6). doi:10.1109/IGCC.2012.6322285

Mues, M. O., Alvarez, A., Espinoza, A., & Garbajosa, J. (2011, July). Towards a distributed intelligent ICT architecture for the smart grid. In *Proceedings of the 2011 9th IEEE International Conference on Industrial Informatics* (pp. 745-749). doi:10.1109/INDIN.2011.6034985

Nafi, N. S., Ahmed, K., Gregory, M. A., & Datta, M. (2016, October). A Survey of Smart Grid Architectures, Applications, Benefits and Standardization. *Journal of Network and Computer Applications, 76*, 1–21. doi:10.1016/j.jnca.2016.10.003

Nanda, A. K., & Panigrahi, C. K. (2016, July). Review on smart home energy management. *International Journal of Ambient Energy, 37*(5), 541–546. doi:10.1080/01430750.2015.1004107

Ndjiongue, A. R., Ferreira, H. C., & Shongwe, T. (2016). Inter-building PLC-VLC integration based on PSK and CSK techniques. In *Proceedings of the 2016 International Symposium on Power Line Communications and its Applications (ISPLC)* (pp. 31-36). IEEE. doi:10.1109/ISPLC.2016.7476254

Nguyen, L.-L., Nguyen, M.-T., Cuong, L. Q., & Nguyen, T.-D. (2016, January). On the design of wireless Smart Grid network for an apartment building based on 868 MHz low power wireless SoC. In *Proceedings of the 2015 International Conference on Advanced Technologies for Communications (ATC)* (pp. 456-461). IEEE.

Nunes, B. A., Mendonca, M., Nguyen, X. N., Obraczka, K., & Turletti, T. (2014). A Survey of Software-Defined Networking: Past, Present, and Future of Programmable Networks. *IEEE Communications Surveys and Tutorials, 16*(3), 1617–1634. doi:10.1109/SURV.2014.012214.00180

Paoletti, G. J., & Herman, G. (2015). Monitoring of electrical equipment failure indicators and zero-planned outages: Past, present and future maintenance practices. In *Proceedings of the IEEE Conference Record of Annual Pulp and Paper Industry Technical Conference*. doi:10.1109/PPIC.2015.7165712

Rani, S., Malhotra, J., Talwar, R., & Ahmed, S. H. (2017, January). Energy Efficient Chain Based Routing Protocol for Underwater Wireless Sensor Networks. *Journal of Network and Computer Applications*.

Salazar-Llinas, A., Ginart, A., & Restrepo, C. (2014). Observer based sensor fault tolerant for grid tied - Solar inverters. In *Proceedings of the IEEE Green Technologies Conference* (pp. 69-74). doi:10.1109/GREENTECH.2014.16

Sangwan, A., Singh, R., & Sawant, P. (2016, April). Coverage and connectivity preserving routing in wireless sensor networks: A new approach. In *Proceedings of the 2016 International Conference on Computing, Communication and Automation (ICCCA)* (pp. 503-509). doi:10.1109/CCAA.2016.7813771

Sanz, A., Pinero, P. J., Idiago, J. M., Esteban, S., & Garcia, J. I. (2014, Nov). Narrowband power line communications evaluation in complex distribution networks. In *Proceedings of the 2014 IEEE International Conference on Smart Grid Communications (SmartGridComm)* (pp. 266-271). doi:10.1109/SmartGridComm.2014.7007657

Saputro, N., Akkaya, K., & Guvenc, I. (2015, October). Privacy-aware communication protocol for hybrid IEEE 802.11s/LTE Smart Grid architectures. In *Proceedings of the 2015 IEEE 40th Local Computer Networks Conference Workshops (LCN Workshops)* (pp. 905-911). doi:10.1109/LCNW.2015.7365945

Sarkar, A., & Senthil Murugan, T. (2016, December). Routing protocols for wireless sensor networks: What the literature says? *Alexandria Engineering Journal, 55*(4), 3173–3183. doi:10.1016/j.aej.2016.08.003

S&C electric company. (2017). *S&C electric company*. Retrieved from Solutions for Self-Healing Grids: https://www.sandc.com/en/solutions/self-healing-grids/

Schmidt, N. P. (1999, October). Comparison between IEEE and CIGRE ampacity standards. *IEEE Transactions on Power Delivery, 14*(4), 1555–1559. doi:10.1109/61.796253

Semedo, S. M., Oliveira, J. E., & Cardoso, F. J. (2014, June). Remote monitoring of high-voltage disconnect switches in electrical distribution substations. In *Proceedings of the 2014 IEEE 23rd International Symposium on Industrial Electronics (ISIE)* (pp. 2060-2064). doi:10.1109/ISIE.2014.6864934

Sentient Energy. (2017). *MM3 Intelligent Sensor*. Retrieved from Sentient Energy: http://www.sentient-energy.com/mm3-intelligent-sensor/

Sha, K., Alatrash, N., & Wang, Z. (2016). A Secure and Efficient Framework to Read Isolated Smart Grid Devices. *IEEE Transactions on Smart Grid*. doi:10.1109/TSG.2016.2526045

Siemens. (2017). *Substation Automation*.

Smith, T. B. (2004). Electricity theft: A comparative analysis. *Energy Policy, 32*(18), 2067–2076. doi:10.1016/S0301-4215(03)00182-4

Song, Y., Zhou, G., & Zhu, Y. (2013). Present status and challenges of big data processing in smart grid. *Power System Technology, 37*, 927–935.

Sood, V. K., Fischer, D., Eklund, J. M., & Brown, T. (2009). Developing a communication infrastructure for the smart grid. In *Proceedings of the 2009 IEEE Electrical Power and Energy Conference*. doi:10.1109/EPEC.2009.5420809

IEEE Std. 2030-2011. (2011, January). *IEEE Guide for Smart Grid Interoperability of Energy Technology and Information Technology Operation with the Electric Power System (EPS), End-Use Applications, and Loads*. Retrieved from http://ieeexplore.ieee.org/stampPDF/getPDF.jsp?arnumber=6018239

Stojkoska, B. L., & Trivodaliev, K. V. (2017, January). A review of Internet of Things for smart home: Challenges and solutions. *Journal of Cleaner Production, 140*, 1454–1464. doi:10.1016/j.jclepro.2016.10.006

Taqqali, W. M., & Abdulaziz, N. (2010, December). Smart Grid and demand response technology. In *Proceedings of the 2010 IEEE International Energy Conference (ENERGYCON 2010)* (pp. 710-715). IEEE. doi:10.1109/ENERGYCON.2010.5771773

The Smart Grid Interoperability Panel. (2010). *Introduction to NISTIR 7628 guidelines for smart grid cybersecurity*. U.S. Department of Energy.

Titouna, C., Aliouat, M., & Gueroui, M. (2016). FDS: Fault detection scheme for wireless sensor networks. *Wireless Personal Communications, 86*(2), 549–562. doi:10.1007/s11277-015-2944-7

US Department of Commerce. (2014). NIST Special Publication 1108.

Vo, M. T., Nguyen, M. T., Nguyen, T. D., Le, C. T., & Huynh, H. T. (2013, Oct). Towards residential smart grid: A practical design of wireless sensor network and Mini-Web server based low cost home energy monitoring system. In *Proceedings of the 2013 International Conference on Advanced Technologies for Communications (ATC 2013)* (pp. 540-545). doi:10.1109/ATC.2013.6698174

Vukojevic, A., Laval, S., & Handley, J. (2015, Feb). An integrated utility microgrid test site ecosystem optimized by an open interoperable distributed intelligence platform. In *Proceedings of the 2015 IEEE Power Energy Society Innovative Smart Grid Technologies Conference (ISGT)*. doi:10.1109/ISGT.2015.7131852

Vyatkin, V., Zhabelova, G., Yang, C. W., McComas, D., & Chouinard, J. (2012, September). Intelligent IEC 61850/61499 logical nodes for smart metering. In *Proceedings of the 2012 IEEE Energy Conversion Congress and Exposition (ECCE)* (pp. 1220-1227). doi:10.1109/ECCE.2012.6342677

Wan, Z., Wang, G., Yang, Y., & Shi, S. (2014, December). SKM: Scalable Key Management for Advanced Metering Infrastructure in Smart Grids. *IEEE Transactions on Industrial Electronics, 61*(12), 7055–7066. doi:10.1109/TIE.2014.2331014

Wang, K., Wang, Y., Sun, Y., Guo, S., & Wu, J. (2016). Green Industrial Internet of Things Architecture: An Energy-Efficient Perspective. *IEEE Communications Magazine, 54*(12), 48–54. doi:10.1109/MCOM.2016.1600399CM

Wei, M., Hong, S. H., & Alam, M. (2016, February). An IoT-based energy-management platform for industrial facilities. *Applied Energy, 164*, 607–619. doi:10.1016/j.apenergy.2015.11.107

Werbos, P. J. (2011, August). Computational Intelligence for the Smart Grid-History, Challenges, and Opportunities. *IEEE Computational Intelligence Magazine, 6*(3), 14–21. doi:10.1109/MCI.2011.941587

Wickelgren, I. J. (1996, September). Local-area networks go wireless. *IEEE Spectrum, 33*(9), 34–40. doi:10.1109/6.535256

Yamunadevi, S. P., Vairam, T., Kalaiarasan, C., & Vidya, G. (2012, March). Efficient comparison of multipath routing protocols in WSN. In *Proceedings of the 2012 International Conference on Computing, Electronics and Electrical Technologies (ICCEET)* (pp. 807-811). doi:10.1109/ICCEET.2012.6203845

Yan, Y., Qian, Y., Sharif, H., & Tipper, D. (2012). A Survey on Cyber Security for Smart Grid Communications. *IEEE Communications Surveys & Tutorials, 14*, 998-1010.

Yan, Y., Qian, Y., Sharif, H., & Tipper, D. (2013). A survey on smart grid communication infrastructures: Motivations, requirements and challenges. *IEEE Communications Surveys and Tutorials, 15*(1), 5–20. doi:10.1109/SURV.2012.021312.00034

Yang, C. W., Zhabelova, G., Vyatkin, V., Nair, N. K., & Apostolov, A. (2012, July). Smart Grid automation: Distributed protection application with IEC61850/IEC61499. In *Proceedings of the IEEE 10th International Conference on Industrial Informatics* (pp. 1067-1072). doi:10.1109/INDIN.2012.6301145

Yang, Y., Lambert, F., & Divan, D. (2007). A survey on technologies for implementing sensor networks for power delivery systems. In *Proceedings of the EEE Power Engineering Society General Meeting* (pp. 1-8). doi:10.1109/PES.2007.386289

Ye, F., Qian, Y., & Hu, R. Q. (2014, Dec). A security protocol for advanced metering infrastructure in smart grid. In *Proceedings of the 2014 IEEE Global Communications Conference* (pp. 649-654). doi:10.1109/GLOCOM.2014.7036881

Yi, S., Hao, Z., Qin, Z., & Li, Q. (2015, Nov). Fog Computing: Platform and Applications. In *Proceedings of the 2015 Third IEEE Workshop on Hot Topics in Web Systems and Technologies (HotWeb)* (pp. 73-78). doi:10.1109/HotWeb.2015.22

Yu, K., Arifuzzaman, M., Wen, Z., Zhang, D., & Sato, T. (2015, August). A Key Management Scheme for Secure Communications of Information Centric Advanced Metering Infrastructure in Smart Grid. *IEEE Transactions on Instrumentation and Measurement, 64*(8), 2072–2085. doi:10.1109/TIM.2015.2444238

Yu, R., Zhang, Y., Gjessing, S., Yuen, C., Xie, S., & Guizani, M. (2011, September). Cognitive radio based hierarchical communications infrastructure for smart grid. *IEEE Network, 25*(5), 6–14. doi:10.1109/MNET.2011.6033030

Zanella, A., Bui, N., Castellani, A., Vangelista, L., & Zorzi, M. (2014, February). Internet of Things for Smart Cities. *IEEE Internet of Things Journal, 1*(1), 22–32. doi:10.1109/JIOT.2014.2306328

Zhang, B., & Baillieul, J. (2016). Control and Communication Protocols Based on Packetized Direct Load Control in Smart Building Microgrids. *Proceedings of the IEEE, 104*(4), 837–857. doi:10.1109/JPROC.2016.2520759

Zhou, B., Li, W., Chan, K. W., Cao, Y., Kuang, Y., Liu, X., & Wang, X. (2016, August). Smart home energy management systems: Concept, configurations, and scheduling strategies. *Renewable & Sustainable Energy Reviews, 61*, 30–40. doi:10.1016/j.rser.2016.03.047

This research was previously published in the International Journal of Embedded and Real-Time Communication Systems (IJERTCS), 8(2); edited by Sergey Balandin, pages 40-65, copyright year 2017 by IGI Publishing (an imprint of IGI Global).

Chapter 17

Smart XSS Attack Surveillance System for OSN in Virtualized Intelligence Network of Nodes of Fog Computing

Shashank Gupta
National Institute of Technology, Kurukshetra, India

B. B. Gupta
National Institute of Technology Kurukshtra, India

ABSTRACT

This article introduces a distributed intelligence network of Fog computing nodes and Cloud data centres for smart devices against XSS vulnerabilities in Online Social Network (OSN). The cloud data centres compute the features of JavaScript, injects them in the form of comments and saved them in the script nodes of Document Object Model (DOM) tree. The network of Fog devices re-executes the feature computation and comment injection process in the HTTP response message and compares such comments with those calculated in the cloud data centres. Any divergence observed will simply alarm the signal of injection of XSS worms on the nodes of fog located at the edge of the network. The mitigation of such worms is done by executing the nested context-sensitive sanitization on the malicious variables of JavaScript code embedded in such worms. The prototype of the authors' work was developed in Java development framework and installed on the virtual machines of Cloud data centres (typically located at the core of network) and the nodes of Fog devices (exclusively positioned at the edge of network). Vulnerable OSN-based web applications were utilized for evaluating the XSS worm detection capability of the authors' framework and evaluation results revealed that their work detects the injection of XSS worms with high precision rate and less rate of false positives and false negatives.

DOI: 10.4018/978-1-5225-5649-7.ch017

1. INTRODUCTION

1.1. Fog Computing

A new virtualized platform (i.e. Fog Computing) is developed that outspreads the infrastructure of cloud platforms to the edge of the network (Bonomi et al., 2012). Fog computing performs the computation of resources in the edge of the network (very close to the ground). It generally performs its computation between the cloud data centres and the network of smart devices. Figure 1 highlights the three-way hierarchy, that clearly highlights the devices of fog computing will be act as an intermediary nodes between the cloud data centres and the network of end smart devices (Stojmenovic et al., 2014). The arrow 'location' highlights the location of smart devices that are positioned at an edge (close to the ground level) of an associated network. The cloud data centres and its related applications are located at the core of the network (which is very far away from the edge of network) (Almorsy et al., 2016; Mather et al., 2009; Modi et al., 2013). The fog devices (possibly a router, a remote machine, etc.) acts as an intermediary between the distributed intelligence network of cloud data centres and smart devices.

1.2. Cross-Site Scripting (XSS) Attack

XSS vulnerabilities are considered to be the topmost threat that have turned out to be a plague for the modern web applications like facebook, twitter, linkedIn, etc. (Gupta et al., 2015a, 2015b, 2014). Such worms steal the sensitive credentials of the active users by injecting the malicious JavaScript code in the form of some posts on such web applications. The statistics of acunetix web application vulnerability report 2015 (Acunetix Web Application Vulnerability Report, 2015) clearly reveals that nearly 38% of web sites were vulnerable to XSS attacks and falls first in the list. In addition, the statistics of 2015 website security statistics report by white hat (Website Security Statistics Report, 2015) undoubtedly discloses that XSS was a significant issue across all platforms of diverse languages utilized by modern web applications. Figure 2 illustrates the simple scenario of exploitation of XSS attack on the web server installed on the backbone of Fog device.

Figure 1. A three-level hierarchy

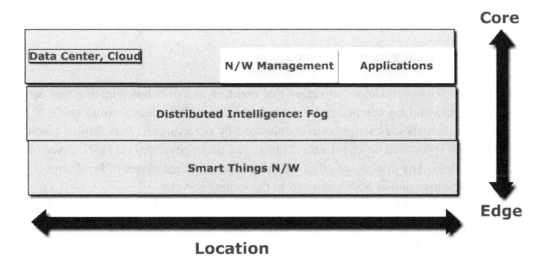

Figure 2. A scenario of XSS attack on fog

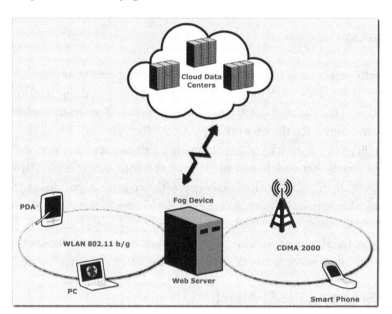

Here, web server is deployed on the node of Fog computing, that acts as an intermediary between the data centres of cloud platforms and the network of smart end devices (placed at the edge of the network). The malicious smart devices can also inject the vulnerable JavaScript code on this Fog device that can also be replicated to the cloud data centres. Later on, such vulnerable piece of JavaScript code will get fetched by the smart devices network. The XSS attack will get exploited on the web browsers of smart devices on the execution of this suspicious JavaScript code (Gupta et al., 2017a, 2017b). The speciality of such vulnerable strings of JavaScript is that they simply replicate themselves onto the different adjacent nodes of Fog network and data centres of Cloud computing. Figure 3 highlights the detailed pattern of exploitation of XSS attack on the OSN web server deployed at the fog computing network. The exploitation of XSS attack will get executed on the web browser of smart devices and the credentials (cookies, password, etc.) of the victim are being re-directed to the attacker's domain.

1.3. Our Contributions

The key contributions of our work are as follows:

- A novel XSS defensive model is introduced that executes in a distributed intelligence network of cloud data centres and fog computing for defending against XSS vulnerabilities on OSN;
- The detection of malicious script code is enhanced by detecting the variation in comments of JavaScript code (produced on cloud data centres) and those generated on OSN server (deployed on the fog device). Any divergence observed in both these values of sets of JavaScript comments will indicate the injection of XSS worms from the remote servers;
- New XSS attack vector repositories are utilized for evaluating the XSS worm injection capability on the tested platforms of OSN-based Web applications. Recent work only refers the XSS cheat sheet for assessing the detection proficiency of malicious script injection on non-OSN-based web applications;

Figure 3. Exploitation of XSS attack on fog devices

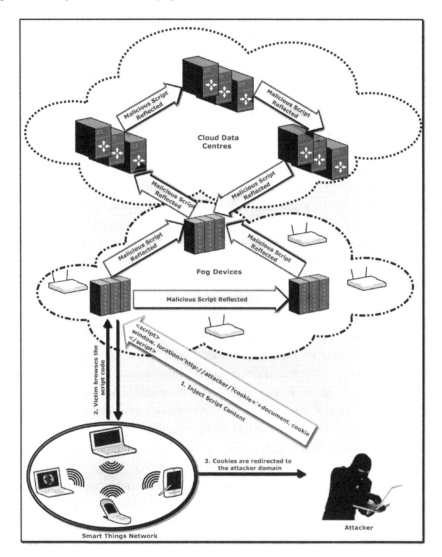

- We also utilized the capabilities of statistical methods (e.g. F-Test and F-Measure) for assessing and validating the XSS worm detection capability of our framework;
- Recent browser-resident XSS filters were utilized for comparing the values of F-Measure on different platforms of Web applications with our framework. Recent techniques only compare the XSS attack detection capability with other work without utilizing such robust statistical methods. In addition, our framework is capable enough to detect HTML5 XSS attack vectors in comparison to recent state-of-art.

The next section discusses our work in detail. The rest of the paper is organized as follows: Section 2 discusses the key contributions of recent related work along with their research gaps that are handled in our work. In section 3, we have introduced our work in detail. Implementation and evaluation of our work are discussed in section 4. Finally, section 5 concludes our work and discusses further scope of work.

2. RELATED WORK

Recently, we proposed two XSS defensive solutions (Gupta et al., 2015c; Gupta et al., 2016a) that detects and mitigates the propagation of XSS worms from different platforms of web applications. The technique repeatedly injects the feature content, generate rules, and insert sanitization routines for the discovery of XSS attacks. However, the totality and accuracy of extracted features of JavaScript could not be assured.

Sanitization of JavaScript attack payloads was considered to be the most effective mechanism for obstructing the exploitation of XSS worms on diverse platforms of web applications (Livshits et al., 2013; Samuel et al., 2011; Gupta et al., 2016d, 2016e). However, our recent work (Gupta et al., 2016b, 2016c) sanitized such malicious payloads by determining their single level of context (Livshits et al., 2013; Samuel et al., 2011; Gupta et al., 2016d, 2016e). They did not determine the nested context of JavaScript variables. Sanitizing the malicious tags/attributes of JavaScript without determining their different nested context is considered to be ineffective as such attributes execute differently in different nested contexts. Nested context-aware sanitization is deliberated as the utmost effective methodology for determining the diverse context of malicious attributes of HTML/JavaScript and accordingly injects the sanitization primitive routines on them. Recently, numerous researchers introduced an efficient method of context-aware sanitization of suspicious variables of JavaScript code. Livshits (Livshits et al., 2013) proposed an automated technique of sanitizer placement by statically analysing the stream of infected data in the program. However, placement of sanitizer was static and sometimes changes to dynamic wherever required. The technique accurately sanitized the string values and shrinks the quantity of nodes that involves the need for instrumentation. This technique presumed every possible source, sinks and sanitizers to be identified in advance, and then tried to position them mutually successfully. Samuel (Samuel et al., 2011) proposed a type-qualifier based method that can be utilized with present templating languages to attain context sensitive auto-sanitization. The proposed system builds an automated scheme that offers a template and a collection of sanitizers, repeatedly sanitizes every untrusted injected input via sanitizer that corresponds to the context in which it is delivered.

The XSS worm detection capability of frameworks of existing literature were usually tested and evaluated by referring the XSS attack vectors from single source repository (i.e. XSS cheat sheet (RSnake, 2008)). However, there are four other XSS attack vector repositories (namely HTML5 Security Cheat Sheet, 523 XSS vectors available, Technical Attack Sheet for Cross Site Penetration Tests, @XSS Vector Twitter Account) (HTML5 Security Cheat, n. d.; 523 XSS vectors available, n. d.; Technical Attack Sheet for Cross Site Penetration Tests, n. d.; @XSS Vector Twitter Account, n. d.) (that includes the list of XSS attack vectors specially designed for OSN platforms) available on the Internet. Therefore, the XSS worm detection capability of robust solution must be evaluated by referring the XSS attack vectors from other four contemporary repositories. Most of the existing XSS defensive solutions were tested and evaluated on the tested bed of open source non-OSN based web applications. In addition, very few existing defensive frameworks were tested on the real-world platforms of OSN-based web applications. On the other hand, some of the recent frameworks demanded major alterations in the existing infrastructure of web applications. Moreover, the setup of existing framework of XSS defensive solutions couldn't be easily integrated in the virtual machines of data centres of Cloud and nodes of Fog computing. Instead of referring the outdated Internet settings for constructing an expensive setup, numerous commercial IT organizations are accessing the services of OSN sites (such as Twitter, Facebook, LinkedIn, etc.) on the cloud platforms. Hence, the infrastructure settings of framework solution must be capable enough to integrate in the settings of virtualized platforms of Fog computing and should evaluate the XSS worm recognition capability on such platforms.

3. PROPOSED SMART XSS ATTACK MONITORING SYSTEM

This article presents an enhanced XSS defensive framework that obstructs the execution of vulnerable JavaScript strings injected in the web applications of OSN that are deployed in the distributed intelligence network of virtualized server nodes of Fog. The key innovation behind our work is that it not only executes the sanitization on the suspicious script code but also computes the comments of JavaScript code in Cloud data centres. Such comments of JavaScript code will get injected in the OSN server of Fog distributed network. The OSN server deployed in the end Fog device will re-compute the comments of JavaScript code embedded in the HTTP response. Any variation reflected in these comments of JavaScript code and those pre-computed comments of JavaScript code will simply indicate the injection of XSS worm in the OSN server deployed in the Fog device. Hereafter, the context of the malicious variables encapsulated in such worms will be determined and subsequently performs the sanitization on them. Finally, the sanitized HTTP response is transmitted to the network of smart devices. The next sub-section discusses the abstract view of our framework.

3.1. Abstract Outline

The proposed framework executes in two modes: learning and online mode. Figure 4 highlights the abstract overview of our framework.

All the four modules (i.e. web page tracing, input field exploration, JavaScript string extraction and JavaScript comment injection) are deployed in the offline cloud data centres. The web page tracing module performs the crawling on different extracted modules of HTML5 web application. The output of this module is a Context Flow Graph (CFG) that will be utilized by input field exploration component for the extraction of vulnerable and hidden injection points. Such points will be explored for the vulnerable JavaScript strings by utilizing the JavaScript string extraction component. The JavaScript comment injection will compute the comments of extracted strings of JavaScript code and append such content in the HTTP response messages. The injection of comments of such JavaScript strings does not alter the behaviour of HTTP response messages. Finally, the JavaScript code with appended comments is injected in the OSN server deployed in the network of Fog device. On the other hand, the OSN server deployed in the distributed network of fog device will re-compute the comments of JavaScript code and inject them in the HTTP response message. Now, this re-computed set of JavaScript will be compared against those computed set (and injected) earlier on the cloud data centre. Any variation observed in both these sets will simple indicate the injection of XSS worm by comment divergence detector. Later on, the taint flow examiner will analyse the tainted flow of variables of JavaScript code. Finally, context-aware sanitization component will determine the different context of such illicit variables of JavaScript code and accordingly performs the sanitization on them for the safe interpretation of HTTP response on the web browsers of smart devices. Figure 5 highlights the detailed execution flow of both the modes of our approach.

Figure 4. Abstract overview of our framework

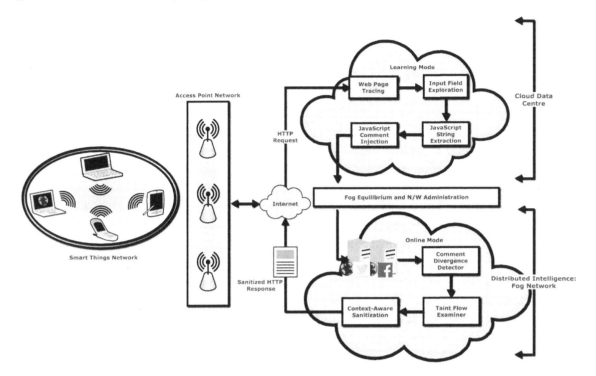

3.2. Smart XSS Surveillance System

In this article, we introduced a smart XSS attack monitoring system that operates in the distributed monitoring infrastructure of virtualized nodes of Fog computing environment and Cloud data centres. Figure 6 highlights the overview of structure of smart XSS attack monitoring system. The key goal of the offline cloud data centres is to calculate and inject the comments of JavaScript code in the existing infrastructure of HTML5 web applications. Here, the cloud data centres will execute in offline mode and will crawl the extracted web application modules for the extraction of vulnerable input fields.

The input fields will be explored for the embedded JavaScript strings of diverse contexts. The cloud data centres will compute the comments of JavaScript strings and append such comments in their source code. Finally, the JavaScript code with injected comments is transmitted to the XSS Attack Detection Server (XSSADS) deployed in the network of end Fog devices. Such end devices will generate the HTTP response (containing JavaScript code with comments) corresponding to the HTTP request and will re-compute the comments of JavaScript code encapsulated in HTTP response messages. This re-calculation is done for the detection of injection of XSS worms on the OSN server integrated in the end devices of fog network. Any variation observed in the JavaScript comments computed on cloud data centres and re-calculated on the XSSADS of fog network will simply indicate the injection of malicious JavaScript code. Finally, XSSADS will find out the context of suspicious variables, subsequently inject the sanitization primitive routines on them and transmit the safe sanitized HTTP response to the edge of the network of smart devices.

Figure 5. Detailed flowcharts of both the modes of our approach

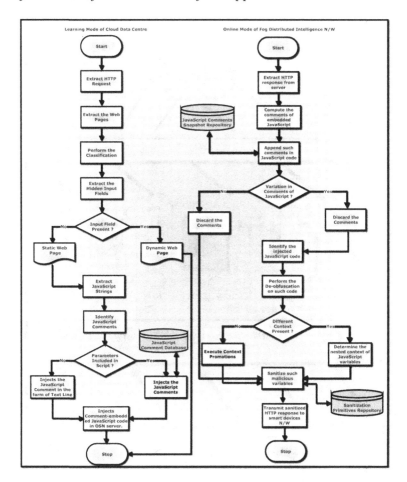

3.3. Modes of Smart XSS Monitoring System

This sub-section discusses the detailed arrangement setup of our distributed intelligence network of Cloud data centres and Fog devices deployed for the smart XSS attack monitoring system on the OSN. Figure 7 highlights the detailed infrastructure-setup of key modules integrated in this network. Here, note that, the modules deployed in the virtual machines of Cloud data centres will operate in learning mode. It completely operates in offline mode for injecting the comments of JavaScript code in the source code of HTML5 web applications. On the other hand, the modules deployed in the end Fog devices of XSSADS will operate in online mode on the reception of HTTP request from the network of smart end devices.

3.3.1. Learning Mode of Cloud Data Centres

This mode operates in offline phase on the virtual machines of Cloud data centres. It manages to perform the scanning on the extracted modules of HTML for extracting the vulnerable input fields and the associated injected JavaScript strings. This mode further calculates the comments of JavaScript code that are non-executable in nature and append them in the source code of web applications. Algorithm 1

Figure 6. Proposed smart XSS attack monitoring system in the virtualized network of fog computing

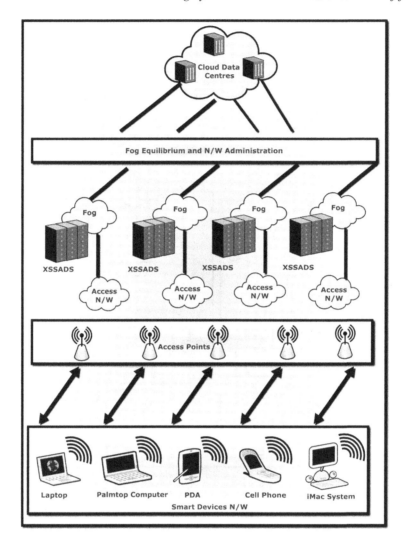

illustrates the detailed execution of this mode executed on the data centres of Cloud platforms. Algorithm 1 operates as follows: Initially, each $HREQ_I$ is provided as a parameter to Web_Page_Scanning () function that will output a graph consisting of 'V' vertices and 'E' edges. This output graph will be passed as an argument to the Input_Field_Analysis() method for the extraction of set of collection of vulnerable input fields IF_log. Such suspicious input fields will be explored for retrieving the strings of JavaScript by passing the address of such fields in the JS_link_Extraction () function. This function will output the collection of JavaScript strings stored in variable JS_L rep. The JavaScript_Comment_Injection () method will take this variable as parameter and compute the comments of associated piece of JavaScript code. This mode also facilitates with the injection of Nonce with each comment identifier. This was done to ensure the uniqueness of injected comments in the OSN server deployed in the distributed network of fog.

Algorithm 1. Learning mode of cloud data centres

Input: HTTP request (HREQ$_1$, HREQ$_2$, ------- HREQ$_N$) extracted from smart things network.
Start
For each extracted HREQ$_I$
Plot_graph(V, E) ← Web_Page_Scanning(HREQ$_I$);
IF_log ← Input_Field_Analysis (Plot_graph(V, E));
JS$_L$_rep ← JS_Link_Extraction(IF_log);
JSL$_I$ ← JavaScript_Comment _Injection (JS$_L$rep);
Cont ← context(JSL$_I$);
Inject (Nonce$_I$, Identifier) at JSL$_I$ in CI_rep;
JS$_L$_rep ← JSL$_I$ ∪ JS$_L$_rep;
End for each
ReturnJS$_L$_rep to the OSN server at Fog network;
End

3.3.2. Online Mode of Virtualized Network of Fog Computing

This mode executes on the distributed intelligence network of Fog computing only after the instrumentation of JavaScript code on the Cloud data centres. It re-calculates the comments of JavaScript code encapsulated in the HTTP response message and compares the pre-calculated value of comments (computed on cloud data centres) with the post-calculated comments (computed in online mode of fog network). The injection of XSS worms on the OSN server (deployed on the fog device) will be detected by observing the variation in these two computed set of JavaScript comments. JavaScript without comments found in the HTTP response message will also indicate the injection of XSS worms on the online mode of fog network. The illicit JavaScript variables embedded in such worms will be determined by analysing their tainted flow and consequently determines their diverse contexts. Finally, the injection of advanced sanitization routine functions will be performed on such suspicious variables of JavaScript code for the safe interpretation of HTTP response on the network of smart devices. Algorithm 2 illustrates the execution flow of online mode of distributed network of Fog computing.

The working of Algorithm 2 is as follows: Initially, Comment_Injection() is invoked by passing an extracted HRES$_I$ from the OSN server. This function will re-calculate the comments of JavaScript strings and inject them in the HRES$_I$. Hereafter, the variation in the JavaScript comments will be detected by invoking the function Comment_Variation_Detector () by simply passing the addresses of two arguments (i.e. HRES$_I$ and JS$_L$rep). JS$_L$rep points to the JavaScript code with embedded comments computed on the modules of cloud data centres. HRES$_I$ points to the JavaScript code with comments calculated on the OSN server during online mode of fog. If no variation is detected, simply transmit the HRES$_I$ (by discarding its comments optionally) to the network of fog devices. Else, the HRES$_I$ will be passed as parameter to the Taint_analyzer () function, that will return the addresses of tainted variables T$_{JS}$ of JavaScript embedded in HRES$_I$. The de-obfuscation () function will decode the value of T$_{JS}$ and store their de-obfuscated version in D$_{JS}$. Now, D$_{JS}$ is passed an argument to the Context_Recognizer () function for determining the diverse context of D$_{JS}$ and store it in a repository Cont. The repository stores

Algorithm 2. Online mode of distributed intelligence network of Fog computing

Input: Set of extracted HTTP request (HREQ$_1$, HREQ$_2$,------ HREQ$_N$)
Output: Sanitized HTTP response (HRES$_1$, HRES$_2$,----------- HRES$_N$)
Start
For each HTTP request as HREQ$_I$
Generate HRES$_I$;
<HRES$_I$, JS$_{L\_}$rep> ← Comment_Injection(H$_{RES}$);
HRES$_I$ ← Comment_Variation_Detector(HRES$_I$,JS$_{L\_}$rep);
If (HRES$_I$ does not contain divergence in JavaScript comments) **then**
return HRES$_I$;
Else
T$_{JS}$ ← Taint_Analyzer(HRES$_I$);
D$_{JS}$ ← de-obfuscation(T$_{JS}$);
Cont ← Context_Recognizer(D$_{JS}$);
S$_{AC}$ ← Sanitization (Cont);
Inject each sanitized variable in HRES$_I$;
return HRES$_I$;
End else
End for each
End

all possible different context of D$_{JS}$. Finally, the injection of sanitization primitive units is carried out by invoking the function Sanitization () on this extracted repository. This function will return the safe sanitized HRES$_I$ (possibly without comments) to the network of end smart devices.

3.4. Components of Smart XSS Monitoring System

The components deployed in the detailed infrastructure setup of our smart XSS monitoring system (shown in Figure 7) executes in learning mode and online mode.

The components deployed in the learning mode of Cloud data centres will execute in offline phase. While, those deployed in the online mode of virtualized network of Fog computing environment will execute in online mode. Following are some of the details of our components deployed in both these modes.

3.4.1. Web Page Scanning

This is the first component that performs the scanning of the HTML5 web application modules for the extraction of all the HTML5 web pages and save them for further classification. It has two key sub-components: crawler and web page classification. The crawler crawls the web application modules with the help of a selenium-based crawler. Initially, it uproots all the internal and external Uniform Resource Identifier (URI) links and then transmits the web pages to web page classification sub-component. The input to this module is an extracted web page retrieved by the crawler. This sub-component again parses

Figure 7. Detailed infrastructure setup of our smart XSS monitoring system

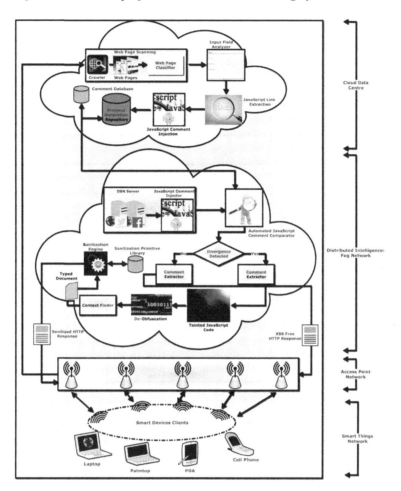

the web page to check whether web page include any input field or not, namely search box, comment field. It main aim is to classify the web page into two categories: dynamic web page and static web page.

If the requested web page falls under the category of dynamic web page then, it is transmitted to the input field analyser module for further processing. Algorithm 3 highlights the algorithm implemented for this module for the extraction of web pages. This algorithm works as follows: URL_rep is the list to store the internal URL links presents in the HTML5 web page, HP_log is a database to hold the HTML5 web pages corresponding to the extracted module. Initially, for each requested M_I, W_I holds the web page. Then, it crawl the web page and extracts the embedded URL link in URL_L, up to the threshold level ψ and stores all extracted URLs in URL_rep. Finally, for each stored $URL_L \in URL\_rep$, we retrieve the web page HPand store them in HP_log. Then, it returns HP_log as its output to the next module (i.e. input field analyser) of the cloud data centre.

Algorithm 3. HTML5 web pages extraction

Input: Series of web application modules (M_1, M_2, M_3, ------ M_N)
Output: Extracted HTML5 web pages
Threshold $\psi \leftarrow 0$;
Start
URL_rep $\leftarrow \varphi$;
HP_log $\leftarrow \varphi$;
For i $\leftarrow$ 1 to ψ
For each extracted M_I
$W_I \leftarrow$ Retrieve web page from crawler;
$URL_L \leftarrow$ Web_Spider(W_I);
URL_rep $\leftarrow URL_L \cup$ URL_rep;
End For Each
For Each $URL_L \in$ URL_rep
HP $\leftarrow$ Retrieve web page $\stackrel{\wedge}{=} URL_L$;
HP_log $\leftarrow$ HP $\cup$ HP_log;
End For each
End
Return HP_log
End

3.4.2. Input Field Analyzer

This module is responsible for the identification of vulnerable input fields in the extracted HTML5 web pages where an attacker may inject malicious code to launch XSS attack. This is achieved by monitoring all malicious contexts in the HTML document with the help of HTML malicious context directory. Algorithm 4 describes the algorithm implemented for accomplishing the functionality of this component. In this algorithm, randomly generated threshold (ψ) is used to crawl different levels of the web pages W_p. It uses URL_rep to store all crawled URLs, IF_log for recording all identified injection points and HP_log to store all the crawled web pages of the web site. URL_rep is initialized with the URL of the W_p. Therefore, for each URL $\in$ URL_rep, it retrieves all HTML5 web pages W_I in HP_Log and stores its URL (URL_J) in URL_rep. Finally, it extracts the entire malicious context as the input fields in the web page W_I and store the input fields (IF_J) in the IF_Log.

Algorithm 4. Suspicious input field detection in HTML5 web pages

Input: URLs of extracted web pages W_p (URL_1, URL_2,------URL_N)
Output: Collection of input fields of retrieved web pages.
Threshold (ψ):= 0
Start
URL_rep $\leftarrow \phi$;
Mal_Con $\leftarrow$ List of different HTML malicious context;
IF_log $\leftarrow \phi$;
HP_log $\leftarrow \phi$;
Initialize:URL_rep $\leftarrow W_p$;
$\psi \leftarrow$ **ranGen();**
$URL_J \leftarrow 0$;
$IF_J \leftarrow 0$;
For J $\leftarrow$ 1 to ψ
For Each URL $\in$ URL_rep
HP_log $\leftarrow W_J$;
Scan suspicious-context(W_I) $\leftrightarrow$ Mal_Con;
$URL_J \leftarrow URL(W_J)$;
$IF_J \leftarrow IF(W_J)$;
URL_rep $\leftarrow URL_J \cup$ URL_rep;
IF_Log $\leftarrow IF_I \cup$ IF_Log
End For Each
End For
Return IF_Log
End

3.4.3. JavaScript Link Extraction

The key goal of this module is to extract the JavaScript code embedded in the extracted input fields. This module is responsible for the extraction of external JavaScript links embedded in the Uniform Resource Identifier (URI) links. Initially, each HTTP response will be checked for embedded parameter values. Such extracted parameter values will be explored for the embedded URI links. The existence of such URI links indicates the remote location of external JavaScript links. It can be usually extracted by transmitting Asynchronous JavaScript XML (AJAX) HTTP request and responses from the remote location of servers.

Algorithm 5 highlights the detailed algorithm of extraction of embedded JavaScript strings. This algorithm restricts the level of crawling of different web pages of the web application, by using a randomly generated threshold (ψ). It maintains JS_L_rep repository to store all crawled URLs. Initially, it retrieves the web page W_p corresponding to the requested URL. Then, it extracts out all the external links embedded in the received web page. Finally, it stores the extracted URLs in the JS_L and produces JS_L_rep as its output.

3.4.4. JavaScript Comment Injection

The key motto of this module is to calculate the comments of JavaScript code embedded in the extracted HTML5 web pages. Algorithm 6 illustrates the algorithm for JavaScript comment injection. This module encapsulates the valid JavaScript code with comment statements that are non-executable. The comment statements comprises of a randomly generated nonce and extracted comments of the valid JavaScript code embedded in the dynamic HTML5 web page. Such comments are wrapped into the protocols and inject such protocols in the comments statement for execution time checking. This module comprises the following key components: Comment Identifier and Protocol Generation. This algorithm works as follows: For each $JSL_i \in JS_L\_rep$, it generates a graphgraph (V, E) by parsing the document.

Then, to extract the JavaScript code comments, firstly, it takes out all embedded JavaScript code. To achieve this, It audits each vertex (v) in the graph (V, E) to check its content. If it is <script> tag, then we extract the content of each node in JS_L_rep that appears during the traversal of unique path, until a

Algorithm 5. Extraction of JavaScript strings embedded in extracted input fields

Input: Set of extracted vulnerable input fields (IF_1, IF_2,-------- IF_N)
Output: JavaScript Links (JS_{L1}, JS_{L2},--------- JS_{LN})
threshold (ψ) :- 0
Start
$JS_L\_rep \leftarrow \phi$;
$\psi \leftarrow$ randomGenerator();
For I $\leftarrow$ 1 to ψ
For each extracted IF_I
$W_p \leftarrow$ webpage $\overset{\wedge}{=} IF_I$
$JS_L \leftarrow$ Web_Spider(W_p); /* traverse internal links*/
$JS_L\_rep \leftarrow JS_L \cup JS_L\_rep$;
End For each
End For
ReturnJS_L_rep;
End

Algorithm 6. JavaScript comment injection in JavaScript strings

Input: Set of extracted JavaScript Links (JS_{L1}, JS_{L2},--------- JS_{LN}
Output: Comment Injected JavaScript Links (CI_rep)
Start
JS_L_rep $\rightarrow$ Extracted JavaScript Link repository;
CI_rep $\rightarrow \varphi$;
JS_L_rep $\rightarrow \varphi$;
For each $JSL_I \in JS_L$_rep
graph(V, E) $\leftarrow$ Parse(JSL_I);
For each $v \in V$
if (v.value != "\<script\>") **then**
Disregard v;
Else
While(v.value!= "\</script\>")
JS_L_rep $\leftarrow$ v.value $\cup$ JS_L_rep;
$v_I \leftarrow$ DFS(v);
End while
End else
End for each
while(JS_L_rep != " ")
For each $JSL_I \in JS_L$_rep
Cont $\leftarrow$ context(JSL_I);
if (Cont == "literal" || Cont == "URI attribute" || Cont == "Obfuscated code") **then**
$Nonce_I \leftarrow$ **random_generator**();
Identifier $\leftarrow$ 1;
Inject ($Nonce_I$, Identifier) at JSL_I in CI_rep;
JS_L_rep $\leftarrow JSL_I \cup JS_L$_rep;
End if
Increment the value of Identifier;
End for each
End for while
End for each
Return CI_rep
End

node with content </script> is found. After this, it starts finding put the unique comments for each extracted JavaScript. For this, it iterates the following process until JS_L_rep is empty. For each $JSL_I \in$ JS_L_rep, it determines the context corresponding to JSL_I. For each context, it firstly generates a random nonce $Nonce_I$ and injects comment comprising $Nonce_I$ and Identifier of the corresponding JavaScript comments. All the modified comments are then stored into JS_L_rep. Finally, it injects the JS_L_rep into the OSN server deployed in the online mode of network of fog devices.

3.4.5. Comment Identifier

It is a component which receives extracted JavaScript code log as its input. The aim of this component is to analyse each script in the log to identify the unique comments. Each JavaScript code string has its own comments to uniquely identify it. These identified comments are then used for the protocol generation. To inject malicious JavaScript code, attacker either modifies the JavaScript function definition written by the programmer or injects a function call to maliciously written function. For instance, consider the code snippet as shown below:

```
<input type="text" name= "username" value="<%request.getParameter("U_name")%>">
```

Here, no filtering mechanism is applied on the username before it is used in the response web page. Thus, this field is vulnerable to the XSS attack. Suppose, an adversary injects a malicious function as: *<script>alert("document.cookie");</script>*. Therefore, the original code becomes *<input type= "text" name= "username" value= "<script>alert("document.cookie");</script>">*. Consequently, when browser renders this response then, cookie information related to the user is shown by an alert box. Therefore, function call and function definition patterns are extracted out from the valid JavaScript code, as its unique feature. Table 1 illustrates some of the examples related to the probable comments of the valid JavaScript code including function call and function definition features.

First example describes the inbuilt function call as Math.pow(4,5), we represent the probable comments as *{pow,2,4,5}*. It means function, named as; pow has 2 parameters 4, 5. Similarly, second example defines a user defined function named active (a, b, c), so the feature is *{active,3,a,b,c}*. Third example shows a nested function call and probable comments for this is *{pro, 2, 3, {pro, 2, 6, 7}}*. Fourth example shows the nested function calling for inbuilt functions. Fifth example shows an anonymous function calling, wherein function pro can be called with the help of a variable X, so, corresponding comment is {X, 2, a, b}. Last example describes function overriding for host object i.e. document.getElementByName and corresponding probable comment is {document.getElementByName, 1, value}.

3.4.5.1. Protocol Generation

It is a server-side component which is responsible for the encapsulation of extracted JavaScript comments in protocol. These protocols are then included in the initial remark statement. This is to ensure that legitimate JavaScript present in the response web page can be properly distinguished from the injected JavaScript code by comparing their comments with ones stored in protocol. Table 2 describes the script code, protocol generation and remark generation. Protocols are stored by using Protocol ID, type, name and paramcount. According to the number of parameters, param field stores the actual parameters. Modified comment statement comprises a nonce and protocol ID as /*N1, 1*/. In function call type, instead of paramcount, we use argcount and arg fields.

Table 1. Extracted probable comments of the valid JavaScript code

Sr. No.	Type	Example	Probable Comments
1.	Inbuilt function call	Math.pow (4,5)	{pow,2,4,5}
2.	User defined function call	function active(a, b, c){..};	{active, 3,a,b}
3.	Nested method call (user defined)	pro(3, pro(6,7))	{pro,2,3,{pro,2,6,7}}
4.	Nested method call (inbuilt)	Math.pow(2, Math.min(3,4))	{pow, 2, 2, {min, 2, 3, 4}}
5.	Anonymous function call	var X= pro (a, b){...};	{X, 2, a, b}
6.	Host object method call	Var ID=document.getElementByName("value"); ID.innerHTML= "hello world";	{document.getElementByName, 1, value}

3.4.5.2. Automated JavaScript Comment Comparator

This module detects the injection of XSS worms from the remote servers by comparing the injected comments embedded in the HTTP response (during online phase) with the comments produced during learning phase at the cloud data centres.

Any variation observed in these two comment sets will simply indicate the injection of malicious JavaScript code. Algorithm 7 illustrates the algorithm for detecting the deviation in injected comment content. This algorithm implements as follows: it receives comment injected HTTP response web page. Firstly, it determines all the input fields I_F present in the web page by parsing the web page. To achieve this, it finds out the malicious context information from Mal_Con which is the list of malicious context. Then, it stores are the identified injection point into IF_log. After this, it extracts the hidden attack vector payload at each IF as M_A and stores each attack vector into JSA_v. Now, for each attack vector, it identifies

Table 2. Protocol generation with modified comment statements

Script Code	Protocol Generation	Modified Comments
<script> var x= product(2,3); </script>	<protocolID>1</protocolID> <type>def</type> <name>product</name> <paramcount>2</paramcount> <param>2</param> <param>3</param>	<script>/*N1, 1*/ var x= product(2,3) /*N1, 1*/ </script>
<body onLoad= "active (a, b)">... </body>	<protocolID>2</protocolID> <type>call</type> <name>active</name> <argcount>2</argcount> <arg>a</arg> <arg>b</arg>	<body onLoad= /*N2, 2*/"active (a, b)" /*N2, 2*/>..</body>
<a href= "javascript:window.alert (document.cookie)">	<protocolID>3</protocolID> <type>call</type> <name>window.alert</name> <argcount>1</argcount> <arg>document.cookie</arg>	<a href= /*N3, 3*/"javascript:window.alert (document.cookie)" /*N3, 3*/>

Algorithm 7. Algorithm for JavaScript comment variation detection

Input: HTTP response embedded with comments of JavaScript code.
Start
IF_log $\rightarrow \phi$;
JSA$_V \rightarrow \phi$;
Mal_Con $\leftarrow$ List of different HTML malicious context;
CJS_rep $\rightarrow$ Injected comments of JavaScript;
For each HRES$_I$ as HTTP response
W$_H \leftarrow$ Web_Spider (HRES$_I$);
I$_F \leftarrow$ Find_Suspicious_Context (W$_H$) $\Longleftrightarrow$ Mal_Con;
IF_log $\leftarrow$ I$_F \cup$ IF_log;
For each I$_F \in$ IF_log
M$_A \leftarrow$ Retrieve Injected Script $\overset{\wedge}{=}$ I$_F$;
JSA$_V \leftarrow$ M$_A \cup$ JSA$_V$;
End for each
For each M$_V \in$ JSA$_V$
C$_{HRES} \leftarrow$ Retrieve comments (M$_A$);
Result $\leftarrow$ compare(C$_{HRES}$, CJS_rep);
if (Result == true) **then**
No Malicious Attack Vector Injection;
Else
Return HRES$_I$;
End if
End for each
End for each
End

the unique comments and performs the comparison with CJS_rep which contains the comments of valid JavaScript code. If no similarity is found, then it means some malicious script is injected, otherwise, it is free from XSS attack.

3.4.6. Context Finder

This module is responsible for the determination of the nested context of the vulnerable strings of JavaScript. It accepts the information provided by the malicious flow decomposer and then exploits it to determine the portion of the web page where vulnerable string value is injected.

Algorithm 8 illustrates the algorithm implemented for this step. This algorithm works as follows: Input to Algorithm 7 is the set of IDs of untrusted source S_ID. CTX_ rep is a log maintained to store

Algorithm 8. Context determination of vulnerable JavaScript strings

Input: Suspicious source identifiers
Output: Different context corresponding to each identifier
Start
Context Identifier: $CI_1 \mid CI_2 \mid \ldots \mid CI_N$;
S_ID $\leftarrow$ Suspicious Sources IDs;
QF_v_rep $\leftarrow \phi$/* list for type qualifier variables*/
For Each $S_I \in$ S_ID
$\quad C_I \leftarrow CI(S_I)$;
CTX_rep $\leftarrow C_I \cup$ CTX_rep;
End For Each
For Each $C_I \in$ CTX_rep
if ($S_I \in$ Regular expression) **then**
$\Lambda \mapsto$ CI: RegExp;
Else if ($S_I \in$ Literal) **then**
$\Lambda \mapsto$ CI: Lit;
$\quad$ **If** ($S_I \in$ String) **then**
$\Lambda \mapsto$ CI: Str;
Else if ($S_I \in$ Numeric) **then**
$\Lambda \mapsto$ CI: Num;
Else if ($S_I \in$ Variable) **then**
$\Lambda \mapsto$ CI: Var;
$\quad$ **End If**
End For Each
QF_v_rep $\leftarrow$ getvalue(C_I);
Return QFV_rep
End

context of each untrusted source. For each tainted source $S_I \in$ S_ID, we attach a context identifier 'CI' in the form as $C_I \leftarrow CI(S_I)$.

The generated output is the internal representation of the extracted JavaScript code embedded with the 'CI' corresponds to each untrusted variable present in it. After this, it is merged with the CTX_rep as CTX_rep $\leftarrow C_I \cup$ CTX_rep. For each $C_I \in$ CTX_rep, we generate and solve the type constraints. Here, Λ represents the type environment that performs the mapping of the JavaScript variable to the 'CI'. In the path sensitive system, variable's context changes from one point to other point. Thus, to handle this issue, untrusted variables are represented through the typing judgments as $\Lambda \mapsto$ e: CI. It indicates that at any program location, e has context identifier 'CI' in the type environment Λ. Finally, all C_I variables have been assigned the context dynamically and produce the modified log QF_V_repas output. This step provides tainted source with their identified context, in which browser interprets it.

3.4.7. Sanitization Engine of Comment-Free JavaScript Code

Sanitization is a process for substituting the untrusted user variable with the sanitized variable. Algorithm 9 illustrates the algorithm for sanitization of untrusted JavaScript code. Comment-free suspicious scripts are sanitized according to the nested context in which they are used in the HTML document. ST_C stores the list of the script templates and S_{AC} is used to store sanitized JavaScript strings. For every template $ST_I \in ST_C$, firstly, it removes placeholders. Then, it searches for the untrusted variable and stores it in the S_V to determine the context (CT_X) and then apply the sanitizer (S_P) according to the context in which S_V is used. Sanitized variable is stored in J_{SP} and then it is appended to the SPR_log for more effective result. Finally, SPR_log is passed as an parameter to the apply_sanitization_routines () function that injects the sanitization routine primitive units and return the sanitized HTTP response S_{HRES} to the web browser of network of smart devices.

Prior to sanitization, the key speciality of our work is to determine the nested context of malicious variables of JavaScript code and accordingly performs the sanitization on them. Recent techniques (Livshits et al., 2013; Samuel et al., 2011) find only the outer context of variables of JavaScript code and subsequently inject the sanitization primitive units on them. In addition, such techniques inject the redundant sanitizers in the source code of web applications that decreases the response time of the web servers. In our work, we determine the nested context of malicious variables of JavaScript code and likewise, execute the injection of sanitization primitive units in such nested contexts of script code. Table 7 highlights the different multiple context of HTML attributes/tags that can be encapsulated in each other context. We explore all such different context (shown in the Table 7) in all the injected attributes/tags of malicious JavaScript code and accordingly inject the sanitization primitive routines in them.

4. IMPLEMENTATION AND EXPERIMENTAL EVALUATION

The prototype of our distributed intelligence network was developed in Java development framework and integrated its settings on the infrastructure of cloud data centres and end fog devices. The key modules utilized for the parsing of HTML5 web application modules and statically determining the nested context of comment injection in the existing source code of such web applications was executed in learning mode. The infrastructure settings of such modules were deployed on the virtual machines of cloud data centres and by utilizing the VMware Workstation 7. This workstation was utilized for altering the existing settings of four virtual desktop systems. The key modules utilized in the learning mode are integrated on such systems with acceptable response time. On the other hand, the modules adjusted in the fog intelligence network executes in online mode on the reception of HTTP request from the network end of smart devices. We utilized the settings of XAMPP server to act as a fog device (named XSSADS) on the behalf of an OSN server. In addition, the functionality of key modules (such as automated JavaScript comment comparator and sanitization engine) was integrated in the XSSADS, which are acting as fog devices.

The parsing of the extracted HTML5 web application modules was executed by utilizing the capabilities of jsoup (Jsoup, n.d.). This parser facilitates the cloud data centres with the full-functional APIs

Algorithm 9. Sanitization engine of comment-free illicit strings of JavaScript code

Input: Different context of retrieved JavaScript code
Output: Sanitized attack vector templates (ST_1, ST_2,------ ST_N)
Start
SPR_log $\Leftarrow$ Sanitization Primitive Routines (SR_1, SR_2, SR_3... SR_N)
$ST_C \Leftarrow$ Set of script templates corresponding to their context
$S_{HRES} \Leftarrow \phi$;
$S_V \Leftarrow \phi$;
$J_{SP} \Leftarrow \phi$;
For Each template $ST_I \in ST_C$
Discaed placeholders (N/S) $\in ST_I$;
$\quad S_V \Leftarrow$ suspicious-variable(ST_I);
$CT_X \Leftarrow$ Context(S_V);
$SPR_I \Leftarrow (S_P \in$ SPR_log) $\cap$ (S_P matches CT_X);
$J_{SP} \Leftarrow SPR_I (CT_X)$;
SPR_log $\Leftarrow J_{SP} \cup$ SPR_log;
End For Each
For Each $SPR_I \in$ SPR_File
$\quad S_{HRES} \Leftarrow$ apply_sanitization_routines(SPR_I);
End For Each
Return S_{HRES};
End

that extract the DOM tree providing the information regarding vulnerable input fields and the embedded JavaScript strings in them. The capabilities of jsoup were also proved to be useful, while computing the comments of JavaScript code. The injection of comments was done on the corresponding script nodes of the DOM tree and saved the addresses of such nodes in the existing infrastructure of web applications. Further, the functionalities of rhino parser (Rhino, n.d.) were also exploited for the better interpretation of modified JavaScript code (Code with injected comments) and for the extraction of injected comments in the script nodes of DOM tree. We found some of the tested platforms of open source web applications, whose settings are deployed on the XAMPP server with backend as MYSQL database server. Table 3 highlights the overview of configuration of such platforms of web applications. Such platforms of web applications undergo the process of parsing by jsoup at learning mode on cloud data centres. These open source platforms of web applications consist of diverse vulnerable injection points embedded with dif-

Table 3. Configuration of different platforms of OSN-based web applications

Application	Version	XSS Vulnerability	Lines of Code
Drupal	7.23	CVE-2012-0826	43835
Humhub	0.10.0	CVE-2014-9528	129512
Elgg	1.8.16	CVE-2012-6561	114735
Joomla	3.2.0	CVE-2013-5738	227351

ferent categories of JavaScript code. We have gathered the statistics of largest number of occurrence of four categories of such code (i.e. local script insertion, event handlers, URL attributes and inline scripts).

Figure 8 highlights the detailed number of such frequently occurring scripts in such web applications. It is clearly reflected from the Figure 8 that the highest number of inline scripts are injected in the vulnerable input field of such web applications. On the other hand, very few local strings of JavaScript code are found in web applications.

We have defined some set of protocols that may vary usually depending on the type of method invocation utilized in such web applications. We have introduced some of the features of JavaScript strings embedded in the vulnerable injection of such web applications. Such features are # of method calls, parameters count, # of host function calls, # of user function calls and # of method definitions. Figure 9 highlights the detailed quantity of such features accumulated and injected in the form of comments on such diverse infrastructures of web applications. We have generated some set of rules for the generation of such features and accordingly inject such features of JavaScript in the form of JavaScript comments and saved such comments in the script nodes of DOM tree. We have injected the feature content in the shape of non-executable comments in numerous vulnerable input fields of such web applications. Table 4 highlights some of the list of gathered malicious input fields of such web applications. In order to assess the XSS attack detection capability on the OSN server integrated in the fog device (i.e. XSSADS), we inject numerous categories of XSS attack vectors. Such malicious attack vectors are easily accessible from the freely available five XSS attack vector repositories. Table 5 highlights some of such categories

Figure 8. Statistics of different categories of JavaScript code

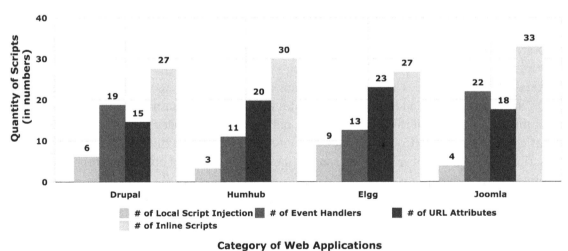

and their example patterns. We have injected the Cascading Style Sheet (CSS)-based attack vectors, HTML5 XSS attack vectors, Scalable Vector Graphics (SVG)-Based vectors, UTF7 and Charset Attack vectors and Malicious Document Object Model (DOM)-Based attack vectors.

These are injected on the OSN server, whose settings are integrated in the fog device. The features of such malicious JavaScript code will be re-calculated on this device and inject such features in the form of comments on the HTTP response message. Hereafter, the XSS attack exploitation was detected by detecting the variation in the injected comments (produced on fog device) with those produced in learning mode on the offline cloud data centres. Any variation observed will simply indicate the exploitation of XSS attack on the web server of fog device.

Figure 10 highlights the XSS attack detection results on all the four platforms of web applications running on the XAMMP server. We injected a total of 127 malicious strings of JavaScript code comprising all the five categories of XSS attack vectors. We injected such strings on the vulnerable input fields of web applications (mentioned in Table 4). In addition, we also injected the features (parameter count, # of user function calls, etc.) in the form of comments in such suspicious input fields.

It is clearly reflected from the Figure 10 that the highest XSS attack exploitation rate (i.e. # of True Positives (FP) is observed in Elgg. On the other hand, acceptable rate of false positives and false negatives is observed in all platforms of web applications. In addition, we calculated the different quantity of features of embedded JavaScript strings and injected them in the form of comments appended with

Figure 9. Statistics of features produced for injection of comments on web applications

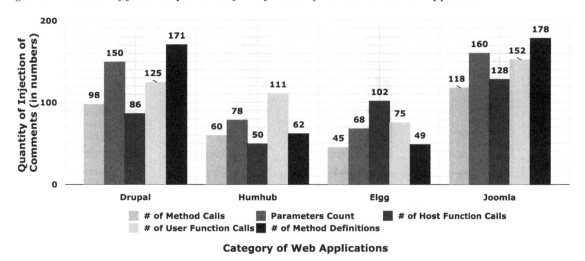

Table 4. Details of suspicious input field of web applications

Web Applications	Suspicious Input Fields
Drupal	Search Text Box, Add Users, Edit Index, Post Comments
Humhub	Create Followers, Add Followers, Add HTML Content, Embed Content
Elgg	User Registration, Add Host, Add Policies, Define Syntax
Joomla	Edit Form, Edit Source Index, Create Page, Add New Configuration

Table 5. Different categories of malicious script code

Category of Attack Vectors	Example Pattern of Attack Vectors
CSS-Based Injection (CBI)	• <a style="-o-link:'javascript:alert(1)';-o-link-source:current">X</a> • <link rel=stylesheethref=data:,*%7bx:expression(write(1))%7d • <style>@import "data:,*%7bx:expression(write(1))%7D";</style> • <style>*[{}@import'test.css?]{color: green;}</style>X
HTML5 Attack Vectors (HAV)	• <form><button formaction="javascript:alert(1)">X</button> • <input onfocus=write(1) autofocus> • <video poster=javascript:alert(1)//></video> • <video onerror="alert(1)"><source></source></video>
SVG-based Attack Vectors (SVG)	• <svgxmlns="http://www.w3.org/2000/svg"><g onload="javascript:alert(1)"></g></svg> • <svg xmlns="http://www.w3.org/2000/svg"><script>alert(1)</script></svg> • <svgonload="javascript:alert(1)" xmlns="http://www.w3.org/2000/svg"></svg>
UTF7 and Charset Attack vectors (UCAV)	• <meta charset="x-mac-farsi">¼script ¾alert(1)//¼/script ¾ • <meta charset="x-imap4-modified utf7">&<script&S1&TS&1>alert&A7&(1)&R&UA;&&<&A9&11/script&X&>
Malicious DOM Attack Vectors (MDAV)	•0?<script>Worker("#").onmessage=function(_)eval(_.data)</script> :postMessage(importScripts('data:;base64,cG9zdE1lc3NhZ2UoJ2FsZXJ0KDEEpJyk')) • <script>crypto.generateCRMFRequest('CN=0',0,0,null,'alert(1)',384,null,'rsa-dual-use')</script>

Figure 10. XSS attack detection results on all platforms of web applications

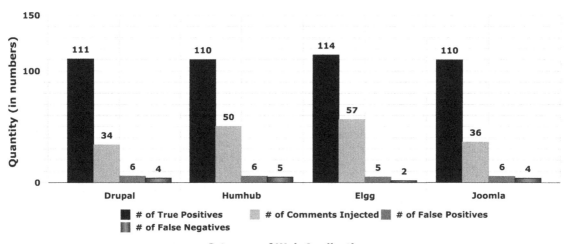

HTTP response message. It must be noted that the performance of our work depends on the comment variation detection capability of automated JavaScript comment comparator. False positive and False negative rate even gets higher, if we get the HTTP response without comments. Therefore, in our work, HTTP response message without comments is also considered as the injection of XSS attack vector from the remote servers.

In addition, the observed rate of false positives and false negatives is acceptable in all the platforms of web applications. We have also calculated the XSS attack payload detection rate of our framework on different platforms of web applications. This is done by dividing the number (#) of True Positives

Table 6. XSS attack detection rate of our framework on all platforms of web applications

XSS Attack Vector Category	Web Applications			
	Drupal	Humhub	Elgg	Joomla
CBI	86	89	94	86
HAV	80	80	90	80
SVG	87	93	80	80
UCAV	91	82	86	95
MDAV	91	86	91	89

(TPs) to the number of malicious script injected for each category of context of attack vectors. Table 6 highlights the detection rate of our framework on five different platforms of web applications w.r.t. individual category of context of attack vectors. It is clearly reflected from the Table 6, the highest malicious JavaScript attack detection rate is observed for Elgg web application.

In order to obstruct the execution of such malicious JavaScript variables, we determine the nested context of variables of JavaScript code and accordingly perform the sanitization on them. Table 7 highlights the list of different possible context of HTML code. HTML data can exist in four different contexts (PCDATA, RCDATA, Tag Name and ATTRIBNAME). Sometimes, such different contexts may be embedded inside other context. For e.g., PCDATA can be embedded inside the RCDATA. The existing sanitization-based XSS defensive solutions (Livshits et al., 2013; Samuel et al., 2011) could not able to determine the nested context of JavaScript variables, hence unable to execute the sanitization on them. In our technique, as soon as, our work detects the variation in comments of JavaScript, it additionally identifies the tainted flow of suspicious variables.

4.1. Performance Analysis

This sub-section discusses a detailed validation and performance analysis of ourcloud-based frameworkby conducting two statistical analysis methods (i.e., F-Score and F-test Hypothesis). We have also compared the suspicious JavaScript detection capability of our proposed framework with other recent XSS defensive methodologies based on some useful metrics. The analysis conducted reveal that our frameworkproduces better results as compared to existing state-of-art techniques.

4.1.1. Performance Analysis Using F-Score

For the binary classification, precision and recall are the values used for evaluations. And F-Score is a harmonic mean of precision and recall:

$$False\ Positive\ Rate\ (FPR) = \frac{False\ Positves\ (FP)}{False\ Positives\ (FP) + True\ Negatives\ (TN)}$$

Table 7. List of HTML elements and their contexts

Elements	Context
HTML	PCDATA
	RCDATA
	Tag Name
	ATTRIBNAME
HTMLATTRIB	Quoted
	Unquoted
JavaScript	String
	REGEX
Cascading Style Sheet (CSS)	ID
	Class
	PROPNAME
	KEYWDVAL
	QUANT
	String
	Quoted URL
	Unquoted URL
URL	Start
	Query
	General

$$False\ Negative\ Rate\ (FNR) = \frac{False\ Negatives\ (FN)}{False\ Negatives\ (FN) + True\ Positives\ (TP)}$$

$$Precision = \frac{True\ Positive\ (TP)}{True\ Positive\ (TP) + False\ Positive\ (FP)}$$

$$Recall = \frac{True\ positive\ (TP)}{True\ Positive\ (TP) + False\ Negative\ (FN)}$$

$$F - Score = \frac{2(TP)}{2(TP) + FP + FN}$$

Here, we calculate the precision, recall and finally F-Score of observed experimental results of our framework on different platforms of web applications. The analysis conducted reveals that our cloud-based framework exhibits high performance as the observed value of F-Score in four platforms of web applications is greater than 0.9. Table 8 highlights the detailed performance analysis of our proposed framework on five real world web applications. It is clearly reflected from the Table that the performance of our work on four different platforms of web applications is almost 97% as the highest value of F-Score is 0.962. In addition to this, the lowest False Negative Rate (FNR) is observed in OsCommerce. This validates the performance of our framework.

4.1.2. Performance Analysis Using F-Test

In order to prove that the number of malicious HTML5 scripts detected (i.e. number of True Positives (TP)) is less than to the number of HTML5 malicious scripts injected; we use the F-test hypothesis, which is defined as:

- **Null Hypothesis:** H_0 = Number of HTML5 malicious scripts detected is less than the number of HTML5 malicious scripts injected ($S1^2 = S2^2$);
- **Alternate Hypothesis:** H_1 = Number of HTML5 malicious scripts injected is greater than number of HTML5 malicious scripts detected ($S1^2 < S2^2$).

The level of Significance is $(\alpha = 0.05)$. The detailed analyses of statistics of XSS attack worms applied and detected are illustrated in the Tables 9 and 10. In our work, we utilized and injected total of 127 XSS attack vectors from the freely available XSS attack repositories in all the five web applications. But here note that, for evaluating and validating the performance of our framework by using F-test, we injected different number of malicious scripts in all different platforms of four web applications:

# of Malicious Scripts Injected

# of Observation (N_1) = 5

Degree of Freedom dof (df_1) = N_1 -1 = 4

# of Malicious Scripts Detected

# of Observation (N_2) = 5

Degree of Freedom dof (df_2) = N_2 -1 = 4

Table 8. Performance analysis of our work by calculating F-Score

Non-OSN Web Application	Total	# of TP	# of FP	# of TN	# of FN	Precision	FPR	FNR	Recall	F-Score
Drupal	127	111	6	6	4	0.948	0.5	0.034	0.965	0.962
HumHub	127	110	6	6	5	0.948	0.5	0.043	0.956	0.958
Elgg	127	114	5	6	2	0.931	0.533	0.035	0.964	0.954
Joomla	127	110	6	7	4	0.948	0.6	0.035	0.964	0.962

Table 9. Statistical analysis of malicious scripts injected

Web Applications	# of Malicious Scripts Injected (X_i)	$(X_i - \mu)$	$(X_i - \mu)^2$	Standard Deviation $S_1 = \sqrt{\sum_{i=1}^{N1}(Xi-\mu)^2 \Big/ (N1-1)}$
Drupal	120	-1	1	
HumHub	124	3	9	
Elgg	122	1	1	2.449
Joomla	118	-3	9	
	$Mean(\mu) = \sum X_i \big/ N1 = 121$		$\sum_{i=1}^{N1}(Xi-\mu)^2 = 24$	

Table 10. Statistical analysis of malicious scripts detected

Web Applications	# of Malicious Scripts Detected (X_i)	$(X_i - \mu)$	$(X_i - \mu)^2$	Standard Deviation $S_2 = \sqrt{\sum_{i=1}^{N1}(Xi-\mu)^2 \Big/ (N1-1)}$
Drupal	115	0	0	
HumHub	118	3	9	
Elgg	118	3	9	2.783
Joomla	112	-3	9	
	$Mean(\mu) = \sum X_i \big/ N1 = 115$		$\sum_{i=1}^{N1}(Xi-\mu)^2 = 31$	

$$F_{CALC} = S_1^2 / S_2^2 = 0.774$$

The tabulated value of F-Test at $df_1 = 4$, $df_2 = 4$ and $\alpha = 0.05$ is:

$$F_{(df1,df2,1-\alpha)} = F_{(9,9,0.95)} = 3.1789$$

We know that the hypothesis that the two variances are equal (Null Hypothesis) is rejected if:

$$F_{CALC} < F_{(df1,df2,1-\alpha)}$$

Since $F_{CALC} < F_{(4, 4, 0.95)}$ therefore, we accept the alternate hypothesis (H1) that the first standard deviation (S_1) is less than the second standard deviation (S_2). Hence it is clear that the number of XSS worms detected is less than number of XSS attack vectors injected and we are 95% confident that any difference in the sample standard deviation is due to random error.

4.1.3. Comparison-Based Analysis With Related Work

On the other hand, we have also compared the performance analysis of existing client-side XSS filter (i.e. IE8 (David, 2008), NoScript (Maone, 2012) and XSSAuditor (Bates, 2010) with our work. Such filters are installed as an extension on the existing infrastructure of web applications. Here also, we have verified the malicious script detection capability of such filters by injecting 127 XSS worms on our four different web applications. Figure 11 highlights the statistics of performance comparison of our framework with existing client-side XSS filters. It can be clearly observed from the Figure 11 that the value of F-Score is decreasing in all the platforms of OSN-based web applications for such filters in comparison to our work.

5. CONCLUSION AND FUTURE WORK

This article introduced a smart XSS attack monitoring system on the contemporary distributed intelligence network of Cloud data centres and Fog computing devices. The key innovation behind this work is to reduce the burden of excessive computation on Cloud data centres deployed on the core of the network. The key goal is to distribute this complex computation on the core end with the virtualized network of Fog computing devices operated on the edge of the network. This distributed network operates in two modes: learning and online mode. The former executes at cloud data centres in offline mode, injects the comments of JavaScript code in the script nodes of DOM tree and save such modified code in source files. The later mode executes in online mode on the Fog computing devices and re-executes the comment injection procedure of JavaScript code in HTTP response message. Any discrepancy observed in both these sets of values of comments will indicate the injection of malicious JavaScript code from the remote servers. Nested context-aware sanitization of illicit variables of JavaScript code will avoid the

Figure 11. Performance comparison of our work with existing XSS filters

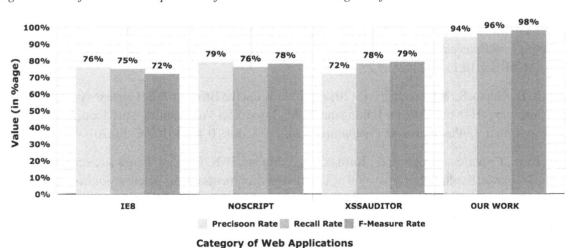

exploitation of XSS worms on the web browsers of smart devices. Detection rate of injection of malicious script code on web server deployed on the Fog computing device was evaluated on tested platforms of open source OSN-based web applications. Evaluation outcomes revealed that the JavaScript comment injection was proved to be very effective in escalating the XSS attack detection rate on such different platforms of web applications with acceptable rate of false positives and false negatives. High precision rate and less performance overhead were observed during the rigorous process of injection of sanitization routines in malicious JavaScript code. We will try to completely shift our learning mode (deployed on the Cloud data centres) to the virtualized nodes of Fog computing devices deployed on the network edge as a part of further work. This complete swing will increase the response time of runtime comment variation detector and hence enhances the XSS worm detection capability our framework.

ACKNOWLEDGMENT

The authors would like to thank the anonymous reviewers for their valuable comments and feedback throughout the reviewing process of this manuscript. We would also like to thank the members of Information and Cyber Security Research Group working in the National Institute of Technology Kurukshetra, India for their valuable feedbacks and worthwhile discussions. This work was financially supported by Ministry of Electronics and Information Technology (MeitY), Government of India and TEQIP-II.

REFERENCES

Acunetix. (2015Acunetix Web Application Vulnerability Report. Retrieved from https://www.acunetix.com/blog/articles/acunetix-web-application-vulnerability-report-2015/

Almorsy, M., Grundy, J., & Müller, I. (2016). An analysis of the cloud computing security problem. arXiv:1609.01107

Bates, D., Barth, A., & Jackson, C. (2010, April). Regular expressions considered harmful in client-side XSS filters. In *Proceedings of the 19th international conference on World wide web* (pp. 91-100). ACM. doi:10.1145/1772690.1772701

Bonomi, F., Milito, R., Zhu, J., & Addepalli, S. (2012, August). Fog computing and its role in the internet of things. In *Proceedings of the first edition of the MCC workshop on Mobile cloud computing* (pp. 13-16). ACM. doi:10.1145/2342509.2342513

Gupta, B. B., Gupta, S., & Choudhary, P. (2017b). Enhancing the Browser-Side Context-Aware Sanitization of Suspicious HTML5 Code for Halting the DOM-Based XSS Vulnerabilities in Cloud. *International Journal of Cloud Applications and Computing*, 7(1), 1–31. doi:10.4018/IJCAC.2017010101

Gupta, B. B., Gupta, S., Gangwar, S., Kumar, M., & Meena, P. K. (2015a). Cross-site scripting (XSS) abuse and defense: Exploitation on several testing bed environments and its defense. *Journal of Information Privacy and Security*, 11(2), 118–136. doi:10.1080/15536548.2015.1044865

Gupta, S., & Gupta, B. B. (2015b). Cross-Site Scripting (XSS) attacks and defense mechanisms: classification and state-of-the-art. *International Journal of System Assurance Engineering and Management*.

Gupta, S., & Gupta, B. B. (2015c). XSS-SAFE: a server-side approach to detect and mitigate cross-site scripting (XSS) attacks in JavaScript code. Arabian Journal for Science and Engineering.

Gupta, S., & Gupta, B. B. (2016a). XSS-secure as a service for the platforms of online social network-based multimedia web applications in cloud. *Multimedia Tools and Applications.*

Gupta, S., & Gupta, B. B. (2016b). *JS-SAN: defense mechanism for HTML5-based web applications against JavaScript code injection vulnerabilities.* Security and Communication Networks.

Gupta, S., & Gupta, B. B. (2016c). XSS-immune: A Google chrome extension-based XSS defensive framework for contemporary platforms of web applications. *Security and Communication Networks, 9*(17), 3966–3986. doi:10.1002/sec.1579

Gupta, S., & Gupta, B. B. (2016d, September). An Infrastructure-Based Framework for the Alleviation of JavaScript Worms from OSN in Mobile Cloud Platforms. In *Proceedings of the International Conference on Network and System Security* (pp. 98-109). Springer International Publishing. doi:10.1007/978-3-319-46298-1_7

Gupta, S., & Gupta, B. B. (2016e, April). Alleviating the proliferation of JavaScript worms from online social network in cloud platforms. In *Proceedings of the 2016 7th International Conference on Information and Communication Systems (ICICS)* (pp. 246-251). IEEE. doi:10.1109/IACS.2016.7476119

Gupta, S., & Gupta, B. B. (2017a). Detection, Avoidance, and Attack Pattern Mechanisms in Modern Web Application Vulnerabilities: Present and Future Challenges. *International Journal of Cloud Applications and Computing, 7*(3), 1–43. doi:10.4018/IJCAC.2017070101

Gupta, S., & Gupta, B. B. (2014). BDS: browser dependent XSS sanitizer. In Cloud-Based Databases with Biometric Applications (pp. 174-191). Hershey, PA: IGI-Global.

HTML 5. (n. d.). HTML5 Security Cheat Sheet. Retrieved from http://html5sec.org/

Jsoup: Java HTML Parser. (n. d.). Retrieved from http://jsoup.org/

Livshits, B., & Chong, S. (2013, January). Towards fully automatic placement of security sanitizers and declassifiers. ACM SIGPLAN Notices, 48(1), 385-398. doi:10.1145/2429069.2429115

Maone, G. (2012). NoScript-JavaScript/Java/Flash blocker for a safer Firefox experience. Retrieved from http://noscript.net

Mather, T., Kumaraswamy, S., & Latif, S. (2009). *Cloud security and privacy: an enterprise perspective on risks and compliance.* O'Reilly Media, Inc.

Modi, C., Patel, D., Borisaniya, B., Patel, A., & Rajarajan, M. (2013). A survey on security issues and solutions at different layers of Cloud computing. *The Journal of Supercomputing, 63*(2), 561–592. doi:10.1007/s11227-012-0831-5

Mozilla. (n. d.). Rhino Parser. Retrieved from http:// www.mozilla.org/rhino

Ross, D. (2008, August). IE 8 XSS filter architecture/implementation. Retrieved from http://blogs.technet.com/srd/archive/2008/08/18/ie-8-xss-filter-architecture-implementation

Rsnake. (2008). XSS Cheat Sheet. Retrieved from http://ha.ckers.org/xss.html

Samuel, M., Saxena, P., & Song, D. (2011, October). Context-sensitive auto-sanitization in web templating languages using type qualifiers. In *Proceedings of the 18th ACM conference on Computer and communications security* (pp. 587-600). ACM. doi:10.1145/2046707.2046775

Stojmenovic, I., & Wen, S. (2014, September). The fog computing paradigm: Scenarios and security issues. In *Proceedings of the 2014 Federated Conference on Computer Science and Information Systems (FedCSIS)* (pp. 1-8). IEEE.

Vulnerability Lab. (n. d.). Technical Attack Sheet for Cross Site Penetration Tests. Retrieved from http://www.vulnerability-lab.com/resources/documents/531.txt

Technomancie.net. (n. d523XSS vectors available. Retrieved from http://xss2.technomancie.net/vectors/

Whitehatsec. (2015) 2015 Stats Report. Retrieved from https://info.whitehatsec.com/rs/whitehatsecurity/images/2015-Stats-Report.pdf

@XSS Vector Twitter Account. (n. d.). Retrieved from https://twitter.com/XSSVector

This research was previously published in the International Journal of Web Services Research (IJWSR), 14(4); edited by Liang-Jie Zhang, pages 1-32, copyright year 2017 by IGI Publishing (an imprint of IGI Global).

Chapter 18
Centralized Fog Computing Security Platform for IoT and Cloud in Healthcare System

Chandu Thota
Infosys Ltd., India

Revathi Sundarasekar
Priyadarshini Engineering College, India

Gunasekaran Manogaran
VIT University, India

Varatharajan R
Sri Ramanujar Engineering College, India

Priyan M. K.
VIT University, India

ABSTRACT

This chapter proposes an efficient centralized secure architecture for end to end integration of IoT based healthcare system deployed in Cloud environment. The proposed platform uses Fog Computing environment to run the framework. In this chapter, health data is collected from sensors and collected sensor data are securely sent to the near edge devices. Finally, devices transfer the data to the cloud for seamless access by healthcare professionals. Security and privacy for patients' medical data are crucial for the acceptance and ubiquitous use of IoT in healthcare. The main focus of this work is to secure Authentication and Authorization of all the devices, Identifying and Tracking the devices deployed in the system, Locating and tracking of mobile devices, new things deployment and connection to existing system, Communication among the devices and data transfer between remote healthcare systems. The proposed system uses asynchronous communication between the applications and data servers deployed in the cloud environment.

DOI: 10.4018/978-1-5225-5649-7.ch018

INTRODUCTION

IoT technology is introduced recently which enables people and objects to interact with each other. IoT is used in the following areas such as smart transport systems, smart cities, smart healthcare, and smart energy. The healthcare world urgently demands the transformation of healthcare from a hospital-centered system to a person-centered environment (Eason et al., 1955). It has been predicted that in the following decades, the way healthcare is currently provided will be transformed from hospital-centered, first to hospital-home-balanced in 2020th, and then ultimately to home-centered in 2030th (Rahmani et al., 2015). In home-based health care the following arrangements are included such as human computer interaction, communications, imaging technologies embattled at diagnosis, treatment and monitoring patients without disturbing the quality of lifestyle. It can be possible the development of a low cost medical devices used for real-time monitoring of patient physical conditions. Significant security solutions are identified to current wireless networks. These approaches are not directly applicable for IoT-based healthcare applications due to following challenges such as 1) Medical sensor nodes can be easily lost or abducted as they are tiny in terms of size, 2) Security solutions must be resource-efficient as medical sensor nodes have limited processing power, memory, and communication bandwidth. Thus, conventional cryptography techniques require heavy computations are infeasible. Due to resource constraints of medical sensors, it is infeasible to utilize conventional cryptography in IoT-based healthcare (Manogaran et al., 2016b; Manogaran et al., 2016c; Manogaran et al., 2017a). The following security protocols DTLS and OpenSSL are used in the proposed approach. DTLS handshake protocol is used to provide security solution for the transport layer in IoT. Open SSL is an open source project for implementing SSL, TLS and various cryptography libraries such as symmetric key, public key, and hash algorithms.

BACKGROUND

IoT Enabling Technologies and Protocols Overview

In recent years, more number of IoT applications is developed for different domains, so we need to develop different protocols and platforms. For example, a number of wearable sensors and devices are developed for continuous monitoring of personal fitness, healthcare, and physical activity awareness (Jawbone Inc, 2015; FitBitInc, 2015). Nowadays, researchers are interested to develop wearable clinical devices in remote health monitoring systems for continuous storage, management and clinical access to the patient's physiological information (Pantelopoulos, 2010; Paradiso, 2005). Wearable clinical devices can give physical routine by a two–three-day periods of continuous physiological monitoring of patient. During this period, sensors would continuously store the patient's physiological data to a database linked with your device (Skourletopoulos et al., 2015).

Applications of IoT with different technologies are explained in this section in detail. These are categorized based on the terms used in the IoT such as Location tracking, sensing, communication, security and identification. Presently, the hardware and software for sensing, communication and decision-making activities have become more versatile and affordable.

Identification Technology

IoT system may include a large number of nodes, where each node is capable of generating data, and any authorized node can access data irrespective of where those are located. To achieve this goal, it is essential to locate and identify the nodes effectively by assign a unique identifier (UID) to a corresponding device, so that the information exchange through this node is un-ambiguous. The Open Software Foundation (OSF) developed the universally unique identifier (UUID) as a part of the Distributed Computing Environment (DCE), which can operate without a centralized coordination. OSF also introduced the Globally Unique Identifier (GUID).

Communication and Location Technologies

In most cases, short-distance communication is based on wireless technologies, including Bluetooth, RFID, Wi-Fi, Infrared Data Association (IrDA), Ultra-wideband (UWB), ZigBee, etc. This paper reviews only on short-distance technologies.

Sensing Technologies

Sensing technology is pivotal to the acquisition of numerous physiological parameters about the patients. Hence, doctor can adequately diagnose the illness and recommend the treatments. Furthermore, new progress of sensing technologies allows a continual data acquisition from patients, facilitating the improvement of treatment outcomes and the reduction of healthcare costs.

Fog Computing

Cisco defines Fog Computing as a paradigm that extends Cloud computing and services to the edge of the network. Fog computing will grow in helping the emerging network paradigms that require faster processing with less delay and delay jitter. Cloud computing would serve the business community meeting their high-end computing demands lowering the cost based on a utility pricing model. By doing so, Fog reduces service latency, and improves QoS, resulting in superior user-experience. Fog Computing supports emerging Internet of Everything (IoE) applications that demand real-time/predictable latency (industrial automation, transportation, networks of sensors and actuators). Fog supports densely distributed data collection points, hence adding a fourth axis to the often-mentioned Big Data dimensions (volume, variety, and velocity) (Thota et al., 2017).

Now there are different approaches are identified to connect the devices with cloud. We could make integration happen on the data level, a point-to-point level where two applications are sharing chunks of data, or at a method level allowing them to share functionality apart from just data. Integration strategy plays vital role in its success in the enterprise ventures. Also, the company needs to have a clear understanding of the requirements specifying what is to be achieved after integrating the applications and database from flog to cloud so that finite goals can be set. A very important and often neglected aspect of integration is the relevance of devices in the integration scheme.

SCOPE OF THE CHAPTER

IoT-based healthcare systems deal with human-related health data. IoT and Cloud computing in Healthcare industry is a combination of Things (devices and sensors), communication technologies, interconnected apps, computing services in cloud, storage services in cloud and people like patients, doctors and care-givers that would function together as one smart system to monitor, track, store, analyze and visualize patients' health information. Security is a major concern wherever networks are deployed at large scales (González-Valenzuela, et al., 2014). Due to direct involvement of humans in IoT-based healthcare appli-cations, providing robust and secure data communication among healthcare sensors, actuators, patients, and caregivers are crucial. Although collected from innocuous wearable sensors, such data is vulnerable to top privacy concerns. In IoT-based healthcare applications, security and privacy are among major areas of concern as most devices and their communications are wireless in nature (Koblitz, 1987).

IOT IN CLOUD ENVIRONMENT

Cloud computing facilitates end-users or small companies to use computational resources such as software, storage, and processing capacities belonging to other companies are calling as cloud service providers. Definition of cloud computing is based on five attributes Multitenancy (Shared Resources), Massive Scalability, Elasticity, Pay as You go and Self-Provisioning of resources. Cloud Providers are companies that offers some component of cloud computing – typically Infrastructure as a Service (IaaS), Software as a Service (SaaS) or Platform as a Service (PaaS) – to other businesses or individuals. Organizations use the Cloud in a variety of different deployment models are Private, Public, and Hybrid. In the cloud deployment model, networking, platform, storage, and software infrastructure are provided as services that scale up or down depending on the demand as required (Shen et al., 2011). Web services are client and server applications that communicate over the World Wide Web's (WWW) and Hypertext Transfer Protocol (HTTP). As described by the World Wide Web Consortium (W3C), web services provide a standard means of interoperating between software applications running on a variety of platforms and frameworks. Web services are characterized by their great interoperability and extensibility, as well as their machine-processable descriptions, thanks to the use of XML. Web services can be combined in a loosely coupled way to achieve complex operations. Programs providing simple services can interact with each other to deliver sophisticated added-value services. In Java EE 6, JAX-RS provides the func-tionality for Representational State Transfer (RESTful) web services. REST is well suited for basic, ad hoc integration scenarios. RESTful web services, often better integrated with HTTP than SOAP-based services are, do not require XML messages or WSDL service–API definitions.

IoT With Cloud Computing and Big Data

Nowadays, big data has been playing a vital role in almost all environments such as healthcare, educa-tion, business organizations and scientific research (Manogaran et al., 2017b; Manogaran et al., 2017c; Manogaran et al., 2017d). There is a strong relationship in big data and IoE. In general, IoT applications are used to capture or observe some specific values to find the hidden values and take better decisions. When the device connected to the Internet it always senses the specific metric and stores those metrics into a connected data stores. This would increase the size of the data stored in a data store (Malan et al.,

2004). Hence, high end devices and scalable storage systems are needed to store such huge size of data. The amount of data to be stored and processed becomes an important problem in real life. Relational data base management system (RDBMS) is generally used to store the traditional data, but day by day the volume, velocity and variety of sensor data is growing towards the Exabyte (Lopez et al., 2014; Lopez et al., 2015; Lopez et al., 2016a; Lopez et al., 2016b) . This requires advanced tools and techniques to store, process and display such large amount of sensor data to the end users. Thus, storing and querying large amount of data requires database clusters and additional resources (Kambourakis et al., 2007). However, storage and retrieval are not the only problem but also extract useful information from huge data (Manogaran et al., 2017e). In order to overcome this issue, cloud computing is used to provide scalable storage systems and high end devices for computation (Koop et al., 2008).

Wireless Sensor Network (WSN) is composed of distributed spatially connected sensor nodes with limited computing power and storage (Lorincz et al., 2004). This chapter consists of an overview of state-of-the-art work on Wireless Sensor-based Cloud Computing (WSCC). Subsequently, integration of WSN and Cloud Computing is highlighted with some insights on how WSN and Clouds can both get benefits from each other. Applications of Wireless Sensors over the cloud are then described. Afterwards, we explain incorporation of mobile sink between WSN and Cloud.

Cloud computing is a type of computing and it is used for the delivery of hosted services over the Internet. In other words, Cloud computing relies on sharing computing resources and hardware's rather than having personal devices or local servers to manage the real-time applications. Mobile cloud can be considered as a marketplace, where the mobile services of the mobile cloud-based system architectures can be leased off via the cloud. In this context, this paper elaborates on a novel fluctuation-based quantification model, which is based on a cost-benefit appraisal, adopting a non-linear and asymmetric approach. The proposed model aims to predict the incurrence and the risk of entering into a new technical debt (TD) in the future and provide insights to inform effective investment decision making. The lease of a cloud-based mobile service was considered, when developing the formula, and the research approach is investigated with respect to the cost that derives from the unused capacity. In general, cloud providers are called as cloud service providers or CSPs. Amazon Simple Storage Service (Amazon S3) is the first cloud offered by Amazon in 2006. There after other cloud providers are developed number of cloud services such as Microsoft, Rackspace, Apple, IBM, Joyent, Google, Cisco, Citrix, Salesforce. com and Verizon/Terremark. Hence, the IoE devices are interconnected with cloud server to store the device generated data. Once the data is stored efficiently into the cloud then there is a need for scalable algorithms to process those data. In order to fulfill the requirements, Amazon Web services provides Elastic MapReduce to process the device generated data.

Fog Computing to Cloud Computing

In this architecture, we are suggesting to store the data into primarily fog servers, which is near edge technology for IoT devices where deployed in IoT applications. Edge computing plays a crucial role in Internet of Things (IoT) (Jara et al., 2009; Jara et al., 2010a; Jara et al., 2010b). Studies related to security, confidentiality and system reliability in the fog computing platform is absolutely a topic for research and has to be discovered. Less demand for bandwidth, as every bit of data's were aggregated at certain points instead of sending over cloud channels. Rather than presenting and working from a central cloud, fog operate on network edge. So, it takes less time. By putting small servers called edge servers in visibility of users, it is possible for a fog computing platform to avoid response time and scalability issues (Hummen, 2014). cloud computing would serve the business community meeting their high-end computing demands lowering the cost based on a utility pricing model. Processing the data of the applications of IoT in Cloud Data centers, we are using the Cloud big data technologies and secure the data by storing the data into different cloud data centers providing by various cloud providers like Amazon, Google, Cisco and Microsoft. Categorize the data of the application and store the data into different data centers as per their categorization as critical, normal, and sensitive and personnel information of the end-users of the applications.

PROPOSING CENTRALIZED FOG COMPUTING SECURITY PLATFORM FOR IOT CLOUD HEALTH SYSTEM

In the paradigms of healthcare IoT, data is collected from smart devices (medical sensors) and transmitted to end-users (caregivers). IoT also enables end-users can access, control, and manage medical sensors through the Internet. Patient data is involved in healthcare IoT applications. Thus, it is necessary to provide secure end-to-end communication between end-users and medical sensors via centralized secure platform. The proposed system has the following tasks to achieve end to end security integration of IoT enabled healthcare system.

Core Functionality of the Proposed System

Identifying the Devices

- **Identifying the Existing Devices in IoT Health System:** The proposed methodology has different tasks to secure the IoT system. First one is to identify the existence of all the devices which are configured and connected in our system. Devices are categorized as wearable and non-wearable, wired and wireless, mobile and non-mobile devices. Above mentioned devices are used to collect, process, transfer the data using internet. These devices use different protocols and technologies to connect and contact each other with wired and wireless communication. Proposed system assigns unique id for each device to identify, track, and find out the existence of device in the system and its connected devices identification. Once the devices are connected, the proposed healthcare system collects the patient information collected from devices (MSNs) and transferring to central Database/Application server (Karlof, 2004). Data should be collected from only identified and existed devices in the system. When intruders and hackers are trying to enter into our system with different devices, the proposed system identifies the unauthorized devices entered into our system using status and history. The proposed methodology continually stores the status and history of each device trying to enter in the system. During the lifecycle of a product, some components could change its unique ID. Hence, it is necessary to maintain the changes of smart devices even when they are reconfigured. Changes in the configuration are critical for maintaining devices, tracking components, and diagnosing failures. In order to overcome the issue the following techniques are followed in the proposed system such as (1) Locate things efficiently based on a global ID scheme, (2) manage identities with the advanced techniques of encoding / encryption, authentication, and repository management, and (3) provide global directory services and IoT service discovery services under diverse UID schemes.

- **Authenticate and Authorize the Devices, Data Identification and Communication Networks:** The privacy of the patients and key negotiation materials should be protected to prevent unauthorized access from learning the contents of the negotiations. It is also important to prevent from malicious activities at the entrance to MSNs. Hence, mutual authentication and authorization of end-users and devices used in healthcare IoT systems is a crucial task (Hill et al., 2004). Proposed architecture performs the authentication and authorization of remote end-users securely and efficiently in the centralized secure platform on behalf of the medical sensors. With the established connection context to the medical sensor nodes, these devices no longer required to authenticate and authorize a remote healthcare center or a caregiver. Thus, any malicious activity can be blocked before entering into a constrained medical domain. The architecture of our proposed centralized secure platform for healthcare IoT monitoring system in home/hospital domain(s) is shown in Figure 2.

Locating and Tracking Devices

- **Locating, Tracking and Connecting Technologies:** Communication technologies support networking services and it can be divided into short-distance and long-distance technologies. However, long-distance technologies mainly involve regular Internet or mobile phones communications. The proposed system properly maintains the locations and track details to efficiently connect the devices in the system. The Global Positioning System (GPS) is a satellite-based navigation system to locate objects under all weather conditions as long as unobstructed lines of sight can be received by four or more satellites. In the healthcare system, the satellite-based positioning system can be used to locate ambulances/transportation network, patients/home network, doctors/hospital network, etc. Since, GPS is insufficient to build an effective healthcare system, it is necessary to compensate GPS with local positioning systems (LPSs) to enhance location accuracy (Rescorla, 2012). LPS locates an object based on the measurement of radio signals travelling among the objects and an array of the pre-deployed receivers. The short-distance communication technologies are essential to implement LPS. For example, UWB radio has a fine temporal resolution, which enables a receiver to estimate the arrival time accurately. Therefore, UWB is an ideal technology for radio-based high-precision positioning.

Mobility Scenario in Healthcare IoT System

- **Identifying, Tracking, Locating and Monitoring for Mobility Devices:** Proposed Architecture is also focusing on identifying the mobile devices identification, which are configured in healthcare system. Tracking and locating the devices to Monitoring the status of the patients, doctors and transport (Moosavi et al., 2016). Mobility support is one of the most important issues in healthcare IoT systems. Improving patients' quality of life is essential in the healthcare system. Continues monitoring of patients is also important when they are walk around the hospital wards. Thus, the connectivity should be good. In addition, when patient to move from his/her base MSN to other rooms/MSN for medical tests they should not lost the connectivity. Mobility can be categorized into two main topics denoted as macro-mobility and micro-mobility. The movement of medical sensors between various medical network domains distinguishes the macro-mobility. Micro-mobility assumes that medical sensors move between different MSNs within the same domain. In this proposed system, where a patient wearing medical sensors decides to move from its room (base network) to other rooms (visited networks). We assume a mobility scenario which consists of several MSNs for remote patient monitoring in a hospital or nursing/home environment. In the considered scenario, patients may roam through the hospital wards or move to other rooms due to take some medical tests (e.g., Laboratory or X-ray). In order to enable seamless transitions of medical sensors, proposed system uses an efficient and robust data handover mechanism to centralized secure platform database. The mobility scenario is discussed in three phases in the following subsections. a) Message exchange in patients' base MSN, b) Entering to a new medical sub network, c) Returning back to the base MSN.

Proposed System Architecture and Its Functionality

Proposed Security Platform Architecture Diagram for end to end Integration of HealthCare system is shown in Figure 1.

Security Methodologies implementation like Authentication/Authorization, PKI Certificate and DTLS Handshake Protocol is shown in Figure 2.

In our proposed methodology, the Security is the major issue while integrating Fog to Cloud environment. The Cloud systems are located within the network by connecting through Internet, with numerous speeds, technologies, topologies and types with no central control. Because of the non-homogeneous and loosely controlled nature of the Internet, there are many issues especially quality of service related ones remain unresolved. One such issue that affects the quality of service severely is network latency. Real time applications with which users directly interact with are badly affected by delay and delay jitter caused by latency in networks (Manogaran et al., 2016a).

Figure 1. Proposing methodology to secure healthcare System in IoT

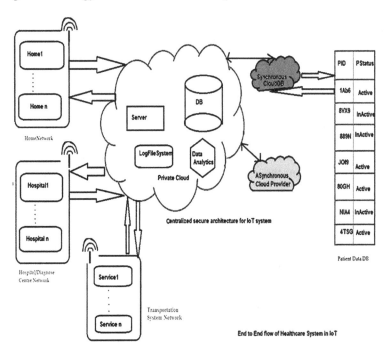

Figure 2. Security architecture for GC architecture for secure integration fog to cloud storage

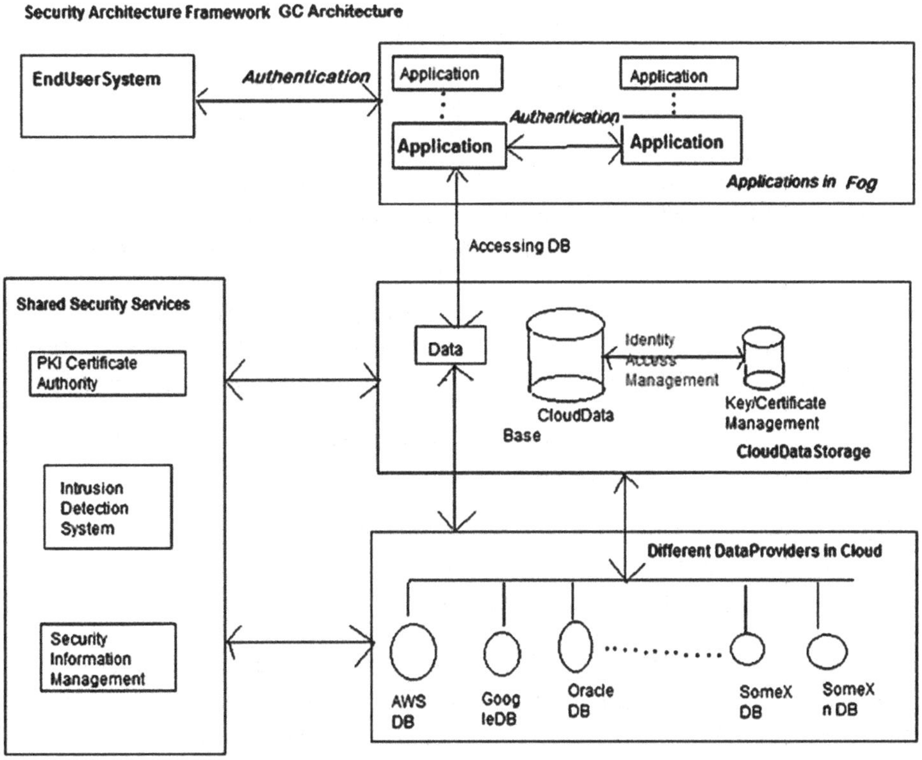

The security architecture here we are providing is uses the existing security terminologies as Public key and private key, encryption and decryption, cryptography Identity Access Management and PKI Certificates Authority. The other major issue confronted with cloud computing is security and privacy. Since the cloud systems have been located with the Internet, user requests, data transmission and system responses need to traverse a large number of intermediate networks depending on the distance between the users and systems. When Patient data is out there in a public cloud, there is a risk of them being compromised of their integrity and confidentiality. Deeper the data inside the Internet, higher the risk as the data has to travel a long distance to and from the user's computer to the cloud system, even if the data is encrypted. Similarly the availability of the cloud systems can also be attacked using various methods. Thus it can be seen that cloud systems at present face various security threats due to very nature of their implementation within the Internet coupled with location independence.

REFERENCES

Eason, G., Noble, B., & Sneddon, I. N. (1955). On certain integrals of Lipschitz-Hankel type involving products of Bessel functions. *Philosophical Transactions of the Royal Society of London A: Mathematical, Physical and Engineering Sciences*, 247(935), 529–551. doi:10.1098/rsta.1955.0005

González-Valenzuela, S., Chen, M., & Leung, V. C. (2011). Mobility support for health monitoring at home using wearable sensors. *IEEE Transactions on Information Technology in Biomedicine, 15*(4), 539–549. doi:10.1109/TITB.2010.2104326 PMID:21216718

Hill, J., Horton, M., Kling, R., & Krishnamurthy, L. (2004). The platforms enabling wireless sensor networks. *Communications of the ACM, 47*(6), 41–46. doi:10.1145/990680.990705

Hummen, R., Shafagh, H., Raza, S., Voig, T., & Wehrle, K. (2014, June). Delegation-based Authentication and Authorization for the IP-based Internet of Things. *Proceedings of the 2014 Eleventh Annual IEEE International Conference on Sensing, Communication, and Networking (SECON)* (pp. 284-292). IEEE.

Jara, A. J., Zamora, M. A., & Skarmeta, A. F. (2009, August). HWSN6: hospital wireless sensor networks based on 6LoWPAN technology: mobility and fault tolerance management. *Proceedings of the International Conference on Computational Science and Engineering CSE'09* (Vol. 2, pp. 879-884). IEEE.

Jara, A. J., Zamora, M. A., & Skarmeta, A. F. (2010a). An initial approach to support mobility in hospital wireless sensor networks based on 6LoWPAN (HWSN6).

Jara, A. J., Zamora, M. A., & Skarmeta, A. F. (2010b, September). Intra-mobility for hospital wireless sensor networks based on 6LoWPAN. *Proceedings of the 2010 6th International Conference on Wireless and Mobile Communications (ICWMC)* (pp. 389-394). IEEE.

Kambourakis, G., Klaoudatou, E., & Gritzalis, S. (2007, April). Securing medical sensor environments: the codeblue framework case. *Proceedings of the Second International Conference on Availability, Reliability and Security ARES '07* (pp. 637-643). IEEE. doi:10.1109/ARES.2007.135

Karlof, C., Sastry, N., & Wagner, D. (2004, November). TinySec: a link layer security architecture for wireless sensor networks. *Proceedings of the 2nd international conference on Embedded networked sensor systems* (pp. 162-175). ACM. doi:10.1145/1031495.1031515

Koblitz, N. (1987). Elliptic curve cryptosystems. *Mathematics of Computation, 48*(177), 203–209. doi:10.1090/S0025-5718-1987-0866109-5

Koop, C. E., Mosher, R., Kun, L., Geiling, J., Grigg, E., Long, S., & Rosen, J. M. et al. (2008). Future delivery of health care: Cybercare. *IEEE Engineering in Medicine and Biology Magazine, 27*(6), 29–38. doi:10.1109/MEMB.2008.929888 PMID:19004693

Li, S., Da Xu, L., & Wang, X. (2013). Compressed sensing signal and data acquisition in wireless sensor networks and internet of things. *IEEE Transactions on Industrial Informatics, 9*(4), 2177–2186. doi:10.1109/TII.2012.2189222

Lopez, D., Gunasekaran, M., Murugan, B. S., Kaur, H., & Abbas, K. M. (2014, October). Spatial big data analytics of influenza epidemic in Vellore, India. *Proceedings of the 2014 IEEE International Conference on Big Data (Big Data)* (pp. 19-24). IEEE.

Lopez, D., & Manogaran, G. (2016b). Big Data Architecture for Climate Change and Disease Dynamics. In *The Human Element of Big Data: Issues, Analytics, and Performance* (pp. 301-331). CRC Press. 10.1007/978-3-319-49736-5_7

Lopez, D., & Sekaran, G. (2016a). Climate change and disease dynamics-A big data perspective. *International Journal of Infectious Diseases*, *45*, 23–24. doi:10.1016/j.ijid.2016.02.084

Lopez, D., & Gunasekaran, M. (2015). Assessment of Vaccination Strategies Using Fuzzy Multi-criteria Decision Making. *Proceedings of the Fifth International Conference on Fuzzy and Neuro Computing (FANCCO-2015)* (pp. 195-208). Springer International Publishing.

Lorincz, K., Malan, D. J., Fulford-Jones, T. R., Nawoj, A., Clavel, A., Shnayder, V., & Moulton, S. et al. (2004). Sensor networks for emergency response: Challenges and opportunities. *IEEE Pervasive Computing*, *3*(4), 16–23. doi:10.1109/MPRV.2004.18

Malan, D., Fulford-Jones, T., Welsh, M., & Moulton, S. (2004, April). Codeblue: An ad hoc sensor network infrastructure for emergency medical care. *Proceedings of the International workshop on wearable and implantable body sensor networks* (Vol. 5).

Manogaran, G., & Lopez, D. (2016b). Health data analytics using scalable logistic regression with stochastic gradient descent. *International Journal of Advanced Intelligence Paradigms*, *9*(1), 1–18.

Manogaran, G., & Lopez, D. (2016c). A survey of big data architectures and machine learning algorithms in healthcare. *International Journal of Biomedical Engineering and Technology*, *23*(4), 1–27.

Manogaran, G., & Lopez, D. (2017b). Disease surveillance system for big climate data processing and dengue transmission. *International Journal of Ambient Computing and Intelligence*, *8*(1), 1–27.

Manogaran, G., & Lopez, D. (2017e). Spatial cumulative sum algorithm with big data analytics for climate change detection. *Computers & Electrical Engineering*, *59*(5), 1–15. doi:10.1016/j.compeleceng.2017.04.006

Manogaran, G., Thota, C., & Kumar, M. V. (2016a). Meta Cloud Data Storage Architecture for Big Data Security in Cloud Computing. *Procedia Computer Science*, *87*, 128–133. doi:10.1016/j.procs.2016.05.138

Manogaran, G., Thota, C., Lopez, D., & Sundarasekar, R. (2017d). Big Data Security Intelligence for Healthcare Industry 4.0. In Cybersecurity for Industry 4.0 (pp. 103-126). Springer International Publishing.

Manogaran, G., Thota, C., Lopez, D., Vijayakumar, V., Abbas, K. M., & Sundarsekar, R. (2017c). Big Data Knowledge System in Healthcare. In *Internet of Things and Big Data Technologies for Next Generation Healthcare* (pp. 133–157). Springer International Publishing.

Manogaran, G., Thota, C., Lopez, D., Vijayakumar, V., Abbas, K. M., & Sundarsekar, R. (2017a). Big data knowledge system in healthcare. In Internet of Things and Big Data Technologies in Next Generation Healthcare. Springer International Publishing.

Moosavi, S. R., Gia, T. N., Nigussie, E., Rahmani, A. M., Virtanen, S., Tenhunen, H., & Isoaho, J. (2016). End-to-end security scheme for mobility enabled healthcare Internet of Things. *Future Generation Computer Systems*, *64*, 108–124. doi:10.1016/j.future.2016.02.020

Rahmani, A. M., Thanigaivelan, N. K., Gia, T. N., Granados, J., Negash, B., Liljeberg, P., & Tenhunen, H. (2015, January). Smart e-health gateway: Bringing intelligence to internet-of-things based ubiquitous healthcare systems. *Proceedings of the 2015 12th Annual IEEE Consumer Communications and Networking Conference (CCNC)* (pp. 826-834). IEEE.

Rescorla, E., & Modadugu, N. (2012). Datagram transport layer security version 1.2.

Shen, W., Xu, Y., Xie, D., Zhang, T., & Johansson, A. (2011, September). Smart border routers for ehealthcare wireless sensor networks. *Proceedings of the 2011 7th International Conference on Wireless Communications, Networking and Mobile Computing (WiCOM)* (pp. 1-4). IEEE. doi:10.1109/wicom.2011.6040606

Skourletopoulos, G., Mavromoustakis, C. X., Mastorakis, G., Rodrigues, J. J., Chatzimisios, P., & Batalla, J. M. (2015, December). A fluctuation-based modelling approach to quantification of the technical debt on mobile cloud-based service level. *Proceedings of the 2015 IEEE Globecom Workshops (GC Wkshps)* (pp. 1-6). IEEE.

Thota, C., Manogaran, G., Lopez, D., & Vijayakumar, V. (2017). Big Data Security Framework for Distributed Cloud Data Centers. Proceedings of the Cybersecurity Breaches and Issues Surrounding Online Threat Protection (pp. 288-310). Hershey, PA: IGI Global. doi:10.4018/978-1-5225-1941-6.ch012

Zheng, K., Yang, Z., Zhang, K., Chatzimisios, P., Yang, K., & Xiang, W. (2016). Big data-driven optimization for mobile networks toward 5G. *IEEE Network*, *30*(1), 44–51. doi:10.1109/MNET.2016.7389830

ADDITIONAL READING

Curran, R. J., & Haskin, R. L. (2010). *U.S. Patent No. 7,840,995*. Washington, DC: U.S. Patent and Trademark Office.

Chandrasekaran, A., & Kapoor, M. (2016). Frost & Sullivan 2011- Market Insight. *Frost.com*. Retrieved 8 January 2016, from http://www.frost.com/prod/servlet/cio/232651119

Gijzen, H. (2013). Development: Big data for a sustainable future. *Nature*, *502*(7469), 38–38. doi:10.1038/502038d PMID:24091969

Hampton, S. E., Strasser, C. A., Tewksbury, J. J., Gram, W. K., Budden, A. E., Batcheller, A. L., & Porter, J. H. et al. (2013). Big data and the future of ecology. *Frontiers in Ecology and the Environment*, *11*(3), 156–162. doi:10.1890/120103

Hashizume, K., Rosado, D. G., Fernández-Medina, E., & Fernandez, E. B. (2013). An analysis of security issues for cloud computing. *Journal of Internet Services and Applications*, *4*(1), 1–13. doi:10.1186/1869-0238-4-5

Hongbing, C., Chunming, R., Kai, H., Weihong, W., & Yanyan, L. (2015). Secure big data storage and sharing scheme for cloud tenants. *Communications, China*, *12*(6), 106–115. doi:10.1109/CC.2015.7122469

Howe, D., Costanzo, M., Fey, P., Gojobori, T., Hannick, L., Hide, W., & Twigger, S. et al. (2008). Big data: The future of biocuration. *Nature*, *455*(7209), 47–50. doi:10.1038/455047a PMID:18769432

Kambatla, K., Kollias, G., Kumar, V., & Grama, A. (2014). Trends in big data analytics. *Journal of Parallel and Distributed Computing*, *74*(7), 2561–2573. doi:10.1016/j.jpdc.2014.01.003

Kayyali, B., Knott, D., & Van Kuiken, S. (2013). *The big-data revolution in US health care: Accelerating value and innovation*. Mc Kinsey & Company.

Kim, G. H., Trimi, S., & Chung, J. H. (2014). Big-data applications in the government sector. *Communications of the ACM, 57*(3), 78–85. doi:10.1145/2500873

Lynch, C. (2008). Big data: How do your data grow? *Nature, 455*(7209), 28–29. doi:10.1038/455028a PMID:18769419

Marchal, S., Jiang, X., State, R., & Engel, T. (2014, June). A Big Data Architecture for Large Scale Security Monitoring. *Proceedings of the 2014 IEEE International Congress on Big Data (Big Data Congress)* (pp. 56-63). IEEE. doi:10.1109/BigData.Congress.2014.18

Mhlanga, F. S., Perry, E. L., & Kirchner, R. (2015). *On Adapting a Military Combat Discrete Event Simulation with Big Data and Geospatial Modeling Toward a Predictive Model Ecosystem for Interpersonal Violence*. Journal Of Information Systems Applied Research.

Pandey, A., & Ramesh, V. (2015). Quantum computing for big data analysis. *History (Historical Association (Great Britain)), 14*(43), 98–104.

Popa, R. A., Stark, E., Valdez, S., Helfer, J., Zeldovich, N., & Balakrishnan, H. (2014). Building web applications on top of encrypted data using Mylar. *Proceedings of the USENIX Symposium of Networked Systems Design and Implementation*.

Reed, D. A., & Dongarra, J. (2015). Exascale computing and big data. *Communications of the ACM, 58*(7), 56–68. doi:10.1145/2699414

Sabahi, F. (2011, May). Virtualization-level security in cloud computing. *Proceedings of the 2011 IEEE 3rd International Conference on Communication Software and Networks (ICCSN)* (pp. 250-254). IEEE. doi:10.1109/ICCSN.2011.6014716

Schmidt, K., & Phillips, C. (2013). *Programming Elastic MapReduce: Using AWS Services to Build an End-to-end Application*. O'Reilly Media, Inc.

Sharma, P. P., & Navdeti, C. P. (2014). Securing big data hadoop: a review of security issues, threats and solution. *Int. J. Comput. Sci. Inf. Technol, 5*.

Shmueli, E., Vaisenberg, R., Elovici, Y., & Glezer, C. (2010). Database encryption: An overview of contemporary challenges and design considerations. *SIGMOD Record, 38*(3), 29–34. doi:10.1145/1815933.1815940

Subashini, S., & Kavitha, V. (2011, October). A metadata based storage model for Securing data in cloud environment. In CyberC (pp. 429-434).

Vayena, E., Salathé, M., Madoff, L. C., & Brownstein, J. S. (2015). Ethical challenges of big data in public health. *PLoS Computational Biology, 11*(2), e1003904. doi:10.1371/journal.pcbi.1003904 PMID:25664461

Wang, W., Chen, L., Thirunarayan, K., & Sheth, A. P. (2012, September). Harnessing twitter" big data" for automatic emotion identification. *Proceedings of the 2012 International Conference on Privacy, Security, Risk and Trust (PASSAT) and 2012 International Conference on Social Computing (SocialCom)* (pp. 587-592). IEEE.

Wang, X., & Sun, Z. (2013). The Design of Water Resources and Hydropower Cloud GIS Platform Based on Big Data. In *Geo-Informatics in Resource Management and Sustainable Ecosystem* (pp. 313–322). Springer Berlin Heidelberg. doi:10.1007/978-3-642-41908-9_32

We Are Social, U. K. (2014). *Global Social Media Users Pass 2 Billion.* Retrieved 8 January 2016, from http://wearesocial.net/blog/2014/08/global-social-media-users-pass-2-billion

KEY TERMS AND DEFINITIONS

Big Data: Big data is high-volume, high-variety and high-velocity information assets that demand cost-effective, innovative forms of information processing that enable enhanced insight, process automation and decision making.

Cloud Computing: Cloud computing is used to connect the computing resources, hardware's and access IT managed services with a previously unknown level of ease.

Hybrid Cloud: Hybrid cloud is a type of cloud computing model which uses a mix of on-premises, private cloud and third-party, public cloud services.

Infrastructure as a Service (IaaS): Infrastructure as a Service (IaaS) is used to deliver the computer infrastructure on an outsourced basis to support enterprise applications.

Platform as a Service (PaaS): Platform as a service (PaaS) is a category of cloud computing model that provides a platform and environment to allow developers to create software applications using tools supplied by the provider.

Private Cloud: A private cloud is a type of cloud computing model that involves a distinct and secure cloud based environment in which only the authorized users can operate.

Public Cloud: A public cloud is a type of cloud computing model, in which a service provider makes resources, such as storage, computing resources and applications available to the all users or the general public over the Internet.

Software as a Service (SaaS): Software as a service (or SaaS) is a software distribution model and it is used to deliver the applications over the Internet as a service.

This research was previously published in Exploring the Convergence of Big Data and the Internet of Things edited by A.V. Krishna Prasad, pages 141-154, copyright year 2018 by Engineering Science Reference (an imprint of IGI Global).

Chapter 19
Privacy Enhanced Cloud– Based Recommendation Service for Implicit Discovery of Relevant Support Groups in Healthcare Social Networks

Ahmed M. Elmisery
Universidad Técnica Federico Santa María, Chile

Mirela Sertovic
University of Zagreb, Croatia

ABSTRACT

Recommending support-groups in healthcare social networks is the problem of detecting for each patient his/her membership to one support-group of relevant patients. The patients in each support-group share some relevant preferences which guarantee that the support-group as a whole satisfies some desired properties of similarity. As a result, forming these support-groups requires the availability of personal data of different patients. This is a crucial requirement for different recommender services. With the increasing trend of service providers to collect a large volume of personal data regarding their end-users, presumably to better serve them. However, a significant part of the data that is typically collected is not essential to the service being offered, or to the completion of the services it was presumably released for. Gathering such unnecessary data can be seen as a privacy threat, and storing it exposes the end-users to further unavoidable risks. In this paper, a privacy enhanced cloud-based recommendation service is proposed for the implicit discovery of appropriate support groups in healthcare social network. A fog based middleware (FMCP) was introduced that runs at patients' sides and allows exchanging of their information to facilities recommending and creating support-groups without disclosing their real preferences to other parties. The membership of patients in various support groups allows receiving highly appropriate and reliable healthcare-related advices. The system utilizes two protocols to attain this goal. Experiments were performed on real dataset.

DOI: 10.4018/978-1-5225-5649-7.ch019

INTRODUCTION

The social networks are fundamentally enhancing the way many people interact with each other. The proliferation of social networks as an efficient gadget to promote the interaction and to facilitate information sharing between members of the network drives the emerging of more purpose driven social networks in different domains. Employing social networks in the healthcare domain had a considerable influence in e-health systems. This in turn aids in raising the term healthcare social networks (HSNs). The emergence of healthcare social networks has facilitated the patient-specialist interaction and allowed the care providers to continuously offer health and wellness services to a wide variety of patients wherever they may be. Currently, the patients utilize healthcare social networks to extract relevant information related to their health conditions from the massive amount of information available online. The Healthcare Social networks hold a substantial value for healthcare providers (Giustini, 2007), since these networks create an interaction space where patients can collaborate together and gather information related to their experiences and observations. Based on a recent statistics, One-third of patients in United States goes online and search for fellow patients who have similar health conditions like them (Elkin, 2008) and 36% of the patients use other patients' opinions and experiences on healthcare social networks before making healthcare related decisions (Levy, 2007). Healthcare Social networks (HSNs) were originally developed to patients with a reduced mobility and/or older adults; however, different healthcare originations and health personnel can participate in it. HSNs accumulate experiences and recommendations for the best practices to deal with certain health conditions. The next generation of the healthcare domain requires applications that have social interaction capabilities. Until now, there have been different paradigms for healthcare social networks such as PatientsLikeMe®, peoplejam®, DailyStrength®, OrganizedWisdom®, and CureTogether®. The biggest healthcare social network is PatientsLikeMe which launched in 2004, and currently has more than 200,000. It allows patients to use ready-made tools to track the progress of their health status and to access health information related to their medical conditions. Patients can benefit from the experiences of other patients with similar health status, share their life-style with likely similar patients and healthcare professionals. PatientsLikeMe® also offers specialized access to anonymized data to various healthcare organizations. Another healthcare social network is CureTogether®, which allows patients to track healthcare related data in an anonymous way to understand their current health status and take considered decisions regarding the required treatments for their conditions. DailyStrength® is a healthcare social network created to support patients-groups. Where patients seek to know other fellow patients to offer emotional support in an open platform that supports discussion of their attempts and useful advices. This network contains numerous online patients-groups regarding different healthcare diseases.

Within healthcare social networks, each patient has his/her own profile that represents his/her preferences in joining different support-groups and in using various services in the social healthcare platform. Support-group's recommendation service is one of these services running on the social healthcare platform and utilizes patient's preferences to provide numerous recommendations to join personalized support-groups out of the large number of candidate support-groups. This kind of cloud-based recommendation service relies on the assumption that patients with related preferences have the same concerns. The extraction of these recommendations depends on the private profiles of these patients, which contain their personal data and sensitive preferences. This service is usually accessible to different kinds of registered patients, which in turn, brings new kinds of threats and problems to the patients from the service provider and other registered patients sides, such as malignant behaviors. For instance, malignant users might perform certain attacks to get one another's personal information, such as current health conditions, place of work and/or relationship status. This kind of attacks could reveal patients' personal information even if it is not supposed to be exposed to the public.

A notable amount of efficient knowledge from diverse areas is available to the users on various Web 2.0 services at anywhere and can be obtained at anytime to offer assistance decision (Zhang et al., 2014). However, most of these versatile services depend on the disclosure of personal information. The potential abuses from unscrupulous service providers that were identified have caused increasing attention among the general public and within the media. Hence, privacy-enhancing techniques (PETs) have emerged to address the concerns of end-users and to allow them to control the use of their personal data. In this regard, several techniques exist in the literature to control the exposure of personal information. One of the most well-known approaches is the utilization of privacy rules to control the flow of private data, a policy engine makes use of these rules to conduct a decision either to liberate or not certain preferences in the user's profile. However, this approach is either coarse-grained or enforces the user to have a detailed understanding of how to construct proper privacy rules, any unsuitable setting may produce unexpected or unplanned exposure of sensitive data. Additionally, this approach is based on a binary philosophy of either permit or denies the publication of specific preferences on the patients' profiles. Once these preferences are published, this process can't be revised and the data owners have no govern over it. This published data can be used later to breach the privacy of the end-users. The malignant parties could employ inference techniques to infer other private preferences that haven't been published by the patients. the authors in (He et al., n.d.) applied inference techniques to deduce private information via social relations. The stronger a relationship between victims in the social network, the higher deduction accuracy could be attained.

In this work, the procedure of discovering and recommending relevant support-groups were laid out at patient side. This approach will attain privacy and helps to embrace the proposed protocols. The published data is concealed using two protocols to exclude the risks of potential privacy breaches. This also attains privacy to patients' data since the sensitive preferences will be available only to the owner in a raw form. During the execution of the proposed protocols, the patterns within patients' data are destroyed. Hence, to facilitate the handling of this concealed data, some selective properties need to be maintained for the recommender algorithm. This research is organized as follows. In Section 2, related works are presented. Section 3 the proposed middleware running at patient's side is described. In section 4, privacy issues in cloud-based recommendation service are presented. Some essential definitions will be introduced in section 5. The protocols used for the implicit discovery of relevant support-groups are explained in detail in section 6. Section 7, experiments and results are reported. Finally, the conclusions and future work are shown in Section 8.

RELATED WORKS

The plurality of the literature on social network analysis highlights the importance of maintaining privacy while outsourcing any information published by the users to external recommendation services, since this is a potential cause of sensitive data leakage as shown in (McSherry & Mironov, 2009). A theoretical framework was proposed in (Aimeur et al., 2008) to maintain the privacy of patrons and the business interests of retailers. A hybrid recommender system was designed in this work, which utilized secure multiparty computation and public key cryptography to attain the required objectives. The authors in

(Hoffmann & Hartman, 2002; Canny, 2002) proposed a privacy preserving distributed recommender system based on peer to peer techniques. In their work, users' communities are formed and an aggregated profile is constructed for each community but not for a single user. The aggregated profile is based on the personal information of each user in the community and it is constructed via peer-to-peer communication and encryption techniques. The recommendations process occurs at user side. The same was approach in (Miller et al., 2004) to store users' information on their side and execute the recommendation process in distributed manner without depending on a centralized entity. In this approach, only the similarity measures are submitted over the peer-to-peer network while the original users' profiles were kept private on their side to attain privacy. This method does not need a centralized recommender service, which was regarded as the main cause of privacy breaches; however, it required high-speed communication channels and greater cooperation between users' devices to generate recommendations in peer-to-peer fashion. In (Koutsabasis et al., 2008) a detailed framework for the personalization of e-businesses aspects especially related to business-to-consumer (B2C) situations was proposed. The proposed framework is related to typical e-business functionality, where it classifies previous research and extends it to provide e-commerce stakeholders with a vocabulary for analyzing e-businesses, for comparing personalization features, and for explaining e-business commerce evaluation results. In (Loureiro et al., 2001) a protocol is presented to preserve the data collected by software agents that are roaming through a group of potentially malignant parties. The proposed protocol is based on a cryptographic system that ensures the integrity of a chain of collected data segments despite of the order of the segment in the chain. In (Polat & Du, 2003), the authors proposed a method for protecting the privacy of users' data in centralized recommender service scenario. In their work, they argue that privacy can be attained by adding ambiguity to the users' profiles using a randomization technique while seeking to maintain the required statistical aggregates for the recommendations techniques. The centralized recommender service will not be able to extract the real profiles of end-users. They presented results of experiments that demonstrate that this method does not extensively reduce the accuracy of the extracted recommendations. A recent work in (Huang et al., 2005) indicates that such methods cannot guarantee a solid privacy levels as previously thought. In (Kargupta et al., 2003) it is revealed that inconsistent randomization does not ensure enough security because it is effortless to breach the privacy preservation it provides. The author utilized spectral filtering techniques to elicit the original users' profile from the randomized one. Their work concluded that randomization techniques offer a limited assurance for safeguarding privacy. Finally, the authors in (Xiao et al., 2015) propose the utilization of participants' sequence of browsing behaviors in generating news recommendation. Additionally, they propose a time-dependent technique to compute the similarity among various participants but their technique did not consider the cold-start and privacy problems.

PROPOSED MIDDLEWARE

With the massive utilization of mobile terminals in mobile medical and social networks (Zhang et al., 2011), patients' health data can be easily collected which greatly encourages the development of cloud-based recommendation service. This research work aims to attain privacy by design approach (Rubinstein, 2011) in which a middleware is proposed to run at patients' devices to govern the data publishing during the support-group discovery process. The patients are no longer forced to select one of two choices, either to publish or not their preferences. However, the patients are now empowered to segregate sensitive information about themselves with different levels of confidentiality (Victor, 2016). In this way, they can unveil themselves gradually. The proposed middleware helps the patients to manage the information they share with different support-groups, and to be enrolled in a specific support-group with a crafted portion of his/her sensitive preferences. The main idea behind the proposed middleware rose from user centric insights, which states that the safest method to protect sensitive information is to not publish it but to keep at patient side. However, to discover relevant support-groups, patients need to reveal their preferences in some manner to enable the group discovery process.

Mobile edge computing (MEC), fog computing (FC), and mist computing (MC) are all new terms that have been introduced in the field of mobile cloud computing (MCC). They all refer to a platform in which a set of devices with limited capabilities can use some nearby resources within nearby devices to accomplish their work (Alsmirat et al., 2016). In the fog computing approach, the fog node is a network edge device that can be depicted as an enhanced access point such as a switch or router operating at the indoor environment of the patient. The fog node is equipped with networking and computing capabilities to facilitate the execution of a dynamic run-time self-reconfiguration mechanism that automatically governs the data collection and usage practices during the group discovery process. The fog node can be considered as the most critical component in the proposed framework as it is responsible for ensuring privacy and anonymity for the patients. Moreover, this component must be trusted for delegation, as the patient must be assured that the fog node will follow the protocols honestly and will not trigger any malicious activities on his/her released health data. Nevertheless, if the patient does not trust the fog node, he/she is not forced to give up the execution of generalization step on any released health data. In other words, the patient can always create a generalized profile before forwarding the released health data to fog node. However, if the patient prefers a double line of privacy preservation to perform privacy guardianship in depth, the fog node can be used as a complement to standard privacy protection measures. Finally, secure transmission channels protect all the traffic between the patient's mobile device and the fog node, such that the patient's released data cannot be eavesdropped or altered by an external attacker before the fog node receives it.

Fog based middleware for cooperative privacy (*FMCP*) is the name of the proposed middleware, which runs on the mobile phones of patients. It consists of different cooperative agents. Each agent has a predefined function as illustrated in Figure 1. The cooperation between these agents is required to attain privacy goals. The learning agent explicitly captures vital sign measurements from the patient's body/home during various physical activities to build three databases, the first one is the vital sign measurements database, and the second one is the metadata database that contains the feature vector for data related to the measurement of the vital. Finally, the last one is the realized activities database. The manager agent is responsible for coordinating between requests and different agents in *FMCP*, such that, the manager agent receives any requests from the cloud-based recommendation service. It then forwards them to the involved agents. It also ensures that the patients' profiles contains the health data required for this particular group discovery process. The local camouflage agent is responsible for generating a generalized profile based on the real sensitive profile of its owner. The masking agent takes as input the generalized profile then executes two cryptographic protocols needed for the discovery process. The first protocol is private relevancy ranking (PRR) which is used to form a virtual society based on patients' profiles. And the second one is private group discovery (PGD) that is utilized to discover support-groups within each virtual society. The trust agent calculates the approximated interpersonal trust between the patients and different fog nodes. The trust computation is done in a decentralized fashion using the entropy definition proposed in (Kim, 2009). Since the database is dynamic in nature, the local camouflage agent periodically conceals the updated vital measurements, and then the synchronize agent forwards them to the cloud-based recommendation service (CRS) or the fog node upon owner permission. Thus, the group discovery can be made on the most recent health data. The synchronize agent is also responsible for calculating and storing parameterized paths in the anonymous network that attains high throughput, which in turn can be used in submitting the patients' profiles anonymously. These parameterized paths are stored in a database called "nodes store". The policy agent is the entity in *FMCP* that has the ability to encode privacy preferences and privacy policies. It also has the responsibility to encode data collection and data usage practices such as P3P policies in the form of XML statements. The policy agent needs to acquire the patient's privacy preferences and express them using APPEL as a set of preferences rules which are then decoded into a set of elements that are stored in a database called "privacy preferences" in the form of tables called "privacy meta-data". These rules contain both privacy policy and an action to be taken for such privacy policy, in this way, it will enable the preference checker to make self-acting decisions on data points that are encountered during the data collection process regarding different P3P policies (e.g.: privacy preferences could include: certain categories of data points should be excluded from health data before submission, refresh rate of vital sign parameters, usage of data points that have been captured during sensitive activities/locations, generalize certain data points in patient's health profile according to defined taxonomy, using synonyms for certain terms or names in patient's profile, suppressing certain data points from the extracted data and insert dummy data points that have the same feature vector like the suppressed ones as described in(Elmisery & Botvich, 2011), limiting the potentially output patterns from the extracted health data etc. in order to prevent the disclosure of sensitive data points in patient's profile). Query Rewriter rewrites the received request constrained by the privacy preferences for its host.

Since, reputation-based services have been widely used in the internet (Wang et al., 2016), extracting an accurate reputation score of fog nodes is an important issue, as it helps in identifying honest fog nodes. Hence, the feedback agent is responsible for anonymously submitting the patient's feedback about the extracted support-groups and discovery process to the cloud-based recommendation service. The feedback agent also reports scores about the different fog nodes and the cloud-based recommendation service to the security authority center (SAC). Finally, the delivery agent is the entity which is responsible for communicating with the external third-party providers in order to provide or fetch meta-data related to the personal life-style to be performed or already performed. *FMCP* utilizes aggregation topologies to organize the accumulation of patients' data; these topologies can be as simple as a ring formation or as complex as a hierarchical formation. The topological formation suits the proposed protocols well. The cloud-based recommendation service (CRS) is a centralized entity that launches the discovery process and stores the extracted support-groups. Additionally, CRS acts as virtual workplace that facilitates any communication between patients. The scenario in this research is as follows: Based on various healthcare themes, the administrator of the healthcare social network creates initial support-groups and requests the patients to join it. Each patient informs his/her *FMCP* to generate a generalized profile that exposes only main topics of his/her sensitive preferences. Patients seek to conceal their current health status and personal information. *FMCP* executes the proposed protocols, and then offers recommendations to enroll in a relevant support-group that its owner may like.

Figure 1. FMCP Components

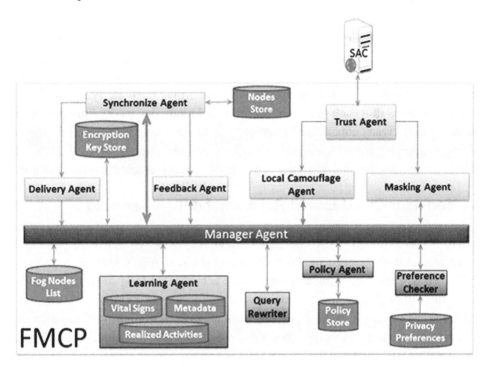

PRIVACY IN THE COULD RECOMMENDATION SERVICE PARADIGM

In the following subsections, we will introduce the definition of privacy, reference model, and security and privacy challenges in cloud-based recommendation service paradigm. In the last subsection, we will state the threat model that has been considered in this work.

Privacy Definition

Privacy is an elusive notion that is hard to symbolize. It is not a fully technical problem but it is connected to aspects of legislation, usage policies, and social norms. Privacy is an adaptable notion which depends on the users' viewpoints. Some users agree to reveal their private data if they are given certain rewards, like a discount coupon, or personalized content. However, when the end-user classifies something as private, this usually means it is something inherently sensitive that he/she desires to hide to avoid discrimination, embarrassment, or harm to his/her professional or personal reputation. The degree to which private information is exposed depends on how external parties conceive this information based on various contexts and time periods. Several viewpoints can be found to fully cover the definition of privacy in this research. However, this subsection is going to only cover fundamental viewpoints that are necessary for proceeding with this work. Warren and Brandeis defined privacy as "the right to be let alone" (Elmesiry, 2014). In the age of information and communication technologies, Westin stated that privacy can be further divided into informational and spatial privacy (Elmesiry, 2014). Informational privacy denotes that the user can control how, when, and to what extent information about him/her is released to others. This is often associated with any personal information such as name, age, phone number, or e-mail.

Further, spatial privacy denotes that the user can exercise control over what information is presented to his/her senses. The authors in (Elmisery, Rho & Botvich, 2016) argue that privacy is neither rule based nor static. Instead, "a fine and shifting line between privacy and publicity exists, and depends on the social context, intention, and the fine-grained coordination between action and the disclosure of that action". A notable work presented in (Elmisery, Rho & Botvich, 2016), in which privacy was defined as permitting services to extract a valid knowledge without learning the underlying users' personal data. At this point, we can state that each privacy enhancing technique has its own privacy definition. The primary concern about privacy enhancing techniques is that services are analyzed for the side effects, which occur due to applying these techniques. Therefore, our definition of privacy is close to previous definition that encompasses the dual goal of meeting privacy requirements and providing valid results.

Reference Model for Cloud-Based Recommendation Services

In this research, it was assumed that cloud-based recommendation service with patients' healthcare devices is built around the reference model proposed in (Union, 2005). Our reference model can be outlined as: The cloud-based recommendation service acts like a living organism, taking advantage of the opportunities afforded by running recommendation services in a cloud infrastructure to connect patients and care providers anywhere and anytime via any network to improve the quality of care, with the patients' healthcare devices, acting as a central nervous system for this model that measures patients' vital statistics, constantly logging their health data and report any abnormalities to the relevant healthcare provider. We consider five main types of entities in our solution. Patients' healthcare devices can be most simply defined as a networked physical device encompassing software, sensors and connectivity, which allows it to collect data about itself, other devices and humans then exchange the collected data with an internal personal gateway (fog node). The fog node accumulates health data then forwards it to the external cloud-based recommendation service in order to discover the relevant support-groups for different patients. Backend recommendation services are hosted in a cloud infrastructure in which patients can share their health related data with the members of his/her support-group to obtain highly personalized, accessible, and on-time healthcare- related information. Patients are the data subjects from which healthcare devices collect health data, this cloud-based recommendation service paradigm is especially important for elderly, disabled and those with chronic conditions by minimizing their need for direct patient-specialist interaction and allowing care providers to deliver more personalized health insights and services. Finally, a digital communication system links various entities together, and uses wired and/or wireless technologies to enable the exchange of data over a point to point or a point to multi-point communication channels.

Threat Model

The proposed middleware maintains privacy in the semi-honest model (Lin et al., 2016). Each party involved in the discovery process is compelled to act in accordance with the protocols but the intermediate values might be stored to later investigate the input of other parties. The cloud-based recommendation service (CRS) is considered to be the untrusted adversary that focuses on collecting the preferences of various patients in order to classify and trace them. This work did not assume that the cloud-based recommendation service to be entirely malignant, which is a sensible assumption, since certain business goals needs to be achieved to increase its profit. The attained privacy is high, only if CRS can't infer any sensitive preferences of the patients.

PROBLEM FORMULATION

In this section, the important notions used in this work will be outlined based on our previous solution in (Elmisery et al., 2012; Elmisery, Doolin, Roussaki, & Botvich, 2012; Elmisery et al., 2011). The patients' preferences are expressed within two types of profiles, a generalized profile and a sensitive profile. The generalized profile is the public version of the sensitive profile, which contain a set of hypernym phrases in the same semantic level of the sensitive preferences. The generalized profile represents the popular data that patients are willing to disclose and accept to be published by *FMCP*. The sensitive profile contains the "personal/secret" preferences that the patients refuse to reveal openly to other patients. Privacy must be respected when detecting relevant members and during the discovery process. It also needs to be maintained when recommending support-groups to the new patients. The data in flux in the discovery process needs to be protected against both of CRS and external third parties. By supporting generalized profiles and guaranteeing that participants are linked through a privacy aware virtual society of social connection, the proposed method reduces problems of cold-start (Zhang et al., 2014). The notion of virtual society in this research can be described:

Definition 1

A virtual society is the set $VS = \{SG_1,\ SG_2,...,SG_n\}$, where n is the total number of support-groups in VS, has the following properties: (1) Each $\forall_{i=1}^{n} SG_i \in VS$ has a 3-tuple $SG = \{I_{sg}, V_{sg}, d_{sg}\}$ such that $I_{sg} = \{i_1, i_2,..., i_l\}$ represents the set of generalized preferences, $V_{sg} = \{v_1, v_2,..., v_k\}$ corresponds to the set of patients, and $d_{sg} \in I_{sg}$ is the main- preferences of SG. (2) For each patient $\forall_{i=1}^{l} v_i \in V_{sg}$, v have the preferences V_{sg}. (3) d_{sg} is the frequent preference in V_{sg} profiles, and it represents the "core-point" of this support-group SG. (4) For any two support-groups SG_a and SG_b $\left(1 \leq a,\ b \leq n \text{ and } a \neq b\right)$ $V_{sg_a} \cap V_{sg_b} = \varnothing$ and $I_{sg_a} \neq I_{sg_b}$.

PROPOSED PROTOCOLS IN *FMCP*

In the proposed approach, *FMCP* enforces and maintains privacy of patients' data (Beil et al., 2002; Fung, 2002; Elmisery, Rho & Botvich, 2015; Elmisery, Rho, & Botvich, 2014, Elmisery, 2015; Elmisery & Botvich, 2011; Elmisery & Botvich, 2012; Elmisery & Botvich, 2011, "An Agent Based"). *FMCP* is running on patients' mobile phones and is arrayed with two cryptographic protocols, namely, private relevancy ranking protocol (PRR) and private group discovery protocol (PGD). *FMCP* facilitates the formation of virtual societies and the discovery of relevant support-groups. Patients sharing the same preferences can exchange their personal knowledge and recommendation to handle the emerging consequence of a certain health problem. Any newly registered patient can search and enroll in any support-group in a privacy-respecting manner.

Private Relevancy Ranking (PRR) Protocol

The main aim of this protocol is to cluster patients' data into numerous virtual societies. Two challenges have been faced while forming those virtual societies. The first one is the representation of such society, i.e., proper intra-society closeness and intra-society segregation need to be attained. The second one is to maintain privacy of sensitive profiles. Hence, the intuition of generalized profiles is essential. The generalized profiles are constructed using public information offered by CRS such as (taxonomy tree and unique public dictionary). The local camouflage agent maps the contents of the sensitive profile into this public information space, which results into the creation of generalized profiles as proposed in (Elmisery et al., 2012; Elmisery, Doolin, Roussaki, & Botvich, 2012; Elmisery et al., 2011). After creating the generalized profiles, *FMCP* incites the masking agent to execute PRR protocol to form the virtual societies. Each virtual society contains the patients who share the same generalized preferences. Any patient can enroll to multiple societies. PRR is performed in a distributed way. PRR begins with organizing a bag of interests that represent generalized preferences based on patients' sensitive preferences. The sensitive preferences are extracted then generalized as stated previously. The generalized preferences of patient V_c are used to create a preference vector $V_c = \left(e_c\left(w_1\right), \ldots\ldots\, e_c\left(w_m\right) \right)$, where m represents the total number of distinct preferences in the patient's profile, and $e_c\left(w_1\right)$ describes the significance of preference w_1 to patient V_c (weighted frequency). The further computation utilizes term frequency inverse profile frequency model (Sebastiani, 2002) as follows:

$$Term - frequency_{V_c}\left(w_i\right) = \# w_i \ in \ V_c \ profile \ / \ \# \ preferences \ in \ V_c \ profile, \ and$$

$$inverse - profile - frequency_{V_c}\left(w_i\right) = log\left(\# \, patient \ / \ \# \, profiles \ contain \ preference \ w_i\right), \ where$$

$$e_c\left(w_1\right) = Term - frequency_{V_c}\left(w_i\right) * inverse - profile - frequency_{V_c}\left(w_i\right)$$

The similarity metric should be tuned appropriately to apprehend the similarity between the generalized preferences of each patient. Dice similarity was employed for this duty. Let $V_c\left(V_d\right)$ be a two preference vectors for patients C and D then:

$$\text{PatientsSimilarity}\left(V_c, V_d\right) = 2\left|V_c \cap V_d\right| / \left|V_c\right|^2 + \left|V_d\right|^2$$

In other words, any two patients C and D are deemed similar to each other if they share many generalized preferences. Hence, these two patients will belong to the same society. The sensitive preferences are kept at patient side. The procedure for PRR is as follows:

1. For every two patients $C, D \in V$ own a set of preference vectors $e_c\left(w_i\right)$ and $e_d\left(w_i\right)$. Each patient employs a hash function h to his/her preference vector to generate $V_c = h\left(e_c\left(w_i\right) \right)$ and $V_d = h\left(e_d\left(w_i\right) \right)$. *FMCP* at patient C produces an encryption key E and decryption key U then sends the encryption key E to patient D. Later, the similarity between these two patients is calculated in two steps. First, computing the numerator, and then the denominator

2. After selecting a fog node as the base for aggregation. A topological formation is created between patients' devices to receive the calculated numerator values.

3. The masking agent at patient D hides V_d by $B_d = \left\{ e_d\left(w_i\right) \times r^D \mid w_i \in V_d \right\}$ where r is a random number for each preference in his/her profile w_i, and then sends B_d to patient C.

4. The masking agent at patient C signs B_d and get the signature S_d, then sends S_d again to D in the same order it was received. *FMCP* at patient reveals preference set S_d using the set of r values and obtains the real signature SI_d, then it implements the hash function h on SI_d to form $SIH_d = H\left(SI_d\right)$.

5. The masking agent at patient C signs the preference set V_c and gets the signature SI_c then implements the same hash function h on SI_c to form $SIH_c = H\left(SI_c\right)$ then submits this to D.

6. The masking agent at patient D compares SIH_d and SIH_c utilizing the knowledge of V_d, D gets the intersection set $IN_{C,D} = SIH_c \cap SIH_d$ that represents $\left|V_c \cap V_D\right|$. *FMCP* at D implements the hash function h on $IN_{C,D}$, and then it encrypts this extracted value along with $\left|V_D\right|$, $\left|V_C\right|$ and patients' pseudonyms identities with the public key of the fog node. This encrypted data is later sent to the fog node of this society.

7. The fog node collects all these intermediate values and decrypts them, then starts to cluster patients into different societies. using S-seeds clustering algorithm (Elmisery et al., 2012).

The above protocol executes these steps on m hashed generalized preferences hosted on m parties without revealing any of these preferences.

Private Group Discovery (PGD) Protocol

The masking agent in *FMCP* implements *PGD* protocol on the virtual societies extracted from PRR protocol. PGD protocol learns in a bilateral way the correlated preferences in the generalized profiles, the final results are used in discovering the relevant support-groups. PGD protocol is based on the work in (Elmisery et al., 2012; Elmisery, Doolin, Roussaki, & Botvich, 2012; Elmisery et al., 2011). The main idea behind PGD is that the sets of frequent preferences shared between the patients should be as large as possible in each support-group. Since, the initial support-groups within these virtual societies have been created by the administrator of the healthcare social network, without any previous knowledge about patients' requirements. *PGD* protocol should be able to operate with the available prior domain knowledge and patients' profiles.

Definition 2 (Frequent Preferences)

"Frequent Preferences" is a notion related to frequent item-sets in association rule mining, it represent a set of preferences that occur jointly in some minimum fraction of patients' profiles. For example, let's consider two frequent preferences, "regulate blood pressure" and "manage blood cholesterol". Profiles containing the preference "regulate blood pressure" may relate to patients suffering from hypertension and information related to its treatment and regulation procedures and Profiles containing the preference "manage blood cholesterol" may relate to lipids disorder treatment and regulation procedures. However, if both preferences occur together in many profiles, then a specific support-group related to "blood disorders" should be identified.

Definition 3 (Global Frequent Preferences)

"Global Frequent Preferences" is a set of preferences that appear together in more than a minimum fraction of the whole patients 'profiles in virtual society VS; a minimum support of the virtual society is specified for this purpose. If this set contains k- preferences, it called global frequent k- preferences such that each preference that belongs to this set is called global frequent preference. Global frequent preference is frequent in specific support-group SG_n if this preference is contained in some minimum fraction of patients' profiles; a minimum support for the support-group is specified for this purpose.

The patients' devices need to be organized into a ring topological formation to discover the relevant support-groups. PGD protocol can be outlined as follows:

1. The PGD protocol is incited by CRS. Patients within the same virtual society negotiate with each other to elect a fog node. The fog node publishes a catalog of 1-candidate frequent preferences. The registered patients execute a local function to extract local frequent preferences using local parameters for the support and closure. The algorithm presented in (Cheung et al., 1996) is utilized to detect global & local frequent preferences for each society.
2. For all patients $\forall_1^n P_i$, patient P_i encrypts the calculated local list with his/her own key and send it to second member P_{i+1} in the society, and so on for all patients.
3. The last patient in the society P_{n-1} sends the received lists to the fog node. The Fog node generates the global support by aggregating the local supports that were received. While, the global closure will be the intersection between the received local closures.
4. The fog node encrypts and publishes the lists of global supports & closures to patient P_{n-1} in random order. Patient P_{n-1} decrypts his/her encrypted contribution from these lists using his/her own private key, and then forwards these lists to the next patient P_{n-2}. The fog node receives these lists back only encrypted with his/her own key. Hence, final results can be obtained.
5. For each neighboring set of global frequent preferences, the fog node creates a basic support-group SG that contains all patients sharing these global frequent preferences; these basic support-groups might be overlapped in the start. PGD will utilize these global frequent preferences as a support-group representative.
6. 6. For each patient's profile V_i, the masking agent determines the best basic support-group $SG\left(c_i\right)$ using a scoring function:

$$\text{SimilarityScore}\left(SG_i \leftarrow V_i\right) = \left[\sum_{w_i} e_r\left(w_i\right) * SG\_support\left(w_i\right)\right] - \left[\sum_{w_i'} e_r\left(w_i'\right) * VS\_support\left(w_i'\right)\right]$$

w_i is the global frequent preference in profile r and this preference is also common in support-group SG_i while w_i' is a global frequent preference in profile r and is not common in support-group SG_i. After implementing this scoring function, each patient will belong to exactly one support-group. The representative is re-calculated based on the current members in each support-group.

7. 7. For each virtual society VS, the fog nodes compile a hierarchical structure of the discovered support-groups. The global frequent k-preferences of each support-group are employed as representatives. Hence, the support-group with k-preferences will become available at level k of this hierarchical structure. The parent support-group at level k-1 is a subset of its child support-group at level k. The scoring function is also utilized to deduce the candidate parent for each child support-group. The fog nodes in various societies share the list of discovered support-groups with one another. This essential step is used to merge similar support-groups together and removes excessively support-groups according to inter-support-group similarity. This new similarity metric is very close to the previous scoring function, the only variation is related to the normalization, which is used to eliminate the effect of changeable number of members in each support-group. This metric is measured as follows:

$$\text{SG\_Similarity}\left(\text{SG}_i \leftarrow \text{SG}_j\right) = \left\lfloor \text{SimilarityScore}\left(\text{SG}_i \leftarrow \forall_{x=1}^n V_x \in \text{SG}_j\right) \middle/ \left[\sum_{w_j} e\left(w_j\right) + \sum_{w_j} e\left(w_j'\right)\right] \right\rfloor + 19.$$

$$Inter\ \text{SG\_}\ similarity\left(SG_i \leftrightarrow SG_j\right) = \left[\text{SG\_}Similarity\left(SG_i \leftarrow SG_j\right) * \text{SG\_}Similarity\left(SG_j \leftarrow SG_i\right)\right].$$

SG_i and SG_j are two support-groups; $\forall_{x=1}^n V_x \in SG_j$ stands for single conceptual profile for the support-groups SG_j. w_j represents a global frequent preference in both SG_i and SG_j while w_j' represent a global frequent preference in only but not in SG_i. $e\left(w_j\right)$ and $e\left(w_j'\right)$ are the weighted frequency of and in support-groups.

8. Finally, any new patient invokes his/her *FMCP* to obtain a list of available support-groups' representatives from CRS. Then executes PRR and PGD protocols on his/her sensitive profile. Finally, *FMCP* measure the similarity with each representative and enroll his/her owner to the support-group with the highest relevancy value.

EXPERIMENTS

The experiments were conducted on two Intel® machines connected via a local network, the lead peer is Intel® Core i7 and the other is Intel® Core 2 Duo. MySQL was used as data storage for the patients' profiles. CRS has been deployed as a web service. *FMCP* has been implemented as an applet to handles the complex interactions between the patient, CRS and other registered patients. Our proposed protocols were implemented using Java and boundycastle© library, RSA key length is set to 512 for all experimental scenarios. The experiments were conducted using a dataset pulled from the SportyPal network that was linked to another dataset containing health parameters (blood pressure, heart rate, electrocardiogram, blood glucose, and respiratory rate) of 6000 students in university of Zagreb in Croatia in the period of 2010 to 2012. To create the generalized profiles based on these profiles we use same method proposed in [29] .

In order to evaluate the attained privacy level and accuracy of results of the proposed solution, precision and recall metrics were utilized as shown in Figure 2. As seen, a good quality is achieved by identifying societies that involve different support-groups, which enables the extraction of accurate recommendations to the patients who share the same preferences. Also, the effect of each preference inside the society can be easily calculated, which allows *FMCP* to detect and remove outlier values that are very far from the generalized preferences. We also evaluated the leaked private preferences of different patients when running the proposed solution. We considered patients, who revealed portion of their sensitive preferences in their generalized profiles, for each of these patients; we tried the attack procedure mentioned in threat model to expose other hidden preferences in their sensitive profiles based on the support-group they are belonging to. The obtained preferences were quantified and the results are shown in Figure 2. As seen, the proposed solution can reduce privacy leakages of exposed private preferences, However, the exposed preferences are only a hashed hypernym phrases based on the sensitive preferences.

In the next experiment, the accuracy of extracted support-groups using PGD protocol was measured. Hierarchical agglomerative clustering was applied on the dataset to identify the natural support-groups from patients' private profiles. The resulting support-groups were utilized for measuring the accuracy of the results produced by the proposed PGD protocol. Each cluster represents a support-group which was assembled from a set of patients' private profiles who share the same specific preferences. To measure the goodness of our results, two error metrics were considered (Cuesta-Frau et al., 2003), which are grouping error (GR) and critical error (CIE). The grouping error (GR), takes into account the number of patients' profiles included in a support-group, but belonging to a topic different from the dominant topic

Figure 2. Recommendations accuracy and privacy

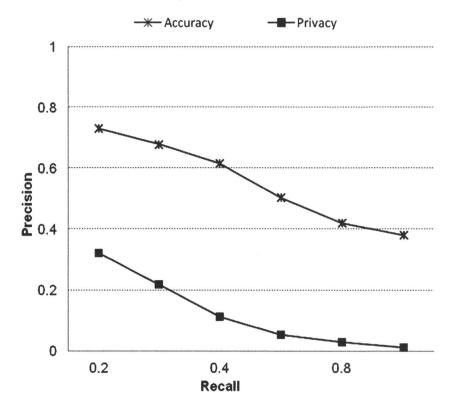

Figure 3. Grouping error (GR) of PGD protocol

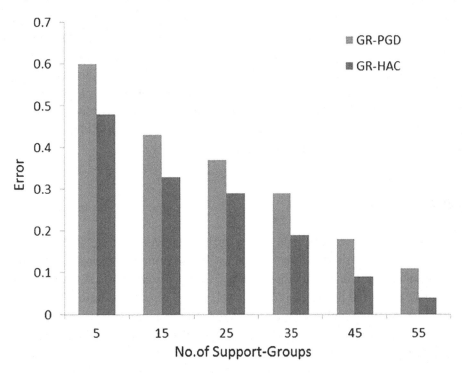

Figure 4. Critical error (CIE) of PGD protocol

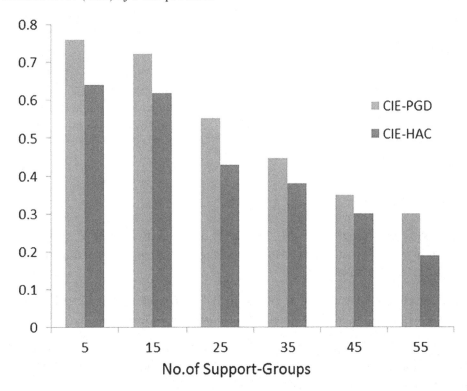

in that support-group. The critical error (CIR) measures the number of patients' profiles belonging to a topic that is not the dominant one in any support-group. The graphs in Figure 3 and Figure 4, contain both GR and CIE values for the results obtained from both hierarchical clustering and PGD protocol for different number of support-groups. This experiment is performed on two versions of our dataset; patients' generalized profiles which were used by the PGD protocol, while hierarchical agglomerative clustering employed patients' private profiles that should kept private in the proposed scenario. We can deduce that both GR and CIE for PGD decrease with the increase in no. of support-groups till reaching natural number of support-groups. This indicates that achieving privacy is feasible and does not severely affect the accuracy of the generated support-group.

CONCLUSION

In this paper, we presented our attempt to develop a fog based middleware (*FMCP*) that runs at patients' sides and allows exchanging of their information to facilities recommending and creating support-groups without disclosing their preferences to other parties. A brief overview of the proposed protocols was given. The performance of the proposed protocols was tested on a real dataset. The experimental and analysis results show attaining higher privacy levels in recommending support-groups is feasible under the proposed approach without reducing the accuracy of the recommendations. For the cloud-based recommendation service, many issues need further investigation. Reputation management techniques should also be involved for support-group's recommendations (Huang et al., 2015). A future research agenda will include utilizing game theory to better formulate virtual societies, multiple preferences release and its impact on patient's privacy.

ACKNOWLEDGMENT

This work was partially financed by the "Dirección General de Investigación, Innovación y Postgrado" of Federico Santa María Technical University- Chile, in the project Private and Secure Mobile Cloud Framework for Medical IoT Devices (UTFSM-DGIP 116.23.3), and by the Microsoft Azure for Research Grant (0518798).

REFERENCES

Aimeur, E., Brassard, G., Fernandez, J. M., Onana, F. S. M., & Rakowski, Z. (2008). *Experimental demonstration of a hybrid privacy-preserving recommender system. Proceedings of ARES '08* (pp. 161–170). doi:10.1109/ARES.2008.193

Alsmirat, M.A. Jararweh, Y. Obaidat, I. & Gupta, B. B. (2016). Internet of surveillance: a cloud supported large-scale wireless surveillance system. *The Journal of Supercomputing*.

Beil, F., Ester, M., & Xu, X. (2002). Frequent term-based text clustering. *Proceedings of the eighth ACM SIGKDD international conference on Knowledge discovery and data mining*, Edmonton, Alberta, Canada (pp. 436-442). doi:10.1145/775047.775110

Canny, J. (2002). *Collaborative filtering with privacy. Proceedings of the IEEE symposium on Security and Privacy* (pp. 45–57).

Cheung, D. W., Han, J., Ng, V. T., Fu, A. W., & Fu, Y. (1996). A fast distributed algorithm for mining association rules. *Proceedings of the fourth international conference on on Parallel and distributed information systems*, Miami Beach, Florida (pp. 31-43). doi:10.1109/PDIS.1996.568665

Cuesta-Frau, D., Pérez-Cortés, J.C., & Andreu-García, G. (2003). Clustering of electrocardiograph signals in computer-aided Holter analysis. *Computer Methods and Programs in Biomedicine, 72*(3), 179-196.

Elkin, N. (2008). *How America Searches: Health and Wellness. iCrossing*.

Elmesiry, A. M. (2014). *Machine Learning based Stochastic Techniques for Collaborative Privacy in Social Recommender Services*. Waterford Institute of Technology.

Elmisery, A. M. (2014). Private personalized social recommendations in an IPTV system. New Review of Hypermedia and Multimedia, 20(2), 145-167. doi:10.1080/13614568.2014.889222

Elmisery, A. M., & Botvich, D. (2011). Privacy Aware Recommender Service for IPTV Networks. Proceedings of the 2011 5th FTRA International Conference on Multimedia and Ubiquitous Engineering (MUE) (pp. 160-166). doi:10.1109/MUE.2011.70

Elmisery, A. M., & Botvich, D. (2011). Enhanced middleware for collaborative privacy in IPTV recommender services. *Journal of Convergence, 2*(2), 10.

Elmisery, A. M., & Botvich, D. (2011). An Agent Based Middleware for Privacy Aware Recommender Systems in IPTV Networks. In J. Watada, G. Phillips-Wren, L.C. Jain & R. J. Howlett (Eds.), *Intelligent Decision Technologies: Proceedings of the 3rd International Conference on Intelligent Decision Technologies (IDT '11)* (pp. 821-832). Springer. doi:10.1007/978-3-642-22194-1_81

Elmisery, A. M., & Botvich, D. (2012). Agent Based Middleware for Maintaining User Privacy in IPTV Recommender Services. In R. Prasad, K. Farkas, A. U. Schmidt, A. Lioy, G. Russello and F. L. Luccio (Eds.), *Security and Privacy in Mobile Information and Communication Systems: Third International ICST Conference MobiSec '11*, Aalborg, Denmark (pp. 64-75). Springer. doi:10.1007/978-3-642-30244-2_6

Elmisery, A. M., & Botvich, D. (2011, October 12-14). Privacy Aware Obfuscation Middleware for Mobile Jukebox Recommender Services. In T. Skersys, R. Butleris, L. Nemuraite & R. Suomi (Eds.), *Building the e-World Ecosystem: 11th IFIP WG 6.11 Conference on e-Business, e-Services, and e-Society*, Kaunas, Lithuania (pp. 73-86). Springer. doi:10.1007/978-3-642-27260-8_6

Elmisery, A. M., Doolin, K., & Botvich, D. (2012). Privacy Aware Community based Recommender Service for Conferences Attendees. IOS press. doi:10.3233/978-1-61499-105-2-519

Elmisery, A. M., Doolin, K., Roussaki, I., & Botvich, D. (2012). Enhanced Middleware for Collaborative Privacy in Community Based Recommendations Services. In Y. Pan, S. Y. Lee, & B. H. Chang (Eds.), *Computer Science and its Applications CSA '12* (pp. 313–328). Dordrecht: Springer Netherlands. doi:10.1007/978-94-007-5699-1_32

Elmisery, A. M., Rho, S., & Botvich, D. (2016). A Fog Based Middleware for Automated Compliance With OECD Privacy Principles in Internet of Healthcare Things. *IEEE Access, 4*, 8418–8441. doi:10.1109/ACCESS.2016.2631546

Elmisery, A. M., Rho, S., & Botvich, D. (2015). Privacy-enhanced middleware for location-based sub-community discovery in implicit social groups. *The Journal of Supercomputing, 72*(1), 247–274. doi:10.1007/s11227-015-1574-x

Elmisery, A. M., Rho, S., & Botvich, D. (2016). Collaborative privacy framework for minimizing privacy risks in an IPTV social recommender service. *Multimedia Tools and Applications, 75*(22), 14927–14957. doi:10.1007/s11042-014-2271-0

Fung, B.C.M. (2002). Hierarchical document clustering using frequent item sets [Master's Thesis]. Simon Fraser University.

Giustini, D. (2007). Web 3.0 and medicine. *BMJ (Clinical Research Ed.), 335*(7633), 1273–1274. doi:10.1136/bmj.39428.494236.BE PMID:18156223

He, J., Chu, W.W., & Liu, Z.V. (2006). Inferring privacy information from social networks. *Proceedings of ISI '06* (pp. 154-165).

Hofmann, T., & Hartmann, D. (2002). Collaborative filtering with privacy via factor analysis. Proceedings of the 2005 ACM symposium on applied computing (pp. 791–795).

Huang, L., Wang, S., Hsu, C.-H., Zhang, J., & Yang, F. (2015). Using reputation measurement to defend mobile social networks against malicious feedback ratings. *The Journal of Supercomputing, 71*(6), 2190–2203. doi:10.1007/s11227-015-1432-x

Huang, Z., Du, W., & Chen, B. (2005). Deriving private information from randomized data. *Proceedings of the 2005 ACM SIGMOD international conference on Management of data*, Baltimore, Maryland (pp. 37-48). doi:10.1145/1066157.1066163

Kargupta, H., Datta, S., Wang, Q., & Sivakumar, K. (2003). On the Privacy Preserving Properties of Random Data Perturbation Techniques. *Proceedings of the Third IEEE International Conference on Data Mining* (pp. 99-106). doi:10.1109/ICDM.2003.1250908

Kim, H. D. (2009). Applying Consistency-Based Trust Definition to Collaborative Filtering. *Transactions on Internet and Information Systems (Seoul), 3*(4), 366–374. doi:10.3837/tiis.2009.04.002

Koutsabasis, P., Stavrakis, M., Viorres, N., Darzentas, J. S., Spyrou, T., & Darzentas, J. (2008). A descriptive reference framework for the personalisation of e-business applications. *Electronic Commerce Research, 8*(3), 173–192. doi:10.1007/s10660-008-9021-1

Levy, M. (2007). *Online health: assessing the risk and opportunity of social and one-to one media* (Vol. 2). Jupiter Research.

Lin, L., Li, S., Li, B., Zhan, J., & Zhao, Y. (2016). TVGuarder: A Trace-Enable Virtualization Protection Framework against Insider Threats for IaaS Environments. *International Journal of Grid and High Performance Computing, 8*(4), 1–20. doi:10.4018/IJGHPC.2016100101

Loureiro, S., Molva, R., & Pannetrat, A. (2001). Secure Data Collection with Updates. *Electronic Commerce Research, 1*(1), 119–130. doi:10.1023/A:1011527713457

McSherry, F., & Mironov, I. (2009). *Differentially private recommender systems: building privacy into the net. Proceedings of KDD '09* (pp. 627–636). doi:10.1145/1557019.1557090

Miller, B. N., Konstan, J. A., & Riedl, J. (2004). PocketLens: Toward a personal recommender system. *ACM Transactions on Information Systems, 22*(3), 437–476. doi:10.1145/1010614.1010618

Polat, H., & Du, W. (2003). Privacy-Preserving Collaborative Filtering Using Randomized Perturbation Techniques. *Proceedings of the Third IEEE International Conference on Data Mining* (pp. 625-628). doi:10.1109/ICDM.2003.1250993

Rubinstein, I. S. (2011). Regulating privacy by design. *Berkeley Technology Law Journal, 26*(3), 1409–1456.

Sebastiani, F. (2002). Machine learning in automated text categorization. *ACM Computing Surveys, 34*(1), 1–47. doi:10.1145/505282.505283

Union, I. (2005). *The Internet of Things. ITU Internet Reports.* International Telecommunication Union.

Victor, N., Lopez, D., & Abawajy, J. H. (2016). Privacy models for big data: A survey. *International Journal of Big Data Intelligence, 3*(1), 61–75. doi:10.1504/IJBDI.2016.073904

Wang, S., Huang, L., Hsu, C.-H., & Yang, F. (2016). Collaboration reputation for trustworthy Web service selection in social networks. *Journal of Computer and System Sciences, 82*(1 Part B), 130-143.

Xiao, Y., Ai, P., Hsu, C., Wang, H., & Jiao, X. (2015). Time-ordered collaborative filtering for news recommendation. *China Communications, 12*(12), 53–62. doi:10.1109/CC.2015.7385528

Zhang, D., Hsu, C. H., Chen, M., Chen, Q., Xiong, N., & Lloret, J. (2014). Cold-Start Recommendation Using Bi-Clustering and Fusion for Large-Scale Social Recommender Systems. *IEEE Transactions on Emerging Topics in Computing, 2*(2), 239–250. doi:10.1109/TETC.2013.2283233

Zhang, D., Zhang, D., Xiong, H., Hsu, C. H., & Vasilakos, A. V. (2014). BASA: Building mobile Ad-Hoc social networks on top of android. *IEEE Network, 28*(1), 4–9. doi:10.1109/MNET.2014.6724100

This research was previously published in the International Journal of Grid and High Performance Computing (IJGHPC), 9(1); edited by Emmanuel Udoh, Ching-Hsien Hsu, and Mohammad Khan, pages 75-91, copyright year 2017 by IGI Publishing (an imprint of IGI Global).

Index

Stay Current on the Latest Emerging Research Developments

Become an IGI Global Reviewer for Authored Book Projects

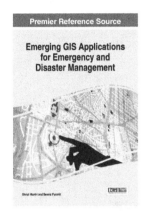

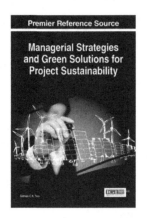

The overall success of an authored book project is dependent on quality and timely reviews.

In this competitive age of scholarly publishing, constructive and timely feedback significantly decreases the turnaround time of manuscripts from submission to acceptance, allowing the publication and discovery of progressive research at a much more expeditious rate. Several IGI Global authored book projects are currently seeking highly qualified experts in the field to fill vacancies on their respective editorial review boards:

Applications may be sent to:
development@igi-global.com

Applicants must have a doctorate (or an equivalent degree) as well as publishing and reviewing experience. Reviewers are asked to write reviews in a timely, collegial, and constructive manner. All reviewers will begin their role on an ad-hoc basis for a period of one year, and upon successful completion of this term can be considered for full editorial review board status, with the potential for a subsequent promotion to Associate Editor.

If you have a colleague that may be interested in this opportunity,
we encourage you to share this information with them.

Printed in the United States
By Bookmasters